Annotated Instructor's Edition

Developing Critical Reading Skills

When he borrowed the book [Robert Frost's book of poems, *North of Boston*] he'd had no idea where this act would lead him. Make no mistake, he said: a true piece of writing is a dangerous thing. It can change your life.

—Tobias Wolff, *Old School*

Annotated Instructor's Edition
Developing Critical Reading Skills

Seventh Edition

Deanne Spears
City College of San Francisco

Boston   Burr Ridge, IL   Dubuque, IA   Madison, WI   New York
San Francisco   St. Louis   Bangkok   Bogotá   Caracas   Kuala Lumpur
Lisbon   London   Madrid   Mexico City   Milan   Montreal   New Delhi
Santiago   Seoul   Singapore   Sydney   Taipei   Toronto

Mc Graw Hill **Higher Education**

DEVELOPING CRITICAL READING SKILLS
Published by McGraw-Hill, a business unit of The McGraw-Hill Companies, Inc., 1221 Avenue of the
Americas, New York, NY, 10020. Copyright © 2006, 2003, 1999, 1995, 1991, 1987, 1983 by The
McGraw-Hill Companies, Inc. All rights reserved. No part of this publication may be reproduced or
distributed in any form or by any means, or stored in a database or retrieval system, without the prior
written consent of The McGraw-Hill Companies, Inc., including, but not limited to, in any network
or other electronic storage or transmission, or broadcast for distance learning.

Some ancillaries, including electronic and print components, may not be available to customers
outside the United States.

This book is printed on acid-free paper.

1 2 3 4 5 6 7 8 9 0 DOC/DOC 0 9 8 7 6 5

ISBN 0-07-298290-X (student edition)
ISBN 0-07-298292-6 (annotated instructor's edition)

Editor in Chief: *Emily Barrosse*
Publisher: *Lisa Moore*
Senior Sponsoring Editor: *Alexis Walker*
Marketing Manager: *Lori DeShazo*
Senior Development Editor: *Jane Carter*
Managing Editor: *Jean Dal Porto*
Senior Project Manager: *Becky Komro*
Manuscript Editor: *Pat Steele*
Art Director: *Jeanne Schreiber*
Associate Designer: *Srdjan Savanovic*

Cover Designer: *Jennifer McQueen*
Associate Art Editor: *Ayelet Arbel*
Photo Research Coordinator: *Natalia C. Peschiera*
Cover Credit: *Superstock/Michael Mortimer Robinson*
Lead Media Project Manager: *Marc Mattson*
Senior Production Supervisor: *Carol A. Bielski*
Permissions Editor: *Marty Granahan*
Composition: *10/12 Stone Serif by Thompson Type*
Printing: *45# New Era Matte, R. R. Donnelley/
Crawfordsville, IN*

Credits: The credits section for this book begins on page A-1 and is considered an extention of the copyright page.

Library of Congress Control Number: 2005049229

The Internet addresses listed in the text were accurate at the time of publication. The inclusion of a Web site does
not indicate an endorsement by the authors of McGraw-Hill, and McGraw-Hill does not guarantee the accuracy of
the information presented at these sites.

www.mhhe.com

ABOUT THE AUTHOR

After receiving a B.A. and an M.A. in Comparative Literature from the University of Southern California, Deanne Spears worked for a management consultant firm as a junior editor. A few months of delivering mail, typing, and correcting the consultants' grammar convinced her that a business career was not for her. She found a long-term substitute teaching job at Los Angeles Valley College, then taught at Rio Hondo Community College, and in 1968 joined the English Department at City College of San Francisco. She has done postgraduate work at San Francisco State University, studying logic, anthropology, and literature. At City College of San Francisco she teaches reading and composition. In addition to this text, she is the author of an intermediate reading book, *Improving Reading Skills* (4th ed.), also published by McGraw-Hill. She is married to a fellow English teacher and jazz musician, David Spears.

DEDICATION

To
David

CONTENTS

PART 3
Discovering Meaning: The Importance of Language 183

CHAPTER 6

Language and Its Effects on the Reader 184

CHAPTER 7

Tone, Point of View, and Allusions 225

C H A P T E R 10

PART 5

PART 6

LIST OF ILLUSTRATIONS

PREFACE

Developing Critical Reading Skills proceeds from the assumption that good reading and clear thinking go hand in hand. For this reason, the text emphasizes practice in sustained, analytical reading. Because learning to read analytically requires concentration and an intense engagement with the text, the text emphasizes the importance of reading with a pencil in one's hand and deliberately omits practice in speed techniques. Students first work with high-quality short passages before moving on to more substantive pieces of greater complexity. The readings explore diverse subjects: anthropology, sports, human behavior, politics, social policy, education, ethics, autobiography, personal reminiscence, the minority and immigrant experience, humor, satire, and so forth. The passages also reflect diverse writing styles, thereby giving students the experience of reading high-level prose by its best practitioners.

This book succeeds if students become more self-assured about their reading and if they recognize that reading well—with confidence, fluency, and enjoyment—is a significant part of their emotional and academic lives. My hope is that students will feel genuine excitement when they encounter a writer who shows them a new way of looking at their lives and at the world. It is this feeling—or inspiration, perhaps, for lack of a better word—that I hope to impart.

Now in its Seventh Edition, the text continues to evolve in response to instructors' concerns, to our students' needs, and to the changing world. The political upheavals resulting from the 2001 terrorist attacks and the shifting political and social landscape in the United States have made it even more imperative for us to be an educated populace, able to read with accuracy and skilled in detecting manipulation, emotional appeals, bias, and propaganda. These events have also made it more important than ever to acquire knowledge about other cultures, particularly about those cultures that have different worldviews and whose members, thus, behave in seemingly incomprehensible ways. Perhaps this book can do a small part to help students—indeed, all of us—to be better thinkers and better citizens, able to participate fully in the democratic process.

■ CHANGES TO THE SEVENTH EDITION

I am indebted to the thoughtful and practical suggestions reviewers have given me, which almost without exception I have incorporated. I hope that these new features will make the Seventh Edition attractive and pedagogically useful. Here is a brief explanation of the changes in this edition:

New Material on Reading Textbooks

- The most significant change in this edition is the addition of **passages from leading lower-division textbooks** in psychology, anthropology, biology, economics, and communications. This material is used both in illustrative passages and in exercise material in Parts 1–3.
- As a corollary, a new section has been added—**Part 6, "Reading and Studying Textbook Material"**—that features an explanation of how to read a textbook using the SQ3R method and a practice selection—a complete chapter—from an introductory psychology text.

New Attention to Visuals

- Because learning to "read" visual information is as crucial in an image-saturated society as reading print, **a wealth of new visual material**—charts, graphs, political and humorous cartoons, photographs, and advertisements—has been added, along with instruction in how to read, interpret, and evaluate these elements.

More on Critical Reading and the World Wide Web

- As in the sixth edition, **Chapter 10, "Evaluating Web Sites,"** offers students the tools necessary to search the Web efficiently, to evaluate Web sites for content and accuracy, and to locate and evaluate information. Chapter 10 now offers **annotated screenshots** of a Web search, to *show* students how best to interpret the results a search yields, and a sample Web site, to help students identify the various features (address, date of creation, authorship, etc.) necessary in determining the reliability of the information it offers.
- **New "On the Web" exercises** follow most long selections in Parts 1–3 and encourage students to refine their Web skills by engaging them in simple research tasks or by having them explore in more depth the subject under discussion.

New Readings

- **Approximately 35–40 percent of the readings are new.** Some writers making an appearance among the new additions are Laura Hillenbrand (with an excerpt from *Seabiscuit*), Barack Obama (from *Dreams from My Father*), Michael Pollan (from *The Botany of Desire*), Sandra Mackey (from *The Saudis: Inside the Desert Kingdom*), Paco Underhill (from *The Call of the Mall*), Matt Ridley (from *Genome*), Joel Best (from *Damned Lies and Statistics*), and Diane Ravitch (from *The Language Police*).

- Some of the readings in this edition reflect **recent world events,** including the 2001 terrorist attacks, the war on terror, and politics in the Middle East. In addition, a few background selections on Arab culture and the Arab worldview are interspersed throughout the text to give students some acquaintance with this important, and, until recently, often academically neglected area of the world.
- The Seventh Edition continues to include **major international writers,** among them Salman Rushdie and Pico Iyer (India and England), Margaret Atwood (Canada), Virginia Woolf (England), Ryszard Kapuściński (Poland), Andrei Codrescu (Romania and the United States), Leo Tolstoy (Russia), Nelson Mandela (South Africa), Milan Kundera (the Czech Republic), and Ryunosuke Akutagawa (Japan).

More on Critical Reading and Persuasion

Chapters 8 and 9 in Part 4, "Reading Critically," present a substantive discussion of the various elements of **critical reading.** In these two chapters, students are taught how to dissect **arguments** in persuasive material representing the entire spectrum of political opinion—conservative, libertarian, liberal, and middle-of-the road. To cite two examples, students can analyze arguments presented by Secretary of Defense Donald Rumsfeld in his defense of the American invasion of Iraq and by the liberal analyst Lewis Lapham in his insistence that America's invasion of Iraq has compromised our nation's stature.

Other Helpful Features

- As in the sixth edition, each chapter begins with an explanation of the **chapter objectives** and a **list of topics** covered in the chapter. Important information and **key terms** throughout the text are boxed for convenient reference.
- An emphasis in the initial chapters on **annotation** shows students how reading with a pencil in one's hand promotes better comprehension, concentration, and retention.
- In Parts 1–3, **short practice exercises** interspersed throughout the text enable students to reinforce the particular skills under discussion. As before, each chapter in Parts 1–3 ends with three short exercises and a longer essay to analyze.
- The introduction to Part 5, "Reading Essays and Articles," now includes a discussion, new to this edition, of **how to paraphrase,** and, as before, an explanation of **how to write a summary.**
- Each of the book's nineteen essays ends with suggestions for further exploration: Features called **"In the Bookstore," "At the Movies,"** or **"On the Web"** point students to relevant books, films, and Web sites thematically connected to the reading, also giving students an opportunity to do simple research tasks related to the reading.
- **Links to the Online Learning Center** appear throughout the text, pointing students to supplementary exercises on the Web site accompanying the text.

ANCILLARY MATERIALS

Supplements
for Instructors

- **Online Learning Center <www.mhhe.com/spears>.** Instructors can find a variety of tests to accompany the text on a password-protected area of the text's Web site. Class-tested sets of exams are available for Chapters 1–2; Chapters 1–5 (midterm); Chapters 6–7; Chapters 8–9; and final examinations. (Click on the book's cover to reach the site.)

- **Computerized Testbank for Developmental Reading (0-07-322267-4).** This free CD-ROM offers instructors hundreds of questions with which to compose tests and quizzes on all the key reading skills.

- **Partners in Teaching Listserv.** From current theory to time-tested classroom tips, this free (and commercial-free) listserv offers insight and support to teachers of developmental English from some of the most experienced voices in the field. To join, send an e-mail message with your name and e-mail address to english@mcgraw-hill.com.

Supplements
for Students

- **Online Learning Center <www.mhhe.com/spears>.** Students will find an extensive array of practice exercises accompanying each chapter of the text's Online Learning Center. (Click on the book's cover to reach the site.)

- *Passport to College Reading* (0-07-310056-0). *Passport to College Reading* is an exciting, new online learning tool designed to support and reinforce key reading skills covered in *Developing Critical Reading Skills* and McGraw-Hill's other best-selling reading textbooks.

- **The McGraw-Hill Textbook Reader** (0-256-88335-1). This free print supplement offers five complete chapters from best-selling McGraw-Hill textbooks, accompanied by questions for reading comprehension, critical thinking, journal writing, and group work.

- **Low-Cost Reference Works.** These Merriam-Webster and Random House reference works are available at low cost when ordered with *Developing Critical Reading Skills*:

  - *Merriam-Webster's Notebook Dictionary.* A compact word resource conveniently designed for three-ring binders, *Merriam-Webster's Notebook Dictionary* includes 40,000 entries for widely used words with concise, easy-to-understand definitions and pronunciations.

  - *The Merriam-Webster Dictionary.* This handy, paperback dictionary contains over 70,000 definitions yet is small enough to carry around in a backpack, so it's always there when it's needed.

  - *Random House Webster's College Dictionary.* This authoritative dictionary includes over 160,000 entries and 175,000 definitions—more than any other college dictionary—and the most commonly used definitions are always listed first, so students can find what they need quickly.

- *Merriam-Webster's Collegiate Dictionary & Thesaurus* **CD-ROM.** This up-to-the-minute electronic dictionary and the-saurus offers 225,000 definitions, 340,000 synonyms and related words, and 1,300 illustrations.
- *Merriam-Webster's Notebook Thesaurus.* Conveniently designed for three-ring binders, *Merriam-Webster's Notebook Thesaurus* provides concise, clear guidance for over 157,000 word choices.
- *Merriam-Webster Thesaurus.* This compact thesaurus offers over 157,000 word choices, and includes concise definitions and examples to help students choose the correct word for the context.
- *Merriam-Webster's Vocabulary Builder.* *Merriam-Webster's Vocabulary Builder* focuses on more than 1,000 words, introduces nearly 2,000 more, and includes quizzes to test the student's progress.
- **Novel Ideas.** These Random House and HarperCollins paperbacks are available at a low cost when packaged with the text:

  Reading Lolita in Teheran (Nafasi); *Waiting* (Ha Jin); *Like Water for Chocolate* (Esquivel); *Beloved* (T. Morrison); *I Know Why the Caged Bird Sings* (Angelou); *Maus,* Vol. 1 (Art Spiegelman); *Things Fall Apart* (Achebe); *The Lone Ranger and Tonto* (Alexie); *Integrity* (Carter); *The House on Mango Street* (Cisneros); *Pilgrim at Tinker Creek* (Dillard); *Love Medicine* (Erdrich); *Their Eyes Were Watching God* (Hurston); *Boys of Summer* (Kahn); *Woman Warrior* (Kingston); *Clear Springs* (Mason); *House Made of Dawn* (Momaday); *Joy Luck Club* (Tan).

For more information or to request copies of any of the above supplementary materials for instructor review, please contact your local McGraw-Hill representative at 1 (800) 338-3987 or send an e-mail message to english@mcgraw-hill.com.

■ ACKNOWLEDGMENTS

No textbook can be created without the assistance of many people. First, I am grateful to the many teachers across the country who read the manuscript for this edition carefully and made many judicious recommendations:

Jesús Adame, El Paso Community College
John Bagnole, Ohio University

Nellie Boyd, Texas Southern University
Flora Brown, Fullerton College
Denise Chambers, Normandale Community College
Robin Clamme, Ivy Tech State College
Peggy Cole, Arapahoe Community College
Janice Hill-Matula, Moraine Valley Community College
Marcy Lee, Mt. Hood Community College
Bonita Miller, Spring Arbor University
Julia Morrissey, Kennesaw State University
Robert Reising, University of North Carolina at Pembroke
Tommy Tyson, Forsyth Tech Community College
Gene Voss, Houston Community College—Central

I am also grateful for the generous help I received from my colleagues at City College of San Francisco who have used the text: Carol Fregly, Pamela Gentile, Michael Hulbert, Elizabeth King, Tore Langmo, Robert Stamps (emeritus), Joan Wilson, Rosalie Wolf (emeritus), and Gloria Yee.

Jill Ramsay continues to ensure the book's accuracy on Canadian matters. My husband's friend, Mac Swanton of El Granada, California, made suggestions derived from his encyclopedic knowledge of film and of political Web sites. And the following people recommended exciting new writers to explore: My daughter, Charlotte Milan, of San Francisco; Naomi Mann, Julia Hansen, and Marlene Mann also of San Francisco; Monilou Carter, of Half Moon Bay, California; Geri McCauley, of Sebastopol, California; and Jennifer Ruddy, of Rockport, Maine.

Warmest thanks to Alexis Walker, my editor at McGraw-Hill, for her abiding encouragement and enthusiasm; to Jane Carter, senior developmental editor, for her many excellent suggestions for ways to improve and reorganize some of the material and for her ability to deal with seemingly dozens of little questions; and to Jesse Hassenger, for his expertise and careful eye regarding Web material. And finally, special thanks to my husband, David, for his boundless good humor and kindness.

Instructors who have comments, suggestions, or questions are invited to contact me via e-mail. The address is *dkspears@comcast.net* or *dkspears@ccsf.edu*. I will do my best to answer within a day or two of receiving messages.

Deanne Spears
City College of San Francisco
San Francisco, California

TO THE STUDENT

A few years ago I was shopping with the man who is now my husband and his 12-year-old daughter in downtown San Francisco. A street musician, whom my husband was acquainted with from his own experience as a musician, was playing the tenor saxophone on a street corner. His name is Clifford, and he had attracted a crowd with his wonderful performance. After he finished, my husband introduced him to me and to Sarah, his daughter. Clifford asked Sarah if she played an instrument, and when she replied that she was taking trumpet lessons and played in her junior high school band, he said, "That's fine, little lady. Learn your instrument well and you can play anything."

Somehow these simple and wise words struck me as fitting not only for an aspiring trumpet player but also for a reader. When you learn to read well, you can read anything you want—not just the daily newspapers and mass circulation magazines, but more difficult reading, such as philosophy, anthropology, film criticism, particle physics, military history—whatever interests you. Your choice of reading would not be limited in any way. Assuming you had the vocabulary—or at least a good dictionary at your side—you could pick up a book or article, concentrate on it, and make sense of the writer's words.

Reading involves more than merely decoding print. It requires internal translation. In other words, you internalize the writer's words so that you take them in, not only to understand their surface meaning but also to understand what they suggest beyond that. Rather than reading passively, sitting back and letting the writer do all the work, in this course you will learn to interact with the text. You will learn to read with a pencil in your hand. When you read, you enter into a peculiar relationship with the writer, a two-way process of communication. Although the writer is physically absent, the words on the page are nonetheless there to be analyzed, interpreted, questioned, perhaps even challenged. In this way, the active reader engages in a kind of silent dialogue with the writer.

Reading instruction in American schools often ends at elementary school, and students may have difficulty as they progress to higher grades. The reading material becomes harder, yet they still must tackle their assignments armed with elementary school reading skills. The result, too often, is frustration and loss of confidence. And the assigned reading in your college courses will be even more demanding than the readings were in high school—both in complexity of content and style and in the amount of reading assigned. *Developing Critical Reading Skills* is designed to accomplish several tasks: to teach you the skills that will enable you to read with greater comprehension and retention, to help you undertake reading assignments with confidence, and to show you how to become an active, fluent reader.

This is the Seventh Edition of *Developing Critical Reading Skills*. With each edition and with each class, I have learned a great deal. You will be the recipient of the many excellent suggestions, which, along with various reviewers' and colleagues' remarks, I have incorporated. You should take some time to look through the table of contents to become familiar with the book's layout and scope. You will begin with basic comprehension skills and gradually move toward the more difficult skills associated with critical reading. In this edition, the readings now more closely duplicate the breadth of reading you do in every part of your daily life, including material from textbooks, newspaper articles and editorials, magazine articles and essays, and of course, both fiction and nonfiction whole works. Also in this edition, I have included visual elements—charts, graphs, cartoons (both humorous and political), photographs, and magazine advertisements—along with a discussion of how to "read" visual elements and, more important, how to evaluate them critically.

As you glance through Parts 1, 2, and 3, you will see that these seven chapters treat the paragraph extensively, including explanations, illustrative passages, and exercises. At first it may seem odd—and perhaps artificial—to devote so much time to single paragraphs that, after all, are seldom read in isolation. Yet my students have found that concentrating on short passages early in the course promotes careful reading.

The paragraph is the basic unit of writing and, in fact, is often referred to as the primary building block of the essay. Studying paragraph structure closely and examining short passages for placement of main idea, methods of development, patterns of organization, inferences, language (especially connotation and figurative language), and tone will teach you how to analyze effectively on a small scale. Certainly it is less intimidating to practice with a hundred-word paragraph than with a five-page essay. Once you become proficient with paragraphs, you will then know how to apply the same analytical skills to longer works.

Specifically, you will learn to identify the main idea and, more important, to put it into your own words; to see relationships between ideas; to determine the writer's tone and purpose; to make accurate inferences; to identify the argument in persuasive prose; to weigh evidence; and to detect bias, unstated assumptions, false appeals, logical fallacies, and distortions.

Much emphasis has been placed on increasing reading speed, on skimming and scanning, on zipping through material simply to get the gist of what the writer is saying. These techniques have their place: A football fan skims through the sports pages to find out if the Green Bay

Packers beat their archrival, an employee scans the help wanted columns to look for a new job, and a student who looks through the electronic card catalog for likely research sources. But skimming is inappropriate for the major part of the reading you will have to do in college. For this reason, *Developing Critical Reading Skills* does not include a discussion of speed-reading techniques.

During the course, as you sharpen your skills, your work should have two results. The first will be an improvement in your own writing. Good reading skills and good writing skills are most certainly interrelated. When you understand how professional writers organize, develop, and support their ideas, you will become more aware of how to deal with your own writing assignments. But more important, you will learn to be a better thinker as well. These skills will serve you well for the rest of your life.

On the Web site accompanying this text, you will find many ancillary exercises where you can get extra practice with the skills taken up in Chapters 1–10. Answers are also provided. The address is www.mhhe .com/spears. Click on the book's cover and then click on Student Resources. If you have comments, suggestions, or questions about the text, you can contact me either on the Web site or by e-mail at *dkspears@ comcast.net* or *dkspears@ccsf.edu*. I will do my best to answer within a day or two of receiving messages.

Deanne Spears

Introduction

The introducton to this book will help you improve your reading by providing:

- An overview of the text and the reading process

- Advice for improving your vocabulary

■ AN OVERVIEW OF THE TEXT AND THE READING PROCESS

Becoming a good reader, rather than merely a competent one, is crucial if you are to do well in your college courses. Students often find their first college academic experience bewildering: They may not know what their instructors expect of them, nor are they sure what to look for when they read or exactly how to proceed with reading assignments, which are more burdensome than those they encountered in high school. *Developing Critical Reading Skills* will help you with all of these matters. You will learn how to look critically and analytically at short passages, essays, and articles and how to discern the parts, the substance, the strengths, and the weaknesses of the writer's prose. As you work through this text, you will find your ability to comprehend difficult prose, your confidence, and most important, your enjoyment in the experience of reading improving. These are admittedly ambitious goals, requiring a closer look at how they can be accomplished.

Defining the Reading Process

The reading process begins with decoding words, that is, deciphering the letters that make up individual words. But reading is more than merely processing letters and sounds. The real meaning of a text lies in the relationship the words have with each other. Reading well requires us to recognize these relationships and to put together the meaning of the text. When you think about everything that goes on simultaneously in the human mind as one reads, the process not only defies easy explanation but also takes on almost magical qualities. Isolating the steps makes the process seem mechanical or reducible to a formula. But nothing about reading is mechanical or formulaic.

In this passage from his book on the modern media, *Amusing Ourselves to Death*, Neil Postman sums up the problems reading poses for the reader:

> [A language-centered discourse] is serious because meaning demands to be understood. A written sentence calls upon its author to say something, upon its reader to know the import of what is said. And when an author and reader are struggling with semantic meaning, they are engaged in the most serious challenge to the intellect. This is especially the case with the act of reading, for authors are not always trustworthy. They lie, they become confused, they over-generalize, they abuse logic and, sometimes, common sense. The reader must come armed, in a serious state of intellectual readiness. This is not easy because he comes to the text alone. In reading, one's responses are isolated, one's intellect thrown back on its own resources. To be confronted by the cold abstractions of printed sentences is to look upon the language bare, without the assistance of either beauty or community. Thus, reading is by its nature a serious business. It is also, of course, an essentially rational activity.

Beyond Decoding—the Requirements of Reading

Reading involves—far beyond decoding the words and knowing their meanings in context—paying attention to these and other elements simultaneously. By working your way through the text, you will learn the following skills:

- Identifying the main idea, the focus or controlling idea, and the writer's purpose (Chapter 1).
- Discerning the relative importance of supporting ideas (major and minor support) as they relate to the main idea (Chapter 1).
- Making accurate inferences, reading between the lines, and identifying what the writer does not explicitly say but surely suggests (Chapter 2).

- Identifying the methods of development, the logical connections between the parts of an essay, and the arrangement of ideas the writer imposes on the subject (Chapters 3, 4, and 5).
- Understanding the denotative and connotative values of words and perceiving instances where language is deliberately misused (Chapter 6).
- Learning how to analyze figurative language like metaphors and similes (Chapter 6).
- Perceiving the writer's point of view and tone, or emotional feeling (Chapter 7).
- Recognizing strategies—both fair and unfair ones—in argumentative and persuasive writing; learning not to believe everything you read just because someone published it or put up a Web site (Chapters 8, 9, and 10).
- Learning to evaluate World Wide Web sites (Chapter 10).

Becoming a First-Rate Reader

The reading process is quite different from watching television, where the images wash over us as we sit like passive automatons. (Note that the pejorative phrase *couch potatoes* applies only to TV watchers, never to readers!) The good reader is engaged with the text and participates fully in the world the writer recreates on the page. However—and this is the magical part—the good reader is unaware of these elements as she reads. They occur involuntarily and effortlessly, the sweep and flow of the words transporting her along and down the page.

Each semester I begin the course by asking students to evaluate their past experiences with reading. We try to determine what makes some readers really good and others merely adequate—decoders of print but not much else. The session helps them focus on what they need to do in the course (as well as over the course of their lives) to become the very best readers they can. Students often write or e-mail me after they have transferred to a four-year university like San Jose State University or UC Davis, typically saying that they are stunned by the amount of reading they are expected to do in their upper-division courses. They report that some courses require them to read as many as 8 or 10 books over a semester. Clearly, unless you are exceptional, the skills that got you through high school won't be up to this job.

A careful reading of an essay assigned in your English class, for example, requires more than a single, cursory reading. Your reading time should be divided into three stages:

1. *Preparing to Read.* This preparatory step enables you to get an overview of the material assigned. Read any chapter objectives or preview questions, turn through the pages, noting the graphic design of the material; noting the appearance of primary and secondary headings (these will be explained later in this introduction); and noting any discussion, review, or study questions at the end.

2. *The First Reading.* Read through the assignment once without stopping. Be sure to keep a pencil in your hand and quickly underline

any unfamiliar words (these you will look up later), and put a question mark next to any passages that are unclear.

3. *The Second Reading.* In this reading, you will not only read the material through again, this time more carefully, but you will also see connections between the various parts, question the writer, look for larger implications, and anticipate discussion or test questions.

The Characteristics of Good Readers

College reading instructors might list these habits as characteristic of good readers:

Good readers:

- Preview the assignment to get an overview of its content (not just to count the pages or look at the pictures).
- Start reading assignments early enough to complete them thoroughly (not at 10 p.m. the night before or on the morning bus ride to campus).
- Underline or circle vocabulary words to look up, and then look them up, in the second go-around (first reading).
- Become actively involved with the text; they read with a pencil in their hands, annotating main points and writing questions marks next to puzzling material (second reading).
- Identify relationships between ideas and examine how the parts of an essay fit together (second reading).
- Question the writer and look beneath the surface for implications (second reading).
- Anticipate questions for quizzes, discussion, or in-class writing assignments (second reading).
- Maintain focus and block out distractions as much as is humanly possible.
- Consider each reading assignment as a challenge and as a way to learn, even if the subject matter is not particularly interesting, and not as an unpleasant task to be put off until the very last minute.

If you have not yet developed these habits or if they sound too daunting and formidable, keep in mind that you will not have to learn everything at once. You will undertake each element singly, with lots of opportunities for practice. And unlike the lonely reader mentioned in Neil Postman's excerpt, you will have the guidance of your instructor to help you through the rough patches. In the meantime, get as much practice as you can outside of class. Most reading teachers recommend that students try to fit in at least an hour per day of reading on their own—not required assignments for your classes but reading for pleasure.

An even more compelling reason to read a lot derives from the results of a recent study done by Dr. Robert Friedland, a professor of neurology at Case Western Reserve University School of Medicine and published in the *Proceedings of the National Academy of Sciences*. Friedland found that "adults with hobbies that exercise their brains—such as reading, jigsaw puzzles, or chess—are 2½ times less likely to develop Alzheimer's, while leisure limited to TV watching may increase the risk."[1]

Types of Texts You Will Read in College

If you are just beginning your college career, you may be unaccustomed to the many types of texts and reading assignments college classes require. Typically, college students aren't assigned just a single textbook, which serves as a sort of academic bible for the semester or quarter. While you will undoubtedly be asked to study from a standard textbook in most of your courses, you may also be asked to complete other types of assignments. For example, your instructor may put together a course reader, a collection of pertinent readings duplicated inexpensively that complement the course material. You may be asked to read articles in magazines or periodicals that the instructor has put on reserve in the library.

In your English and humanities classes, you will surely be asked to read fiction, both novels and short stories, and perhaps poetry. In your introductory composition courses, you will be assigned nonfiction prose—articles and essays by writers who are generally considered masters, whether for their observations and perceptions of the human condition or world affairs, the clarity of their expression, or their use of various rhetorical devices. For all of these types of reading assignments, *Developing Critical Reading Skills* will help you develop the skills you need to navigate them. Working through this text and faithfully completing the exercises will teach you the skills you need to read any texts.

How to Read This Textbook (and Other Textbooks)

In this edition, a short section on how to read textbooks (Part 6, "Reading and Studying Textbook Material," pp. 482–504) is included. But consider that *Developing Critical Reading Skills* is itself a textbook, and like all textbooks, it reflects features common to the genre. As you should with any other textbook, take a few minutes to become familiar with the features and structure of *Developing Critical Reading Skills*. Unlike essays and articles, which usually consist only of straight, unembellished text, textbooks (like this one) provide considerable help for students. A textbook chapter typically includes chapter objectives to give you something to guide your reading; various types of headings to indicate the relative importance of the various types of material; tables, boxes, and charts to provide data succinctly; often photographs or drawings to reinforce ideas or provide visual examples; self-quizzes and study or review questions to aid in review and mastery—all in addition to the text.

[1]Paul Recer, "Brain Teasers May Delay Alzheimer's," Associated Press, March 6, 2001. The abstract of this study is worth reading. You can access it from the homepage of the Proceedings of the National Academy of Sciences. Go to www.pnas.org. Click on "Archives," and then locate March 6, 2001. Scroll down the alphabetical list to Robert Friedland.

Let us consider this matter of headings. Look at the first two pages of this introduction, which appear below in reduced form:

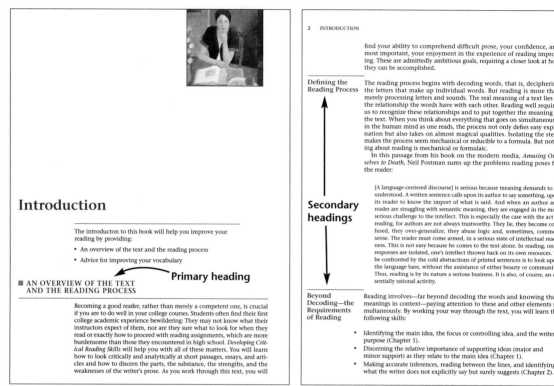

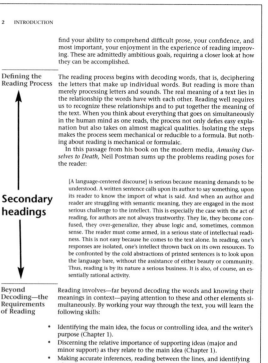

Primary heading

The first, primary-level heading is set in all capital letters. The secondary headings look different: They're printed in boldfaced, lower-case letters, instead. These graphic distinctions organize the material around key points and enable you to see the relative importance of each section.

To practice previewing this textbook, answer the following questions, which will require you both to examine the table of contents on pages vii–xii and to look at specific sections within the text.

1. How many parts does the book contain? <u>seven parts</u>
2. How many chapters are there in Part 1? What are their titles?

    <u>two chapters: Chapter 1 is titled Reading for the Main Idea and</u>

    <u>the Author's Purpose; Chapter 2 is titled Reading Between the</u>

    <u>Lines: Making Accurate Inferences.</u>
3. Open the text to the first page of any chapter in Parts 1, 2, or 3. What comes at the very beginning? <u>a list of chapter objectives</u>

4. What type of material comes at the end of Chapters 1 through 7?

    <u>chapter exercises, a practice essay, and information on relevant</u>

    <u>books, movies, or Web sites</u>

5. Look again at the table of contents. In which chapter will you learn about evaluating Web sites? <u>Chapter 10, Evaluating Web</u>

    <u>Sites</u>

6. Look at the first essay in Part 5, "An Ethnic Trump" by Gish Jen on page 399. What information is provided before the essay begins?

    <u>There is a biographical headnote, a small thumbnail photo of the</u>

    <u>writer, and preview questions to think about before you read.</u>

7. Notice that the pages are perforated. What might be the reason for this design feature? <u>Perforated pages enable students to remove</u>

    <u>pages neatly from the text if the instructor requires them to</u>

    <u>submit homework.</u>

If you have another textbook for a class, examine its table of contents, graphic elements, and organization in the same way that you did for this textbook.

To read this textbook and to gain maximum benefit from it, look over each chapter before beginning to read it, and study the chapter objectives, which give you an overview of the various topics that are taken up. *Most important,* study the explanatory section in relation to each illustrative passage. Be sure you understand how the illustrative passage relates to the explanation, and if you are unsure, ask your instructor for clarification.

Reading with a Pencil

Let us illustrate the first skill mentioned earlier: annotating a text. If you have trouble concentrating or are easily distracted by the passing world around you, reading with a pencil in your hand will go a long way toward helping you comprehend better, maintain focus, and stay on track. Annotating means making brief marginal notations, specifically, writing questions to raise in class, underlining important points, and circling words to look up.

Reprinted here is a short excerpt from a book that caused a stir in zoological circles and in the popular press when it was published in 1995. The thesis of *When Elephants Weep* by Jeffrey Masson and Susan McCarthy is that animals feel emotions and that we can observe these feelings. (Hard scientists usually reject human attempts to interpret animal behavior in anthropomorphic terms.) The chapter from which the excerpt is taken is entitled "Grief, Sadness, and the Bones of Elephants," which is a fair indication of its contents; the subsection is called "Imprisonment."

Captive animals are sad

[1]Even when captive animals are not confined in solitude, their imprisonment may make them sad. It is often said of zoo animals that the way to tell if they are happy is to ask whether the young play and the adults breed. Most zookeepers would not accept this standard of happiness for themselves. As Jane Goodall noted, "Even in concentration camps, babies were born, and there is no good reason to believe that it is different for chimpanzees."

Goodall—chimps breed in captivity?

[2]Captivity is undoubtedly more painful to some animals than others. Lions seem to have less difficulty with the notion of lying in the sun all day than do tigers, for example. Yet even lions can be seen in many zoos pacing restlessly back and forth in the stereotyped motions seen in so many captive animals. The concept of *funktionslust,* the enjoyment of one's abilities, also suggests its opposite, the feeling of frustration and misery that overtakes an animal when its capacities cannot be expressed. If an animal enjoys using its natural abilities, it is also possible that the animal *misses* using them. Although a gradual trend in zoo construction and design is to make the cages better resemble the natural habitat, most zoo animals, particularly the large ones, have little or no opportunity to use their abilities. Eagles have no room to fly, cheetahs have no room to run, goats have but a single boulder to climb.

Animals suffer b/c can't do natural activities, even in good zoos

"Possible" suggests speculation, not fact

[3]There is no reason to suppose that zoo life is not a source of sadness to most animals imprisoned there, like displaced persons in wartime. It would be comforting to believe that they are happy there, delighted to receive medical care and grateful to be sure of their next meal. Unfortunately, in the main, there is no evidence to suppose that they are. Most take every possible opportunity to escape. Most will not breed. Probably they want to go home. Some captive animals die of grief when taken from the wild. Sometimes these deaths appear to be from disease, perhaps because an animal under great stress becomes vulnerable to illness. Others are quite obviously deaths from despair— near-suicides. Wild animals may refuse to eat, killing themselves in the only way open to them. We do not know if they are aware that they will die if they do not eat, but it is clear that they are extremely

Most likely sad, not grateful for good care

Can't move naturally, esp. hard on large species

Negative side effects—no breeding, stress causes illness or death; may starve on purpose

Note other "hedge" words ("probably")

Gorilla in 1913 died of "broken heart"

unhappy. In 1913 Jasper Von Oertzen described the death of a young gorilla imported to Europe: "Hum-Hum had lost all joy in living. She succeeded in living to reach Hamburg, and from there, the Animal Park at Stellingen, with all her caretakers, but her energy did not return again. With signs of the greatest sadness of soul Hum-Hum mourned over the happy past. One could find no fatal illness; it was as always with these costly animals: 'She died of a broken heart.'"

1913? Why no recent ex?

Note obvious anthropomorphic slant

Marine mammals in captivity—high death rate; not enough room to roam

[4]Marine mammals have a high death rate in captivity, a fact not always apparent to visitors at marine parks and oceanariums. A pilot whale celebrity at one oceanarium was actually thirteen different pilot whales, each successive one being introduced to visitors by the same name, as if it were the same animal. It takes little reflection to see the great difference in a marine mammal's life when kept in an oceanarium. Orcas grow to twenty-three feet long, weigh up to 9,000 pounds, and roam a hundred miles a day. No cage, and certainly not the swimming pools where they are confined in all oceanariums, could possibly provide satisfaction, let alone joy. They are believed to have a life expectancy as long as our own. Yet at Sea World, in San Diego, the oceanarium with the best track record for keeping orcas alive, they last an average of eleven years.

What is life span for orcas in wild?

[5]If a person's life span were shortened this much, would one still speak of happiness? Asked whether their animals were happy, a number of marine mammal trainers all said yes: they ate, engaged in sexual intercourse (it is extremely rare for an orca to give birth in captivity), and were almost never sick. This would mean that they were not depressed, but does it mean they were happy? The fact that people ask this question again and again indicates a (malaise) perhaps profound guilt at subjecting these lively sea travelers to unnatural confinement.

Would we want this for ourselves? No!

Jeffrey Masson and Susan McCarthy,
When Elephants Weep

Three words in this excerpt might be unfamiliar to you: *"funktionslust"* in paragraph 2; "vulnerable" in paragraph 3; and "malaise" in paragraph 5. Notice that the German word *funktionslust* is defined by the phrase that follows it: "the enjoyment of one's abilities."

Similarly, the meaning of *vulnerable* should be evident from the context. Of these four dictionary definitions, which best fits the way the writers use the word?

1. _____ capable of or susceptible to being wounded or hurt physically or emotionally.
2. _____ susceptible to temptation or corrupt influence.
3. _____ open to or defenseless against criticism or moral attack.
4. _____ open to assault; difficult to defend.

For this context, the best answer is number 1.

The dictionary lists two definitions for *malaise*. Again, in context, which of the two definitions seems to fit? (Remember that the writers are discussing *human,* not animal, reactions to keeping marine mammals in captivity.)

1. _____ a vague feeling of bodily discomfort, as at the beginning of an illness.
2. _____ a general sense of depression or unease.

The better choice seems to be number 2.

Now, list two or three questions that occurred to you as you read the excerpt.

_____

_____

_____

Here are a few that occurred to me, along with some tentative answers:

1. *Have the writers proved their point that captive animals are sad? What evidence is offered? Is it sufficient, relevant, and up-to-date?* Certainly, some of the behaviors exhibited by zoo animals (pacing, repetitive actions, infrequent breeding) suggest unhappiness and stress. The fact that zoos often resort to artificial insemination to breed their captives adds credence to the writers' observation, though they do not mention this. The discussion in paragraph 2 is more speculative or theoretical, and the authors admit as much by using the "hedge" word *possible* in explaining that an animal misses using its natural abilities.
2. *Why haven't the writers used a more current example of an animal's having "died of a broken heart" than that of the gorilla observed in 1913, nearly a century ago?* This question is unanswerable but still justified. Does the use of this example suggest that the writers couldn't locate one more recent than almost nine decades old? Also, the phrase "to die of a broken heart" is anthropomorphic; while we can surely

identify with the emotion, the diagnosis is emotional, not scientific. Additionally, one's interpretation of this passage depends a great deal on one's worldview. Readers who avoid zoos because the sight of caged animals depresses them would probably be more likely to accept Masson and McCarthy's observations than would readers who think zoos are important educational institutions.

3. *The writers suggest that zookeepers would not accept for themselves the level of happiness afforded captive animals. Does the Jane Goodall quotation at the end of paragraph 1 support this contention?* Since no one is proposing that zookeepers be "confined in solitude" as zoo animals are, the statement about an unacceptable level of happiness is moot. Goodall's quotation is more puzzling, however. If babies were born in concentration camps—to prisoners who lived in unspeakable conditions—isn't that an indication of rising above one's misery rather than giving in to it? If Goodall's remark is supposed to reinforce the idea that chimpanzees can breed in captivity, then Masson and McCarthy contradict themselves in paragraph 3 when they write that most captive animals "will not breed."

4. *Is the evidence based on fact or on speculation, or is it a combination of both?* Notice that most evidence is general rather than specific: "Eagles have no room to fly, cheetahs have no room to run"; "Most take every possible opportunity to escape"; and so on. The writers cite only one example of a specific animal at a specific zoo. I noted the adjective *possible* in paragraph 2; paragraph 3 uses similar words, suggesting that these remarks are theoretical: "*Probably* they want to go home"; "these deaths *appear* to be from disease"; "Wild animals *may* refuse to eat," and so forth. These words suggest that the writers are trying to protect themselves from attack.

Despite the flaws and the absence of hard scientific research, the discussion is nonetheless compelling because Masson and McCarthy make us feel empathy. If we would not like to live in such conditions, as they say, why do we suppose that animals would?

This exercise illustrates the analytic method of reading undertaken in this textbook. As you work through it, you will be asked to read passages, longer ones than this, using these techniques. But critical analysis and questioning on this level are possible only as a result of careful reading and annotation. Skimming through a passage quickly will enable you to get its drift but not to have full understanding.

■ IMPROVING YOUR VOCABULARY

A good vocabulary is probably the single most important prerequisite for good reading. Every other skill—comprehension, retaining information, making inferences, drawing appropriate conclusions, evaluating—

depends on whether you know what the words on the page mean in relation to each other and in their context. After all, if you don't know what the words on the page mean, you cannot know what you are reading. Sometimes it is possible to wing it, getting the general idea without having a complete understanding. Most often, however, and especially with the analytical reading you will do in this course, your understanding of a passage may hinge solely on the meaning of a single word, a situation where guessing is hazardous.

E. D. Hirsch, a professor of education and humanities at the University of Virginia, offers these remarks on vocabulary and its relationship to reading comprehension:

> Vocabulary experts agree that adequate reading comprehension depends on a person already knowing between 90 and 95 percent of the words in a text. Knowing that percentage of words allows the reader to get the main thrust of what is being said and therefore to guess correctly what the unfamiliar words probably mean. (This inferential process is of course how we pick up oral language in early childhood and it sustains our vocabulary growth throughout our lives.)[2]

One of my colleagues characterizes the problem of not looking up important words in a reading selection as the "swiss-cheese" approach to reading—as if the text has holes scattered through it, like the holes in a slice of swiss cheese.

Clearly, then, ignoring new words in your reading assignments, hoping that they don't really matter, or assuming you know what a word means when you really don't may impair your comprehension. An incident that occurred in one of my classes illustrates these risks. The class had been discussing a *New York Times* editorial written by an Orthodox Jewish student at Yale University. The writer was defending a lawsuit he had filed against the university; his argument was that Yale should exempt him and some other Orthodox Jewish students from the requirement that freshmen and sophomores live in dormitories. He and his fellow students had objected to the permissive sexual environment of the dorms. In one sentence the student quotes the president of Yale, who states that the university is proud of not having any "parietal rules." When I asked the students in the class what *parietal* means, one young man responded that it meant that Yale didn't have any rules such as parents might make.

Despite their similar appearance, *parietal* and *parental* have nothing to do with each other. *The American Heritage Dictionary* defines parietal

---

[2]E. D. Hirsch, Jr., "Reading Comprehension Requires Knowledge—of Words and the World," *American Educator,* Spring 2003. The entire article is available at www.aft.org. Click on "Publications," then on "American Educator," and then on "Previous Issues." Scroll down to Spring 2003. The issue is devoted to articles on reading comprehension and vocabulary acquisition.

rules as those "governing the visiting privileges of members of the opposite sex in college or university dormitories." In other words, Yale has *no rules* governing its students' sexual conduct or visiting privileges. The student's inaccurate guess resulted in his misconstruing Yale's position and misinterpreting part of the editorial.

In the real world, failing to check the meaning of words in the dictionary may have serious financial repercussions. In 1997, Reebok, the athletic shoe manufacturing company, had to discard 53,000 pairs of a new line of women's running shoes called "Incubus." Although the shoes had been on the market for a year with no customer complaints, ABC, upon learning about the name of the shoe line, put the story on the evening news. It seems that no one at the company had bothered to check in the dictionary to see that an incubus is a male demon who comes to a woman and makes love to her while she sleeps. Reebok suffered a corporate red face and lost a lot of money.

Vocabulary in Perspective

The process of acquiring vocabulary is a lifelong pursuit, and it is both naive and unrealistic to think that a single course in reading or in English can remedy your vocabulary weaknesses. At first, learning dozens of new words may seem like a discouraging, perhaps an even overwhelming, prospect, but it *is* possible. Everyone has to start somewhere, and even the best reader comes across words in his or her daily reading that require looking up. (The fourth edition of *The American Heritage Dictionary* lists 350,000 words, 16,000 of them new.)

To see the dimensions of acquiring an adult-level vocabulary, consider the findings of Richard C. Anderson and William E. Nagy, authorities in reading and educational theory. They estimate that there are approximately 88,000 words in what they call "school English" (compiled from 1,000 items of reading materials from elementary through high school). When they added proper nouns, compound words, multiple meanings of homonyms (words that sound alike but that have different spellings and meanings), and idioms, they estimated that "there may be 180,000 distinct vocabulary items in school English and that an average high school senior may know eight thousand of them."[3] The sheer number of words in the language partly explains why acquiring a good vocabulary takes so long. Obviously, a college student is expected to know even more than the numbers of words that Anderson and Nagy cite, since college reading assignments are more difficult than those in high school. Many studies point to American students' diminished vocabulary, demonstrating the importance of getting your level up to par at the beginning of your college career.[4]

---

[3]Richard C. Anderson and William E. Nagy, "The Vocabulary Conundrum," *American Educator,* Winter 1992.
[4]From *Harper's* Index for August 2000: "Average number of words in the written vocabulary of a 6- to 14-year-old American child in 1945: 25,000. Average number today: 10,000." The source for these sobering statistics is Gary Ingersoll of Indiana University.

Daily Reading and Vocabulary Improvement

An exhaustive treatment of vocabulary acquisition is not within the scope of this book, and many excellent vocabulary guides are available. Simply memorizing lists of words in isolation is tempting but inefficient; you simply won't remember many of them. The very best way to learn new words is to read as much as you have time for. Certainly, the reading you will do in this book will expose you to hundreds of college-level vocabulary words. Most of the words you recognize in your reading you know because of prior exposure. New words are best learned—and retained—when you encounter them in your reading. Reading for pleasure an hour a day—or if that is not possible, a half hour a day—will pay big dividends.

As a personal sidenote, I can attest to the benefits of daily reading as an aid to building vocabulary. For the past year and a half, I have been taking intensive Italian courses. Someone once observed that picking up a new language as an adult is as simple as picking up a truck—an apt metaphor, to be sure. Yet I have found that reading little short stories or articles online from one of the major Italian newspapers—for an hour a day or even for just a half an hour a day—along with looking up most of the unfamiliar words and writing them in a notebook have paid off handsomely. In Italian, there is a phrase, *piano piano,* meaning "slowly, slowly": Acquiring new reading vocabulary occurs little by little. The process can't be rushed, and though the progress one makes in a single day may not seem very significant, over a period of weeks or months, the gains add up, and eventually the results become apparent.

Suggestions for Vocabulary Improvement

My students have benefited from implementing these ideas:

- *Invest in a new hardback dictionary.*   If you do not have an unabridged dictionary published recently, buy one. It will be money well spent. A new dictionary will last well beyond your college years. Some good dictionaries are listed in the next section (see p. 16).

- *Develop an interest in words and their origins.*   When you look up a new word in an unabridged dictionary, look at its **etymology,** or history; many English words have unusual origins. The etymology of a word is usually printed in brackets following the definitions; it explains and traces the derivation of the word and gives the original meaning in the language or languages the word is derived from.

  For instance, one dictionary traces the history of the word *villain* like this: [Middle English *vilein,* feudal serf, person of coarse feelings, from Old French, from Vulgar Latin *villanus,* feudal serf, from Latin *villa,* country house]. You can easily see how far this word, now denoting a bad guy, has deviated from its earlier meanings.

  Here is another example. The word *curfew* comes from medieval French. Because most houses in France during the medieval period were made of wood and had thatched roofs, the danger of fire was always great, particularly at night. Every evening residents had to put out their candles when a bell was rung, signaling the order "cover fire." The French word *couvrefeu,* meaning "cover fire," brought to England by the Norman French conquerors, later evolved into today's word *curfew.*

- *Learn the most common prefixes and roots.* Approximately 60 percent of the words in English come from Latin and around 15 percent come from Greek. Therefore, learning Latin and Greek prefixes and roots can add to your vocabulary stock. For example, the Greek prefix *mono,* meaning "one" can be seen in *monogamy* (sexual relations with only one person at a time); *monotheism* (the belief in one god); *monocle* (a single-lens eyeglass); *monolingual* (speaking one language); and *monopoly* (control over producing and selling by one group). The Latin root *spirare,* meaning "to breathe," for example, gives us the English words *inspire, respiration, perspiration, conspiracy* (literally, to "breathe with"), *aspire,* and *expire.* A question on a recent *Jeopardy!* episode went something like this: "*Spiracles* are openings on butterflies that allow them to do this." The answer: "What is to breathe?" Even if you know nothing about the anatomy of a butterfly, knowing the Latin root gets you the right answer.

www. mhhe. com/ spears

For a comprehensive list of Latin and Greek prefixes and roots, click on the "Student Resources" button on the Web site.

- *Devise a system for learning important new words.* Some students like to write new words in a small notebook or on index cards. Some instructors recommend the three-dot method, which works like this: When you look up a new word in the dictionary, place a small dot with a pencil next to it. The next time you look it up, add a second dot. The third time, add a third dot and learn the meaning of the word.

- *Subscribe to one or more Word-of-the-Day Web sites.* These sites offer a painless, entertaining way to learn new words. Try two or three of those listed in the box on page 16 to see which you prefer. You can either visit the sites every day, or more conveniently, subscribe to their service, which sends the word of the day to your e-mail address. Most offer interesting, relatively challenging words; most include—besides the obvious definitions—the etymology and some illustrative sentences using the word. Some include hyperlinks taking you to other sites of interest relevant to the word of the day. All are free, though most do have banner ads. The box below lists a variety of sites and includes a representative word from each site.[5]

[5]As with all Web sites and URLs quoted in this text, I cannot guarantee that these sites will remain available or that the URL will remain the same for the life of this edition. If you can't find a site mentioned here, perform a search with your favorite search engine. (For more on searching the World Wide Web, see Chapter 10, pp. 366–380.)

Name of Site	World Wide Web URL	Sample Word
dictionary.com	dictionary.reference.com/wordoftheday/	apotheosis
Merriam-Webster's Word of the Day	www.m-w.com/cgi-bin/mwwod.pl	cajole
WordCommand's Word of the Day	www.wordcommand.com/ wordoftheday.htm	alacrity
Wordsmith.org	wordsmith.org/awad/index.html	zany

Using the Dictionary

Traditional (Print) Dictionaries

No electronic device, no matter how flashy, can surpass the convenience and the abundance of information in a good print dictionary. You should have two: an abridged (or shortened) paperback edition for class and an unabridged (complete) to use at home. Both should be up to date. (Using your father's tattered dictionary from the 1970s is a foolish economy; it will not reflect the wealth of new words that have entered the language even during the past decade.) Ask your instructor to recommend one, or choose one from this list. All are available in less expensive college editions.

- *The American Heritage Dictionary of the English Language*
- *The Random House Webster's College Dictionary*
- *Webster's New World Dictionary*
- *Webster's Collegiate Dictionary*

If you are unsure about how current your dictionary is, first see how many of these current words and phrases you know. Then check to see how many your dictionary contains.

sound bite	arm candy	pashmina
McMansion	fatwa	trophy wife
reverse mortgage	luminaria	fat farm
chick lit	bling bling	comb-over
blog	brewsky	identity theft
zine or 'zine	sweat equity	bum's rush

Online Dictionaries

The computer revolution has extended to the world of dictionaries. As I proofread this list in the spring of 2005, these are the best known currently available:

Merriam-Webster Online Dictionary   www.m-w.com/
The American Heritage Dictionary   www.bartleby.com/61/
  of the English Language
yourDictionary.com   www.yourdictionary.com
AllWords.com   www.allwords.com

Each site works a little differently, and it is worth spending time with each one to see which best suits your needs. Having surveyed these dictionaries and having put them through their paces with a few sample words and phrases, I see advantages and disadvantages to their use. These remarks also apply to electronic dictionaries, such as the various Franklin electronic spellers, which feature *Merriam-Webster's Collegiate Dictionary.*

Advantages of Online Dictionaries

- Entries are not cluttered with confusing symbols and multiple definitions.
- Some texts on Web sites have links to the *American Heritage* or *Merriam-Webster's* dictionaries, so that you can click on a word and be taken immediately to the online dictionary entry.
- Many offer other amenities, such as word games, word puzzles, and links to other sites for word lovers.
- The sites are free, though you should expect advertisements; registration is typically not required.

Disadvantages of Online Dictionaries

- Only the very most common senses are listed; therefore, if the word you are looking up is used in an unusual way, you may not find the definition you need.
- Obsolete and archaic forms may not be listed.
- Most do not offer variant forms (although American Heritage and Merriam-Webster's do). Are both *benefited* and *benefitted* correct?
- Most do not provide usage notes, although the *American Heritage* site does. For example, that site explains why using *debut* as a verb is not considered good usage as in, the movie debuted in July; YourDictionary.com alludes to a usage problem, but doesn't explain what it is.
- The etymology (or language of origin) is not always provided. If it is, usually only the source language is provided but not the original meaning or an analysis of the word parts.
- Searching for phrases produces unpredictable results. Try, for example, searching for the definitions for the phrases *trophy wife* and *catbird seat.*
- Unless you have a high-speed connection, access to Web sites can be slow.

- Looking up a word on your laptop (assuming you have one) isn't convenient while riding on the subway or waiting at a doctor's office. A paperback dictionary is more portable.
- Popup and banner ads are annoying and intrusive.
- During a blackout, you're out of luck!

It seems clear that online dictionaries have their uses, but to rely on one for all one's college work seems impractical.

Dictionary Features

The dictionary—the traditional print variety—can provide the curious reader with a wealth of information beyond listing spellings and definitions. We can only scratch the surface in this introduction, but it would be good idea to read through your dictionary's introductory pages and to become acquainted with its myriad features, particularly the way the dictionary arranges multiple definitions.

Order of Definitions

You may have been taught that the first definition is probably the one you want. This is bad advice, especially because some dictionaries organize their definitions historically rather than by frequency of meaning. In the *Random House Webster's College Dictionary* and *American Heritage Dictionary,* the most common meanings generally come before those that are encountered less frequently. However, the *Merriam-Webster's Collegiate Dictionary* and *Webster's New World Dictionary* typically order the senses historically.

Choosing the Right Definition

Students often complain, and with good reason, that the dictionary lists so many definitions, it's hard to figure out which is the best one. Unfortunately, there is no easy remedy for this complaint, but here are a few suggestions:

- Become familiar with the way your dictionary organizes its definitions.
- Study the context of the sentence or paragraph you are reading to see the word's part of speech and its likely meaning.
- Substitute the definition you chose in the sentence to see if it makes sense.
- If you are unsure about which definition works best, ask your instructor for help.
- Realize that sometimes a word may straddle two definitions.

Here are the opening sentences of Albert Camus's essay, "Reflections on the Guillotine." (This essay was so influential when it was published in 1960 that the French government was persuaded to ban capital punishment.)

> Shortly before the war of 1914, an assassin whose crime was particularly repulsive (he had slaughtered a family of farmers, including the children) was condemned to death in Algiers. He was a farm worker who had killed in a sort of bloodthirsty frenzy but had *aggravated* his case by robbing his victims. The affair created a great stir. It was generally thought that decapitation was too mild a punishment for such a monster.[6]

Which of these two dictionary definitions best suits the way Camus uses *aggravated*?

1. To make worse or more troublesome.
2. To rouse to exasperation or anger.

Only the first definition works because one can substitute it for the original word: had made his case worse, *not* had roused his case to exasperation or anger.

Even seemingly easy words can cause difficulty, as this example from Rosalie Pedalino Porter's book *Forked Tongue: The Politics of Bilingual Education* illustrates:

> My family was poor, so the first necessity was for us to gain the economic means to survive. We children did not *enjoy* the middle-class luxury of a choice of schooling or careers.

Which of these two definitions for *enjoy* from the *American Heritage Dictionary* is right for this context?

1. To receive pleasure or satisfaction from.
2. To have the use or benefit of.

Number 2 is the better choice: Since her family was poor, they could not have the benefit of choices available to middle-class families.

Parts of Speech

A knowledge of grammar helps when you look up unfamiliar words, because many words in English fall into more than one grammatical category (part of speech). The dictionary labels parts of speech using abbreviations (n. = noun; v. = verb; adj. = adjective; adv. = adverb; and so on.) The word

---

[6]From *Resistance, Rebellion, and Death,* Trans. Justin O'Brien (Knopf, 1960).

temper is one example of a word that crosses over grammatical lines. Here are a few definitions for the word "temper" from the *Random House Webster's College Dictionary.*

> **tem · per** (tem′ pər). *n.* **1.** a particular state of mind or feelings. **2.** habit of mind, esp. with respect to irritability or patience; disposition: *an even temper* . . . *v.t.* **9.** to moderate: *to temper justice with mercy.* **10.** to soften or tone down. **11.** to make suitable by or as if by blending. **12.** to work into proper consistency, as clay or mortar. **13.** to impart strength or toughness to by heating and cooling. **14.** to tune (a keyboard instrument) so as to make the tones available in different keys or tonalities.

Write the definition number and part of speech of for each use of *temper* in these four sentences.

1. Senator Jackson *tempered* his remarks about his opponent after the polls showed that his attacks had cost him voters.   <u>9 or 10   verb</u>
2. Most county building inspectors require a homeowner to install *tempered* glass windows if they are low enough to the floor for someone to fall through them. <u>13   verb</u>
3. Professor Wilson appears to be in a bad *temper* tonight; perhaps she is disappointed in our test scores. <u>1   noun</u>
4. Our neighbor's *temper* is so predictably calm that even little Johnny's home run hit through his living room window didn't upset him. <u>2   noun</u>

Using Context Clues

Although a good dictionary is indispensable, it is unrealistic to think that you must look up every unfamiliar word you come across. If you are unable to figure out a word's meaning by analyzing its word parts, the **context**—the way the word is used in its particular setting—may yield a reasonably accurate meaning. (The word *context* comes from Latin, "to weave together.")

Relying on context clues is not a substitute for looking up exact meanings in the dictionary, nor will every sentence with unfamiliar words necessarily provide you with a clue. But if one is there, a clue is a useful shortcut toward efficient reading, especially when the word is not absolutely crucial to your understanding the text.

> *Types of Context Clues*
>
> - Synonyms
> - Antonyms
> - Examples and illustrations
> - Opinion and tone

Synonyms

The most frequently used context clue is a **synonym,** a word or phrase similar in meaning to the unfamiliar word. Although the synonym may not have the exact meaning, it may be close enough to give you an approximate definition. For example,

> The candidate for student body president was having difficulty. When called upon to give a campaign speech, he was so *reticent* that his long silences made everyone uncomfortable.

The phrase, "long silences," is the context clue, from which you could probably figure out that "reticent" means "unwilling to speak." Consider this example:

> The *prototype* for the original Apple computer was put together in a Cupertino, California, garage.

Prototype most likely means

  (a) basic design.
  (b) the first working model.
  (c) a knock-off or cheap imitation.
  (d) the final product.

Circle the word that provides the synonym clue. "*original*"

Antonyms

When a sentence suggests a contrast or a contradiction, the context clue may be in the form of an **antonym,** a word or phrase that means the opposite of the word in question. If you know the antonym, then you may be able to figure out the new word. For example,

> Because Professor Sanchez wants his writing students to develop a concise writing style, Melvin often receives low grades on his papers as his style is too *verbose*.

Since it is obviously being contrasted with *concise,* a word with which you are probably familiar, *verbose* means the opposite, "overly wordy." Here is another example:

> A well-known writer was most upset when he learned that his publisher planned to release his new novel, which contained profanity and steamy sex scenes, in an *expurgated* version. Instead, he canceled the contract and found a company that would publish the book without removing the objectionable parts.

"Expurgated" most likely means

(a) thoroughly revised.
(b) (having offensive material removed.)
(c) simplified, made easier to understand.
(d) made more concise.

Circle the phrase that serves as the antonym clue. "without removing

the objectionable parts"

Examples and Illustrations

The meaning of an unfamiliar word may be suggested by nearby examples and illustrations. In this case, no single word or phrase implies the definition, but taken together, the examples help us infer the meaning. Try this sentence:

> The *squalid* conditions of many American inner cities—with their burned-out buildings, crumbling schools, and garbage-filled vacant lots—pose a problem for parents trying to raise their children in such grim circumstances.

From the examples printed between the dashes, you can probably determine that *squalid* means "wretched and neglected." Now try this one:

> Professor Dyer applies *stringent* rules for his students' papers: Margins have to be exactly one and a quarter inches on all sides (he even measures them), and after the third sentence fragment or spelling error he assigns a failing grade.

Stringent most likely means

(a) unnecessary.
(b) useful.
(c) (severe.)
(d) unusual.

The two examples (precise margins and a failing grade for excessive fragments) suggest the meaning.

Opinion and Tone

This last kind of context clue is less direct and consequently more difficult to rely on. The writer's **tone**—that is, his or her attitude toward the subject or the **opinions** the writer expresses—may give you a clue for an unfamiliar word. Study this example:

Some critics of mass media blame daytime television talk shows for their *insidious* influence on the viewing public, because these programs parade their guests' bizarre and deviant behaviors and create an unhealthy appetite for ever more grotesque revelations.

The obvious critical nature of this sentence suggests that *insidious* is something bad, and indeed it is, since it means "progressing or spreading in a harmful way."

Consider one last example:

Charley is an *ardent* champion of the poor. His dedication to helping poverty-stricken people get jobs and to qualify for low-cost medical treatment is admirable.

Ardent most likely means

(a) careful.
(b) merely competent.
(c) (passionate.)
(d) consistent.

Circle the noun and the adjective that cast a glowing impression on Charley's activities. "dedication" and "admirable"

Practice Exercise 1

Now try your hand at using context clues to determine the meaning of words in some selected passages. Read each passage and study the context. If possible, try to break the word down into its component parts. Choose the definition that best fits the italicized word.

A. This passage concerns the origin of the classic children's book *Charlotte's Web* by E. B. White, published in 1952.

"Charlotte was a story of a friendship, life, death, salvation," wrote E. B. White. His creation, a brown spider who taught the pig Wilbur the meaning of life, has become one of the most beloved of all children's books. White found his source on the grounds of this own home in Brooklin, Maine, where he moved in 1928. He had been living in New York and working at *The New Yorker,* but he yearned for life outside the *confines* of a great urban environment. Brooklin, halfway up the coast of Maine, provided him with the setting and surroundings he needed to write and to live a good life. There he had some animals: some sheep, some geese, and a young pig named Wilbur. As he later noted, an old rat and a spider arrived uninvited. He had been *mulling over* a new book about animals aimed at children. One day, while headed through the orchard to feed Wilbur, he realized that a spider he had noticed in his barn might provide him with his story. He studied her for about a year, watching her spin her web and catch flies and even bear young. And he read any book he could find about spiders, a species he had never much cared for but, after close inspection, found he liked very much. He named the live spider Charlotte, finding her to have a precise, disciplined New England-like air about her, and she soon inhabited his book. White told his publisher that his spider would not appeal to those looking for a Disney version of animals. Life is stark in nature; animals eat each other, and they die, as Charlotte did. But White cared deeply for her, and for all the animals he came to see and know about his place, in the essential nature of their animal life. *Anthopomorphizing* Charlotte would not have produced the real creature we have come to love. (The book's illustrator, Garth Williams, originally drew Charlotte as a spider with a woman's face, a move White quickly rejected. He sent Williams to various spider guides, especially pointing out the species *Aranea cavatica* as much more suitable, and much less Disneyfied.)

André Bernard, "Charlotte," *Madame Bovary, C'est Moi!*

1. *Confines* most likely means
    (a) neighborhoods.
    (b) limits, borders.
    (c) stimuli, influences.
    (d) cultures.
2. The phrase *mulling over* most likely means
    (a) planning carefully.
    (b) writing.
    (c) thinking about.
    (d) researching.
3. *Anthropomorphizing* most likely means
    (a) giving human characteristics to something nonhuman.
    (b) drawing realistically.
    (c) making an idealized version of something.
    (d) portraying something as a cartoon character.

B. The author of this passage, Bernard Lewis, is a renowned Middle East scholar.

In the course of human history, many civilizations have risen and fallen—China, India, Greece, Rome, and before them, the ancient civilizations of the Middle East. During the centuries that in European history are called medieval, the most advanced civilization in the world was undoubtedly that of Islam. Islam may have been equalled—or even, in some ways, surpassed—by India and China, but both of those civilizations remained essentially limited to one region and to one ethnic group, and their impact on the rest of the world was correspondingly restricted. The civilization of Islam, on the other hand, was *ecumenical* in its outlook, and explicitly so in its aspirations. One of the basic tasks *bequeathed* to Muslims by the Prophet was jihad. This word, which literally means "striving," was usually cited in the Koranic phrase "striving in the path of God" and was interpreted to mean armed struggle for the defense or advancement of Muslim power. In principle, the world was divided, into two houses: the House of Islam, in which a Muslim government ruled and Muslim law prevailed, and the House of War, the rest of the world, still inhabited and, more important, ruled by *infidels*. Between the two, there was to be a perpetual state of war until the entire world either embraced Islam or submitted to the rule of the Muslim state.

Bernard Lewis, "The Revolt of Islam," The New Yorker

1. *Ecumenical* most likely means concerned with
    (a) restricting access to a particular religion.
    (b) promoting unity among religions.
    (c) causing divisiveness among religions.
    (d) limiting people to a particular region and ethnic group.
2. *Bequeathed* most likely means
    (a) assigned or required.
    (b) aspired to or desired.
    (c) emphasized, stressed.
    (d) passed or handed down.
3. *Infidels* most likely means those who
    (a) are unbelievers of a particular religion.
    (b) conservative or orthodox members of a particular religion.
    (c) are faithful to a particular religion.
    (d) are militaristic in their defense of a particular religion.

Practice Exercise 2

In this last exercise, each of the italicized words has a fairly obvious context clue. Study the context. Then in the first space write a definition for each italicized word. Then look the word up in the dictionary and in the second space write the definition. See how close you were to the correct definition. The author of this passage lived in Saudi Arabia for several years during the 1970s and 1980s. The subject is the structure and role of the family in Saudi Arabia.

Clustered in family or tribe, the Bedouins refuse to surrender to outside authority. Their support can be bought but their loyalty is anchored in the family. In the past, each desert family was alone, separated from the rest of society by the sparseness of the vegetation needed to support the animals on which their very lives depended. From this isolation in family units there developed over many centuries an intense feeling that an individual had no protection beyond that of the family. Of the various values the Bedouins have bestowed on modern Saudi Arabia, the primacy of the family is among the most important.

Saudis live in large extended families. It is one of their significant differences from Western culture that, for the Saudis, the concept of individuality is absent. A Saudi sees himself in the context of his family and, to a lesser degree, the tribe.

His duty is never to himself but to the group. Within the family, there is a strong sense of *patrilineal* descent, for a man is considered to be a descendant only of his father and his paternal grandfather but never his mother or maternal grandfather. He belongs only to his father's group, which claims his entire, undivided loyalty. This is why the most sought-after marriages are first cousin marriages between children of brothers. By sharing the same grandfather, the all-important group solidarity is ensured.

There is within the family a rigid *hierarchy* made up of the male members of the family in descending order of age. The oldest male member decides what is in the best interests of the family and dictates the role each individual is to play in the group's general goal. For the individual, this determines whom he marries, where he lives, whether he pursues an education, and what his occupation is. I never became accustomed to the answer I often got from young Saudis, male and female, to my question "Are you going abroad to study?" The response was, "I do not know. My father has not decided."

This idea is anathema to Westerners steeped in the intense individualism of Western society. But to a Saudi, the absence of any independent choice is in no way perceived as doing damage to the individual. The *docile* acceptance of decisions made by the *patriach* results from the way the Saudi family perceives itself in relation to the rest of the world. The world outside the family is viewed as an *inimical* place, where a family must be ready to defend itself even against its neighbor. In the last part of the twentieth century, even educated Saudis harbor a deep fear of the world outside the home. Well-to-do families live in houses clustered together in compounds that are walled off from the rest of the world. Modest homes and the new apartment houses are built with small windows that seem to shut out everyone but those admitted through the iron gate or locked metal door that stands in front of all Saudi dwellings. So *insulated* is the family that Saudi social life is markedly different from that of other Middle Easterners. A pattern of socializing among village women is absent. The men do frequent the coffee houses on occasion, but otherwise there is almost no social infrastructure for cultural reenforcement through festivals, dances, or drama. Socializing among Saudis is almost exclusively within the kinship group. As a result, without the support and approval of his family, a Saudi is lost. With no other alternative, a Saudi willingly pays the price for family support—the strict conformity to the group's demands.

Sandra Mackey, *The Saudis: Inside the Desert Kingdom*

1. *patrilineal*
   Your definition _____
   Dictionary definition   <u>tracing a family's ancestry through the father</u>
2. *hierarchy*
   Your definition _____
   Dictionary definition <u>categorization of a group by ability or status</u>
   <u>(or in this case, by age)</u>

3. *docile*

Your definition _____

Dictionary definition <u>yielding to supervision, direction, or management</u>

4. *patriarch*

Your definition _____

Dictionary definition <u>a man who rules a family, clan, or tribe (in this</u> <u>case, a family)</u>

5. *inimical*

Your definition _____

Dictionary definition <u>unfriendly, hostile</u>

6. *insulated*

Your definition _____

Dictionary definition <u>describing a detached or isolated position</u>

www. mhhe. com/ spears

For additional exercises in using the dictionary and in using context clues, click on "Student Resources" and scroll down to Dictionary Exercise and Context Clues Exercises.

Reading for Understanding: Practice in Basic Comprehension Skills

1

Reading for the Main Idea and Author's Purpose

CHAPTER OBJECTIVES

This first chapter will help you improve your reading comprehension by showing you how to identify the:

- Main idea in paragraphs

- Placement of the main idea

- Implied main ideas

- Major and minor supporting details

- Author's purpose and modes of discourse

■ THE MAIN IDEA OF THE PARAGRAPH

In the first five chapters of this book, the focus of our study is on the individual paragraph. It might seem odd—and perhaps artificial—to devote so much time to paragraphs. After all, the text of essays, articles, and text-book chapters consist of long strings of paragraphs, and we seldom read paragraphs just by themselves. Yet focusing on shorter passages, at least initially, promotes careful reading and analysis. To learn what to look for in nonfiction prose, it is less intimidating to analyze a 100-word para-graph than a 10-page essay.

In nonfiction prose, the paragraph is the fundamental unit of written thought. Simply put, a paragraph is a group of related sentences that de-velop and support one idea. It may be any length as long as it keeps to that one idea. The main idea of a paragraph is a general statement telling the reader what it is about; the main idea may be explicitly stated in a sentence that *often* appears at or near the beginning of the paragraph. As you will see, however, many writers of adult prose do not adhere to this pattern.

Main Idea and Controlling Idea In elementary school, you were probably taught that the first sentence of a paragraph is the topic sentence. This rule is convenient but mislead-ing; to assume that the first sentence is the main point may result in in-accurate comprehension, since professional writers frequently violate this principle. For this reason, I prefer the term **main idea.**

If one is present, a main-idea sentence consists of two parts: the **topic** and the **controlling idea.** The topic is the general subject the paragraph is about (though not necessarily the grammatical subject). The control-ling idea—often a descriptive word or phrase—limits, qualifies, or nar-rows the topic to make the larger subject manageable. Diagrammed, then, a typical main-idea sentence might look like this:

> Topic + Controlling Idea = Main Idea

Consider this sentence:

> The World Wide Web has revolutionized the way we obtain and retrieve information.

In this example, the topic—"The World Wide Web"—is underlined once, and the controlling idea—"has revolutionized the way we obtain and re-trieve information"—twice. Stated another way, the controlling idea re-stricts the writer to only that information, and every subsequent sentence in a well-constructed paragraph is limited to that phrase. But if the writer shifted direction and changed the controlling idea, the focus of the para-graph would change:

> Spending hours a day surfing the World Wide Web, according to some social critics, may isolate users from reality and damage their ability to form social relationships.

And here is a third example, showing yet another controlling idea and thus a different direction:

> The World Wide Web, where users move quickly from one link to another and view flashy graphics, may alter users' ability to concentrate on sustained reading of printed matter.

Note that you do not need to label irrelevant information, as this example suggests:

> Although some diehard writers like Danielle Steel still use a typewriter to write, the widespread availability of inexpensive personal computers has revolutionized and simplified the writing process.

The first part of the sentence (beginning with "Although") will probably not be discussed, because the writer is not interested in the *disadvantages* of using a typewriter. The writer mentions this fact only to concede a truth and to avoid generalizing. The controlling idea points to only positive results of the computer revolution—"has revolutionized and simplified the writing process." Thus, the controlling idea serves as a sort of umbrella for the remainder of the paragraph. Identifying the topic and controlling idea keeps you on track as you read.

Although this pattern—**topic + controlling idea**—is the typical one, the elements may be reversed. Whether the topic precedes the controlling idea or follows it, the meaning is still the same.

> The writing process has been revolutionized and simplified because of the widespread availability of inexpensive personal computers, although some diehard writers like Danielle Steel still use a typewriter to write.

Although the meaning is the same, the effect is not. Which version, the first or the second, better emphasizes the controlling idea?

Occasionally, a writer may ease into the actual main idea, as these two sentences from Robert Coles's book, *The Moral Intelligence of Children,* illustrates. Which sentence represents the main idea to be developed—the first or the second? Underline the topic and controlling idea in the sentence you choose.

> "Moral intelligence" isn't acquired only by memorization of rules and regulations, by dint of abstract classroom discussion or kitchen compliance. We grow morally as a consequence of learning how to be with others, how to behave in this world, a learning prompted by taking to heart what we have seen and heard.

**Practice
Exercise 1**

Label these main-idea sentences by underlining the topic once and the controlling idea twice. Start with these easier examples.

1. The bathroom is the most dangerous room in the house.
2. The most dangerous room in the house is the bathroom.
3. The Australian cattle dog, sometimes referred to as the blue or red heeler, is an extraordinarily intelligent and loyal breed of dog.
4. An extraordinarily intelligent and loyal breed of dog is the Australian cattle dog, sometimes called the blue or red heeler.
5. Powell's City of Books occupies an entire city block in Portland, Oregon, and it is so large that patrons must use a map to find their way around; it is regarded by book lovers as the most comprehensive bookstore in the entire United States.
6. One result of the Bush Administration's decision to invade Iraq in March 2003 was that we alienated many of our traditional European allies.
7. Part of the appeal of popular music, from the emergence of rock 'n' roll in the early 1950s to contemporary music like punk rock, death metal, and gangsta rap, is its ability to irritate adults.
8. As Greg Critser explains in his recent book *Fat Land,* the reasons that Americans are the most obese people in the world are varied and complex and go beyond the usual culprits, the fast-food industry with its supersized meals.

Now try these more difficult main-idea sentences, which are taken from published material, some of which you will encounter later in this book.

9. Skating [skateboarding] is a narcotic that offers release and a negation of self that defies analysis. (Jocko Weyland, *The Answer Is Never: A Skateboarder's History of the World*)
10. . . . [C]offee is the second most valuable exported legal commodity on earth (after oil), providing the largest jolt of the world's most widely taken psychoactive drug. (Mark Pendergrast, *Uncommon Grounds*)
11. Computer modeling has made it possible to study traffic not only as a physical system but as a social system. . . . (John Seabrook, "The Slow Lane")
12. Such a simple invention, or discovery, the compass. (Jonathan Raban, *Passage to Juneau*)
13. Much of the wildlife is nocturnal and it creeps through the nights, poisonous and alien. (Luis Alberto Urrea, *The Devil's Highway*)
14. Corals are among the simplest of invertebrate animals, composed of little more than a hollow tube, the gastric cavity, surrounded by a fringe of stinging tentacles with which they capture prey. (Julia Whitty, "Shoals of Time")

15. The most successful campaign of all, of course, was for the Marlboro, an upscale cigarette for ladies that Philip Morris reintroduced in 1954 in a filtered version for the mainstream. (Jonathan Franzen, *How to Be Alone*)

Placement of the Main Idea

In your academic textbooks, the main ideas are generally fairly easy to spot. Contemporary textbook publishers often use graphic elements such as boldface or italic type to make the main ideas more conspicuous. For example, consider this paragraph from a standard economics text:

> ### *Gross Domestic Product*
>
> The primary measure of the economy's performance is its annual total output of goods and services or, as it is called, its *aggregate output*. Aggregate output is labeled **gross domestic product (GDP):** *the total market value of all final goods and services produced in a given year.* GDP includes all goods and services produced by either citizen-supplied or foreign-supplied resources employed within the country. The U.S. GDP includes the market value of Fords produced by an American-owned factory in Michigan and the market value of Hondas produced by a Japanese-owned factory in Ohio.
>
> Campbell R. McConnell and Stanley L. Brue,
> *Economics: Principles, Problems, and Policies*

Notice that the heading is printed in colored boldface, the key term, "gross domestic product (GDP) is in black boldface, and the definition is in italics, making it easy to identify. Of course, remembering it is another matter.

As a college reader, you must learn to cope with diverse writing styles and techniques, requiring you to rewrite some of the rules you may have been taught in the past. Adult nonfiction (nontextbook) prose is not as neatly formulaic as students would like it to be, and the careful reader has to be alert for variations. The main idea may be delayed, buried in the middle of the paragraph, it may be at the end, it may occur in bits and pieces throughout the paragraph, or to complicate matters, it may only be implied, not stated explicitly. Let us examine a few paragraphs to see the location of the main idea, beginning with a passage from Laura Hillenbrand's book about the famous racehorse, Seabiscuit. Study my annotations:

main idea

dominant idea
throughout—
a thoroughbred
racehorse runs
at impressive
speeds & is
born to run

A Throughbred racehorse is one of God's <u>most impressive engines</u>. Tipping the scales at up to 1,450 pounds, he can sustain *speeds* of forty miles per hour. Equipped with reflexes much faster than those of the most quick-wired man, he <u>swoops</u> over as much as twenty-eight feet of earth in a single stride, and corners on a dime. His body is a paradox of mass and lightness, crafted <u>to slip through air with the ease of an arrow</u>. His mind is impressed with a single command: <u>run</u>. He pursues <u>speed</u> with superlative courage, pushing beyond defeat, beyond exhaustion, sometimes beyond the structural limits of bone and sinew. In flight, he is nature's ultimate wedding of form and purpose.

Laura Hillenbrand, *Seabiscuit: An American Legend*

The underlined words and phrases all reinforce the controlling idea, "most impressive machines." Rather than repeating the word *speeds,* Hillenbrand uses several synonymous words and phrases. Everything works together to create "a network of interlocking ideas," as Richard Marius has described the paragraph.[1] Reading in this way makes it easier to follow the chain of ideas.

In addition to identifying the main-idea sentence—assuming that one is present—an even more important skill is to paraphrase the main point by putting it into your own words. I cannot stress how crucial this skill is: The ability to read a passage and to say what it is about in your own words will serve you well in your academic and work life, and throughout this chapter you will have ample opportunity to practice this skill. Here is an example of a paraphrased main idea of the preceding paragraph:

> Thoroughbred racehorses are built for incredible speed and endurance.

A third way to test your ability to identify the main idea is to devise an appropriate title for a passage. A title is written as a phrase rather than as a complete sentence, and it should contain both the topic and the controlling idea. In addition, a good title should be neither too broad nor too narrow and must encompass the scope of the entire paragraph. Which of these four choices seems like the most appropriate title for the Hillenbrand paragraph?

(a) Impressive Machines
(b) Thoroughbred Racehorses: An Overview
(c) The Racehorse: Paradox or Machine?
(d) The Extraordinary Speed of Thoroughbred Racehorses

Although the phrase "impressive machines" appears in the passage, Answer A is misleading, because it suggests that the topic is actually machines rather than horses. Answer B is too general, and Answer C, although present in the passage, misses the main point. Only Answer D encompasses both the topic (racehorses) and the controlling idea (their incredible speed).

However, not all paragraphs are organized so simply as this passage on the racehorse, with the main idea stated at the beginning. In the next paragraph, which sentence represents the main idea in this paragraph? After you identify it, restate the main idea in your own words.

[1]Biology is destiny—or at least more and more people seem ready to believe that it is. [2]Perhaps this is because recent scientific advances—gene splicing,

---

[1]*A Writer's Companion,* 4th edition, McGraw-Hill Inc., 1998.

in vitro fertilization, DNA identification of criminals, mapping the human genome—have been repeatedly echoed and amplified by popular culture. [3]From science fact to science fiction (and back again), the gene has become a pervasive cultural symbol. [4]It crops up not just in staid scientific journals and PBS documentaries, but also with increasing regularity in political discourse, popular entertainment, and advertising.

Jeff Reid, "The DNA-ing of America," *Utne Reader*

Main idea sentence: <u>sentence 3</u>

Main idea paraphrased: <u>The gene as a symbol has permeated</u>
<u>our culture.</u>

And in this one? Again, restate the main idea in your own words after you make your choice.

[1]The Bear Paw Mountains, a low-slung range south of Chinook, Montana, get their name from an Indian tale of a hunter who ventures into a land of giant bears in order to feed his starving family. [2]When he kills a deer, an angry bear grabs him. [3]In a flash, the Creator severs the bear's paw. [4]Another version tells of an Indian girl who comes to bathe in a virginal lake. [5]A bear bewitched by her beauty reaches out, and the Creator saves her in the same way. [6]The naming of these mountains, like all Indian naming, is poetically exact. [7]From the High Plains, they appear magically inviting, and also remarkably like the just severed paw of a giant bear, its knuckles rippling across the horizon.

Mark Stevens, "Chief Joseph's Revenge," *The New Yorker*

Main idea sentence: <u>sentence 6</u>
A good title:

(a) (Indian Naming of the Bear Paw Mountains)
(b) The Bear Paw Mountains of Montana
(c) Traditional Uses for Poetry
(d) A Native American Bear Legend

Main idea restated: <u>The Native Americans named geographic</u>

<u>features like Montana's Bear Paw Mountains poetically yet</u>

<u>realistically.</u>

Occasionally, the main idea of a passage emerges in bits and pieces. Read this short passage, look at the underlined words and phrases, and then write a main-idea sentence for it. The subject of the passage, the Ohlone

Indians, were Native Americans who inhabited the San Francisco and Monterey Bay areas prior to the arrival of the Europeans.

> The <u>Ohlones</u>, like all other California Indians, were a "<u>Stone-Age</u>" <u>people</u>. Their arrows were tipped with flint or obsidian, their mortars and pestles were of stone, and other tools were made of bone, shell, or wood. To fell a tree they hacked away at it with a chert blade, pausing now and then to burn out the chips before they renewed their hacking. They used no metal, had no agriculture (at least as we understand it), wove no cloth, and did not even make pottery. They lived entirely by <u>hunting and gathering</u>.
>
> <u>But</u> while the <u>Ohlones were a Stone-Age people</u>, hunting was not just a matter of bludgeoning an animal to death with a club, as it is sometimes pictured. <u>Hunting,</u> especially deer hunting, was <u>among the most important things in a man's life</u>. The <u>hunter pursued and killed deer</u> without pity, but <u>never without reverence</u>. Deer were spiritually powerful animals in a world in which animals were still gods, and <u>deer hunting was an undertaking</u> surrounded at every step with <u>dignity, forethought, and ritual</u>.

Malcolm Margolin, The Ohlone Way

Main Idea: <u>Although the Ohlone Indians were Stone-Age people</u>

<u>with only primitive tools at their disposal, they treated deer</u>

<u>hunting with reverence.</u>

Implied Main Ideas

When a writer suggests the main idea by providing various details, the main idea is **implied** and not explicitly stated. Study the underlined words and phrases. Then choose the main idea sentence that best represents the point of the paragraph.

> There are some 16,000 species of <u>lichens</u> in the world. All are <u>slow-growing</u>, but <u>those that encrust the rocks</u> of <u>mountain peaks</u> are <u>particularly so</u>. At high altitudes, there may be only a single day in a whole year when growth is possible and a lichen may take as long as 60 years to cover just one square centimeter. Lichens as big as plates, which are very common, are therefore likely to be hundreds if not thousands of years old.

David Attenborough, The Living Planet

1. There are 16,000 species of lichens in the world.
2. Lichens, especially those found in mountainous areas, are slow-growing.
3. Some lichens grow as large as plates.
4. Lichens are unusual plants that everyone should learn to identify.

Notice that Answer 2 contains all of the important elements. Answers 1 and 3 are too narrow; and answer 4 is not mentioned. Underline the key words in this paragraph.

Sagebrush covers 58,000 square miles of Wyoming. The biggest city has a population of fifty thousand, and there are only five settlements that could be called cities in the whole state. The rest are towns, scattered across the expanse with as much as sixty miles between them, their populations two thousand, fifty, or ten. They are fugitive-looking, perched on a barren, windblown bench, or tagged onto a river or a railroad, or laid out straight in a farming valley with implement stores and a block-long Mormon church. In the eastern part of the state, which slides down into the Great Plains, the new mining settlements are boomtowns, trailer cities, metal knots on flat land.

Gretel Ehrlich, *The Solace of Open Spaces*

Now decide which of these statements best represents Ehrlich's implied main idea.

1. Wyoming towns are forlorn-looking.
2. There are only five cities in Wyoming.
3. Wyoming's sparse population lives in towns scattered across the state.
4. There is more sagebrush in Wyoming than there are people.

Answer 1 is too specific; answer 2 is a small detail; answer 4 focuses too much on the minor detail of sagebrush. Only answer 3 incorporates all the essential elements of the paragraph.

Practice Exercise 2

Read these paragraphs and then complete the main-idea exercise as directed.

A. Hannah Nyala has been a ranger and tracker of lost people in California's Joshua Tree National Monument for several years.

Simply *getting* lost doesn't necessarily pose a problem, because with clear thinking one's steps can be retraced fairly quickly. But clear thinking is usually the first trait to go when someone looks around and sees nothing at all that is familiar. Hurried movement, instinctive as it may be, compounds the trouble. And considering the desert fashions that some visitors favor (bikinis, sandals, no hat) and their lack of preparation (failure to bring water or sunscreen, for instance), the survival of anyone who steps off the trail and gets lost in the Mojave Desert may be immediately threatened. Contrary to folklore, coaxing potable drinking water from a barrel cactus is all but impossible without a chainsaw. Hot daytime temperatures, which suck moisture out of the body at noon, plummet at dusk, summoning hypothermia. Cactus, snakes, and rough terrain easily become serious hazards when you are tired, hungry, and thirsty, cold or hot, and above all frightened. And where a lost child is concerned, abduction is always a possibility. For the tracker, who is often one of dozens of searchers, every move is grimly dogged by the knowledge that success or failure may equal life or death for the lost person.

Hannah Nyala, Point Last Seen

A good title for this paragraph is

    (a) The Importance of Clear Thinking When Hiking in the Desert
    (b) How to Avoid Getting Lost in the Desert
    (c) How to Track Lost People in the Desert
    (d) (The Hazards of Being Lost in the Desert)

    B.

It is, after all, only a berry, encasing a double-sided seed. It first grew on a shrub—or small tree, depending on your perspective or height—under the Ethiopian rain forest canopy, high on the mountainsides. The evergreen leaves form glossy ovals and, like the seeds, are laced with caffeine.

Yet coffee is the second most valuable exported legal commodity on earth (after oil), providing the largest jolt of the world's most widely taken psychoactive drug. From its original African home, coffee propagation has spread in a girdle around the globe, taking over whole plains and mountainsides between the Tropics of Cancer and Capricorn. In the form of a hot infusion of its ground, roasted seeds, coffee is consumed around the world for its bittersweet bouquet, its mind-racing jump start, and social bonding. At various times it has been prescribed as an aphrodisiac, enema, nerve tonic, and life-extender.

Coffee provides a livelihood (of sorts) for over twenty million human beings. It is an incredibly labor-intensive crop, with all but a tiny percentage requiring the individual human hand. Calloused palms plant the seeds, nurse the seedlings under a shade canopy, transplant them to mountainside ranks, prune and fertilize, spray for pests, irrigate, harvest, and lug 200-pound bags of coffee cherries. Laborers regulate the complicated process of removing the precious bean from its covering of pulp and mucilage. Then the beans must be spread to dry for several days (or heated in drums), the parchment and silver skin removed, and the resulting green bean (*café oro,* or "golden coffee," as it is known in Latin America) bagged for shipment, roasting, grinding, and brewing around the world.

Mark Pendergrast, Uncommon Grounds

A good title for this paragraph would be

    (a) (Coffee as a Valuable Commodity)
    (b) Where Coffee Is Propagated Worldwide
    (c) Coffee: Berry or Drug?
    (d) The Varied Uses of Coffee

C.

Boring vs. Interesting Instruction   Academic subject matters such as ancient history and science are to be withheld from children in the early grades on the grounds that true education proceeds from the child's interest rather than from an external imposition. Children learn best when new knowledge is built upon what they already know (true), and it is further claimed that the child's interest in a subject will derive from its connection with his or her immediate experiences and home surroundings. Early schooling should therefore teach subjects that have direct relevance to the child's life, such as "my neighborhood" and similar "relevant" topics. Yet every person with enough schooling to be reading these words knows that subject matters by themselves do not repel or attract interest, and that an effective teacher can make almost any subject interesting, and an ineffective one can make almost any subject dull. The presumption that the affairs of one's neighborhood are more interesting than those of faraway times and places is contradicted in every classroom that studies dinosaurs and fairy tales— that is, in just about every early classroom in the nation. The false polarity between "boring" and "interesting" or "relevant" and "irrelevant" really conceals an anti-intellectual, antiacademic bias.

E. D. Hirsch, Jr., *The Schools We Want and Why We Don't Have Them*

Write a complete sentence in your own words that states the main idea of the paragraph. <u>The presumption that one can't teach children subjects</u>

<u>outside of their own experiences and surroundings is both false and</u>

<u>anti-intellectual.</u>

D.

The threat of warfare was always present in the Ohlone world, and when war broke out it was occasionally bloody. In the heat of anger there were ambushes and raids, invariably followed by reprisals. In such all-out warfare, men were killed, children were killed, women were raped and kidnapped, and in rare cases whole villages were destroyed. Torture and corpse mutilation were practiced. Scalps were taken, hoisted onto poles, and carried among the villages of the victors for wild celebrations. If the slain warrior had been particularly brave or powerful, his enemies might eat a small piece of his flesh to acquire (or perhaps neutralize) some of his power.

The most savage practices of warfare were part of Ohlone life. But they were a very occasional part. Most of the time hostility was contained, always simmering under the more or less placid surface of daily life, but only rarely boiling over into the open. As virtually every early visitor testified, the Ohlones were in no way a warlike people—not when compared with other cultures. They never developed the elaborate institutions or instruments of war that the Plains Indians or some of the Eastern tribes developed. Their only weapons were hunting weapons—bows and arrows, sometimes spears. They had no tomahawks, no war clubs, no body armor, no shields painted with magical war emblems. Their war chiefs were chosen for warfare only and had no other power within the tribe-let. Their society was not built around booty, slavery, war rituals, or the worship of war heroes. Adolescents did not attain manhood by killing an enemy or "counting coup." There were no Romans or Aztecs anywhere in Central California: indeed, complete subjugation, territorial conquest, a system of widespread domination and empire—such things were totally foreign to the Ohlone world.

Malcolm Margolin, The Ohlone Way

Write a complete sentence in your own words that states the main idea of the paragraph. <u>Although the Ohlone Indians occasionally engaged in</u>

<u>brutal and bloody warfare, they were not a particularly warlike people,</u>

<u>nor did they develop warlike institutions in comparison to other Native</u>

<u>American groups or to members of earlier civilizations.</u>

Levels of Support

Now we can turn our attention to the paragraph's supporting sentences and the importance of being able to distinguish between **major supporting statements** and **minor supporting statements.** Although good readers probably don't consciously label sentences as will be demonstrated in this section, learning to separate major and minor support is an important thinking skill. Briefly, **major** statements directly relate to and develop the main idea, whereas **minor** ones further explain, illustrate, or otherwise develop the major ones. Analysis of levels of support trains you to think logically because you must weigh the relative importance of ideas in relation to the main idea. In an ideally constructed paragraph, a diagram of the supporting sentences might look like this:

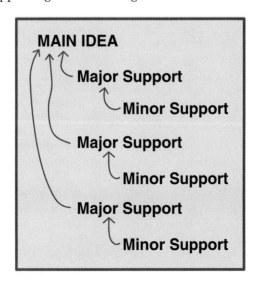

The following paragraph by Mortimer Adler, who was a prominent American educator and thinker, exemplifies this ideal construction. The paragraph's six sentences reinforce the main idea, stated in the first sentence. Notice that the major supporting sentences identify each of the three types of book owner, and the minor supporting sentences comment on each type, using parentheses. (In Chapter 4, you will learn that this paragraph is developed by a method called classification.)

[1]There are three kinds of book owners. [2]The first has all the standard sets and best-sellers—unread, untouched. [3](This deluded individual owns wood-pulp and ink, not books.) [4]The second has a great many books—a few of them read through, most of them dipped into, but all of them as clean and shiny as the day they were bought. [5](This person would probably like to make books his own, but is restrained by a false respect for their physical appearance.) [6]The third has a few books or many—every one of them dog-eared and dilapidated, shaken and loosened by continual use, marked and scribbled in front to back. [7](This man owns books.)

Mortimer Adler, "How to Mark a Book," *Saturday Review*

The following paragraph varies this pattern. It is by Alexander Petrunkevitch, who was one of this country's foremost arachnologists (an expert in spiders). Notice that the first two sentences consist of introductory descriptive details; they are minor descriptive details.

[1]The entire body of a tarantula, especially its legs, is thickly clothed with hair. [2]Some of it is short and woolly, some long and stiff. [3]Touching this body hair produces one of two distinct reactions. [4]When the spider is hungry, it responds with an immediate and swift attack. [5]At the touch of a cricket's antennae the tarantula seizes the insect so swiftly that a motion picture taken at the rate of 64 frames per second shows only the result and not the process of capture. [6]But when the spider is not hungry, the stimulation of its hairs merely causes it to shake the touched limb. [7]An insect can walk under its hairy belly unharmed.

Alexander Petrunkevitch, "The Spider and the Wasp," *Scientific American*

This paragraph is printed again on the next page, this time in graphic form showing the relative importance of the supporting details in relation to the main idea:

Main idea:
Touching this body hair produces one of two distinct reactions. [sent. 3]

Major support:
When the spider is hungry, it responds with an immediate and swift attack. [sent. 4]

Minor support:
At the touch of a cricket's antennae the tarantula seizes the insect so swiftly that a motion picture taken at the rate of 64 frames per second shows only the result and not the process of capture. [sent. 5]

Major Support:
But when the spider is not hungry, the stimulation of its hairs merely causes it to shake the touched limb. [sent. 6]

Minor support:
An insect can walk under its hairy belly unharmed. [sent. 7]

Just because we label minor details "minor" does not mean they are of no importance. Without them, we would not know how fast the spider's rate of capture is when hungry nor the spider's indifference to the presence of prey when not hungry. As you can see, supporting sentences operate on two different levels—some general, some more specific—suggesting two considerations: Supporting sentences have relative significance, and they are not all equally important. Unfortunately, not every paragraph is balanced as this one is, nor does every paragraph follow this alternating pattern. Still, the ability to distinguish between the two helps you see the *texture* (for want of a better word) good writers try hard to achieve; good readers unconsciously sort out these details as they read. In summary, the most important part of the paragraph is the main idea, and two types of supporting details are there to buttress and reinforce this main idea.

Practice Exercise 3	Try your hand at distinguishing between the two kinds of support in this paragraph by American novelist and essay writer Jonathan Franzen. The subject is cigarette companies' advertising campaigns, specifically the original Marlboro campaign. Although cigarettes are no longer allowed to advertise on television, Franzen's remarks apply equally to contemporary magazine and billboard advertisements. In the space before each sentence, indicate whether the sentence represents the main idea (MAIN), major support (MA), or minor support (MI). Finally, for the main idea, underline the topic once and the controlling idea twice.

__MAIN__   The most successful campaign of all, of course, was for the Marlboro, an upscale cigarette for ladies that Philip Morris reintroduced in 1954 in a filtered version for the mainstream. __MA__ Like all modern products, the new Marlboro was intensively designed. __MI__ The tobacco blend was strengthened so as to survive the muting of a filter, the "flip-top" box was introduced to the national vocabulary, the color red was chosen to signal strong flavor, and the graphics underwent endless tinkering before the final look, including a fake heraldic crest with the motto *Veni, vidi, vici,*[2] was settled on; there was even market-testing in four cities to decide the color of the filter. __MA__ It was in Leo Burnett's ad campaign for Marlboro, however, that the real genius lay. __MA__ The key to its success was its transparency. __MI__ Place a lone ranch hand against a backdrop of buttes at sunset, and just about every positive association a cigarette can carry is in the picture: rugged individualism, masculine sexuality, escape from an urban modernity, strong flavors, the living of life intensely. __MA__ The Marlboro marks our commercial culture's passage from an age of promises to an age of pleasant, empty dreams.

Jonathan Franzen, "Sifting the Ashes," *How to Be Alone*

■ THE AUTHOR'S PURPOSE AND MODES OF DISCOURSE

The last skill we will take up in this chapter is identifying the **mode of discourse,** which refers to the kind of writing in nonfiction prose. These modes are closely related to the **author's purpose**—why the writer is writing and what he or she wants to accomplish. There are four modes: (1) **narration,** to tell a story; (2) **description,** to show what something looks or feels like; (3) **exposition,** to inform, explain, or set forth; and (4) **persuasion,** to convince the reader to adopt the writer's point of view. The following box shows the relationship between mode of discourse and author's purpose.

Author's Purpose ⟶	*Mode of Discourse*
• To tell a story ⟶	Narration
• To show what something looks like or feels like ⟶	Description
• To inform, to set forth, to explain, to discuss ⟶	Exposition
• To convince the reader to adopt the writer's point of view ⟶	Persuasion

[2]"Veni, vidi, vici" is a famous phrase from Julius Caesar's account of his conquering of Gaul (now France) in his memoir, *Gallic Wars.* In English the phrase translates to "I came, I saw, I conquered." The appropriation of this phrase as a motto for Marlboro cigarettes seems ironic in light of the cigarette companies' recent revelation that a cigarette is deliberately designed to be a "drug-delivery system." In other words, the Philip Morris design of Marlboro was intentionally designed to win over its victims.

Narration

Narration is the most easily recognized mode of discourse; it means simply to tell a story. A writer uses narration to relate events, either real or imagined, in chronological order, not to entertain, but to provide evidence for some larger truth, as Lewis Thomas does in this passage:

> We may be about to rediscover that dying is not such a bad thing to do after all. Sir William Osler took this view: he disapproved of people who spoke of the agony of death, maintaining there was no such thing.
>
> In a nineteenth-century memoir on an expedition in Africa, there is a story by David Livingston about his own experience of near-death. He was caught by a lion, crushed across the chest in the animal's great jaws, and saved in the instant by a lucky shot from a friend. Later, he remembered the episode in clear detail. He was so amazed by the extraordinary sense of peace, calm, and total painlessness associated with being killed that he constructed a theory that all creatures are provided with a protective physiologic mechanism, switched on at the verge of death, carrying them through in a haze of tranquillity.
>
> Lewis Thomas, "The Long Habit," *Lives of a Cell*

State the main idea that this little narrative supports. We think of death as being painful, but an experience that David Livingston relates suggests that this may be a misconception.

Description

The mode of discourse called **description** shows what someone or something looks like or what something feels like. The author wants to show a visual picture of a *particular* scene, not a generalized one based on a composite of many such scenes. Descriptive writing typically relies on details that appeal to the five senses. It may also use figures of speech (imaginative comparisons such as metaphors and similes, which are covered in Chapter 6). Although a descriptive passage by itself usually does not have a sentence stating the main idea, there usually is a **dominant impression,** revealed little by little as the details accumulate. The following passage is by Jason Elliott, a British writer who traveled extensively in Afghanistan in the late 1990s. In it, he describes Afghan buses. The wealth of detail suggests that they are very different from their North American counterparts. Underline the key details as you read.

> Afghan buses are full of character, and are fastidiously maintained by the men who risk their lives daily by driving them. They run until they disintegrate, after which they are frequently reborn in mutated incarnations, their various parts salvaged from scrapyards and lovingly reassembled. Loose bodywork is reinforced with riveted sheet metal. There was one bus with its engine housing built entirely from timber, and the frame of was another patched with strips of Russian field runway. I once saw a bus in a Kabul street

that had been run over by a tank. 'We'll have it back on the road in a few days,' joked the undaunted owner.

Floral ironwork, with more whorls than a Provençale bell-tower, decorates rear windows, or is welded to roofs to serve as an anchor for mountains of luggage. Sometimes chains and metal pendants, which jangle musically with a rocking chassis—the modern vestiges, perhaps, of the caravan's camel bells—are draped on their sides in the manner of a necklace. Fertility symbols—a pair of fishes is the most common motif—are stitched into the leather of radiator-grille covers. Buses as well as trucks are often lovingly painted. I saw several idyllic alpine scenes, complete with Swiss chalets and cotton-wool clouds; others bore images of budgerigars, leaping lions and moonlit water-gardens, and above their wind-screens in big multicoloured letters: 'Hero Bus', 'Welcome to Bus', 'Modern Bus', 'King of the Road', 'Good Your Journey', or 'We Trust In God'. Always the driver's cockpit is festooned with tassels, tinsel, extra mirrors and plastic flowers, stickers of eyes, the slender hand of a woman, cars and animals. Each has a talismanic and protective significance, as does the traditional religious paraphernalia of dangling pendants carved in the name of God, the Prophet, and his Caliphs, and stick-on verses of the Qur'ān[3] or pictures of the Ka'bah at Mecca.

Sometimes the destinations are painted on the sides of the buses; more often you listen for the voice of a driver shouting out the name of the place you are going. There is no schedule; the bus leaves when the driver decides it is full enough. Even as it pulls away the driver's teenage accomplice hangs from the wing mirror yelling the destination in the hope of sweeping up a few extra passengers.

Jason Elliott, An Unexpected Light: Travels in Afghanistan

In your own words, write a sentence summarizing the dominant impression that the details in the passage suggest.   Despite their

sometimes jerry-built construction, buses in Afghanistan are not only

distinctive and well maintained but are also elaborately decorated.

Exposition	**Exposition,** or expository writing, is the most common kind of reading you will encounter in your college courses. Expository readings very likely make up the bulk of the reading in your freshman English anthology and in your textbooks. Exposition is essentially objective writing with a straightforward purpose: to inform, to explain, to make clear, to discuss, or to set forth. Expository writing is usually *factual,* consistent with its purpose to provide information. By its very nature then, exposition presents subject matter without trying to influence our opinions or emotions or to criticize or argue. In this first example, Julia Whitty informs the reader about the nature of corals and how coral reefs are formed.

---

[3]A variant spelling of the Koran.

Corals are among the simplest of invertebrate animals, composed of little more than a hollow tube, the gastric, cavity, surrounded by a fringe of stinging tentacles with which they capture prey. Reef-building corals secrete external limestone skeletons—the coral rock—pockmarked with tiny depressions where each individual animal—the polyp—resides. Related polyps are connected by living tissue through which they share digested food. Generation after generation of new corals grow atop the limestone skeletons of dead corals, until a reef is formed. Although the growth is incremental, less than one inch per year, the colonies can live a thousand years or more. Measurements in some Pacific atolls show the skeletons of dead corals stretching nearly a mile below the living reef.

In this way, working together, depositing up to 880 tons of limestone per acre per year, coral colonies construct the largest architecture on the planet. Australia's Great Barrier Reef has grown to 92,000 square miles, bigger than anything humans have ever built. Visible from space, it has conceivably already informed distant, alien intelligences that this planet harbors life.

Julia Whitty, "Shoals of Time," *Harper's Magazine*

Textbooks, or academic discourse, employ exposition to explain difficult concepts, to trace historical events, and to provide information. Examine this passage from an introductory anthropology textbook, which explains the term *multiculturalism*. Notice that the author presents the information and examples objectively, without alluding to the controversy surrounding this word in the so-called culture wars.

Multiculturalism views cultural diversity in a country as something desirable and to be encouraged. The multicultural model contrasts sharply with the assimilationist model, in which minorities are expected to abandon their traditions, replacing them with those of the majority population. Multiculturalism encourages the perception and practice of many ethnic traditions. A multicultural society socializes individuals not only into the dominant (national) culture but also into an ethnic culture. Thus, in the United States, millions of people speak both English and another language. They eat both "American" foods (apple pie, steak, hamburgers) and "ethnic" cuisine (e.g., Chinese, Cambodian, Armenian). They celebrate both national (July 4, Thanksgiving) and ethnic-religious holidays. And they study both national and ethnic-group histories. Multiculturalism works best in a society whose political system promotes free expression and in which there are many and diverse ethnic groups.

In the United States and Canada, multiculturalism is of growing importance. This reflects awareness that the number and size of ethnic groups have grown dramatically in recent years. If this trend continues, the ethnic composition of the United States will change dramatically. . .

Because of immigration and differential population growth, whites are now outnumbered by minorities in many urban areas. For example of 8,008,278 residents of New York City in 2000, 27 percent were black, 27 percent Hispanic, 10 percent Asian, and 36 percent other—including non-Hispanic whites. The comparable figures for Los Angeles (3,694,820 people) were 11 percent black, 47 percent Hispanic, 9 percent Asian, and 33 percent other—including non-Hispanic whites (Census 2000, www.census.gov).

Conrad Phillip Kottak, *Anthropology: The Exploration of Human Diversity*

Persuasion

The terms *persuasion* and *argumentation* are often used interchangeably, though technically there is a difference. **Argumentation** traditionally refers to writing that is supported by logical evidence in defense of a specific issue. In contrast, **persuasion** is an attempt to change another person's feelings or opinions by using emotional or ethical appeals. For now, the distinction is not particularly important. A writer persuades when he or she wants to *convince* the reader that an idea or opinion is worth holding or to win the reader over to a certain viewpoint. Unlike exposition, persuasion more typically deals with controversial issues. In addition, persuasive writing may use facts, but these facts will be used to support an opinion. By definition, opinions are subjective, meaning that they exist in the mind, influenced as it is by experience and opinion, rather than in external, objective reality. The distinction between fact and opinion is an important one, as you will see in another excerpt from Julia Whitty's article on coral reefs. As you read through the passage, identify the sentences that are persuasive and those that are purely factual.

The worldwide trade in aquarium fish—currently worth $200 million per year and fueled mostly by demand among home aquarists in the United States, Europe, and Japan—is badly in need of transformation. The collection methods are brutal. Using poisons, primarily sodium cyanide, poor people destroy entire ecosystems in order to capture the few stunned fish surviving on the perimeters. The sodium cyanide begins to kill corals and fish within thirty seconds of contact. A handful of fish at the outermost edge of the destruction, disabled but not dead, are then collected by hand.

With each purchase of a lionfish or butterflyfish, the home aquarist, obliviously or uncaringly, funds this devastation

Julia Whitty, "Shoals of Time," *Harper's Magazine*

State the writer's argument in a sentence. <u>The brutal methods used to</u> <u>collect aquarium fish need to be completely changed.</u>

Mixed Modes of Discourse

Thus far, each passage you have read in this section represents one dominant mode. But in nonfiction prose like an essay or article, writers often combine two or more modes. In this excerpt from his entertaining and informative book on the world of skateboarding, Jocko Weyland, a lifetime skater who grew up in Southern California, shifts back and forth between all four modes of discourse. See if you can determine where these shifts occur. Then write a sentence expressing the main idea of the entire passage.

I was thirteen when I acquired the half-pipe. The summer before that, I spent hours each day riding a twenty-foot stretch of sidewalk in front of our town's municipal pool, where until recently I had swum back and forth countless times in swim practice. Even though I was only skating a narrow sidewalk surrounding a rock garden, I had already fallen under the spell. Skating was all that mattered. My former swim coach would come out to talk, shaking his head at my folly and asking me when I was going to return to the fold. No time soon, I'd reply. Actually, never. He had ridden skateboards in the clay-wheel era of the sixties and liked to tell a story about two friends of his who had been riding down a sidewalk, one sitting on the shoulders of the other.

"They hit a crack," he'd tell me, "and they stopped dead. They ate it. The guy on top went flying onto his face. We looked down and saw two white lines on the sidewalk."

"Yeah, what was it?" I would ask.

"It was his two front teeth, they were ground down to his gums."

The story resonated; it was riveting and oddly inspirational, and there was something about the dental carnage that skating had wrought on that poor unfortunate that was powerful and enticing. I'd laugh with my ex-coach and then push off to attack the sidewalk for the hundredth time that day.

Twenty years later I'm still at it. I'm not entirely sure why, though I do have some theories. The primary one is that there is an inexpressible freedom in the act of skating and also in the culture of skateboarding. It has influenced and affected many of the choices I've made in my life, informing almost everything I've done. I'm under the spell of an athletic activity that lies at a unique junction of sport and art. There are no coaches, no rules, no one telling you what to do. It is a solitary pursuit that engenders intense camaraderie. There are no limits to what can be done or imagined except for the ones you impose on yourself, because skating is open-ended and always evolving. It can be done anywhere there is concrete, and reconfigures the public spaces of modern architecture, using constructed areas in imaginative ways that become second nature to the skater but are not understood by the nonpractitioner. Skating is a narcotic that offers release and a negation of self that defies analysis. Skating is different.

But what really matters is actually riding. So at the age of thiry-three, I'm skating alone in front of a building in downtown Manhattan that has a set of five steps I'm trying to ollie over. The ollie is the basis of almost every move in street skating; it involves popping the tail of the board off the concrete so the board is propelled upwards into the air, its path directed by the feet of the skater without any hand-to-board contact. After ten tries I manage it, flying six feet out before landing on the sidewalk and rolling off the curb into the street, where an oncoming garbage truck almost runs me over. I then try to ollie onto a foot-high cube of concrete and wheelie across it, falling on my face in front of the tourists and business people, oblivious to passersby. I try again and again but keep falling, chasing my board when it shoots into traffic and getting scraped up and grimy from my bodily encounters with the cement.

Jocko Weyland, *The Answer Is Never: A Skateboarder's History of the World*

In a passage like this, it is difficult to isolate a dominant mode of discourse. Considering Weyland's purpose, however, which of the four modes of discourse do you think predominates? _Answers will vary, but_

persuasion seems to dominate the narrative and expository elements.

In nonfiction writing, some maintain that everything is an argument.

Main idea _The unique activity of skateboarding merges sport and_

art and appeals to free spirits seeking freedom and release from

convention.

Practice Exercise 4

For the first four passages, first identify the dominant mode of discourse and then write a complete sentence stating the main idea in your own words. (For descriptive passages, write the dominant impression.) For the last passage, identify two modes of discourse.

A.

American front lawns are a symbol of man's control of, or superiority over, his environment. Americans have moved from regional landscapes based on local vegetation and climate to a national landscape based on an aesthetic that considers grassy front yards necessary to domestic happiness. The philosopher Yi-Fu Tuan suggests that the garden, and by extension the lawn, is a pet. Man manages to dominate nature in order to create the lawn and thus makes a pet out of it, lavishing it with care and attention. Lawns must be maintained thoughtfully and systematically and, to be perfect, require constant attention. Otherwise they will revert to nature. Man's attempt to control nature has also been called "the Western way—in which the individual lives in alienation from his environment, competing with it, exploiting it, resisting it, or ignoring it." Lawns, however, often represent man's failure to achieve the perfect green velvety carpet. Despite the chemical and biological warfare that has raged for the past century, crabgrass and dandelions continue to flourish in most neighborhoods. Many homeowners have not learned the aesthetic lessons, have not been totally socialized. Good front lawns never have been completely the norm.

Virginia Scott Jenkins, The Lawn: A History of an American Obsession

Mode of discourse <u>exposition</u>

Main idea or dominant impression <u>The American front lawn</u>

<u>symbolizes man's attempt to dominate nature.</u>

B. The subject of this paragraph is Afghanistan.

It was a beautiful road. At the edges of the plain, enclosing a fertile band of cultivated land several miles wide, high snow-draped mountains rose to ten thousand feet. In the fields alongside, old men walked barefoot in the furrows of their winter ploughings. Children and women were loading boxes of grapes on trucks bound for Pakistan. On either side there were countless ruined buildings that had once been tiny villages. Even in ruin, made from the same soil out of which they appeared to grow, they retained a certain dignity, more like places abandoned quietly than the victims of modern battles. Only the inverted tank turrets lying in the fields nearby, or the hollow rusting carcasses onto which they had once fitted, betrayed the unnatural origins of the destruction.

Jason Elliott, An Unexpected Light: Travels in Afghanistan

Mode of discourse <u>description</u>

Main idea or dominant impression <u>Despite evidence of destruction</u>

<u>as a result of war, the country road, fields, and mountains the</u>

<u>writer observed were still beautiful.</u>

C.

What alarms so many life historians is not that extinctions are occurring but that they appear to be occurring at a greater rate than they have at all but a few times in the past, raising the specter of the sort of wholesale die-offs that ended the reign of the dinosaurs. Do we want, they ask, to exile most of our neighbors to posterity? Exactly how much of our planet's resources do we mean to funnel into people-making? Such questions are serious; they involve choosing among futures, and some of these futures are already with us, in the form of collapsing international fisheries, rich grasslands gnawed and trampled into deserts, forests skeletonized by windborne acids, and so forth. Thus high rates of extinction are seen as a symptom of major problems in the way our species operates—problems that may, if we're not careful, be solved for us. A new word has been coined to define the value most threatened by these overheated rates: "biodiversity." As species disappear, biodiversity declines, and our planet's not-quite-limitless fund of native complexities—so some argue—declines with it.

Thomas Palmer, "The Case for Human Beings," The Atlantic Monthly

Mode of discourse <u>persuasion</u>

Main idea or dominant impression <u>To preserve biodiversity and to</u>

<u>prevent a future catastrophic die-off, we need to decide how best</u>

<u>to stop the accelerating trend of species becoming extinct.</u>

D.

By trial and error animals figure out—sometimes over eons, sometimes over a single lifetime—which plants are safe to eat and which forbidden. Evolutionary counterstrategies arise too: digestive processes that detoxify, feeding strategies that minimize the dangers (like that of the goat, which nibbles harmless quantities of a great many different plants), or heightened powers of observation and memory. This last strategy, at which humans particularly excel, allows one creature to learn from the mistakes and successes of another.

The "mistakes" are, of course, especially instructive, as long as they're not your own or, if they are, they prove less than fatal. For even some of the toxins that kill in large doses turn out in smaller increments to do interesting things—things that are interesting to animals as well as people. According to Ronald K. Siegel, a pharmacologist who has studied intoxication in animals, it is common for animals deliberately to experiment with plant toxins; when an intoxicant is found, the animal will return to the source repeatedly, sometimes with disastrous consequences. Cattle will develop a taste for locoweed that can prove fatal; bighorn sheep will grind their teeth to useless nubs scraping a hallucinogenic lichen off ledge rock. Siegel suggests that some of these adventurous animals served as our Virgils in the garden of psychoactive plants. Goats, who will try a little bit of anything, probably deserve credit for the discovery of coffee: Abyssinian herders in the tenth century observed that their animals would become particularly frisky after nibbling the shrub's bright red berries. Pigeons spacing out on cannabis seeds (a favorite food of many birds) may have tipped off the ancient Chinese (or Aryans or Scythians) to that plant's special properties. Peruvian legend has it that the puma discovered quinine: Indians observed that sick cats were often restored to health after eating the bark of the cinchona tree. Tukano Indians in the Amazon noticed that jaguars, not ordinarily herbivorous, would eat the bark of the yaje vine and hallucinate; the Indians who followed their lead say the yaje vine gives them "jaguar eyes."

Michael Pollan, The Botany of Desire

Mode of discourse <u>exposition</u>

Main idea or dominant impression <u>Both animals and humans benefit</u>

<u>from observing what plants are safe to eat, what plants are</u>

<u>poisonous, and what plants may have medicinal or curative</u>

<u>properties.</u>

E.   The last passage represents two modes of discourse. The subject of the passage is the Devil's Highway, the desert area of southern Arizona between Yuma and Tucson, which illegal immigrants must traverse after sneaking across the border from Mexico.

The plants are noxious and spiked. Saguaros, nopales, the fiendish chollas. Each long cholla spike has a small barb, and they hook into the skin, and they catch in elbow creases and hook forearm and biceps together. Even the green mesquite trees have long thorns set just at eye level.

Much of the wildlife is nocturnal, and it creeps through the nights, poisonous and alien: the sidewinder, the rattlesnake, the scorpion, the giant centipede, the black widow, the tarantula, the brown recluse, the coral snake, the Gila monster. The kissing bug bites you and its poison makes the entire body erupt in red welts. Fungus drifts on the valley dust, and it sinks into the lungs and throbs to life. The millennium has added a further danger: all wild bees in southern Arizona, naturalists report, are now Africanized. As if the desert felt it hadn't made its point, it added killer bees.

Luis Alberto Urrea, *The Devil's Highway*

Modes of discourse <u>description and exposition</u>

Main idea or dominant impression <u>The plants and wildlife in this</u>

<u>desert are poisonous and otherwise harmful to those who come in</u>

<u>contact with them.</u>

■ CHAPTER EXERCISES

Selection 1   [1]It will not do to blame television for the state of our literacy. [2]Television watching does reduce reading and often encroaches on homework. [3]Much of it is admittedly the intellectual equivalent of junk food. [4]But in some respects, such as its use of standard written English, television watching is acculturative. [5]Moreover, as Herbert Walberg points out, the schools themselves must be held partly

responsible for excessive television watching, because they have not firmly insisted that students complete significant amounts of homework, an obvious way
to increase time spent on reading and writing. **6**Nor should our schools be ex-
cused by an appeal to the effects of the decline of the family or the vicious circle
of poverty, important as these factors are. **7**Schools have, or should have, children for six or seven hours a day, five days a week, nine months a year, for thirteen years or more. **8**To assert that they are powerless to make a significant
impact on what their students learn would be to make a claim about American
education that few parents, teachers, or students would find it easy to accept.

E. D. Hirsch, Jr., *Cultural Literacy: What Every American Needs to Know*

A. Vocabulary

For each italicized word from the selection, choose the best definition according to the context in which it appears.

1. *encroaches on* [sentence 2]:
   (a) substitutes for.
   (b) makes irrelevant.
   (c) intrudes upon.
   (d) is more important than.
2. *acculturative* [4]: Describing the process of
   (a) acquiring new ideas.
   (b) accumulating material goods.
   (c) restructuring and reshaping the culture.
   (d) learning about and adopting cultural traits.
3. *assert* [8]:
   (a) complain about.
   (b) declare, claim.
   (c) accuse, blame.
   (d) debate both sides of an issue.

B. Content and Structure

Complete the following questions.
1. A good title for this paragraph would be
   (a) "Television and Our Children's Literacy."
   (b) "Homework vs. Television: How Much Is Too Much?"
   (c) "The Importance of Homework."
   (d) "Our Powerless Schools."
2. What is the state of our literacy, according to what the author
   suggests? _____

   What word or phrase helped you arrive at your answer? _____

   _____

3. The mode of discourse is
   (a) narration.
   (b) description.
   (c) exposition.
   (d) persuasion.
4. Look again at sentences 1–3. Then label the next three sentences according to whether they represent major support (MA) or minor support (MI):

   _____ sentence 4   _____ sentence 5   _____ sentence 6
5. Whom or what does Hirsch criticize *most* for the state of our literacy?
   (a) television itself for the poor programming quality.
   (b) children, who watch television rather than doing homework or reading.
   (c) parents, who do not limit their children's television viewing.
   (d) schools, which do not demand enough work from children.
6. Which of the following is the most accurate paraphrase of sentence 6? The decline of the family and poverty are factors that
   (a) explain children's poor performance in school.
   (b) cannot be dismissed, although schools should not use them as an excuse to require little work from their students.
   (c) make it impossible for many teachers to teach effectively.
   (d) explain why affluent schools produce better educated students than poor schools.

Answers for Selection 1

A. Vocabulary

1. (c)   2. (d)   3. (b)

B. Content and Structure

1. (a)
2. The state of our literacy is poor, suggested by the word "blame" in sentence 1.
3. (d)
4. Sentence 4: MA; sentence 5: MI; sentence 6: MI
5. (d)
6. (b)

Selection 2

[1]Over the last three decades, fast food has infiltrated every nook and cranny of American society. [2]An industry that began with a handful of modest hot dog and hamburger stands in southern California has spread to every corner of the nation, selling a broad range of foods wherever paying customers may be found.

[3]Fast food is now served at restaurants and drive-throughs, at stadiums, airports, zoos, high schools, elementary schools, and universities, on cruise ships, trains, and airplanes, at K-Marts, Wal-Marts, gas stations, and even at hospital cafeterias. [4]In 1970, Americans spent about $6 billion on fast food; in 2000, they spent more than $110 billion. [5]Americans now spend more money on fast food than on higher education, personal computers, computer software, or new cars. [6]They spend more on fast food than on movies, books, magazines, newspapers, videos, and recorded music—combined.

[7]Pull open the glass door, feel the rush of cool air, walk in, get in line, study the backlit color photographs above the counter, place your order, hand over a few dollars, watch teenagers in uniforms pushing various buttons, and moments later take hold of a plastic tray full of food wrapped in colored paper and cardboard. [8]The whole experience of buying fast food has become so routine, so thoroughly unexceptional and mundane, that it is now taken for granted, like brushing your teeth or stopping for a red light. [9]It has become a social custom as American as a small, rectangular, hand-held, frozen, and reheated apple pie.

Eric Schlosser, *Fast Food Nation: The Dark Side of the All-American Meal*

A. Vocabulary

For each italicized word from the selection, write the dictionary definition most appropriate for the context.

1. fast food has *infiltrated* [sentence 1]: <u>surreptitiously penetrated</u>

2. every *nook and cranny* [1]: <u>an expression meaning every corner and</u>
   <u>small area</u>

3. so thoroughly *unexceptional* [8]: <u>usual, ordinary</u>

4. so thoroughly *mundane* [8]: <u>commonplace, ordinary</u>

B. Content and Structure

Complete the following questions.
1. Which two modes of discourse are represented in the passage?
   (a) narration.
   (b) description.
   (c) (exposition.)
   (d) (persuasion.)
2. A good title for this paragraph would be
   (a) "$6 Billion for Fast Food Every Year."
   (b) "Why Americans Eat So Much Fast Food."

    (c) ("The Pervasiveness of Fast Food Restaurants.")
    (d) "A McDonald's or a Burger King on Every Block."
3. Sentences 3–6, taken together, support the idea that
    (a) (fast food has made inroads in every part of American life and accounts for a large amount of our yearly expenditures.)
    (b) Americans spend more money at fast food restaurants than at traditional restaurants.
    (c) the fast food industry has set a bad precedent for Americans' dining habits.
    (d) the fast food industry is the largest growing segment in the American economy today.
4. Read sentence 7 again, which suggests that
    (a) teenagers are exploited in the fast food industry.
    (b) fast food restaurants are clean and sanitary.
    (c) (fast food restaurants are uniform, and they all operate alike.)
    (d) fast food restaurants offer inexpensive food served quickly.
5. Label the following sentences from paragraph 1 as follows: MAIN (main idea); MA (major support); or MI (minor support).

MAIN sentence 1   MAIN sentence 2   MA sentence 3

MA sentence 4   MA sentence 5   MA sentence 6

Selection 3

[1]Ambivalence about the death penalty is an American tradition. [2]When the Republic was founded, all the states, following English law, imposed capital punishment. [3]But the humanistic impulses that favored democracy led to questions about whether the state should have the right to kill the citizens upon whose consent government was erected. [4]Jefferson was among the earliest advocates of restricting executions. [5] In 1846, Michigan became the first American state to outlaw capital punishment, except in the case of treason, and public opinion has continued to vacillate on the issue. [6]Following the Second World War and the rise and fall of a number of totalitarian governments, Western European nations began abandoning capital punishment, but their example is of limited relevance to us, since our murder rate is roughly four times the rate in Europe. [7]One need only glance at a TV screen to realize that murder remains an American preoccupation, and the concomitant questions of how to deal with it challenge contending strains in our moral thought, pitting Old Testament against New, retribution against forgiveness.

Scott Turow, "To Kill or Not to Kill," *The New Yorker*

A. Vocabulary

For each italicized word from the selection, write the dictionary definition most appropriate for the context.

1. *Ambivalence* about the death penalty [sentence 1]   <u>uncertainty,</u>

   <u>indecisiveness, being of two minds</u>

2. the earlier *advocates* [4] <u>supporters, those who argue for a cause</u>

3. public opinion has continued to *vacillate* [5] <u>waver, fluctuate</u>

4. *totalitarian* governments [6] <u>characterizing a central government</u>

   <u>that has absolute control over all aspects of life and that</u>

   <u>suppresses free political thought or expression</u>

5. the *concomitant* questions [7] <u>those that exist concurrently</u>

6. *retribution* against forgiveness [7] <u>repayment, vengeance, punishment</u>

B. Content and Structure

Complete the following questions.

1. The first sentence of the paragraph represents Turow's main point. Which of the following is correct?
   (a) "Ambivalence about the death penalty" is the main idea and "an American tradition" is the controlling idea.
   (b) "An American tradition" is the main idea and "ambivalence about the death penalty" is the controlling idea.

2. The writer's purpose in the paragraph is to
   (a) relate a historical event.
   (b) examine the reasons the death penalty is part of our judicial system.
   (c) explain our long-standing ambivalence toward the death penalty.
   (d) persuade the reader that the death penalty is immoral and should be abolished.

3. According to Turow, what is the primary reason that Americans have questioned whether or not the death penalty was defensible?
   (a) The country was established on humanistic and democratic impulses, which seemed contrary to the idea of imposing a death penalty.
   (b) The country was following the lead of European nations, which gradually eliminated the death penalty.
   (c) Michigan outlawed the death penalty except in cases of treason, and that action got people thinking.

    (d) America did not want to follow in the footsteps of totalitarian regimes, which often used the death penalty to stifle political dissent.

4. What does Turow mean in the last part of sentence 3 when he writes, "whether the state should have the right to kill the citizens upon whose consent government was erected"?
    (a) It would be more humane for the government to sentence such criminals to life in prison rather than to execute them.
    (b) The state exists because all the citizens, even those who commit serious crimes, consent to it; thus, by definition, the state cannot exist to harm its own citizens.
    (c) No one who commits a crime deserving of capital punishment would willingly consent to be executed.
    (d) The state was erected on the principle of the death penalty, and its citizens consented to that principle.

5. The reference to the Old and the New Testament and to "retribution against forgiveness" in the last sentence suggests that
    (a) the ambivalence Americans feel about capital punishment is rooted in religious tradition.
    (b) Americans are close to resolving their ambivalence toward capital punishment.
    (c) America's religious groups are predominantly opposed to capital punishment.
    (d) American ambivalence toward capital punishment will soon be resolved by the courts.

■ PRACTICE ESSAY

From *Seabiscuit: An American Legend* "How Jockeys Controlled Their Weight"
Laura Hillenbrand

Laura Hillenbrand's best-selling 2001 book about the legendary racehorse, Seabiscuit, not only introduces the reader to the world of Thoroughbred horse racing, but also examines the social and cultural forces at work during the 1930s and the dark years of the Depression when America needed a diversion from its economic woes. Seabiscuit, an ungainly and not particularly attractive horse, represented one such diversion, as he won race after race and astonished the nation with his incredible speeds. Since 1989 Laura Hillenbrand has been writing about Thoroughbred racing for Equus *magazine. She has also published widely in other magazines, among them* The Blood-Horse, Thoroughbred Times, The Backstretch, Turf, *and* Sport Digest. *The genesis for her best-selling book was a 1998 article published in* American Heritage, *which won the Eclipse Award for Magazine Writing.*

Preview Questions

1. What do you know about horse racing? Have you ever attended a horse race or watched one of the nation's premier horse races on television (i.e., the Kentucky Derby, the Preakness, the Belmont Stakes)? What are some reasons that horse racing has been a popular pastime for Americans?

2. Why must racing jockeys be small? What is a handicap, and how is one determined?

1   They called the scale "the Oracle," and they lived in slavery to it. In the 1920s and 1930s, the imposts, or weights horses were assigned to carry in races, generally ranged from 83 pounds to 130 or more, depending on the rank of the horse and the importance of the race. A rider could be no more than 5 pounds over the assigned weight or he would be taken off the horse. Some trainers trimmed that leeway down to just a half pound. To make weight in anything but high-class stakes races, jockeys had to keep their weight to no more than 114 pounds. Riders competing in ordinary weekday events needed to whittle themselves down another 5 pounds or so, while those in the lowest echelons of the sport couldn't weigh much more than 100. The lighter a rider was, the greater the number of horses he could ride. "Some riders," wrote Eddie Arcaro,[1] "will all but saw their legs off to get within the limit."

2   A few riders were naturally tiny enough to make weight without difficulty, and they earned the burning envy of every other jockey. Most of them were young teenagers whose growth spurts lay ahead of them. To ensure that they didn't waste time and money training and supporting boys who would eventually grow out of their trade, contract trainers checked the foot size of every potential bug boy,[2] since a large foot is a fairly good sign of a coming growth spurt. Many also inspected the height and weight of a potential bug boy's siblings. Trainer Woody Stephens, who began his racing career as a bug boy in the late 1920s, always felt he got lucky in this respect. In vetting him for the job, his trainer neglected to look at his sister, a local basketball phenom.

3   Virtually every adult rider, and most of the kids, naturally tended to weigh too much. Cheating, if you did it right, could help a little. One pudgy 140-pound rider earned a place in reinsman legend by fooling a profoundly myopic clerk of scales by skewing the readout to register him at 110. No one is exactly sure how he did it, but it is believed that either he positioned his feet on a nonregistering part of the scale or his valet

[1]Eddie Arcaro was a famous American jockey who won the Kentucky Derby five times and won the Triple Crown twice during his long career.

[2]A bug boy is an apprentice jockey who gets a weight allowance to compensate for his inexperience.

stuck his whip under his seat and lifted up. He made it through an entire season before someone caught him.

4   Most jockeys took a more straightforward approach: the radical diet, consisting of six hundred calories a day. Red Pollard[3] went as long as a year eating nothing but eggs. Sunny Jim Fitzsimmons confessed that during his riding days a typical dinner consisted of a leaf or two of lettuce, and he would eat them only after placing them on a windowsill to dry the water out of them. Water, because of its weight, was the prime enemy, and jockeys went to absurd lengths to keep it out of their systems. Most drank virtually nothing. A common practice was to have jockey's room valets open soda cans by puncturing the top with an ice pick, making it impossible to drink more than a few drops at a time. The sight and sound of water became a torment; Fitzsimmons habitually avoided areas of the barn where horses were being washed because the spectacle of flowing water was agonizing.

5   But the weight maximums were so low that near fasting and water deprivation weren't enough. Even what little water and calories the body had taken in had to be eliminated. Many riders were "heavers," poking their fingers down their throats to vomit up their meals. Others chewed gum to trigger salivation; Tommy Luther could spit off as much as half a pound in a few hours. Then there were the sweating rituals, topped by "road work." This practice, used by both Red Pollard and George Woolf, involved donning heavy underwear, zipping into a rubber suit, swaddling in hooded winter gear and woolen horse blankets, then running around and around the track, preferably under a blistering summer sun. Stephens remembered seeing jockeys in full road-work attire gathering at a bowling alley, so lathered that sweat spouted from their shoes with each step. After road work, there were Turkish baths, where jockeys congregated for mornings of communal sweating. The desiccation practices of jockeys were lampooned by turf writer Joe H. Palmer in a column written on jockey Abelardo DeLara: "DeLara has to sweat off about two pounds a day to make weight. Last year, by his own estimate, he lost 600 pounds this way. Since he weighs about 110, it is a mere matter of arithmetic that he would be a bit more than 700 pounds if he hadn't reduced so regularly."

A. Comprehension

Choose the answer that best completes each statement. Do not refer to the selection while doing this exercise.

---

[3]Red Pollard and George Woolf (mentioned later in paragraph 5) both rode Seabiscuit. Sunny Jim Fitzsimmons was another well-known jockey in the late 1930s.

1. In the 1920s and 1930s, jockeys had to maintain a weight of no more than
    (a) 95 pounds.
    (b) 100 pounds.
    (c) (114 pounds.)
    (d) 145 pounds.
2. Jockeys called the scales they had to weigh themselves on
    (a) ("the Oracle.")
    (b) "the Career Breaker."
    (c) "the Monster."
    (d) "the Master."
3. Horse trainers did not want to waste their time training bug boys (young apprentice jockeys) if eventually they would
    (a) grow bored with racing and drop out.
    (b) prove not to be winners.
    (c) (grow to be too big to ride.)
    (d) leave and sign on with another trainer.
4. Because it added weight to their bodies, most jockeys did everything they could to avoid
    (a) eating vegetables.
    (b) drinking alcohol.
    (c) eating bread or other carbohydrates.
    (d) (drinking water.)
5. To ensure that they would meet weight restrictions, many jockeys
    (a) performed exhausting workouts in the gym.
    (b) (underwent various types of sweating rituals.)
    (c) became anorexic.
    (d) lied about their weight or cheated.

B. Vocabulary

For each italicized word from the selection, choose the best definition according to the context in which it appears. You may refer to the selection to answer the questions in this section and in all the remaining sections.

1. needed to *whittle* themselves *down* to [paragraph 1]:
    (a) (reduce gradually.)
    (b) gain self-respect.
    (c) develop their muscles.
    (d) learn to handle a horse under dangerous circumstances.
2. those in the lowest *echelons* [1]:
    (a) social classes.
    (b) (ranks, levels.)
    (c) weight categories.
    (d) abilities or skills.

3. a profoundly *myopic* clerk [3]:
   (a) nearly blind.
   (b) (near-sighted.)
   (c) far-sighted.
   (d) color blind.
4. the *desiccation* practices [5]:
   (a) retention.
   (b) starvation.
   (c) weight loss.
   (d) (removing moisture.)
5. the practices were *lampooned* [5]:
   (a) severely criticized.
   (b) (made fun of.)
   (c) exaggerated.
   (d) questioned.

C. Structure

Complete the following questions.

1. The predominant mode of discourse in the passage as a whole is
   (a) narration.
   (b) description.
   (c) (exposition.)
   (d) persuasion.
2. Why do you think that jockeys referred to the weight scale as "the Oracle"?   An oracle both predicts the future and dispenses wise

   counsel. Thus, the scale would be the final word in determining

   their future as jockeys: Whether they would race or not depended

   on whether they maintained the proper weight.
3. Hillenbrand emphasizes that the ideal weight for a jockey was around 100 pounds because this weight ensured that
   (a) heavier jockeys would hurt the horses.
   (b) they would look good in their jockey outfits.
   (c) (they could ride a horse no matter what it weighed.)
   (d) they could ride in any state in the nation, including championship races like the Kentucky Derby.
4. Look again at paragraph 5. Write a main-idea sentence for it. Jockeys

   went to often absurd lengths to keep their weight down.

5. Read the end of paragraph 5 again, where the turf writer Joe H. Palmer commented on the weight lost by the jockey Abedlardo DeLara. What point was Palmer trying to make?
   (a) DeLara had exaggerated about all the weight he had lost by sweating.
   (b) DeLara was not a very good jockey.
   (c) DeLara had a serious weight problem that often kept him from racing.
   (d) The usual fasting and water deprivation hadn't worked for DeLara.

D. Questions for Discussion and Analysis

1. What might be the reason that racehorses carry imposts, or weights? What do these imposts have to do with the subject of this essay, jockeys' attempts to keep their weights at certain prescribed levels?
2. Why might teenage boys coming of age during the Depression have been attracted to horse racing?

ON THE WEB

Read reviews of the book from which this passage is taken, *Seabiscuit: An American Legend,* at www.powells.com or www.amazon.com.

2

Reading Between the Lines: Making Accurate Inferences

CHAPTER OBJECTIVES

Chapter 2 will help you improve your reading skills by showing you how to make inferences and by acquainting you with the following topics:

- Facts and inferences

- Definition of inference

- Problems with inferences

- Explaining sample inferences

- Making open-ended inferences

- Making inferences with visual material

■ FACTS AND INFERENCES

We must first distinguish inferences from facts. A fact is a verifiable piece of information; that is, it can be duplicated, measured, confirmed in other sources, demonstrated, or proved. If I say that our living room is 20 feet long, the matter can easily be proved or disproved with a tape measure. Here are three more facts:

- Eucalyptus trees are native to Australia.
- The gestation period for an elephant is 18 months.
- Watermelon contains more vitamin C than oranges.

Inferences are *derived* from facts. From the above facts, we might infer the following:

- Eucalyptus trees probably grow well in Australia.
- The size of an animal determines the length of gestation. (For this inference, we draw on common knowledge: The gestation period for humans, who are smaller than elephants, is only nine months.)
- Watermelon is a better source of vitamin C than oranges. Another inference is that we should eat more watermelon.

In the real world, we use inferences to help us organize our lives and to solve everyday problems. Let's say we are planning a wedding reception. After measuring the reception area adjoining the church, we determine that the hall is 60 feet long and 40 feet wide. We are inviting only 25 people to the ceremony and reception. From these two sets of facts, we might draw these inferences:

- The reception hall is too large for such a small crowd.
- People generally feel lost when they are forced to congregate in a large space.
- We should choose a smaller location that would be more suitable for such a small group.

Notice that the first inference is derived directly from the first fact; the second inference is derived both from the first fact and from our experience. The third inference, however, is a **conclusion,** another type of inference that is derived from the facts but that also points to a solution. Inferences, then, proceed from facts.

■ INFERENCES DEFINED

As the preceding examples show, we make inferences all the time. William Lutz has defined an inference as "a statement about the unknown based on the known."[1] In reading, the inference-making process involves reading between the lines, connecting facts to make sense of them when no explanation is offered, or drawing a conclusion about a future course of action based on the facts. In this chapter, you will practice making inferences with several passages of varying levels of difficulty.

Practice Exercise 1

Carefully read the following report and the observations based on it. On the basis of the information presented, indicate whether you think the observations are true, false, or doubtful. Circle "T" if the observation is definitely true, circle "F" if the observation is definitely false, and circle "?" if the observation may be either true or false. Judge each observation in order.[2]

A well-liked college teacher had just completed making up the final examinations and had turned off the lights in the office. Just then a tall, broad figure with dark glasses appeared and demanded the examination. The professor opened the drawer. Everything in the drawer was picked up and the individual ran down the corridor. The dean was notified immediately.

1.	The thief was tall, broad, and wore dark glasses.	T	F	?
2.	The professor turned off the lights.	T	F	?
3.	A tall, broad figure demanded the examination.	T	F	?
4.	The examination was picked up by someone.	T	F	?
5.	The examination was picked up by the professor.	T	F	?
6.	A tall, broad figure appeared after the professor turned off the lights in the office.	T	F	?
7.	The man who opened the drawer was the professor.	T	F	?
8.	The professor ran down the corridor.	T	F	?
9.	The drawer was never actually opened.	T	F	?
10.	In this report three persons are referred to.	T	F	?

Answers

1. **?** There is no evidence that there was a thief.
2. **?** Are the college teacher and the professor the same person?
3. **T** There is an exact statement in the story that proves this to be true.
4. **?** There is no mention of the examination being or not being picked up by someone.

[1]William Lutz is a professor of English at Rutgers University in New Jersey. This definition comes from his essay "Abstracting Our Way into Doublespeak," from *The New Doublespeak* (1996).
[2]This exercise is adapted from Joseph A. DeVito, *General Semantics: Guide and Workbook.* The test is based on one developed by William Honey, *Communication and Organizational Behavior,* 3rd ed. (Irwin, 1973).

5. **?** We don't know if anyone picked up the examination.
6. **?** We don't know who turned off the lights.
7. **?** We don't know if the professor was a man or a woman.
8. **?** We don't know who ran down the corridor.
9. **F** The drawer was opened.
10. **?** There could have been three or four people: We don't know if the professor and the college teacher were the same person.

■ PROBLEMS WITH INFERENCES

The foregoing exercise reveals these difficulties with inferences:

- Our assumptions often get in the way of making accurate inferences.
- We may not read carefully enough or pay close enough attention to the language.
- We may indulge in stereotyping. This problem is particularly evident in question 7, if we incorrectly infer that a professor is more likely to be a man than a woman.

In the real world, as well, the more we get carried away with our assumptions and make inferences based on facts we do not have, on an isolated fact, or on facts that we ignore, the less probable it is that our inferences are correct.

It is the same in reading. We should not "read into" the author's words *beyond what they suggest or imply.* Because our own experiences are necessarily limited, relying on them when we read may lead us astray from the writer's real intentions. The result may be that we misread or misinterpret. Thus, in this textbook, it is safer to restrict your answers to only what the writer suggests, and not base them on something you have read or experienced outside the text.

■ USING EVIDENCE TO MAKE INFERENCES

In the first part of this chapter, you are asked to label inference questions in three ways.

- **Probably accurate (PA).** This kind of inference follows from the facts presented or is strongly implied by the author's words. We have enough information to say that the inference is most likely accurate.
- **Probably inaccurate (PI).** An inaccurate inference misstates or distorts the writer's words and observations.
- **Not in the passage (NP).** These are inferences that you can't reasonably make because they're not implied in the passage. Either there is

insufficient evidence or the information in the passage is insufficient to determine accuracy or inaccuracy.

Of course, when you read your textbook chapters and other assigned college material, you would not label a writer's ideas in this way. You are asked to do so here only for practice in distinguishing between appropriate and inappropriate inferences. To begin, read these two short passages and label the inference statements. Then study the answers and explanations that follow. The first is a little parable titled "Trucks." (A parable is a little story written to illustrate a moral truth.)

> A customs officer observes a truck pulling up at the border. Suspicious, he orders the driver out and searches the vehicle. He pulls off panels, bumpers, and wheel cases but finds not a single scrap of contraband, whereupon, still suspicious but at a loss to know where else to search, he waves the driver through. The next week, the same driver arrives. Again the official searches, and again finds nothing illicit. Over the years, the official tries full-body searches, X rays, and sonar, anything he can think of, and each week the same man drives up, but no mysterious cargo ever appears, and each time, reluctantly, the customs man waves the driver on.
>
> Finally, after many years, the officer is about to retire. The driver pulls up.
>
> "I know you're a smuggler," the customs officer says. "Don't bother denying it. But damned if I can figure out what you've been smuggling all these years. I'm leaving now. I swear to you I can do you no harm. Won't you please tell me what you've been smuggling?"
>
> "Trucks," the driver says.
>
> Todd Gitlin, "Trucks,"
Media Unlimited: How the Torrent of Images and Sounds Overwhelms Our Lives

On the basis of the evidence in the parable, label these inferences as follows: PA (probably accurate), PI (probably inaccurate), or NP (not in the passage).

1. _____ The customs officer made a lifetime career out of trying to catch the truck driver smuggling illegal goods.

2. _____ The first time the customs officer encountered the truck driver, he had good reason to be suspicious.

3. _____ The truck driver had been smuggling illicit goods for many years, but they were so cleverly hidden that the customs officer never found them.

4. _____ Sometimes in their fixation on observing small details, people miss the obvious.

Here are the answers. Question 1 should be marked PA. The phrases "over the years" and "after many years" suggest that this inference is a safe one. Question 2 is NP. The author does not offer any particular reason that would have made the customs officer suspicious. Perhaps he was just naturally suspicious as the result of his contact with other smugglers. Question 3 should be marked PI. After all those years of careful searches, if something illegal had been concealed in the truck, the officer surely would have spotted it. The last question is PA, because this represents a logical conclusion or lesson that parable is meant to exemplify.

The second passage is a slightly more difficult fable:

Death speaks:

[1]There was a merchant in Bagdad who sent his servant to market to buy provisions and in a little while the servant came back, white and trembling, and said, Master, just now when I was in the market-place I was jostled by a woman in the crowd and when I turned I saw it was Death that jostled me. [2]She looked at me and made a threatening gesture; now, lend me your horse and I will ride away from this city and avoid my fate. [3]I will go to Samarra and there Death will not find me. [4]The merchant lent him his horse, and the servant mounted it, and he dug his spurs in its flanks and as fast as the horse could gallop he went. [5]Then the merchant went down to the market-place and he saw me standing in the crowd and he came to me and said, Why did you make a threatening gesture to my servant when you saw him this morning? [6]That was not a threatening gesture, I said, it was only a start of surprise. [7]I was astonished to see him in Bagdad, for I had an appointment with him tonight in Samarra.

W. Somerset Maugham, "Death Speaks," *Sheppey*

On the basis of the evidence in the fable, label these inferences as follows: PA (probably accurate), PI (probably inaccurate), or NP (not in the passage).

1. _____ The servant misinterpreted Death's gesture in the market-place.
2. _____ The merchant thought his servant was foolish to go to Samarra.
3. _____ The time and place of our death are predetermined before we are born.
4. _____ The servant thought he could outwit Death.
5. _____ Ironically, in trying to escape Death, the servant sealed his own fate.

Here are the answers: (1) PA; (2) PI; (3) NP; (4) PA; (5) PA. Let us examine the reasoning behind them.

The first inference is clearly *accurate* based on the information in sentences 6 and 7; however, to make this inference, we must accept Death's explanation for her gesture and reject the servant's explanation. The second inference should be marked *probably inaccurate;* sentence 4 implies that the merchant willingly lent his horse, suggesting that he agreed with his servant's decision to flee Death's threatening gesture. Further evidence is that later the merchant scolded Death for frightening his servant. Also, a good master would not want his servant to die. Thus the original inference statement misinterprets the events of the story.

The third inference should be marked *not in the passage* for the following reasons: Death says that she already knew in advance that the servant would be in Samarra, implying that the servant's death was predetermined; however, the fable says nothing about our own death being predetermined, much less predetermined before our birth.

Last, inferences 4 and 5 should be labeled *probably accurate:* In attempting to outwit Death and escape his fate, the servant, instead, sealed his own fate. We and the narrator, Death, know what the servant does not. (This fable nicely illustrates the concept of dramatic irony.)

As should be plain by now, these inference questions make you think. Although some of these inferences may seem trivial or even nit picky, they do force you to look carefully at a passage and to exercise care in considering the evidence. Practicing with inferences will help you become both an active, questioning reader and a better thinker, seeing implications beyond the writer's literal words. Because these inference questions are quite challenging, be sure to look back at the text to find the phrase or sentence that pertains to each question. Try not to jump to conclusions or to intrude your own assumptions, stereotypes, or personal beliefs. Remember that in making inferences, you may encounter a gray area—that is, you may not be wholly certain that the inference is verifiably true, only that it is *probably* accurate or *probably* inaccurate. If you disagree with an answer, try to determine by yourself where you went wrong; if you are still unsure, ask your instructor for help.

As you saw in the two preceding examples, making inferences requires the reader to connect details, to infer explanations when the writer offers none, and to draw logical conclusions. These skills require you to examine the evidence—the information within the passage—that leads to the inference. Here are two more passages for you to practice with. For each, try to locate the evidence that leads to the inference. The first passage is an excerpt from Tobias Wolff's engaging autobiography, *This Boy's Life.* In it Wolff describes the grades he received while attending the public high school in Concrete, a town in eastern Washington State.

> I brought home good grades at first. They were a fraud—I copied other kids' homework on the bus down from Chinook and studied for tests in the hallways as I walked from class to class. After the first marking period I didn't bother to do that much. I stopped studying altogether. Then I was given C's instead of A's, yet no one at home ever knew that my grades had fallen. The report cards were made out, incredibly enough, in pencil, and I owned some pencils myself.

Tobias Wolff, *This Boy's Life*

On the basis of the evidence in the paragraph, mark these statements as follows: PA (probably accurate), PI (probably inaccurate), or NP (not in the passage).

1. _PI_ Students at the high school in Concrete had to work hard to receive A's.
2. _PA_ The narrator continued to receive good grades only because he erased the teacher's marks and changed them to higher ones.
3. _PA_ The teachers were naive to record students' grades in pencil.

The second excerpt is from a broadcasting and media textbook and is part of a section titled "Media Sharing: Napster and Peer-to-Peer Servers."

Technology can create new possibilities and immense problems simultaneously. Napster, a music swapping service, began operating in June 1999 and quickly revolutionized the way people sought out and acquired music. The Napster program, created by then-college-freshman Shawn Fanning, allowed people to perform a music search and then swap music and multimedia files stored on their computers. By typing in a title or artist, the Napster user could call up a list of potential servers where a person could download the file. Clicking on the song title would cause the file to be "shared" or transferred from computer to computer. When "members" joined Napster, the contents of their hard drive were made available to other Napster users via a central directory. Soon (and we mean almost immediately) college students around the country started swapping songs.

By December 1999, the Recording Industry Association of America (RIAA), worried that record sales could be hurt, sued for copyright infringement. Metallica and other performers threatened suit as well. In spring 2000, many universities tried to ban Napster because student use was overwhelming college servers and as summer ended, a U.S. District Court ordered Napster to shut down. Napster was ultimately ordered to block 100 percent of all copyrighted material. Unable to meet the requirements of the court order, Napster ceased operations in 2001 and then filed for bankruptcy some months later.

Joseph R. Dominick, Fritz Messere, and Barry L. Sherman,
Broadcasting, Cable, the Internet, and Beyond: An Introduction to Modern Electronic Media

For each question, choose the most accurate inference.

1. The idea of swapping music files appealed to Napster users because
    (a) it allowed students to download music using superfast connections.
    (b) the music obtained through such swapping was free.
    (c) they enjoyed using a service created by Shawn Fanning, whom they considered a peer.
    (d) their computer hard drives could store far more music than they could store on CDs.

2. Universities tried to ban students from using Napster because
    (a) students were spending so much time swapping music that their grades were suffering.
    (b) the universities thought that file swapping was unethical.
    (c) the universities no longer had control over what their students were doing.
    (d) the music sharing was so prevalent that it interfered with the universities' computer systems.

Practice Exercise 2

In this section are three short passages arranged from least difficult to most difficult. Answer the questions as directed.

A. This excerpt describes the poet Gary Soto's first experiences in elementary school.

For four years I attended St. John's Catholic School where short nuns threw chalk at me, chased me with books cocked over their heads, squeezed me into cloak closets and, on slow days, asked me to pop erasers and to wipe the blackboard clean. Finally, in the fifth grade, my mother sent me to Jefferson Elementary. The Principal, Mr. Buckalew, kindly ushered me to the fifth grade teachers, Mr. Stendhal and Mrs. Sloan. We stood in the hallway with the principal's hand on my shoulder. Mr. Stendhal asked what book I had read in the fourth grade, to which, after a dark and squinting deliberation, I answered: *The Story of the United States Marines*. Mr. Stendhal and Mrs. Sloan looked at one another with a "you take him" look. Mr. Buckalew lifted his hand from my shoulder and walked slowly away.

Gary Soto, *Living Up the Street*

1. Which of the following can you infer about the author?
    (a) He was a model student.
    (b) He had a reputation among teachers for being a troublemaker.
    (c) He had been asked to leave Catholic school.
    (d) He enjoyed public school more than Catholic school.
2. What inference can you make about the book Soto says he read in fourth grade, *The Story of the United States Marines?*
    (a) It was assigned reading at his former school.
    (b) He probably hadn't read it.
    (c) He probably had read it.
    (d) There is no way to tell whether he had read it or not.
3. What inference can you make about his new teachers, Mr. Stendhal and Mrs. Sloan?
    (a) They were impressed with Soto's answer.
    (b) Soto ended up in Mrs. Sloan's class.
    (c) Soto ended up in Mr. Stendhal's class.
    (d) They both thought Soto was something of a wise guy.

B. The author describes a job interview with William Shawn, the legendary editor of *The New Yorker* magazine.

When I was nineteen, William Shawn interviewed me for a summer job at *The New Yorker*. To grasp the full import of what follows, you should know that I considered *The New Yorker* a cathedral and Mr. Shawn a figure so godlike that I expected a faint nimbus to emanate from his ruddy head. During the course of our conversation, he asked me what other magazines I hoped to write for.

"Um, *Esquire*, the *Saturday Review*, and—"

I wanted to say *"Ms.,"* but my lips had already butted against the *M*—too late for a politic retreat—when I realized I had no idea how to pronounce it. Lest you conclude that I had been raised in Ulan Bator, I might remind you that in 1973, when I met Mr. Shawn, *Ms.* magazine had been published for scarcely a year, and most people, including me, had never heard the word *Ms.* used as a term of address. (Mr. Shawn had called me Miss Fadiman. *He* was so venerated by his writers that "Mister" had virtually become part of his name.) Its pronunciation, reflexive now, was not as obvious as you might think. After all, *Mr.* is not pronounced "Mir," and *Mrs.* is not pronounced "Mirz." Was it "Mzzzzz"? "Miz"? "Muz"?

In that apocalyptic split second, I somehow alighted on "Em Ess," which I knew to be the correct pronunciation of *ms.*, or manuscript.

Mr. Shawn didn't blink. He gave no indication that I had said anything untoward. In fact, he calmly proceeded to discuss the new feminist magazine—its history, its merits, its demerits, the opportunities it might offer a young writer like myself—for four or five minutes *without ever mentioning its name*.

Anne Fadiman, "The His'er Problem," Ex Libris

1. Which of the following can you accurately infer about Mr. Shawn?
   (a) He had never heard of *Ms.* magazine.
   (b) He didn't want to hire Fadiman for a job at *The New Yorker*.
   (c) He didn't know how to pronounce the title of *Ms.* magazine himself.
   (d) He didn't want to embarrass Fadiman by pronouncing *Ms.* correctly.
2. Which of the following can you accurately infer about Anne Fadiman?
   (a) She finally got a job at *The New Yorker*.
   (b) She was impressed with Mr. Shawn's good manners.
   (c) She was raised in Ulan Bator, the capital of Mongolia.
   (d) She did not really want to write for *Ms.* magazine.

C. In this passage from Bill Bryson's *Notes from a Small Island,* a book about traveling in England, he relates an experience that happened to him in Calais, France, the small city where one catches a ferry to cross the English Channel to England.

For reasons that I have never understood, the French have a particular genius when it comes to tacky religious keepsakes, and in a gloomy shop on a corner of the Place d'Armes, I found one I liked: a plastic model of the Virgin Mary standing with beckoning arms in a kind of grotto fashioned from seashells, miniature starfish, lacy sprigs of dried seaweed, and a polished lobster claw. Glued to the back of the Madonna's head was a halo made from a plastic curtain ring, and on the lobster claw the model's gifted creator had painted an oddly festive-looking *"Calais!"* in neat script. I hesitated because it cost a lot of money, but when the lady of the shop showed me that it also plugged in and lit up like a fun-fair ride at Blackpool, the only question in my mind was whether one would be enough. *"C'est très jolie,"*[3] she said in a kind of astonished hush when she realized that I was prepared to pay real money for it, and bustled off to get it wrapped and paid for before I came to my senses and cried, "Say, where am I? And what, pray, is *this* tacky piece of Franco-*merde*[4] I see before me?"

"C'est très jolie," she kept repeating soothingly, as if afraid of disturbing my wakeful slumber. I think it may have been some time since she had sold a Virgin Mary with Seashells Occasional Light. In any case, as the shop door shut behind me, I distinctly heard a whoop of joy.

Bill Bryson, *Notes from a Small Island*

1. When Bryson refers to the maker of the religious keepsake as a "gifted creator," we can infer that he
   (a) truly admired the artist's talent.
   (b) is being sarcastic.
   (c) wanted to see more of the artist's work.
   (d) personally knew the artist.
2. We can accurately infer that the shopkeeper let out a "whoop of joy" after Bryson left because she
   (a) thought Bryson was a sucker for buying such a tacky object.
   (b) had made an expensive sale and was celebrating her good fortune.
   (c) knew Bryson would be back to buy more items the next day.
   (d) had charged him twice what it was worth, and she had fooled him.
3. Concerning Bryson, we can also infer that he
   (a) is a deeply religious person.
   (b) delights in buying tacky tourist souvenirs.
   (c) wanted to give the Virgin Mary to a religious friend at home.

[3]*C'est très jolie:* French for "It's very pretty."
[4]*Merde:* French for "shit."

■ MAKING OPEN-ENDED INFERENCES

The term *open-ended inference* means that you draw your own inferences and state them in your own words, which is a more realistic way of making inferences in your everyday reading. Study this first example, in which the writer John Hildebrand is describing a horse named Blue.

> Not much bigger than a pony, Blue stood fourteen hands high and weighed 950 pounds. His mother was a bucking horse bought from a rodeo, mean and ornery as they come, her history written in overlapping brands that covered her flanks.
>
> John Hildebrand, *Mapping the Farm*

Why did Blue's mother have so many brands? The overlapping brands suggested that she had had several owners, each of whom had branded her.

(Making the correct inference here depends on your knowing the meaning of the word *brand* as it pertains to livestock. If you are unsure, check the dictionary.)

The second example is from David Lamb's book, *Over the Hills,* in which he describes a cross-country bicycle trip he made from Virginia to California. Here he contrasts the typical overweight American's concern with dieting and his own nutritional intake while on the road.

> Between 1980 and 1991—when the diet business was in full bloom—the average adult American put on eight pounds. That, says the National Center for Health Statistics, is the equivalent of an extra one million tons of fat on the waistline of a nation where one in three persons is certifiably overweight. Ironically, the more we spend trying to get thin—$15 billion a year on diet soft drinks alone, another $4 billion on stuff like Lean Cuisine and pseudo-food appetite suppressants—the plumper we become. Something is clearly out of whack. These contradictions were of no concern to me, however, because I had learned the secret of gluttony without guilt. Day after day I started the morning with French toast or pancakes, enjoyed apple pie with double scoops of ice cream during pre-noon coffee breaks, drank milk shakes, Hawaiian Punch and chocolate milk by the bucketful, snacked on three or four candy bars in the afternoon and often had room for a hot dog or two before I started thinking about dinner. Unlike the rest of America, the more I ate, the less I weighed. I could eat two pieces of coconut custard pie at 11 A.M. and within an hour on the road burn off the 450 calories and then some. By the time I reached western Arkansas, the love handles on my waist had disappeared and I had to tighten my belt an extra notch to keep my pants up.
>
> David Lamb, *Over the Hills*

According to Lamb's experiences (and aside from overeating), why are so many Americans overweight? <u>They don't exercise enough.</u>

Practice Exercise 3

Answer each inference question in your own words.

A. California's Golden Gate Bridge, which connects San Francisco and Marin County, has been the site of over 1,000 suicides since it opened in 1937. In a lengthy *New Yorker* article about the bridge, Tad Friend ends with this anecdote.

The bridge comes into the lives of all Bay Area residents sooner or later, and it often stays. Dr. Jerome Motto, who has been part of two failed suicide-barrier coalitions, is now retired and living in San Mateo. When I visited him there, we spent three hours talking about the bridge. Motto had a patient who committed suicide from the Golden Gate in 1963, but the jump that affected him most occurred in the seventies. "I went to this guy's apartment afterward with the assistant medical examiner," he told me. "The guy was in this thirties, lived alone, pretty bare apartment. He'd written a note and left it on his bureau. It said, 'I'm going to walk to the bridge. If one person smiles at me on the way, I will not jump.'"

Motto sat back in his chair. "That was it," he said. "It's so needless, the number of people who are lost."

Tad Friend, "Jumpers," *The New Yorker*

What can you infer about the reason Dr. Motto's patient committed suicide? <u>The anecdote implies that no one smiled at the victim on his way to the bridge.</u>

Why do you think the author ends his article with this anecdote? <u>The anecdote is emotionally affecting and leaves the reader with something to think about. It shows how tenuous the line between life and death is.</u>

B. Probably all of us have heard the truism that no two snowflakes are identical. Cullen Murphy explains where this idea originated and comments on its accuracy.

For all the scientific awareness of the symmetrical character of snow crystals, the ubiquity of their popular image—the one we see in children's paper cutouts and on bags of ice and signs for motels that have air-conditioning—is a relatively recent phenomenon. What snowflakes actually looked like was not widely known until the middle of the nineteenth century, when the book *Cloud Crystals,* with sketches by "A Lady," was published in the United States. The lady had caught snowflakes on a black surface and then observed them with a magnifying glass. In 1885 Wilson Alwyn ("Snowflake") Bentley, of Jericho, Vermont, began taking photographs of snowflakes through a microscope. Thousands of Bentley's photomicrographs were eventually collected in his book *Snow Crystals* (1931). The fact that not one of the snowflakes photographed by Bentley was identical to another is probably the basis for the idea that no two snowflakes are ever exactly the same—an idea that is in fact unverifiable.

Cullen Murphy, "In Praise of Snow,"
The Atlantic Monthly

The author ends by saying "the idea that no two snowflakes are ever exactly the same" is "in fact unverifiable." Why is this statement likely to be true?

What evidence in the paragraph suggests it? The "thousands" of snow-flakes in Bentley's book is a limited number relative to the total number of snowflakes that fall in even a single snowstorm. One could never observe all the snowflakes that fall in the world, nor all the snowflakes that have ever fallen, making this "fact" unverifiable.

◼ MAKING INFERENCES WITH VISUAL MATERIAL

Political Cartoons

Cartoons, especially political cartoons, often require one to make inferences.[5] A cartoon strips a situation down to its essential elements, and the careful reader must piece these elements together to make connections, especially if the cartoon doesn't include a caption. Political cartoons on the editorial page of major metropolitan newspapers are especially effective at molding public opinion and commenting on the news of the day in a humorous or ironic way. Following is a cartoon that offers a cynical interpretation of the announcement in June 2004 by George Tenet, director of the CIA, that he would resign. The White House stated that Tenet's resignation letter cited "personal reasons" for his departure. However, the CIA, along with the FBI, had been widely criticized by the 9/11 Commission investigating the government's response to the attacks on the World Trade Center for not anticipating a major attack by Al Qaeda operatives, as well as for other serious lapses. What specifically is the artist implying in this cartoon?

[5]For further instruction in interpreting visual elements like the cartoon in this section and the graphs in the next section, see pages 291–292 and 346 in Chapters 8 and 9.

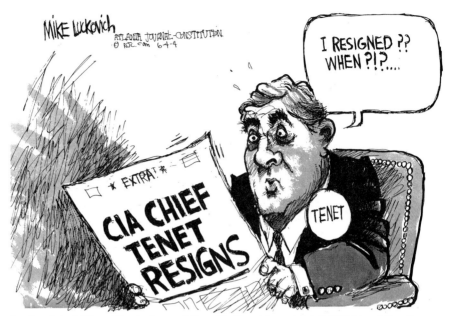

Luckovich, Mike. *Atlanta Journal-Constitution.* Copyright © 2004 by Atlantic Journal-Constitution. Reproduced with permission.

What is the artist implying about Tenet's resignation as CIA director?

His "resignation" was not voluntary. The cartoon implies that Tenet was

forced to resign.

Graphs and Charts

In June 2004, U.S. District Court Judge Martin Jenkins granted class-action status to 1.6 million women—former and current employees—who are suing the nation's biggest retailer, Wal-Mart, for sex discrimination in wages and promotion. This lawsuit will probably be the biggest class-action suit in the history of the United States. The article examining Judge Jenkins's ruling was accompanied by the graphics on the next page; the pie chart and bar graph show a statistical breakdown between gender and earnings at Wal-Mart using figures from 2001.

1. First consider the following question: Should men and women be paid the same wages for performing the same work? Explain your thinking.

   Answers will vary.

2. In a large corporation such as Wal-Mart, with 3,566 stores throughout the United States, without discrimination, would the number of management and hourly employees be roughly split between men and women? Why or why not? Answers will vary.

Women and Wal-Mart

On average, women working for Wal-Mart Stores Inc. in 2001 earned less than men in various job categories, according to a statistician's analysis of company data supplied to the court.

Gender breakdown

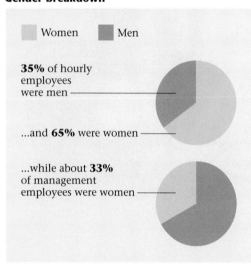

35% of hourly employees were men

...and **65%** were women

...while about **33%** of management employees were women

Average earnings
Full-time employees working at least 45 weeks

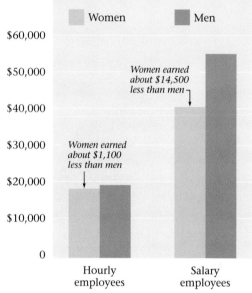

Source: Copyright © 2005 Associated Press. All rights reserved. Distributed by Valeo IP. Reprinted by permission.

3. Now study the pie chart on the left. What inference can you make about gender and the Wal-Mart workplace?   There is a pattern of discrimination concerning the numbers of hourly and management employees. Hourly employees are disproportionately women, while management employees are disproportionately men.

4. Next study the bar graph on the right. What inference can you make from this chart? Because the bulk of hourly employees were women and because they earned on average of $1,100 per year less than men, a pattern of discrimination seems to exist among the lowest paid workers. The difference in annual salary—$14,500—between men and women in management positions is even more pronounced.

5. What conclusion can you draw from these two charts about the way Wal-Mart operates in terms of its corporate culture? <u>Again, answers</u>

<u>will vary, but it seems evident that the charts support the judge's</u>

<u>decision, which was that "a strong corporate culture . . . includes</u>

<u>gender stereotyping."</u>

6. What other information would you need to know before deciding on the worth of this case? <u>How do other large retailers compare in</u>

<u>terms of gender and earnings? Also is other evidence available—</u>

<u>either statistical or anecdotal—to support the charge that Wal-</u>

<u>Mart fostered a culture of male dominance in management</u>

<u>positions? How many women applied for management positions and</u>

<u>were turned down, and on what basis? How much turnover is there</u>

<u>among women?</u>

■ CHAPTER EXERCISES

Selection 1

The author, who lived in Belgium before World War II, had a childhood fascination with the Lowara band of Gypsies who camped every year near his village and who earned their livelihood by horsetrading. At the age of 12, in the 1930s, he asked his parents if he could leave home and live with the Gypsies, for at least part of each year, and incredibly, they agreed. This is the opening paragraph of his book recounting his experiences.

[1]As I approached the Gypsy camp for the first time, yellow, wild-looking stiff-haired dogs howled and barked. [2]Fifteen covered wagons were spread out in a wide half circle, partly hiding the Gypsies from the road. [3]Around the campfires sat women draped in deep-colored dresses, their big, expressive eyes and strong, white teeth standing out against their beautiful dark matte skin. [4]The many gold pieces they wore as earrings, necklaces and bracelets sharpened their color even more. [5]Their shiny blue-black hair was long and braided, the skirts of their dresses were ankle-length, very full and worn in many layers, and their bodices loose and low-cut. [6]My first impression of them was one of health and vitality. [7]Hordes of small barefoot children ran all over the campsite, a few dressed in rags but most nearly naked, rollicking like young animals. [8]At the far end of the encampment a number of horses, tethered to long chains, were grazing; and of course there were the ever-present half-wild growling dogs. [9]Several men lay in the shade of an oak tree. [10]Thin corkscrews of bluish smoke rose skyward and the pungent,

penetrating smell of burning wood permeated the air. [11]Even from a distance the loud, clear voices of these Gypsies resounded with an intensity I was not accustomed to. [12]Mingling with them, farther away, were the dull thuds of an ax, the snorting and neighing of horses, the occasional snapping of a whip and the high-pitched wail of an infant, contrasting with the whisper of the immediate surroundings of the camp itself.

Jan Yoors, *The Gypsies*

A. *Vocabulary*

For each italicized word from the selection, choose the best definition according to the context in which it appears.

1. *vitality* [sentence 6]:
   (a) laziness.
   (b) enthusiasm.
   (c) curiosity.
   (d) energy.
2. *rollicking* [7]:
   (a) rolling.
   (b) prancing.
   (c) behaving.
   (d) romping.
3. *pungent* [10]:
   (a) sweetish.
   (b) sharp.
   (c) sickening.
   (d) familiar.
4. *permeated* [10]:
   (a) perfumed.
   (b) polluted.
   (c) wafted through.
   (d) spread throughout.

B. *Content and Structure*

Complete the following questions.

1. Find the two nouns that Yoors uses to state his dominant impression of

   these Gypsies. _____
2. Yoors uses many words that appeal to our senses. Which sense is *not* emphasized? Words pertaining to
   (a) sight.
   (b) smell.

      (c) sound.
      (d) touch.
  3. Yoors most likely found these Gypsies to be
      (a) weird.
      (b) fascinating.
      (c) alien.
      (d) lazy.
  4. A good title for this paragraph would be
      (a) "A Study of Gypsy Life."
      (b) "The Survival of the Gypsies."
      (c) "I Decide to Become a Gypsy."
      (d) "First Impressions of a Gypsy Camp."

C. Inferences

On the basis of the evidence in the paragraph, mark these statements as follows: PA (probably accurate), PI (probably inaccurate), or NP (not in the passage).

1. _____ The Gypsy camp the author came across was in America.
2. _____ The writer had been to the Gypsy camp many times before.
3. _____ Gypsies are persecuted in many European countries.
4. _____ Gypsy culture, at least the culture represented by this group, is essentially nomadic.
5. _____ In Gypsy culture, the women do all the work while the men lie around, enjoying themselves.
6. _____ Despite the children's ragged appearance, they appeared to be happy.

Answers for Selection 1

A. Vocabulary
1. (d)   2. (d)   3. (b)   4. (d)

B. Content and Structure
1. health and vitality (sentence 6)
2. (d)   3. (b)   4. (d)

C. Inferences
1. NP   2. PI   3. NP   4. PA   5. NP   6. PA

Selection 2

[1]In California, the discovery of gold in 1848 took place two years before the territory was admitted to statehood and even before a peace treaty had been signed in the Mexican War. [2]The news about Sutters's Mill spread through the

neighboring communities in short order and almost emptied out San Francisco within a few weeks. **3**With no radios, television, or Internet, however, word reached the rest of the country more slowly. **4**The first deposit of gold from California at the U.S. Mint did not arrive until December 8, 1848, at which point it was greeted by one periodical as "the new mistress."

5The big rush did not begin until 1849, after President Polk mentioned it in his State of the Union address to Congress, which is why the prospectors (and the San Francisco football team) came to be known as the Forty-Niners rather than the Forty-Eighters. **6**The long delay between the discovery and Polk's announcement was the primary impetus for the first revolution in telecom—the establishment of the Western Union Company and the wiring of the entire United States for telegraphy. **7**By 1853, over one hundred thousand people had swarmed into California, including 25,000 Frenchmen and twenty thousand Chinese, and annual gold production approached eighty metric tons; production would peak as early as 1853 at around 95 tons.

Peter Bernstein, *The Power of Gold: The History of an Obsession*

A. Vocabulary

For each italicized word from the selection, write the dictionary definition most appropriate for the context.

1. *in short order* [sentence 2]: _with no delay, quickly._

2. The primary *impetus* [6]: _driving force, stimulus._

B. Content and Structure

Complete the following questions.

1. A good title for this passage is
    (a) "The Discovery of Gold."
    (b) "Why the Forty-Eighters Became the Forty-Niners."
    (c) "Gold: The New Mistress."
    (d) "Some Effects of the 1848 California Gold Rush."
2. The main idea of the passage is that
    (a) The Gold Rush brought instant wealth to those who prospected for gold in California.
    (b) The discovery of gold in California in 1848 was responsible for major changes in both the United States and in California.
    (c) The discovery of gold led to the establishment of the Western Union Company.
    (d) News traveled slowly in the middle of the nineteenth century.
3. The mode of discourse in the passage is
    (a) narration.
    (b) description.

    (c) exposition.
    (d) persuasion.

4. Gold was referred to in one periodical as "the new mistress" probably because
    (a) prospectors became obsessed with it and abandoned themselves to it.
    (b) prospecting for gold often replaced the prospectors' normal social life.
    (c) prospecting for gold led one to invest in a lot of expensive equipment.
    (d) gold could be made into jewelry for prospectors' wives or mistresses.

C. Inferences

Answer these inference questions.

1. Which of the following can we accurately infer from the passage?
    (a) Despite all the rumors, there wasn't very much gold to be found in California.
    (b) After 1853, gold production declined in California.
    (c) California would not have been admitted to statehood if gold had not been discovered there.
    (d) The discovery of gold became an issue during the Mexican War.

2. The author evidently sees a strong connection between the discovery of gold and
    (a) statehood for California.
    (b) the end of the Mexican War.
    (c) new techniques for locating and producing gold.
    (d) the increased need for a speedy way to get news via telegraphy.

3. The term "Gold Rush" is used because it describes
    (a) a system for locating gold in the ground.
    (b) a large number of people eagerly moving someplace.
    (c) the hurried way in which word spread about the discovery of gold.
    (d) the name of the first gold mine.

Selection 3

[1]In Japan, specially licensed chefs prepare the rarest sashimi delicacy: the white flesh of the puffer fish, served raw and arranged in elaborate floral patterns on a platter. [2]Diners pay large sums of money for the carefully prepared dish, which has a light, faintly sweet taste, like raw pompano. [3]It had better be carefully prepared, because, unlike pompano, puffer fish is ferociously poisonous. [4]You wouldn't think a puffer fish would need such chemical armor, since its main form of defense is to swallow great gulps of water and become so bloated it is too large for most predators to swallow. [5]And yet its skin, ovaries, liver, and intestines contain tetrodotoxin, one of the most poisonous chemicals in the world, hundreds of times more lethal than strychnine or cyanide. [6]A shred small enough to fit under one's fingernail could kill an entire family. [7]Unless the poison is completely removed by a deft, experienced chef, the diner will die mid-meal. [8]That's the appeal of the dish; eating the possibility of death, a fright your

lips spell out as you dine. [9]Yet preparing it is a traditional art form in Japan, with widespread aficionados. [10]The most highly respected *fugu* chefs are the ones who manage to leave in the barest touch of the poison, just enough for the diner's lips to tingle from his brush with mortality but not enough to actually kill him. [11]Of course, a certain number of diners do die every year from eating *fugu*, but that doesn't stop intrepid *fugu*-fanciers. [12]The ultimate *fugu* connoisseur orders *chiri*, puffer flesh lightly cooked in a broth made of the poisonous livers and intestines. [13]It's not that diners don't understand the bizarre danger of pufferfish toxin. [14]Ancient Egyptian, Chinese, Japanese, and other cultures all describe *fugu* poisoning in excruciating detail: It first produces dizziness, numbness of the mouth and lips, breathing trouble, cramps, blue lips, a desperate itchiness as of insects crawling all over one's body, vomiting, dilated pupils, and then a zombielike sleep, really a kind of neurological paralysis during which the victims are often aware of what's going on around them, and from which they die. [15]But sometimes they wake. [16]If a Japanese man or woman dies of *fugu* poison, the family waits a few days before burying them, just in case they wake up. [17]Every now and then someone poisoned by *fugu* is nearly buried alive, coming to at the last moment to describe in horrifying detail their own funeral and burial, during which, although they desperately tried to cry out or signal that they were still alive, they simply couldn't move.

Diane Ackerman, *A Natural History of the Senses*

A. Vocabulary

For each italicized word from the selection, choose the best definition according to the context in which it appears.

1. *deft* [sentence 7]:
   (a) skillful.
   (b) efficient.
   (c) clever.
   (d) well-trained.
2. *aficionados* [9]:
   (a) customers.
   (b) trendsetters.
   (c) gourmets.
   (d) enthusiastic followers.
3. *intrepid* [11]:
   (a) serious.
   (b) courageous.
   (c) foolish.
   (d) stubborn.
4. *ultimate* [12]: representing the
   (a) farthest extreme.
   (b) the first in a sequence.

(c) the last in a sequence.

(d) the largest.

5. *connoisseur* [12]:

    (a) a newcomer, novice.

    (b) a daredevil.

    (c) a person who does not understand the consequences of his or her actions.

    (d) (a person who has knowledge of food, wine, or other esthetic matters.)

6. *excruciating* [14]:

    (a) (intensely painful and exact.)

    (b) overly simplified.

    (c) boring, monotonous.

    (d) nauseating, sickening.

B. *Content and Structure*

Complete the following questions.

1. With regard to puffer fish, Ackerman's purpose in writing is

    (a) to persuade and encourage the reader to sample it.

    (b) to warn the reader about the dangers of eating it.

    (c) (to explain the fundamentals of preparing puffer fish and its appeal.)

    (d) to describe its appearance.

2. The main idea of the paragraph is stated in

    (a) sentence 2.

    (b) sentence 5.

    (c) (sentence 8.)

    (d) sentence 13.

3. In sentence 3 what does Ackerman mean when she compares the puffer fish's poison to armor? <u>The armor—the poison—protects the</u>

<u>puffer fish from predators.</u>

4. Why does Ackerman characterize diners who eat *chiri* the "ultimate *fugu* connoisseur"? <u>*Chiri* contains a double dose of poison—in the</u>

<u>broth and in the meat.</u>

5. As the headnote indicates, this passage comes from Ackerman's book, *A Natural History of the Senses.* Each section of the book takes up one of the five senses. Which section does this passage most likely appear in?

    <u>taste</u>

6. Which of the following best describes the author's attitude toward puffer fish connoisseurs?

    (a) She thinks they are weird.

    (b) She thinks they are foolish.

    (c) She thinks they are admirable.

    (d) (Her attitude is not evident from the passage.)

C. Inferences

On the basis of the evidence in the paragraph, mark these statements as follows: PA (probably accurate), PI (probably inaccurate), or NP (not in the passage).

1. _PA_ *Fugu* is another word for puffer fish.
2. _PI_ The puffer fish is poisonous only when it is served raw as sashimi.
3. _PA_ It would be risky to eat puffer fish prepared by an inexperienced or novice chef.
4. _PA_ People who eat puffer fish seek the thrill of the possibility of being poisoned.
5. _PI_ Eating puffer with a tiny amount of poison left it makes one's entire body feel tingly.
6. _NP_ The author has sampled puffer fish.

PRACTICE ESSAY

"Potlatching"
Conrad Phillip Kottak

This excerpt is from a leading anthropology textbook, *Anthropology: An Exploration of Human Diversity*. The author, Conrad Phillip Kottak, has taught anthropology at the University of Michigan since 1968. In addition to this text, he has published numerous other books and articles in the field. According to the "About the Author" section in the text, "His general interests are in the processes by which local cultures are incorporated—and resist incorporation—into larger systems." He has done ethnographic field work both in Brazil and in Madagascar. The subject of this excerpt is an unusual and often misunderstood practice called *potlatch*.

Preview Questions

1. Why do North Americans entertain? That is, why do they throw parties or other celebrations? What do they expect to receive in return for their efforts?
2. What examples of conspicuous consumption and seemingly deliberately wastefulness are you familiar with in American culture?

1   One of the most thoroughly studied cultural practices known to ethnography is the **potlatch,** a festive event within a regional exchange system among tribes of the North Pacific Coast of North America, including the Salish and Kwakiutl of Washington and British Columbia and the Tsimshian of Alaska. . . . Some tribes still practice the potlatch, sometimes as a memorial to the dead (Kan 1986, 1989). At each such event, assisted by members of their communities, potlatch sponsors traditionally gave away food, blankets, pieces of copper, or other items. In return for this they got prestige. To give a potlatch enhanced one's reputation. Prestige increased with the lavishness of the potlatch, the value of the goods given away in it.

2   The potlatching tribes were foragers, but atypical ones. They were sedentary and had chiefs. And unlike the environments of most other recent foragers, theirs was not marginal. They had access to a wide variety of land and sea resources. Among their most important foods were salmon, herring, candlefish, berries, mountain goats, seals, and porpoises (Piddocke 1969).

3   If classical economic theory is correct that the profit motive is universal, with the goal of maximizing material benefits, then how does one explain the potlatch, in which wealth is given away? Many scholars once cited the potlatch as a classic case of economically wasteful behavior. In this view, potlatching was based on an economically irrational drive for prestige. This interpretation stressed the lavishness and supposed wastefulness, especially of the Kwakiutl displays, to support the contention that in some societies people strive to maximize prestige at the expense of their material well-being. This interpretation has been challenged.

4   Ecological anthropology, also known as *cultural ecology,* is a theoretical school in anthropology that attempts to interpret cultural practices, such as the potlatch, in terms of their long-term role in helping humans adapt to their environments. A different interpretation of the potlatch has been offered by the ecological anthropologists Wayne Suttles (1960) and Andrew Vayda (1961/1968). These scholars see potlatching not in terms of its apparent wastefulness, but in terms of its long-term role as a cultural adaptive mechanism. This view not only helps us understand potlatching, it also has comparative value because it helps us understand similar patterns of lavish feasting in many other parts of the world. Here is the ecological interpretation: Customs like the potlatch are cultural adaptations to alternating periods of local abundance and shortage.

5   How does this work? The overall natural environment of the North Pacific Coast is favorable, but resources fluctuate from year to year and place to place. Salmon and herring aren't equally abundant every year in a given locality. One village can have a good year while another is experiencing a bad one. Later their fortunes reverse. In this context, the potlatch cycle of the Kwakiutl and Salish had adaptive value, and the potlatch was not a competitive display that brought no material benefit.

6   A village enjoying an especially good year had a surplus of subsistence items, which it could trade for more durable wealth items, like blankets, canoes, or pieces of copper. Wealth, in turn, by being distributed, could be converted into prestige. Members of several villages were invited to any potlatch and got to take home the resources that were given away. In this way, potlatching linked villages together in a regional economy—an exchange system that distributed food and wealth from wealthy to needy communities. In return, the potlatch sponsors and their villages got prestige. The decision to potlatch was determined by the health of the local economy. If there had been subsistence surpluses, and thus a buildup of wealth over several good years, a village could afford a potlatch to convert its food and wealth into prestige.

7   The long-term adaptive value of intercommunity feasting becomes clear when we consider what happened when a formerly prosperous village had a run of bad luck. Its people started accepting invitations to potlatches in villages that were doing better. The tables were turned as the temporarily rich became temporarily poor and vice versa. The newly needy accepted food and wealth items. They were willing to receive rather than bestow gifts and thus to relinquish some of their stored-up prestige. They hoped their luck would eventually improve so that resources could be recouped and prestige regained.

8   The potlatch linked local groups along the North Pacific Coast into a regional alliance and exchange network. Potlatching and intervillage exchange had adaptive functions, regardless of the motivations of the individual participants. The anthropologists who stressed rivalry for prestige were not wrong. They were merely emphasizing motivations at the expense of an analysis of economic and ecological systems.

9   The use of feasts to enhance individual and community reputations and to redistribute wealth is not peculiar to populations of the North Pacific Coast. Competitive feasting is widely characteristic of nonindustrial food producers. But among most foragers, who live, remember, in marginal areas, resources are too meager to support feasting on such a level. In such societies, sharing rather than competition prevails.

10   Like many other cultural practices that have attracted considerable anthropological attention, the potlatch does not, and did not, exist apart from larger world events. For example, within the spreading world capitalist economy of the 19th century, the potlatching tribes, particularly the Kwakiutl, began to trade with Europeans (fur for blankets, for example). Their wealth increased as a result. Simultaneously, a huge proportion of the Kwakiutl population died from previously unknown diseases brought by the Europeans. As a result, the increased wealth from trade flowed into a drastically reduced population. With many of the traditional sponsors dead (such as chiefs and their families), the Kwakiutl extended the right to give a potlatch to the entire population. This stimulated very intense competition for prestige. Given trade, increased wealth, and a decreased population, the Kwakiutl also started converting wealth into pres-

tige by destroying wealth items such as blankets, pieces of copper, and houses (Vayda 1961/1968). Blankets and houses could be burned, and coppers could be buried at sea. Here, with dramatically increased wealth and a drastically reduced population, Kwakiutl potlatching changed its nature. It became much more destructive than it had been previously and than potlatching continued to be among tribes that were less affected by trade and disease.

11   In any case, note that potlatching also served to prevent the development of socioeconomic stratification, a system of social classes. Wealth relinquished or destroyed was converted into a nonmaterial item: prestige. Under capitalism, we reinvest our profits (rather than burning our cash), with the hope of making an additional profit. However, the potlatching tribes were content to relinquish their surpluses rather than use them to widen the social distance between themselves and their fellow tribe members.

References

Kan. S. 1986. The 19th-Century Tlingit Potlatch: A New Perspective. *American Ethnologist* 13:191–212.

Kan. S. 1989. *Symbolic Immortality: The Tlingit Potlatch of the Nineteenth Century.* Washington, D.C.: Smithsonian Institution Press.

Piddocke, S. 1969. The Potlatch System of the Southern Kwakiutl: A New Perspective. In *Environment and Cultural Behavior,* ed. A. P. Vayda, pp. 130–156. Garden City, NY: Natural History Press.

Suttles, W. 1960. Affinal Ties, Subsistence, and Prestige among the Coast Salish. *American Anthropologist* 62: 296–395.

Vayda, A. P. 1968 (orig. 1961). Economic Systems in Ecological Perspective: The Case of the Northwest Coast. In *Readings in Anthropology,* 2d ed., vol. 2, ed. M. H. Fried, pp. 172–178. New York: Crowell.

A. *Comprehension*

Choose the answer that best completes each statement. Do not refer to the selection while doing this exercise.

1.   Which sentence best represents the main idea of the essay?
     (a) The potlatch was an example of lavish wastefulness, which was intended to cement the power and prestige of the tribal leaders.
     (b) The potlatch is an interesting area for cultural ecologists to study to learn how cultures adapt.
     (c) The potlatch festive events were confined to the North Pacific Coast of North America.
     (d) The potlatch was a way for a culture to adapt to the environment and to alternating periods of abundance and shortage.

2. Classical economic theory says that
    (a) the impulse to entertain and to throw large parties is universal.
    (b) the impulse to show off is universal.
    (c) (the profit motive is universal.)
    (d) all cultures try to maximize their prestige.

3. An important consideration for anthropologists studying potlatch is understanding how
    (a) (humans adapt to their environment.)
    (b) why potlatches took place during certain times of the year.
    (c) why other cultures in similar environments did not give potlatches.
    (d) tribes exhibit apparent wastefulness when they can ill afford it.

4. In the Pacific Northwest, the potlatch tradition served to
    (a) (link groups into regional alliances and exchange networks.)
    (b) create more divisiveness, as tribes competed with each other to see which could throw the more lavish potlatch.
    (c) increase a healthy economic competition among tribes.
    (d) equalize the prestige and material wealth during times of abundance as well as during times of scarcity.

5. Competitive feasting, like the potlatches in the North Pacific Coast, is evident primarily among people who are
    (a) skilled in hunting, trapping, and fishing.
    (b) (nonindustrial food producers.)
    (c) needy economically and who therefore must depend on the charity of other, richer, tribes.
    (d) eager for the prestige that results from acquiring and giving away immense amounts of goods.

B. Vocabulary

For each italicized word from the selection, write the definition most appropriate for the context. You may refer to the selection to answer the questions in this section and in all the remaining sections.

1. they were *sedentary* [paragraph 2]: _fixed in location, not migratory_

2. cultural *ecology* [4]: _the relationship between people and their environments._

3. resources *fluctuate* from year to year [5]: _vary irregularly, rise and fall_

4. *subsistence* surpluses [6]: _describing a situation of having barely enough to survive_

5. to *relinquish* [7]: _give up, let go of_

6. resources could be *recouped* [7]: <u>recovered, got back</u>

7. the development of socioeconomic *stratification* [11]: <u>separation into</u> <u>different classes and social levels.</u>

C. *Inferences*

Complete the following questions.

1. Look at paragraph 2 again. Why did anthropologists have difficulty reconciling the potlatch ceremony with classical economic theory? <u>The</u> <u>potlatch appeared at first to work against the idea of a universal</u> <u>profit motive, which suggests that people will not engage in an</u> <u>activity that damages their material well-being.</u>

2. Look at paragraph 3 again. What adjective suggests that potlatches weren't as wasteful as anthropologists originally thought? <u>"supposed"</u> <u>(wastefulness)</u>

3. How can the potlatch be regarded as cyclical as a cultural adaptation? (See paragraphs 4 and 7.) <u>When a group has an abundance of items,</u> <u>the potlatch would help groups suffering from bad luck; conversely,</u> <u>when a previously rich village suffered a shortage, their generosity</u> <u>would be reciprocated by those whom they had helped earlier.</u>

4. Read paragraph 10. What was the *initial impetus* in the nineteenth century that led to increasingly destructive potlatches among the Kwakiutl? <u>contact with Europeans</u>

5. According to paragraph 11, what is the primary difference between a potlatching culture and a capitalistic one? <u>A capitalistic culture</u> <u>widens the gap between social classes as wealth (surplus or profit)</u> <u>is converted into more wealth. Such social distinctions do not occur</u> <u>as much in potlatching cultures.</u>

D. Structure

Complete the following questions.

1. The mode of discourse in the passage is
   (a) narration.
   (b) description.
   (c) (exposition.)
   (d) persuasion.
2. What is the purpose of paragraph 3?
   (a) It offers several interpretations of potlatch ceremonies.
   (b) It attempts to reconcile a universal economic theory to a seemingly bizarre practice that doesn't fit.
   (c) It describes a typical potlatch ceremony.
   (d) It shows that anthropologists cannot agree on the meaning of the potlatch.
3. A good title for paragraph 6 would be
   (a) "Potlatches Now and Then"
   (b) "The Decision to Potlatch"
   (c) "Potlatch: The Path to Prestige"
   (d) ("Potlatch: A Regional Economic System")

E. Questions for Discussion and Analysis

1. Does the potlatch resemble any other custom or ritual in North American culture?

2. Americans like to think of themselves as being members of an advanced technological society, where science can solve all human problems. For foragers, the day-to-day existence seems decidedly harsh and difficult. Imagine for a moment what it would be like to have to survive by your wits day to day, rather than having a permanent shelter and the local Safeway to do your shopping.

ON THE WEB

Using your favorite search engine, do some research on cultures that still practice the potlatch system. To avoid turning up many unrelated sites, use the "advanced search" settings to limit the pages returned to those with the domain ".edu" or ".org." (If you don't know what a site's "domain" is or if you need help using a search engine, see Chapter 10, "Evaluating Web Sites," on pp. 368–371.

PART

Discovering Meaning:
The Importance of Form

3

Four Methods of Paragraph Development

CHAPTER OBJECTIVES

In this chapter, you will learn four methods of paragraph development, including:

- Facts and statistics

- Examples, illustration, and significant details

- Process analysis (directive and informative)

- Comparison and contrast

▨ MODES OF DISCOURSE
AND METHODS OF DEVELOPMENT COMPARED

In Chapter 1 you were introduced to the four modes of discourse—narration, description, exposition, and persuasion—the predominant forms of writing in nonfiction prose. In Chapters 3 and 4 you will study the methods of paragraph development. These methods refer to various kinds of *evidence*. A main idea cannot be left unexplored; it must be examined, supported, proved, explained, illustrated, or defined as befits the subject. You will recall from Chapter 1 that a mode of discourse is a rather general term referring to a particular type of nonfiction writing. Usually in a longer piece, one mode predominates, though as you saw in the Jocko Weyland excerpt on pages 49–50, a longer piece may reflect mixed modes.

On the other hand, the term **methods of development**[1] refers to evidence—ways of supporting an idea *within* a paragraph. In a typical essay, then, a writer might use several methods of development. One paragraph might be developed with facts and statistics, another with the definition of an ambiguous word, a third with contrasting information. The choice of method depends on the writer's assessment of how best to clarify and support the main assertion. It also depends on the mode of discourse: These methods of development are most typically found in expository and persuasive prose. As you will see, identifying these various methods in an essay will make you a more analytical reader and teach you blueprints for thinking logically. An equally important skill is the ability to *predict* what method of development a writer is likely to use.

www. mhhe. com/ spears

For a practice exercise on predicting methods of development by examining main-idea sentences, click on Chapter 3 and scroll down to "Predicting Methods of Development."

▨ METHODS OF PARAGRAPH DEVELOPMENT

This chapter introduces you to the four most easily recognizable methods of paragraph development; Chapter 4 takes up the remaining ones. As you study each type and the accompanying illustrative passage, you will see that although the majority are expository, writers may use them in persuasive or argumentative writing, as well.

---

[1]Although some teachers of reading use the term "organizational patterns," I have followed the terminology used in the majority of rhetorically arranged introductory-level composition readers. Since the terms "methods of development" and "expository rhetorical modes" are familiar to students in composition courses, I have adhered to this terminology to avoid confusion.

| Facts and Statistics | As you recall from Chapter 2, a **fact** is a piece of objective information. Facts are verifiable: One can prove their truth by scientific measurement, by personal observation, by duplication, and so on. **Statistics** are data in the form of numbers, derived from research studies, polls, census figures, or other similar sources. The use of statistics is the simplest method of development to recognize.[2] |

The evidence in this first paragraph by William Langewiesche consists of a series of facts regarding how camels store and use water.

> Camels do not store water in their humps. They drink furiously, up to twenty-eight gallons in a ten-minute session, then distribute the water evenly throughout their bodies. Afterward, they use the water stingily. They have viscous urine and dry feces. They breathe through their noses, and keep their mouths shut. They do sweat, but only as a last resort, after first allowing their body temperatures to rise 10 degrees Fahrenheit. As they begin to dehydrate, the volume of their blood plasma does not at first diminish. They can survive a water loss of up to one-third of their body weight, then drink up and feel fine. Left alone, unhurried and unburdened, they can live two weeks between drinks.
>
> William Langewiesche, *Sahara Unveiled*

The next paragraph in this section uses both facts and statistics. In it, Tom Chaffin, a teacher of U.S. history at Emory University, traced the Oregon Trail from its beginning in St. Louis to the mouth of the Columbia River in Oregon. As he traveled, he stood in the same places that the explorer John C. Frémont had written about in his journal. This particular stopping point was in former Sioux Indian territory along the South Fork of Nebraska's Platte River. (Meta is Chaffin's wife; Zoie is their dog.)

> Although the bloodiest chapters of the U.S. wars with the plains Indians were decades away, Frémont's maps and journals anticipated, and in some ways precipitated, the violence to come. "Good guard ought to be kept all the way," Frémont warns of this section of the trail. "Sioux Indians are not to be trusted." A decade after Frémont published his report, the U.S. Army began its thirty-year campaign against the tribes of the plains—a campaign that was, in the long run, horrendously successful. Perhaps nothing so distinguishes the West that Frémont explored from the wilderness preserves and impoverished ranch land through which Meta, Zoie, and I drove as this: In 1842, Native Americans still controlled nearly all of the territory west of

---

[2]Ironically, however, statistics are capable of leading readers astray or of presenting false information. One can find numbers to fit any theory, and statistics can easily be manipulated. A recent book by Joel Best, *Damned Lies and Statistics,* explains this problem. A short excerpt from this book is included at the end of Chapter 9.

the Mississippi and north of the Rio Grande; by 1895, the U.S. had obtained, by chicanery, massacre, diplomacy, and theft, some 90 million acres, or 95 percent, of these lands. Although elsewhere tribes have in recent years reclaimed lost territory and treaty rights, in Nebraska—one third of which Congress had set aside for the Indians in the 1830s—tribes now control a mere 100 square miles, or one tenth of one percent of the entire state. The only sign of Sioux to be found along this stretch of the Platte today is the occasional billboard for the Rosebud Casino & Quality Inn, located on the Lakota reservation, 150 miles north of here on the South Dakota border.

Tom Chaffin, "How the West Was Lost:
A Road Trip in Search of the Oregon Trail," *Harper's Magazine*

What is the main point Chaffin wants to convey in this paragraph?
Frémont's journals describing his experiences with Indians foreshadow the violence later perpetrated by the U.S. Army in its battles to exterminate the Plains Indians and to take away their land.

Identify the piece of evidence that best supports this point. The 90 million acres, or 95 percent, of Indian land confiscated during the 30-year campaign.

Examples and Illustration

An **example** is a specific instance of a more general concept. Suppose you come across this sentence in a magazine article:

Miss Plum's Ice Cream Shop in Rockport, Maine, offers a wide variety of exotic flavors.

If the sentence stands alone, the writer is asking the reader to supply his or her own examples. A more careful writer would add three or four examples of "exotic flavors"—perhaps mango-mango, peanut butter toffee, mandarin orange-strawberry, and coconut-pineapple-rum.

A writer may support a general idea by citing two or three specific examples—specific instances—of the main idea or by using a single longer, extended example called an **illustration.** The methods function in the same way: Both point to typical and concrete instances of a more general idea. The only difference between them is that examples are short and are usually found in clusters, whereas an illustration typically involves a little narrative, in effect an extended and more detailed discussion.

In the following passage, Marjorie Garber develops the main idea with three short examples. Study my annotations to see where each new example begins.

At a time when "universal" ideas and feelings are often compromised or undercut by group identities, the dog tale still has the power to move us. Paradoxically, the dog has become the repository of those model human properties which we have cynically ceased to find among human beings. On the evening news and in the morning paper, dog stories supply what used to be called "human interest." There was the story of <u>Lyric</u>, for instance—<u>the 911 dog</u>, who <u>dialled emergency services to save her mistress</u>, and wound up the toast of Disneyland. Or the saga of <u>Sheba</u>, the <u>mother dog in Florida who rescued her puppies</u> after they were buried alive by a cruel human owner. His crime and her heroic single-motherhood were reliable feature stories, edging out mass killings in Bosnia and political infighting at home. Here, after all, were the family values we'd been looking for as a society—right under our noses.

1—Lyric dialed 911

2—Sheba rescued puppies

Indeed, at a time of increasing human ambivalence about human heroes and the human capacity for "unconditional love," dog heroes—and dog stories—are with us today more than ever. Near the entrance to Central Park at Fifth Avenue and Sixty-seventh Street stands the statue of <u>Balto</u>, the <u>heroic sled dog</u> who led a team <u>bringing medicine to diphtheria-stricken Nome</u>, <u>Alaska</u>, in <u>the winter of 1925</u>. Balto's story recently became an animated feature film, joining such other big-screen fictional heroes as Lassie, Rin Tin Tin, Benji, and Fluke.

3—Balto brought medicine in diphtheria outbreak

Marjorie Garber, "Dog Days," *The New Yorker*

Write a sentence stating the main idea of the passage. <u>Because humans so often disappoint us in our lives, stories of heroic dogs affect us profoundly.</u>

In this next paragraph, Jeffrey Masson and Susan McCarthy use a single dramatic illustration in support of the main idea, which occurs in the first sentence.

Tenderness may also cross the species barrier, with some animals showing distinct pleasure in caretaking. When a young sparrow crash-landed in the chimpanzee cage at the Basel Zoo, one of the apes instantly snatched it in her hand. Expecting to see the bird gobbled up, the keeper was astonished to see the chimpanzee cradle the terrified fledgling tenderly in a cupped palm, gazing at it with what seemed like delight. The other chimpanzees gathered and the bird was delicately passed from hand to hand. The last to receive the bird took it to the bars and handed it to the astounded keeper.

Jeffrey Masson and Susan McCarthy, *When Elephants Weep*

Illustration in Textbooks

At this point in the course, you should also be noting how these expository methods of development are manifest in your other textbooks. Illustration is a common method of development that textbook writers use to reinforce and add interest to the discussion of otherwise abstract concepts. For example, in a complicated discussion of long-term memory (LTM) and short-term memory (STM), the author of a leading psychology textbook augments the text with this illustrative passage titled "The Tip-of-the-Tongue Phenomenon":

The Tip-of-the-Tongue Phenomenon

We have all had the maddening experience of trying to recall a fact that we can *almost* remember—it's on the "tip of my tongue." Fortunately, there is a lesson in this on the nature of retrieval from LTM. The tip-of-the-tongue phenomenon was investigated by Harvard University psychologists Roger Brown and David NcNeil (1966) by giving definitions of uncommon words to college students and asking them to recall the words. For example, they might be read the definition of *sampan* ("a small boat used in shallow water in Asia that is rowed from behind using a single oar"). Often, the students could recall the word *sampan*. Sometimes, though, they could not quite recall the word, and the researchers were able to create the tip-of-the-tongue sensation in these students. When this happened, the students found that they were able to recall some information about the word ("It starts with *s*" or "It sounds like *Siam*") or recall something about the thing the word referred to ("It looks a little like a junk"), even when they could not retrieve the word. Then, moments later, the word would pop into memory for some students, proving that it was there all the time but just could not be retrieved for the moment. Studies suggest that about half of the things that we can't remember, but are on the tip of our tongues, are recalled within a minute or so (Schachter, 1999), but you can drive yourself nuts for hours trying to remember the other half!

Benjamin B. Lahey, *Psychology: An Introduction*

Process

Process is the next method of development. There are two kinds of process writing, and both use step-by-step or chronological (time) order. In the **directive** process method, the author explains the steps that *one must follow* to perform a task, such as how to make a pizza, how to do an Internet search, or how to lose 10 pounds. Process writing is found most often in laboratory or technical manuals and in how-to and self-help books. Here is an example of a paragraph developed using a directive process.

. . . pasta is far easier to cook than to classify. Choose a good brand made exclusively from durum wheat. Boil water, add coarse salt, toss in the pasta, and stir to prevent sticking. Check regularly by biting a piece in two. Chew attentively, testing for firmness without a hint of granularity against the teeth—perfectly cooked pasta is al dente, literally "to the tooth." Then scan the remaining section for that faint white trace in the middle that some Italians call the anima, the soul, of perfectly cooked pasta. Don't add oil to the water or on any account throw a strand of pasta against the wall to see if it sticks. Italians have never heard of these bizarre practices, mutations probably born in the 19th-century United States that are about as Italian as canned elbow macaroni.

Tom Mueller, "Cultural Icon," *Hemispheres*

In the **informative** process method, the writer describes a phenomenon—how something works, how something developed, or how it came into existence. The informative process, like the directive process, uses chronological order, but the underlying purpose is different: The writer does not expect us to duplicate the process, perhaps because it would be impossible (or dangerous) to do so. An especially good example of an informative process occurs in this paragraph, in which Ruth Brandon describes the "Substitution Trunk," a trick performed by the famous magician and master of illusion, Harry Houdini. For this paragraph, number each step of the process.

The very first trick ever performed by Houdini on the professional stage was a simple but effective illusion known generally as the "Substitution Trunk," though he preferred to call it "Metamorphosis." Houdini and his partner would bring a large trunk onto the stage. It was opened and a sack or bag produced from inside it. Houdini, bound and handcuffed, would get into the sack, which was then sealed or tied around the neck. The trunk was closed over the bag and its occupant. It was locked, strapped and chained. Then a screen was drawn around it. The partner (after they married, this was always Mrs. Houdini) stepped behind the screen which, next moment, was thrown aside—by Houdini himself. The partner had meanwhile disappeared. A committee of the audience was called onstage to verify that the ties, straps, etc., around the trunk had not been tampered with. These were then laboriously loosened; the trunk was opened; and there, inside the securely fastened bag, was—Mrs. Houdini!

Ruth Brandon, *The Life and Many Deaths of Harry Houdini*

What phrase serves as the controlling idea for the paragraph? <u>"a simple but effective illusion"</u>

Comparison and Contrast

The method of **comparison and contrast** is used to explain similarities and differences between two subjects. **Comparison** discusses *similarities,* often between two apparently dissimilar things, for example, how building a house is like writing an essay. But comparison can also be used to examine two related things. If a writer in an automotive magazine, for example, were to compare two cars, two Japanese imported cars—say, Toyotas and Hondas—he or she would focus on insightful or significant similarities, rather than on obvious ones. That both types of car have steering wheels, engines, brakes, and other necessary equipment is hardly worth pointing out. In trying to recommend which make to buy, the writer would note the significant similarities in body styling, structural workmanship, and fuel efficiency. He or she might then assess the differences, the contrasting points.

In this clever passage, surgeon-writer Richard Selzer examines the close relationship between two improbable professions—medicine and writing—by relating only insightful similarities.

> At first glance, it would appear that surgery and writing have little in common, but I think that is not so. For one thing, they are both sub-celestial arts; as far as I know, the angels disdain to perform either one. In each of them you hold a slender instrument that leaves a trail wherever it is applied. In one, there is the shedding of blood; in the other it is ink that is spilled upon a page. In one, the scalpel is restrained; in the other, the pen is given rein. The surgeon sutures together the tissues of the body to make whole what is sick or injured; the writer sews words into sentences to fashion a new version of human experience. A surgical operation is rather like a short story. You make the incision, rummage around inside for a bit, then stitch up. It has a beginning, a middle and an end. If I were to choose a medical specialist to write a novel, it would be a psychiatrist. They tend to go on and on. And on.
>
> Richard Selzer, "The Pen and the Scalpel," *The New York Times*

Write a main-idea sentence for this paragraph.   <u>Surgery and writing</u>

<u>have more in common than one might think.</u>

Contrast properly refers to a discussion of the *differences* between two or more related or like things—for example, the presidential terms of George Bush and of his son, George W. Bush; the three *The Lord of the Rings* movies; or the German import the VW Passat and the American-made Toyota Camry. Comparison and contrast may be used together or singly, depending on the subject and the writer's purpose. Contrast is the dominant method of development in this next passage by Paco Underhill, an expert in shopping center design and shopping habits. In it, he examines the differences in shopping styles between men and women. How many points of contrast does he include?

> A recent study of how men and women differ when it comes to the mall turned up this fact: Men, once you get them in the door, are much more interested in the social aspect of malls than the shopping part, whereas women say the social aspect is important but shopping comes first. Men enjoy the mall as a form of recreation—they like watching people and browsing around in stores more than shopping. Maybe they'll spend fifteen minutes in a bookstore or a stereo store and leave without buying a thing. They treat it like an information-gathering trip. Men also like the nonretail parts—the rock-climbing walls, the food courts, anything that doesn't actually require them to enter stores and look at, try on, or buy merchandise. Women, of course, are there for *exactly* those things. The only females who truly love the nonshopping aspects of the mall are teenage girls. They love shopping, of course, but they also love the food courts and video arcades and all that stuff, too. And that's probably because the mall is the only non-home, nonschool environment they have. But they outgrow that by the time they're in college. From then on, they're at malls to shop.
>
> Paco Underhill, *Call of the Mall*

A paragraph developed by comparison or contrast does not have to give equal treatment to the two subjects under discussion. Read, for example, this excerpt by Luis Alberto Urrea.

> One of the most beautiful views of San Diego is from the summit of a small hill in Tijuana's municipal garbage dump. People live on that hill, picking through the trash with long poles that end in hooks made of bent nails. They scavenge for bottles, tin, aluminum, cloth; for cast-out beds, wood, furniture. Sometimes they find meat that is not too rotten to be cooked.
>
> This view-spot is where the city drops off its dead animals—dogs, cats, sometimes goats, horses. They are piled in heaps six feet high and torched. In that stinking blue haze, amid nightmarish sculptures of charred ribs and carbonized tails, the garbage-pickers can watch the buildings of San Diego gleam gold on the blue coastline. The city looks cool in the summer when heat cracks the ground and flies drill into their noses. And in the winter, when windchill drops night temperatures into the low thirties, when the cold makes their lips bleed, and rain turns the hill into a gray pudding of ash and mud, and babies are wrapped in plastic trash bags for warmth, San Diego glows like a big electric dream. And every night on that burnt hill, these people watch.
>
> Luis Alberto Urrea, *Across the Wire: Life and Hard Times on the Mexican Border*

Why does Urrea focus more on the Tijuana side of the border than on the American side? The audience is likely to be Americans who would already be familiar with typical American affluence; readers might not be aware of the severe poverty in Tijuana.

Comparison and Contrast in Textbooks	In textbook material, contrast is a useful way to distinguish between easily confused concepts or between a correct and an incorrect interpretation. This latter case is demonstrated in this discussion from a leading anthropology textbook: The selection contrasts Darwinian evolution (the scientific belief that species were transformed through genetic mutation over the centuries) with the earlier Lamarckian theory (that traits change through the animals' own efforts and are then passed on). In this particular excerpt, the author uses the example of the giraffe's neck to contrast evolutionary belief (the process of natural selection) with the Lamarckian view of "the inheritance of acquired characteristics."

Natural selection is the process by which nature selects the forms most fit to survive and reproduce in a given environment. For natural selection to work on a particular population, there must be variety within that population, as there always is. Natural selection operates when there is competition for *strategic resources* (those necessary for life), such as food and space, between members of the population. Organisms whose attributes render them most fit to survive and reproduce in their environment do so in greater numbers than others do. Over the years, the less fit organisms gradually die out and the favored types survive.

The giraffe's neck can be used to illustrate how natural selection works on variety within a population. In any group of giraffes, there is always variation in neck length. When food is adequate, the animals have no problem feeding themselves with foliage. But in times when there is pressure on strategic resources, so that dietary foliage is not as abundant as usual, giraffes with longer necks have an advantage. They can feed off the higher branches. If this feeding advantage permits longer-necked giraffes to survive and reproduce even slightly more effectively than shorter-necked ones, the trait will be favored by natural selection. The giraffes with longer necks will be more likely to transmit their genetic material to future generations than will giraffes with shorter necks.

An incorrect alternative to this (Darwinian) explanation would be the inheritance of acquired characteristics. That is the idea that in each generation, individual giraffes strain their necks to reach just a bit higher. This straining somehow modifies their genetic material. Over generations of strain, the average neck gradually gets longer through the accumulation of small increments of neck length acquired during the lifetime of each generation of giraffes. This is not how evolution works. If it did work this way, weight lifters could expect to produce especially muscular babies. Workouts that promise no gain without the pain apply to the physical development of individuals, not species. Instead, evolution works as the process of natural selection takes advantage of the variety that is already present in a population. That's how giraffes got their necks.

Conrad Phillip Kottak, *Anthropology: The Exploration of Human Diversity*

Even though there are no markers like *in contrast* or *however* or *nevertheless,* the transitional sentence at the beginning of the third paragraph suggests the contrast method.

Practice Exercise 1

Read the following paragraphs. First, decide which of the following methods of development predominates.

- Facts and statistics
- Example or illustration
- Process (directive or informative)
- Comparison and contrast

Then write a sentence stating the main idea in your own words.

A.

Some animals have senses humans do not possess, capacities only recently discovered. Other animal senses may remain to be discovered. By extension, could there be feelings animals have that humans do not, and if so, how would we know? It will take scientific humility and philosophical creativity to provide even the beginning of an answer.

A mother lion observed by George Schaller had left her three small cubs under a fallen tree. While she was away, two lions from another pride killed the cubs. One male ate part of one of the cubs. The second carried a cub away, holding it as he would a food item, not as a cub. He stopped from time to time to lick it and later nestled it between his paws. Ten hours later, he still had not eaten it. When the mother returned and found what had happened, she sniffed the last dead cub, licked it, and then sat down and ate it, except for the head and front paws.

This mother lion was acting like a lion, not like a person. But in understanding what lions do, what she felt is part of the picture. Maybe she felt closer to her dead offspring when it was part of her body once again. Maybe she hates waste, or cleans up all messes her cubs make, as part of her love. Maybe this is a lion funeral rite. Or maybe it is something only a lion can feel.

Jeffrey Masson and Susan McCarthy, *When Elephants Weep*

Method of development: <u>illustration</u>

Main idea: <u>Even if we were aware of animal feelings, we might not</u>

<u>be able to understand them.</u>

B.   The writer of this passage, Lewis H. Lapham, confesses to having smoked for over 50 years. In an editorial, Lapham complains about a policy enacted in March 2003 prohibiting patrons of restaurants and bars in New York City from smoking. Arguing that the ban on smoking is a ban on freedom of expression, Lapham observes this:

The preferred attitude toward smoking accords with the canon of political correctness that has arisen over the last twenty years in concert with the government's pretensions to imperial grandeur—the new media cleansed of strong language and imperfect hair, the authors of standardized college tests inoculated against infection of dangerous adjectives and subversive nouns. Among the topics deemed inadmissible on its roster of searching essay questions, The Princeton Review now lists, in no particular order, war, drugs, sex, alcohol, tobacco, junk food, socioeconomic advantages (swimming pools, expensive vacations), divorce, religion, Halloween, anything "disrespectful" or "demeaning." Diane Ravitch's new book, *The Language Police,* takes note of the same fastidiousness governing the assembly of high school textbooks, and as examples of the words and images deleted in the interest of a risk-free intellectual environment she mentions Mickey Mouse and Stuart Little (both rodents and therefore suggestive of rats in slums), depictions of a mother cooking dinner for her children (gender stereotype), dinosaurs (their presence lending credibility to the theory of evolution), owls (in some cultures associated with death). Because the committees buying the freshly laundered lesson plans seek "multidimensional companionship" with the censors on the Christian right (who compose pictures of an idealized, nonexistent past) and the censors on the liberal left (who compose pictures of an idealized, nonexistent future) the books provide the students with the comfort of a fairy tale.

Lewis H. Lapham, "Notebook: Social Hygiene," Harper's Magazine

Method of development: <u>example</u>

Main idea: <u>The canon of political correctness has gone beyond</u>

<u>contempt for smoking, now having infiltrated the media, college</u>

<u>admissions testing, and textbooks.</u>

C.

Broadly posed, the trick of weaponizing anthrax is to make it breathable. A clump of infected soil might contain billions of anthrax spores, but a clump of soil is unlikely to be inhaled. So the first task in weaponizing anthrax is to purify it, producing a concentration of spores. This is done by creating a suspension, in which the anthrax spores are separated from the material surrounding them in the sample—water, material from the growth medium, and so on. No particle of anything much bigger than five microns is likely to get past the mucous membranes and reach deep into the lungs, and each anthrax spore is itself less than two microns in size. Purifying and concentrating the spores requires real laboratory skill.

Purification and concentration, however, is not enough. In even the purest concentrate, anthrax spores, like most small particles, will clump together, owing to natural electrostatic force. "If you just grow up spores in a test tube and then you remove the liquid, you'll have a kind of a clump," says Philip S. Brachman, a legendary epidemiologist and an old anthrax hand. "Now, that clump won't go anywhere—it'll fall to the ground." The next grand step in weaponizing anthrax is to cause those purified spores to separate, like individual sprinkles of fine powder, so they can linger in the air and be inhaled.

Peter Boyer, "The Ames Strain," The New Yorker

Method of development: <u>informative process</u>

Main idea: <u>To make anthrax breathable, a scientist must follow</u>

<u>several steps.</u>

D.

By the end of the century, supersizing—the ultimate expression of the value meal revolution—reigned. As of 1996 some 25 percent of the $97 billion spent on fast food came from items promoted on the basis of either larger size or extra portions. A serving of McDonald's french fries had ballooned from 200 calories (1960) to 320 calories (late 1970s) to 450 calories (mid-1990s) to 540 calories (late 1990s) to the present 610 calories. In fact, everything on the menu had exploded in size. What was once a 590-calorie McDonald's meal was now . . . 1550 calories. By 1999 heavy users—people who eat fast food more than twenty times a month . . . —accounted for $66 billion of the $110 billion spent on fast food. Twenty times a month is now McDonald's marketing goal for every fast-food eater. The average Joe or Jane thought nothing of buying Little Caesar's pizza "by the foot," of supersizing that lunchtime burger or supersizing an afternoon snack. Kids had come to see bigger everything—bigger sodas, bigger snacks, bigger candy, and even bigger doughnuts—as the norm; there was no such thing as a fixed, immutable size for anything, because anything could be made a lot bigger for just a tad more.

Greg Critser, Fat Land: How Americans Became the Fattest People in the World

Method of development: <u>facts and statistics</u>

Main idea: <u>Supersizing of meals became the dominant trend in the</u>

<u>fast-food industry during the 1990s, leading to a huge increase in</u>

<u>the number of calories consumed.</u>

Combination of Methods	Finally, you should recognize that, like many of life's challenges, the task of reading is a complex undertaking. Not all paragraphs can be as neatly categorized as those you have examined here. Although some writers use an easily recognizable method of development, many do not. In particular, within an essay or article, a writer may use several different methods from paragraph to paragraph or within the same passage. In the following passage, Michael Specter examines the technology called G.P.S., which stands for "Global Positioning System," now available on some makes of automobiles. As you read it, try to identify the various expository methods of development it encompasses.

> The satellites function as reference points—the way stars once did for mariners—and not since the twelfth century, when the compass came into use, has a navigational tool promised to more fundamentally alter the way we live. Within a few years, every cell phone, quartz watch, and laptop computer may come with a tiny G.P.S. receiver embedded in it. In fact, by December 31, 2002, federal law will require cellular carriers to be able to locate the position of every user making a 911 call. That should eventually make it possible for emergency personnel to find anyone in America who calls 911.

> Though there are earthbound means of complying with the new "E911" mandate, many carriers will rely on G.P.S. technology. The National Park Service is already using G.P.S. to map trails, keep their snowplows on the road, and even track bears. Air routes routinely have a geographical tag and so do coastal waterways and shipping lanes. It is even possible to rig a driver's air bag so that, as it is deployed, it activates a G.P.S. device that reports the car's location to the nearest ambulance. Our children may never fully understand the word "lost"—just as few people under the age of ten have any idea what it means to "dial" a phone number.

Michael Specter, "No Place to Hide," The New Yorker

List the methods of development. (I counted three.) <u>informative</u>

<u>process, examples, facts</u>

Practice Exercise 2	Read the following passages. Next choose the two dominant methods of development from the choices provided. Then write a sentence stating the main idea in your own words.

A.

Few words evoke as many images of ancient decadence, glory and prophetic doom as does "Babylon." Yet the actual place—50 miles south of Baghdad—is flat, hot, deserted and dusty. Next to a crumbling small-scale reconstruction of the Ishtar Gate, its once-vivid blue tiles faded and its parade of animal reliefs scarred and broken, a forlorn gift shop offers miniature plastic statues of the famous Lion of Babylon and T-shirts bearing faux cuneiform. The real Ishtar Gate, built by Nebuchadnezzar II around 600 B.C., was hauled off to Berlin by archaeologists a century ago. Visitors must visualize among the low mounds of rubble a vast and cosmopolitan city, holy as Mecca, wealthy as Zurich, as magnificently planned as Washington. The Tower of Babel is now a swampy pit. Looming above the sad heaps of brick is an imperious palace built in 1987 by Saddam Hussein, who often expressed a kinship with Nebuchadnezzar.

Andrew Lawler, "Saving Iraq's Treasures," *Smithsonian*

Choose the two predominant methods of development.
    (a) comparison   (c) (significant details)
    (b) (contrast)   (d) informative process

Main idea: The contrast between ancient Babylon with its wealth and splendor and the crumbling, rubble-filled Babylon of today is remarkable.

B.

The death of the cowboy as a vital figure has been one of my principal subjects, and yet I'm well aware that killing the *myth* of the cowboy is like trying to kill a snapping turtle: no matter what you do to it, the beast retains a sluggish life. . . . The Marlboro man is a last survival of the Western male in the heroic mode. In Marlboro ads the West is always the mountain West, the high, rich country that runs from Jackson Hole around to Sheridan, Wyoming, where the Queen of England sometimes goes to buy her racehorses. The West of those ads is the familiar, poeticized, pastoral West—the Marlboro men themselves need to do little other than light up. Perhaps they swing their ropes at a herd of horses that are thundering toward a corral.

Horses only, mind you—never cattle. The image of horses running is perhaps the most potent image to come out of the American West: cattle running produce a far less graceful, far less appealing picture. The fact is, cows are hard to poeticize—even longhorns. They tend to seem ugly, stupid, and slow, which they are; images of cows are unlikely to loosen the pocketbooks of smokers in Japan or elsewhere where the Marlboro man and his horses are seen, and they are seen everywhere. No image out of the American West is so ubiquitous, and they are images that are entirely male—Marlboro country is a woman-free zone. Sometimes there is a cabin in the snow, with a wreath of smoke coming out of the chimney. The running horses may be making for this cabin. But if there is a woman in there, cooking for her man, we don't see her: we just see the rugged male, riding the high country forever.

Larry McMurtry, *Walter Benjamin at the Dairy Queen*

Choose the two predominant methods of development.
(a) facts and statistics   (c) comparison
(b) (examples)   (d) (contrast)

Main idea: The image of the Western male survives in Marlboro

ads, with the Western landscape dominated by horses (never

cattle) and with women conspicuously absent.

▨ CONCLUSION: METHODS OF DEVELOPMENT AND PATTERNS OF THOUGIIT

The methods of development you have just studied parallel the ways we impose order on our thought processes. Consider these real-life situations, and decide which method of development underlies the mental process involved.

1.   You want to build a new cabinet for your CD player, TV, and DVD player.   directive process

2.   Are flat-panel computer screens really better than the conventional kind?   contrast

3.   How are the other students in my section of Physics 1 performing in the class?   statistics; perhaps comparison and contrast

4.   A friend from Arkansas decides she wants to move to Chicago, where you live. She writes, asking you about apartment rents in various parts of the city.   examples, statistics

5.   Your 10-year-old niece asks you how babies are born.

     informative process

■ CHAPTER EXERCISES

Selection 1

[1]Certainly, imported diseases have recently caused problems for small numbers of people in wealthy countries. [2]Increased travel between rich and poor countries exposes travelers to the unsolved problems of the poorer countries. [3]The blood of visitors to sub-Saharan Africa has a good chance of acquiring the malaria parasites that annually kill a million people in poor countries. [4]The intestinal tracts of travelers to almost any poor country have a good chance of becoming hosts to the waterborne viruses, bacteria, and protozoa that annually kill millions of people by causing diarrhea.

[5]Every day, travelers bring these pathogens into JFK and Los Angeles International Airport, fresh from the poorer countries. [6]These infected travelers may serve as the source for a few additional infections that arise within our borders, but by and large these chains of infection peter out, largely because the infrastructure of rich countries inhibits their spread.

[7]Consider dengue. [8]The dengue virus is continually slipping across the Texas border from Mexico, but it does not spread within the United States, probably because people on the Texas side spend most of their time in mosquito-proof houses, cars, and workplaces. [9]By keeping people inside mosquito-proof structures, computers and televisions may help curb the spread—the virus becomes stranded like a traveler in an airport in which all flights have been canceled.

Paul W. Ewald, *Plague Time*

A. Vocabulary

For each italicized word from the selection, choose the best definition according to the context in which it appears.

1. bring these *pathogens* [sentence 5]:
   (a) germs.
   (b) disease-causing agents.
   (c) hosts for microorganisms.
   (d) infectious diseases.
2. these chains of infection *peter out* [6]:
   (a) break out into serious epidemics.
   (b) spread throughout the population.
   (c) disappear as mysteriously as they appear.
   (d) slowly diminish and die out.
3. the *infrastructure* of rich countries [6]:
   (a) facilities and services that help a community function.
   (b) natural resources used in manufacturing.
   (c) advanced medicine and technology.
   (d) economic distribution system.

B. *Content and Structure*

Complete the following questions.

1. The main idea of the passage is best stated in
   (a) sentence 1.
   (b) sentence 2.
   (c) sentences 1 and 2 together.
   (d) sentence 5.
2. A good title for this passage is
   (a) "How the Dengue Virus Spreads."
   (b) "Travel and the Spread of Disease."
   (c) "Disease in Rich and Poor Countries."
   (d) "How Pathogens Travel."
3. The mode of discourse in the passage is
   (a) narration.
   (b) description.
   (c) exposition.
   (d) persuasion.
4. Which method of development is used in the paragraph comprising sentences 7 to 9?
   (a) directive process.
   (b) comparison.
   (c) facts and statistics.
   (d) illustration.
5. From sentences 7 to 9 we can infer that the dengue virus is caused by
   (a) increased travel between Mexico and the United States.
   (b) mosquitoes.
   (c) poor sanitation.
   (d) a virus that has not yet been identified.
6. Sentence 6 alludes to the "infrastructure." What is an example of such infrastructure in the passage?
   (a) large airports like JFK and Los Angeles International Airports.
   (b) borders between nations like Mexico and the United States.
   (c) mosquito-proof houses, cars, and workplaces.
   (d) increased travel to poor countries.

Answers for
Selection 1

A. *Vocabulary*

   1. (b)   2. (d)   3. (a)

B. *Content and Structure*

   1. (c)   2. (b)   3. (c)   4. (d)   5. (b)   6. (c)

Selection 2

[1]So many disturbing traits, once you look into them—with a somewhat morbid curiosity, I'd begun prowling around the University Science Library,[3] an airy new building with gestures toward native construction materials, a self-conscious sensitivity to the surrounding redwoods, and the rational and antiseptic calm of too many quantitative minds padding silently down well-carpeted corridors. [2]A few tidbits: sharks are the world's only known *intrauterine cannibals;* as eggs hatch within a uterus, the unborn young fight and devour each other until one well-adapted predator emerges. [3](If the womb is a battleground, what then the sea?) [4]Also, without the gas-filled bladders that float other fish, sharks, if they stop swimming, sink. [5]This explains their tendency to lurk along the bottom like twenty-one-foot, 4,600-pound benthic land mines with hundred-year life spans. [6]Hard skin bristling with tiny teeth sheathes their flexible cartilage skeletons— no bone at all. [7]Conical snouts, black eyes without visible pupils, black-tipped pectoral fins. [8]Tearing out and constantly being replaced, their serrated fangs have as many as twenty-eight stacked spares (a bite meter embedded in a slab of meat once measured a dusky shark's bite at eighteen tons per square inch). [9]And all of the following have been found in shark bellies: a goat, a tomcat, three birds, a raincoat, overcoats, a car license plate, grass, tin cans, a cow's head, shoes, leggings, buttons, belts, hens, roosters, a nearly whole reindeer, even a headless human in a full suit of armor. [10]Swimming with their mouths open, great whites are indiscriminate recyclers of the organic—my sensitive disposition, loving family and affection for life, my decent pickup, room full of books, preoccupation with chocolate in the afternoons, and tendency to take things too personally: all immaterial to my status as protein.

Daniel Duane, *Caught Inside: A Surfer's Year on the California Coast*

A. Vocabulary

For each italicized word from the selection, write the dictionary definition most appropriate for the context.

1. *morbid* [sentence 1]: <u>gruesome, preoccupied by unwholesome</u>

   <u>thoughts</u>

2. *lurk* [5]: <u>lie in wait</u>

3. *serrated* [8]: <u>sharply notched like the edge of a saw</u>

B. Content and Structure

Complete the following questions.

1. Locate the topic of the paragraph. <u>sharks</u>

[3]The library Duane refers to is at the University of California at Santa Cruz.

Then write the controlling idea. <u>"so many disturbing traits"</u>

2. Consider again the phrase you wrote for the preceding question. Which of the following methods of development in the remainder of the paragraph is most evident as support for that phrase?
   (a) comparison.
   (b) contrast.
   (c) (example.)
   (d) illustration.

3. Paraphrase Duane's parenthetical remark from sentence 3: "If the womb is a battleground, what then the sea?" <u>If sharks are</u>

   <u>cannibals, killing and eating each other before they are born, an</u>

   <u>intended victim in the ocean doesn't have much of a chance.</u>

4. Why must sharks constantly swim? <u>They lack a gas-filled bladder.</u>

5. Look again at sentence 5, in which Duane imaginatively compares the shark to "a benthic land mine." (Benthic is an adjective referring to benthos, or organisms that live on ocean or lake bottoms.) What does Duane intend to suggest in this comparison? <u>The shark can behave</u>

   <u>explosively; it can strike without warning at any time and cause</u>

   <u>enormous damage.</u>

6. From the information given in sentences 9 and 10, we can conclude that sharks
   (a) (can and will eat anything, whether it is food or not.)
   (b) prefer humans to any other food.
   (c) are basically carnivorous.
   (d) are able to digest inorganic objects.

7. Consider again the list of items found in sharks' stomachs. Now read sentence 10 again and locate the phrase that best describes sharks' function in the ocean. <u>"indiscriminate recyclers of the organic"</u>

Selection 3

Suketu Mehta, the writer of the following passage, was born in Calcutta, India, and grew up in Bombay. Mumbai, the new official name of Bombay, is the biggest city in India, with a population of over 12 million people. Understanding the impact of this passage requires a little background about India's caste system. A caste is a social hierarchy. In traditional Indian society, Brahmins were at the top, followed by four different Hindu castes, then Muslims, and finally, the so-called untouchables, the lowest caste, who performed menial jobs such as sweeping streets and collecting garbage. The caste system has been officially illegal for many years, and discrimination based on one's caste is prohibited. Yet the system remains ingrained in behavior, and remnants persist. Mehta's passage presents a rather different version of human behavior.

1   The manager of Bombay's suburban railway system was recently asked when the system would improve to a point where it could carry its five million daily passengers in comfort. "Not in my lifetime," he answered. Certainly, if you commute into Bombay, you are made aware of the precise temperature of the human body as it curls around you on all sides, adjusting itself to every curve of your own. A lover's embrace was never so close.

2   One morning I took the rush hour train to Jogeshwari. There was a crush of passengers, and I could only get halfway into the carriage. As the train gathered speed, I hung on to the top of the open door. I feared I would be pushed out, but someone reassured me: "Don't worry, if they push you out they also pull you in."

3   Asad Bin Saif is a scholar of the slums, moving tirelessly among the sewers, cataloguing numberless communal flare-ups and riots, seeing first-hand the slow destruction of the social fabric of the city. He is from Bhagalpur, in Bihar, site not only of some of the worst rioting in the nation, but also of a famous incident in 1980, in which the police blinded a group of criminals with knitting needles and acid. Asad, of all people, has seen humanity at its worst. I asked him if he felt pessimistic about the human race.

4   "Not at all," he replied. "Look at the hands from the trains."

5   If you are late for work in Bombay, and reach the station just as the train is leaving the platform, you can run up to the packed compartments and you will find many hands stretching out to grab you on board, unfolding outward from the train like petals. As you run alongside you will be picked up, and some tiny space will be made for your feet on the edge of the open doorway. The rest is up to you; you will probably have to hang on to the door frame with your fingertips, being careful not to lean out too far lest you get decapitated by a pole placed close to the tracks. But consider what has happened: your fellow passengers, already packed tighter than cattle are legally allowed to be, their shirts drenched with sweat in the badly ventilated compartment, having stood like this for hours, retain an empathy for you, know that your boss might yell at you or cut your pay if you miss this train and will make space where none exists to take one more person with them. And at the moment of contact, they do not know if the hand that is reaching for theirs belongs to a Hindu or Muslim or Christian or Brahmin or untouchable or whether you were born in this city or arrived only this morning or whether you live in Malabar Hill or Jogeshwari; whether you're from Bombay or Mumbai or New York. All they know is that you're trying to get to the city of gold, and that's enough. Come on board, they say. We'll adjust.

Suketu Mehta, "Mumbai: A Lover's Embrace," *Granta*

A. *Vocabulary*

For each italicized word from the selection, write the dictionary definition most appropriate for the context.

1. *cataloguing* numerous flare-ups [paragraph 3]: <u>recording as a list</u>

2. numerous *flare-ups* [3]: <u>sudden outbursts of anger</u>

3. retain an *empathy* for you [5]: <u>emotional identification</u>

B. *Content and Structure*

Complete the following questions.

1. Look again at the significant details in paragraphs 1 and 2. What overall impression of Bombay's railway system do they convey? <u>The subway</u>

   <u>system is crowded and uncomfortable.</u>

2. The behavior of the railway passengers on the trains leading to Bombay has led Asad Bin Saif, the "scholar of the slums" mentioned in paragraph 3, to be
   (a) optimistic about the human race.
   (b) pessimistic about the human race.
   (c) antisocial and isolated from the human race.
   (d) indifferent, callous toward the human race.

3. What method of development is represented in paragraph 5?
   (a) process.
   (b) comparison.
   (c) contrast.
   (d) illustration.
   (e) facts.

4. What emotion or motivation governs those already on the trains to pull latecomers on board? <u>empathy—all the passengers look out for each</u>

   <u>other's welfare</u>

5. In paragraph 4, locate the verb phrase "retain an empathy for." Then, in the same sentence, locate the *subject* that goes with this verb phrase and write it in the space. <u>"your fellow passengers"</u>

6. What is the point, the larger lesson, of the story related in paragraph 5?

   <u>Caste, religious, and racial distinctions are immaterial when people</u>

   <u>are united in a common goal, in this case reaching the "city of gold."</u>

PRACTICE ESSAY

"Book of Dreams: The Sears Roebuck Catalog"
Rose Del Castillo Guilbault

In 1993 Sears Roebuck & Company announced that it would stop publishing its mail-order catalog, a venerable institution begun in 1886. For generations Americans had shopped at home with the catalog, especially farm families, who made infrequent trips to town.

Rose Guilbault was born in Mexico and later immigrated with her family to the United States, where they settled in the Salinas Valley, an agricultural area in central California. She writes of her childhood that she discovered books early on, but she never had enough books to read. The local library allowed children to check out only two books at a time, and her father could take her to town only twice a month. Guilbault has had a varied career in journalism: She formerly wrote a column for the Sunday *San Francisco Chronicle,* called "Hispanic, USA"; she worked in community relations, public relations, and production for three Bay Area television stations; currently, she is vice president of corporate communications and public affairs for the California State Automobile Association.

Preview Questions

1. How do you define the American dream?
2. If your family immigrated to the United States recently, what was the impetus for their immigration? If your family immigrated a few generations ago, how would you go about investigating the reasons for their coming to this country?
3. For Rose Guilbault, the Sears Roebuck catalog was an important part of her childhood. Is there a similar publication that represents a significant influence in your childhood?

1   The news that Sears is closing 113 stores and folding its 97-year-old catalog sent me scurrying through the basement in search of one of my favorite possessions, a 1941 Sears Roebuck & Company catalog. I was relieved to find it, still inside a metal filing cabinet, underneath a jumble of old Chronicles and a 1939 *Liberty* magazine.

2   I've always had an affinity for the 1940s. I love the Big Band music, the movies and the fashions. As a child I sat mesmerized, listening to my mother's stories about dances under the stars where local groups played and my young mother and her sisters flirted the night away.

3   But that's not the only reason I've held onto this ragged catalog through college, marriage, children and numerous moves. It symbolizes the America my parents and I believed in when we arrived in this country from Mexico. An America where everything you could possibly want was in an emporium inside a book. A book that came to your home from which you could leisurely, conveniently choose items that would be delivered to your doorstep. The concept was amazing to us. This wasn't about accumulating goods but about obtaining a piece of the American pie.

4   Many of today's immigrants are easily caught in this country's web of materialism, easy credit and easy debt. But in the early '60s, the values in rural areas were different. These "wish books" were a metaphor for America's bounty and what could be had with hard work.

5   Every new catalog was savored. We all had our own dream sections. Papa, eyes sparkling, would ease himself into his chair after dinner and briskly examine the tools, hunting rifles and cameras. Then he'd pass the catalog to Mama, who—for what seemed to me to be hours—studied the pretty dresses, household appliances, dishes and plants.

6   By the time the catalog made its way into my hands, my palms itched with anxiety. At Easter time, I would lose myself in pages of frilly, pastel dresses with matching hats and purses. In the Christmas season, which brought my favorite edition of the year, I would sit for hours, staring glassy-eyed at the pages of toys, dolls and games.

7   But nothing frivolous was ever ordered. We lived on a farm in the Salinas Valley, miles and miles from a big city and miles from the nearest small town. To get there, you'd turn off the main paved road onto a bumpy dirt trail that led to two farmhouses—one big one where the boss and his family lived, and a small, four-room cottage where we lived. The inside was sparsely furnished, mostly with hand-me-down furniture from the boss, except for the spindly TV and a cheap, forest-green nylon sofa set my father bought my mother as a wedding gift.

8   Extravagances were unaffordable. Only the most practical and necessary items would be given consideration—my mother's first washing machine, a school coat for me, and thick, dark denim overalls to keep Papa warm in the frostiest of dawns.

9   The Sears catalog had other uses. I'd cut out the models and use them as paper dolls. My mother would match English words with pictures, *"Y estas ollas? Seran "pots" en ingles?"* And in my most desperate hours of boredom, when only sports programs dominated afternoon television, rain fell outdoors, and absolutely nothing interested me indoors, I'd pick up the thick catalog, sit in the bedroom with the faded cabbage-rose print linoleum and spin fantasies about living the good life I imagined the Americans in the catalogs lived.

10   In the front of my 1941 Sears catalog are two stories about typical Sears customers. One profiles the Browns of Washington state, who arrived there as homesteaders, lived in a tent with their children, until their farm produced enough for them to build a two-room shack, and eventually build a

comfortable white clapboard farmhouse on their land. Photos show Mr. and Mrs. Brown with their new cream separator, daughter Evelyn with her new Elgin bicycle, and the whole family listening to their silver-tone radio-phonograph—all from Sears, of course.

11   The second article describes the Yeamens of Glendale, in Los Angeles County. Mr. Yeamen works at Lockheed Aviation, a mile and a half commute from their "modern, five-room bungalow . . . with a barbecue grill in the back yard and a view of the mountains from every window." Photographs show the various family members with their Sears products: Dad relaxing on a glider swing in the back yard, Mom putting avocado sandwiches in lunch boxes and the kids romping in their stylish clothes.

12   The Browns and Yeamens, the catalog summarizes, are what all of us want to be—good, solid, dependable Americans.

13   As corny and blatantly commercial as these stories are, I like reading them. It reminds me of the America of my youth, or perhaps of my imagination. Even though my family of Mexican immigrants probably didn't have a whole lot in common with the Browns and the Yeamens, we all shopped from that Sears catalog—a book that made us believe everything was reachable, and ours to have.

14   My family prospered too. Not in great leaps and bounds like the Browns of Washington state, but little by little. Our progress was marked by the occasional splurge from the Sears catalog.

15   When I got to the point where I had to own my own clarinet or drop out of the school band—there was a limit to how long we could borrow from the music department—my family had to make a choice. I was not a great musician; we all knew that. But the band was a wholesome activity that integrated me into school life, into America. One evening after dinner, my parents called me into the living room. I searched their faces for a clue, but they remained mysteriously impassive until my father brought out a wrinkled brown package from behind his back.

16   My heart began pounding when I saw the Sears return address. Out came a compact gray and white case, and inside it, lying on an elegant bed of royal blue rayon velvet, were the pieces of a brand-new ebony clarinet. Never in my stolen afternoons with the Sears catalog had I imagined possessing something so fine!

17   Somehow I can't envision today's kids reminiscing about a Lands' End or Victoria's Secret catalog. Times have changed, and so have demographics. People in rural America no longer need a catalog. They now have Kmarts or Wal-Marts in their own mini-malls.

18   Newspaper articles reporting on the Sears closures have described the catalog as "the best record of American material culture." But to many of us, this catalog wasn't about materialism at all. It was about making dreams come true.

A. *Comprehension*

Choose the answer that best completes each statement. Do not refer to the selection while doing this exercise.

1. For Guilbault, the Sears Roebuck catalog primarily represented
   (a) an unobtainable vision of America for her and her family.
   (b) the possibility of obtaining a piece of the American pie.
   (c) a simpler, less stressful life.
   (d) a convenient way to shop for necessities at home.
2. For the author and her family, the most important American virtue was
   (a) a competitive spirit.
   (b) generosity.
   (c) hard work.
   (d) the desire for an education.
3. Guilbault's mother looked at the catalog both to enjoy the pictures of clothing and household items and to
   (a) get ideas for gifts.
   (b) practice English.
   (c) covet the possessions of the wealthier families depicted.
   (d) help choose farm equipment with her husband.
4. The catalog's description of the model families—the Browns and the Yeamans—suggested that
   (a) her family was just like them.
   (b) America was not really the land of opportunity.
   (c) it was important to buy one's belongings from Sears.
   (d) everything in America was reachable.
5. Guilbault remembers one especially memorable acquisition, a clarinet. Aside from marking her family's economic prosperity, this purchase also
   (a) meant that she could reach her dream of becoming a great musician.
   (b) improved her social status at school.
   (c) allowed her to be integrated into American life.
   (d) contributed to the family's love of music.

B. *Vocabulary*

For each italicized word from the selection, choose the best definition according to the context in which it appears. You may refer to the selection to answer the questions in this section and in all the remaining sections.

1. an *affinity* for the 1940s [paragraph 2]:
   (a) natural attraction.
   (b) obsession.
   (c) slight interest in.
   (d) reaction.

2. an *emporium* inside a book [3]:
   (a) playground.
   (b) educational center.
   (c) imaginary toyland.
   (d) large retail store.
3. a metaphor for America's *bounty* [4]:
   (a) high reputation.
   (b) amalgamation of goods and services.
   (c) generosity, liberality in giving.
   (d) treasure chest.
4. nothing *frivolous* was ever ordered [7]:
   (a) insignificant, trivial.
   (b) attractive, esthetically pleasing.
   (c) expensive, costly.
   (d) of good quality.
5. they remained mysteriously *impassive* [15]:
   (a) silent, withdrawn.
   (b) showing no emotion.
   (c) excited, jubilant.
   (d) embarrassed, uncomfortable.
6. times have changed, so have *demographics* [17]: The study of
   (a) social values.
   (b) populations and their characteristics.
   (c) ethnic and minority groups.
   (d) social classes.

C. *Structure*

Complete the following questions.

1. This article has a clear beginning, middle, and end. Locate the major divisions in the essay and indicate the appropriate paragraph numbers.

   Introduction: paragraphs 1 to 4

   Body: paragraphs 5 to 16

   Conclusion: paragraphs 17 and 18

2. With respect to her childhood and the role the Sears Roebuck catalog played in her family, what is the author's point of view?
   (a) nostalgic.
   (b) objective.
   (c) envious.
   (d) philosophical.
   (e) self-pitying.

3. What method of development is used in paragraph 4?
   (a) example.
   (b) process.
   (c) comparison.
   (d) (contrast.)
4 What primary method of development is used in paragraphs 5 to 9?
   (a) (example.)
   (b) comparison.
   (c) contrast.
   (d) process.
5. What is the relationship between paragraph 14 and paragraphs 15 and 16?
   (a) They all represent steps in an informative process.
   (b) Paragraph 14 includes a term to be defined, and the other two define it.
   (c) Paragraphs 15 and 16 offer a contrast to paragraph 14.
   (d) (Paragraph 14 makes a general statement, and paragraphs 15 and 16 serve as a supporting illustration.)

D. Questions for Analysis and Discussion

1. In paragraph 4, Guilbault implicitly criticizes today's culture for its emphasis on materialism, yet it is clear that the Sears catalog, too, promoted materialism. Guilbault suggests a difference, however. What is it?

2. In paragraph 17, Guilbault writes, "Somehow I can't envision today's kids reminiscing about a Lands' End or a Victoria's Secret catalog." What does she mean? Do you agree with her?

IN THE BOOKSTORE

Luis Alberto Urrea's recent book, *The Devil's Highway,* relates the true story of 14 Mexican men who died trying to sneak into the United States by crossing a portion of the Arizona desert near the U.S.–Mexico border. Promised by a human smuggler (called a "coyote") that they would be conducted safely to towns and cities where they would blend in, they were betrayed. Abandoned in the desert, they confronted a terrible wasteland of harsh landscape, no water, and a pitiless sun. Urrea writes with sympathy and compassion.

Four More Methods of Paragraph Development

In Chapter 4 you will learn four more methods of paragraph development common to exposition and persuasion, including:

- Cause and effect

- Classification and analysis

- Definition

- Analogy

■ METHODS OF PARAGRAPH DEVELOPMENT: THE SECOND GROUP

The next four methods of paragraph development—cause and effect, classification, definition, and analogy—are commonly found in essays and articles, whether by professional writers, academics, or college students.

Cause and Effect The **cause-and-effect method** of development is related to reasons and consequences, or results. A writer may provide *reasons* (*causes*) to explain events, problems, or issues and the *consequences* (*effects*) of those events, problems, or issues. Like the comparison and contrast method, which can be used singly or in combination, a writer may discuss only causes or only effects or both, and the causes and effects can be used in either order. Read the following passage; then identify the cause–effect connection in the spaces below.

> When two friends meet and talk informally they usually adopt similar body postures. If they are particularly friendly and share identical attitudes to the subjects being discussed, then the positions in which they hold their bodies are liable to become even more alike, to the point where they virtually become carbon copies of each other. This is not a deliberate imitative process. The friends in question are automatically indulging in what has been called Postural Echo, and they do this unconsciously as part of a natural body display of companionship.
>
> There is a good reason for this. A true bond of friendship is usually only possible between people of roughly equal status. This equality is demonstrated in many indirect ways, but it is reinforced in face-to-face encounters by a matching of the postures of relaxation or alertness. In this way the body transmits a silent message, saying: "See, I am just like you"; and this message is not only sent unconsciously but also understood in the same manner. The friends simply "feel right" when they are together.
>
> Desmond Morris, *Manwatching: A Field Guide to Human Behaviour*

Cause: True friendship can exist only if both people are of equal status.

Effect: The result is called the Postural Echo, an unconscious but deliberate imitation of body movements between two good friends.

Next, read this paragraph by William Langewiesche on the terrorist attacks on the World Trade Center of September 11, 2001. As you read, make a note in the margin of each cause and effect.

Causes: why towers fell—bldgs. filled with jet fuel; hit by powerful missiles; stairwells built too close together

Effects: people were trapped causing more than 1,000 unnecessary deaths

Everyone understood the deal. The attack on the World Trade Center was an act of war. Despite the occasional chatter in the press about shoddy steel or substandard fireproofing, the towers were as well designed, built, and maintained as could have reasonably been expected in America in the late twentieth century. But the context had changed now. The towers fell because they were severely maimed and sprayed with burning jet fuel; they fell as any building will, no matter how resilient, if it is hit by the next bigger missile in the escalating progression of war. In retrospect, their greatest failing was so obvious that it hardly required discussion: the stairwells had been clustered too closely together, and their simultaneous destruction had trapped people above the impact zones, causing more than a thousand unnecessary deaths. This was an error that would have to be avoided in future designs. But there was no point in wishful thinking here. Civilians die in wars, and always will.

William Langewiesche,
"American Ground: Unbuilding the World Trade Center," *The Atlantic Monthly*

In this final passage, Jocko Weyland begins by establishing his credibility as a skateboarder. In the second paragraph, he varies the cause–effect pattern by examining (1) an effect, (2) a cause, (3) a more general effect. See if you can identify these three elements.

The skating of ramps, pools, marble plazas, handrails, ledges, curbs and every other skateable terrain has been an ever present element in my life for the last twenty years. I have skateboarded all over the world—parks in Colorado, drainage ditches on Oahu, backyard pools in California, the streets of London. New York, St. Petersburg, Russia, and Santa Margherita Ligure in Italy. I've even skated in Cameroon. There is so much concrete and wood in the world that riding a skateboard is possible almost anywhere.

Why skating has had such a profound effect on so many people might be because it is a kind of play that defies any practical purpose—that is, it's fun. Play is a manifestation of an atavistic legacy that can be traced back to the propensity for the animals of all higher species to cavort and roughhouse. Humans inherited these impulses and used early transportation like rafts, chariots and wagons for more than just practical purposes from the time of their invention. Then they came careering down snow on skis and riding waves on surfboards. At some point in the middle of the twentieth century, the apple cart broke off the front of some anonymous kid's homemade scooter and the skateboard was born. Skating has now progressed from these humble beginnings to Hawk's and Rowley's[1] feats, and along the way, what began as a toy gained tens of millions of adherents, spawned magazines and would change our culture, influencing music, fashion, art and film.

Jocko Weyland, *The Answer Is Never: A Skateboarder's History of the World*

[1]Hawk and Rowley are X Games champion skateboarders.

Cause and Effect in Visual Material

The following chart, "Don't Fence Me In," accompanied an article by Mark Derr titled "Big Beasts, Tight Space and a Call for Change" (*New York Times,* October 2, 2003).[2]

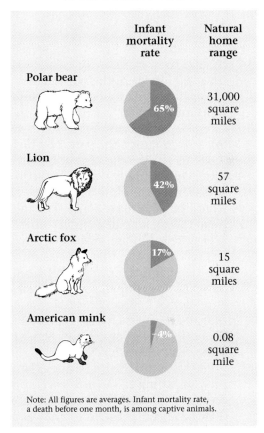

Don't fence me in

	Infant mortality rate	Natural home range
Polar bear	65%	31,000 square miles
Lion	42%	57 square miles
Arctic fox	17%	15 square miles
American mink	4%	0.08 square mile

Note: All figures are averages. Infant mortality rate, a death before one month, is among captive animals.

Source: Copyright © 2003 by Associated Press. All rights reserved. Distributed by Valeo IP. Reprinted by permission.

1. What cause-and-effect relationship does the chart show? <u>The chart shows a correlation between infant mortality in animals and captivity.</u>

[2]For further instruction in interpreting visual elements, see pages 291–292 and 346 in Chapters 8 and 9.

2. Look again at the four species of animals listed. What conclusion can you draw about the relationship between animal species and the size of their natural home range? <u>Larger species of animals</u>

    <u>require a larger territory.</u>

3. Which species of animal has the highest infant mortality rate in captivity? <u>the polar bear</u>

Classification and Analysis

Classification and analysis are traditionally considered together. Although they are actually separate methods, their underlying purpose is the same. In each, the writer takes apart a larger subject and examines its separate parts to see how each relates to the whole. With the **classification** method, a writer puts *several* things (or ideas) into classes or categories, following a consistent system. **Analysis** is different, involving a *single* entity, the parts of which are examined one at a time.

Let us look at classification first. In the real world, we classify all the time. For example, if you decide to reorganize your CD collection, you would first determine a *system* for grouping them; of course, the system would have to make sense. You might organize them by type of music (hard rock, jazz, blues, and so on) or alphabetically by band name. Whatever system you use, it must remain consistent to avoid confusion and to be useful. Passages that use classification often begin with a sentence like this one from an economics textbook: "There are three *types* of unemployment: frictional, structural, and cyclical." (Campbell R. McConnell and Stanley L. Brue, *Economics: Principles, Problems, and Policies.*) Notice that the key word, *types,* is printed in italics, providing easy identification of the types of unemployment. The remainder of the passage goes on to examine each type.

But with analysis, a writer examines the various elements that comprise *one* thing to see how each contributes to the whole. For example, one can evaluate a political speech by using analysis. Let's suppose a student has been assigned to analyze Richard Nixon's famous "Checkers" speech, one often studied by politicians and communications students. She would examine Nixon's purpose, the ideas he presented, his delivery, the logical fallacies he committed, and the emotional appeals he used. Performing this analysis enables her to examine the parts of the speech in terms of how they relate to the whole.

Let us now look at some examples of paragraphs using these methods. Although the topic of this paragraph is a bit grisly, it illustrates the classification method clearly. In a chapter describing the horrors inflicted on residents of the Central African Republic by its former leader Bokassa, Alex Shoumatoff classifies cannibalism into four types.

> There are many kinds of cannibalism. Revenge cannibalism—the gloating, triumphant ingestion of a slain enemy's heart, liver, or other vital parts—is common at the warring-chiefdom stage of social evolution. Emergency can-

nibalism was resorted to by the Uruguayan soccer team whose plane crashed in the Andes.[3] Ritual endocannibalism is practiced by certain tribes like the Yanonamo of northern Amazonia, whose women drink the pulverized ashes of slain kin mixed with banana gruel before their men go off on a raiding party. In the Kindu region of Zaire there are to this day leopard men who wear leopard skins, smear their bodies with leopard grease (which protects them even from lions), chip their teeth to points, and attack and eat people. Among their victims were some Italian soldiers who were part of the U.N. peace-keeping force during the turbulence after independence in 1960. The rarest kind of cannibals are gustatory cannibals—people who are actually partial to the taste of human flesh.

Alex Shoumatoff, "The Emperor Who Ate His People," African Madness

What is the basis for the author's classification system?   _____

As stated earlier, analysis examines a *single* idea and looks at its separate parts. Consider this paragraph by Robert N. Bellah and his co-authors from their study of American values. Here they analyze the cowboy—his characteristics and his importance in American culture.

America is also the inventor of that most mythic individual hero, the cowboy, who again and again saves a society he can never completely fit into. The cowboy has a special talent—he can shoot straighter and faster than other men—and a special sense of justice. But these characteristics make him so unique that he can never fully belong to society. His destiny is to defend society without ever really joining it. He rides off alone into the sunset like Shane, or like the Lone Ranger moves on accompanied only by his Indian companion. But the cowboy's importance is not that he is isolated or antisocial. Rather, his significance lies in his unique, individual virtue and special skill and it is because of those qualities that society needs and welcomes him. Shane, after all, starts as a real outsider, but ends up with the gratitude of the community and the love of a woman and a boy. And while the Lone Ranger settles down and marries the local schoolteacher, he always leaves with the affection and gratitude of the people he has helped. It is as if the myth says you can be a truly good person, worthy of admiration and love, only if you resist fully joining the group. But sometimes the tension leads to an irreparable break. Will Kane, the hero of *High Noon*, abandoned by the cowardly townspeople, saves them from an unrestrained killer, but then throws his sheriff's badge in the dust and goes off into the desert with his bride. One is left wondering where they will go, for there is no longer any link with any town.

Robert N. Bellah et al., Habits of the Heart

---

[3]The experiences of the Uruguayan soccer team have been recorded in a fine book by Piers Paul Read, *Alive!*, which was made into a 1993 film of the same name.

Analysis in Textbooks

The analytical method is particularly useful in textbook material that must clarify how the parts of a whole work together. For example, consider this passage from a biology textbook that shows the function of each part of a flower:

> Although flowers vary widely in appearance, most have certain structures in common. The **peduncle,** or flower stalk, expands slightly at the tip into a **receptacle,** which bears the other flower parts. These parts, called **sepals, petals, stamens,** and **carpels,** are attached to the receptacle in whorls (circles). The sepals, collectively called the **calyx,** protect the flower bud before it opens. The sepals may drop off or may be colored like the petals. Usually, however, sepals are green and remain attached to the receptacle. The petals, collectively called the **corolla,** are quite diverse in size, shape, and color. The petals often attract a particular pollinator. Each stamen consists of a saclike **anther,** where pollen is produced, and a stalk called a **filament.** In most flowers, the anther is positioned where the pollen can be carried away by wind or a pollinator. One or more carpels is at the center of a flower. A carpel has three major regions: ovary, style, and stigma. The swollen base is the **ovary,** which contains from one to hundreds of ovules. The **style** elevates the **stigma,** which is sticky or otherwise adapted for the reception of pollen grains. Pollen grains develop a pollen tube that takes sperm to the female gametophyte in the ovule. Glands located in the region of the ovary produce nectar, a nutrient that is gathered by pollinators as they go from flower to flower.
>
> Sylvia S. Mader, *Biology*

Definition

Unlike the other methods, **definition** is often associated with other methods of development. As a method it is nearly self-explanatory, but the purposes of the definition method may differ, as we shall see in this section. Definition is useful when a writer wants to clarify a term because it may be open to varying interpretations (or to misinterpretation) or because he or she is using a word in a subjective or personal way. Definition is especially useful for abstract terms like *machismo, feminism, honor, racism,* or *patriotism.* Even when we think we know what a word means, not every one may share that definition.

The expository method of development used in paragraphs, and occasionally in entire essays, is called an **extended** definition. In the examples that follow, besides definition, each writer also uses a secondary method; definition is commonly used with other expository methods, most typically example or illustration, comparison and contrast, and analysis. In the first passage, writer Jon Katz writes a **personal** definition, an idiosyncratic list of characteristics in order to define the word *geek.*

Geek:

A member of the cultural elite, a pop-culture-loving, techno-centered Community of Social Discontents. Most geeks rose above a suffocatingly unimaginative educational system, where they were surrounded by obnoxious social values and hostile peers, to build the freest and most inventive culture on the planet: the Internet and World Wide Web. Now running the systems that run the world.

Tendency toward braininess and individuality, traits that often trigger resentment, isolation, or exclusion. Identifiable by a singular obsessiveness about the things they love, both work and play, and a well-honed sense of bitter, even savage, outsider humor. Universally suspicious of authority. In this era, the Geek Ascension, a positive, even envied term. Definitions involving chicken heads no longer apply.

Jon Katz, *Geeks*

Besides definition and contrast, what other method of development is evident? cause and effect

Now look up the word "geek" in an unabridged dictionary. Explain what Katz's reference to chicken heads in the last sentence means. The word "geek" is an old-fashioned circus word, referring to a performer who engaged in bizarre acts, for example, biting the heads off live chickens.

A **stipulated** definition is one where the writer stipulates, or specifies, the way he or she intends to use the word. In this passage, the writer, an emergency room physician, answers the question "When is someone dead?" by stipulating how a physician defines death.

The answer to the question "When is someone dead?" has changed during my professional career. At the beginning, we would pronounce a person dead when he or she had no heartbeat and no spontaneous breathing. Now, with drugs and devices to sustain the heart and circulation, and ventilators and oxygen to substitute for breathing, we look to the brain to determine if someone is dead. Patients with untreatable structural damage to their brains—provided they have no drugs or metabolic abnormalities that might cause coma, and are not hypothermic or in shock—are brain-dead when: there is no response to painful stimulation, no spontaneous breathing, and there are no reflexes from the brain stem, which is the headquarters for primitive but vital physiological functions. Absence of electrical activity from the brain on an electroencephalogram is an additional requirement in some states. Brain-dead patients have no blood flow to their brains, and their hearts will cease beating within hours or, at most, a few days, even with cardiorespiratory support.

John F. Murray, *Intensive Care: A Doctor's Journal*

Another type of extended definition is definition by **etymology,** which establishes the meaning of a word by examining its language or languages of origin. In this example, Charles Earle Funk, the editor in chief of *Funk & Wagnalls Dictionary,* examines the various connotations of the English word *fascination* by looking at the concept of the evil eye and at the meaning of the Latin word *fascinatio,* from which our word is derived.

From earliest times, and even today among superstitious people, it has been believed that certain persons, if so inclined, have the power to injure or even kill other persons or animals or to destroy crops or commit other injury by no more than a malignant glance. Such a person is held to possess the "evil eye." In ancient Greece, the power of the evil eye was called *baskania,* in Rome *fascinatio.* Because no one knew who that he might meet had the power and the wish to do him injury, it was an almost universal custom, in olden times, to wear an amulet of some kind which was believed to protect the wearer. Even the cattle were sometimes so adorned. Children were thought to be especially susceptible to the power of the evil eye, and no Roman mother, in classical days, would permit a child of hers to leave the house without first suspending from its neck, under the robe, a certain amulet called *fascinum.* Actually, therefore, our word "fascinate," when first brought into English use, meant to cast the evil eye upon one, to put one under the spell of witchcraft. We use the word rarely now in such a literal sense, but employ it rather to mean to hold one's attention irresistibly or to occupy one's thoughts exclusively by pleasing qualities.

Charles Earle Funk, "Fascinate," *Thereby Hangs a Tale*

Besides definition, what are two other methods of development in this passage? _example and contrast_

The last type of definition uses **contrast** to differentiate between easily confused words. In this passage, education writer Diane Ravitch distinguishes between the words *censorship* and *selection:*

The word *censorship* refers to the deliberate removal of language, ideas, and books from the classroom or library because they are deemed offensive or controversial. The definition gets fussier, however, when making a distinction between censorship and selection. Selection is not censorship. Teachers have a responsibility to choose readings for their students, based on their professional judgment of what students are likely to understand and what they need to learn. Librarians, however, unlike teachers, are bound by a professional code that requires them to exclude no publication because of its content or point of view. It is also important to remember that people have a First Amendment right to complain about textbooks and library books that they don't like.

Censorship occurs when school officials or publishers (acting in anticipation of the legal requirements of certain states) delete words, ideas, and topics from textbooks and tests for no reason other than their fear of controversy. Censorship may take place before publication, as it does when publishers utilize guidelines that mandate the exclusion of certain language and topics, and it may happen after publication, as when parents and community members pressure school officials to remove certain books from school libraries or classrooms. Some people believe that censorship occurs only when government officials impose it, but publishers censor their products in order to secure government contracts. So the result is the same.

Diane Ravitch, *The Language Police*

Of the two words, *censorship* and *selection,* which one is Ravitch most interested in defining in the passage?   **censorship**

Definition in Textbooks

Key terms in textbooks are usually printed in boldfaced or italic type. Notice that in this excerpt from a psychology textbook, the key terms *sociocultural perspective* and *culture* are set in boldfaced print; their definitions follow.

An important perspective that has emerged in psychology in recent years is termed the **sociocultural perspective.** Like social learning theory, the sociocultural approach is based on the assumption that our personalities, beliefs, attitudes, and skills are learned from others. The sociocultural approach goes further, however, in stating that it is impossible to fully understand a person without understanding his or her culture, ethnic identity, gender identity, and other important sociocultural factors (Miller, 1999; Phinney, 1996).

For example, we are all shaped by our culture and must be understood in that context. **Culture** is defined as the patterns of behavior, beliefs, and values that are shared by a group of people. Culture includes everything—from language and superstitions to moral beliefs and food preferences—that we learn from the people with whom we live. When I worked in Miami for 3 years, I met many persons who were born in Cuba and had moved to the United States. They brought with them all of the beliefs, attitudes, and ways of Cuban culture, but they are now part of the culture of the United States. To fully understand my Miami friends, you would need to understand the ways in which Cuban and U.S. cultures are similar and different and how each has influenced their lives.

Benjamin B. Lahey, *Psychology: An Introduction*

Analogy

The last method of development, **analogy** is the most sophisticated and therefore the hardest to interpret. An analogy is an *extended metaphor* in which the writer discusses the literal subject in terms of something else. In an imaginative yoking of two unlike things, shared characteristics are emphasized and a fresher insight ensues. A writer, for instance, might explain the functioning of a human eye in terms of the way a camera works—in other words, by comparing the eye to a more familiar object. The analogy starts with a metaphor:

> A : B
> A (the subject) is compared to B (the metaphor)
> The human eye : A camera

Unlike a simple metaphor, however, the analogy is *sustained,* typically over a few sentences or—less commonly—even throughout an essay.

Consider the following passage in which the writer, the owner of a small orchard in California's Central Valley, uses an inventive analogy to compare weeds to an advancing army.

I used to have armies of weeds on my farm. They launch their annual assault with the first warm weather of spring, parachuting seeds behind enemy lines and poking up in scattered clumps around the fields.

They work underground first, incognito to a passing farmer like me. By the end of winter, dulled by the holidays and cold fog, I have my guard down. The weeds take advantage of my carelessness.

The timing of their assault is crucial. They anticipate the subtle lengthening of each day. With exact calculation they germinate and push upward toward the sunlight, silently rooting themselves and establishing a foothold. The unsuspecting farmer rarely notices any change for days.

Then, with the first good spring rain, the invasion begins. With beachheads established, the first wave of sprouting creatures rises to boldly expose their green leaves. Some taunt the farmer and don't even try to camouflage themselves. Defiantly they thrust their new stalks as high as possible, leaves peeling open as the plant claims more vertical territory. Soon the concealed army of seeds explodes, and within a week what had been a secure, clear territory is claimed by weeds. They seem to be everywhere, no farm is spared the invasion.

Then I hear farmers launching their counterattack. Tractors roar from their winter hibernation, gunbarrel-gray exhaust smoke shoots into the air, and cold engines churn. Oil and diesel flow through dormant lines as the machines awaken. Hungry for work, they will do well when let loose in the fields. The disks and cultivators sitting stationary throughout winter rains await the tractor hitch. The blades are brown with rust stains, bearings and gears cold and still since last fall. But I sense they too may be anxious to cleanse themselves in the earth and regain their sleek steel shimmer.

David Mas Masumoto, *Epitaph for a Peach*

Good analogies like this one are effective and compelling: They are more than a mere attention-getting device, however, because they provide a new way of looking at a subject.

A writer may use an analogy to help us understand complex ideas. Science writer David Perlman employs a homely analogy to explain the concept of the "Hubble Constant," which he characterizes as a "mysterious and controversial number." He begins the discussion by describing the movement of galaxies: "[E]very galaxy in the universe is now speeding away from every other galaxy at a rate that increases by 160,000 miles an hour for every 3.3 light-years that each galaxy finds itself away from Earth's own Milky Way." Then he continues:

Considering that a single light-year is equal to about 6 trillion miles, such speeds are almost inconceivable. Even harder to grasp is the fact that the Milky Way itself is part of this vast explosion. What that means is that we're not at the center of the universe, after all; instead, we're like a single raisin in a vast lump of dough that is rising in an oven where all the other raisins are moving away from each other, faster and faster as the oven gets hotter and hotter.

That rate of expansion for the universe, known as the Hubble Constant, is named after Edwin Hubble, who first found evidence for the expansion in 1929. Since then, other astronomers have used the Hubble Constant to estimate the age of the universe as anywhere from 10 billion to 20 billion years old.

David Perlman, "At 12 Billion Years Old, Universe Still Growing Fast,"
San Francisco Chronicle, May 26, 1999

Analogies can also be fanciful and whimsical, as is the case in this opening paragraph of an article about golf:

> I fell in love with golf when I was twenty-five. It would have been a healthier relationship had it been an adolescent romance or, better yet, a childhood crush. Though I'd like to think we've had a lot of laughs together, and even some lyrical moments, I have never felt quite adequate to her demands, and she has secrets she keeps from me. More secrets than I can keep track of; when I've found out one, another one comes out, and then three more, and by this time I've forgotten what the first one was. They are sexy little secrets that flitter around my body—a twitch of the left hip, a pronation of the right wrist, a cock of the head one way, a turn of the shoulders the other—and they torment me like fire ants in my togs; I can't get them out of my mind, or quite wrap my mind around them. Sometimes I wish she and I had never met. She leads me on, but deep down I suspect—this is my secret—that I'm just not her type.
>
> John Updike, "An Ode to Golf," *The New Yorker*

What, literally, do the "secrets" refer to? <u>the finer points of the game</u>

<u>that eluded him</u>

What does Updike mean when he writes in the last sentence that "I'm just not her type"? <u>Golf really isn't the right game for him to play.</u>

For some exercises in verbal analogies, click on Chapter 4.

Practice Exercise 1

Read the following paragraphs and decide which method of development predominates.

- Cause and effect
- Definition
- Classification and analysis
- Analogy

Then write a sentence stating the main idea in your own words.

A.

Paragraphs are a modern invention. Greek and Latin writers did not use them. Until the nineteenth century, written English scarcely noticed them. The word *paragraph* originally meant a pi mark like this π placed at the head of a section of prose to announce that the subject of the discourse was changing slightly. After the mark, the section might go on for several pages. Eventually the paragraph mark was replaced by an indented line. Even then, the indentation might introduce a long section of unbroken prose. The paragraphs of John Stuart Mill and Charles Darwin, both great prose writers in the nineteenth century, ran on for several pages. Only gradually did the paragraph assume its modern form—a fairly short block of prose introduced by an indentation, organized so that every sentence in it contributes to a limited subject.

Richard Marius, A Writer's Companion

Method of development: <u>definition</u>

Main idea: <u>The idea of breaking up text to form paragraphs is a</u>

<u>recent invention.</u>

B.

The censorship that has spread throughout American education has pernicious and pervasive effects. It lowers the literacy level of tests because test makers must take care to avoid language as well as works of literature and historical selections that might give offense. It restricts the language and the ideas that may be reproduced in textbooks. It surely reduces children's interest in their schoolwork by making their studies so deadly dull. It undermines our common culture by imposing irrelevant political criteria on the literature and history that are taught.

Diane Ravitch, The Language Police

Method of development: <u>cause and effect</u>

Main idea: <u>The censorship that has permeated our schools has</u>

<u>several dangerous effects.</u>

C.

Instruction manuals that come with new gadgets are notoriously frustrating. They never seem to have the one piece of information you need, they send you round in circles, they leave you high and dry, and they definitely lose something in the translation from Chinese. But at least they do not insert, just when you are getting to the bit that matters, five copies of Schiller's "Ode to Joy" or a garbled version of a set of instructions for how to saddle a horse. Nor do they (generally) include five copies of a complete set of instructions for how to build a machine that would copy out just that set of instructions. Nor do they break the actual instructions you seek into twenty-seven different paragraphs interspersed with long pages of irrelevant junk so that even finding the right instructions is a massive task. Yet that is a description of the human retinoblastoma gene and, as far as we know, it is typical of human genes: twenty-seven brief paragraphs of sense interrupted by twenty-six long pages of something else.

Mother Nature concealed a dirty little secret in the genome. Each gene is far more complicated than it needs to be, it is broken up into many different "paragraphs" (called exons) and in between lie long stretches (called introns) of random nonsense and repetitive bursts of wholly irrelevant sense, some of which contain real genes of a completely different (and sinister) kind.

The reason for this textual confusion is that the genome is a book that wrote itself, continually adding, deleting and amending over four billion years. Documents that write themselves have usual properties. In particular, they are prone to parasitism. Analogies become far-fetched at this point, but try to imagine a writer of instruction manuals who arrives at his computer each morning to find paragraphs of his text clamouring for his attention. The ones that shout loudest bully him into including another five copies of themselves on the next page he writes. The true instructions still have to be there, or the machine will never be assembled, but the manual is full of greedy, parasitic paragraphs taking advantage of the writer's compliance.

Matt Ridley, *Genome*

Method of development: <u>analogy</u>

Main idea: <u>Because of the way the human genome developed, each genome contains a great deal of irrelevant and nonsense material.</u>

D.

Why do organisms need scientific names? And why do scientists use Latin, rather than common names, to describe organisms? There are several reasons. First, a common name will vary from country to country because different countries use different languages. Second, even people who speak the same language sometimes use different common names to describe the same organism. For example, the Louisiana heron and the tricolored heron are names for the same bird found in southern United States. Furthermore, between countries, the same common name is sometimes given to different organisms. A "robin" in England is very different from a "robin" in the United States, for example. Latin, on the other hand, is a universal language that not too long ago was well known by most scholars, many of whom were physicians or clerics. When scientists throughout the world use the same Latin binomial name, they know they are speaking of the same organism.

Sylvia S. Mader, *Biology*

Method of development: <u>cause and effect</u>

Main idea: <u>There are several reasons that scientists use Latin scientific names to describe organisms.</u>

E.

The first law of gossip is that you never know how many people are talking about you behind your back. The second law is thank God. The third—and most important—law is that as gossip spreads from friends to acquaintances to people you've never met, it grows more garbled, vivid, and definitive. Out of stray factoids and hesitant impressions emerges a hard mass of what everyone knows to be true. Imagination supplies the missing pieces, and repetition turns these pieces into facts; gossip achieves its shape and amplitude only in the continual retelling. The best stories about us are told by perfect strangers.

Tad Friend, "The Harriet-the-Spy Club," *The New Yorker*

Method of development: <u>analysis</u>

Main idea: <u>There are three laws of gossip.</u>

F.

Those who learn that they have been lied to in an important matter—say, the identity of their parents, the affection of their spouse, or the integrity of their government—are resentful, disappointed, and suspicious. They feel wronged; they are wary of new overtures. And they look back on their past beliefs and actions in the new light of the discovered lies. They see that they were manipulated, that the deceit made them unable to make choices for themselves according to the most adequate information available, unable to act as they would have wanted to act had they known all along.

Sissela Bok, *Lying: Moral Choices in Public and Private Life*

Method of development: <u>cause and effect</u>

Main idea: <u>People who have been lied to about an important matter</u>

<u>feel resentful, disappointed, and mistrustful.</u>

Combination of Methods

As discussed at the end of Chapter 3, a writer may use a mix of expository methods of development. In this selection, Paco Underhill, an expert in shopping center design, uses a combination of methods to examine a phenomenon we have probably observed unconsciously: The entrances to shopping malls are populated with what he calls "the least attractive tenants."

You might think that retailers would fight to be nearest the entrances. But take a look at what's here, just inside the doorway. A hair salon on one side and a store that sells exercise equipment on the other. The beauty parlor is nearly full, although you can bet these are regular customers, not mall shoppers who have decided on impulse to get a cut and color. The exercise store is empty, which makes sense—how many treadmills does the average consumer buy? If the shop sells one or two it's a good day. You'll sometimes find banks in these locations, another low-profile tenant. Post offices. Video game arcades. Why is it that the least attractive tenants get these high-traffic positions?

Call it the mall's decompression zone. The fact is that when we enter any building, we need a series of steps just to make the adjustment between out there and in here. You need to slow your walk a little, allow your eyes to adjust to the change in lighting, give your senses a chance to detect changes in temperature and so on. You walk through any door and suddenly your brain has to take in a load of new information and process it so you'll feel oriented. You're not really ready to make any buying decisions for the first ten or fifteen feet. This transition stage is one of the most critical things we've learned in two decades of studying how shoppers move through retail environments. Nothing too close to the door really registers. If there's a sign, you probably won't read it. If there's a display of merchandise, you'll barely notice it. Some stores have the bad habit of stacking shopping baskets just inside the doorway. People zoom right past them.

Because of this transition zone, the best stores in the mall are never near the entrance. The reasoning is simple—the mall owner charges every tenant a flat rent based on space plus a percentage of sales. So it's in the mall's own interest to have the hottest stores in the prime locations, inside. Because this particular doorway feels like a secondary entrance, only a small portion of all shoppers will even see these shops. Fewer eyeballs equals fewer bucks. That equation is the basis for all mall math. And that's why underachievers go nearest the door. When entering a mall, your eye is immediately drawn way up ahead, to the heart of the place. That's where you want to be. So let's join everybody else speeding past the ladies under the hair dryers. We've got a date.

Paco Underhill, *The Call of the Mall*

In this passage, Underhill uses a combination of methods: definition (to show us what the term *decompression zone* means); examples (to illustrate the types of stores found at mall entrances); and cause and effect (to explain the rationale behind the placement of stores within a mall).

Practice Exercise 2

Read the following passage and select the methods of development from the choices provided. Then write a sentence stating the main idea in your own words.

If you ask someone to draw a whale, she will probably draw a sperm whale, the bulbous-headed whale made famous in Melville's *Moby Dick,* a book that is as much a treatise on whales as it is a piece of fiction. But whales come in many shapes, sizes, and colors. There are two basic groups: the toothed whales (Odontoceti, from the Latin for "tooth" and "whale") and the baleen whales (Mysticeti, from the Latinized Greek word for "whale"). Toothed whales include the sperm whale, the dolphin, and the orca, or killer whale, and they have a single external blowhole, which in the course of evolution has migrated to the top of the head. They echolocate just as bats do, using sonar to scan their world, find their prey, and map their underwater landscape. And they have teeth, which they use to hold on to such prey as fish, squid, and shrimp. Whales swallow their prey whole, so the teeth are for grasping rather than for chewing.

In contrast, baleen whales don't have teeth but hundreds of tightly packed, springy baleen plates (made of keratin, the same substance as human fingernails), which grow down from the upper gums. Baleen whales have paired blowholes—nostrils, in fact—which are on the top of the head. Some baleen species graze peacefully as they move through the water, rolling slowly through the surface with their mouths yawning open. Because the baleen has a smooth outside edge and a bristly inside edge, water can flow freely through the whale's mouth, but krill, plankton, and small schooling fish get caged inside.

Diane Ackerman, *The Moon by Whale Light*

Choose the three predominant methods of development.
- (a) (example)
- (b) definition
- (c) (analysis and classification)
- (d) analogy
- (e) comparison
- (f) (contrast)

Main idea: The two basic types of whales—toothed and baleen—can be distinguished according to the structure of their mouths and the way they catch prey.

■ CONCLUSION: METHODS OF DEVELOPMENT AND PATTERNS OF THOUGHT

As I pointed out at the end of Chapter 3, it helps to think of methods of development as relating to patterns of thought in the real world. For example, which methods of development covered in this chapter would be appropriate for these situations?

1. You have just moved to a new apartment. In your kitchen are three drawers, one on top of the other. You have a couple of large boxes of kitchen utensils to store in these drawers.   <u>classification</u>

2. Why did the founders of *www.google.com*—a popular and eminently useful World Wide Web search engine—choose that name?

   <u>definition (from Googol, the number 10 raised to the 100th power,</u>

   <u>in other words, the number 1 followed by 100 zeroes)</u>

3. Your English teacher said in class that the eyes are the window of the soul. What does that mean?   <u>analogy</u>

4. You are considering quitting school for a year and working full-time. What impact would that decision have on your life?

   <u>cause-effect</u>

5. Your literature instructor has assigned you to write a paper on the unique characteristics of science fiction as a literary genre.

   <u>analysis</u>

■ CHAPTER EXERCISES

Selection 1

The writer of this passage, James E. Rosenbaum, is professor of sociology, education, and social policy at Northwestern University. [4]

New Dreams, New Misconceptions

[1]The past 40 years brought three radical social transformations that together have dramatically increased the percentage of students who want to attend college. [2]First, the earnings advantage of college graduates has grown (Grubb, 1996). [3]Second, college—especially community college (a minor factor in the prior generation)—has become much more accessible. [4]In the past four decades, while enrollments at four-year colleges doubled, enrollments increased five-fold at community colleges (NCES, 1999). [5]Third, and perhaps most remarkably, virtually all community colleges adopted a revolutionary policy of open admissions. [6]Unlike many four-year colleges, virtually all two-year colleges opened their doors to admit all interested high school graduates, regardless of students' prior academic achievements. [7]Even high school graduates with barely passing grades are routinely welcomed because almost all two-year colleges offer a wide array of remedial courses. [8]Indeed, in many

[4]The entire article from which this excerpt comes, is available online at www.aft.org. Click on "Publications" and then click on *American Educator,* Spring 2004.

cases, students do not even have to be high school graduates because most two-year colleges offer these students access to some non-credit courses, including GED courses.

[9]These three transformations have dramatically altered the rules of college attendance and given students remarkable new opportunities. [10]However, as with all revolutions, there are also unintended consequences. [11]The revolutions spawned a set of myths—we'll call them misconceptions—that combined to send a message to students: Don't worry about high school grades or effort; you can still go to college and do fine. [12]This message has not been sent to high achievers aiming for prestigious colleges, where grades and scores matter—and the students headed there know it. [13]But it is the message that students who know little about college have received—particularly those whose parents did not go to college. [14]These students (and their parents) are being misled with disastrous consequences. [15]Their motivation to work hard in high school is sapped; their time to prepare for college is wasted; their college savings are eaten up by remedial courses that they could have taken for free in high school; and their chances of earning a college degree are greatly diminished. [16]Further, the effect on many colleges has been to alter their mission and lower their standards.

James E. Rosenbaum, "It's Time to Tell the Kids: If You Don't Do Well in High School, You Won't Do Well in College (or on the Job)," *American Educator*

A. *Vocabulary*

For each italicized word from the selection, choose the best definition according to the context in which it appears.

1. these revolutions *spawned* a set of myths [sentence 11]:
   (a) produced.
   (b) described.
   (c) contradicted.
   (d) emphasized.

2. their motivation to work hard is *sapped* [15]:
   (a) strengthened, energized.
   (b) misunderstood, misinterpreted.
   (c) depleted, weakened.
   (d) welcomed, praised.

B. *Content and Structure*

Complete the following questions.

1. Write a sentence stating the main idea of the passage. _____

_____

2. Study the two paragraphs again. What is the relationship between them?
   (a) term to be defined and a definition.
   (b) cause and effect.
   (c) comparison and contrast.
   (d) classification.

3. In the first paragraph, what seems to be the writer's attitude toward community college's policy of open-door admissions? _____

   _____

4. Whom does the writer blame for sending the wrong message to high school students that accounts for the "disastrous consequences" many students face in college?
   (a) the students themselves for wasting their precious high school years.
   (b) the high schools for not requiring enough work of their students and allowing them to slack off.
   (c) American society in general, for fostering the idea that a college degree guarantees success.
   (d) colleges, and especially community colleges, for opening their doors to all students regardless of their academic background.

5. How many of the following recommendations would the writer *probably* support?
   (a) No student should be admitted to a community college without being a high school graduate.
   (b) Community colleges should tighten up their admissions standards by revising their open-door policy.
   (c) High school teachers and counselors should do a better job of educating students about the realities they will face in college.
   (d) High schools should establish trade and technical programs for students who are not college bound.
   (e) Colleges should stop looking at high school grades and focus only on standardized test scores as a better predictor of college success.
   (f) Community colleges offer a helpful second chance for students if they are willing to work hard and show effort.

The article was accompanied by several charts, among them the one on the next page dating from 1982.

In the class of 1982, 86 percent of college-bound students with poor grades didn't graduate from college.

AVERAGE HIGH SCHOOL GRADES	As	Bs	Cs OR LOWER	ALL
Percentage attaining A.A. or higher	63.9	37.1	13.9	37.7
Percentage not attaining any degree	36.1	62.9	86.1	62.3

Seniors with college plans (A.A. or higher) who complete an A.A. degree or higher within 10 years of high school graduation.
Source: Beyond College for All; High School and Beyond data.

6. Write a sentence stating the relationship between high school grades and the attainment of a college degree that these figures convey.

   _____

7. What information in the chart explains why the chart uses seemingly old figures from 1982? _____

   _____

Answers for Selection 1

A. **Vocabulary**

1. (a)   2. (c)

B. **Content and Structure**

1. The transformations in American society that increased the percentage of students who want to attend college have often had unintended and negative consequences.
2. (b)
3. He suggests that the open-door admissions policy is a mistake.
4. (d)
5. (b), (c), and (f)
6. The chart shows that students who have A or B averages in high school have a much better chance of graduating from college with an AA or higher.
7. The students were given 10 years after graduation (from 1982 to 1992) to attain a degree.

Selection 2

[1]Coffee has never been just a drink, but has always been loaded with social and political consequence as well. [2]The desire for it helped spur French, British, and Dutch colonial expansion. [3]Its infusion into 18th-century life helped create a

nightlife culture and provided a social context in which political dissidents gathered to discuss the issues of the day. **4**Historians have ascribed to it at least partial responsibility for the Enlightenment—a period that valued alert and rational thought. **5**"The powers of a man's mind are directly proportional to the quantity of coffee he drank" wrote the 18th-century Scottish philosopher Sir James MacKintosh in one of the many pamphlets that circulated through London's coffeehouses in a raging war of arguments for and against the new drink. **6**It was celebrated as a substance that would lengthen the workday and provide stimulation to those engaged in the new sedentary occupations that accompanied the Industrial Revolution, according to Wolfgang Schivelbusch, a German social scientist and author of *Tastes of Paradise: A Social History of Spices, Stimulants and Intoxicants.* **7**"Not to drink coffee," writes Schivelbusch, "[was] almost as great a sin for the puritanical bourgeoisie as wasting time itself."

8Most importantly, it was egalitarian in its easy accessibility to all social classes. **9**In Britain, 17th-century coffeehouses were the first gathering places where ability to pay the bill was far more important than social class in gaining access; tradesmen joined with gentry in consuming the new brew.

10That tradition continued in the United States: American colonists heaved tea over the side of a British schooner in Boston Harbor, and coffee became a symbol of defiance against the British. **11**George Washington signed the British terms of surrender to American rebels in a still-operating coffeehouse/tavern in New York. **12**Everywhere they opened, coffeehouses became the centers of political intrigue and philosophical discussion, fostering the concepts of individual liberty and freedom of opinion in the budding republic. **13**Some analysts even claim that coffee has been key to the development of the urban work ethic. **14**"Coffee," says Irene Fizer, a scholar who teaches a course called "Caffeine Culture" at New York's New School, "has been keyed to the construction of a rigidified work life. **15**The urban workaday economy would be unthinkable without coffee."

Mark Schapiro, "Muddy Waters," *Utne Reader*

A. Vocabulary

For each italicized word from the selection, write the dictionary definition most appropriate for the context.

1. *infusion* [sentence 3]:   introduction

2. *dissidents* [3]:   those who disagree with the current political situation

3. *ascribed* [4]:   attributed

4. *sedentary* [6]:   requiring much sitting

5. *bourgeoisie* [7]:   the middle class

6. *egalitarian* [8]:   political and social equality for all

7. *gentry* [9]:   the upper or ruling class

8. *intrigue* [12]:   secret plots, schemes

B. *Content and Structure*

Complete the following questions.

1. Which sentence expresses the main idea of the first paragraph?

    <u>sentence 1</u>

    In the sentence you chose, write the topic of the first paragraph.

    <u>"coffee"</u>

    Write the controlling idea. <u>"has always been loaded with social and</u>

    <u>political consequences"</u>

2. Which sentence expresses the main idea of the *second* paragraph?

    <u>sentence 8</u>

    The topic is the same in this paragraph as for the first paragraph, but
    what is the controlling idea? <u>"egalitarian in its easy accessibility to</u>

    <u>all social classes"</u>

3. Which *two* methods of development are used in the paragraph?

    <u>cause effect and example</u>

4. The author evidently sees a connection between the increasing popu-
    larity of coffee and
    (a) the beginning of unions to protect laborers from exploitation.
    (b) the evils of colonialism.
    (c) a rigid workday.
    (d) (the increasing importance of democracy and social equality.)

5. The writer suggests that Americans drank coffee rather than tea
    because
    (a) coffee tastes better.
    (b) coffee has more caffeine than tea.
    (c) coffeehouses, not teahouses, became gathering places to discuss
         politics.
    (d) (drinking coffee was a way of rebelling against British rule.)

Selection 3   **1**   Sexually transmitted pathogens take on secretive and even sinister strategies.
The underlying reason is that people have sex with new partners less frequently
than they come within sneezing or coughing distance. The sporadic opportunities for sexual transmission put sexually transmitted pathogens in a difficult situation. They have to stay viable within a person until the person has a new sexual
partner. They have to persist in the face of an immune system that is superb at
recognizing and destroying foreign invaders. Then they must be transmissible to

the next sexual partner when the opportunity arises. And that is just to break even. To make a profit, the pathogens must meet these challenges for at least another round of partner change—the more rounds, the better their competitive advantage. Respiratory pathogens typically reproduce to the point of contagiousness and then get wiped out or at least sequestered by the immune system within a week or two. A sexually transmitted pathogen using such a strategy would be cut out of the competition. To evade this fate, sexually transmitted pathogens must employ sneaky tricks.

2   Sexually transmitted pathogens must act like criminals living in a town that is heavily patrolled by police. Like human criminals, they have developed a variety of strategies for evading recognition, surveillance, and capture. Because the immunological police soon become very familiar with their appearance, most sexually transmitted pathogens keep a low profile.

3   The bacteria that cause syphilis persist by stripping off many of the external molecules that would make them recognizable to the immune system. They are like criminals who sand off their fingerprints.

4   HIV impersonates a police officer, wrapping itself in the immune cell's own membrane when it buds off a cell. To stay ahead of the current mug shot, it frequently modifies its telltale features by mutating and recombining its genetic instructions—genetically engineered plastic surgery.

5   The bacteria that cause gonorrhea are quick-change artists, wearing different external molecules from day to day to avoid being tracked down after they are recognized. They also hide out away from the areas of most active surveillance, causing damage to the reproductive tract but not so much that it generates a sweeping immunological assault.

Paul Ewald, *Plague Time*

A. Vocabulary

For each italicized word from the selection, choose the best definition according to the context in which it appears.

1. get wiped out or at least *sequestered* [1]
   (a) imprisoned.
   (b) isolated, set apart.
   (c) arranged in a particular sequence.
   (d) put into chronological order.
2. modifies its telltale features by *mutating* [4]:
   (a) disguising itself.
   (b) going into hiding.
   (c) adapting to a new environment.
   (d) transforming itself.

B. Content and Structure

Complete the following questions.

1. The mode of discourse in the passage is
   (a) narration.
   (b) description.
   (c) (exposition.)
   (d) persuasion.
2. Locate the sentence that states the main idea of the passage. Identify the topic and the controlling idea.

   Topic: "sexually transmitted pathogens"

   Controlling idea: "take on secretive and even sinister strategies"

3. In relation to the main idea of the passage, what is the function of the *last* sentence of paragraph 1?
   (a) It offers contrasting information to the information contained in the main idea.
   (b) It defines a key term contained in the main idea.
   (c) (It restates the main idea in different words.)
   (d) It states the effect of the cause expressed in the main idea.
4. This passage uses a combination of methods of development. Which *three* predominate?
   (a) directive process.
   (b) (classification.)
   (c) definition.
   (d) (analogy.)
   (e) facts and statistics.
   (f) (cause and effect.)
5. Explain in your own words the reason that sexually transmitted pathogens have to "take on secretive and even sinister strategies."

   These pathogens have limited opportunities to infect the victim,

   and the human immune system works well to repel them.

6. The reader can logically infer from the passage that
   (a) an increase in the number of sexual partners has little impact on the transmission of sexual diseases.
   (b) an increase in the number of sexual partners increases the likelihood of sexual diseases being transmitted.
   (c) sexually transmitted pathogens behave erratically, so whether a person becomes infected or not is largely a matter of chance.
   (d) sexually transmitted pathogens mutate so frequently that new drugs cannot keep up with them or prevent victims from being infected.

PRACTICE ESSAY

"In Praise of the Humble Comma"
Pico Iyer

Pico Iyer has built his reputation primarily as a travel writer. His best-known books are *Video Night in Kathmandu: And Other Reports from the Not-So-Far East* (1989) and *Falling Off the Map: Some Lonely Places of the World* (1994). He has most recently served as editor of a collection of travel writing first published for Salon.com, *Salon.com Wanderlust: Real-Life Tales of Adventure and Travel* (2000). "In Praise of the Humble Comma," first published in *Time* magazine in 1988, examines the significance of punctuation in writing.

Preview Questions

1. Have you received extensive instruction in grammar and punctuation?

2. Do you pay attention to punctuation when you read, for example, noting when a writer uses a colon or a semicolon? Refer to the Web site mentioned at the end of the essay for further help and clarification in the rules for punctuation and for the influence of punctuation on a writer's style.

3. Why are marks of punctuation, aside from periods, so hard to master in writing? Which marks of punctuation are you uncomfortable or unsure about using? What might be some ways to remedy this problem—assuming that it is one—and expand your proficiency in this area?

1   The gods, they say, give breath, and they take it away. But the same could be said—could it not?—of the humble comma. Add it to the present clause, and, of a sudden, the mind is, quite literally, given pause to think; take it out if you wish or forget it and the mind is deprived of a resting place. Yet still the comma gets no respect. It seems just a slip of a thing, a pedant's tick, a blip on the edge of our consciousness, a kind of printer's smudge almost. Small, we claim, is beautiful (especially in the age of the microchip). Yet what is so often used, and so rarely recalled, as the comma—unless it be breath itself?

2   Punctuation, one is taught, has a point: to keep up law and order. Punctuation marks are the road signs placed along the highway of our communication—to control speeds, provide directions and prevent head-on collisions. A period has the unblinking finality of a red light; the comma is a flashing yellow light that asks us only to slow down; and the semicolon is a stop sign that tells us to ease gradually to a halt, before gradually starting up again. By establishing the relations between words,

punctuation establishes the relations between the people using words. That may be one reason why schoolteachers exalt it and lovers defy it ("We love each other and belong to each other let's don't ever hurt each other Nicole let's don't ever hurt each other," wrote Gary Gilmore[1] to his girlfriend). A comma, he must have known, "separates inseparables," in the clinching words of H.W. Fowler, King of English Usage.

3   Punctuation, then, is a civic prop, a pillar that holds society upright. (A run-on sentence, its phrases piling up without division, is as unsightly as a sink piled high with dirty dishes.) Small wonder, then, that punctuation was one of the first proprieties of the Victorian age, the age of the corset, that the modernists threw off: the sexual revolution might be said to have begun when Joyce's Molly Bloom[2] spilled out all her private thoughts in 36 pages of unbridled, almost unperioded and officially composed press; and another rebellion was surely marked when E.E. Cummings[3] first felt free to commit "God" to the lower case.

4   Punctuation thus becomes the signature of cultures. The hot-blooded Spaniard seems to be revealed in the passion and urgency of his doubled exclamation points and question marks ("*¡Caramba! ¿Quien sabe?*"), while the impassive Chinese traditionally added to his so-called inscrutability by omitting directions from his ideograms. The anarchy and commotion of the '60s were given voice in the exploding exclamation marks, riotous capital letters and Day-Glo italics of Tom Wolfe's[4] spray-paint prose; and in Communist societies, where the State is absolute, the dignity   and divinity—of capital letters is reserved for Ministries, Sub-Committees and Secretariats.

5   Yet punctuation is something more than a culture's birthmark; it scores the music in our minds, gets our thoughts moving to the rhythm of our hearts. Punctuation is the notation in the sheet music of our words, telling us when to rest, or when to raise our voices; it acknowledges that the meaning of our discourse, as of any symphonic composition, lies not in the units but in the pauses, the pacing and the phrasing. Punctuation is the way one bats one's eyes, lowers one's voice or blushes demurely. Punctuation adjusts the tone and color and volume till the feeling comes into perfect focus: not disgust exactly, but distaste; not lust, or like, but love.

---

[1]Gary Gilmore committed a murder in Utah, for which he was subsequently executed. His story is superbly detailed in Norman Mailer's classic study of crime and punishment, *The Executioner's Song.*

[2]Molly Bloom is a character in the 1922 novel *Ulysses,* written by Irish writer James Joyce. Bloom is famous in literature for her frank soliloquy using the stream-of-consciousness technique.

[3]e. e. cummings (Edward Estlin Cummings) was a twentieth-century American poet known for unconventional punctuation and uncapitalized words, as you can see in his name.

[4]In *The Electric Kool-Aid Acid Test,* a nonfiction work about Ken Kesey and the Merry Pranksters, Tom Wolfe indulged his penchant for the startling use of punctuation and for other typographical oddities.

6   Punctuation, in short, gives us the human voice, and all the meanings that lie between the words. "You aren't young, are you?" loses its innocence when it loses the question mark. Every child knows the menace of a dropped apostrophe (the parent's "Don't do that" shifting into the more slowly enunciated "Do not do that"), and every believer, the ignominy of having his faith reduced to "faith." Add an exclamation point to "To be or not to be . . ." and the gloomy Dane[5] has all the resolve he needs; add a comma, and the noble sobriety of "God save the Queen" becomes a cry of desperation bordering on double sacrilege.

7   Sometimes, of course, our markings may be simply a matter of aesthetics. Popping in a comma can be like slipping on the necklace that gives an outfit quiet elegance, or like catching the sound of running water that complements, as it completes, the silence of a Japanese landscape. When V.S. Naipaul,[6] in his latest novel, writes, "He was a middle-aged man, with glasses," the first comma can seem a little precious. Yet it gives the description a spin, as well as a subtlety, that it otherwise lacks, and it shows that the glasses are not part of the middle-agedness, but something else.

8   Thus all these tiny scratches give us breadth and heft and depth. A world that has only periods is a world without inflections. It is a world without shade. It has a music without sharps and flats. It is a martial music. It has a jackboot rhythm. Words cannot bend and curve. A comma, by comparison, catches the gentle drift of the mind in thought, turning in on itself and back on itself, reversing, redoubling and returning along the course of its own sweet river music; while the semicolon brings clauses and thoughts together with all the silent discretion of a hostess arranging guests around her dinner table.

9   Punctuation, then, is a matter of care. Care for words, yes, but also, and more important, for what the words imply. Only a lover notices the small things: the way the afternoon light catches the nape of a neck, or how a strand of hair slips out from behind an ear, or the way a finger curls around a cup. And no one scans a letter so closely as a lover, searching for its small print, straining to hear its nuances, its gasps, its sighs and hesitations, poring over the secret messages that lie in every cadence. The difference between "Jane (whom I adore)" and "Jane, whom I adore," and the difference between them both and "Jane—whom I adore—" marks all the distance between ecstasy and heartache. "No iron can pierce the heart with such force as a period put at just the right place," in Isaac Babel's[7] lovely words; a comma can let us hear a voice break, or a heart. Punctuation, in fact, is a labor of love. Which bring us back, in a way, to gods.

[5]The "gloomy Dane" is a reference to Hamlet, Prince of Denmark, celebrated in Shakespeare's play of the same name.
[6]V. S. Naipaul is a British writer, born in Trinidad.
[7]Isaac Babel was a twentieth-century Russian short-story writer.

A. Comprehension

Choose the answer that best completes each statement. Do not refer to the selection while doing this exercise.

1. Choose the sentence that best represents the main idea of the essay.
   (a) Punctuation rules must be consistently applied to make the reader's task easier.
   (b) Punctuation marks determine both the meanings and rhythms of a writer's words as well as our emotional responses to them.
   (c) Use of punctuation marks in the twentieth century has become more daring and unorthodox.
   (d) Each culture has a unique system of punctuating to determine meaning.
2. Iyer labels the comma a "humble" mark of punctuation because
   (a) its appearance is so insignificant.
   (b) there are too many rules governing its use.
   (c) it should be used only when the reader takes a breath or pauses.
   (d) it lacks the authority and finality of other marks of punctuation.
3. The writer compares punctuation marks to road signs to emphasize their
   (a) shape.
   (b) difficult rules.
   (c) use as controls over our reading.
   (d) ease of recognition.
4. Iyer states that by "establishing the relations between words," punctuation
   (a) establishes a relationship between the writer and the reader.
   (b) establishes a relationship between the writer and his or her publisher.
   (c) serves as an agreed-upon system for distinguishing between important and less important ideas.
   (d) establishes the relations between people using words.
5. Iyer characterizes a world with "only periods" as one without
   (a) love and affection.
   (b) inflections and shade.
   (c) music.
   (d) interest or enthusiasm.

B. Vocabulary

For each italicized word from the selection, write the dictionary definition most appropriate for the context. You may refer to the selection to answer the questions in this section and in all the remaining sections.

1. a *pedant's* tick [paragraph 1]: <u>referring to a person who pays</u>

   <u>excessive attention to learning and rules</u>

2. schoolteachers *exalt* it [2]: <u>glorify</u>

3. the first *proprieties* [3]: <u>customs of polite society</u>

4. his so-called *inscrutability* [4]: <u>difficulty of understanding</u>

5. the *ignominy* of having his faith reduced [6] <u>great personal dishonor</u>

6. double *sacrilege* [6]: <u>disrespect for something sacred</u>

7. the silent *discretion* [8]: <u>freedom to act on one's own</u>

8. to hear its *nuances* [9]: <u>subtle shades of meaning</u>

C. Inferences

On the basis of the evidence in the paragraph, mark these statements as follows: PA (probably accurate); PI (probably inaccurate); or NP (not in the passage).

1. <u>PI</u> Good writers would be wise never to break the rules of punctuation.
2. <u>PI</u> Punctuation marks are more important than the words on the page for determining meaning.
3. <u>PI</u> Punctuation is closer to music than it is to any other art form.
4. <u>PA</u> Without punctuation marks, words would be dead and lifeless and lacking rhythm and nuance.
5. <u>NP</u> Iyer teaches grammar and punctuation at a university.

D. Structure

Complete the following questions.

1. Which of these sentences *best* states the thesis or main idea of the essay?
   (a) "Punctuation, one is taught, has a point: to keep up law and order."
   (b) "Punctuation, then, is a civic prop, a pillar that holds society upright."
   (c) "Punctuation thus becomes the signature of culture."
   (d) "Punctuation, in short, gives us the human voice, and all the meanings that lie between the words."

2. Which *three* methods of paragraph development are evident in the essay? <u>example, definition, analogy</u>

3. Read paragraph 3 again. Then write a sentence in your own words stating the main point Iyer makes in it. <u>One characteristic of the modern age is rebellion, and modern writers rebelled against repressive systems by boldly experimenting with punctuation.</u>

4. If you are unsure of its meaning, look up the word "jackboot" (paragraph 8). Then explain why this word is appropriate for this context.

<u>The word "jackboot" has highly negative associations: It conjures up militaristic forces marching and trampling human liberties. There would be no subtlety or nuance when a jackbooted army marches, and it would be the same monotony if only periods were used.</u>

5. In calling punctuation marks "tiny scratches" (see paragraph 8), Iyer emphasizes their
    (a) apparent lack of purpose.
    (b) seeming insignificance.
    (c) odd appearance.
    (d) lack of grace and elegance.

E. Questions for Discussion and Analysis

1. Look through Iyer's essay and point to sentences whose use of punctuation reinforces his meaning, whose use "scores the music in our minds," as he writes in paragraph 5.

2. Another task: Identify all of the analogies and figures of speech (imaginative comparisons) Iyer uses to explain his subject.

ON THE WEB

Students have found the Web site titled "Guide to Grammar and Writing" to be an invaluable aid in mastering grammar, usage, and punctuation rules. The site provides instruction, lots of examples, quizzes, and answers. The URL is http://webster.commnet.edu/grammar/.

www. mhhe. com/ spears

For a discussion of how punctuation affects meaning, click on "Student Resources." There you will find a discussion of all of the marks of punctuation along with illustrations of their uses.

Patterns of Paragraph Organization

CHAPTER OBJECTIVES

In Chapter 5 you will study the ways writers arrange ideas within paragraphs and the devices they use to achieve coherence, including:

- Patterns of paragraph organization

- Coherence in paragraphs

■ PATTERNS OF ORGANIZATION DEFINED

The **patterns of organization** refer to the various ways that a paragraph's sentences can be arranged. As you have seen, the paragraph is remarkably flexible; nevertheless, we can identify four standard patterns:

- Chronological
- Spatial

- Deductive
- Inductive

The first and second patterns are found most often in narrative and descriptive writing; the other two are found more often in expository or persuasive writing.

Chronological Order

Chronological (or time) order, the easiest pattern to recognize, refers to the order in which events happen. It is used to tell a story, to relate an incident, to recount a historical event, or to describe the steps in a process. In this excerpt, William Langewiesche relates the collapse of the two World Trade Center Towers as a result of the terrorist attacks of September 11, 2001.

> When the Twin Towers collapsed, on the warm, bright morning of September 11, 2001, they made a sound heard variously around New York as a roar, a growl, or distant thunder. The South Tower was the first to go. At 9:59 its upper floors tilted briefly before dropping, disintegrating, and driving the building straight down to the ground. The fall lasted ten seconds, as did the sound. Many people died, but mercifully fast. Twenty-nine minutes later the North Tower collapsed just as quickly, and with much the same result. Somehow a few people survived. For an instant, each tower left its imprint in the air, a phantom of pulverized concrete marking a place that then became a memory. Prefabricated sections of the external steel columns tumbled down onto lesser buildings, piling onto terraces and rooftops, punching through parking structures, offices, and stores, inducing secondary collapses and igniting fires. The most catastrophic effects were eerily selective: with the exception of Saint Nicholas, a tiny Greek Orthodox church that dissolved in the rain of steel, the only buildings completely wrecked were those that carried the World Trade Center label. There were seven of them, and ultimately none endured. Not even the so-called World Trade Center Seven, a relatively new forty-seven-floor tower that stood independently across the street from the complex, was able to escape the fate associated with its name. Though it did not seem seriously wounded at first, it burned persistently throughout the day, and that evening became the first steel-frame high-rise in history to fall solely because of fire.

> William Langewiesche,
> "American Ground: Unbuilding the World Trade Center," *Atlantic Monthly*

Spatial Order

The term **spatial** is related to the word *space.* Spatial order refers to the arrangement of objects in an environment. Most often used in descriptive writing, spatial order helps a writer organize descriptive details and present them so that the reader can visualize the scene. Without spatial order, the details would be a helter-skelter assembly of impressions, and the scene would be difficult to recreate in our minds.

Some typical ways writers arrange details spatially are from left to right or right to left, near to far or far to near, top to bottom or bottom to top. The transitions showing movement from one part of a scene to another—often in the form of prepositional phrases like "from a distance" or "on the left"—enable us to visualize the whole. This passage by Sallie Tisdale describes a cabin her family owned in the Klamath National Forest of southern Oregon. Tisdale's process is almost photographic, as if she were holding a movie camera and filming the scene, beginning with outside of the cabin, then moving to the first floor, then to the staircase, and finally to the second floor.

> The cabin was a small, boxy two-story building with a deck, which we called the porch, perched on stilts outside the front door—a room-size platform with a rail on three sides and a dusty porch swing in constant shade. On the first floor was a long, narrow kitchen, which was lined—floor, walls, and ceiling—with a wood so old that it was black from years of lamp-oil and wood smoke. Across from it was a square open stairway, which led to a single room twice as large as the kitchen and extending up the stretch of a hill. To the right at the top of the stairs was the bathroom; the floor of the shower was always gritty with sand, and the shower head yielded no more than a drizzle of cold water. Over the kitchen, facing the river, was a sleeping porch—a narrow screened room with several iron beds, each one piled with musty, lumpy mattresses two or three deep. I slept on them in perfect peace.
>
> Sallie Tisdale, "The Pacific Northwest," *The New Yorker*

In this second example, Kenneth Boulding uses spatial order in an unusual way: to locate himself first in his narrow environment and then to locate Earth in the larger universe. By repeating the key preposition *beyond,* Boulding enables us to follow his mind's journey. (A basic knowledge of world geography also helps.)

> As I sit at my desk, I know where I am. I see before me a window; beyond that some trees; beyond that the red roofs of the campus of Stanford University; beyond them the trees and the roof tops which mark the town of Palo Alto; beyond them the bare golden hills of the Hamilton Range. I know, however, more than I see. Behind me, although I am not looking in that direction, I know there is a window, and beyond that the little campus of the Center for the Advanced Study in the Behavioral Sciences; beyond that the Coast Range; beyond that the Pacific Ocean. Looking ahead of me again, I know that beyond the mountains that close my present horizon, there is a broad valley; beyond that a still higher range of mountains; beyond that other mountains, range upon range, until we come to the Rockies; beyond that the Great Plains and the Mississippi; beyond that the Alleghenies; be-

yond that the eastern seaboard; beyond that the Atlantic Ocean, beyond that is Europe; beyond that is Asia. I know, furthermore, that if I go far enough I will come back to where I am now. In other words, I have a picture of the earth as round. I visualize it as a globe. I am a little hazy on some of the details. I am not quite sure, for instance, whether Tanganyika is north or south of Nyasaland.[1] I probably could not draw a very good map of Indonesia, but I have a fair idea where everything is located on the face of this globe. Looking further, I visualize the globe as a small speck circling around a bright star which is the sun, in the company of many other similar specks, the planets. Looking still further, I see our star the sun as a member of millions upon millions of others in the Galaxy. Looking still further, I visualize the Galaxy as one of millions upon millions of others in the universe.

Kenneth Boulding, *The Image*

Aside from his unusual geography tour, what is the central philosophical point Boulding makes? <u>Earth is an infinitesimally small part of the universe, and in a parallel point, human life is insignificant when put into that perspective.</u>

Deductive Order In Chapter 1 you learned that paragraphs often begin with a main idea, which is reinforced by specific supporting sentences. This pattern of organization, the most common pattern in the English paragraph, is called **deductive** order; for this reason, deductive order is sometimes called **general-to-specific** order. This term actually refers to a pattern of thinking, which you will read about in more detail in Chapter 9 (pp. 316–319). In a paragraph, deductive order is determined by the placement of the main idea. You can better visualize deductive order if you imagine an inverted triangle with the base at the top:

[1]Tanganyika and Zanzibar joined together and are now called Tanzania; Nyasaland is now called Malawi.

Typically, expository paragraphs use deductive order, as Lewis Thomas does in the first example. Notice that the main idea in sentence 1 is supported with a single effective illustration.

> Animals seem to have an instinct for performing death alone, hidden. Even the largest, most conspicuous ones find ways to conceal themselves in time. If an elephant missteps and dies in an open place, the herd will not leave him there; the others will pick him up and carry the body from place to place, finally putting it down in some inexplicably suitable location. When elephants encounter the skeleton of an elephant out in the open, they methodically take up each of the bones and distribute them, in a ponderous ceremony, over neighboring acres.
>
> Lewis Thomas, *Lives of a Cell*

In this second passage, Joan Acocella uses deductive order to examine the "wealth of imagination," the "sheer, shining fullness" of the Harry Potter books written by J. K. Rowling.

> The great beauty of the Potter books is their wealth of imagination, their sheer, shining fullness. Rowling has said that the idea for the series came to her on a train trip from Manchester to London in 1990, and that, even before she started writing the first volume, she spent years just working out the details of Harry's world. We reap the harvest: the inventory of magical treats (Ice Mice, Jelly Slugs, Fizzing Whizbees—levitating sherbet balls) in the wizard candy store; the wide range of offerings (Dungbombs, Hiccup Sweets, Nose-Biting Teacups) in the wizard joke store. Hogwarts is a grand, creepy castle, a thousand years old, with more dungeons and secret passages than you can shake a stick at. There are a hundred and forty-two staircases, some of which go to different places on different days of the week. There are suits of armor that sing carols at Christmas time, and get the words wrong. There are poltergeists—Peeves, for example, who busies himself jamming gum into keyholes. We also get ghosts, notably Nearly Headless Nick, whose executioner didn't quite finish the job, so that Nick's head hangs by an "inch or so of ghostly skin and muscle"—it keeps flopping over his ruff—thus, to his grief, excluding him from participation in the Headless Hunt, which is confined to the thoroughly decapitated.
>
> Joan Acocella, "Under the Spell," *The New Yorker*

Inductive Order   **Inductive** order, the opposite of deductive order, is sometimes called **specific-to-general** order. Inductive order derives from a kind of thinking called induction, which will also be taken up in Chapter 9 (see pp. 316–319). For now, it is enough to know that inductive order involves a series of specific observations leading to a generalization (the main idea) that the reader can validly infer from those statements.

A diagram of an inductively arranged paragraph looks like this:

Study this excerpt from George Orwell's classic semi-autobiographical book, *Down and Out in Paris and London.*

> It was a very narrow street—a ravine of tall, leprous houses, lurching toward one another in queer attitudes, as though they had all been frozen in the act of collapse. All the houses were hotels and packed to the tiles with lodgers, mostly Poles, Arabs, and Italians. At the foot of the hotels were tiny *bistros,* where you could be drunk for the equivalent of a shilling. On Saturday nights about a third of the male population of the quarter was drunk. There was fighting over women, and the Arab navvies who lived in the cheapest hotels used to conduct mysterious feuds, and fight them out with chairs and occasionally revolvers. At night the policemen would only come through the street two together. It was a fairly rackety place. And yet amid the noise and dirt lived the usual respectable French shopkeepers, bakers and laundresses and the like, keeping themselves to themselves and quietly piling up small fortunes. It was quite a representative Paris slum.
>
> George Orwell, *Down and Out in Paris and London*

Which sentence states the main idea?   <u>the last one</u>

Practice Exercise 1

Read the following paragraphs. First, decide which pattern of organization each represents.

- Chronological order
- Deductive order
- Spatial order
- Inductive order

Then write a sentence stating the main idea in your own words.

A.

Pawn is one of the oldest and most basic of financial transactions. A customer presents an item to a pawnbroker as collateral on a loan. The customer then has a fixed period of time in which to repay the loan, plus interest, or forfeit the item. The amount of the loan is usually between 10 and 50 percent of what the broker believes he can sell the merchandise for, should the customer not return to claim it. In Nevada, the maximum interest rate a pawn broker can charge is 10 percent a month (or 120 percent a year). The customer has 120 days in which to repay the loan before the pawned item becomes the property of the broker.

Joe Heim, "Pawnshops," *The Real Las Vegas: Life beyond the Strip*

Pattern of organization: <u>deductive order</u>

Main idea: <u>Pawning items is an old form of financial transaction.</u>

B.

Atlanta is a city of contradictions. It is home to the largest concentration of black universities in the United States, has a rich and educated black middle class, and has been run by black mayors for the last twenty-four years; it is referred to as Black Mecca. But the Confederate battle flag still flies over the Georgia state-house. Between 1915 and 1945, the city was the official headquarters of the Ku Klux Klan, and yet in the fifties and sixties it became the cradle of the civil-rights movement. Atlanta seems obsessed with its history: the heroes of the old Con-federacy—Jefferson Davis, Robert E. Lee, and Stonewall Jackson—stand watch over the city from their perch on the side of Stone Mountain, Atlanta's version of Mt. Rushmore. When people in Atlanta speak about "the war," they are talking not about Vietnam or any of the wars of the last hundred years but about "the war of Northern aggression." Yet Atlanta is also an upstart city: it is much younger than Richmond, Charleston, or Savannah, and has a brash, openly commercial nature. While Savannah basks in its former glory, having chosen historic preser-vation over economic growth, Atlanta has become the boomtown of the fastest-growing region of the United States, going from one million to three and a half million people in about thirty years. Unfortunately, in its drive to become a major capital, it has lost much of its regional character, and looks remarkably like every other new American city: it could be Phoenix, Houston, Denver, or Seattle.

Alexander Stille, "Who Burned Atlanta?" *The New Yorker*

Pattern of organization: <u>deductive order</u>

Main idea: <u>Both in its attitudes toward race and toward history,</u>

<u>Atlanta is a city of many contradictions.</u>

C.   The following passage was written after the writer's visit to the world's largest pile of used tires in California's Stanislaus County.

Aerial crop dusters use burning tires as wind socks. To attract fish, tires are piled in oceans as artificial reefs. Tires are amassed around harbors as porous breakwaters. In Guilford, Connecticut, Sally Richards grows mussels on tires. Tires are used on dairy farms to cover the tarps that cover silage. They stabilize the shoulders of highways, the slopes of drainage canals. They are set up as crash barriers, dock bumpers, fences, and playground tunnels and swings. At Churchill Downs, the paving blocks of the paddock are made of scrap tires. Used tires are used to fashion silent stairs. They weigh down ocean dragnets. They become airplane shock absorbers. They become sandals. Crumbled and granulated tires become mud flaps, hockey pucks, running tracks, carpet padding, and office-floor anti-fatigue mats. Australians make crumb rubber by freezing and then crushing tire chips. Japanese have laid railroad track on crumbled tires. Dirt racetracks seeded with crumbled tires are easier on horses. Crumbled tires added to soil will increase porosity and allow more oxygen to reach down to grass roots. Twelve thousand crumbled tires will treat one football field. In Colorado, corn was planted in soil that had been laced with crumbled tires. The corn developed large, strong roots. A mighty windstorm came and went, and the tire-treated field was the only corn left standing in that part of Colorado. All such uses, though, as imaginative and practical as they may be, draw down such a small fraction of the tires annually piled as scrap that while they address the problem they essentially do not affect it.

John McPhee, *Irons in the Fire*

Pattern of organization: <u>inductive order</u>

Main idea: <u>Despite the myriad practical and clever ways old tires</u>

<u>have been put to use, they still present a serious problem.</u>

D.

Monday, August 6, 1945, began like any other wartime day in Japan. By 8 A.M. most Hiroshima office workers were at their desks, children were at school, soldiers were doing physical exercises, high-school students and civilian work gangs were busy pulling down wooden houses to clear more firebreaks. During the night, there had been two air-raid alerts—and then all-clears. At 7:09 A.M., there was another alert, as a B-29 on a last weather check approached the city, and, at 7:31 A.M., another all-clear as it turned away. Minutes after eight, watchers in the city saw two B-29s approaching from the northeast: these were an observation plane and the Enola Gay. (Colonel Paul Tibbets, the pilot, had only the day before named the bomber after his mother.) The Enola Gay, in the lead, held its course straight and level for ten miles; at eight-fifteen, it let fall its single bomb. Immediately, the other B-29 banked hard to the left, the Enola Gay to the right; both quit the scene. Released at thirty one thousand six hundred feet, or nearly six miles, the bomb fell for forty-three seconds and was triggered (by a barometric switch) by heavily symbolic chance nineteen hundred feet directly above a small hospital that was two hundred and sixty yards from the aiming point, the T-shaped Aoio Bridge.

Murray Sayle, "Letter from Hiroshima: Did the Bomb End the War?" *The New Yorker*

Pattern of organization: <u>chronological order</u>

Main idea: <u>Although August 6, 1945, began like any other day in</u>
<u>Japan, that was the day the Americans dropped an atomic bomb on</u>
<u>Hiroshima.</u>

E.   The narrator is describing a landscape in Burma.

They rode out of the clearing on a trail that paralleled the river. By the sun, Edgar reckoned they were heading southeast. They passed through a small grove of willows that stretched up from the riverbed. The foliage was thick and low and Edgar had to duck his head to keep from being knocked from the saddle. The path turned uphill and slowly rose above the willows, giving way to a drier brush. On the ridge that sheltered the camp, they stopped. Below, to the northeast, a wide valley stretched out, covered with small bamboo settlements. To the south, a small series of hills pushed up through the slope of the land, like the vertebrae of a disinterested skeleton. In the far distance, higher mountains were barely discernible for the glare of the sun.

Daniel Mason, *The Piano Tuner*

Pattern of organization: <u>spatial</u>

Main idea: <u>From the river, the character followed a path that</u>
<u>eventually took him to a vista where he could see a valley and,</u>
<u>farther away, a range of mountains.</u>

◼ COHERENCE IN PARAGRAPHS

With the patterns you just studied, how do writers ensure that you stay on track, no matter which of the patterns they use? As you learned in Chapter 1, careful writers try to help the reader follow the main idea by ensuring that the paragraph has *unity,* or singleness of purpose. In good writing, there should be no irrelevant or extraneous sentences to lead you astray. But in addition to unity, well-constructed paragraphs also have **coherence,** literally, the quality of "sticking together." Coherence means that each sentence leads logically and smoothly to the next, the sentences in effect forming a chain of interconnected thoughts. Writers achieve coherence through three primary techniques: by using transitions, by repeating key words, and by using pronouns.

Transitions

Transitions are signposts or markers that indicate a logical relationship or a shift in direction. Transitions can be single words or phrases; occasionally, an entire paragraph can serve as a bridge between the major sections of an essay. Although transitions may appear at the beginning of sentences, this is not a hard and fast rule. Paying attention to transitions will improve your concentration and comprehension and will help you see the logical *connections* between ideas. Sometimes a good understanding of a passage may depend on a seemingly unimportant little word like "but" or "for" or "as." To show you how crucial transitions are, this paragraph by George Orwell is printed with the transitions omitted:

> After getting into the water the toad concentrates on building up his strength by eating small insects. He has swollen to his normal size again. He goes through a phase of intense sexiness. All he knows, at least if he is a male toad, is that he wants to get his arms round something. If you offer him a stick, or even your finger, he will cling to it with surprising strength and take a long time to discover that it is not a female toad. One comes upon shapeless masses of ten or twenty toads rolling over and over in the water, one clinging to another without distinction of sex. They sort themselves out into couples, with the male duly sitting on the female's back. You can distinguish males from females. The male is smaller, darker, and sits on top, with his arms tightly clasped round the female's neck. The spawn is laid in long strings which wind themselves in and out of the reeds and soon become invisible. The water is alive with masses of tiny tadpoles which rapidly grow larger, sprout hind legs, then forelegs, then shed their tails. The new generation of toads, smaller than one's thumbnail but perfect in every particular, crawl out of the water to begin the game anew.

Obviously, something is wrong here. Reading this paragraph is like reading a novel with every tenth page missing, or like trying to put a bicycle together when the manufacturer has left out some of the necessary screws. It just does not hold together, and the sentences sound monotonous and choppy. Here is the actual version, this time printed with the transitions restored and italicized, making it much less tedious to read.

> *For a few days* after getting into the water the toad concentrates on building up his strength by eating small insects. *Presently* he has swollen to his normal size again, *and then* he goes through a phase of intense sexiness. All he knows, at least if he is male toad, is that he wants to get his arms round something, *and if* you offer him a stick, or even your finger, he will cling to it with surprising strength and take a long time to discover that it is not a female toad. *Frequently* one comes upon shapeless masses of ten or twenty toads rolling over and over in the water, one clinging to another without distinction of sex. *By degrees, however,* they sort themselves out into couples, with the male duly sitting on the female's back. You can *now* distinguish males from females, *because* the male is

smaller, darker and sits on top, with his arms tightly clasped round the female's neck. *After a day or two* the spawn is laid in long strings which wind themselves in and out of the reeds and soon become invisible. A *few more weeks, and* the water is alive with masses of tiny tadpoles which rapidly grow larger, sprout hind legs, then forelegs, then shed their tails; *and finally, about the middle of the summer,* the new generation of toads, smaller than one's thumbnail but perfect in every particular, crawl out of the water to begin the game anew.

George Orwell, "Some Thoughts on the Common Toad," *The Orwell Reader*

The boxes in this section of the chapter present the various transitions according to their function, followed by a few examples of words or phrases indicating the logical relationship they bring to the sentences they join. An example is provided for each category of transition.

Transitions Signaling an Additional Statement (usually of equal importance)

and, in addition (to), additionally, as well as, besides, furthermore, moreover

---

Example: The house was badly neglected: the windows were broken, *and* the paint was blistered. *Moreover,* what had once been a well-tended lawn was now only an overgrown weed patch.

Transitions Signaling a Contrast

but, yet, however, nevertheless, nonetheless, while, whereas, on the other hand, in contrast (to), contrary to

---

Example: Basset hounds and St. Bernards are known for their placid and friendly natures; *in contrast,* terriers are often high-strung and highly excitable.

Transitions Signaling an Example or Illustration

for example, as an example, to illustrate, as an illustration, for instance, namely, specifically, a case in point, consider the following

---

Example: Many residents of urban neighborhoods believe that an influx of national franchise stores can ruin local businesses and destroy a neighborhood's unique quality, resulting in a homogenized, bland environment. *For instance,* neighbors of Larchmont Boulevard, a two-block street in Los Angeles lined with trees and small independent businesses, fought, unsuccessfully, to preserve its local character from intrusion by Payless Drugs, Noah's Bagels, Koo Koo Roo (a local fast-food chain), and Starbucks.

Transitions Signaling Steps in a Process of Chronological Order

first, second, third, next, the next step, further, then, before, after that, finally, last, in July, last week, in a few days, in 2005

Example: To use the spell-check function in Microsoft Word, *first* pull down under the "Tools" menu to "Spelling and Grammar." The computer will *then* scan through the document to identify any misspelled or questionable words. *After* each word is flagged, select the correct spelling. *Finally,* be sure to save the changes in your file.

Transitions Signaling Emphasis

indeed, in fact, certainly, without a doubt, undoubtedly, admittedly, unquestionably, truly

---

Example: The level of violence and intimidation directed at abortion clinics and the physicians who perform abortions has seriously escalated in recent years. *In fact,* in the 1990s, two abortion providers were killed, and protestors have posted abortion providers' names and addresses on antiabortion Web sites.

Transitions Signaling a Concession (an admission of truth)

although, even though, in spite of, despite, after all

Example: Although chimpanzee society is characterized by power displays, especially among males, the social hierarchy is usually quite stable. (In this sentence, the first clause *concedes* a truth. Another way to think of a concession is to substitute "regardless of the fact that" or "even though this is true, this is also true.")

Transitions Signaling a Conclusion

therefore, thus, then, to conclude, in conclusion, in summary, to summarize, consequently, hence

Example: Charley spent two hours a day working in the reading laboratory, and he looked up every unfamiliar word he encountered. *As a result,* there was a dramatic improvement in his reading comprehension by the end of the semester.

Transitions Signaling Spatial Order

above, below, to the right, to the left, nearby, from afar, beyond, farther on, up the road, on top, underneath

---

Example: "Where the mountains meet the sea" is the official motto of Camden, Maine, a New England village known for its splendid harbor. No wonder. *Behind the harbor, not far from* where the schooners, sailboats, and cabin cruisers are anchored, Ragged Mountain rises precipitously. *Near the peak of the mountain* one can find Maiden Cliffs, where, according to legend, an Indian maiden leaped to her death because of an unhappy love affair. *At the base of the mountain* is Lake Megunticook, a local swimming hole for midcoast Maine residents.

Repetition of Key Words and Phrases

Another way writers achieve coherence—producing a chain of interconnected thoughts—is by repeating key words and phrases, which help keep the reader on track and maintain focus. Readers who want to improve their concentration, which seems a fundamental goal of reading students, will gain mastery over their reading by learning to identify such repetitions.

Read this paragraph taken from former South African president Nelson Mandela's autobiography. In it, he explains the significance of the circumcision tradition in Xhosa culture. As you read it, follow the links between the circled words to see how a good writer achieves coherence.

When I was sixteen, the regent decided that it was time that I became a man. In Xhosa tradition, this is achieved through one means only: circumcision. In my tradition, an uncircumcised male cannot be heir to his father's wealth, cannot marry or officiate in tribal rituals. An uncircumcised Xhosa man is a contradiction in terms, for he is not considered a man at all, but a boy. For the Xhosa people, circumcision represents the formal incorporation of males into society. It is not just a surgical procedure, but a lengthy and elaborate ritual in preparation for manhood. As a Xhosa, I count my years as a man from the date of my circumcision.

Nelson Mandela, *Long Walk to Freedom*

Mandela's paragraph is easy to read because of the repetition of key words and use of synonyms to substitute for those key words.

Practice Exercise 2

A. Read this paragraph about Lyndon Baines Johnson, former president of the United States, and circle all of the pronouns that refer to him. The source from which this excerpt is taken, *Vietnam: A History,* is a leading textbook on the Vietnam War.

Lyndon Baines Johnson, a consummate politician, was a kaleidoscopic personality, forever changing as he sought to dominate or persuade or placate or frighten his friends and foes. A gigantic figure whose extravagant moods matched his size, he could be cruel and kind, violent and gentle, petty, generous, cunning, naive, crude, candid, and frankly dishonest. He commanded the blind loyalty of his aides, some of whom worshiped him, and he sparked bitter derision or fierce hatred that he never quite fathomed. And he oscillated between peaks of confidence and depths of doubt, constantly accommodating his lofty ideals to the struggle for influence and authority. But his excesses reflected America's dramas during his lifetime, among them the dramas he himself created.

Stanley Karnow, *Vietnam: A History*

B. Circle and link the words and phrases concerning *taste, smell,* and *aging* that Olga Knopf uses to achieve paragraph unity and coherence. Underline the transitional words and phrases.

Taste and smell are also affected by aging, but their changes are less understood and appreciated. People who are in contact with the elderly will tell you they have two major complaints—food and their children. The complaint about food is easily explained when one considers how the taste buds work. Distributed over the tongue, they last no longer than a few days each and then are replaced. In keeping with the general slowing-down process, they are renewed more slowly than they are used up. This means that the total number of taste buds declines, and, therefore, food tastes less savory. Extensive dentures that cover a large portion of the oral cavity diminish the perception of taste even further. In addition, there is the close interrelationship between smell and taste. Anyone who has ever had a cold can testify to the fact that while the cold lasts, not only is the sense of smell reduced, but food loses its taste as well. There is a similar deterioration in the sense of smell as a result of the process of aging.

Olga Knopf, *Successful Aging*

■ CHAPTER EXERCISES

Selection 1

This passage is about the custom or requirement for Saudi women to cover themselves from head to toe when they are in public. Saudi women wear high-necked dresses down to the floor and long sleeves. In addition, they cover their hair completely with an *abaaya,* a black cloak that hangs completely over the head. Women who live in the cities also wear a veil over their faces attached at the top to the *abaaya.* It is important to note that the Koran, the sacred text of Islam containing Mohammed's teachings, does not command women to wear the veil.

[1]The origin of the veil in Saudi Arabia is unknown. [2]Face veiling in the Middle East is recorded as far back as the Assyrians (1500 B.C.), followed by a brief revival about the time of the Crusades. [3]The most accepted theory about the specific veiling practices in Saudi Arabia is that when the eastern coastal areas were under Turkish control, women of high social standing wore veils, probably to protect their complexions against the brutality of the desert sun. [4]The desire for status—an overpowering emotional need among Arabs—decreed, therefore, that every woman wear a veil so everyone could lay claim to being upper class. [5]Another theory is that when Bedouin tribes[2] made war on each other and raided the livestock of the rival tribe, the women were veiled so that the beautiful ones would not be carried off with the goats. [6]Others say Bedouin women were such fierce fighters in these raids that, by a code of desert chivalry, women were veiled as a form of identity and kept out of battle so the intrepid men were spared the risk of fighting them.

[7]Regardless of the veil's origins, today few Saudi women are allowed by their men outside the house without a veil. [8]The rule applies to women in all social classes, from those sharing the back of a pickup truck with shaggy sheep to those stepping from limousines at chic boutiques. [9]In public, women lose all personality and individuality to become so many black blobs gliding down the street. [10]Each is covered in black, her face masked behind impenetrable black gauze. [11]In the eyes of a Westerner, the veil is starkly symbolic of a woman's subservience to man in all areas of Saudi life. [12]It sets the tone of a woman's confinement and states her total dependence on the male members of her family, who regulate her ability to function as a member of society.

Sandra Mackey, *The Saudis: Inside the Desert Kingdom*

A. Vocabulary

For each italicized word from the selection, choose the best definition according to the context in which it appears.

[2]Bedouins are members of nomadic tribes that inhabit the desert in various Middle Eastern countries. They subsist as herders, typically of camels, sheep, and goats.

1. The desire for status *decreed* [sentence 4]:
    (a) inspired copying.
    (b) ordered authoritatively.
    (c) weakened, undermined.
    (d) became apparent.
2. the *intrepid* men were spared [sentence 6]:
    (a) fearless.
    (b) jealous.
    (c) chivalrous.
    (d) honorable.
3. symbolic of a woman's *subservience* [sentence 11]:
    (a) arrogance, haughtiness.
    (b) isolation, alienation.
    (c) station, status in life.
    (d) submissiveness, inferiority.

B. *Content and Structure*

Complete the following questions.

1. A good title for this passage is
    (a) "Saudi Arabian Women."
    (b) "The Veil in Saudi Arabia: Myth and Reality."
    (c) "A Mysterious Tradition."
    (d) "The Origin and Significance of the Veil for Saudi Women."
2. The mode of discourse in the passage is
    (a) narration.
    (b) description.
    (c) exposition.
    (d) persuasion.
3. The pattern of organization in both paragraphs is
    (a) chronological.
    (b) spatial.
    (c) deductive.
    (d) inductive.
4. Look again at the first sentence in paragraph 1, which represents the main idea. In the same paragraph, locate three unifying phrases that provide coherence and write them in the spaces provided.

_____

_____

_____

5. The transitional phrase in sentence 7, "regardless of the veil's origins," suggests that the various theories that account for the requirement that Saudi women wear the veil
   (a) are interesting perhaps but are not particularly important in relation to the reality of Saudi women's position in society.
   (b) have changed so much throughout history that no one theory is conclusive.
   (c) are important to understand the role that the veil plays in Saudi society.
   (d) show that attitudes toward the veiling requirement are changing.

6. Look again at sentences 11 and 12. Whose point of view is represented in the concluding sentences?
   (a) Saudi women's
   (b) Saudi men's
   (c) Westerners'
   (d) all of the above

Answers for Selection 1

A. *Vocabulary*

1. (b)   2. (a)   3. (d)

B. *Content and Structure*

1. (d)   2. (c)   3. (c)
4. "the most accepted theory," "another theory," "others say"
5. (a)   6. (c)

Selection 2

The subject of this passage is the impact of invasive (nonnative) species of animals and plants on the environment.

[1]What do fire ants, zebra mussels, Asian gypsy moths, tamarisk trees, maleleuca trees, kudzu, Mediterranean fruit flies, boll weevils, and water hyacinths have in common with crab-eating macaques or Nile perch? [2]Answer: They're *weedy* species, in the sense that animals as well as plants can be weedy. [3]What that implies is a constellation of characteristics: They reproduce quickly, disperse widely when given a chance, tolerate a fairly broad range of habitat conditions, take hold in strange places, succeed especially in disturbed ecosystems, and resist eradication once they're established. [4]They are scrappers, generalists, opportunists. [5]They tend to thrive in human-dominated terrain because in crucial ways they resemble *Homo sapiens:* aggressive, versatile, prolific, and ready to travel. [6]The city pigeon, a cosmopolitan creature derived from wild ancestry as a Eurasian rock dove (*Columba livia*) by way of centuries of pigeon fanciers whose coop-bred birds occasionally went AWOL, is a weed. [7]So are those species that, benefiting from human impacts upon landscape, have increased grossly in abun-

dance or expanded their geographical scope without having to cross an ocean by plane or by boat—for instance, the coyote in New York, the raccoon in Montana, the white-tailed deer in northern Wisconsin or western Connecticut. [8]The brown-headed cowbird, also weedy, has enlarged its range from the eastern United States into the agricultural Midwest at the expense of migratory songbirds. [9]In gardening usage the word "weed" may be utterly subjective, indicating any plant you don't happen to like, but in ecological usage it has these firmer meanings. [10]Biologists frequently talk of weedy species, meaning animals as well as plants.

David Quammers, "Planet of Weeds," Harper's Magazine

A. Vocabulary

For each italicized word from the selection, write the dictionary definition most appropriate for the context.

1. a *constellation* of characteristics [sentence 3]:   <u>a group of related</u>

    <u>things</u>

2. they are *scrappers* [4]:   <u>organisms that are full of fight</u>

3. they are *opportunists* [4]:   <u>those who take advantage of favorable</u>

    <u>circumstances</u>

4. versatile, *prolific* [5]:   <u>capable of producing many offspring</u>

5. a *cosmopolitan* creature [6]:   <u>widely distributed in the whole world</u>

6. occasionally went *AWOL* [6]:   <u>an acronym meaning "absent without</u>

    <u>leave"</u>

B. Content and Structure

Complete the following questions.

1. Explain the logical relationship between sentences 1 and 2. <u>Sentence 1</u>

    <u>lists examples, and sentence 2 provides a general definition.</u>

2. In relation to the main idea, what is the function of sentence 10?
    (a) It restates the main idea.
    (b) It draws a conclusion.
    (c) It states a warning for the future.
    (d) It presents an effect of several causes.

3. The author's main point is that
   (a) invasive plants and animals must be eradicated at all costs.
   (b) invasive animal species thrive in a wide variety of habitats.
   (c) weedy animals are amazingly similar to humans.
   (d) (in ecological terms, both animals and plants can be weedy.)
4. The pattern of organization in the paragraph is
   (a) chronological.
   (b) spatial.
   (c) (deductive.)
   (d) inductive.
5. What method of development is most evident in sentences 2 to 5?
   (a) analogy.
   (b) informative process.
   (c) example.
   (d) (definition.)
6. We can accurately infer that weedy animal species
   (a) are a purely modern phenomenon.
   (b) probably would not have occurred to such a great extent without human inventions or human settlement.
   (c) is a problem only in developed nations like the United States.
   (d) are the target of government eradication programs.

Selection 3

1 The term "asteroid" means "like stars," stars being what earlier humankind most often mistook asteroids for. When an asteroid breaches Earth's atmosphere it becomes a meteor; when it strikes Earth's surface it is called a meteorite. A "shooting star" is typically envisioned as a midsized burning chunk of speeding rock, when in fact most shooting stars are no bigger than a grain of sand. The speed at which they travel, and the opposing force of Earth's atmosphere, cause the particles to explode. The streaks of light we see in the night sky are these particles' violently released energy.

2 The solar system's primary asteroid repository whirls in a formation known as the asteroid belt, which lies between Mars and Jupiter, the latter possessing our system's second most powerful gravitational force, after the sun. Most asteroids are the fragmentary remains of the same cosmic *deus ex nihilo*[3] that discharged rock and matter across the galaxy several billion years ago. In our solar system alone, as many as a trillion pieces of debris once floated around the perpetually contained hydrogen explosion we know as the sun, most of which were bashed into oblivion by collisions. Only nine of these space rocks were large enough to form atmospheres, and only one is known to have developed complex forms of life. This did not make them invulnerable. A Mars-sized object slammed into the nascent Earth billions of years ago, for instance, and the drama of its effect can be appreciated by the fact that it threw off a huge, wounded, molten glob that

[3]A Latin phrase for "god from nothingness"

froze, was captured by Earth's gravity, and eventually became the moon. Because of this ancient demolition derby, the solar system is presently a much more open place, and collisions are far less frequent.

Tom Bissell, "A Comet's Tale," *Harper's Magazine*

A. Vocabulary

For each italicized word from the selection, choose the best definition according to the context in which it appears. You may refer to the selection to answer the questions in this section and in all the remaining sections.

1. when an asteroid *breaches* Earth's atmosphere [paragraph 1]:
   (a) duplicates.
   (b) causes an explosion in.
   (c) breaks through.
   (d) separates from.
2. the solar system's primary asteroid *repository* [2]:
   (a) a place that contains a store of something.
   (b) point of origination.
   (c) structure and formation.
   (d) a place that is undetectable by the ordinary eye.
3. bashed into *oblivion* by collisions [2]:
   (a) a state of forgetfulness.
   (b) nothingness.
   (c) small fragments.
   (d) a transformed shape.
4. slammed into the *nascent* Earth [2]:
   (a) describing an impenetrable shell.
   (b) still evolving, changing.
   (c) prehistoric.
   (d) emerging, newly formed.

B. Content and Structure

Complete the following questions.

1. A good title for this passage would be
   (a) "Asteroids and Meteors."
   (b) "The History of the Universe."
   (c) "How Asteroids Shaped the Solar System."
   (d) "A Cosmic *Deus Ex Nihilo.*"
2. In paragraph 1, what method of development is most evident?
   (a) example and illustration.
   (b) informative process.
   (c) definition.
   (d) analogy.

3. In paragraph 2, what pattern of organization is most evident?
   (a) chronological order.
   (b) deductive order.
   (c) inductive order.
   (d) spatial order.

4. The author explains that Earth's moon was formed by
   (a) Mars slamming into Earth after a hydrogen explosion.
   (b) rocks and other matter which were discharged into the atmosphere and which bombarded Earth.
   (c) an asteroid the size of Mars that slammed into Earth.
   (d) a large rock that became trapped in Earth's gravity.

5. In paragraph 2, locate the imaginative comparison that describes the collisions in the solar system from asteroids.   "this ancient demolition derby"

6. We can logically conclude that, without asteroids, the solar system would be
   (a) much more crowded with planets and other objects closer together.
   (b) relatively undeveloped, without the complex forms of life it has today.
   (c) free from the danger of collisions with its attendant loss of life and destruction of the atmosphere.
   (d) filled with much more debris in the form of rocks and other matter.

PRACTICE ESSAY

"Surviving Deer Season: A Lesson in Ambiguity"
Castle Freeman

A resident of Newfane, Vermont, Castle Freeman is an essayist and short story writer. He is the author of *The Bride of Ambrose and Other Stories* (1987) and *Spring Snow: The Seasons of New England from* The Old Farmer's Almanac (1995). This article was first published in *The Atlantic Monthly*.

Preview Questions

1. Do you or any member of your family hunt? If so, what reasons do you have for the practice?

2. In the modern era of supermarkets and the ready availability of meat, is hunting more of an anachronism than a necessity?

1   The foothills of southeastern Vermont were once dairy country, although by the time I arrived, twenty years ago, dairying was mostly finished. One farm in the neighborhood still kept a few milkers, though, and it was there that I became acquainted with a particular local custom that is, I find, rarely celebrated in articles on endearing rural ways through the seasons. Their authors will tell you how to tap a maple in March, mow hay in June, and make cider in October, but by failing to touch on the subject I refer to, they neglect a passage in the turning year that is as venerable as these but darker and more pointed.

2   One morning in November, looking into my neighbor's pasture, I observed an uncanny thing: on the nearest of his animals the word COW had been painted with whitewash in letters two feet high. A further look revealed that the entire herd had been painted the same way. What was this? Was the herd's owner perhaps expecting a visit from city people in need of rural education? Was his tractor painted TRACTOR, his barn BARN? I asked him.

3   "Well, you know what tomorrow is," my neighbor said.

4   "Saturday?" I said.

5   "You're new around here," he said. "You'll see."

6   I saw, all right. More precisely, I heard. The next morning Vermont's two-week deer-hunting season began. Just before dawn the slumbering woods erupted with the fell echo of small arms. Single gunshots, doubles, volleys of three or four, came from all points of the compass, some far off, others seemingly in the living room. By eleven the fire had mounted to a fusillade worthy of Antietam.[1] Across the road, however, my neighbor's cows survived. They hugged the earth fearfully, like Tommies[2] at the Somme,[3] but they were alive. After all, no deer hunter who could read would shoot a cow.

7   Since then I have become a close student of the lengths to which people go each year on the eve of deer season to provide a margin of safety for themselves, their loved ones, their livestock, their pets. This is the season when dogs wear brightly colored bandannas around their necks, like John Wayne and Montgomery Clift in *Red River*. Cats and smaller dogs, as far as I can tell, have to take their chances along with the deer, although I don't know why the kind of elegant dog vest to be seen on the Pekingeses of Park Avenue shouldn't be produced in hunter orange for the greater safety of their country cousins.

---

[1]Antietam was a major Civil War battle.

[2]British slang for "soldiers," short for Tommy Atkins, the name used in sample official British army forms.

[3]The site of the devastating Battle of the Somme during World War I (1916).

8   That same hunter orange, a hideous toxic color, suddenly appears everywhere in mid-November, like the untimely bloom of an evil flower. Hunters themselves, of course, wear hunter orange to make it less likely that they'll be shot by their peers. But civilians, too, turn up in hunter-orange caps, vests, sweaters, and jackets, as they go about their business outdoors during this uneasy fortnight in the year.

9   Uneasy indeed. Are you a hiker, a birder, an idle tramper through the woods? In deer season you think twice before setting out—think twice and then stay home. If you're a nonhunter, it's painful to avoid the woods and fields as though they were a deserted street in the South Bronx. There is also the trouble of preparing for deer season. It's not as though you don't have enough to do to get the place ready for winter without having to find time to paint the cow, flag the dog, pray for the cat, and plan two weeks' worth of useful projects to do in the cellar.

10   The heaviest demand that deer season makes on the nonhunter, however, it makes not on his time but on his mind. You have to reflect. You have to collect your thoughts. You don't want to move into deer season without having examined your responses, your beliefs.

11   I don't object to deer hunting: let everyone have his sport, I say. I don't for a moment doubt the value, importance, and dignity of hunting for those who do it. Deer hunting teaches skill, discipline, and patience. More than that, it teaches the moral lesson of seriousness—that certain things must be entered into advisedly, done with care, and done right. That hunting provides an education I am very willing to believe. And yet deer season is for me a sad couple of weeks. Because with all its profound advantages for the hunter, the fact remains that deer season is a little tough on the deer.

12   Suddenly deer turn up in strange places: thrown down in the backs of pickup trucks; roped on top of cars; hanging in front of barns; flopped in blood across platform scales in front of country stores and gas stations. It's hard to recognize in those abject, inert cadavers the agile creatures you surprise along the roads at night or see sometimes in the woods picking their way on slender legs and then bounding off, the most graceful animals in North America. It's hard to see them so defeated, so dead.

13   It's particularly hard for children, those instinctive animal lovers, to see deer season's bloody harvest hauled out of the woods. It's especially hard to explain to them why it isn't wrong to kill deer—or, if it is wrong, why nobody can stop it, and how it is that the hunters themselves, who are also your friends and neighbors, are otherwise such familiar, decent, innocent people. It's a lesson in ambiguity, I guess—a lesson in tolerance.

14   I had a number of conversations along these lines with my children when they were young, inconclusive conversations with on their side conviction and passion, and on my own . . . nothing satisfactory. What do you tolerate, why, and how? How do you separate the act from the friend, and condemn the one but not the other? Not an easy matter at any age, in any season.

15   We don't have those talks anymore. The children are older now. They know that with some things all you can do is figure out how you will conduct your own life and let others do the same. Perhaps they have learned this in part from deer season. If so, I'm content. Let the gunners fire at will—and as for the nonhunters, good luck to them, too. It's not only hunters who can learn from hunting.

A. *Comprehension*

Choose the answer that best completes each statement. Do not refer to the selection while doing this exercise.

1. One farmer protected his cows at the beginning of deer season by
    (a) moving them into barns.
    (b) moving them into pastures away from the woods.
    (c) painting "COW" on each animal.
    (d) putting brightly colored bandannas around their necks.
2. During deer season, to prevent themselves from accidentally being shot, people wear clothing in
    (a) hunter green.
    (b) neon green.
    (c) neon yellow.
    (d) hunter orange.
3. For the author, deer season requires him to
    (a) examine his beliefs carefully.
    (b) join his friends in hunting.
    (c) write letters protesting the hunting season.
    (d) join antihunting organizations.
4. For Freeman, deer hunting, both for himself and for his children, represents
    (a) a chance to bond with the neighbors.
    (b) a lesson in ambiguity and tolerance.
    (c) a chance to learn new skills.
    (d) the loss of one's innocence.
5. Freeman is very much concerned with how to separate
    (a) the hunter's professed reason for killing deer and the actual reason.
    (b) the pros and cons of hunting as a sport.
    (c) the activity of hunting from the affection he feels for a friend who hunts.
    (d) the activity of hunting from the hostility he feels for a friend who hunts.

B. *Vocabulary*

For each italicized word from the selection, write the dictionary definition most appropriate for the context. You may refer to the selection to answer the questions in this section and in all the remaining sections.

1. as *venerable* as [paragraph 1]: <u>worthy of respect</u>

2. an *uncanny* thing [2]: <u>uncomfortably strange</u>

3. those *abject,* inert cadavers [12]: <u>miserable</u>

4. those abject, *inert* cadavers [12]: <u>unmoving</u>

5. a lesson in *ambiguity* [13]: <u>uncertainty with regard to interpretation</u>

C. Inferences

Complete the following questions.

1. At the end of paragraph 1, Freeman writes that Vermonters describe many annual rituals associated with rural living but that they neglect to write about hunting season. What can you infer is the reason for this neglect?
   (a) There is no need to write articles about hunting because the practice is so ingrained and accepted in the community.
   (b) Vermonters are ashamed of their fondness for hunting.
   (c) Vermonters do not want to call attention to the sport for fear of angering the antihunting and antigun lobbies.
   (d) One cannot accurately infer a reason.

2. We can infer from nonhunters' behavior during deer season, as described in paragraphs 7 to 9, that
   (a) innocent animals and people have been shot by accident.
   (b) nonhunters are too intimidated to speak out against hunting.
   (c) hunters are very careful about who or what they shoot.
   (d) nonhunters are so accustomed to the sport that they take no special precautions.

3. The subtitle of this essay is "A Lesson in Ambiguity." Another good subtitle would be
   (a) "Autumn Vermont Customs."
   (b) "Why I Am Opposed to Deer Hunting."
   (c) "A Lesson in Tolerance."
   (d) "How to Avoid Danger and Survive during Hunting Season."

D. Structure

Complete the following questions.

1. The author's purpose is to
   (a) criticize hunting as a sport.
   (b) analyze the advantages and disadvantages of hunting as a sport.
   (c) examine the ambiguities hunting presents to a nonhunter.
   (d) explain the positive benefits of hunting.

2. Read footnotes 4, 5, and 6 again. In the context of the discussion, how do these allusions, references to historical material, reinforce Freeman's main point? _Because they all refer to military matters, they_

   reinforce the idea that hunting is violent; they suggest that

   hunting is a kind of warfare—man against defenseless deer.

3. The pattern of organization in paragraphs 2 to 6 is
   (a) chronological.
   (b) spatial.
   (c) deductive.
   (d) inductive.

4. What is the purpose of paragraph 10? It serves as
   (a) background information.
   (b) a transition from the background to the main point.
   (c) a conclusion from the earlier paragraphs.
   (d) a cause–effect connection.

5. With respect to the essay as a whole, what is the purpose of paragraph 11?

   It serves as a concession, discussing the positive features of

   hunting, thereby ensuring that the essay isn't one-sided.

6. Locate the transitional phrase "and yet" in paragraph 11. What two logical relationships does it signify?
   (a) steps in a process.
   (b) a contrast.
   (c) a conclusion.
   (d) emphasis.

7. The pattern of organization in paragraph 12 is
   (a) chronological.
   (b) spatial.
   (c) deductive.
   (d) inductive.

8. The emotional attitude of the writer in the essay can best be described as
   (a) contemplative, regretful, and sad.
   (b) sentimental, maudlin.
   (c) intolerant, biased.
   (d) unsure, hesitant, and indecisive.

E. Questions for Discussion and Analysis

1. Discuss your own experience with and/or thinking about hunting as a sport. Has this essay changed your thinking in any way?

2. It can be argued that in earlier stages of American history, hunting was a necessity if homesteaders and pioneers wanted to eat. But the practice seems less defensible today. Freeman writes of the skill and patience hunting requires. Does the sport have any other virtues?

3. Freeman writes this essay as much to show the importance of tolerance as he does to show his concerns about the sport of hunting. What is another practice that, fundamentally, you do not accept but that you have developed tolerance for? How did you achieve this tolerance?

ON THE WEB

Read about gun enthusiasts' and hunters' perspectives on a variety of issues relating to gun laws, hunting restrictions, and weapons culture at these two sites.

- The Guns Network Forums
  The Guns Network General Discussion Board
  www.gunsnet.net/forums/
- The National Rifle Association
  http://mynra.com

3

Discovering Meaning: The Importance of Language

Language and Its Effects on the Reader

CHAPTER OBJECTIVES

In this chapter, we will be concerned with language in prose writing—with words and the effect the writer intends them to have on us. We will examine these elements of language:

- Denotation and connotation

- Figurative language (metaphors, similes, and personification)

- Language misused and abused

■ DENOTATION AND CONNOTATION

Good writers choose their words carefully. Most strive to recreate as precisely as possible the thoughts and emotions in their heads as words on the printed page. Gustave Flaubert, the nineteenth-century French writer, was the consummate craftsman. He agonized over his words, always searching for what he called "the right word" *(le mot juste)* and often spending an entire day working and reworking his sentences. On some days he would produce for his efforts only a single page. Much of our pleasure in reading derives from savoring the emotional associations such efforts afford us. An understanding of these associations will significantly improve your literal understanding and enhance your enjoyment of reading.

In the first section, we will study **word choice,** or **diction.** Some words are meant to arouse positive feelings, some are meant to be neutral or literal, while others are meant to convey a negative impression. The following chart shows the difference between **denotation** and **connotation,** the two elements in word choice.

Denotation vs. Connotation

Denotation: The literal or explicit meaning of a word; often called the dictionary definition.

> Examples: *Home*—one's residence; the place where one
>   lives
>   *Lemon*—a sour, yellow-skinned, citrus fruit

Neither of these words implies any particular judgment or suggests an emotional attitude.

Connotation: The cluster of suggestions, ideas, or emotional associations a word conjures up.

> Examples: *Home*—a place of safety, privacy, comfort,
>   nurturing
>   *Lemon*—a piece of defective equipment, usually
>   a car

These two examples show that connotative values refer to an emotional response, in this case, one positive, the other negative.

Connotation extends the meaning beyond the denotative. As Richard Altick, author of *Preface to Critical Reading,* has written: "Nothing is more essential to intelligent, profitable reading than sensitivity to connotation." However, no one can teach you this sensitivity. It comes from wide reading and a willingness to consult the dictionary definitions and the accompanying usage notes for help. This sensitivity may take years to develop. After all, the process of acquiring new words is a lifetime commitment, and learning the connotations of words is part of that commitment.

Connotation and Synonyms

The English language contains an irksome number of words that appear to be synonymous but that, upon closer examination, are not. (It is this feature of the English language that makes its study so difficult and yet so gratifying.) Consider, for example, these near synonyms: *ask, inquire, interrogate,* and *grill.* Are these words really synonyms? *Ask* and *inquire* seem neutral, with *inquire* a bit more formal than *ask. Interrogate,* because of its association with police or FBI interrogations, seems decidedly more negative, often carrying the unpleasant connotation of harshness or intimidation. *Grill* is less formal than *interrogate,* but it also suggests that the questioning is relentless, and the dictionary definition of *grill* bears this observation out.

How would you rank these near-synonyms for their connotative values?

stingy   thrifty   cheap

For one last example, let's look at the verb *walk.* It is clearly neutral, denoting a forward movement by putting one foot in front of the other. But what of these related verbs: *stride, saunter, stroll, meander, glide, mince, lumber, plod, trudge, stagger, lurch, stomp, waddle, slither,* and *march*? Study their associations and try to visualize the motion each suggests.

Variations on the Verb "Walk"

Stride: To walk purposely or resolutely.

Saunter, stroll: To walk in a leisurely, unhurried way.

Meander: To walk in no particular direction; to wander here and there with no fixed destination.

Glide: To walk in an elegant, graceful manner, often said of fashion models.

Mince: To walk in little steps with exaggerated affectation or primness.

Lumber: To walk heavily and/or clumsily; often reserved for describing the movements of large, bulky animals such as bears.

Plod, trudge: To walk in a heavy or laborious way; may suggest discouragement or defeat.

Stagger, lurch: To walk in an unsteady manner, whether because of illness, drunkenness, or some other affliction; *stagger* is stronger than lurch.

> *Stomp:* To walk with purposeful steps, often in anger.
>
> *March:* To walk as in a regiment, in describing a military person; used in an ordinary way, it suggests walking purposefully or steadily.
>
> *Waddle:* To walk in a slow, swaying, or side-to-side manner; often used to describe the way ducks or obese people walk.

Practice Exercise 1

For the following pairs of words, mark the word that carries a positive connotation with a plus sign and the word that carries a negative connotation with a minus sign.

chubby –	plump +
assertive +	aggressive –
shopping binge –	shopping spree +
faux +	fake –
childish –	childlike +
loiter –	wait + or neutral
Frankenfoods –	genetically-altered foods + or neutral
modest +	prudish –
lurk –	hide + or neutral
follow + or neutral	stalk –
surgeon + or neutral	sawbones –
slumlord –	real estate magnate +
conservative + or neutral	reactionary –

Connotation and Levels of Language

Levels of language, which relate to a writer's style, are also influenced by connotation. A writer can employ an *informal* or casual style by using ordinary words that are part of everyone's spoken and reading vocabulary; a writer can employ a *formal* style if the word choice is elevated, scholarly, perhaps even pretentious, by using words derived from Latin and Greek.

Practice Exercise 2

Study these pairs of synonyms. Label one *informal* (ordinary) and the other *formal* (elevated). If you are unsure of the meanings, check a dictionary.

osculate	formal	kiss	informal
door	informal	portal	formal
particle	formal	smidgeon	informal
salty	informal	saline	formal
quotidian	formal	daily	informal
house	informal	domicile	formal

Connotative Restrictions

In addition to the positive or negative "charge" that words can convey, some words in English are restricted to describe a particular group. For example, the word *spry* usually applies to old people or animals. The *American Heritage Dictionary* usage notes states that *spry* suggests "unexpected speed and energy of motion," traits that would be more characteristic of an old person or an old dog than they would be of, say, a six-year-old child. Similarly, the denotative meaning of the adjective *debonair* is "handsome, suave, and worldly." However, its connotation suggests that the word is better applied to a man than to a woman. Although neither of my two dictionaries suggests this distinction, I have inferred this distinction from the many contexts in which I have encountered this word. A woman may be handsome, attractive, elegant, and so on, but not debonair.

Consider the word *demure*.

What is the word's denotative meaning?   _modest and reserved in_

manner and behavior

Is its connotation positive or negative? _positive_

To which gender is it more generally applied? _a female_

Does it suggest any particular age? (Hint: Which person would you describe as demure—a fifty-year-old man or a thirteen-year-old girl?)

a young girl or woman

Words are powerful. Armed as they are with these associative values, words can arouse passions, dreams, hostility, or any other strong emotion. This is borne out when considering the labels people choose to describe themselves (race or ethnicity), which may carry connotative value. In the United States, there is a significant debate about whether people of Mexican descent should be called *Hispanic* or *Latino*. (The term *Hispanic* was added to the U.S. Census in 1970.) When Mexican-American novelist Sandra Cisneros walked into a San Antonio bookstore titled Valenzuela's Latino Bookstore, she was thrilled to find an independent bookstore specializing in Latino writers. However, when she noticed that a section was devoted to "Hispanic" writers, she became upset. Why the emotional reaction? For Cisneros, and for many Mexican-Americans, *Hispanic* refers specifically to the white descendants of those who came from the Iberian peninsula (Spain and Portugal), whereas *Latino* refers to people descended from the indigenous Indians (brown-skinned) of Central and South America who were conquered by Spain. (Darryl Fears, "The Power of a Label," *The Washington Post National Weekly Edition,* September 1–7, 2003.)

How does one learn these connotative restrictions and values? As noted at the beginning of the chapter, experience and practice help. Let us begin with a short reading passage. As you read it, pay particular attention to the circled words and phrases.

> The (persistent cloud cover,) the almost (constant patter of rain,) are (narcotic.) They seem to (seal) Seattle inside (a damp, cozy cocoon,) (muffling reality) and (beckoning) residents (to snuggle up) with a good book and a cup of coffee or a glass of wine. (Mary Bruno, "Seattle Under Siege," *Lear's*)

Taken together, do these words and phrases have a positive or a negative connotation?   <u>positive</u>

Once you establish that, does the writer intend the word *narcotic* to have a positive or negative connotation? <u>positive</u>

Explain your thinking. How is she using the word here? <u>narcotics</u>

<u>soothe and make one feel tranquil; they relieve pain</u>

How Denotation and Connotation Work Together   When examining a passage for denotative and connotative words, look first at the major words: nouns, verbs, adjectives, and adverbs. Obviously, nouns are necessary to identify the thing or person or idea being talked about. The connotative words are apt to be verbs, adjectives, and adverbs. Read this passage from Sebastian Junger's best-selling nonfiction book, *The Perfect Storm.* Underline each word that is purely denotative and circle the connotative words. The first two sentences have been done for you.

> <u>Swordfish</u> are not (gentle) <u>animals</u>. They <u>swim</u> through schools of <u>fish</u> (slashing) (wildly) with their <u>swords</u>, trying to (eviscerate) as many as possible; then they (feast.) <u>Swordfish</u> have (attacked) <u>boats</u>, pulled <u>fishermen</u> to their deaths, (slashed) <u>fishermen</u> on deck. The scientific <u>name</u> for <u>swordfish</u> is <u>*Xiphias gladius*</u>; the first word means "sword" in Greek and the second word means "sword" in Latin. "The scientist who named it was evidently impressed by the fact that it had a sword," as one guidebook says.
>
> The <u>sword</u>, which is a bony extension of the upper jaw, is (deadly sharp) on the sides and can grow to a length of four to five feet. Backed up by five hundred pounds of (sleek,) (muscular) <u>fish</u>, the <u>weapon</u> can do quite a bit of <u>damage</u>. <u>Swordfish</u> have been known to (drive) their <u>swords</u> right through the hulls

of boats. Usually this doesn't happen unless the fish has been hooked or harpooned, but in the nineteenth century swordfish attacked a clipper ship for no apparent reason. The ship was so badly damaged that the owner applied to his insurer for compensation, and the whole affair wound up in court.

Sebastian Junger, The Perfect Storm

Studying just the first two sentences reveals a pleasing and effective balance between denotative and connotative words. The verbs "slashing," "eviscerate," and "feast"—taken together—suggest an incredibly strong fish ("not gentle," as the first sentence so eloquently states), and the rest of the passage bears this out.

Connotation in Fiction

In fiction, a writer may use descriptive details that are designed to evoke in the reader a particular emotional response to the characters. These details help you both visualize and assess the character. In this paragraph from *David Copperfield,* Charles Dickens introduces the reader to a character named Miss Murdstone. As you read it, underline the descriptive words associated with metal and with unpleasantness.

> It was Miss Murdstone who was arrived, and a gloomy-looking lady she was: dark, like her brother, whom she greatly resembled in face and voice, and with very heavy eyebrows, nearly meeting over her large nose, as if, being disabled by the wrongs of her sex from wearing whiskers, she had carried them to that account. She brought with her two uncompromising hard black boxes, with her initials on the lids in hard brass nails. When she paid the coachman she took her money out of a hard steel purse, and she kept the purse in a very jail of a bag which hung upon her arm by a heavy chain, and shut up like a bite. I had never, at that time, seen such a metallic lady altogether as Miss Murdstone was.

Charles Dickens, David Copperfield

Consider the words and phrases you underlined; then write a sentence explaining what these connotative words and phrases suggest about Miss Murdstone's character.   *She is an inflexible, unpleasant, and*

unapproachable woman.

To complete this discussion of connotation, let us examine the names of recent battles, which was the subject of many articles at the beginning of the war in Iraq. Just as the war was getting under way, the *San Jose Mercury News* published a list of names of several battles involving the U.S. military. Here is a small sampling. What is the connotative value of each name?

World War II:	Operation Overlord (the 1944 Normandy invasion)
The Korean War:	Operations Thunderbolt, Roundup, Killer, Audacious (all used to inspire troop morale)
Vietnam War:	Operation Rolling Thunder, Operation Flaming Dart (retaliatory strikes against the North Vietnamese)
The U.S. invasion of Grenada (1983):	Operation Urgent Fury
Gulf War:	Operation Desert Shield (initial deployment of troops to Kuwait to prevent Saddam Hussein from annexing that country)
Post–September 11:	Operation Infinite Justice (the name of the original war on terrorism), Operation Enduring Freedom (this term replaced Operation Infinite Justice)
The invasion of Iraq:	Operation Iraqi Freedom

(Quoted in "The Language of War: Battle Names Try to Convey Purpose, Power, Benevolence," March 23, 2003.)

◾ FIGURATIVE LANGUAGE

Next, we come to the most difficult, but perhaps the most inventive and interesting use of language. **Figurative language** or the use of a **figure of speech** refers to the use of language not in its literal sense, but in a metaphorical or imaginative way. Although you may associate figures of speech primarily with poetry, many prose writers also employ them to give immediacy or drama to their writing, to create a mental image, to establish a mood, or to clarify a difficult concept. Here is a summary of the kinds of figurative language we will take up in this section of the chapter:

- **Metaphors:** A direct and imaginative comparison
- **Similes:** An imaginative comparison using "like" or "as"
- **Personification:** A comparison in which something nonliving is described as if it were human

Metaphors and Similes

Metaphors and **similes** are closely enough related that we should treat them together. Both represent imaginative comparisons between two *essentially unlike* things. This point is important. The sentence "My house looks like your house" is not figurative; because houses are in the same class, there is no imaginative comparison. A good definition of metaphor can be found in the charming and poignant film *Il Postino (The Postman)*. The main character, a semiliterate postman, wants to write a love poem to the barmaid Beatrice, the object of his affections. He asks the great Chilean poet, Pablo Neruda, who lives in his town, how to go about writing such a thing. Neruda says that love poems must have lots of metaphors, which he defines as "a way of describing something by comparing it to something else."

A **metaphor** refers to a *direct* comparison, in which a particular quality or characteristic of one thing (the figurative) is transferred to another (the literal). Although literally, such transfer of meaning does not make sense, the reader knows to interpret it as imaginative. For example, consider this sentence:

> The farmer's leathery, lined face revealed years of toil in the sun.

The writer is directly comparing the farmer's skin to leather (in other words, transferring directly the characteristics of leather to skin), suggesting that the man's skin is browned, thick, and tough.

A **simile,** in contrast, is an imaginative comparison stated *indirectly,* usually with the words "like," "as," "as though," "as if," and occasionally "seem." In the above example, a change in the wording would result in a simile:

> The farmer's lined face looked like leather, revealing years of toil in the sun.

Therefore, metaphors are considered stronger than similes, if only because the two things—literal and metaphorical—are joined without the reader's being *told* that they are similar. Let us examine a few figures of speech in detail before you analyze some on your own. Because they are easier to identify, we will begin with similes. In the first, from the novel *The Kitchen God's Wife* by Amy Tan, the narrator is describing her mother's house:

> The front of her place is Day-Glo pink, the unfortunate result of her being talked into a special deal by a longtime customer, a painting contractor. And because the outside is bumpy stucco, the whole effect looks like Pepto-Bismol poured over cottage cheese.

To analyze any figure of speech, you first must know what is being compared to what. In this case, the garish pink color of the narrator's house is being compared to the color of Pepto-Bismol, and the bumpy surface texture of the exterior stucco is compared to the texture of cottage cheese. This amusing simile presents a striking visual image.

Here is another from John Berendt's novel, *Midnight in the Garden of Good and Evil,* describing the main character, Jim:

> He was tall, about fifty, with darkly handsome, almost sinister features: a neatly trimmed mustache, hair turning silver at the temples, and eyes so black they were like the tinted windows of a sleek limousine—he could see out, but you couldn't see in.

The word "sinister" at the beginning of the passage is reinforced by the simile, comparing his black eyes to a limousine's tinted windows. The simile also suggests a certain coldness, a deliberate attempt to separate himself from other people, which is precisely why celebrities travel in limousines with tinted glass. In this case, Berendt uses the familiar to explain the unfamiliar.

Now let us examine a metaphor with the literal and figurative elements underlined. The selection below is from Gabriel García Marquez's novel *Love in the Time of Cholera:*

> The death of his mother left Florentino Ariza condemned once again to his maniacal pursuits: the office, his meetings in strict rotation with his regular mistresses, the domino games at the Commercial Club, the same books of love, the Sunday visits to the cemetery. It was the <u>rust</u> of <u>routine</u>, which he had despised and feared so much, but which had protected him from an awareness of age.

We see first the catalog of Ariza's humdrum weekly activities; then García Marquez ingeniously compares his routine to "rust." The pairing is brilliant. Rust or corrosion usually results from disuse or neglect, but in this case, it results in Ariza's rusting away; he does the same thing week after week, and his life has become corroded by routine, just as disuse eventually rusts metal.

Uses of Metaphors and Similes

Metaphors and similes have a wide range of uses. Study these purposes (in italics) and the accompanying examples (below):

- *To provide a visual image.*

  Consuelo was easy to distinguish even from a distance, her long red hair like a whip of fire against the eternal green of that landscape. (Isabel Allende, *Eva Luna*)

- *To establish a mood or situation.*

  Like a frog at the bottom of a well, she had seen nothing beyond the circle of blue sky that meant freedom. (Ruthanne Lum McCunn, *A Thousand Pieces of Gold*)

- *To reinforce an observation.*

  Phoenix is among the five fastest-growing metropolises in the country, and few places are as relentlessly suburban in character.

It has a downtown so exiguous that a pedestrian outside its biggest office building at 9 on a weekday morning is a phenomenon as singular as a cow in Times Square. (Jerry Adler, "Paved Paradise," *Newsweek*)

- *To clarify a difficult scientific concept.*

  Astronomers have followed the motion of stars circling a hugely massive black hole at the center of the Milky Way, shedding new light on one of our galaxy's greatest mysteries. For decades, astronomers have theorized that a black hole must lie at the center of the galaxy like some dark and deadly spider, its gravity so enormous that it sucks all nearby gas and stars into it until they disappear with a final flash of energy. (David Perlman, "New Clues to What Lies at Center of Earth's Galaxy," *San Francisco Chronicle*)

- *To persuade or convince.*

  We have waited for more than 340 years for our constitutional and God-given rights. The nations of Asia and Africa are moving with jetlike speed toward gaining political independence, but we still creep at horse-and-buggy pace toward gaining a cup of coffee at a lunch counter. (Martin Luther King, Jr., "Letter from Birmingham Jail," 1963)

Not all figures of speech can be classified in these ways, nor should you worry about which of the foregoing classes a metaphor or simile belongs to. Some figures of speech are simply inventive and thoughtful, as is this example from Jason Elliott's nonfiction book about Afghanistan. (Kabul is the capital of that country.)

Kabul is a mountain-ringed history book written in the faces of its people. Walking through the streets of the city you read the traces of the millennia in the features of its men and women and remember you have entered an unrivalled meeting-place of bloods. (Jason Elliott, *An Unexpected Light: Travels in Afghanistan*)

Playful Aspects of Figurative Language

Not all figures of speech are used in service of such serious purposes. Some writers simply like to play with language, relishing the chance to show off or to dazzle the reader with ingenious comparisons. One writer who often indulges in daring, even bizarre figures of speech is T. C. Boyle. (His short story "Chicxulub" is included in Part 7.) In a story titled "Beat," Boyle tells of a teenager who embarks on a fictional journey to meet Jack Kerouac, writer of the 1960s cult novel *On the Road*. The narrator runs away from his home in California and travels to New York, locates Kerouac's house, and finally musters enough courage to knock on the front door. Here is his description of the woman, supposedly Kerouac's mother, who answers the door.

> My first surprise was in store. It wasn't Jack who answered the door but a big blocky old lady with a face like the bottom of a hiking boot. She was wearing a dress the size of something you'd drape over a car to keep the dust off it. . . . She gave me the kind of look that could peel the tread off a recapped tire.

Taken together, what impression of Kerouac's fictional mother do these figures of speech suggest? <u>She is huge, unattractive, and unpleasant.</u>

Personification

The last figure of speech we will consider in this chapter is **personification,** in which something inanimate or nonhuman—for example, objects, animals, plants, or concepts—is given human attributes or feelings. Here are a few examples:

> I must say a word about fear. It is life's only true opponent. Only fear can defeat life. It is a clever, treacherous adversary, how well I know. It has no decency, respects no law or convention, shows no mercy. It goes for your weakest spot, which it finds with unerring ease. (Yann Martel, *The Life of Pi*)

Personification here gives fear the human qualities associated with a fierce opponent or adversary.

> Fairhaven is a smaller version of New Bedford, which sits half a mile away across the Acushnet River. Both cities are tough, bankrupt little places that never managed to diversify during the century-long decline of the New England fishing industry. If Gloucester is the delinquent kid who's had a few scrapes with the law, New Bedford is the truly mean older brother who's going to kill someone one day. (Sebastian Junger, *The Perfect Storm*)

What literal comparison is Junger making between Gloucester and New Bedford? <u>Gloucester is a tough and gritty town, but New Bedford is</u>

<u>significantly more dangerous.</u>

> Spc. David Johnson considers himself a patriotic man. But after a year in Iraq, the 47-year-old California National Guardsman finds he isn't looking forward to the nation's birthday this year. "Here it is Fourth of July, people are setting off fireworks, M-80s—I take a defensive position," the tall, fit San Jose native said. "Then I pick myself up and say, 'What am I doing?'" After a year of driving trucks across Iraq under fire, Johnson came home in May only to find that the war had come with him, hitchhiking in the darkened

recesses of his mind. (Quoted in Matthew B. Stannard, "War Vets Suffering Stress, Study Says," *San Francisco Chronicle,* July 1, 2004.)

What is the literal idea and how is it personified (to what is it compared) in this passage? The war in Iraq is compared to a hitchhiker.

Spc. Johnson has carried the horrors of the war home with him,

like a hitchhiker he can't get rid of.

Practice Exercise 3

Here are several short passages containing figurative language to analyze. Use a separate sheet of paper for your answers. First, decide whether the excerpt uses simile, metaphor, or personification. Then decide what the literal subject is and what it is metaphorically being compared to. Finally, briefly explain the meaning. Start with these relatively easy ones.

1. It was a big cemetery, windy and flat and anonymous. The stones were laid out in rows like tract homes. (Donna Tartt, *The Secret History*)
    Simile. In comparing the headstones to tract homes, the narrator emphasizes their uniform size, shape, and spacing.

2. America is a large, friendly dog in a very small room. Every time it wags its tail, it knocks over a chair. (Arnold Toynbee)
    Metaphor. America is compared to a large, friendly dog. The nation is clumsy in foreign affairs but also displays good humor and desire to be liked.

3. We set our backpacks on the ground and stood there saying nothing, trying to get our bearings. Below us a slender ribbon of silver river wound its way through the valley, both banks covered with dense green forest. (Haruki Murakami, *The Wild Sheep Chase*)
    Metaphor. The visual figure "ribbon" refers to the river; it complements and extends the adjective "slender" and emphasizes its narrowness.

4. [In this excerpt, the narrator's wife is in labor and is about to deliver her child.]
    With the other hand she clasped his, squeezing tighter as the contraction gained in intensity, in this way communicating its progress. She was prepared, she was controlling her breathing, making steady, rhythmic exhalations that accelerated into shallow panting as she approach the peak. She was off on this second journey alone, all he could do was run along the shore and call encouragement. (Ian McEwan, *The Child in Time*)
    Metaphor. As every woman who has ever been in labor knows, it is a solitary journey. Her husband's role was simply to encourage her, but she would have to do the hard work all by herself.

5. Thinking such worrying thoughts of poor huntsmanship and its con-
    sequences, Ada made troubled progress up the slope. . . . She set
    each foot down slowly, letting the snow muffle her steps, and she was
    glad she wore britches, for trying to be stealthy in long skirts and their
    underlying petticoats would be impossible, like walking through the
    woods flapping a bed quilt around. (Charles Frazier, *Cold Mountain*)
    Simile. *Walking in long skirts in the snow would be awkward and
    clumsy, like trying to walk while wearing a bedspread.*

6. Regret grew only more insistent. She didn't just wait on his stoop any
    longer, she began to rap her icy knuckles against the door. (Andrew
    Dubus III, *The House of Sand and Fog*)
    Personification. *Regret is compared to an insistent and cold woman.*

7. In the mornings, before it was too hot, Ultima and I walked in the hills
    of the llano, gathering the wild herbs and roots for her medicines. We
    roamed the entire countryside and up and down the river. I carried a
    small shovel with which to dig, and she carried a gunny sack in which
    to gather our magic harvest. "¡Ay!" she would cry when she spotted a
    plant or root she needed, "what luck we are in today to find la yerbo
    del manso!" Then she would lead me to the plant her owl-eyes had
    found. (Rudolfo A. Anaya, *Bless Me, Ultima*)
    Metaphor. *Ultima's eyes are compared to those of an owl, a bird
    known for its keen ability to spot prey from afar.*

The next group is slightly more difficult. Some passages may contain more
than one figure of speech.

8. It seems that Father had learned some painful lessons about prejudice
    while searching for an apartment in Paterson [New Jersey]. Not until
    years later did I hear how much resistance he had encountered with
    landlords who were panicking at the influx in Latinos into a neighbor-
    hood that had been Jewish for a couple of generations. But it was the
    American phenomenon of ethnic turnover that was changing the
    urban core of Paterson, and the human flood could not be held back
    with an accusing finger. (Judith Ortiz Cofer, *Silent Dancing*)
    Metaphor. *The huge increase in the number of immigrants coming
    into Paterson is compared to a flood, suggesting an influx of
    people that can't be stopped.*

9. Up and up I and my horses and my dreams went, toward the angle of
    slope beneath the center of Roman Reef. Eventually a considerable
    sidehill of timber took the trail from sight, and before Pony and Bub-
    bles [his horses] and I entered the stand of trees. I whoaed us for a last
    gaze along all the mountains above and around. They were the sort of
    thing you would have if every cathedral in the world were lined up
    along the horizon. (Ivan Doig, *English Creek*)
    Metaphor. *The narrator compares the mountains he observes at
    the horizon to all the cathedrals of the world, emphasizing their
    great height and beauty and also their domination of the skyline.*

10. Parker's wife was sitting on the front porch floor, snapping beans. Parker was sitting on the step, some distance away, watching her sullenly. She was plain, plain. The skin on her face was thin and drawn as tight as the skin on an onion and her eyes were grey and sharp like the points of two toothpicks. (Flannery O'Connor, "Parker's Back")
Similes. Her skin is compared to the skin on an onion, meaning that it looked tight. Her eyes are compared to the points of toothpicks—small, piercing, and cold.

11. And his marriage, too, what was that if not shattered glass? Jesus Christ, he loved her, but they were as opposite as two people could get and still be considered part of the same species. Lauren was into theater and books and films Sean couldn't understand whether they had subtitles or not. She was chatty and emotional and loved to string words together in dizzying tiers that climbed and climbed toward some tower of language that lost Sean somewhere on the third floor. (Dennis Lehane, *Mystic River*)
Metaphors. First, Sean and Lauren's marriage is not just broken; it's shattered, like little pieces of broken glass that can't be put back together. Lauren's command of language is compared to a high tower; her articulateness goes way beyond Sean's comprehension.

12. An old lady with a kerchief was hanging clothes on a rooftop now that the rain had ceased. Old men with flat caps gathered in an alleyway to play *boules*. Amid such homespun normalities I felt vicariously part of the city. Seeing a city out of season is like finding a woman at home in her bathrobe without makeup: there is a feeling both of intimacy and letdown in which you may learn something vital. (Robert Kaplan, *Mediterranean Winter*)
Simile. Kaplan tells us what this figure of speech means. In comparing a new city to a woman who shows her true self—not dressing or making herself up for the outside world—one feels at home in the city and yet ready to learn something beyond the façade.

13. [The writer is describing the weather in Wyoming.]
Spring weather is capricious and mean. It snows, then blisters into heat. There have been tornadoes. They lay their elephant trunks out in the sage until they find houses, then slurp everything up and leave. (Gretel Ehrlich, "The Solace of Open Spaces")
Metaphor. The tornado funnel cloud is compared to the elephants' trunks. Funnel clouds and elephants' trunks are the same shape and the same color of gray. Both suck everything up before moving on.

14. The man who has not the habit of reading is imprisoned in his immediate world, in respect to time and place. His life falls into a set routine; he is limited to contact and conversation with a few friends and acquaintances, and he sees only what happens in his immediate neighborhood. From this prison there is no escape. (Lin Yu-T'ang, "The Art of Reading")

Metaphors. The man who doesn't read is compared to a prisoner who is further isolated by his inability to learn about anything outside his immediate world. Or, a life that doesn't include reading is compared to life in prison.

Finally, see how well you can do with these more difficult figures of speech.

15. Snaking diagonally across the top of Arizona, the Grand Canyon is a stupendous, 277-mile rent in the planet's hide that functions as a formidable natural barrier, effectively cutting off the northwestern corner from the rest of the state. This isolated wedge of backcountry—almost as big as New Jersey, yet traversed by a single paved highway—is known as the Arizona Strip, and it has one of the lowest population densities in the forty-eight conterminous states. (Jon Krakauer, *Under the Banner of Heaven*)
Metaphors. The Grand Canyon is compared to a tear ("rent") in the earth's surface (its "hide"). The shape of the canyon is like a wedge.

16. Wyoming had been dry as a quart of sand for three years and Elk Tooth was in the heart of the drought disaster zone. Those ranchers who had held on to their herds hoping for rain were caught like mice. As the summer drew to its stove-lid end, the most precious commodity to those in the cow business was hay, and the prices demanded for it matched the prices for rubies. (Annie Proulx, "The Trickle-Down Effect," *The New Yorker*)
Metaphors. Sand is dry and contains no moisture; hence the comparison with Wyoming's drought to sand. The farmers who hadn't sold their cattle are compared to mice caught in a mousetrap, implying that they were ruined financially. The summer's oppressive heat is compared to the lid on an old-fashioned stove, which covers the burning wood inside. Finally, the price of hay was so high that she compares it to the price of precious jewels.

17. [The narrator is describing an early-morning reaction to her lover.]
And then, abruptly, she woke up beside him in her own bed one early spring morning and knew she loathed him and couldn't wait to get him out of the house. She felt guilty, but guilty in the way one feels guilty when about to discommode some clinging slug that has managed to attach itself to one's arm or leg. (Gail Godwin, "Amanuensis," *Mr. Bedford and the Muses*)
Simile. In the phrase, "guilty in the way one feels guilty," "in the way" replaces the more usual "as" or "as though" usually associated with similes. The narrator's feelings of repugnance and guilt are compared to the way someone might feel about getting rid of a disgusting slug that she finds on her leg. In other words, the guilt she feels is minimal.

18. . . . a new business in town, the Something for Nothing Floating Casino Corporation, ran an announcement that the boat was hiring for

"certain positions." . . . Wayne sat in the glass guardhouse at the edge of the parking lot sniffing the dye in his new gray uniform. Down the bank in the Mississippi River, the *Something for Nothing* floated in the greasy current looking like a wedding cake decorated by a lunatic. The roofline of every deck was crowded with blowtorch-made, serpentine gingerbread, a turquoise-and-lavender pattern repeated on the boxy landing building and along the top of the parking-lot fence. (Tim Gautreaux, "Something for Nothing," *Harper's Magazine*)

Simile. The narrator compares the floating casino's architecture to a wedding cake designed by a lunatic, because of its odd colors and bizarre features. (Gingerbread is an architectural term meaning elaborate and often tasteless ornamentation, not a type of cake, and therefore in this sense is not figurative.)

19. The logic that pointed to the death of writing and reading was compelling. Each new medium was more visually and sensually rich than the last: movies gave way to talking movies, which gave way to round-the-clock talking color television. In that context, words just hung around looking glum, with hardly enough energy left to compose themselves into sentences. (Adam Gopnik, "The Return of the Word," *The New Yorker*)

    Personification. Gopnik facetiously refers to predictions of gloom about the death of reading and writing. Words are here compared to a glum person who has so little energy left in the face of all the competition from movies, videos, television, and the like that he can hardly do his job.

20. [This excerpt describes Marco, a character who has left home to live in a hippie commune.]

    There were times, hefting his pack, sticking out his thumb, waking in a strange bed or in some nameless place that was exactly like every other place, when it infected him with a dull ache, like a tooth starting to go bad, but mostly now his parents were compacted in his thoughts till they were little more than strangers. He'd skipped bail. There was a warrant out for his arrest, the puerile little brick of a misdemeanor compounded by interstate flight and the fugitive months and years till it had become a towering jurisdictional wall—with a charge of draft evasion cemented to the top of it. Home? This was his home now. (T. C. Boyle, *Drop City*)

    Simile. His alienation is compared to the first stages of a toothache. Metaphor. Having skipped bail, Marco has compounded his problems, so that his original misdemeanor offense is now compared to a huge wall that will be nearly impossible to surmount.

21. Martin Luther King, Jr., went to Birmingham, Alabama, in 1963, to organize a black boycott of white businesses. In so doing, King, the president of the Southern Christian Leadership Conference, had been accused of being an outsider coming in to cause trouble. Here is part of his defense.]

. . . I am cognizant of the interrelatedness of all communities and states. I cannot sit idly by in Atlanta and not be concerned about what happens in Birmingham. Injustice anywhere is a threat to justice everywhere. We are caught in an inescapable network of mutuality, tied in a single garment of destiny. (Martin Luther King, Jr., "Letter from Birmingham Jail")

Metaphor. "Destiny," referring to the future relations of blacks and whites, is compared to a single garment composed of individual threads woven together to form a single item of clothing; he means that blacks and whites must work together for the common good.

22. As a final challenge, try to unravel the meaning of this linguistic puzzle, a poem titled "Metaphors" by Sylvia Plath.[1]

I'm a riddle in nine syllables.

An elephant, a ponderous house,

A melon strolling on two tendrils.

O red fruit, ivory, fine timbers!

This loaf's big with its yeasty rising.

Money's new-minted in this fat purse.

I'm a means, a stage, a cow in calf.

I've eaten a bag of green apples,

Boarded the train there's no getting off.

www. mhhe. com/ spears

For further exercises in analyzing figures of speech, click on Chapter 6.

▨ LANGUAGE MISUSED AND ABUSED

From one edition of this book to the next, deceptive and manipulative uses of the language have proliferated and become even more entrenched. For easier reference, I have alphabetized the misuses and abuses in this section. The examples here come from writers, politicians, the new breed of political advisors called "spin doctors," advertising copywriters, and others. Most writers, at least those who write for mainstream, legitimate publications, are ethical and honest. They adhere to

[1]Answer: pregnancy

the rules of good journalism, strive for integrity in their reporting, and resist the temptation to inject personal bias. But not all writers are so honest, and advertising and politicking have become so cutthroat that manipulative and deceptive language is commonly condoned or ignored. It's like elevator music: It's there, but we no longer hear how awful—and how unlike good music—it is.

Some writers are sloppy or lazy and use imprecise, ambiguous, or clichéd language. Others—particularly (and unfortunately)—government officials try to put the best "spin" on their proposals or on world events or to soften the impact of an idea that might otherwise be more realistically or harshly interpreted. An unscrupulous writer may use language to exploit the reader, to incite or inflame passions. As a critical reader, you should be particularly alert to language that seeks to influence you by the clever misuse of words. In this section, we will examine several types of misused language, including:

- **Clichés:** Tired, overused expressions.
- **Code words:** Secret words or phrases that mean something special to insiders but something different to outsiders.
- **Doublespeak:** Language used to twist, to deceive, or to misrepresent the truth.
- **Euphemisms:** Inoffensive language used as a substitute for possibly offensive terms.
- **Jargon:** Specialized language used by a particular group.
- **Politically correct language:** Language that attempts to avoid insensitivity related to diversity, historical injustices, racism, and the like.
- **Sneer words:** Words with strong negative, derogatory connotations.

Do not worry if some of these terms appear to overlap because, in fact, they occasionally may. As with becoming aware of the connotative values of words, experience and wide reading will help you develop increased sensitivity to words and to see through linguistic sleaze and sludge when you encounter it. What follow are many examples of language abuses so that you can learn to identify them readily.

Clichés

Clichés—tired, overused expressions—tell the careful reader that a lazy writer is at work. Good writers avoid clichés because these fossilized expressions long ago lost their effectiveness; many no longer make sense: for example, "That speech is like grist to the mill," "Let's get down to brass tacks," or "to fight someone tooth and nail." Some clichés probably sounded clever the first time, but now, at the beginning of the twenty-first century, many sound quaint or ridiculous. In the first box are some standard clichés. See how many you recognize as clichés. (Note, of course, that if you have never heard a phrase labeled as clichéd, it is hard to identify it as such!)

> ### Common Clichés
>
> | | |
> |---|---|
> | as fresh as a daisy | as rich as Croesus |
> | to come to a grinding halt | to be up in arms |
> | as smart as a whip (referring to intelligence) | as cool as a cucumber |
> | | to leave no stone unturned |
> | a labor of love | a chip off the old block |
> | as clear as mud | a peaches-and-cream complexion |
> | to be slower than molasses in January | |

Merle Rubin, a book reviewer, makes the following observation about clichés:

> There are certain words and phrases that creep into our daily lives, taking over our patterns of speech until it seems as if they are almost indispensable. They are often trite and misleading, and yet they will not go away. Indeed, they seem to grow stronger with repetition, making everyday conversation a special kind of ordeal. (Quoted in "A Nightmare of Cliché," *The Wall Street Journal,* June 8, 2001.)

She cites these as examples: "closure," "getting on with my life," "I'll always be there for you," "support," "judgmental," "issues," and "deal with it." Here are some others that I have compiled over the past few months. For fun, you might begin your own list of clichés to add to this one:

> ### Contemporary Clichés
>
> | | |
> |---|---|
> | to think outside the box | to wake up and smell the coffee |
> | at the end of the day | to be (or not to be) a happy camper |
> | it's not rocket science | |
> | plain vanilla (describing computers or other equipment) | been there, done that |
> | | to give someone a heads up |
> | to play telephone tag | all the bells and whistles |
> | to tweak | to get one's ducks in a row |
> | a go-to guy | it's a no-brainer |
> | | to push the envelope |

Code Words

Like club members who share secret handshakes or passwords, **code words** are secret words or phrases that mean one thing to those in the know—to insiders—and something different to those on the outside. The term "inner city," which to the uninitiated might sound like the downtown area of a metropolis, is usually regarded as a code phrase for minority neighborhoods. Similarly the term "gated community" is considered a code word for a wealthy white enclave. "Prolife" is a code word to describe an abortion opponent without using the word "abortion."

Doublespeak

The term **doublespeak** combines the words *doublethink* and *newspeak,* coined by George Orwell in his novel *1984.* In the novel, he describes a future in which the government twists words to manipulate its citizens' thoughts. In that novel, the totalitarian government indoctrinated its citizens with these three slogans: "War is peace, ignorance is strength, slavery is freedom." William D. Lutz, a member of Rutgers University's English department, for many years edited the *Quarterly Review of Doublespeak,* a periodical dedicated to publishing especially egregious examples of doublespeak. He has compared doublespeak to "an infection that sickens the language through the pollution of words carefully chosen." In the introduction to his recent book, *The New Doublespeak: Why No One Knows What Anyone's Saying Anymore,* Lutz writes:

> Doublespeak is language that pretends to communicate but really doesn't. It is language that makes the bad seem good, the negative appear positive, the unpleasant appear attractive or at least tolerable. Doublespeak is language that avoids or shifts responsibility, language that is at variance with its real or purported meaning.

Doublespeak is further described as language that is "grossly deceptive, evasive, euphemistic, confusing or self-contradictory" with the potential for "pernicious social or political consequences." Doublespeak may or may not involve *euphemism* (see next section). Below are some examples to illustrate these deceptions.

Britain's Plain English Campaign annually bestows a "Foot in Mouth" prize for the most baffling statement by a public official. In 2003, Donald Rumsfeld, Secretary of Defense in the Bush administration, gave a press briefing on Iraq in which he said:

> Reports that say that something hasn't happened are always interesting to me, because as we know, there are known knowns, there are things we know we know. We also know there are known unknowns, that is to say we know there are some things we do not know. But there are also unknown unknowns—the ones we don't know we don't know. (Quoted in Sue Leeman, Associated Press, December 3, 2003.)

On another occasion, Rumsfeld was giving a press conference in Brussels. When asked by some European journalists for proof that Iraqi president Saddam Hussein had weapons of mass destruction, Rumsfeld replied: "The absence of evidence is not evidence of absence." (Quoted in Lewis H. Lapham, "Cause for Dissent," *Harper's Magazine,* April 2003.)

Another example of defensive arguments and clever language occurred in 2002 when President George W. Bush publicized a plan called the Healthy Forests Initiative; as Elizabeth Kolbert wrote, "in spite of its cheery, public-spirited name, represents an attempt to open up more national forestland to the timber industry." (Quoted in "Sound of a Tree Falling," *The New Yorker,* November 18, 2002.)

A variation of doublespeak is **waffling,** where, for example, a political candidate's views on current issues undergo constant shifts, making it difficult to see what he or she really stands for. On April 22, 2004, several news sources reported some fancy linguistic footwork on Senator John Kerry's part while he was campaigning for the presidency. In a conference call to reporters, Kerry urged Americans to buy fuel-efficient cars and declared his support for raising fuel economy standards to 36 miles per gallon by 2015, thereby reducing America's dependence on foreign oil. During the conference call, reporters asked whether he owned a Chevrolet Suburban. Kerry replied: "I don't own an SUV. The family has it. I don't have it." (Quoted on the Web site www.boston.com/news/politics/kerry/articles/2004.)

Here are some more recent examples of doublespeak from a variety of fields:

Military Doublespeak ("Pentagonese")

Civilian irregular defense soldiers	mercenaries paid for by the U.S. government during the Vietnam War
Force packages	bombs
Visit the site	bomb the site
Revisit the site	bomb the site again
Suppression of assets	bombing of both civilian and military targets during Operation Desert Storm
Ethnic cleansing	genocide as practiced by Serbians against ethnic Albanians in Kosovo
Collateral damage	civilians killed as a result of military actions. This term was used by NATO to refer to bombs that killed refugees and Serbian civilians during the 1999 war in Kosovo; Timothy McVeigh, convicted and executed for the Oklahoma City bombing of the federal building, used this term in reference to the 19 children killed among the 168 victims; the U.S. military used the term to refer to civilian deaths in Iraq.

Miscellaneous Examples of Doublespeak

Retrievable storage site	a nuclear fuel dump
Uncontrolled contact with the ground	a safety expert's term for an airplane crash
Runway incursion	the FAA's term for planes and airport vehicles that stray off course and cause a hazard or collision
Water landing	United Airlines term for a crash in the ocean
Therapeutic misadventure	the medical profession's term for a doctor's incompetence that results in a patient's death
Negative employee retention	corporate doublespeak for employee layoffs
Frame-supported tension structure	Defense Department term for a tent
Manually powered fastener-driving impact device	Defense Department term for a hammer

Euphemisms

A **euphemism** is an inoffensive word or phrase substituted for what might be a more offensive (or sometimes a more humdrum) one. Writers use euphemisms to soften our perception of unpleasant events, to change our beliefs, or perhaps even to cover up wrongdoing. Because euphemisms pervade our culture, you should learn to spot them readily and to recognize the intent behind them.

Here are a few examples. A trendy restaurant in Los Angeles refers to toast as "grilled peasant bread." The winner of the Miss America pageant no longer "reigns" (which sounds too royalist and elitist); now she does "a year of service." When Justin Timberlake either accidentally or purposefully ripped off part of Janet Jackson's costume during the 2004 Super Bowl halftime entertainment, exposing her right breast on national television, he later referred to the incident as a "wardrobe malfunction." When former president Bill Clinton was asked about his relationship with young White House intern Monica Lewinsky, he replied with these euphemisms: "I had an 'inappropriate encounter'" and "I met with her alone." Look at this Dilbert cartoon for a spoof on euphemisms used to describe real estate:

© by Scott Adams. Reprinted by permission of United Feature Syndicate, Inc.

While some may find these linguistic abuses more amusing than dangerous, what of the phrase, "regime change," which the Bush administration used to describe the invasion of Iraq and the military's overthrowing of Saddam Hussein? "Regime change" sounds nicer, more neutral, and certainly blander than a military invasion intended to topple a dictator.

As may be apparent, doublespeak may involve euphemism (though not all euphemisms involve doublespeak), and sometimes the line between them is hard to see. The difference is that doublespeak is *deliberately* and grossly deceptive, whereas the motives for using euphemisms are typically less nefarious. One's interpretation of such phrases perhaps depends on one's worldview (see Chapter 8, pp. 272–273). The American public routinely refers to the Korean and Vietnam Wars, even though Congress never actually declared war in either instance. Still, the U.S. military's insistence that these wars and invasions be termed "conflicts" or "operations" seems to bear out the observation that the line between doublespeak and euphemism is often blurry.

Jargon

Jargon refers to the specialized language members of a particular trade, group, or profession use. Like doublespeak and euphemisms, jargon can be used to deceive, but in this case, its purpose is more often to make the writer or speaker sound more intelligent or learned than if he or she used ordinary language. In and of itself, jargon is not necessarily harmful, at least not in the way the other kinds of misused language we have examined are. All specialists—whether they're plumbers, neurosurgeons, or college reading teachers—have their own special terminology that nonspecialists or the ordinary lay audience might not understand.

For example, stockbrokers often refer to the "dead-cat bounce," a phrase describing a trading session when the market makes a modest comeback after a day or two of serious price declines. (The phrase comes from the fact that even a dead cat bounces, though not very high.) Comic book artists use the term "ashcan" to refer to a few sample pages of the first version of a comic book—sort of like a partial prototype—because they often wind up in the trash. When ice skaters finish performing in the Olympics or other major competitions, they go to a section off the ice called the "kiss-and-cry," where they exchange hugs and kisses with the coach and await the judge's decision. The "cry" refers to the tears they shed if the judges scored them lower than they expected.

These are inoffensive—even colorful—uses of jargon that the reader might be able to figure out from the context, but even if he or she can't figure out its meaning, the intention is not to hoodwink. At its best, jargon is useful, providing a verbal shorthand between people who are fluent in the terminology and the subject. At its worst, however, jargon is pretentious, obscure, and impossible to read. What is one to make of this sentence?

> The artist's employment of a radical visual idiom serves to decontextualize both conventional modes of representation and the patriarchal contexts on

which such traditional hegemonic notions as representation, tradition, and even conventional contextualization have come to be seen as depending for their privileged status as aestheto-interpretative mechanisms. (Quoted in David Foster Wallace, "Tense Present: Democracy, English, and the Wars over Usage," *Harper's*, April 2001.)

Even the most skilled reader would have trouble translating this.

Like doublespeak, jargon can sometimes be employed to mislead. In 2000, the giant online bookseller Amazon.com announced a new strategy called "dynamic pricing." This term sounded positive, as if consumers could compare deals on merchandise with a mouse click. But what consumers didn't know was that Amazon intended to use the information about their buying habits and their geographical location (determined by their zip code) to charge *different prices to different customers* based on their likely financial status. Fortunately, the jargon was exposed for what it actually referred to and Amazon dropped the plan. (Quoted in David Streitfeld, "Amazon Flunks Its Pricing Test," *The Washington Post*, September 28, 2000.)

Politically Correct Language

During the 1980s, a movement called **political correctness** grew out of increased sensitivity to diversity in the country. Briefly, this movement was an attempt by liberals to purge the language of words and phrases that might be considered insensitive or racially charged or that called into question people's differences. Thus evolved a whole new vocabulary of **politically correct ("PC") language.** *The Official Politically Correct Dictionary and Handbook* suggests some semantic labels for dealing with race, gender, and people typically considered "disadvantaged." Here are a few examples. On the left is the conventional term; on the right is the new preferred PC term.

Members of minority groups	Use *people of color, emergent groups, traditionally underrepresented,* or *members of the world's majorities*
Chairman	Use *chairperson* or *chair*
Mankind	Use *humanity* or *humankind*
Handicapped	Use *physically challenged* or *differently abled*
Prostitute	Use *sex worker*
Old person	Use *mature person, senior,* or *chronologically gifted*

Despite the sometimes humorous substitutions that PC language has created, many attempts to replace insensitive terms have validity. For example, in Maine, the state legislature was pressured by Native Americans to purge the word "squaw" from place names in that state (Maine has a Squaw Pond, Squaw Bay, and Big and Little Squaw Townships). Donna

Loring, a representative of the Penobscot Nation addressed the legislature: "I can say with 99% certainty, if you are a native woman and live on a reservation, you have heard the word and felt the sting and pain." (Quoted in "Maine to Decide If 'Squaw' Is Offensive," *San Francisco Examiner,* March 5, 2000.)

Explain the parody of political correctness in this cartoon:

"As an animal lover, I find these images disturbing."

Sneer Words

As we learned in the section on euphemisms, a writer can shape our perception of events, making things seem less bad than they actually are. Similarly, a writer can intensify an already bad situation by using **sneer words,** words with strong negative connotations suggesting derision and scorn. Environmentalists often refer to farmers, ranchers, and corporate executives who are opposed to environmental protections as "toad stabbers"; environmentalists, in turn, are sometimes called "tree huggers" or "wolf worshipers" by their opponents. The sneer-word label, "card carrying" (as in "a card-carrying member of the ACLU" or a "card-carrying member of the John Birch Society") is meant to cast derision on members of those groups.

Here are some other examples of sneer words:

Neocon	Short for "neo-conservative," what liberals call the new conservatives
Appeasers	Liberals who opposed the U.S. invasion of Iraq
Agenda	Term used to describe the thinking of a group one dislikes (i.e., the gay-rights agenda, the Christian agenda, the liberal agenda, and so on)

Lackey	A servant; also a fawning, servile follower who serves as a master's yes-man
Flyover states	The states between the East and West coasts; the states one flies over when traveling between the two coasts, implying that these states don't have much influence on American culture
Girlie-men	A term used humorously by California governor Arnold Schwarzenegger to describe Democratic legislators who opposed his budget

---

Practice Exercise 4

Read the following passages. Then decide which type of misuse or abuse of language is being used—cliché, code words, doublespeak, euphemism, jargon, PC language, or sneer words.

1. When Maryland beat Stanford in the NCAA basketball tournament in March 2001, one television sportswriter noted that Stanford had suffered an "agonizing defeat." cliché

2. In 1998 President Clinton appeared before Kenneth Starr's committee and was asked questions about answers he had given earlier to the grand jury. That group had asked Clinton whether he had had sexual relations with Monica Lewinsky. Before Starr's committee, Clinton characterized his earlier answers as "legally accurate." doublespeak

3. Real-estate agents often use the following to describe property for sale: "cozy" to mean "very small"; a "fixer-upper" or "handyman's special" to mean a house in a horrendous state of disrepair; and "close to transportation" to mean right next to the train tracks. euphemism

4. When diplomats or union and management officials engage in sensitive negotiations, they often talk to the press afterwards. Often the representatives say that "the talks were productive." The diplomats or other officials know that this sentence really means that nothing happened. code words

5. The American Hair Loss Council prefers that toupees (men's hairpieces) now be called "hair systems." euphemism

6. Former secretary of state during the Nixon administration, Alexander Haig: "Because of the fluctuational predispositions of your position's productive capacity as juxtaposed to government standards, it would be momentarily injudicious to advocate an increment." doublespeak

7. In elementary schools today, multiple-choice answers on a test are called "selected responses," an essay test is called "extended constructed responses," the day's lesson in subtracting is called "modeling efficient subtraction strategies," and the detention room for misbehaving students is called either the "alternative instruction room" or the "reflection room." (Quoted in Joel Kotkin, "GOP Wiped Out in Land of Reagan," *The Wall Street Journal*, Nov. 6, 1998.) jargon and euphemism

8. A brochure for a cemetery advertises its services with this message: "It must be wise to protect yourself and your family AGAINST THE ONE EVENT THAT MOST CERTAINLY WILL HAPPEN. AND WHAT is the event? It is the same day—it is never a question of IF, only a question of WHEN . . . you will have a break in your family circle and as a result have to make hurried decisions for final arrangements, and we sincerely hope that the need is a remote one." (Brochure for Skylawn Memorial Park, San Mateo, California) _euphemisms_

9. Employees at Sea World in Orlando, Florida, are instructed to use a particular vocabulary, especially when answering park visitors' questions. Here are some examples: "enclosure" (not "cage"); "controlled environment" (not "captivity"); "natural environment" (not "wild"); and "acquired" (not "captured"). (Quoted in "Chickens of the Sea," *Harper's*.) _euphemisms or doublespeak_

10. An animal-rights organization called In Defense of Animals lobbied the Berkeley City Council to go on record as opposing the term "pet owner" because it suggests that an animal is "property." The new term approved by the council is "pet guardian." _politically correct_

   language

11. A television commercial shown in early 2004 sponsored by the Conservative Club for Growth attacked Vermont governor Howard Dean, who was then running in the Democratic presidential primaries with these words: "take his tax-hiking, government-expanding, latte-drinking, sushi-eating, Volvo-driving, *New York Times*-reading, body-piercing, Hollywood-loving, left-wing freak show back to Vermont, where it belongs." (Quoted in Thomas Frank, *What's the Matter with Kansas: How Conservatives Won the Heart of America*.) _sneer words_

12. At the First International Conference of Love and Attraction, delegates came up with the following definition for "love": "The cognitive-affective state characterized by intrusive and obsessive fantasizing concerning reciprocity of amorant feeling by the object of amorance."
   jargon

Finally, consider the Doonesbury cartoon by Garry Trudeau (May–June 2003), which appears on the next page. It parodies nearly all of the language abuses we have been discussing in this chapter. List the abuses parodied and give examples from the cartoon. _clichés ("as you leave today,"_

"Be assured that you have the tools," "Will there be challenges on the

way?"), jargon ("de-conflict the workspace"), and especially doublespeak

("high-value assets," "denied environments," "threat conditions,"

"blowback," "mission creep," "friendly fire," "shock and awe")

DOONESBURY. Copyright © 2003 by G. B. Trudeau. All rights reserved.
Reprinted with permission of Universal Press Syndicate.

■ CHAPTER EXERCISES

Selection 1   The writer, reminiscing about his days as a high-school student, is describing the role TV played in his household.

[1]To all of us, TV was something like a third parent. [2]We had grown up with it. [3]At my house, the first person up on any given morning flipped on the set, which stood dead-center in our upstairs-apartment living room, and the magic box hummed, hollered, sang, wept, flattered, and cajoled all day and well into the night, often with one or two or three or four of us there gazing, but often not. [4]Often the TV sounded and flashed away to an audience of no one in particular. [5]Did the cave dwellers extinguish their communal fire when they weren't actually warming their hands in front of it? [6]Then why should we flip off the box when we weren't actually watching?

Mark Edmundson, Teacher: The One Who Made the Difference

A. Content and Structure

Complete the following questions.

1. In describing the TV in Edmundson's household as being "something like a third parent," the writer means that it
   (a) took the place of his parents, who were seldom around.
   (b) had always been in his household, just as his parents had been.
   (c) was used as a convenient babysitter when they were too busy to look after their children.
   (d) taught him and his siblings values just as parents would.
2. Read sentences 5 and 6 again, which suggest that in Edmundson's household,
   (a) the TV functioned as the social center of the household, just as a communal fire did for cave dwellers.
   (b) it was too much effort to turn the TV off, just as communal cave dwellers did not extinguish their fire because they did not have the technology to recreate it easily.
   (c) the TV played a practical role for the family, just as the communal fire did.
   (d) the TV had more symbolic value than practical value, similar to the communal fire.
3. Which of these is an accurate statement based on the paragraph?
   (a) Only the children watched TV; the parents seldom did.
   (b) Every member of the family watched TV avidly whenever they were home.
   (c) The TV was the source of constant arguments within the family.
   (d) The TV was on all day and most of the night, whether anyone was watching or not.
4. The writer's attitude in sentences 5 and 6 might be described as slightly
   (a) adolescent, juvenile.
   (b) smart-alecky, cheeky.
   (c) informative, straightforward.
   (d) hostile, angry.

B. *Language Analysis*

Complete the following questions.

1. Look again at this portion of sentence 3: "the magic box hummed, hollered, sang, wept, flattered, and cajoled." This figure of speech is
   (a) a metaphor.
   (b) a simile.
   (c) personification.
2. If you are unsure of the meaning of the word "cajole," look it up. How would you characterize this word in the context?
   (a) It probably has a positive connotation.
   (b) It probably has a negative connotation.
   (c) It is purely denotative.
3. What do you think Edmundson is referring to specifically when he says that the TV "cajoled"? _____

Answers for Selection 1

A. *Content and Structure*

1. (b)   2. (a)   3. (d)   4. (b)

B. *Language Analysis*

1. (c)   2. (a)
3. He is probably referring to television advertisements, which coax people to buy things they might otherwise not want to buy; another possibility is the sort of lessons children's programs like *Sesame Street* include—for example, teaching children what the sign "danger" means.

Selection 2

The writer of this passage is Canadian.

[1]I liked the oddness of Winnipeg, its paradoxes, its nonchalant complexity. [2]I admired the extravagance of its history and the abundance of its rivers: the Red, the Assiniboine, the Seine, the La Salle and a dribble of creeks, one of which rises on the international airport. [3]I appreciated the city's refusal to disclose its character and secrets at first sight. [4]Though I wasn't sure about its motto—"Commerce, Prudence, Industry"—I was happy to find that a city with such a slogan could produce a ghoulish rock group called Bunnies From Hell.

[5]Winnipeg is the only inescapable place on the prairies. [6]Farther west, Calgary and Edmonton have boomed to a slightly larger population (above 600,000) and sprawl across an even greater space; yet somehow those cities are optional, not essential. [7]You can avoid one of them and still gain a sense of the character of Alberta or the psychology of the west. [8]But Winnipeg stands where the white west began, and for a long time it was the only metropolis between the Pacific and Lake Ontario. [9]It dominates its province, its political hinterland, more than any city on the continent. [10]Three-fifths of Manitoba's people live here; no other

city is even seven per cent as large. [11]The province, as a result, has an ungainly, unbalanced feel, as though its makers had joined the head of a moose to the body of a raccoon.

Mark Abley, *Beyond Forget: Rediscovering the Prairies*

A. Content and Structure

Complete the following questions.

1. A good title for this passage would be
    (a) "Canadian Cities."
    (b) "Winnipeg: A City on the Prairie."
    (c) "Winnipeg: An Unusual and Complex City."
    (d) "A Lesson in Canadian Geography."
2. Which of these statements accurately interprets sentence 3?
    (a) Winnipeg is a difficult city to get to know.
    (b) Winnipeg at first glance is an unappealing city that eventually grows on the visitor.
    (c) Winnipeg needs to be explored until it reveals its true character.
    (d) Winnipeg is not an especially welcoming city to those who don't know it well.
3. What specifically is Abley contrasting in the details provided in sentence 4?

    Although Winnipeg's slogan suggests a business-friendly, rather

    conservative city, there is still evidence of a counterculture.

4. The passage as a whole, but especially sentences 5 to 9, describe Winnipeg's
    (a) odd appearance in comparison to other cities.
    (b) importance as a major metropolis, unlike Calgary and Edmonton.
    (c) position as the biggest population center in all of Canada.
    (d) essential role in the Canadian economy.
5. What can we infer about Winnipeg from the passage?
    (a) It is the capital of Alberta.
    (b) It is the capital of Ontario.
    (c) It is the capital of Manitoba.
    (d) It is as large as Calgary and Edmondton.

B. Language Analysis

Complete the following questions.

1. In sentences 1 and 2, how would you characterize these words: "paradoxes," "nonchalant," "complexity," "extravagance," and "abundance"?
    (a) They have positive connotations.
    (b) They have negative connotations.
    (c) They are purely denotative.

2. The word "ghoulish" in sentence 4 typically means "gruesome" or "ghastly." What value does Abley intend it to have in this context—describing a rock band?
   (a) It has a positive connotation.
   (b) It has a negative connotation.
   (c) It is purely denotative.
3. What figure of speech is included in sentence 11?
   (a) a metaphor
   (b) a simile
   (c) personification
4. In this same figure of speech, what specifically is being compared to this strange creature?
   (a) the province that includes Winnipeg
   (b) the city of Winnipeg
   (c) the Canadian prairie
   (d) the white west

Selection 3

1   The noses of a great many Canadians resemble Porky Pig's. This comes from spending so much time pressing them against the longest undefended one-way mirror in the world. The Canadians looking through this mirror behave the way people on the hidden side of such mirrors usually do: They observe, analyze, ponder, snoop and wonder what all the activity on the other side means in decipherable human terms.

2   The Americans, bless their innocent little hearts, are rarely aware that they are even being watched, much less by the Canadians. They just go on doing body language, playing in the sandbox of the world, bashing one another on the head and planning how to blow things up, same as always. If they think about Canada at all, it's only when things get a bit snowy, or the water goes off, or the Canadians start fussing over some piddly detail, such as fish. Then they regard them as unpatriotic; for Americans don't really see Canadians as foreigners, not like the Mexicans, unless they do something weird like speak French or beat the New York Yankees at baseball. Really, think the Americans, the Canadians are just like us, or would be if they could.

3   Or we could switch metaphors and call the border the longest undefended backyard fence in the world. The Canadians are the folks in the neat little bungalow with the tidy little garden and the duck pond. The Americans are the other folks, the ones in the sprawly mansion with the bad-taste statues on the lawn. There's a perpetual party, or something, going on there—loud music, raucous laughter, smoke billowing from the barbecue. Beer bottles and Coke cans land among the peonies. The Canadians have their own beer bottles and barbecue smoke, but they tend to overlook it. Your own mess is always more forgivable than the mess someone else makes on your patio.

4   The Canadians can't exactly call the police—they suspect that the Americans are the police—and part of their distress, which seems permanent, comes from their uncertainty as to whether or not they've been invited. Sometimes they do drop by next door, and find it exciting but scary. Sometimes the Americans drop by their house and find it clean. This worries the Canadians. They worry a lot. Maybe that Americans want to buy up their duck pond, with all the money they seem to have, and turn it into a cesspool or a water-skiing emporium.

Margaret Atwood, "The View from the Backyard," *The Nation*

A. *Content and Structure*

Complete the following questions.

1. In your own words, write a sentence stating Atwood's main idea.

   Canadians and Americans distrust each other, but for different

   reasons.

2. When Atwood writes at the beginning of paragraph 2, in referring to Americans, "bless their innocent little hearts," she is being
   (a) honest.
   (b) scornful.
   (c) sarcastic.
   (d) religious.
   (e) admiring.

3. From what Atwood implies in paragraph 2, explain what Americans think about Canadians. Americans think that Canadians envy them—

   and that Canadians pay too much attention to environmental issues.

4. From the information in paragraph 4, why specifically do Canadians "worry a lot" about their southern neighbor? They are afraid the

   Americans will overrun them economically.

5. What are the broader implications of Atwood's passage? What is the central inference you can make about the relationship between Canada and the United States? Relations between the two countries are

   cordial but strained.

B. *Language Analysis*

Complete the following questions.

1. Read paragraph 1 again. Why do Canadians' noses resemble Porky Pig's?

<u>They spend so much time watching the activities on the other side</u>

<u>of the border by "pressing [their noses] against the . . . one-way</u>

<u>mirror" that their noses are flattened, like a pig's.</u>

2. What does Atwood mean when she refers to the border between Canada and the United States as a "one-way mirror"? What does this metaphor say about Canadians? <u>The Canadians watch the Americans</u>

<u>and wonder what the Americans are up to. Because the mirror is</u>

<u>one-way, Americans don't pay attention to the Canadians.</u>

3. How would you characterize the word "snoop" in the context it is used toward the end of paragraph 1? It suggests a
   (a) neutral, denotative meaning.
   (b) positive connotation.
   (c) (negative connotation.)
   (d) cliché.

4. Atwood says in paragraph 2 that Americans go on "playing in the sandbox of the world, bashing one another on the head and planning how to blow things up, same as always." What does the sandbox metaphor refer to? <u>America is a playground bully.</u>

   Explain what the metaphor means. <u>America bosses other countries</u>

   <u>around and meddles in their affairs.</u>

5. In paragraph 3, Atwood switches metaphors, comparing the border between Canada and the United States to "the longest undefended backyard fence in the world." In your own words, explain Atwood's thinking about how these neighboring nations get along. Specifically, try to determine what she means when she refers to the Canadians' "neat little bungalow," the Americans' "sprawly mansion," and the "perpetual party" with the "raucous laughter" and the beer bottles and Coke cans thrown in the peonies. <u>Canadians are neat and</u>

   <u>orderly; Americans are loud and brash. Americans pollute.</u>

6. In paragraph 4, what is the literal meaning of these sentences? "Sometimes they do drop by next door, and find it exciting but scary. Sometimes the Americans drop by their house and find it clean." <u>When</u>

   <u>Canadians visit the United States, they are enthralled by all that</u>

   <u>they see, but they are also skeptical and worry that the attrac-</u>

   <u>tions might find their way across the border. When Americans</u>

   <u>visit Canada, they are charmed by its beauty.</u>

PRACTICE ESSAY

"The Death of the Moth"

Virginia Woolf

Virginia Woolf (1882–1941) was one of the most important British writers of the twentieth century. Known for her unconventional lifestyle and experimental novelistic methods, Woolf remains widely read in American and British universities today. Her best-known novels are *Mrs. Dalloway* and *To the Lighthouse.* "The Death of a Moth" is one of Woolf's most famous essays; indeed, it is often reprinted in English anthologies as a model of descriptive non-fiction prose.

Preview Questions

1. How can a writer—using only words on a blank page—create images of life and of vitality? As you read this essay, note, in particular in the first half of the essay, how Woolf captures the very essence of life, not just in the moth's struggles to survive its entrapment against the window, but also in the images she describes outside of the window.

2. Some students and critics say that Woolf exhibits cruelty—or at least indifference to the moth's suffering—in her attempts to right the moth with a pencil. What do you think? What is your reaction?

1   Moths that fly by day are not properly to be called moths; they do not excite that pleasant sense of dark autumn nights and ivy-blossom which the commonest yellow-underwing asleep in the shadow of the curtain never fails to rouse in us. They are hybrid creatures, neither gay like butterflies nor sombre like their own species. Nevertheless the present specimen, with his narrow hay-coloured wings, fringed with a tassel of the same colour, seemed to be content with life. It was a pleasant morning, mid-September, mild, benignant, yet with a keener breath than that of the summer months. The plough[2] was already scoring the field opposite the window, and where the share[3] had been, the earth was pressed flat and gleamed with moisture. Such vigour came rolling in from the fields and the down[4] beyond that it was difficult to keep the eyes strictly

[2]British spelling for *plow.*
[3]Short for *plowshare,* or the cutting blade of a plow.
[4]A down, sometimes used in the plural as in paragraph 2, is a grassy expanse where cattle graze.

turned upon the book. The rooks[5] too were keeping one of their annual festivities; soaring round the tree tops until it looked as if a vast net with thousands of black knots in it had been cast up into the air; which, after a few moments sank slowly down upon the trees until every twig seemed to have a knot at the end of it. Then, suddenly, the net would be thrown into the air again in a wider circle this time, with the utmost clamour and vociferation, as though to be thrown into the air and settle slowly down upon the tree tops were a tremendously exciting experience.

2   The same energy which inspired the rooks, the ploughmen, the horses, and even, it seemed, the lean bare-backed downs, sent the moth fluttering from side to side of his square of the window-pane. One could not help watching him. One was, indeed, conscious of a queer feeling of pity for him. The possibilities of pleasure seemed that morning so enormous and so various that to have only a moth's part in life, and a day moth's at that, appeared a hard fate, and his zest in enjoying his meagre opportunities to the full, pathetic. He flew vigorously to one corner of his compartment, and, after waiting there a second, flew across to the other. What remained for him but to fly to a third corner and then to a fourth? That was all he could do, in spite of the size of the downs, the width of the sky, the far-off smoke of houses, and the romantic voice, now and then, of a steamer out at sea. What he could do he did. Watching him, it seemed as if a fibre, very thin but pure, of the enormous energy of the world had been thrust into his frail and diminutive body. As often as he crossed the pane, I could fancy that a thread of vital light became visible. He was little or nothing but life.

3   Yet, because he was so small, and so simple a form of the energy that was rolling in at the open window and driving its way through so many narrow and intricate corridors in my own brain and in those of other human beings, there was something marvellous as well as pathetic about him. It was as if someone had taken a tiny bead of pure life and decking it as lightly as possible with down and feathers, had set it dancing and zigzagging to show us the true nature of life. Thus displayed one could not get over the strangeness of it. One is apt to forget all about life, seeing it humped and bossed and garnished and cumbered so that it has to move with the greatest circumspection and dignity. Again, the thought of all that life might have been had he been born in any other shape caused one to view his simple activities with a kind of pity.

4   After a time, tired by his dancing apparently, he settled on the window ledge in the sun, and, the queer spectacle being at an end, I forgot about him. Then, looking up, my eye was caught by him. He was trying to resume his dancing, but seemed either so stiff or so awkward that he could only flutter to the bottom of the window-pane; and when he tried to fly across it he failed. Being intent on other matters I watched these

[5]Rooks are crows.

futile attempts for a time without thinking, unconsciously waiting for him to resume his flight, as one waits for a machine, that has stopped momentarily, to start again without considering the reason of its failure. After perhaps a seventh attempt he slipped from the wooden ledge and fell, fluttering his wings, on to his back on the window sill. The helplessness of his attitude roused me. It flashed upon me that he was in difficulties; he could no longer raise himself; his legs struggled vainly. But, as I stretched out a pencil, meaning to help him to right himself, it came over me that the failure and awkwardness were the approach of death. I laid the pencil down again.

5   The legs agitated themselves once more. I looked as if for the enemy against which he struggled. I looked out of doors. What had happened there? Presumably it was midday, and work in the fields had stopped. Stillness and quiet had replaced the previous animation. The birds had taken themselves off to feed in the brooks. The horses stood still. Yet the power was there all the same, massed outside indifferent, impersonal, not attending to anything in particular. Somehow it was opposed to the little hay-coloured moth. It was useless to try to do anything. One could only watch the extraordinary efforts made by those tiny legs against an oncoming doom which could, had it chosen, have submerged an entire city, not merely a city, but masses of human beings; nothing, I knew had any chance against death. Nevertheless after a pause of exhaustion the legs fluttered again. It was superb this last protest, and so frantic that he succeeded at last in righting himself. One's sympathies, of course, were all on the side of life. Also, when there was nobody to care or to know, this gigantic effort on the part of an insignificant little moth, against a power of such magnitude, to retain what no one else valued or desired to keep, moved one strangely. Again, somehow, one saw life, a pure bead. I lifted the pencil again, useless though I knew it to be. But even as I did so, the unmistakable tokens of death showed themselves. The body relaxed, and instantly grew stiff. The struggle was over. The insignificant little creature now knew death. As I looked at the dead moth, this minute wayside triumph of so great a force over so mean an antagonist filled me with wonder. Just as life had been strange a few minutes before, so death was now as strange. The moth having righted himself now lay most decently and uncomplainingly composed. O yes, he seemed to say, death is stronger than I am.

A. Comprehension

Choose the answer that best completes each statement. Do not refer to the selection while doing this exercise.

   1. The main idea of the essay is that, for Woolf,
      (a) the death of the moth illustrated the cruelty of nature.
      (b) rural life is the scene of daily tragedies and triumphs.

    (c) observing death up close makes the observer more accepting and reflective of this inevitability.

    (d) the little moth embodied life itself, but it could not overcome death's power.

2. The sentence, "It was as if someone had taken a tiny bead of pure life and decking it as lightly as possible with down and feathers, had set it dancing and zigzagging," shows

    (a) what moths look like and how they fly.

    (b) the strangeness of insect life.

    (c) the true nature of life.

    (d) how pathetic and insignificant the moth was.

3. Woolf views the little moth with pity because

    (a) his shape so limited his activities.

    (b) he would not survive the heat of the day.

    (c) his death would be unnoticed by everyone but her.

    (d) he would live for only one day.

4. In the moth's death, Woolf sees

    (a) an admirable yet futile struggle to survive death's superior force.

    (b) a foreshadowing of her own death.

    (c) a rebellion against and a refusal to accept death's inevitability.

    (d) a triumph over a force greater than life itself.

5. In observing the little moth, Woolf concludes that

    (a) life and death are inextricably linked.

    (b) death's triumph over the forces of life was both strange and moving.

    (c) all organisms have an innate desire to triumph over death.

    (d) its death shows the impersonality and indifference of the universe.

B. Vocabulary

For each italicized word from the selection, choose the best definition according to the context in which it appears. You may refer to the selection to answer the questions in this section and in all the remaining sections.

1. a pleasant morning, . . . *benignant* [paragraph 1]:

    (a) mild, gentle.

    (b) promising good fortune.

    (c) hot, humid.

    (d) inactive, lazy.

2. his zest in enjoying his *meagre* opportunities (British spelling of *meager*) [2]:

    (a) unusual, different.

    (b) limitless, abundant.

    (c) paltry, limited.

    (d) curious, strange.

3. to move with the greatest *circumspection* [3]:
   (a) care, watchfulness.
   (b) frenzy, frantic activity.
   (c) grace, elegance.
   (d) curiosity, inquisitiveness.
4. triumph . . . over so mean an *antagonist* [5]:
   (a) victor.
   (b) opponent.
   (c) instigator of trouble.
   (d) bearer of bad tidings.

C. *Language Analysis*

Complete the following questions.

1. Read paragraph 1 again. In her description of the ploughman, the rooks, and the horses, the dominant mood and atmosphere she establishes are
   (a) sleepy and languid.
   (b) full of life, energy, and vigor.
   (c) mournful, somber.
   (d) exciting, adventurous.
2. In paragraph 1, Woolf figuratively compares the rooks to <u>the knots in</u>
   <u>a black net that is thrown into the air, sinks down onto the trees,</u>
   <u>and is thrown into the air again.</u>
3. This figure of speech is meant to illustrate
   (a) the birds' movement and energy.
   (b) the great clamor the birds were making.
   (c) the birds' mating habits.
   (d) the birds' disruption by the ploughman and his horses.
4. Read paragraph 2 again, which emphasizes that, despite its insignificant size and simple activities, the moth
   (a) represented all the energy and life in the world.
   (b) longed to be more than merely insignificant.
   (c) reflected the same energy as the rooks and the horses.
   (d) had probably been injured somewhere before flying into the house.
5. What realization does Woolf come to when she considers trying to help the struggling moth with her pencil? <u>The moth's death is inevitable:</u>
   <u>human intervention is of no use.</u>
6. Consider this excerpt from paragraph 5: "One could only watch the extraordinary efforts made by those tiny legs against an oncoming doom which could, had it chosen, have submerged an entire city, not

merely a city, but masses of human beings. . . ." Explain what Woolf means in your own words.   _Although the moth was struggling_

valiantly, his efforts were no match for the power of death.

D. Questions for Discussion and Analysis

1. Explain in detail why Woolf feels such pity for the little moth.

2. Go through the essay and comment on the mood established in each paragraph. What devices contribute to it? How is it achieved?

IN THE BOOKSTORE AND AT THE MOVIES

Michael Cunningham's novel *The Hours,* loosely based on both Virginia Woolf's life and on the novel *Mrs. Dalloway,* is an imaginative and compelling book. The film, based on the novel and starring Nicole Kidman, Meryl Streep, and Julianne Moore, received much critical praise.

Tone, Point of View, and Allusions

CHAPTER OBJECTIVES

In Chapter 7 several elements you have studied thus far come together. In this second chapter dealing with the importance of language, you will enhance and deepen your understanding of what you read by studying some rather sophisticated elements, including:

- Point of view

- Tone

- Allusions

- Special effects

■ POINT OF VIEW

The phrase **point of view** refers to the writer's attitude toward or position on a subject—his or her **stance.** A writer's point of view—especially with regard to controversial matters—can be favorable, unfavorable, neutral, or ambivalent. This point of view leads to the other important elements in writing: mode of discourse (a subject you studied in Chapter 1, pp. 44–50); diction, or word choice (the subject of the preceding chapter); and **tone** (which we examine in this chapter).

Let us illustrate these connections with a paragraph about the Central Intelligence Agency. After the terrorist attacks of September 11, 2001, both the CIA and the FBI were criticized harshly by the 9/11 Commission for failing to take seriously the warnings about impending terrorist attacks. Although the article from which the paragraph is taken was written before the attacks, the writer presents several different accusations about the agency's failures. As you read it, pay attention to the circled words and phrases and be sure to look up any unfamiliar words.

> In an era when citizens are upset about (needless government agencies) the Central Intelligence Agency may stand out as the ultimate example of a (bureaucracy) whose lifespan has been (pointlessly prolonged.) Long after its original mission ceased to matter, a combination of (iniquity and inertia) has kept the CIA intact.
>
> Unlike other controversial government agencies that merely (squander) taxpayers' money, the Central Intelligence Agency is (a sinister enterprise,) with (a long criminal record.) Its sole rationale—engaging (in shadowy combat) with its equally nefarious communist counterparts—crumbled at about the same time the Berlin Wall did. Without a Cold War to wage, the CIA has become (a dinosaur desperate to avoid extinction.)

> Kevin J. Kelley, "R.I.P. for the CIA?" *Utne Reader*

Follow the arrows from element to element in the circle below to see how they all work together.

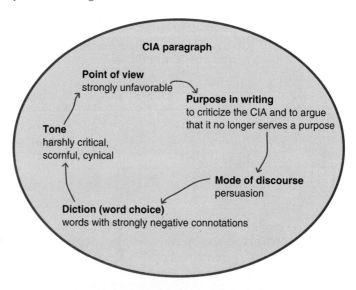

In summary, the writer's unfavorable **point of view** toward the CIA leads to his **purpose** in writing: to convince the reader that the agency has outlived its usefulness. Persuasion is the **mode of discourse** appropriate for both the point of view and the purpose, and Kelley's word choice—with the strong negative connotations—reflects all three elements. Taken together, these elements produce the harsh, scornful tone, and we come full circle—to point of view. As you practice with this chapter's exercises, analyze each reading in this way.

■ AN OVERVIEW OF TONE

Let us begin with a real-life workplace situation that nicely illustrates why ascertaining tone can be so tricky. These opening paragraphs are from an article titled "Misunderstandings @ the Office," written by Sarah Schafer, a staff writer for *The Washington Post.*

> The e-mail seemed so innocent. "Betty, hi," he remembers cheerfully typing to his colleague. "I haven't been successful reaching you by phone, so I'll try e-mail instead." And so Bill Lampton—then an employee of a large hospital—dashed off the rest of his note on some trivial office matter and hit the send button.
>
> Betty never got past the greeting.
>
> "I have no idea what you mean about my not returning phone calls," Lampton recalls Betty firing back. "To have you accuse me of ignoring your calls is unthinkable and inexcusable. . . . As to the purpose of the e-mail that you sent me, I prefer not to respond, as I dislike dealing with anyone who assumes the worst of me."

A few paragraphs later, Schafer writes:

> In a recent survey of 1,000 workers, Vault [vault.com, a New York workplace research firm] found that 51 percent of respondents said that the tone of their e-mails is often perceived—as angry, or too casual or abrupt, for example. One survey respondent said, "I wrote a question to [my boss] one day; she thought I was being insubordinate by the tone. I almost lost my job!"
>
> "Misunderstandings @ the Office,"
> *The Washington Post National Weekly Edition,* November 13, 2000

Schafer's observation brings up an important consideration: **Tone**—the feeling, mood, or emotional quality of a piece of writing—is hard to perceive on paper, or perhaps more accurately, it is easy to *mis*perceive. In conversation, a speaker's tone is readily apparent with gestures, tone of voice, vocal pitch (the voice's rise and fall), facial expression, and body language, in addition to the actual words spoken. However, when we read, visual and vocal cues are absent; all we have are the black words on the white page (or screen). Determining tone goes beyond a literal comprehension of the ideas. The reader must infer the tone from the writer's words and their connotative values, from the details included, from the rhythms and cadences of the sentence structure, and, of course, from the writer's point of view or attitude toward the subject. Identifying tone requires you to duplicate the "sound" of the sentences as the writer intended you to hear them. Richard Altick defines tone as "the total emotional and intellectual effect of a piece of writing." It's a complicated undertaking but one worth mastering.

As you will see, tone can run the gamut of human feelings or moods, reflecting the complex beings we humans are. The remainder of this chapter will illustrate a few of the infinite possibilities. The following box represents some of the more common and easy-to-recognize tones. (A second group of more difficult ones is taken up later.) Check an unabridged dictionary if you are unsure of any of these words' meanings. (Sometimes students have difficulty articulating the tone of a passage because they lack the vocabulary to express the emotion it embodies.) For ease of learning, they are grouped into clusters of similar tones showing gradations in meaning, so that the first one is typically mild; the second one, stronger; and so on. For example, in the second cluster below, "approving" is more neutral than its more positive cousin "admiring," while "laudatory" is even more strongly admiring.

Common Varieties of Tone

Informative, impartial, instructive
Approving, admiring, laudatory
Sincere, honest, candid
Serious, somber, grave
Philosophical, reflective, pensive
Eager, fervent, passionate, zealous
Questioning, skeptical, cynical
Amusing, funny, humorous
Sorrowful, mournful, lamenting
Nostalgic, wistful, melancholy
Critical, fault-finding, disparaging
Complaining, aggrieved, whining
Harsh, mean-spirited, nasty
Provocative, shrill, rabble-rousing, inflammatory
Sentimental, gushy, maudlin, mawkish

Space limitations make it impossible for us to examine each of these tones; for now it is sufficient just to know that they exist and that you will encounter them throughout your reading. Because complete objectivity, even in expository prose, is nearly impossible for a writer to achieve (even assuming it were desirable), the careful reader must be alert to the subtle nuances that contribute to a selection's tone. Finally, as you will see in some of the illustrative passages in this chapter, a passage may reflect conflicting or multiple tones, depending on the complexity of the material and of the writer's emotions regarding it.

Tone in Textbooks

The textbooks that you read in your academic courses typically reflect an objective and impartial tone. Reading academic discourse is different from reading newspapers, popular magazines, novels, or other leisure reading. Textbooks are not forums for controversy or for arousing emotions. The tone corresponds to the writer's purpose—to convey factual information—and academic discourse is typically characterized by an unemotional, straightforward, and objective tone. A glance at a chapter in any of your current textbooks and at the textbook passages in this text will confirm this observation. However, textbook material, particularly the material in the explanatory sidebars, may exhibit an identifiable tone. Economics texts are known for their rather dry tone, but in this passage, the author adopts a particular tone toward the subject—ticket scalping.

Some Market Transactions Get a Bad Name That Is Not Warranted.

Tickets to athletic and artistic events are sometimes resold at higher-than-original prices—a market transaction known by the term "scalping." For example, the original buyer may resell a $50 ticket to a college bowl game for $200, $250, or more. The media often denounce scalpers for "ripping off" buyers by charging "exorbitant" prices. Scalping and extortion are synonymous in some people's minds.

But is scalping really sinful? We must first recognize that such ticket resales are voluntary transactions. Both buyer and seller expect to gain from the exchange. Otherwise, it would not occur! The seller must value the $200 more than seeing the event, and the buyer must value seeing the event more than the $200. So there are no losers or victims here: both buyer and seller benefit from the transaction. The "scalping" market simply redistributes assets (game or concert tickets) from those who value them less to those who value them more.

Does scalping impose losses or injury on other parties, in particular the sponsors of the event? If the sponsors are injured, it is because they initially priced tickets below the equilibrium level. In so doing, they suffer an economic loss in the form of less revenue and profit than they might have otherwise received. But the loss is self-inflicted because of their pricing error.

That mistake is quite separate and distinct from the fact that some tickets are later resold at a higher price.

What about spectators? Does scalping deteriorate the enthusiasm of the audience? Usually not! People who have the greatest interest in the event will pay the scalper's high prices. Ticket scalping also benefits the teams and performing artists, because they will appear before more dedicated audiences—ones that are more likely to buy souvenir items or CDs.

So is ticket scalping undesirable? Not on economic grounds. Both seller and buyer of a "scalped" ticket benefit, and a more interested audience results. Event sponsors may sacrifice revenue and profits, but that stems from their own misjudgment of the equilibrium price.

Campbell R. McConnell and Stanley L. Brue,
"Ticket Scalping: A Bum Rap?" *Economics: Principles, Problems, and Policies*

Despite the negative connotation of the term *ticket scalping,* with its unfortunate reference to a barbaric form of killing or torturing, the authors' tone—at least in this excerpt—is clearly favorable and positive.

Tone in Fiction

In short stories and novels, a writer's tone depends largely on the characters and their relation to the environment they live in and to the other characters. Just to cite one example, in Jeffrey Eugenides' three-generational novel, the main character, or protagonist (Callie), is sent to a private girls' school in Grosse Point, Michigan, called the Baker & Inglis School for Girls. (Grosse Point is a wealthy suburb near Detroit, where many executives in the automobile industry live.) In this excerpt, Callie is describing a group of girls—a clique—whom she refers to as the Charm Bracelets.

The Charm Bracelets: they were the rulers of my new school. They'd been going to Baker & Inglis since kindergarten. Since pre-kindergarten! They lived near the water and had grown up, like all Grosse Pointers, pretending that our shallow lake was no lake at all but actually the ocean. The Atlantic Ocean. Yes, that was the secret wish of the Charm Bracelets and their parents, to be not Midwesterners but Easterners, to affect their dress and lock-jaw speech, to summer in Martha's Vineyard, to say "back East" instead of "out East," as though their time in Michigan represented only a brief sojourn away from home.

What can I say about my well-bred, small-nosed, trust-funded schoolmates? Descended from hardworking, thrifty industrialists (there were two girls in my class who had the same last names as American car makers), did they show aptitudes for math or science? Did they display mechanical ingenuity? Or a commitment to the Protestant work ethic? In a word: no. There is no evidence against genetic determinism more persuasive than the children of the rich. The Charm Bracelets didn't study. They never raised their hands in class. They sat in the back, slumping, and went home each day carrying the prop of a notebook. (But maybe the Charm Bracelets understood more about life than I did. From an early age they knew what little value the world placed in books, and so didn't waste their time with them. Whereas I, even now, persist in believing that these black marks on white paper bear the greatest significance, that if I keep writing I might be able to catch the rainbow of consciousness in a jar. The only trust fund I have is this story, and unlike a prudent Wasp, I'm dipping into principal, spending it all . . .)

Jeffrey Eugenides, Middlesex

Most readers can probably identify with Callie's feelings about the Charm Bracelets. All high schools have such groups, the "rulers" of the school. How would you characterize her tone in this passage? She is clearly scornful and resentful of their social standing, their shallowness, their arrogance, their refusal to study, the fact that they know that they don't need to study. Even at a young age, she is aware of her own role in life—her need to write, to accomplish something. So we might say that her tone toward the end of the passage is one of resignation to her fate. The tone is complex and not easily reduced to a single feeling.

Tone in Nonfiction Prose

The majority of the readings in this text are from nonfiction prose. In this section, we will start with two easy examples and work our way up to a more difficult one. The first excerpt is from a fine little book, *The Year 1000,* in which the authors recount a month-by-month appraisal of what life was like at the end of the first millennium.

Before leaving the month of February, let us spare a nod for Valentinus—the third-century priest who was martyred in Rome in the reign of the Emperor Claudius and whose feast day was celebrated on February 14, as it has been ever since. The details of St. Valentine's life are obscure, and ecclesiastical experts have been unable to discover any reason why he should have become the patron saint of lovers and romance. Historians note that mid-February was the occasion of the licentious Roman fertility festival of Lupercalia, when women sought cures for sterility, while folklorists trace the modern orgy of card-sending and candle-lit dinners back to the old country belief that birds commence coupling on February 14. Either or both of these explanations may be correct, and they would seem to illustrate the cleverness with which the early church appropriated heathen superstitions for its own purposes. But there is no Christian reason why St. Valentine should be the only saint in the calendar whose feast is celebrated with universal ardour today.

Robert Lacey and Danny Danziger, The Year 1000

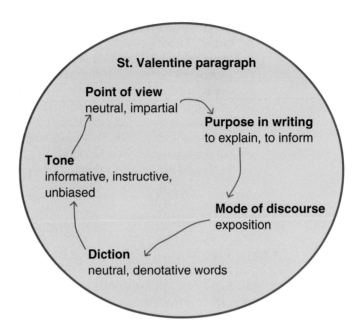

In the next example, Harvard biologist Edwin O. Wilson discusses indigenous people's contributions to the world's food supply. Circle the connotative words as you read it.

From the mostly unwritten archives of native peoples has come a wealth of information about wild and semicultivated crops. It is a remarkable fact that with a single exception, the macadamia nut of Australia, every one of the fruits and nuts used in western countries was grown first by indigenous peoples. The Incas were arguably the all-time champions in creating a reservoir of diverse crops. Without the benefit of wheels, money, iron, or written script, these Andean people evolved a sophisticated agriculture based on almost as many plant species as used by all the farmers of Europe and Asia combined. Their abounding crops, tilled on the cool upland slopes and plateaus, proved especially suited for temperate climates. From the Incas have come lima beans, peppers, potatoes, and tomatoes. But many other species and strains, including a hundred varieties of potatoes, are still confined to the Andes. The Spanish conquerors learned to use a few of the potatoes, but they missed many other representatives of a vast array of cultivated tuberous vegetables, including some that are more productive and savory than the favored crops. The names are likely to be unfamiliar: achira, ahipa, arracacha, maca, mashua, mauka, oca, ulloco, and yacon. One, maca, is on the verge of extinction, limited to 10 hectares in the highest plateau region of Peru and Bolivia. Its swollen roots, resembling brown radishes and rich in sugar and starch, have a sweet, tangy flavor and are considered a delicacy by the handful of people still privileged to consume them.

Edwin O. Wilson, The Diversity of Life

Now complete the following items:

Point of view: <u>favorable</u>

Purpose in writing: <u>to inform, to explain</u>

Mode of discourse: <u>exposition</u>

Diction: <u>some words with favorable connotations</u>

Tone: <u>informative; also admiring, laudatory</u>

Did you circle these positive connotative phrases—"a wealth of information," "a remarkable fact," "arguably the all-time champions," "a reservoir of diverse crops," "a sophisticated agriculture," "abounding crops," and "vast array of cultivated tuberous vegetables"? Besides word choice, the content Wilson offers—especially the impressive list of foods he provides—also suggests both an informative and admiring tone, since these foods were grown "[w]ithout the benefit of wheels, money, iron, or written script," inventions that seem like essential prerequisites for agriculture.

Abraham Lincoln's "Farewell at Springfield" was delivered to a vast audience of his fellow citizens on February 11, 1861, as he was leaving for Washington to assume the duties of president. Keep in mind as you read it that Lincoln's primary goal was to preserve the Union.

> My friends—No one not in my situation, can appreciate my feeling of sadness at this parting. To this place, and the kindness of these people, I owe everything. Here I have lived a quarter of a century, and have passed from a young to an old man. Here my children have been born, and one is buried. I now leave, not knowing when, or whether ever, I may return, with a task before me greater than that which rested upon Washington. Without assistance of that Divine Being, who ever attended him, I cannot succeed. With that assistance I cannot fail. Trusting in Him, who can go with me, and remain with you and be everywhere for good, let us confidently hope that all will yet be well. To His care commending you, as I hope in your prayers you will commend me, I bid you an affectionate farewell.

Apart from the obviously strong religious tone, Lincoln's tone can also be described as

1. nostalgic, almost melancholy and dejected.
2. eloquent, yet modest and unassuming.
3. sorrowful, mournful, lamenting.
4. irritable, complaining, aggrieved.

For a completely different type of writing, read these opening sentences from travel writer Paul Theroux's recent book on Africa. In this passage, he is describing Addis Ababa, the capital of Ethiopia.

> My first impression of Addis Ababa: handsome people in rags, possessed of both haughtiness and destitution, a race of aristocrats who had pawned the family silver. Ethiopia was unique in black Africa for having its own script, and therefore its own written history and a powerful sense of the past. Ethiopians are aware of their ancient cultural links with India and Egypt and the religious fountainhead of the Middle East, often claiming to be among the earliest Christians. When your barbarian ancestors were running around Europe bare-assed, with bellies painted in blue woad, elaborately clothed Ethiopians were breeding livestock and using the wheel and defending their civilization against the onslaught of Islam, while piously observing the Ten Commandments.
>
> Paul Theroux, *Dark Star Safari*

Before determining the tone in this passage, be sure you understand what Theroux is saying. Which of the following best states the main idea?

1. Although Western European cities are now more technologically advanced than a city like Addis Ababa, the city retains a strong sense of its own history and destiny.
2. Although Addis Ababa is now a proud but destitute city, Ethiopia had an illustrious past, and when Western Europe was still barbaric, Ethiopian culture was flourishing.
3. Ethiopia was Christian long before the countries of Western Europe were.

Did you choose Answer 2?

What does Theroux mean when he writes of the Ethiopians that they are "a race of aristocrats who . . . pawned the family silver"?

1. Ethiopia has always been financially dependent on other countries for aid.
2. Ethiopia was culturally rich at one time, though now the country has fallen on hard times.

3. Ethiopia was rich in precious metals, but they squandered their resources.

Again, did you mark Answer 2?

Now we can turn to the tone of the passage. In your own words, identify Theroux's tone, first toward Ethiopia and then toward European ancestors. <u>The tone in the first part is admiring (Ethiopians); the tone</u>

<u>in the second part is slightly mocking because many people of European</u>

<u>ancestry are convinced of their cultural superiority.</u>

A Special Case: Sentimentality

In the earlier list of tones at the beginning of the chapter, the final group is "sentimental, gushy, maudlin, mawkish." Each merits a little discussion. *Sentimentality* is an umbrella word describing a tone that appeals to one's tender emotions. My dictionary defines *gushy* as showing excessive displays of sentiment or enthusiasm. A maudlin tone is embarrassingly or tearfully sentimental, and mawkishness is even stronger—referring to sentimentality so overdone that it is objectionable, almost sickening.

Sentimentality can be genuine or fake, depending on the writer's motive and care in writing. And it can be both effective and affective. A writer may appeal to our tender and compassionate instincts and win us over. Many readers enjoy reading about those who have overcome serious obstacles, found true love, or conquered grave illnesses. Such stories ennoble us, give us hope, and inspire us to muddle through our daily lives and to cope with our fears and our shortcomings. The immense popularity of the *Chicken Soup for the Soul* books is a testimony to this observation.

What can go wrong with the sentimental point of view? If the writer deliberately plays to our heartstrings with counterfeit emotions and clichés, the effect is offensive or ludicrous. We see through the fakery. Richard D. Altick and Andrea A. Lunsford in their excellent textbook, *Preface to Critical Reading,* explain that writers may lapse into sentimentality because most of the important things in life—love, loss, the innocence of childhood, old age and death, for example—have already been written about, making it difficult to say anything new about them. Altick and Lunsford explain further that sentimentality is cliché-ridden; sentimental prose tries to elicit emotion from readers without giving readers a good reason for feeling it.

The writers then go on to illustrate the difference between sentimentality and a genuine emotional tone. The two examples they offer differ in point of view—the first comes from a social worker's case file; the second, from a local newspaper report following a fire that destroyed the home of the family the social worker discussed. Which report is sentimental? How can you tell?

The unfinished frame summer-kitchen addition to the dilapidated farmhouse Mrs. Denby occupies on the outskirts of Birchdale is a mute reminder of the ambition Mr. Denby had entertained to remodel the property and make it more habitable: an ambition interrupted last autumn by his fatal three-month illness. He left his family in sorry straits. There are five children, the youngest only fourteen months old. They must live on their Mother's Assistance Fund grant of $155 a month. Mrs. Denby's house is kept clean, but, with the exception of a shining new electric refrigerator in one corner of the kitchen, it is poorly furnished.

One of Mrs. Denby's elder sons was badly burnt in an accident some years ago and missed a year and a half of school. His sister, Elizabeth, is now living with Mr. Denby's relatives nearby, an arrangement which Mrs. Denby is willing to tolerate at least temporarily, although she has no truck with her numerous "in-laws."

Mr. Denby, the oldest of fifteen children, left school to go to work. He held various jobs, but not for long. He was a notoriously poor provider, Mrs. Denby says, but despite this shortcoming her life with him was serene.

Their son George is said by his teachers to be retarded in his school work. He has not had an intelligence test, but his native ability seems possibly lower than average. He will have some difficulty in keeping up with his age group.

Widow Sobs as Flames Destroy All

A 38-year-old widow, mother of five children, poked aimlessly through the fire-blackened ruins of her little home at Center Road and Delaney Street yesterday and wept bitter tears of utter hopelessness.

"What are we to do?" Mrs. Hannah S. Denby sobbed. "The fire took everything except the clothes on our backs. It even burned my pictures of my husband . . . and he died only six months ago."

And for Mrs. Denby, the loss of that picture seemed even harder to bear than the destruction of all but a few pieces of their furniture in the blaze which broke out Sunday afternoon shortly after the family had returned from church.

For her tow-headed five-year-old daughter, Beth, the fire had meant another heart-rending loss, for her only doll and her doll coach were consumed by the flames.

And for 17-year-old Frank, now the man of the family, for 11-year-old James and seven-year-old George, the fire meant the end of the happiness they had just started to recapture in family life since the death of their father.

Only 16-month-old Robert was unaware of the feeling of family tragedy. He cooed gaily in his mother's arms.

For the time being the widow and her children have found a home with her sister. "But she is very ill," Mrs. Denby said, "and it is hardly fair for us to stay there. I wish I knew what we could do, where we could turn. Perhaps the good Lord will find a way. . . ."

Richard D. Altick and Andrea L. Lunsford,
Preface to Critical Reading, 6th edition

Note the use of clichéd images (like the little girl's burned doll) and clichéd language ("bitter tears," "man of the family").

Practice Exercise 1

Here are some passages for you to practice with. As before, pay careful attention to word choice (especially to connotation) and to the sound of the prose. Underline key words and phrases. Determine how point of view, mode of discourse, and diction point to the writer's tone. Then decide which of the four choices best represents the writer's tone.

A.

I'm as sick of work as the next guy, but I'm still practical enough to recognize the need for it. Without work, where would all the new breed of millionaires that I read about in *Time* Magazine get their dry cleaning done? Who would fix their cars? Who would strip for them when they unload their trophy wives for the evening and go out for a night on the town? Us, the ununited workers of the world. I get the newspaper and dig through the classifieds.

It's the same old crap. "CAREER OPPORTUNITY!!!" screams an ad for a $6.25 an hour warehouse clerk. They mention that they drug test. Who are they kidding? They're discouraging their target market. Who but a crack head would want an opportunity like that? Opportunity, my ass. Why is it so difficult for the people who write these ads to present their jobs in a realistic and readable fashion? Why am I always looking at classifieds that say "FUN EXCITING PLACE TO WORK" and show up to see a bunch of desk jockeys a blink away from quitting, or suicide.

All the ads are like this. There's an ad that reads "NO MULTI-LEVEL MARKETING OR COLD CALLING SALES" for a company that, a friend of mine who applied there informs me, sticks you at a desk to do cold calling, only you're not supposed to actually sell anything to the people; you get the lead for the salesman. Therefore, they've made an end run around the phrase "no cold calling sales." How brilliant. How delighted are the people going to be when they show up, fill out an application, get hired, and find out that the company they've just joined has, instead of providing them with a job they might want, carefully worded its ad to get through a verbal loophole? Then the people quit after a day, a day they've wasted when they could have been looking for something worthwhile. Does this benefit the company? Perhaps. With this endless supply of new marketing companies, a lot of them have a workforce that is expected only to last until they figure out they've been duped. If the new-hires work at the phones one morning, that's fine for the marketers. The next morning they've got a new batch. And none of these people even show up to pick up their nineteen dollar paychecks, so they have a labor force every morning that's on the house.

Iain Levison, *A Working Stiff's Manifesto: A Memoir*

Levison's tone is

1. arrogant, egotistical.
2. (humorously scornful.)
3. serious, stern.
4. critical, fault-finding.

B.   The author is a chef and restaurant owner in New York City.

People who order their meat well-done perform a valuable service for those of us in the business who are cost-conscious: they pay for the privilege of eating our garbage. In many kitchens, there's a time-honored practice called "save for well-done." When one of the cooks finds a particularly unlovely piece of steak—tough, riddled with nerve and connective tissue, off the hip end of the loin, and maybe a little stinky from age—he'll dangle it in the air and say, "Hey, Chef, whaddya want me to do with *this?*" Now, the chef has three options. He can tell the cook to throw the offending item into the trash, but that means a total loss, and in the restaurant business every item of cut, fabricated, or prepared food should earn at least three times the amount it originally cost if the chef is to make his correct food-cost percentage. Or he can decide to serve that steak to "the family"—that is, the floor staff—though that, economically, is the same as throwing it out. But no. What he's going to do is repeat the mantra of cost-conscious chefs every-where: "Save for well-done." The way he figures it, the philistine who orders his food well-done is not likely to notice the difference between food and flotsam.

Anthony Bourdain, "Don't Eat before Reading This," *The New Yorker*

Bourdain's tone is

1. (honest, candid, frank.)
2. critical, fault-finding, disparaging.
3. philosophical, reflective.
4. approving, admiring, laudatory.

C.

Lost in the cities of America, the immigrant Jews succumbed to waves of nostalgia for the old world. "I am overcome with longing," wrote an early immigrant, "not only for my Jewish world, which I have lost, but also for Russia." Both the handful of intellectuals and the unlettered masses were now inclined to re-create the life of the old country in their imaginations, so that with time, distance and suffering, the past they had fled took on an attractive glow, coming to seem a way of rightness and order. Not that they forgot the pogroms, not that they forgot the poverty, but that they remembered with growing fondness the inner decorums of *shtetl* life. Desperation induced homesickness, and homesickness coursed through their days like a ribbon of sadness. In Russia "there is more poetry, more music, more feeling, even if our people do suffer appalling persecution. . . . One enjoys life in Russia better than here . . .

"There is too much materialism here, too much hurry and too much prose—and yes, too much machinery." Even in the work of so sophisticated a Yiddish poet as Moshe Leib Halpern, who began to write after the turn of the century, dissatisfaction with the new world becomes so obsessive that he "forgets that his place of birth was very far indeed from being a paradise." "On strange earth I wander as a stranger," wrote Halpern about America, "while strangeness stares at me from every eye."

Irving Howe, *World of Our Fathers*

Howe's tone is

1. angry, hostile, bitter.
2. honest, candid.
3. informative, instructive.
4. (nostalgic, melancholy.)

    D. This poem was published on a Web site devoted to Mother's Day poems.

Happiness is like a sunny day:
All one's bitterness is drowned in light.
Praise be the light, though it must pass away,
Perhaps because compassion needs the night.
Yet when one feels like swallowing barbed wire,
More or less does nothing for the pain.
Old memories return as if on fire,
Tormenting one with unforgiving shame.
How can I, who love you, come inside,
Each wound to bind up with an ointment rare,
Restoring the once effervescent bride
   'Neath misery no happiness can spare?
So shall I sing to you of all life's beauty,
Doing through the night my daytime duty.
A song of love may not bring back your noon,
Yet in your darkness, let me be your moon.

Nicholas Gordon, "Happiness Is Like a Sunny Day"[1]

---

[1] Available at www.members.aol.com/nickgo5/happi7.html, Mother's Day Poems by Nicholas Gordon.

The tone of the poem is

1. philosophical, reflective, pensive.
2. sincere, honest, candid.
3. (sentimental, maudlin.)
4. nostalgic, melancholy.

E.   Considered a rising star in the Democratic party, Barack Obama is an African-American civil rights lawyer and community organizer in Chicago. In 2004, he ran successfully for the U.S. Senate representing Illinois. In this passage, he discusses the difference between studying the history of the civil rights movement and the realities of community organizing.

At the time, about to graduate from college, I was operating mainly on impulse, like a salmon swimming blindly upstream toward the site of his own conception. In classes and seminars, I would dress up these impulses in the slogans and theories that I'd discovered in books, thinking—falsely—that the slogans meant something, that they somehow made what I felt more amenable to proof. But at night, lying in bed, I would let the slogans drift away, to be replaced with a series of images, romantic images, of a past I had never known.

They were of the civil rights movement, mostly, the grainy black-and-white footage that appears every February during Black History Month, the same images that my mother had offered me as a child. A pair of college students, hair short, backs straight, placing their orders at a lunch counter teetering on the edge of riot. SNCC workers standing on a porch in some Mississippi backwater trying to convince a family of sharecroppers to register to vote. A county jail bursting with children, their hands clasped together, singing freedom songs.

Such images became a form of prayer for me, bolstering my spirits, channeling my emotions in a way that words never could. They told me (although even this much understanding may have come later, is also a construct, containing its own falsehoods) that I wasn't alone in my particular struggles, and that communities had never been a given in this country, at least not for blacks. Communities had to be created, fought for, tended like gardens. They expanded or contracted with the dreams of men—and in the civil rights movement those dreams had been large. In the sit-ins, the marches, the jailhouse songs, I saw the African-American community becoming more than just the place where you'd been born or the house where you'd been raised. Through organizing, through shared sacrifice, membership had been earned. And because membership was earned—because this community I imagined was still in the making, built on the promise that the larger American community, black, white, and brown, could somehow redefine itself—I believed that it might, over time, admit the uniqueness of my own life.

Barack Obama, *Dreams from My Father: A Story of Race and Inheritance*

The tone of the passage is

1. (philosophical, fervent, inspiring.)
2. hesitant, confused, ambivalent.
3. sorrowful, mournful, lamenting.
4. nostalgic, wistful, melancholy.

■ TONE CONTINUED: MORE DIFFICULT VARIETIES

In this section, you will study a more difficult group of tones. Cultural, social, and political observers point to an increased cynicism in our culture, an increased skepticism about the American dream and about the country's role in the world political arena. The increasing polarization between political parties and economic classes, especially over issues like abortion, immigration, outsourcing of jobs, gay marriage, environmental protection, coupled with the terrorist attacks of September 11, 2001, the war on terrorism, and the U.S. invasion and occupation of Iraq—all of these considerations have led to increased uncertainty and skepticism. On both sides of the spectrum, there is less trust in our institutions, more pessimism, more stridency—and these attitudes are reflected in popular magazines and on our newspapers' editorial pages. Beyond these brief observations, there are other reasons that account for our new insecurities that are too complex to delve into here; suffice it to say, however, that you will frequently encounter these tones in your everyday reading:

> Witty, playful, droll
> Ironic, tongue-in-cheek
> Sarcastic, scornful, sardonic
> Pessimistic, cynical
> Mocking, satirical

In the following section, we will examine and illustrate them one by one.

Wit

A **witty** tone reveals the writer's mental keenness and sense of playfulness and an ability to recognize the comic elements of a situation or condition. Unlike sarcasm, with its obvious mean streak, wit succeeds because it is humorous, brief, clever in its use of words, and pointedly perceptive in describing human frailty and folly. Notice that some of these witticisms demonstrate a clever turn of phrase or a play on words.

- Mark Twain defined golf as a good walk ruined.
- Samuel Johnson, the eighteenth-century English man of letters, commented on a friend's rather hasty remarriage by saying: "A second marriage is the triumph of hope over experience."

- Mae West, a famous American actress of the 1930s and 1940s, a "blonde bombshell" type known for her risqué remarks: "I was as pure as the driven snow—but I drifted."
- From Zsa Zsa Gabor, a Hungarian-American actress known for her many marriages to rich men: "No rich man is ugly," and another, "A man in love is incomplete until he is married. Then he is finished."
- Ambrose Bierce, nineteenth-century American writer: "War is God's way of teaching Americans about geography."
- Movie director and actor Woody Allen: "It's not that I'm afraid to die— I just don't want to be there when it happens."

Irony

Irony serves many masters. An ironic tone occurs when a writer deliberately says the opposite of what he or she really means or points to the opposite of what one would typically expect to occur. This unexpected contrast results in a curious heightening of intensity about the real subject. Irony can be used to poke fun at human weaknesses and inconsistencies, or more seriously, to criticize, to encourage reform, or to cast doubt on someone's motives. The writer assumes that the reader will see through the pretense and recognize that the words mean something different from their literal meaning.

Consider this real-life example of irony. A *Washington Post* newspaper article describing a state visit to England by President George W. Bush in November 2003 began like this: "President Bush arrived here [London] Tuesday night for a four-day state visit with plans to tell skeptical Europeans that they must join the United States in spreading democracy, by force if necessary." (Quoted in Dana Milbank and Glenn Frankel, "Bushes Arrive in Britain, Bunk at Buckingham Palace," *The Washington Post,* November 19, 2003.) Political commentators made much of this idea—that democracy, which is supposed to reflect the will of the people, can (or should be) imposed by force.

Sometimes, one can predict an ironic tone just from a title. For example, before the 2000 presidential election, *Harper's* magazine published a decidedly unflattering story written by Joe Conason, a political columnist for salon.com. The article dug into the background of George W. Bush, then governor of Texas, and his oil and baseball cronies. The title was "Notes on a Native Son: The George W. Bush Success Story"; the subtitle was "A Heartwarming Tale about Baseball, $1.7 Billion, and a Lot of Swell Friends" (*Harper's,* February 2000). The article was indeed an unflattering portrait of financial bailouts by Bush's rich Texas friends before he ran for his first term as president.

Irony is at the heart of many jokes. In the following example, Page Smith uses irony to illustrate memory failure in older people. An old man and his wife are sitting on their front porch:

Wife: "I certainly would appreciate a vanilla ice cream cone."
Husband: "I'll hobble right down to the drugstore and get you one, dear."
Wife: "Now, remember, I want vanilla. You always get chocolate. Write it down. Vanilla."
Husband: "I can certainly remember vanilla. The store is only two blocks away."

Husband comes back with a hamburger and hands it to his wife. She looks at it disgustedly. "I knew you'd forget the mustard," she says.

Page Smith, "Coming of Age: Jokes about Old Age,"
San Francisco Chronicle

Irony often is present in cartoons, as well. Study this *New Yorker* cartoon drawn by Harry Bliss. Then see if you can identify the irony underlying the situation depicted.

Explain the irony. The cartoon depicts the Grim Reaper, the traditional personification of death, and his apartment, which is presumably in a large city like New York. The five-lock system is typical of urban residents who protect themselves from a burglary or break-in. The cartoon's irony is that we wouldn't expect the Grim Reaper to be afraid of crime.

Sarcasm

Sarcasm derives from the Latin words for "flesh-cutting," and this etymology will help you remember its purpose. The *American Heritage Dictionary* defines *sarcasm* as "a form of wit intended to taunt, wound, or subject another to ridicule or contempt." Although it often involves irony, instead of merely saying the opposite of what one means, the intention of a writer who uses sarcasm is to mock and to sneer at the victim. Sometimes the line between irony and sarcasm is hard to discern. The best way to separate the two is to consider the writer's intent. If the intent is a personal and heavy-handed insult, the tone is more likely sarcastic than ironic. Consider these examples:

- From a television review of an NBC drama called *Titans* produced by Aaron Spelling; the subject is Yasmine Bleeth's acting performance:

  Bleeth is first glimpsed—opening scene of the show—in a white bikini that you could stash in a bottle cap and still have extra space for character development. That space won't be used." (Quoted in John Carman, "'Titans' Emerge as a Giant Race of Idiots," *San Francisco Chronicle,* October 4, 2000, p. E2.)

- Every Sunday, the *San Francisco Chronicle* Datebook section runs a question-and-answer column called "Ask Mick LaSalle," in which readers write LaSalle and ask him questions about movies. (LaSalle is known for his humorously caustic style.) Here is one excerpt:

  Hey Mick: What gives? You review a movie with Amanda Peet in it ("Something's Gotta Give") and barely mention her. Sure, [Jack] Nicholson and [Diane] Keaton are the deal here. But my gosh!

  —Tim Coats, Berkeley

  Hey Tim: You're right. I should have said something, and thanks for the opportunity to correct that oversight. Here's a sentence about Amanda Peet in "Something's Gotta Give" that I worked on just for you, and I hope you like it: "As for Amanda Peet, she's also in the movie." (*San Francisco Chronicle,* December 28, 2003)

- It was the habit of Winston Churchill, prime minister of England during World War II, to drink a quart of brandy every day. One evening a woman at a dinner party told Churchill that he was drunk. Churchill replied: "And you, madam, are ugly. But tomorrow I shall be sober."
- A final example, again from Churchill: The playwright George Bernard Shaw once sent Churchill two tickets for the opening night of one of his new plays, noting, "Bring a friend—if you have one." Churchill wrote back to say that he was otherwise engaged on opening night but that he would appreciate tickets for the second performance—"if there is one." (Quoted in Joseph Epstein, *A Line Out for a Walk*)

Cynicism

The generation who came of age during the Watergate scandal and the Vietnam War often identify those two pivotal eras as the source of the **cynicism** that infects modern attitudes. The *Random House College Dictionary* definitions of *cynical* are helpful:

- Distrusting or disparaging the motives or sincerity of others
- Sneeringly distrustful, contemptuous, or pessimistic

A cynic detects falseness in others and recognizes impure motives. Politicians are sometimes described as cynical because they underestimate the intelligence of the voting public. The cynical tone is sneering, just as sarcasm is, but it is on a deeper level and from a different motive: Cynicism suggests a questioning and distrusting of people's stated motives or virtues. It may or may not involve irony. Here are three examples, all of which have in common the element of distrust and the desire to expose foolishness:

- Mort Sahl, American comedian, was quoted as saying during the 1996 presidential campaign: "God bless Bob Dole and Bill Clinton. Long may they waver."
- Voltaire, the eighteenth-century writer and philosopher said, "The first clergyman was the first rascal who met the first fool."
- L. Ron Hubbard, founder of the religion Scientology: "The best way to get rich in this country is to start a religion."

Satire

A **satire** is a type of writing that seeks to expose folly or wickedness, to hold human behavior up to ridicule, and to show the reader that certain actions or behavior would be more desirable. Satire typically relies on exaggeration and imitation of real literary forms. Muriel Spark, twentieth-century British novelist was once quoted as saying: "Satire is far more important, it has a more lasting effect, than a straight portrayal of what is wrong. I think that a lot of the world's problems should be ridiculed, but ridiculed properly rather than, well, wailed over." (Quoted in Hal Hager, "About Muriel Spark," *The Prime of Miss Jean Brodie.*)

Here is one example. In his book *Dave Barry's Complete Guide to Guys*, humorist Dave Barry includes a chapter titled "Tips for Women: How to Have a Relationship with a Guy." One of Barry's rules is this: "Don't make the guy feel threatened," which he follows with this advice in the form of a table, on the next page:

SITUATION	THREATENING RESPONSE	NONTHREATENING RESPONSE
You meet a guy for the first time.	"Hello."	"I am a nun."
You're on your first date. The guy asks you what your hopes for the future are.	"Well, I'd like to pursue my career for a while, and then get married and maybe have children."	"A vodka Collins."
You have a great time on the date, and the guy asks you if you'd like to go out again.	"Yes."	"Okay, but bear in mind that I have only three months to live."
The clergyperson asks you if you take this man to be your lawful wedded husband, for richer and poorer, in sickness and in health, etc., 'til death do you part.	"I do."	"Well, sure, but not *literally.*"

Source: Dave Barry, *Dave Barry's Complete Guide to Guys*

Practice Exercise 2

Read the following passages. Then, keeping in mind the writer's purpose and intent, decide which of the following tones is most accurately reflected in each excerpt:

- Witty
- Ironic
- Sarcastic
- Cynical
- Satirical

A.

The Kim Basinger movie *I Dreamed of Africa* bombed at the box office last weekend. It wasn't supposed to be that way. It was originally expected to bomb way back in September.

Tom King, "Waiting for Their Closeups," *The Wall Street Journal,* May 12, 2000

The tone of this selection is <u>ironic or sarcastic.</u>

B.

From Oscar Wilde, Irish playwright: "Bigamy is having one wife too many. Monogamy is the same."

The tone of this definition is <u>witty.</u>

C.

Samuel Johnson's recipes for cucumbers: "A cucumber should be well sliced, and dressed with pepper and vinegar, and then thrown out, as good for nothing."

The tone of this statement is   <u>witty.</u>

    D.   From a review of Bolt of Fate by Tom Tucker, a biography of
          Benjamin Franklin

. . . a new book argues that the legend on which Franklin's reputation rests is
dubious. There was no kite, no key, no bolt, no knuckle, no charge. He let people
believe he had been places he never went, done things he never did, and seen
things that never happened. No wonder he's been called the father of American
journalism.

Adam Gopnik, "American Electric: Did Franklin Fly the Kite?" *The New Yorker*

The tone of this excerpt is   <u>cynical.</u>

    E.

If Superman were real, here's how the Iraq war could have been avoided: At the
request of the U.N., the Man of Steel rockets to Iraq, scans for weapons of mass
destruction with his X-ray vision and, upon finding some, flings them into the
sun. Instant disarmament.

Jeff Jensen, "Cape Cowed," *Entertainment Weekly*

The tone of this passage is   <u>cynical.</u>

    F.   The writer of this letter to the editor is a Roman Catholic priest.
          As the passage indicates, Gene Robinson was appointed to be an
          Episcopal bishop in New Hampshire; the controversy arose be-
          cause Robinson is openly homosexual. In 1534, King Henry VIII
          of England broke from the Roman Catholic Church because the
          Pope would not allow him to divorce his first wife, Catherine
          of Aragon. This break is the origin of the Anglican (Episcopal)
          Church.

Editor—A brief e-mail from a priest friend greeted me Wednesday morning: "The
consecration of Gene Robinson as bishop of the New Hampshire Diocese of the
Episcopal Church is an affront to Christians everywhere. I am just thankful that
the church's founder, Henry VIII, and his wife Catherine of Aragon, and his wife
Anne Boleyn, and his wife Jane Seymour, and his wife Anne of Cleeves, and his
wife Katherine Howard, and his wife Catherine Parr are no longer here to suffer
through this assault on traditional Christian marriage."

Fr. Larry N. Lorenzoni, S.D.B.

San Francisco

San Francisco Chronicle, December 5, 2003

The tone of this letter is   <u>witty and ironic.</u>

G.

With the appearance in movie theaters of *Daredevil,* we have now officially arrived at the bottom of the comic-book pile. There we find Ben Affleck, flattened in every aspect except his chin, which is gargantuan, and his bangs, which are as poofy as a poodle's.

As it turns out, Daredevil really isn't much of a superhero, and in Affleck, he has the perfect person to play him, because he really isn't much of an actor. Together, this deadly duo now seeps across the floor of the American multiplex, waiting to be scraped off the bottom of your feet.

Daredevil comes from the frighteningly inexhaustible line of Marvel Comics franchises that includes *Spider-Man* and *X-Men,* and his story is very similar to theirs, except, of course, that he is neither mutant nor mutation—he's a lawyer! An incredibly solemn, blind lawyer, whose other senses all have been sharpened by the loss of his sight. The same cannot be said of the common sense of the people who made this movie.

Bruce Newman, "Affleck Takes a Dare," *San Jose Mercury News,* February 14, 2003

The tone of this movie review is sarcastic.

■ ALLUSION

An **allusion** is a pointed and meaningful reference to something outside the text; such references to past associations serve to illuminate today's ideas. The reference may be from any field, but these sources are the most common:

- The Bible or other religious texts
- History
- Literature
- Greek, Roman, or other mythology

Indeed, although allusions can come from any discipline, they generally come from works or events that educated readers are familiar with. The reader who misses the connections allusions provide misses out not only on the literal meaning but on the deeper connotative meaning as well. The ability to recognize allusions—without having to turn to reference books—takes years to develop, but it is attainable through wide reading and exposure to our cultural traditions. In the meantime, ask your instructor to explain unfamiliar allusions or use reference books or the Internet to figure them out. Any good unabridged dictionary will indicate most of the allusions you will encounter in your everyday reading.

Here is an allusion used to good effect in the introduction to a newspaper article on the Sacramento River in Glenn County, California:

From a drift boat, this stretch of the Sacramento is remarkably bucolic, particularly at this time of year.

The water is green and swift, and cottonwoods and willows crowd the shore. The sky is a piercing blue, and the air crisp as a winesap apple. Alarmed beavers slap their tails at the approach of the boat, and wood ducks and great blue herons rise from backside eddies.

It's easy to imagine you're in another time, when the trees were a lush, almost impenetrable forest that extended for miles beyond this river's banks.

But this is not the Sacramento River of 1870. Magnificent as they are, the trees are merely a thin buffer strip, a kind of Potemkin village, obscuring the huge agricultural complex that lies beyond. Just past the levees are thousands of acres of orchards and rice fields.

Glen Martin, "Wetlands, Birds and Salmon Returning to the Sacramento," *San Francisco Chronicle*

The allusion to a Potemkin village underscores Martin's main point. The original Potemkin village originated during Catherine the Great's reign over Russia in the eighteenth century. Upon learning of her wish to tour the countryside, Grigori Potemkin, her lover and an army officer, designed elaborate fake villages that the czarina could observe from her carriage. These façades would hide the reality of grinding poverty of Russia's peasant villages. The *American Heritage Dictionary* defines *Potemkin village* as "something that appears elaborate and impressive but in actual fact lacks substance." What is Martin saying, then, about the trees along today's Sacramento River? As splendid as they are, they are nowhere nearly as impressive as they used to be, since they merely obscure the realities of modern agriculture just behind them.

Can you explain the allusion in this recent *New Yorker* cartoon? (Hint: If you are unable to figure out the allusion, go to your favorite search engine and type in "Dolly the sheep.")

"I agree—the idea of cloning humans is disgusting."

■ SPECIAL EFFECTS

In this final section of the chapter, we will briefly look at some **special effects** that contribute to tone.

Special Effects

- Understatement
- Hyperbole (deliberate exaggeration)
- Alliteration
- Repetition for effect
- Unusual sentence structure

Understatement Actually a form of irony, **understatement** involves deliberate restraint, downplaying a situation to heighten its significance. Consider this little excerpt from an article about increased attendance at "mega-budget" movies from the summer of 1999:

> "Even those of us who thought it would a big summer never thought it could be this big," says Tom Sherak, who chairs the motion picture group for 20th Century Fox. His studio had a little movie called *Star Wars: Episode 1—The Phantom Menace*. It has taken in $420 million in the United States and about $300 million abroad. That makes it the second most successful movie in history, after *Titanic*.
>
> Sharon Waxman, "Summer Films Broke Rules," *The Washington Post*

Locate the one word that creates the understatement. "little"

Hyperbole Pronounced hī-pûr'-bə-lē, **hyperbole** is a figure of speech using deliberate exaggeration for effect. Consider this passage from Mark Edmundson's memoir of the 1960s and the life-altering influence of a high school teacher named Frank Lears. In this excerpt, Edmundson refers to the images he and his classmates projected to Lears:

> What he saw when we sat still and tried to listen was also in some measure the world created by TV, for we looked like nothing so much as people who aspired to be in family sitcoms, aspired, that is, to a certain wholesomeness, fed as we were on American cheese and Wonder Bread, with Fluffer-Nutter sandwiches and sloppy joes on the weekends. The girls wore jumpers and pleated skirts and had their hair militantly lacquered into imposing helmets. What our school alone used in hair spray would have been enough to burn a considerable hole in the ozone.
>
> Mark Edmundson, *Teacher: The One Who Made the Difference*

Alliteration

Alliteration—the repetition of initial consonant sounds in words—is more often associated with poetry than with prose. A repetition of sibilant ("s") sounds, for example, can be used to create a sinister mood. One section of Martin Luther King, Jr.'s, classic essay "Letter from Birmingham Jail" discusses the burdens prejudice has placed on African Americans. King uses alliteration—a sequence of initial "d" and "b" consonants—to create a heavy, brooding mood. Here is one illustrative sentence, which should be read out loud for the full effect.

> Like so many experiences of the past we were confronted with blasted hopes, and the dark shadow of a deep disappointment settled on us.

Repetition for Effect

Repeating key words, phrases, or clauses brings about a pleasing balance and calls attention to important ideas. Such is the effect of this excerpt from Todd Gitlin's study of the media and its influence on our culture. He introduces this excerpt by commenting on Americans' dependence on television, writing that on September 11, 2001, Americans "turned to television not only for facts but for rituals of shared horror, grief, sympathy, reassurance, and the many forms of solidarity":

> In a society that fancies itself the freest ever, spending time with communications machinery is the main use to which we have put our freedom. All human beings play, but this civilization has evolved a particular form of play: wedding fun to convenience by bathing ourselves in images and sounds. The most fun important thing about the communications we live among is not that they deceive (which they do); or that they broadcast a limiting ideology (which they do); or emphasize sex and violence (which they do); or convey diminished images of the good, the true, and the normal (which they do); or corrode the quality of art (which they also do); or reduce language (which they surely do)—but that with all their lies, skews, and shallow pleasures, they saturate our way of life with a promise of feeling, even if we may not know exactly how we feel about one or another batch of images except that they are *there,* streaming out of screens large and small, or bubbling in the background of life, but always coursing onward. To an unprecedented degree, the torrent of images, songs, and stories streaming has become our familiar world.
>
> Todd Gitlin, *Media Unlimited*

Unusual Sentence Structure

Writers not only choose words carefully, but they also endeavor to create sentences that reinforce both the content and the mood of the piece. Here are three examples of distinctive sentence structure. The first is the beginning of an article on the 2002 *Star Wars* movie and the hype that surrounded its release:

> Out on the cold concrete, where the faithful have gathered yet again to wait all night for that which must be waited for, the awful rumor has begun to circulate and take hold. The rumor that must not be acknowledged. The rumor of the blasphemers. The rumor that the new *Star Wars* movie, opening in a few hours, just might not be very good. The rumor, more insistent than the heavy breathing of Darth Vader, is spreading on the sidewalk and in the parking lot outside the Coronet Theater on Geary Boulevard, the sacred space of the steadfast and true.

> Steve Rubenstein, "Faith in the Force," *San Francisco Chronicle,* May 15, 2002

The deliberate use of incomplete sentences (fragments) and the repetition of the word "rumor" create an unusual effect.

Short sentences have a quite different effect in this paragraph in which the author describes the preparations of Harry Houdini, the famous magician, to jump from a bridge while manacled.

> Picture the scene as Houdini performs one of his bridge jumps, so often described with such unvarying excitement. The excited crowd, several thousand strong, jostles around. Houdini and his team arrive. <u>A silence falls.</u> Houdini strips to his bathing suit and climbs onto the parapet. The attention of all these thousands of people is focused upon him—a small man, slightly bow-legged, very muscular. The local chief of police comes forward carrying handcuffs, often two sets; leg-irons. Houdini allows himself to be manacled. He stands there, waiting until he "hears the voice." <u>Then he jumps. The crowd surges forward. It is waiting for—what</u>? What it sees, in a minute or so, is Houdini, swimming strongly for the bank or the boat, brandishing the irons in one hand. It is slightly disappointed, but also satisfied. Death has been defeated once more.

> Ruth Brandon, *The Life and Many Deaths of Harry Houdini*

Underline the short sentences to see how they heighten suspense and contribute to the dramatic effect.

This final example, by Sherman Alexie, a Coeur d'Alene Indian from Washington state, is the opening paragraph of his 1996 novel *Indian Killer.* In it he describes an Indian Health Service hospital. The sentence fragments, taken together, create a series of impressions, almost as if he were sketching the hospital scene with charcoal rather than with words. What dominant impression of the hospital does the reader come away with?

> The sheets are dirty. An Indian Health Service hospital in the early sixties. On this reservation or that reservation. Any reservation, a particular reservation. Antiseptic, cinnamon and danker odors. Anonymous cries up and down the hallways. Linoleum floors swabbed with gray water. Mop smelling

like old sex. Walls painted white a decade earlier. Now yellowed and peeling. Old Indian woman in a wheelchair singing traditional songs to herself, tapping a rhythm on her armrest, right index finger tapping; tapping. Pause. Tap, tap. A phone ringing loudly from behind a thin door marked PRIVATE. Twenty beds available, twenty beds occupied. Waiting room where a young Indian man sits on a couch and holds his head in his hands. Nurses' lounge, two doctors' offices and a scorched coffee pot. Old Indian man, his hair bright white and unbraided, pushing his IV bottle down the hallway. He is barefoot and confused, searching for a pair of moccasins he lost when he was twelve years old. Donated newspapers and magazines stacked in bundles, months and years out of date, missing pages. In one of the exam rooms, an Indian family of four, mother, father, son, daughter, all coughing blood quietly into handkerchiefs. The phone still ringing behind the PRIVATE door. A cinder-block building, thick windows that distort the view, pine trees, flagpole. A 1957 Chevy parked haphazardly, back door flung open, engine still running, back seat damp. Empty now.

Sherman Alexie, *Indian Killer*

Practice Exercise 3

Identify the allusion or special effect in these short selections. If an allusion is evident, explain its meaning. Choose your answer from one of these elements:

- Allusion (be sure to explain the allusion's meaning)
- Understatement
- Hyperbole
- Repetition for effect

A.

In 2004, the September 11 Commission, investigating the government's preparedness for terrorist attacks, requested that Condoleezza Rice, national security advisor, appear before the commission and give testimony about what she knew before the attacks. However, initially, Rice refused to testify, citing that to do so would compromise the constitutional powers of the executive branch. (Eventually, Rice did testify, but not until after several weeks of controversy.) Rice's initial refusal to testify was puzzling in light of her frequent appearances on national television. Richard Ben-Veniste, a member of the 9/11 Commission, was quoted as saying, "Dr. Rice has appeared everywhere except my local Starbucks."

Allusion (and meaning) or special effect: hyperbole (the Ben-Veniste

quotation)

B.

My parents' marriage was, it's safe to say, less than happy. They stayed together for the sake of their children and for want of hope that divorce would make them any happier. As long as my father was working, they enjoyed autonomy in their respective fiefdoms of home and workplace, but after he retired, in 1981, at the age of sixty-six, they commenced a round-the-clock performance of *No Exit* in their comfortably furnished suburban house. I arrived for brief visits like a U.N. peacekeeping force to which each side passionately presented its case against the other.

Jonathan Franzen, "My Father's Brain," *How to Be Alone*

(Hint: Go to www.google.com and look up *No Exit*.)

Allusion (and meaning) or special effects: Allusion—*No Exit*, the existentialist play by Jean Paul Sartre, depicts a modern vision of hell set in a living room where three people—a man and two women who can't stand each other—are condemned to live for eternity.

C. The writer is an Italian journalist who lived for several years in the United States.

Americans candidly admit that they "go gaga" over kiddies. My dictionary says this means they "become excessively enthusiastic." Children—especially those between the ages of two and four—enjoy absolute impunity in America. Let your small son loose in a university bookstore (I have actually done this) and everyone—students, faculty, and bookshop staff—will vie with each other to make him happy. Outrageous demands (a desire to embrace fifteen fluffy toy dogs at once) will be accepted as perfectly legitimate. Acts of underage violence (kicking the aforementioned toy dogs up and down the aisles) are smiled upon.

Beppe Severgni, *Ciao, America*

Allusion (and meaning) or special effects: hyperbole (the examples of a child's behavior and others' reactions)

D. The article from which this excerpt comes was published on the day of the 2004 Belmont Stakes race. It concerns the phenomenal rise to fame of a horse named Smarty Jones and his jockey, Stewart Elliott, who had already won the Preakness and the Kentucky Derby. Winning the Belmont Stakes race would have meant winning the Triple Crown. (Smarty Jones lost.)

In a battered, weight-interrupted, booze-hampered, peripatetic career, Stewart Elliott has managed to win 3,286 races, but even in his best year, one of the recent ones at Philadelphia Park, the 39-year-old Elliott never earned as much as $300,000. Then in six weeks this year, Elliott rode Smarty Jones to a couple of wins at Oaklawn Park in Arkansas, tacked on a victory in something called the Kentucky Derby, and—presto!—more than $600,000 came his way.

Bill Christine, "Elliott Is Cashing In Big on Smarty Jones,"
Los Angeles Times, May 31, 2004

Allusion (and meaning) or special effect: <u>understatement</u>

<u>("something called the Kentucky Derby")</u>

E.   A New York trial involved an off-duty policeman named Frantz Jerome and a gang member named Darryl Barnes, who had been caught carrying an illegal Tec-9 submachine gun on a street near Yankee Stadium. Jerome fired his gun three times at Barnes, and left him paralyzed from the waist down. According to a magazine article about civilians suing New York City,

Barnes sued the city, claiming that Jerome had used excessive force to subdue him. His case went well: in 1998, a jury awarded Barnes $76.4 million in damages.

Jeffrey Toobin, "Payday," *The New Yorker*

Allusion (and meaning) or special effect: <u>understatement ("the case</u>

<u>went well")</u>

F.

A few years after I began teaching, it occurred to me that being a teacher—not being a student—provides the best education. "To teach is to learn twice," wrote Joubert, in a simple-sounding maxim that could have several different meanings. It could mean that one first learns when getting up the material one is about to teach and then tests and relearns it in the actual teaching. It could mean that being a teacher offers one a fine chance for a second draft on one's inevitably inadequate initial education. It could mean that learning, like certain kinds of love, is better the second time around. It could mean that we are not ready for education, at any rate of the kind that leads to wisdom, until we are sixty, or seventy, or beyond. I favor this last interpretation, for its accounts for the strange feeling that I have had every year of my adult life, which is that only twelve months ago I was really quite stupid.

Aristides (pseudonym of Joseph Epstein), "To Learn Twice," *The American Scholar*

Allusion (and meaning) or special effect: <u>repetition for effect ("it</u>

<u>could mean . . .")</u>

G. The writer is describing the departure of tourists from Ft. Lauderdale's airport on their way to Caribbean cruise ships. This one has two elements you have studied.

Apparently Ft. Lauderdale Airport is always just your average sleepy midsize airport six days a week and then every Saturday resembles the Fall of Saigon.

David Foster Wallace, *A Supposedly Fun Thing I'll Never Do Again*

Allusion (and meaning) or special effect: <u>hyperbole; also an allusion to</u> <u>the 1975 invasion by North Vietnamese troops, which brought</u> <u>about the collapse of the South Vietnamese government and the</u> <u>American evacuation of Saigon.</u>

■ CHAPTER EXERCISES

Selection 1   This passage comes from a chapter on the American government's mistreatment of various Indian tribes during the nineteenth century.

The most famous removal of Indians, of course, was the removal of the Cherokee from Georgia westward to Indian Territory in 1838 and 1839. There are many accounts of the forced march that came to be known as the Trail of Tears—of the Cherokee's previous peaceableness and prosperity on their lands in Georgia; of the Georgia settlers' hatred of Indians and desire for those lands; of the mercilessness of President Andrew Jackson; of Supreme Court Justice John Marshall's ruling that the removal was illegal; of Jackson's response: "He has made his law. Now let him enforce it"; of the opposition of people as diverse as Ralph Waldo Emerson and Davy Crockett to the removal; of the U.S. soldiers' roundup of the Georgia Cherokee; of the Cherokee's suffering in the stockades and along the trail; of the death of more than four thousand Cherokee, about a third of the population of the tribe, before the removal was through. The Cherokee had their own written language, with an alphabet devised by the Cherokee leader Sequoyah during the 1820s. But their success at following the ways of the whites proved no defense. As would happen again elsewhere, building houses and farms only gave the Indians more to lose when government policy changed.

Ian Frazier, *On the Rez*

A. *Content and Structure*

1. A good title for this paragraph would be
   (a) "A Sad Day in American History."
   (b) "A History of the Cherokee Indians."

   (c) "Forced Removals in American History."
   (d) "The Cherokee and the Trail of Tears."

2. The author suggests that the Cherokee
   (a) were envied for their prosperity by the Georgia settlers.
   (b) had waged wars with the Georgia settlers.
   (c) had little public support for remaining in Georgia.
   (d) were removed because of past broken treaties with the government.

3. Concerning the Cherokees' experiences along the Trail of Tears, what seems to be Frazier's central concern?   _____

   _____

4. Frazier also suggests that the Cherokee
   (a) were singled out for retribution for trying to emulate whites.
   (b) were somewhat unusual among Indian tribes for having a written language.
   (c) had brought much of their misfortune upon themselves.
   (d) only (a) and (b).
   (e) (a), (b), and (c).

B. *Language and Tone Analysis*

1. Frazier's tone and his attitude toward the Cherokee can be best described as
   (a) complaining, aggrieved.
   (b) informative, instructive.
   (c) sad, lamenting.
   (d) critical, fault-finding.

2. When President Jackson responded to Supreme Court Justice Marshall's ruling, "He has made his law. Now let him enforce it," we can interpret Jackson's tone as
   (a) honest, candid.
   (b) defiant, insolent.
   (c) complaining, aggrieved.
   (d) nostalgic, wistful.

3. A special effect evident in the paragraph is
   (a) hyperbole.
   (b) understatement.
   (c) alliteration.
   (d) repetition for effect.

Answers for Selection 1

A. Content and Structure

1. (d)   2. (a)
3. The Cherokees' mistreatment and suffering at the hands of the U.S. government
4. (d)

B. Language and Tone Analysis

1. (c)   2. (b)   3. (d)

Selection 2

[1]Human beings find the most ingenious ways to protect their privacy, even under conditions of near-constant physical proximity to others. [2]In many cultures, even minimal control over physical access can be hard to come by in the midst of communal and family life. [3]Some villages have huts with walls so thin that sounds can easily be heard through them; others have no walls at all separating couples, or families. [4]Many ways are then devised to create privacy. [5]Villagers may set up private abodes outside the village to which they go for days or even months when they want to be alone or with just one or two others. [6]Many cultures have developed strict rules of etiquette, along with means of dissimulation and hypocrisy that allow certain private matters to remain unknown or go unobserved. [7]In such ways, it is possible to exercise some control over one's openness to others even in the midst of communal life or crowds.

[8]An arresting example of how such control can be maintained is provided by the Tuareg men of North Africa who wear blue veils and long robes of indigo cotton, so that little of them shows except their hands, their feet, and the area around their eyes. [9]The veil is worn at home as well as outside, even when eating or smoking. [10]Some wear it even when asleep. [11]It is raised to cover the face most completely in the presence of highly placed persons or family members granted special respect, such as in-laws. [12]One observer noted that the veil protects ceremonial reserve and allows a "symbolic withdrawal from a threatening situation."

[13]The veil, though providing neither isolation nor anonymity, bestows facelessness and the idiom of privacy upon its wearer and allows him to stand somewhat aloof from the perils of social interaction while remaining a part of it.

Sissela Bok, *Secrets: On the Ethics of Concealment and Revelation*

A. Vocabulary

For each italicized word from the selection, write the dictionary definition most appropriate for the context.

1. the most *ingenious* ways [sentence 1]: <u>clever, imaginative</u>

2. near-constant physical *proximity* [1]: <u>physical closeness</u>

3. means of *dissimulation* [6]: <u>disguise, concealment</u>

4. the veil *bestows* facelessness [13]: <u>confers, presents</u>

B. Content, Structure, and Tone

Complete the following questions.

1. The main idea of the paragraph is that
   (a) privacy is a universal concern.
   (b) loss of personal privacy may have serious emotional consequences.
   (c) clothing can sometimes establish one's privacy.
   (d) human beings have devised ingenious ways to protect their privacy.
2. The primary method of paragraph development is
   (a) example.
   (b) analysis.
   (c) definition.
   (d) cause–effect.
3. The reader can infer that maintaining privacy is
   (a) more difficult in economically developed nations.
   (b) impossible to achieve or maintain in communal societies or in large families.
   (c) more important to cultures in North Africa than it is to Americans or Europeans.
   (d) a special problem in cultures where people live in close proximity.
4. Sentences 12 and 13 suggest that the veil allows the wearer to
   (a) withdraw from society whenever he wants to escape annoyances.
   (b) protect himself from enemies.
   (c) escape threatening situations while still being a part of the group.
   (d) adopt a modest position in front of highly placed officials or other important persons.
5. The author's tone can best be described as
   (a) philosophical, reflective.
   (b) admiring, laudatory.
   (c) informative, instructive.
   (d) ironic, amusing.

Selection 3

The chimpanzee who is the subject of this passage, Cholmondeley—or Chumley as he was known to his friends—was being donated to the London Zoo. The author had promised the owner to take the chimp back to England on his way home from Africa.

1He arrived in the back of a small van, seated sedately in a huge crate. **2**When the doors of his crate were opened and Chumley stepped out with all the ease and self-confidence of a film star, I was considerably shaken; standing on his bow legs in a normal slouching chimp position, he came up to my waist, and if he had straightened up his head would have been on a level with my chest. **3**He had huge arms and must have measured at least twice my size round his hairy chest. **4**Owing to bad tooth growth, both sides of his face were swollen out of all proportion, and this gave him a weird pugilistic look. **5**His eyes were small, deep-set, and intelligent; the top of his head was nearly bald, owing, I discovered later, to his habit of sitting and rubbing the palms of his hands backward across his head, an exercise which seemed to afford him much pleasure and which he persisted in until the top of his skull was quite devoid of hair. **6**This was no young chimp such as I had expected, but a veteran about eight or nine years old, fully mature, strong as a powerful man, and, to judge by his expression, with considerable experience of life. **7**Although he was not exactly a nice chimp to look at (I had seen handsomer), he certainly had a terrific personality; it hit you as soon as you set eyes on him. **8**His little eyes looked at you with great intelligence, and there seemed to be a glitter of ironic laughter in their depths that made one feel uncomfortable.

9He stood on the ground and surveyed his surroundings with a shrewd glance, and then he turned to me and held out one of his soft, pink-palmed hands to be shaken, with exactly that bored expression that one sees on the faces of professional hand-shakers. **10**Round his neck was a thick chain, and its length drooped over the tailboard of the lorry[2] and disappeared into the depths of his crate. **11**With an animal of less personality than Chumley, this would have been a sign of his subjugation, of his captivity. **12**But Chumley wore the chain with the superb air of a Lord Mayor; after shaking my hand so professionally, he turned and proceeded to pull the chain, which measured some fifteen feet, out of his crate. **13**He gathered it up carefully into loops, hung it over one hand, and proceeded to walk into the hut as if he owned it. **14**Thus, in the first few minutes of arrival, Chumley had made us feel inferior; he had moved in, not, we felt, because we wanted him to, but because he did. **15**I almost felt I ought to apologize for the mess on the table.

Gerald Durrell, "The Life and Death of Cholmondeley"

A. *Vocabulary*

For each italicized word from the selection, choose the best definition according to the context in which it appears.

---

[2] *Lorry* is the British word for truck.

1. *sedately* [sentence 1]:
   - (a) calmly, in a dignified manner. ⟵
   - (b) nervously, apprehensively.
   - (c) arrogantly, haughtily.
   - (d) uncomfortably, awkwardly.
2. *pugilistic* [4]: Having the appearance of a
   - (a) military officer.
   - (b) movie star.
   - (c) fighter. ⟵
   - (d) vicious animal.
3. *ironic* [8]: In this context,
   - (a) cynical, distrustful.
   - (b) satirical, ridiculing.
   - (c) sarcastic, suggesting a superior attitude. ⟵
   - (d) nasty, cruel.
4. *subjugation* [11]:
   - (a) boredom, indifference.
   - (b) defeat, enslavement. ⟵
   - (c) cooperative spirit.
   - (d) subjectivity, introspective nature.

B. Content, Structure, and Tone

Complete the following questions.

1. The dominant impression of Chumley that Durrell wants to convey is his
   - (a) weird appearance.
   - (b) large size.
   - (c) maturity.
   - (d) superior attitude. ⟵
2. The passage contains three metaphors that describe Chumley's behavior. Identify each in the space provided.

   Sentence 2: "with all the ease and self-confidence of a film star"

   Sentence 9: "with exactly that bored expression that one sees on

   the faces of professional handshakers"

   Sentence 12: "Chumley wore the chain with the superb air of a

   Lord Mayor"
3. These three figures of speech, taken together, suggest that Chumley was accustomed to "being the center of attention, of being treated

   like a celebrity."

4. Which of the following is an accurate inference?
   (a) Durrell had never seen a chimp before.
   (b) Chumley was embarrassed by the chains used to tether him to his crate.
   (c) Chumley insisted on having his surroundings be clean and orderly.
   (d) Durrell had expected Chumley to be an ordinary chimp.
5. The tone of the passage can best be described as
   (a) ironic, wry, and amused.
   (b) sarcastic, ridiculing.
   (c) serious, earnest.
   (d) sentimental, maudlin

PRACTICE ESSAY

"Making the Grade"
Kurt Wiesenfeld

Each week *Newsweek* publishes a column titled "My Turn," in which people in various professions express personal viewpoints. "Making the Grade" is one such article. This particular column written by Kurt Wiesenfeld, a professor of physics since 1997 at Georgia Institute of Technology in Atlanta, caused much discussion among college students and teachers after its publication in the June 17, 1996, issue.

Preview Questions

1. Are you familiar with the term "grade inflation"? In your experience, does a final grade of "A" mean superior achievement in a course?

2. What do you consider an average grade? A "B"? A "C"? Examine your thinking.

3. If grade inflation exists in American colleges and universities today, what might be some reasons to account for it?

1   It was a rookie error. After 10 years I should have known better, but I went to my office the day after final grades were posted. There was a tentative knock on the door. "Professor Wiesenfeld? I took your Physics 2121 class? I flunked it? I wonder if there's anything I can do to improve my grade?" I thought: "Why are you asking me? Isn't it too late to worry about it? Do you dislike making declarative statements?"

2   After the student gave his tale of woe and left, the phone rang. "I got a D in your class. Is there any way you can change it to 'Incomplete'?" Then the e-mail assault began: "I'm shy about coming in to talk to you, but I'm not shy about asking for a better grade. Anyway, it's worth a try." The next day I had three messages from students asking *me* to call *them*. I didn't.

3   Time was, when you received a grade, that was it. You might groan and moan, but you accepted it as the outcome of your efforts or lack thereof (and, yes, sometimes a tough grader). In the last few years, however, some students have developed a disgruntled-consumer approach. If they don't like their grade, they go to the "return" counter to trade it in for something better.

4   What alarms me is their indifference toward grades as an indication of personal effort and performance. Many, when pressed about why they think they deserve a better grade, admit they don't deserve one but would like one anyway. Having been raised on gold stars for effort and smiley faces for self-esteem, they've learned they can get by without hard work and real talent if they can talk the professor into giving them a break. This attitude is beyond cynicism. There's a weird innocence to the assumption that one expects (even deserves) a better grade simply by begging for it. With that outlook, I guess I shouldn't be as flabbergasted as I was that 12 students asked me to change their grades *after* the final grades were posted.

5   That's 10 percent of my class who let three months of midterms, quizzes and lab reports slide until long past remedy. My graduate student calls it hyperrational thinking: if effort and intelligence don't matter, why should deadlines? What matters is getting a better grade through an unearned bonus, the academic equivalent of a freebie T-shirt or toaster giveaway. Rewards are disconnected from the quality of one's work. An act and its consequences are unrelated, random events.

6   Their arguments for wheedling better grades often ignore academic performance. Perhaps they feel it's not relevant. "If my grade isn't raised to a D I'll lose my scholarship." "If you don't give me a C, I'll flunk out." One sincerely overwrought student pleaded, "If I don't pass, my life is over." This is tough stuff to deal with. Apparently, I'm responsible for someone's losing a scholarship, flunking out or deciding whether life has meaning. Perhaps these students see me as a commodities broker with something they want—a grade. Though intrinsically worthless, grades, if properly manipulated, can be traded for what has value: a degree, which means a job, which means money. The one thing college actually offers—a chance to learn—is considered irrelevant, even less than worthless, because of the long hours and hard work required.

7   In a society saturated with surface values, love of knowledge for its own sake does sound eccentric. The benefits of fame and wealth are more obvious. So is it right to blame students for reflecting the superficial values saturating our society?

8   Yes, of course it's right. These guys had better take themselves seriously now, because our country will be forced to take them seriously

later, when the stakes are much higher. They must recognize that their attitude is not only self-destructive, but socially destructive. The erosion of quality control—giving appropriate grades for actual accomplishments—is a major concern in my department. One colleague noted that a physics major could obtain a degree without ever answering a written exam question completely. How? By pulling in enough partial credit and extra credit. And by getting breaks on grades.

9   But what happens once she or he graduates and gets a job? That's when the misfortunes of eroding academic standards multiply. We lament that school children get "kicked upstairs" until they graduate from high school despite being illiterate and mathematically inept, but we seem unconcerned with college graduates whose less blatant deficiencies are far more harmful if their accreditation exceeds their qualifications.

10   Most of my students are science and engineering majors. If they're good at getting partial credit but not at getting the answer right, then the new bridge breaks or the new drug doesn't work. One finds examples here in Atlanta. Last year a light tower in the Olympic Stadium collapsed, killing a worker. It collapsed because an engineer miscalculated how much weight it could hold. A new 12-story dormitory could develop dangerous cracks due to a foundation that's uneven by more than six inches. The error resulted from incorrect information being fed into a computer. I drive past that dorm daily on my way to work, wondering if a foundation crushed under kilotons of weight is repairable or if this structure will have to be demolished. Two 10,000-pound steel beams at the new natatorium collapsed in March, crashing into the student athletic complex. (Should we give partial credit since no one was hurt?) Those are real-world consequences of errors and lack of expertise.

11   But the lesson is lost on the grade-grousing 10 percent. Say that you won't (not can't, but won't) change the grade they deserve to what they want, and they're frequently bewildered or angry. They don't think it's fair that they're judged according to their performance, not their desires or "potential." They don't think it's fair that they should jeopardize their scholarships or be in danger of flunking out simply because they could not or did not do their work. But it's more than fair; it's necessary to help preserve a minimum standard of quality that our society needs to maintain safety and integrity. I don't know if the 13th-hour students will learn that lesson, but I've learned mine. From now on, after final grades are posted, I'll lie low until the next quarter starts.

A. Comprehension

Choose the answer that best completes each statement. Do not refer to the selection while doing this exercise.

1. Wiesenfeld states that some college students do not consider grades a measure of their
   (a) mastery of the subject.
   (b) (personal performance and effort.)
   (c) ability to organize their time wisely.
   (d) performance in relation to other students' performance in the class.
2. Some students try to get high grades by
   (a) cheating.
   (b) cramming at the last minute.
   (c) (begging and pleading.)
   (d) threatening the instructor.
3. The students described in the article receive low grades because they
   (a) attend class.
   (b) are unprepared academically for the course work.
   (c) work too many hours, which interferes with their studies.
   (d) (let an entire semester's work slide without doing anything.)
4. The idea that students deserve high grades without working for them reflects
   (a) parental pressure for them to succeed.
   (b) (the superficial values of the larger society.)
   (c) the importance of getting into a good graduate school.
   (d) grade inflation.
5. One particularly serious consequence of undeserved grades in science and engineering courses is that
   (a) educational standards in other disciplines are also weakened.
   (b) (unsafely designed buildings and structures can result in loss of lives.)
   (c) graduates expect similar undeserved rewards when they enter the working world.
   (d) professors feel as if they are under siege.

B. Vocabulary

For each italicized word from the selection, write the dictionary definition most appropriate for the context. You may refer to the selection to answer the questions in this section and in all the remaining sections.

1. the e-mail *assault* [paragraph 2]: attack, offensive

2. a *disgruntled*-consumer approach [3]: discontented

3. *hyperrational* thinking [5]: The prefix *hyper-* means excessive

4. *wheedling* better grades [6]: using flattery or cajolery

5. sincerely *overwrought* student [6]: highly agitated

6. *intrinsically* worthless [6]: essentially

7. illiterate and mathematically *inept* [9]:   <u>incompetent</u>

8. less *blatant* deficiencies [9]: <u>offensively conspicuous</u>

9. *eroding* academic standards [9]: <u>deteriorating, wearing down</u>

10. maintain safety and *integrity* [11]: <u>state of being complete and sound</u>

C. *Inferences*

On the basis of the evidence in the paragraph, mark these statements as follows: PA (probably accurate), PI (probably inaccurate), or NP (not in the passage).

1. <u>PA</u> Many students equate good grades with high salaries rather than with knowledge acquired.
2. <u>NP</u> It is not only science and engineering students who plead for higher grades; liberal arts students do as well.
3. <u>PI</u> Parental pressure and the large financial investment college entails may account for some students begging for grades they do not deserve.
4. <u>NP</u> The engineers who designed the defective bridge and the Olympic Stadium light tower probably received higher grades than they should have in their college engineering courses.
5. <u>PI</u> Giving partial or extra credit on examinations or projects is a good way to measure students' learning; even if they don't get the entire answer right, at least they should be rewarded for getting some of it right.
6. <u>PI</u> Professors should understand that today's students are under tremendous pressure and grade more leniently.

D. *Structure*

Complete the following questions.

1. The mode of discourse represented in this article is
   (a) narration.
   (b) description
   (c) exposition
   (d) persuasion.

2. From the information in paragraph 1, explain the "rookie error" that Wiesenfeld made. <u>His error was in returning to his office after</u>

   <u>final grades were posted.</u>

3. Write a main-idea sentence in your own words for paragraph 4.

    <u>Because they don't equate grades with personal effort and per-</u>

    <u>formance, many students want good grades whether or not they</u>

    <u>deserve them or have done the work.</u>

4. With respect to the practices of giving partial credit for incomplete answers or giving easy grades, the purpose of paragraphs 7 to 10 is to
    (a) warn the reader about the long-term consequences of this practice.
    (b) explain their origins.
    (c) prove how widespread they are.
    (d) present the students' point of view.

5. Consider carefully all of the elements in paragraph 1 again. How would you characterize the tone, with regard to Wiesenfeld's attitude toward the student quoted?
    (a) witty
    (b) ironic
    (c) neutral or objective
    (d) sarcastic

6. Now characterize the tone of the entire article.
    (a) haughty, self-righteous
    (b) critical, fault-finding
    (c) mildly and humorously critical
    (d) provocative, inflammatory

E. Questions for Discussion and Analysis

1. Do you see any contradiction in Wiesenfeld's explanation of what grades mean to many students today and what they should mean? (See paragraphs 3 and 4, in particular the writer's phrase "their indifference toward grades.")

2. Is Wiesenfeld accurate in his criticism of today's students and their attitude about grades? Do you detect any bias? Does he avoid generalizing about his students, and if so, how?

3. From your experience as a student and your observation of your fellow students' attitudes toward grades, comment on his most significant points.

4. Finally, study the chart on the next page, which shows the progression of inflated grades. It was prepared by Stuart Rojstaczer, a professor of geology, environment, and engineering at Duke University:[1]

---

[1]Go to www.gradeinflation.com for the complete study.

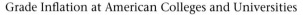

Grade Inflation at American Colleges and Universities

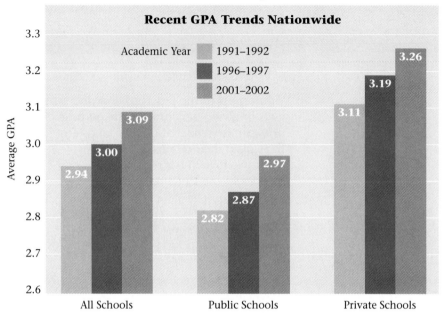

Source: Rojstaczer, Stuart. From chart entitled, "Grade Inflation at American Colleges and Universities: Recent GPA Trends Nationwide." www.gradeinflation.com. Reprinted with permission.

What conclusions can you draw from the three sets of figures? Which type of college reveals more obvious grade inflation? Can you offer any explanation for this phenomenon?

Reading Critically

C H A P T E R 8

Elements of Critical Reading

CHAPTER OBJECTIVES

In this chapter, the first of three chapters dealing with reading critically, you will learn to analyze and evaluate claims and evidence in arguments, building on the analytical skills developed in Parts 1, 2, and 3. The readings in Part 4 represent the persuasive or argumentative mode of discourse—nonfiction prose that expresses a writer's subjective opinion, whether it's a newspaper or magazine editorial, a letter to the editor, a political speech, a political cartoon, a position paper, or an article on a World Wide Web site. Here you will learn:

- What critical reading is

- What the reader's responsibilities are

- How to develop a worldview

- How arguments are constructed

- How to take arguments apart

- How to analyze visual images

CRITICAL READING DEFINED

In the term **critical reading,** *critical* does not mean tearing down or finding fault. Critical reading is the most deliberate and thorough kind of reading. It goes beyond literal comprehension. It means judging, evaluating, weighing the writer's words carefully, and applying your reasoning powers. It requires keeping an open mind and developing a healthy skepticism, not accepting unquestioningly what you read just because it is in print, but also not rejecting ideas simply because they are different from your beliefs. Critical reading goes beyond literal and inferential comprehension—it means judging the worth of what you read, its legitimacy as argument, as well as its accuracy, fairness, reliability, and significance. Critical reading may also require you to suspend judgment and put aside your prejudices until you get more information or read other points of view on an issue. Critical reading involves detecting fallacious arguments, whether from deliberate manipulation, deceptive appeals to emotion, logical fallacies (errors in reasoning), or bias. And finally, critical reading extends to visual material—advertisements, charts, graphs, photographs, cartoons, and other visual images.

Recent terrorist attacks on American soil and around the world, as well as political developments, have undermined Americans' security. The important issues our society faces have become more complicated and more difficult to interpret. The foundation of a democratic society is the right to think freely for oneself; the way to accomplish that is to read widely on the issues. With the wealth of information available from both traditional and electronic sources, the necessity of reading that information critically has become even more necessary—as always, to protect our pocketbooks, but also to safeguard our right to question and to decide for ourselves the answers to the day's important issues.

THE READER'S RESPONSIBILITIES

If the writer's task is to muster convincing and fair evidence in support of an argument and to adhere to the rules of logic, then the reader's responsibility is to read carefully and thoughtfully. When we misread and misinterpret, the reason is sometimes laziness. We may not take the trouble to comprehend accurately, being content to graze over the contents with no more concentration than if we were checking out the newspaper's sports pages. Laziness may keep us from looking up the definitions of important words. Consider, for example, this sentence:

> The defense attorney used a *meretricious* argument to ensure his client's acquittal.

A lazy student who encounters this sentence might think, *"Meretricious* sounds sort of like *merit,* and I remember from high-school French that *mère* is the French word for 'mother,' so *meretricious* probably means something good." Unfortunately, this conclusion is way off the mark; *meretricious* means "attracting attention in a vulgar manner."

Another form of laziness occurs when we merely skim through an article instead of reading it carefully because we already agree with the author's point of view. However, the author's position may be weak, supported by flimsy or flawed evidence. The position may not really be worth holding or may not stand up to scrutiny. Haphazard reading never reveals these defects. Even worse, we may glance at an article and not read it because we know in advance that we *don't* agree with the author, thus missing an important part of the intellectual experience—examining the worth of opinions we do not share.

Another form of intellectual laziness is letting prejudice or bias, narrow personal experience or parochial values interfere with a clear-headed appraisal. Critical readers try—insofar as it is humanly possible—to suspend their biases and personal prejudices so they do not interfere with accurate comprehension. A willingness to see events from another perspective is an essential component of critical reading and of the intellectual experience; all these skills should be developed during the college years when you are exposed to a wide assortment of political, social, and philosophical ideas. In the years following college, you can refine your thinking and call upon these skills in every aspect of your lives. Although it is impossible for human beings to be wholly free of bias and prejudice, ascertaining why we believe as we do helps us interpret what we read.

■ DEVELOPING A WORLDVIEW

One obstacle to critical thinking is **ethnocentrism,** the belief that one's nation or social group is superior, that it is at the center of the universe, and that a different way of perceiving events is wrong or flawed, as if everyone else in the world should look at issues and problems the same way you do.

Sorting out the opinions that you are exposed to in your college experience is difficult. But as you grow intellectually and reflect on what you have read, learned, and experienced firsthand, you will develop a **worldview**—a perspective on the world, the way you see and interpret events and issues. Too often we are content to hang on to our opinions because examining other viewpoints is too much trouble; then, too, our opinions are comfortable, providing us with a ready-made set of beliefs. These may be sufficient for day-to-day life experiences, but they may fall short with serious social, economic, or political issues.

Where does your worldview come from? Obviously, from the many influences during your formative years: parents, siblings, teachers, friends, acquaintances, members of the clergy, and co-workers, to name a few. To these we add personal experience, observation of the world around you, and the reading you have done. But your worldview is also formed by intangibles like the value system you were raised with; your family's economic status, level of education, racial or ethnic background, and expectations; and your religious and moral foundation. All these influences leave their imprint on you and shape your interpretation of the world around you.

Our worldview undergoes constant change as part of the educational process afforded by contact with the intellectual world and with the everyday world. Note that the verb *educate* derives from Latin and literally refers to "a leading out" (from the prefix *e*, meaning "from," and the root *ducare*, meaning "leading.")

To characterize your worldview, begin by questioning why you think the way you do. Consider your upbringing and the people who influenced you most. To what extent does your thinking conform to the way you were raised? To your education? Becoming an independent thinker and reader involves developing one's *own* worldview, not adopting uncritically someone else's views. Worldviews are personal and unique, and they should be respected, provided that they derive from careful thought and conviction, rather than from an automatic, conditioned response. A recent television advertisement for Fujitsu expresses the idea of a worldview well: "No two eyes see the same world." What does all this have to do with reading? A good critical reader determines if a writer's claim accords with his or her worldview. As we read and reflect, our worldview may subtly alter over time.

Practice Exercise 1	The previous section listed *ethnocentrism* as one impediment to critical thinking. With the Middle East so much in the news—more than a half-century of strife between the Palestinians and the Israelis, the first Gulf War, the 2003 U.S. invasion of Iraq and its aftermath, the instability of Saudi Arabia, the West's dependence on Middle Eastern oil, the recent terrorist attacks, and the war on terrorism—it might be profitable, at least briefly, to examine the Arab worldview. To be sure, the Arab world is not monolithic—meaning that there is diversity of thought and opinion in the various Islamic societies; nonetheless, it is instructive to examine some of the fundamental tenets of the Arab worldview and to contrast them with our own. We will do this with two excerpts from recent publications.

The first excerpt is from Sandra Mackey's excellent study of Saudi Arabian society. Mackey, an American writer, lived in Saudi Arabia during the 1970s and early 1980s, but she updated her study in light of the war on terror. In this passage Mackey examines the way that Saudis view themselves in relation to the rest of the world and, by extension, to other Arab nations:

> One must understand how Saudi Arabia views the world to appreciate the importance the Saudis attach to their standing among other Arabs. The Saudis see the world as a series of concentric circles, with Saudi Arabia in the center, surrounded by the Arab world, surrounded by the Islamic world. In this scheme, the world is largely bipolar—Moslem and non-Moslem. Central to this concept of bipolarization is an acute consciousness of being a member of the second ring, the Arab nation, a consciousness shared by all Arabs. Yet there exists an enormous gap between the ideal of Arab brotherhood and the national interests and ambitions of the individual countries. Consequently, all relations between Arab countries are conducted on the basis of unity and discord. Although profoundly confusing to Westerners, this is not contradictory to Arabs, who view Arab nations much like a family. Furthermore, the rules worked out for the survival of the Arab family are applied to the Arab nation: I against my brothers; I and my brothers against my cousins; I and my cousins against the world. Within this psychological context, all conflicts are viewed as temporary and any unity as permanent.
>
> Sandra Mackey, *The Saudis: Inside the Desert Kingdom*

1. Summarize the Arab worldview as Mackey describes it. _A series of concentric circles, with Saudi Arabia at the center, with the other Arab nations in the second circle, and the circle containing the Islamic world outside that, creates an us-against-them worldview. This accounts for the "bipolarization"—or the division of the world into Moslem and non-Moslem—sometimes described as a conflict between the Islamic world and the "infidels," or those who do not follow Islam._

2. How do you think the Western view of the world differ from the series of concentric circles Mackey describes here? _Answers will vary, but certainly Western culture is more open, more fluid, and less inclined to see the world in such an us-vs.-them fashion._

The next excerpt was published just after the September 11, 2001, terrorist attacks on the World Trade Center and the Pentagon. Initially, when President George W. Bush declared the war on terrorism, he characterized the war as a "crusade." (That term was quickly dropped, for reasons that the article explains.) For Americans, this word *crusade* has a positive connotation; the Islamic world had a completely different reaction:

> The average American probably thinks of the Crusades—if he thinks of them at all—as a dimly recalled page in a high school history book, possibly overlaid with images from the 1935 Cecil B. De Mille film epic starring Jason Robards Sr. and Loretta Young.
>
> In the Islamic world, it's not like that.
>
> Arab societies "have a very fluid sense of time," explains Mary-Jane Deeb, adjunct professor at American University and Middle East specialist. "For them, events like the Crusades, a thousand years ago, are as immediate as yesterday. And they are very, very powerful events in the Arab mind. A lot of Islamic rhetoric revolves around the crusaders."
>
> The reasons why are part history, part culture, part linguistics. When President Bush on Sept. 15 declared that "this crusade, this war on terrorism, is going to take a while," Muslims were stung.
>
> The president was using "crusade" in its Western sense of "any vigorous action in behalf of a cause." But many Muslims, particularly Arabs, recognize no such usage. To them "crusade," even uncapitalized, is a profoundly loaded term. It evokes not just a war against their people, who were hacked apart, man and child, 1,000 years ago, until the streets of Jerusalem and other cities ran deep in blood. It evokes an unprovoked war against their religion and their every way of life—a war they see mirrored today in the steady corrosion of Islamic values by a globalizing Western culture they believe undermines their families, trivializes learning and profanes their God.
>
> When Islam is under attack, the Koran justifies a *jihad,* or holy war, against unbelievers. To many in the Muslim world, Islam has been under attack by the West at least since the 11th century and the First Crusade.
>
> "It's not simply a matter of religion as Westerners understand it," Deeb explains. "Conservative Muslims see the West imposing an entire system of economic, political and social values which strike at the heart of the Islamic way of life. Westerners would consider most of these values secular, but to conservative Muslims almost nothing is secular. The Koran governs everything, including banking and politics. All is Islam."
>
> To appreciate the sense of cultural violation many Muslims feel toward the West, it helps to remember that Islam, in its early centuries, was quite tolerant of Christians and Jews.

Ken Ringle, "A Thousand Years of Bad Memories,"
The Washington Post National Weekly Edition, October 29–November 4, 2001

1. List two significant elements of the Islamic worldview you derived from this excerpt. <u>(1) For Arabs, historical events are as immediate as today's events. (2) The values in the Muslim world tend to come from the religious teachings in the Koran. (3) Islamic law condones a *jihad* against unbelievers who are perceived as attacking their culture.</u>

2. Now list three ways that the West differs in its worldview. <u>Answers will vary, but here are some possibilities: (1) We tend to view historical events as remote, especially those that occurred more than 1,000 years ago; (2) our values come from a variety of sources, both secular and religious; (3) the way we deal with our enemies may involve waging war, but it may also involve diplomacy, economic sanctions, propaganda, or plain old-fashioned arm-twisting.</u>

3. How does this information help you better understand the reason for the recent terrorist attacks? <u>Answers will vary.</u>

_____

_____

_____

■ TWO WORLD MAPS—TWO WORLDVIEWS

To what extent are our worldview and our perception of our country's status in the world influenced by its geography or by the image we have in our minds by its geographical position? Here are two maps of the world. The first map shows the world with North and South America toward the right, Africa in the center, and Eurasia and Australia toward the left; Antarctica (not shown) would be at the top. The second map shows North and South America in the center, with Eurasia split and Australia at the bottom left; Antarctica (again, not shown) would be at the bottom.

1. First locate North America (Canada, the United States, and Mexico) on both maps. Which map most closely reflects the image you have of the United States, either from your social studies classes or from your exposure to television news?

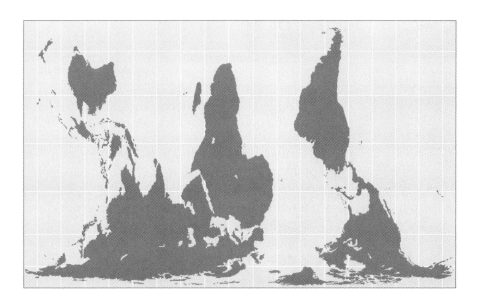

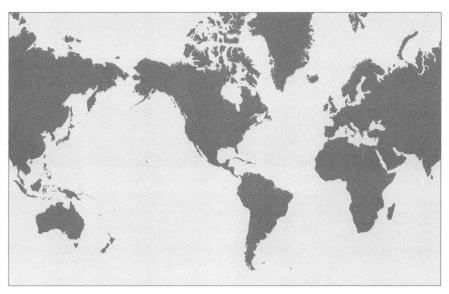

2. Comment on the difference in the two maps with regard to the position of the United States in the Western Hemisphere and in the world, particularly in relation to the continents of Asia and Africa.

3. How might the second map affect one's perception of America's size and influence in the world?

4. Does studying the first map in any way change your worldview with regard to America's role as the dominant superpower in world affairs?

■ THE STRUCTURE OF ARGUMENTS

According to rules established by rhetoricians in ancient Greece, a sound argument had to conform to a rigid format. Through the centuries, these rules have been relaxed so that the argumentative form today is as varied as any other kind of nonfiction writing. A conventional argument includes these elements, although they may not appear in the order presented here:

- The claim (also called the thesis or proposition)—the writer's main idea or point
- Evidence to support the claim
- A refutation, sometimes called the concession—the writer's discussion of opposing viewpoints
- A conclusion, which might be a restatement of the claim or a recommendation for future action

■ THE TEST OF A GOOD ARGUMENT

Some of what is published is very good, some is mediocre, and some is awful. How do you learn to tell the difference? What criteria should you use to determine whether a persuasive or argumentative piece of writing is good or bad, sound or unsound? Here are some simple standards for judging what you read.

- The writer should have some competence or expertise in the area; in other words, he or she should be considered an **authority.**
- The central **claim**—the **argument** or **proposition**—should be clearly stated, or at least clearly implied.
- **Key words** should be **defined,** especially abstract words open to subjective interpretation (like *honor, responsibility, evil, censorship*). The language should be clear and unambiguous.
- The **supporting evidence** should be logically organized, relevant to the main idea, and sufficient to support the claim credibly. Moreover, the discussion should appeal to our intelligence and to our reason, not solely to our emotions.
- Ideally, the persuasive writer should include a **refutation,** in which he or she examines one or two of the opposition's strongest arguments and disproves or finds fault with them.

■ TAKING ARGUMENTS APART

The remainder of this chapter is concerned with how to break down an argument into its constituent elements. Since the process is complicated, we will take up these steps one at a time:

- Evaluating the writer as an authority
- Identifying the type of claim
- Stating the claim or argument in a sentence
- Ascertaining any unstated assumptions
- Evaluating the supporting evidence
- Locating the refutation, if one is present

The Question of Authority

An **authority** is defined in the dictionary as "an accepted source of expert information or advice." The writer of persuasive prose should have firsthand knowledge of and/or experience with the topic. The writer may be a college or university professor, a scientific researcher, or a person with practical experience in the field. However, these are not hard-and-fast requirements, since ordinary citizens may be experts on various issues by virtue of their experience in the world, and they may express their opinions on these issues in the letters-to-the-editor section of newspapers, in chat rooms, and in other venues. And although print journalists may not be experts in the strict sense of the word, they do often specialize in a subject; they are also experienced at delving into an issue and intelligently presenting their findings. When a writer establishes his credibility (or at least the reason for his interest in the subject), we can deem the information reliable. Knowing that the writer is an authority inspires our confidence. It does not mean, however, that we need to accept the argument, just that we give it our consideration.

The debate over stem cell research was an issue in the 2004 presidential campaign. During his presidency, George W. Bush severely limited the number of stem cell lines available for researchers; John Kerry, his Democratic opponent, promised to fund stem cell research, arguing that the scientific community and the public both support an end to the restrictions. In August 2004, First Lady Laura Bush criticized Kerry's stand on the stem-cell issue, saying, "We don't even know that stem cell research will provide cures for anything—much less that it's very close." She went on to say, "I hope that stem cell research will yield cures. But I know that embryonic stem cell research is very preliminary right now, and the implication that cures for Alzheimer's are around the corner is just not right, and it's really not fair to people who are watching a loved one suffer with this disease." (Quoted in Ron Fournier, "Laura Bush Raps Kerry over Stem Cell Debate," Associated Press, August 10, 2004.)

Laura Bush is surely entitled to voice her opinions, but her heartfelt remarks are those of an ordinary citizen, not an authority on genetics whose claim that research is still "preliminary" and not certain to yield medical breakthroughs to cure diseases is questionable. (The critical reader will also note the irony in her remarks: Stem cell research remained preliminary because of the 78 stem cell lines suitable for study, President George W. Bush limited researchers to only 21. Scientists have argued that the 100 additional stem cell lines worldwide be made available for study.)

Practice Exercise 2

Read through this list of writers. If the person appears to be an authority on the subject noted, write "A" in the space. If the person appears *not* to be an authority, write "N." If you are unsure, write a question mark.

1. ___A___ Emeril Legasse, owner of two restaurants, one in New Orleans and the other in New York City, cookbook author, and celebrity chef on Food Network, judging a chili-cooking contest in Missouri.

2. ___A___ Larry Sabato, professor of political science at the University of Virginia, commenting on American presidential politics.

3. ___A___ David Innes, senior minister of the Hamilton Square Baptist Church in San Francisco, writing an editorial about why Christians should oppose gay marriage.

4. ___N___ Ernie Goldthorpe, a community college English teacher, sounding off about the government's ban on cloning human beings.

5. ___A___ George Abraham Thampy, a 12-year-old boy who, along with his siblings, has been home-schooled all his life, writing on the virtues of home schooling.

6. ___A___ Randy Jackson, a former bassist with John Fred and His Playboy Band and with Journey and an artist-and-repertoire record executive for CBS Records and MCA, now a judge on *American Idol.*

7. ___A___ Simon Cowell, frequent actor and television performer, who served as a judge for *Pop Idol* in the United Kingdom and now *American Idol.* According to his official Web site, Cowell says that the first time he gave a criticism was at age four when he looked at his mother's white fuzzy pillbox hat and remarked "Mummy, you look like a poodle."

8. ___A___ Paula Abdul, formerly a cheerleader for the Los Angeles Lakers and a pop recording star, now a judge on *American Idol.*

9. ___N___ Louis Freeh, former director of the FBI, explaining the mechanical failures that caused the crash of a TWA jet off Long Island in 1997.

10. ___A___ Jo Laster, a 15-year employee of Dell Computer who commutes daily from Round Rock to Austin, Texas, writing a letter to the daily newspaper to complain about traffic congestion on the local interstate highway.

11. ___A___ Cynthia Tucker, an African-American journalist and editor of the *Atlanta Journal and Constitution* opinion page, writing about race issues in America. (The paper is Atlanta's leading daily newspaper.)

12. __N__ Florence Henderson, the TV actress best known for playing Carol Brady on *The Brady Bunch,* doing a TV infomercial for a new antiaging cosmetic.

13. __A__ Former rapper and manufacturer of a line of men's clothing, P. Diddy Combs, commenting on the latest fashions for black urban males.

14. __A__ John R. Lott, Jr., a fellow at the University of Chicago Law School and author of *More Guns, Less Crime,* writing on common myths associated with gun-control laws.

15. __A__ Kathy Snow Guillermo, author of a book on the animal-rights movement and a writer for PETA (People for the Ethical Treatment of Animals), arguing that circuses should ban animal acts.

16. __N__ Deepak Chopra, author of many self-help books and consciousness-raising guru, discussing the child molestation scandals in the Catholic Church on *Larry King Live.*

Try to explain why Ernie Goldthorpe, Louis Freeh, Florence Henderson, and Deepak Chopra are not authorities on these particular subjects. (Whether or not the judgments Randy Jackson, Paula Abdul, and Simon Cowell make about *American Idol* performances are expert seems to be a matter of personal opinion.)

Identifying Claims

As stated above, the **claim** is the idea to be proved, the proposition. Claims can be divided into three types: **claims of fact, claims of value,** and **claims of policy.** Keep in mind that persuasive writing involves controversy, it is subject to speculation, and its essence is subjectivity. We begin with some simple examples:

Claims of fact:
- Blueberries contain high amounts of antioxidants that help prevent cancer.
- Long-term cigarette smoking is responsible for serious illnesses, including cancer and heart disease.
- Cantaloupe contains more vitamin C than oranges.

These claims can be proved by citing factual evidence and the results of scientific research.

Claims of value:
- Chocolate ice cream tastes better than vanilla.
- Compared to the first two *Lord of the Rings* films, the final film in the series, *The Return of the King,* is by far the best.
- Adoption is morally more defensible than abortion for unmarried pregnant women who choose not to keep their babies.

These claims are harder to prove because they involve matters of taste, morality, opinion, and ideas about right and wrong. The support would have to be in the form of reasons, examples, and personal experience.

Claims of policy:
- Public libraries ought not to censor Internet sites for their patrons.
- To reduce air pollution, the government should require SUVs to meet the emission standards of automobiles rather than light trucks.
- Danbury State University should encourage the use of vanpools and other forms of public transit for both employees and students.

These claims indicate a course of action, a proposal for change, or a problem that requires a remedy. These claims can be supported by citing good reasons and the likely effects if the proposal is implemented. Note that claims of policy usually include a verb like *should, ought, need,* and *must.*

Practice Exercise 3

Label each of these arguments according to whether it represents a claim of fact, value, or policy.

1. _fact_   English 100 improved my writing skills.
2. _policy_   All college freshmen should be required to take English 100.
3. _value_   English 100 is a more challenging and useful course than English 50.
4. _policy_   The countries of the world should unite in banning human cloning.
5. _fact_   Cloned animals may be more susceptible to illness and genetic defects than ordinary animals.
6. _value_   Making homosexual marriage legal is the mark of an advanced society concerned about guaranteeing equal protection under the law for all citizens.
7. _policy_   A marriage between gays permitted in one state like Massachusetts should not be recognized in other states.
8. _value_   Broccoli tastes better than brussels sprouts.
9. _value_   Animal acts in circuses constitute a barbaric type of entertainment.
10. _fact_   To quell their critics who claim that animals are mistreated, more and more circuses are abandoning their traditional animal acts.

Identifying Claims in Editorials

The exercise you just completed consisted only of one-sentence claims. In reality, however, claims do not appear in isolation. As noted before, prose writers—no matter what mode of discourse they choose—may place the main idea wherever it best suits their purpose. With editorial or opinion pieces, it is the same. However, it is possible to isolate three *likely* positions:

- At the very beginning—the direct-announcement approach. (This placement results in a **deductive argument,** because the claim or proposition, a general statement, is followed by the supporting evidence; for more on deductive reasoning, see Chapter 9, pp. 316–317.)
- In a sentence immediately after the introductory "hook"—a telling anecdote, an attention-grabbing set of statistics, some relevant background. (This placement is sometimes referred to as the funnel pattern; see the introduction to Part 5 on pp. 383–384, for further explanation.)
- At the very end, following all of the supporting evidence. This placement is called an **inductive argument** because the claim or proposition derives from the specific evidence. (For more on inductive reasoning, see Chapter 9, pp. 316–318.)

Practice Exercise 4

In this next exercise you are asked to locate and isolate the claim. Reprinted here are the beginning portions of six representative opinion pieces one might encounter in newspapers or periodicals. First, identify the type of claim (fact, value, or policy). You will see that some excerpts seem to straddle two types of claims; for these, indicate the secondary type of claim as well. Then, write a sentence stating the writer's claim or argument. Do not include evidence or support in your argument sentence.

A.

One of the small thrills of public school is picking which foreign language to study. It's like getting an airplane ticket to a faraway place—a chance to leave campus every day and see Berlin, Paris, Tokyo, Moscow or Mexico City through the mind's eye.

Make that Mexico City only. If trends continue, Spanish will be the only language taught in most Oregon high schools within a decade or two. That would be an educational travesty.

Many Oregon high schools are dropping their German or French programs, as *The Oregonian*'s Aimee Green reported Sunday. Others have lost Latin, Russian or Japanese. Many middle schools are dropping their foreign-language programs altogether. Most of these losses are because of budget cuts.

In many Oregon schools, Spanish is it. And while it makes demographic sense for Spanish to dominate, it's senseless for a high school to offer only one foreign language.

"A Smaller World, After All," *The Sunday Oregonian*, October 26, 2003

Type of claim: <u>value</u>

Argument: <u>For Oregon public schools to limit their foreign-</u>
<u>language offerings to Spanish would be an educational travesty.</u>

B.

For decades, cigarette smoking was cool. It suggested being grown up, sophisticated, macho, virile, sexy, sensuous, and even romantic. Cigarettes dangled from the lips of every movie star. Humphrey Bogart said in *Casablanca,* "Here's looking at you, kid," and millions played Bogey by lighting up.

We were had. The cigarette companies perverted or concealed the truth. Who can forget advertising slogans such as "Not a cough in a carload"? Even after 1964, when the surgeon general spelled out the risks, the cigarette companies kept pretending. Now hardly a month goes by without another study being released that conveys even worse news about smoking. Let the tobacco interests try to blow away these facts: Smoking is the most preventable cause of disease and death in the United States.

> Morton B. Zuckerman, "Let's Snuff Out Coffin Nails," *U.S. News & World Report,*
> October 19, 1998. (Zuckerman is editor-in-chief of *U.S. News and World Report.*)

Type of claim: <u>fact</u>

Argument: <u>Cigarette smoking is this country's most preventable</u>
<u>cause of disease and death.</u>

C.

"The idea that there is some pristine place—whether in the Pacific or the Caribbean or some other place in the Third World—where tourists can come and spend their money and have a fantasy 14-day rest from the maniacal life of the First World is false," says activist and Hawaiian studies professor Haunani-Kay Trask in *The Progressive* (Dec. 2000). "My advice is, if you're thinking about Hawaii, don't come. Stay right where you are. If you do come, remember that you're contributing to the oppression of a native people in their home country."

While businesses in Hawaii benefit from tourism, not all its residents do. Foreign investment in the tourist economy has driven up inflation—and the cost of living. As a result, nearly one-fifth of Hawaii's resident population is classified as near homeless.

> Karen Olson, "Please Stay Home," *Utne Reader,* July–August 2001

Type of claim: <u>policy; secondary claim—fact</u>

Argument: <u>Don't go to Hawaii on your vacation.</u>

Secondary argument: <u>Native people are harmed by foreign</u>

<u>investment in tourism, which raises the standard of living.</u>

D.

It's a corny joke that goes back a million years. A man riding on the old Erie Railroad spots a bug crawling across his Pullman bed. Irate, he writes a letter complaining to the railroad.

He receives a letter from the president of the railroad apologizing and stating that this has never happened in the history of the railroad. Unfortunately, accidentally clipped to the letter is a note that the president had only intended for his secretary to see. It reads: "Send this guy the bug letter."

No one even gets the courtesy of "the bug letter" these days.

These days, what the consumer mostly gets is neglect. Firestone sells apparently defective tires but refuses to acknowledge responsibility. United Airlines cancels flights without notice; when weather grounds a flight, the airline holds you hostage on the runway with soft drinks and packets of peanuts to sustain you. Then, to make amends, it announces that it plans to cut down on the number of regular flights. Its new slogan, I guess, would be, "United Airlines . . . Fewer flights to fewer places, but it beats sitting on the runway for 12 hours."

Consumers feel as if they have no power. . . . In the shadow of these behemoths, the consumer is reduced to a tiny figure crying in the wilderness. More often than not, his protests go unheard—literally.

> Jerry Della Femina, "They've Got Us Where They Want Us,"
> *The Washington Post National Weekly Edition,* October 9, 2000
> (Jerry Della Femina is chairman of an advertising agency in New York.)

Type of claim: <u>fact</u>

Argument: <u>American corporations are ignoring consumer</u>

<u>complaints.</u>

E.

One argument against gay marriage is that most Americans oppose it. It has never been condoned by common law. Many Americans view homosexuality as immoral and contrary to God's law. They believe, and sometimes cite allegedly scientific evidence to show, that children raised by gay or lesbian parents fare worse than those raised by a mother and a father.

One difficulty with such argumentation is that much the same was true, earlier in U.S. history, of interracial marriage. It was illegal in most states. Many or most Americans believed it to be wrong, unnatural and perhaps contrary to God's law. Volumes of scientific data were marshaled to prove that children resulting from such marriages were deficient.

Before we spur a truckload of indignant letters, let us be clear: We are not equating the African American experience with the experience of gays and lesbians, nor are we saying that because a majority of people believe something it must be wrong. We are saying that public unreadiness for or opposition to a censured social arrangement is not sufficient proof that the new structure must be immoral. It has to be examined on its merits—on the basis of fairness, justice and practicality. By those measures, it has seemed to us that the arguments are strong for allowing committed gay and lesbian couples to enjoy the benefits and obligations that accrue to civil marriage. How religions deal with this matter is their business. But society already allows such couples to live together openly and to raise children. To then purposely make life more difficult for them in dozens of ways—from trust law to hospital bedsides to children's medical care—is neither right nor logical.

"The Merits of Gay Marriage," *The Washington Post National Weekly Edition,*
December 1–7, 2003

Type of claim: _value; secondary claim—policy_

Argument: _The question of gay marriage must be evaluated on its_

own merits; denying gays the right to marry is neither fair nor

logical.

F.   This cartoon was published during the Summer Olympic Games in August 2004.

Copyright © Steve Benson.
Reprinted by permission of
United Features Syndicate,
Inc.

Type of claim: <u>claim of fact</u>

Argument: <u>The American Olympic teams have been tainted by the</u>

<u>accusations that some athletes have taken steroids or other</u>

<u>performance-enhancing drugs.</u>

Unstated Assumptions

Another analytical skill is uncovering the **unstated assumptions** underlying arguments. In our daily lives, we operate from assumptions all the time, most of which we never bother to articulate. For example, if you tell your friend that you will meet him at Gino's Pizza at 6:00 p.m. after your last final exam, your statement implies several obvious assumptions, such as:

- You will both be alive tomorrow.
- The bus you rely on to get you to Gino's Pizza by 6:00 p.m. will arrive on time.
- Your final exam will end in enough time for you to get to Gino's by 6:00.
- Gino's will be open for business.

Unlike this situation where we can safely take the unstated assumptions for granted, argumentative writing demands that we separate the argument from the assumptions that underlie it. These assumptions are seemingly self-evident beliefs that the writer assumes we share. Separating them out is more difficult than it sounds, and it takes some practice. For example, consider this sentence from a film review: "The unusual special effects in 'Pearl Harbor' make it an especially good movie." The writer implicitly connects the argument—*Pearl Harbor* is a good movie (a claim of value)—with the presence of unusual special effects as an essential component. Can we accept this assumption? If yes, then we can accept the argument; if not, then we can reject it, or at least expect the reviewer to justify it. One way to ascertain unstated claims is to ask these questions:

- For whom is the writer writing?
- What allegiances does the writer seem to have?
- Does he or she appear to favor one group over another? Who would benefit from our accepting the argument?

Review the last editorial excerpt from the *Washington Post* in Practice Exercise 4. The writer's unstated assumption seems to be that homosexuals deserve equal protection and treatment under the law, including the right to marry. The connection between this unstated assumption and the evidence—a discussion of fairness under the legal system—is sometimes called a **warrant**—a guarantee that the evidence cited supports the claim and leads to an appropriate conclusion.

How important is it that the evidence used to back up an argument be connected to the claim? Here is one example: President Bush and his advisors got themselves into deep political trouble after the weapons of mass destruction (WMDs) that Saddam Hussein supposedly had stockpiled failed to turn up despite extensive U.N. inspections and searches during the American occupation of Iraq. It seemed that Congress had declared war based on flawed intelligence. The Bush administration's claim—that Hussein needed to be overthrown because his WMDs posed a serious threat to other nations—was not backed up by physical evidence. One newspaper article summarized the problem succinctly: "The United States went to war with Iraq on the basis of flawed intelligence assessments that 'either overstated or were not supported by' the underlying evidence on Baghdad's weapons programs, according to a scathing report released by the Senate Intelligence Committee. . . . The report documented sweeping and systematic failures of the CIA and other U.S. intelligence agencies that led to erroneous conclusions that Iraq had stockpiles of chemical and biological weapons and was reconstituting its efforts to build a nuclear bomb." (Quoted in Greg Miller and Mary Curtius, "CIA Iraq 'Failures' Condemned," *Los Angeles Times,* July 10, 2004.)

Unstated assumptions in persuasive writing are not necessarily bad or manipulative. In fact, they are necessary if the argument is not to bog down into mind-numbing tedium, the certain result if a writer spelled out every idea underlying the discussion. In other words, they represent a kind of shorthand. However, if the assumptions are invalid or if they don't accord with your thinking, then you do not have to accept the argument.

Practice Exercise 5

Study these arguments. Then write down at least one assumption that underlies the discussion. The first one has been done for you.

1. School districts should not spend precious funds on expensive computer equipment at the expense of programs like art and music programs.

   Unstated assumption(s): Money allotted to school districts is limited. Or: It is more important that students learn to appreciate art and music than that they develop computer expertise.

   Note: Reminder—always ask yourself whether you accept the unstated assumptions. In this case, consider whether it's true that districts must fund either art and music *or* computer equipment. Could the dilemma be resolved if school districts stopped wasting money on frivolous expenditures? (In Chapter 9, p. 331, you will learn to recognize that this argument rests upon the either-or fallacy.)

   Start first with these easy arguments.

2. Many parents prefer to educate their children at home so that they can enter college at a younger age than their peers who attend traditional schools.

   Unstated assumption(s): <u>Attending college at a younger age is</u>

   <u>desirable.</u>

3. Of course, Tom Brokaw's memoir about growing up in South Dakota, *A Long Way from Home,* is a good book. It was the number 1 book on the *New York Times* bestseller list last week.

   Unstated assumption(s): <u>If a book is popular, it must be good.</u>

4. A college English teacher asked her students to read a non-fiction book and write a critique of it. One student chose Truman Capote's *In Cold Blood,* but the instructor rejected the choice, saying that a made-for-TV movie based on the book was going to be aired in the next few days. The teacher thought that the student would simply watch the movie and not read the book.

   Unstated assumption(s): <u>Students will cheat if they think they can</u>

   <u>get away with it. Students are lazy and will look for the easy way</u>

5. Vegans follow a healthy diet. They eat only fruits, vegetables, and nuts. No animal products are allowed.

   Unstated assumption(s): <u>Eating animal products is unhealthy.</u>

Now move on to these more difficult arguments:

6. Marriage should be restricted to a union between a man and a woman. Marriage was intended to offer a foundation for procreation and for the raising of children.

   Unstated assumption(s): <u>Only a man and a woman can satisfy this</u>

   <u>requirement.</u>

7. Advertising slogan for Stetson's Men's Cologne: "What man has never been a cowboy?"

   Unstated assumption(s): <u>All men have the desire to be cowboys.</u>

8. The government should not require food producers to list evidence of health claims on their labels, nor provide warnings about possible hazards in eating their products.

Unstated assumption(s):   <u>Consumers aren't interested in such</u>

<u>information. If they are interested, they can do the research</u>

<u>themselves.</u>

Now go back through these arguments and test each against your own experience and worldview. Which rest on unstated assumptions that you can accept? Which would you reject as being untenable or indefensible?

The Importance of Definition in Arguments	Earlier in the chapter, you learned that one characteristic of good argumentative prose is the definition of key words, particularly abstract words open to subjective interpretation or words used in a personal or idiosyncratic way. But good critical readers know that they must subject the definitions in arguments to the same scrutiny that they subject misstated assumptions to.

For example, consider this argument:

> This much is undisputed: Soybeans do not lactate. So soy producers should not be calling their beverages "milk," according to the National Milk Producers Federation, which filed a complaint with the Food and Drug Administration this month seeking to banish the terms "soy milk" and "soymilk" from grocery shelves and dairy cases.

The article goes on to cite the testimony of Rob Byrne, the milk federation's vice president of regulatory affairs: "We don't want them using milk's good name for their product." (Quoted in Cindy Skrzycki, "Dairy Group Tells FDA Soy Milk Is Full of Beans," February 29, 2000.)

The dairy federation is relying on a narrow definition of "milk" in support of its argument: Milk comes from the "lacteal secretion" of cows; soybeans come from the ground and don't lactate. Do you accept this definition of *milk*? If you look the word up in an unabridged dictionary, you will find three definitions, one referring to the liquid produced by female mammals used to nourish their offspring, one referring to the milk of cows and goats used by humans as food, and one referring to "a liquid, such as coconut milk, milkweed sap, plant latex, or various medical emulsions, that is similar to milk in appearance."

When you find that an argument includes a definition that you don't think holds up to careful scrutiny, consider the motive of the person or group offering that definition. In the case of the National Milk Federation, the motive is loss of sales. After health-conscious consumers began using soy products to replace the high fat and cholesterol found in cow's milk, milk sales declined. The milk producers may not like the inroads soy products are making in their profits, but the dictionary does not bear out their restrictive use of the word *milk*. There is a better way to argue this point. (Also if soymilk isn't milk, what then should we call the liquid inside coconuts?)

■ ANALYZING VISUAL IMAGES

In this portion of Chapter 8, we will examine the following types of visual images:

- Charts and graphs
- Photographs

Photographs, illustrations, charts, and graphs reinforce the message and help us learn. So it's important to study carefully any visuals that accompany the text.

Charts and Graphs

The same skills that you have been practicing with editorial material can be used to evaluate and interpret graphs and charts, which often accompany articles in newspapers and magazines (and material in textbooks, too). Graphs and charts show changes over time or how different items relate to one another. Used to enhance and to offer support for the ideas expressed, or to present complicated statistics in an easily comprehensible form, charts and graphs also make an argument: they try to persuade a reader to accept connections in the data presented. So it is just as important to subject a graph to careful scrutiny as it is to scrutinize the article that includes it. When evaluating a chart or graph, start by considering:

- What the title of the graph or chart is.
- What the vertical axis measures; what the horizontal axis measures.
- What relationship the graph or chart shows.
- Whether the chart or graph is accompanied by an illustration.

Then consider the data provided in the graph:

- What years does the data cover? Is it recent enough to be reliable?
- Does the data seem complete? Are there any obvious gaps? For example, are any years or relevant groups missing?
- What is the source of the data? Does the source have an agenda to promote or is the source likely to be impartial?

Next consider how the graph or chart relates to the text:

- Does the graph or chart support the point the text is trying to make?
- If the graph includes an illustration, what point does the illustration seem to suggest? Does the illustration relate to the text's main point? (See the material on interpreting photographs on pp. 297–298.)

With these considerations in mind, study this simple line graph from a *Wall Street Journal* article titled "After Years Off, Women Struggle to Revive Careers" (May 6, 2004). To read this graph, examine these elements:

- The title of the graph and the brief explanation of the subject
- The row of vertical numbers on the left side depicting percentages
- The horizontal row at the bottom depicting a range of years
- The line representing the trend in percentages within a range of years
- The accompanying photograph

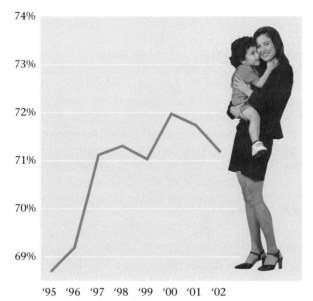

Working Moms
Labor-force participation of mothers with children under 18.
Source: Bureau of Labor Statistics.

Now answer these questions.

1. What is the subject of the graph? The graph shows the
   percentage of mothers with children under 18 who work.

2. Explain the overall trend as depicted in the line graph from 1995 to 2002. The number of working mothers in the last five years of
   the twentieth century was around 70 percent. The number climbed
   sharply from 1995 to 2000, after which it began to level off.

3. In what year was the percentage of working mothers highest?
   2000

4. What is the significance of the photograph accompanying these figures? Look at how woman is dressed. Note the expression on her and her child's face. In what way does this photograph represent a claim? The photograph shows a professional woman

 dressed in business attire. The happy smiles on both faces

 suggest that the child is not suffering from her mother's working.

 The photo represents a claim of value: Working mothers can do

 both: have a job and a happy child.

5. Is there any information missing from this graph that would be useful to understand the statistics better? Answers will vary, but

 here are two possibilities. The figures do not reveal how many

 working mothers have very young children, say below the age of

 six, nor do they indicate exactly what "labor-force participation"

 means—fulltime employment, parttime employment, or a

 combination.

Practice Exercise 6

The issue of childhood obesity has been in the news in recent months. One article explained that Arkansas became the first state in the nation to tackle the problem in an unusual way: mailing annual health report cards to schoolchildren's parents informing them of their children's weight and offering health and lifestyle advice. According to the article, "The Arkansas Center for Health Improvement, which is responsible for analyzing the weight data, found that 40% of Arkansas' children are either overweight or at risk of becoming so—10% more than the federal government had estimated for 2001 for this region." Researchers analyzed BMI (body mass index[1]) measurements for 276,783 students, or more than half of the students in Arkansas public schools. The chart that appears on the following page accompanied the article by Rosie Mestel, "Arkansas Schoolchildren Getting Weight Report Cards," *Los Angeles Times*, June 4, 2004.

[1]BMI is calculated by taking a person's weight in pounds multiplied by 703 and then divided by the height in inches squared. Nutritionists classify people with a BMI of between 25 and 29.9 as overweight; those with a BMI of 30 or more are classified as obese.

A Growing Problem

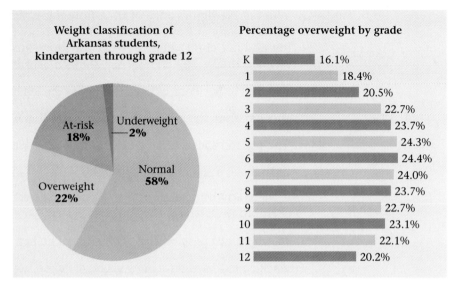

Weight classification of Arkansas students, kindergarten through grade 12

At-risk **18%**
Underweight **2%**
Overweight **22%**
Normal **58%**

Percentage overweight by grade

K 16.1%
1 18.4%
2 20.5%
3 22.7%
4 23.7%
5 24.3%
6 24.4%
7 24.0%
8 23.7%
9 22.7%
10 23.1%
11 22.1%
12 20.2%

Source: Copyright © 2005 by Associated Press. All rights reserved. Distributed by Valeo IP.

1. Locate the authority. What is the source of the information? <u>The state</u> <u>of Arkansas, though the article cites the Arkansas Center for</u> <u>Health Improvement.</u>

2. What is the primary claim represented in the graph? <u>Claim of fact:</u> <u>About a quarter of Arkansas children in grades K through 12 are</u> <u>overweight.</u>

3. Can you identify any unstated assumptions from the graphic material? <u>Being overweight as a child constitutes a serious health problem.</u>

4. What is the supporting evidence? <u>Two types of evidence are pre-</u> <u>sented: (1) the percentage of the total Arkansas student popula-</u> <u>tion that are of normal weight, are overweight, are at-risk, and are</u> <u>underweight; and (2) showing the percentage of children who are</u> <u>overweight by grade.</u>

5. Are key terms defined? <u>Neither graph clarifies exactly what is meant</u> <u>by "overweight" or "at-risk"; nor do the graphs explain what consti-</u> <u>tutes a normal BMI or what is considered to be overweight or obese.</u> <u>(The accompanying article does not provide this information either.)</u>

6. Is any information missing that would help you interpret the illustration? <u>The graphs show that fifth- and sixth-graders are</u> <u>more overweight than older adolescents or younger children, but</u> <u>the graph (and the article) don't explain why. What steps can</u> <u>schools take to help students maintain a healthy weight? Is mailing</u> <u>a health report card to parents a good idea or not? Do some</u> <u>investigation on your own. What is your local school district doing,</u> <u>if anything, to combat the problem of childhood obesity?</u>

Practice Exercise 7

This line graph is reprinted from a basic college communications textbook, *Broadcasting, Cable, the Internet, and Beyond* by Joseph R. Dominick, Fritz Messere, and Barry L. Sherman. It appears in a chapter titled "TV Programming." The source of the figures is not provided. As before, study the graph carefully by looking at the percentages presented on the vertical axis, the range of years presented on the horizontal axis, and the lines representing statistics for the five items listed as sources of news.

Sources of News, 1959–1997, with Percentage of People Naming Various Media as Their Source of Most News

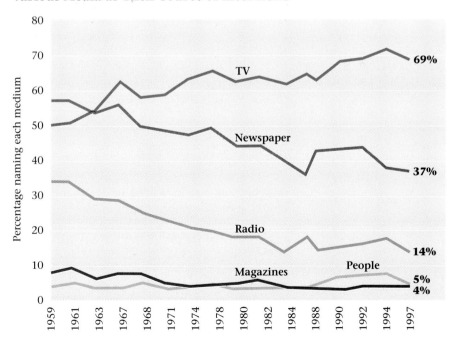

Source: Dominick, Joseph R.; Messere, Fritz; and Sherman, Barry L. From *Broadcasting, Cable, The Internet and Beyond: An Introduction to Modern Electronic Media*. Copyright © 2003 by McGraw-Hill. Reprinted by permission of The McGraw-Hill Companies.

1. What is the subject of the graph?   The graph depicts the percentages of people and the sources for most of their news.

2. In 1959 what percentage of people received most of their news from
   these media?

   from newspapers? about 50 percent

   from television? about 58 percent

   from radio? about 35 percent

3. About 40 years later, in 1997, what percentage of people received most
   of their news from these media?

   from newspapers? 37 percent

   from television? 69 percent

   from radio? 14 percent

4. Summarize the overall trends that this chart represents.   The percentage of people who get their news from newspapers has declined
   significantly in the 40-year period from 1959 to 1997, as has radio
   news, while the percentage of people who get their news from
   television has increased dramatically. News from magazines was
   never a strong medium for news coverage, and readership seems
   to have stayed nearly flat.

5. If this chart were redone now, what other medium would be included
   that was apparently not a factor in 1997? the Internet

   Can you speculate about the impact this medium would have on these
   figures? This is impossible to answer, but a survey of reading habits
   I did in three classes where this textbook is used revealed that
   these students receive at least 25 percent of their news from the
   Internet, around 50 percent from television, and only around
   10 percent from newspaper.

6. What do these figures suggest about the ability of the American people to understand the complex issues of the day?   <u>Answers will vary, but</u>

<u>the figures are troubling. Despite the obvious appeal of television,</u>

<u>the nature of the medium renders it incapable of presenting the</u>

<u>complexities of difficult issues facing the world today.</u>

Photographs

Like graphs and charts, photographs present information—the content of the image—but they also convey a sense of character or place and often evoke an emotional response in the reader. Because photographs can be so powerful, it's crucial to analyze them carefully. When analyzing photographs, consider these following elements:[2]

- When was the photograph taken? Under what circumstances was it taken? What is the historical context?
- What is the subject of the photograph? What or who is being depicted?
- How are the figures or objects arranged? Does one particular figure or object dominate the photograph? Are there background elements that are of interest?
- What activity is being depicted? Of what significance is this activity?
- Examine the faces of the person or people depicted. What emotions or feelings do their faces reveal? What do they seem to be thinking?
- What are the people in the photograph wearing? Does their clothing reveal anything about them—their position, status, occupation, or any other relevant information?
- Does the photograph appeal to your emotions or to your sense of justice?
- How do you think the photographer intended you to respond to the image?
- What is the larger significance of the photograph? What is it meant to represent?

War photographs have always aroused emotions and affected public opinion. As Kenny Irby of the Poynter Institute for Media Studies wrote recently, "It is true that a picture can be worth 1,000 words. And it's also true that some pictures are worth 1,000 pictures. Especially in war, certain pictures have a unique way of changing the course of history." (Quoted in Kenny Irby, "War Photography's Power: Shocking Iraq Photos Spark Media Debate over Taste vs. Truth," *San Jose Mercury News,* May 9, 2004.)

---

[2]I am indebted to Robert Keith Miller whose "Establishing a Framework for Analysis" in *Motives for Writing,* 4th edition, clearly lays out an extensive system for analyzing visual material. I have adapted and simplified some of his criteria.

One photograph taken during the war in 2004 was published, first, in the *Seattle Times* and, then, in several major newspapers around the country. The photo showed the interior of a cargo plane filled with rows of coffins draped in American flags containing the bodies of American soldiers who had died in Iraq. Since 1991, the Defense Department has prohibited the media from taking photographs of coffins containing American soldiers who have died in combat. The woman whose photograph was published in the *Seattle Times* was fired from her job with a Defense Department contractor. However, after a citizen filed a request under the Freedom of Information Act, the Pentagon was obligated to turn over several hundred photos. (A large collection of these photos can be seen at www.thememoryhole.org.)

Here is one of the photos. Study it carefully and then analyze it according to the criteria outlined here.

What is your reaction to this photograph? What message do the images of coffins draped in American flags send to the viewer? Answers will vary, but notice that the flag-draped coffins dominate the photo and that the uniformed soldiers in the background are relatively indistinct. Also, the images of the coffins humanize the statistics published in the paper or on the evening news of the numbers of war dead. The photograph is a sobering reminder of the Americans dying in war.

**Practice
Exercise 8**

Again using the criteria listed on p. 297, analyze these two iconic photographs.

A. In its landmark 1954 decision in *Brown v. the Board of Education,* the Supreme Court ruled that segregation in public schools was illegal. This photograph from the *Arkansas Democrat Gazette* archives shows a student shouting at Elizabeth Eckford, one of nine students who attempted to attend the all-white Central High School in Little Rock, Arkansas, in 1957. Eckford and a group of black students had sought admission to the high school, but were turned away from the school by the Arkansas National Guard.

How effective is this photograph at showing the racial division that existed 50 years ago in the United States? What was the photographer's intent? What emotions does this photograph arouse in the viewer?   Answers will

vary, but it is clear that the white student yelling at the young black

student is a symbol of pure racial hatred. The photograph is meant to

arouse sympathy in us and represent the injustices of racial segregation.

🖱 ON THE WEB

Do an Internet search on the so-called "Little Rock Nine," the group of black students who tried to integrate Little Rock's Central High. In 1997, the group had a 40th anniversary, which is commemorated in a Web site. In 2007, they will celebrate their 50th anniversary. See what became of these brave young African Americans who were at the forefront of the U.S. civil rights movement.

B.   In June 1989, pro-democracy protestors staged an uprising in Beijing's Tiananmen Square. Chinese troops sent in tanks to quell the disturbance and restore order. This photograph shows a solitary man carrying only two shopping bags who confronted a convoy of approaching tanks and refused to move. To this day, the man's identity and fate remain a mystery. This showdown lasted for several minutes until he was finally pulled from danger by some onlookers.

Comment on the effectiveness of this photograph. What is its particular larger significance? What emotions does this photograph arouse in the viewer? _Answers will vary, but this photograph suggests the power one_

lone citizen can exercise even in the face of overwhelming military

power and government repression.

Evaluating Evidence

The term **evidence** refers to any information or support used to back up a claim. (Before continuing with this section, it might help to review Chapters 3 and 4 on methods of paragraph development.) The type of evidence can be used by itself or in combination. The types of evidence are

- Facts and statistics, including survey or poll results.
- Examples and illustrations from observation, personal experience, or reading.
- Good reasons (part of the cause-effect pattern).
- Historical analysis or citing of precedents from history.
- Testimony of experts and authorities in the field.
- Analogy.

In judging the worth of an argument, note the main supporting points; it is especially helpful to annotate them in the margin. Then ask if the evidence is relevant to the claim and if it is sufficient to persuade you to accept the claim. If statistics are used, are they current?

Practice Exercise 9

Examine these excerpts from editorials and opinion pieces. First, write a sentence stating the writer's argument. Then identify the type(s) of evidence used to support the claim.

A. Abraham Lincoln made this statement in a speech responding to critics who complained that the government was allowing the Civil War to drag on too long.

Gentlemen, I want you to suppose a case for a moment. Suppose that all the property you were worth was in gold, and you had to put it in the hands of Blondin, the famous rope-walker, to carry across the Niagara Falls on a tight rope. Would you shake the rope while he was passing over it, or keep shouting to him, "Blondin, stop a little more! Go a little faster!"? No. I am sure you would not. You would hold your breath as well as your tongue, and keep your hand off until he was safely over. Now, the Government is in the same situation. It is carrying an immense weight across a stormy ocean. Untold treasures are in its hands. It is doing the best it can. Don't badger it! Just keep still, and it will get you safely over.

Abraham Lincoln

Argument: The government is in too dangerous a position to speed
up the war effort.

Type(s) of evidence: analogy

B.   Albert Hunt is a political analyst for *The Wall Street Journal.*

I am a convert to accepting gay marriages. But as a political issue it's a time bomb for both sides.

This is evident in this week's *Wall Street Journal*/NBC News national survey. Americans are evenly split on the question of civil unions, or granting spousal benefits to gay and lesbian partners; but solidly against gay marriages. Only marginally, however, does the public support a constitutional amendment to ban gay marriages. . . .

Bob Teeter, who conducts the poll with Peter Hart, believes gay unions is "becoming the number-one social issue in the country" with "fascinating" cross-currents: "The country and young people especially are becoming much more tolerant of gays. However much of the country also is religious and considers marriage a sacrament. . . . My instinct is the public will stay divided for a while." . . .

The WSJ—NBC News poll shows that younger voters—18 to 34-year olds—by an overwhelming 68% support civil unions, and a majority even supports gay marriages. As was also true during the drive for civil rights a generation or two ago, younger Americans are not encumbered with many of the hang-ups and prejudices of their elders; the tide is with change.

Note: This editorial is accompanied by the following statistical chart:

Divided

	FAVOR	OPPOSE
Civil unions	43%	44%
Gay marriage	32%	56%
Constitutional amendment	48%	44%

Albert R. Hunt, "Public Ambivalence on Gay Unions," *The Wall Street Journal,* December 18, 2003.

Argument: <u>Although the public is more supportive of civil unions,</u>
<u>it remains divided on the issue of gay marriage.</u>

Type(s) of evidence: <u>statistics, national poll results</u>

C.

Suppose there's an alligator in your neighborhood. He's been around for years, and he hangs out at the far end of your street, feeding on chickens that the local children bring him. The alligator's been there so long, and caused such little inconvenience, that he's receded to a small place in your mind; you casually leave food out on the porch, and the backdoor's wide open. But while your thoughts are elsewhere, the alligator is tripling in size. One day those chickens aren't enough, and he sets off for your bedroom.

I'm reduced to spinning metaphors like this by the spectacle in Congress two weeks ago. The House passed a corporate tax bill so expensive and so bad that there's only one way to explain it: Congress has just plain forgotten that we are racking up a national debt that may eventually devour us. The subject of budget deficits is so eyerollingly tedious, and we've survived so cheerfully until now, that nobody cares anymore. Well, think of it this way: The House bill is the equivalent of dunking your head in the alligator's favorite sauce and going to sleep next to him.

Sebastian Mallaby, "Deficits' Bite,"
The Washington Post National Weekly Edition, June 28–July 11, 2004

Argument: <u>Congress's recent corporate tax bill reveals a shocking</u>

<u>indifference to the massive national debt.</u>

Type(s) of evidence: <u>analogy</u>

D. Rubin is professor of computer science and technical director of the Information Security Institute at Johns Hopkins University.

In August 2003, a large portion of the Northeast United States, including all of New York City, suffered a two-day blackout because of a software glitch in one of the power grid control systems.

Last Sunday, thousands of airline passengers on American Airways and US Airways were stranded in airports across the country because of a software glitch. US Airways was down for two hours; American was down for three. More than 200 flights were canceled. "This has never happened before," said Tim Wagner of American Airlines. "We were unaware that there was the potential for this to happen."

Software glitches are no surprise to computer scientists. Software in highly complex, and large, computerized systems often fail in unexpected ways.

Experienced computer experts cringe at the thought of relying on fully automated systems for critical operations. Nowhere is this more perilous than in voting.

There is a reason that the vast majority of the computer-science community, the very people who dedicate their lives to pushing the envelope of technology, are in almost uniform opposition to the rapidly growing phenomenon of fully electronic, paperless voting. It is not because the computer-science community has suddenly decided that computers are bad. Rather, those who deal with technology daily know that there are risks associated with electronic systems that are not as apparent to those with less experience.

Even limited exposure to computers, however, gives some appreciation of the dangers. Who hasn't lost data because of corrupt files? Who hasn't experienced a hard-disk failure, or data loss due to an operating-system crash? "Our computers are down; please call back later," is a recognized excuse. We've all heard it.

Unseen Failures

When considering voting technology, it is important to remember that the worst problems we are likely to encounter have probably never been experienced. Advocates for fully electronic, or Direct Recording Electronic, machines say that these systems have never experienced a failure. Unfortunately, regardless of whether this is true, it does not matter. The most horrendous system failures are ones that have never been encountered before.

The question to ask is whether there is a potential for catastrophic breakdown of the system, not whether a particular failure has been experienced. And the answer is that every fully electronic system has that potential.

What happens in a case where the results of an election appear questionable after the fact? Two weeks ago, in Miami-Dade County, Fla., a group of citizens requested copies of the ballot images from the 2002 race for governor where DRE machines were used. The request was prompted by the fact that the number of reported votes was suspiciously lower than the number of people who signed the registers at the polls. At issue was whether the voting machines failed to count some of the votes.

Unfortunately, when officials looked for the data, they discovered that it had been wiped out because of a system crash. For a few days, it seemed that the electronic voting system had faltered. Then, luckily, a CD was found with a copy of the data.

Hidden Problems

The lesson from Miami-Dade is not that the CD was found. Rather, it is that electronic data is fragile and easily corrupted or deleted. . . .

Avi Rubin, "The Perils of Electronic Voting," *San Jose Mercury News,* August 8, 2004

Argument: <u>Using an electronic, paperless voting system is too</u>

<u>risky when so much is at stake.</u>

Type(s) of evidence: <u>analogy, examples, good reasons, historical</u>

<u>precedents</u>

The Refutation   The final element in analyzing arguments is to look for a **refutation**—a section in the editorial or opinion piece that anticipates the opposition and offers a counterargument. Sometimes called a **concession,** the refutation forces the writer to look at the other side or sides and to explain where the opposition falls short. Even though many editorial writers—for whatever reason (ignorance, space considerations, laziness)—do not include a refutation section, a sound persuasive or argumentative piece should include one, even if it is just a sentence or a short paragraph. To examine an effective use of refutation, here is the beginning section of an opinion piece that Donald Rumsfeld, secretary of defense in George W. Bush's administration, wrote one month after the fall of Baghdad. In it, he defends America's invasion. As you read it, locate the two paragraphs that serve as his refutation.

1   WASHINGTON—I recently returned from Baghdad, where I had the opportunity to meet with the troops who liberated Iraq. Notwithstanding death squads and dust storms, they crossed hundreds of miles to reach the gates of Baghdad in less than two weeks, toppling Saddam Hussein's regime in less than a month—a remarkable achievement.

2   But just as remarkable as what they accomplished are all the things that did not happen. Because of the speed of the execution of the war plan, the regime did not attack its neighbors with SCUD missiles; the vast majority of Iraq's oil fields were not destroyed and an environmental disaster was averted; key bridges, roads and rail lines were secured; dams were not broken; villages were not flooded; the infrastructure of the country is largely intact; there were no large masses of refugees fleeing across borders into neighboring countries, and the coalition took great care to protect the lives of innocent civilians as well as important holy sites.

3   These accomplishments have provided a strong foundation on which to build the peace. Unlike Europe after World War II, for the most part the people of Iraq do not have to rebuild from war, even as they work to rebuild their country and society after decades of dictatorship.

* * *

4   There are still difficulties in Iraq, to be sure—crime, inflation, gas lines, unemployment. But the fact that such difficulties exist should come as no surprise: No nation that has made the transition from tyranny to a free society has been immune to the difficulties and challenges of taking that path—not even our own.

5   The years after our war of independence involved a good deal of chaos and confusion. There were uprisings such as Shays' Rebellion, with mobs attacking courthouses and government buildings. There was rampant inflation caused by the lack of stable currency and the issue of competing paper monies by the various states. There were regional tensions between mercantile New England and the agrarian South. There was looting and crime and a lack of an organized police force. There were supporters of the former regime whose fate had to be determined. Our first effort at a governing charter—the

Articles of Confederation—failed miserably, and it took eight years of contentious debate before we finally adopted our Constitution and inaugurated our first president. And, unlike the people of Iraq, we did not face the added challenge of recovering from the trauma of decades of brutal rule by a dictator like Saddam Hussein.

6   The point is this: It is now just seven weeks since Iraq's liberation—and the challenges are there. As Thomas Jefferson put it, "we are not to expect to be translated from despotism to liberty in a featherbed." It took time and patience, but eventually our Founders got it right—and we hope so will the people of Iraq, over time.

7   We have a stake in their success. For if Iraq—with its size, capabilities, and resources—is able to move to the path of representative democracy, the impact in the region and the world could be dramatic. Iraq could conceivably become a model—proof that a moderate Muslim state can succeed in the battle against extremism taking place in the Muslim world today.

8   We are committed to helping the Iraqi people get on that path to a free society. We do not have an American "template" we want to impose: Iraqis will figure out how to build a free nation in a manner that reflects their unique culture and traditions. . . .

Donald H. Rumsfeld, "Core Principles for a Free Iraq,"
The Wall Street Journal, May 27, 2003

1. Which two paragraphs serve as the refutation? <u>paragraphs 4 and 5</u>

2. What type(s) of evidence does Rumsfeld use? <u>good reasons,</u>

<u>historical precedent</u>

**Practice
Exercise 10**

Look again at the editorial excerpts in Practice Exercise 4, on pp. 283–286. Identify the sentence or paragraph in which a refutation appears.

■ CHAPTER EXERCISES: EVALUATING EDITORIALS

The following five editorials will give you practice in putting everything together that you have learned in this chapter. These passages, from the op-ed pages of major newspapers and from a magazine, discuss controversial issues. For each selection that your instructor assigns (or that you read on your own), consider these issues:

- Who is the writer? Does he or she represent an authority? On what basis?
- What type of claim does the argument represent?

- What is the writer's main argument or claim? Be sure that you can state it in your own words.
- If possible, list one or two unstated assumptions underlying the argument.
- What type(s) of evidence does the writer provide in support of the argument? Is the evidence relevant to the argument? Is it sufficient to support the claim adequately? List two or three of the main supporting points.
- Is there a refutation?
- Is the argument, as the author presents it, convincing or at least worth considering?
- Do you accept the argument? Why or why not? What other information would you need before you could accept it?

Selection 1

I'm not a vegetarian; I eat fish and fowl. I don't oppose experimenting on animals when necessary for medical research. I like zoos. I have no moral objection to wearing fur or leather. I think it's OK to keep pet dogs on a leash and birds in a cage. And I am no supporter of PETA (People for the Ethical Treatment of Animals) or its fanatic agenda.

But I do think sport fishing is cruel.

By sport fishing I mean catch-and-release fishing—fishing for fun and adventure, not for food. I have no quarrel with the man who takes a salmon or trout out of the water and eats it for dinner. What appalls me is fishing for its own sake. I don't doubt that it can be thrilling to drag a fish through the water by a barbed hook in its mouth, or that there is pleasure in making it struggle frantically, or that it is exciting to force a wild creature to exhaust itself in a desperate effort to get free. I don't deny the allure of it all. But finding gratification in the suffering of another isn't sport. It's sadism.

One of PETA's billboards shows a dog with a hook through its lip, and asks: "If you wouldn't do this to a dog, why do it to a fish?" PETA's analogies are frequently tasteless and morally repugnant, but this one is exactly right.

Writing a few years ago in Orion, a magazine about nature and culture, essayist and outdoorsman Ted Kerasote opened a piece about the ethics of catch-and-release fishing with a quote from a fellow outdoorsman, "the philosopher, mountaineer, and former angler Jack Turner."

"Imagine using worms and flies to catch mountain bluebirds," Turner told him, "or maybe eagles and ospreys, and hauling them around on 50 feet of line while they tried to get away. Then, when you landed them, you'd release them. No one would tolerate that sort of thing with birds. But we will for fish because they are underwater and out of sight."

I can hear the indignant reply of countless anglers: Fish are different. Fish don't feel pain. The hook doesn't hurt them.

But there is mounting evidence that fish do feel pain. A team of biologists at Edinburgh's Roslin Institute make the case in a paper just published by the Royal Society, one of Britain's leading scientific institutes. Their experiments with rainbow trout prove the presence of pain receptors in fish, and show that fish undergoing a "potentially painful experience" react with "profound behavioral and physiological changes . . . comparable to those observed in higher mammals."

Other studies have demonstrated the responses of fish to painful conditions, from rapid respiration to color changes to the secretion of stress hormones. Does this mean that a fish feels pain in the way that we do, or that its small brain can "understand" the painful event? No. It does mean that the ordeal of being hooked through the mouth, yanked at the end of a fishing line and prevented from breathing each time its body leaves the water is intensely unpleasant and distressing.

Anglers tell themselves that catch-and-release fishing is more humane and nature-friendly than catching fish and killing them. That strikes me as a conscience-salving fib.

"We angle because we like the fight," Kerasote writes. "Otherwise all of us would be using hookless (flies) and not one angler in 10,000 does. The hook allows us to control and exert power over fish, over one of the most beautiful and seductive forms of nature, and then, because we're nice to fish, releasing them 'unharmed,' we can receive both psychic dispensation and blessing. Needless to say, if you think about this relationship carefully, it's not a comforting one, for it is a game of dominance followed by cathartic pardons, which . . . is one of the hallmarks of an abusive relationship."

I'm not blind to the beauty of fishing. But any sport that depends for its enjoyability on forcing an animal to fight for its life is wrong. Wrong for what it does to the fish. Even more for what it does to the fisher.

Jeff Jacoby, "Fishing for Sport Is Cruel, Inhumane," *The Boston Globe,* May 11, 2003

Selection 2

Several years ago, the college where I teach created an electronic "quick mail" system to reduce our use of paper and to increase our efficiency. Electronic communication is now standard in most organizations. The results, however, are mixed at best. The most obvious is a large increase in the sheer volume of stuff communicated, much of it utterly trivial.

I have also witnessed a manifest decline in the grammar, literary style, and civility of communication. People are less likely these days to stroll down the hall or across campus to converse. Our conversations, thought patterns, and institutional clockspeed are increasingly shaped to fit the imperatives of technology. Not surprisingly, more and more people feel overloaded by the demands of incessant "communication." But to say so publicly is to run afoul of the technological fundamentalism that is now dominant virtually everywhere.

By default and without much thought, it has been decided for us that communication ought to be cheap, easy, and quick. Accordingly, more and more of us are instantly wired to the global nervous system with cell phones, beepers; pagers, fax machines, and e-mail. Though this wiring is useful in real emergencies, the overall result is to homogenize the important with the trivial, making everything an emergency and making an already frenetic civilization even more so. We are drowning in unassimilated information, most of which fits no meaningful picture of the world. In our public affairs and in our private lives we are increasingly muddleheaded because we have mistaken volume and speed of information for substance and clarity.

It is time to consider the possibility that—for the most part—communication ought to be somewhat slower, more difficult, and more expensive than it is now. Beyond some relatively low threshold, the rapid movement of information works against the emergence of knowledge, which requires time to mull things over, to test results, to change perceptions and behavior. The clockspeed of genuine wisdom, which requires the integration of many different levels of knowledge, is slower still. Only over generations, through a process of trial and error, can knowledge eventually congeal into cultural wisdom about the art of living well within the resources, assets, and limits of a place.

David Orr, "The Speed of Sound," *EarthLight,* Spring 2001

Selection 3

The merits of reducing the college degree to three years from four are being broadly discussed in academic circles. The debate was started by Fred Starr, the president of Oberlin, and is being fueled by a Stanford University curriculum re-examination that considers whether the time it takes to earn a baccalaureate degree should be reduced to three years.

The idea is appealing on the surface. At a time when college tuitions are soaring, cutting a year from undergraduate study would appear to reduce costs 25%. But like many other academic exercises, it is out of touch with reality.

The idea is not new. Harvard had a three-year degree in the 1640s. Its second president got into a battle royal with his board of trustees when he turned it into a four-year degree. Periodically in the years since, both the debate and "new" three-year degree have reappeared. Most recently, in the early 1970s, the Carnegie Corporation supported the creation of three-year programs at colleges and universities across the country. Nearly all of those programs are now gone. There was too little student interest to justify their continuation.

If anything, three-year degree programs probably would be even less successful now than they were then. There are several reasons:

First, student academic skills have declined since the late 1960s. More than a third of undergraduates report that they are in need of remedial courses. In short, students appear to need more education today, not less.

Second, the average time required to earn a college degree is actually increasing. A growing proportion of students are taking five years of classes, particularly at large public universities, which the majority of students now attend.

Third, a majority of college students work today while attending college. Most work 20 hours or more a week to be able to pay their tuition. The promise of not paying a fourth year of tuition would not eliminate their need to work. As a consequence, the notion of extending the college year or even the college day is impractical.

Fourth, eliminating the final year of college would be a financial disaster for most institutions, which are heavily dependent on tuition or enrollments to fund their operations. Schools would lose a quarter of their student bodies. Outside the West and the South, the demographics of the nation are such that the loss of students simply could not be made up. Colleges might have to raise tuition substantially to compensate.

However, there is a much larger problem for the three-year degree than any mentioned so far: It does not make educational sense. The four-year degree is entirely arbitrary. And so is the three-year degree. Degree time measures how long students sit in class. It is not a measure of how much they learn.

Imagine taking your clothes to a laundry and having the proprietor ask, "How long do you want me to wash them: three hours or four?" The question would be absurd. We don't care how long the clothes are washed. We want them clean. We want the launderer to focus on the outcome of his washing, not the process.

Education should operate similarly. Colleges and universities should define the skills and knowledge a student needs to possess in order to earn a baccalaureate degree, rather than the number of hours of lectures and classes a student should attend to earn a degree.

Students enrolled in college now are more heterogeneous than ever before. More than half of all high-school graduates are going on to some form of post-secondary education, and the fastest-growing group attending college is older adults. As a result there is a greater range of knowledge, skills and experience among college students than in the past. Many will require more than four years of instruction to earn a degree. Others will come to college with such rich backgrounds that they will be able to complete a degree in less than four years and perhaps less than three. For these reasons, it is a mistake for colleges to tie in their degrees to time served.

Arthur Levine, "College—More Than Serving Time," *The Wall Street Journal*, December 21, 1993 (Arthur Levine is president of Teachers College at Columbia University.)

Selection 4

It wasn't even close. The U.S. Senate easily shut down debate last week over a proposed constitutional amendment banning gay marriage.

Democrats were joined by a handful of Republicans—including Arizona's John McCain—who remember the cornerstone of conservatism: Government has no business regulating citizens' private lives. As McCain put it, the amendment "strikes me as antithetical in every way to the core philosophy of Republicans."

With that ugly business behind us perhaps it will be possible now to have a legitimate discussion about the dire state of heterosexual marriage. People of goodwill—those of all faiths and those with none—ought to be able to dispense with the lies and illogic that have poisoned the debate so that we can concentrate on the changed cultural expectations that bedevil modern marriage.

The two-career couple; the wife who earns more than her husband; disagreements over religion, money and child-rearing; old-fashioned adultery and betrayal—those are the challenges that confront contemporary couples. Not to mention a destabilizing factor embedded in 21st-century romance—the idealized Hollywood marriage, which gives young couples a false premise on which to base a lifetime pledge. (As a divorcee, I know something about the dilemmas that doom so many heterosexual marriages.)

As commonplace as those problems are, you haven't heard much about them in debate over "saving" traditional unions. Instead, narrow-minded preachers and pandering politicians have propagated a lot of foolish notions; among the most foolish is the idea of a connection between the faltering state of traditional marriage and the growing movement for gay rights. Jennifer Lopez, Britney Spears and Trista and Ryan—who married in a televised cereomony after she spent a few weeks culling him from a herd of unattached males on a so-called reality show—have contributed to the decline of heterosexual marriage. Gays and lesbians have had nothing to do with it.

Conservative activists have also fostered the false premise that marriage has always been defined as a union between one man and one woman. Nonsense. During 100,000 years of history of homo sapiens, marriage has been a union between one man and as many women as he could afford. The Bible tells us that King Solomon had a thousand wives and concubines. If you've read the record of any ancient civilization—whether the history of the ancient Israelites or the history of the ancient Greeks—you know that women were considered property, first of their fathers, later of their husbands, to be treated as the men saw fit.

In other words, there is a good reason that traditional marriage is in trouble. Many of those traditions were deeply flawed. If you don't understand the laws and traditions that have governed the treatment of women for thousands of years, you cannot possibly appreciate the ways in which cultural change has shaken the foundations of marriage.

Nor does the more traditional philosophy still preached by many conservative Christian churches—that the man should be the unquestioned head of his household—seem to make those unions stronger than others in which the man and woman share power. According to a study released three years ago by the Barna Research Group Ltd., "born-again Christians are just as likely to get divorced as non-born-again adults." And 90 percent of those divorces occurred "after they accepted Christ, not before."

(Gay and lesbian unions, by the way, encounter the same difficulties and evidence the same variety that heterosexual unions have shown. Some are loving and stable unions that last a lifetime. Many are not. How could it be otherwise, since gays are subject to the same cultural forces that affect the rest of us?)

It may be that, in the broad sweep of human history, traditional marriage is doomed. As human beings live longer and longer lives, the idea that one partner can satisfy our desire for love, stability and happiness forever may come to seem quaint.

But I still believe in the institution of marriage, still believe it is worth saving. Whatever else it has been, it has functioned as a building block of civilization. And a loving and stable marriage remains, I believe, the best institution for bringing well-adjusted children into adulthood.

The institution deserves at least an honest debate. It hasn't gotten that. We cannot begin to work on restoring heterosexual marriage unless we are candid about the cultural changes—starting with the Enlightenment and its emphasis on the individual—that have contributed to its decline. This vicious and vulgar business of blaming gays and lesbians gets us nowhere.

Cynthia Tucker, "Our Opinion: Marriage Needs Straight Talk," *Atlanta-Journal Constitution,* July 18, 2004 (Tucker is editorial page editor of the *Atlanta-Journal Constitution.*)

Selection 5

The murder of 20-year-old Raul Tinajero at the Los Angeles County Jail in April focused national attention on the violence that dominates much of the American correctional system. Mr. Tinajero had testified for the prosecution at a murder trial and had been guaranteed special protection that never materialized. The inmate against whom he testified roamed the jail for hours on a forged pass, the authorities say, until he entered Mr. Tinajero's cell and strangled him in front of his cellmates.

This marked the fifth murder of an inmate at the Los Angeles County Jail in seven months. Battered by public criticism, the jail opened its doors to reporters, who could see right away that violence was far from the only hazard associated with life behind bars. *The Times*'s Charlie LeDuff reported that the jail commonly housed as many as six prisoners in a single cell, which meant two slept on floors wet with toilet seepage.

A staph infection was raging through the cellblocks, and inmates crowded at the bars to show their lesions. These infections are especially dangerous to people with compromised immune systems, a category that includes many prisoners. The Centers for Disease Control and Prevention has cited the Los Angeles County Jail for an outbreak of drug-resistant strains of staph, which are especially aggressive and difficult to treat.

Staph can be partly contained by giving inmates access to soap and hot water and making sure that the laundry is thoroughly washed and dried. But jails that cannot organize themselves well enough to provide clean sheets stand little chance of success against the heavyweight infectious diseases that have become endemic behind bars today. Among them are H.I.V., tuberculosis and hepatitis C. Complications from hepatitis kill 25,000 people each year.

The diseases that incubate behind bars don't just stay there. They come rushing back to the general population—and to the overburdened public health system—with the nearly 12 million inmates who are released each year.

Some states have responded to the danger of prison epidemics by gearing up to test, treat and counsel inmates. But most of the system is not so forward looking. Faced with tight budgets, many jails and prisons have backed away from testing inmates for fear that they will be required to pay for treatment.

This approach was shown to be penny wise but pound foolish when the country experienced an epidemic of drug-resistant tuberculosis—driven mainly by former prison inmates—during the 1990's. Though expensive, testing and treatment for TB cases behind bars are more efficient and cost-effective than mounting a full-scale assault on the disease once it hits the streets. A similar pattern has emerged with AIDS as infected inmates leave prison and infect people outside, who then turn to the public health system.

The prison health problem registered in Congress, which in 1997 held hearings and instructed the Justice Department to perform the country's first nationwide study of the health environment of jails and prisons. The study, a groundbreaking work entitled "The Health Status of Soon-to-Be-Released Inmates," was completed in 2000.

Critics of the government say that the report was shelved for two years before being made public—without the imprimatur of the Justice Department, which had worked on the project. Once released, the study sank so swiftly from view that even members of Congress seemed unaware that it existed.

"The Health Status of Soon-to-Be-Released Inmates" is available on the Web site of the National Commission on Correctional Health Care, which worked with the government on the project. It offers a sobering view of the corrections system, which has clearly become a major conduit for infectious disease. The rate of transmission for sexually transmittable disease behind bars is roughly 10 times that in the world outside. In any given year, 17 percent of people with AIDS, 35 percent of people with tuberculosis and nearly a third of those with hepatitis C pass through the corrections system.

This system represents a gaping hole in the public health network, thanks in part to the fact that prisoners become ineligible for Medicaid assistance while they're behind bars. Inmates who have the misfortune of being housed in jails and prisons without serious medical programs often have no choice but to cease treatment, which means that they get sicker and continue to pose an infection risk to others. Once released, these same inmates spend months trying to re-enroll in the Medicaid program and get care.

The United States would experience less infectious disease—which means fewer deaths and less strain on the health system—if the public health apparatus were fully extended into the jails and prisons. The health status report argues convincingly for a rigorous program of testing, treating and counseling that would slow the spread of disease and alert inmates to illnesses before they reached the crisis stage and became prohibitively expensive to handle.

These ideas are perfectly consistent with what we know about the importance of preventive medicine. But applying them to prison inmates will be difficult until we begin to see them not as outcasts who deserve to be cut off from the public largess, but as fellow citizens with whom we will eventually share a common fate.

Brent Staples, "Treat the Epidemic Behind Bars Before It Hits the Streets," *The New York Times,* June 22, 2004 (Staples is on the editorial board of *The New York Times.*)

C H A P T E R

9

Evaluating Arguments: Problems in Critical Reading

Building on the primary skills from Chapter 8, this chapter examines more complex elements of argumentation, specifically, how to identify flaws and weaknesses in persuasive writing. Learning to recognize deceptive techniques—whether they are intentional or unintentional—will sharpen your critical reading skills and safeguard your ability to think independently. The chapter ends with some readings on manipulative techniques in advertising, in the media, and in the use of statistics. Thus, in this chapter you will learn:

- What inductive and deductive reasoning are

- The problems associated with inductive and deductive reasoning

- The emotional appeals in arguments

- Common logical fallacies

- Bias and other deceptive techniques

■ INDUCTIVE AND DEDUCTIVE REASONING

Chapter 8 introduced you to the basic difference between deductive and inductive arguments. It's worth learning more about these two forms of reasoning, as problems in persuasive writing can result from faulty inductive or deductive reasoning.

Inductive Reasoning

As you recall from the discussion of patterns of organization in Chapter 5, in inductive reasoning the argument moves from the specific to the general. An **inductive argument** is built upon a set of facts derived from observation or experience that serve as evidence and that lead to a conclusion. Inductive arguments are sometimes called **probability arguments** because the conclusion is only probable, not certain. Consider this example:

Evidence:	The Krispy Kreme doughnut store in Akron has been a phenomenal success.
Evidence:	The Krispy Kreme doughnut shop in Pittsburgh is doing a booming business.
Evidence:	The Krispy Kreme outlet in the Erie location has been a big hit since the day it opened.
Conclusion:	Krispy Kreme donuts are very popular.

Although it is based on three pieces of evidence, the conclusion—a **generalization**—is only probable, because other conclusions are possible—maybe all kinds of donuts are popular in this region. However, the more instances of successful Krispy Kreme outlets one provides, the stronger the probability that the conclusion is true.

Deductive Reasoning

Unlike inductive arguments, a **deductive argument** moves from reason to conclusion or to a specific application with certainty. For example, if you know that your textbook is in your backpack and you know that your backpack is in your car, then you can logically deduce that your textbook is in your car. This is a logical conclusion that necessarily proceeds from the two pieces of evidence, called **premises.** Taken together, the two premises and the conclusion derived from them constitute a **syllogism:**

Premise 1:	My textbook is in my backpack.
Premise 2:	My backpack is in my car.
Conclusion:	Therefore, my textbook is in my car.

As long as the argument follows the prescribed form of the syllogism, it is *logically valid;* further, if the premises are true, then the argument is considered to be *sound* or reliable.

These two forms of reasoning are the foundation of persuasive writing. In an inductive argument, the reasons *suggest* that the conclusion is true, and as more evidence accumulates, the conclusion becomes stronger. Yet an inductive argument always involves a leap from the evidence to the conclusion—the matter of *probability.* But in a deductive argument, there is no leap or question of probability. Another way to keep the two forms of reasoning straight is this: Induction is more of an argument of *content,* whereas deduction is an argument of *form,* by virtue of the syllogism.

■ PROBLEMS WITH INDUCTIVE ARGUMENTS

With this background in mind, we can now turn to errors in reasoning that these two patterns of thinking sometimes lead to.

Hasty Generalizations and Stereotyping

The two most common types of errors in inductive thinking result from conclusions derived from insufficient or unrepresentative evidence. A **hasty generalization** is an all-inclusive statement made in haste, without allowing for exceptions and qualifiers. For example:

> If you're in the market to buy a dog, don't get a Shetland collie. All of them are too nervous and high-strung. My friend, Pamela Gentile, has a miniature collie, and that dog yaps at every little sound even when the phone rings. He jumps all over people, too.

This generalization stems from an observation of only one Shetland collie and leaves no room for exceptions. Producing even one calm Shetland collie negates the argument. A careful writer might qualify this statement by saying, "some," "often," "the one Shetland I have observed," and so forth. Notice, too, that a characteristic like nervousness is relative, calling for a subjective judgment. What some people might call nervous and high-strung, others might call spirited or playful.

Stereotyping is similar to the hasty generalization, except that it results in generalizations about people because of their gender, age, ethnic background, race, attire, or other characteristics.

> In my college math classes, I have observed that there are more Asians than any other group. Asians are really good in math, and that makes it hard for the rest of us who have to struggle just to pass.

This stereotype places all Asian students into a category based on a supposedly shared characteristic. If the observation is true—that math classes tend to have more Asians than members of other races—there may be other reasons to account for the observation besides the questionable assertion of inherent ability.

Incorrect Sampling	Inductive arguments often include a **sampling** of a larger group which, if done incorrectly, can produce a flawed conclusion. Consider the results of this study based on a sample: In 2000 a team of scientists at the University of California–Berkeley published a study in the science journal *Nature* saying that differences in finger lengths might yield clues to sexual orientation. In brief, the researchers found that lesbians had more "masculine" hands than heterosexual women. Supposedly, the index fingers of lesbians—unlike those of heterosexual women—are significantly shorter than their ring fingers. The researchers concluded that "homosexual women were exposed to greater levels of fetal androgen than heterosexual women." (Quoted in Carl T. Hall, "Finger Length Points to Sexual Orientation," *San Francisco Chronicle,* March 30, 2000.) This article was picked up by the national media and had women all over the country measuring their index fingers.

However, the method of sampling was problematic: The scientists had set up booths at gay pride events in Berkeley and San Francisco. Then they offered willing participants a free $1 lottery ticket if they agreed to have their hands measured and to answer a detailed questionnaire. The team examined the hands of 720 adults. Why is this an example of faulty inductive reasoning? Wouldn't 720 pairs of hands be enough evidence to lead to a valid conclusion?

No, the fact that female attendees at gay pride events are likely to be lesbian is also problematic. The number of hands isn't a large enough sample from which to draw such a conclusion. A researcher should examine several thousand pairs of hands from a diverse population before reaching a conclusion.

■ PROBLEMS WITH DEDUCTIVE REASONING

A flawed deductive argument is termed *unsound* if one of the premises is untrue or if it is a generalization. It is interesting to note, however, that the argument can still be *valid* as long as the syllogism is properly constructed and follows the prescribed form. The following is a valid but unsound syllogism:

Major Premise:	All Frenchmen are good lovers.
Minor Premise:	Michel is French.
Conclusion:	Therefore Michel is a good lover.

Because Michel has been placed in a class in which all the members are said to share the same characteristic, the statement is valid. Therefore, we can deduce (arrive at the conclusion) that he shares that characteristic. Yet the argument is *unsound* because the major premise—that all Frenchmen are good lovers—is obviously untrue, representing a generalization that could be easily invalidated by only one unromantic Frenchman. Note that the major premise above is the *conclusion* of an unreliable *inductive* argument:

Evidence: Claude is a romantic lover who has left behind a string of broken hearts.

Evidence: André is such a good lover that he has all the women swooning.

Evidence: Jules is a connoisseur of romance and is an excellent lover.

Conclusion: Therefore, all Frenchmen are good lovers.

Faulty deductive reasoning can also proceed from an unsound or unacceptable assumption. For example, consider this argument:

Major Premise: Only English speakers should be allowed to vote.

Minor Premise: This group of people cannot speak English.

Conclusion: These people should not be allowed to vote.

Here, the major premise rests upon a restrictive statement that not everyone would accept. While there are other ways in which syllogisms can be invalid or unsound, they lie outside the scope of this text. Suffice it to say that the careful reader should be alert to arguments either proceeding from generalizations (faulty deductive arguments) or arising from generalizations (faulty inductive arguments).

Practice Exercise 1	All the arguments in this exercise are faulty. First, determine if the argument proceeds by inductive or by deductive reasoning. Then explain the error in reasoning in each argument.

1. The city of Seattle surveyed a thousand residents who regularly commute by bicycle to work. Nearly 75 percent of the bicyclists felt that the city should build no new freeways. <u>inductive argument; small sample</u>

2. Heinrich at Plaza VW Motors repairs my Jetta. He's German, and Germans are the best car mechanics. <u>deductive argument;</u>

   <u>generalization</u>

3. Sue Jensen is against abortion. She must be a member of the National Pro-Life Coalition. <u>deductive argument; rests on a generalization</u>

   <u>that all who oppose abortion are members of the coalition *or*</u>

   <u>inductive argument; small unrepresentative sample</u>

4. It's no wonder the security personnel at Denver International Airport took a passenger aside for a more thorough search before allowing him to board my flight. He looked distinctly Middle Eastern. <u>inductive</u>

    <u>argument; stereotyping</u>

5. I don't see why people get so upset about small children seeing violent movies. Before the new codes went into effect, I took my seven-year-old nephew to see horror movies all the time, and he turned out all right. You don't see him committing violent crimes! <u>deductive</u>

    <u>reasoning; hasty generalization</u>

6. A college instructor with five years of experience observes that students who sit in the front rows of a classroom get A's and B's, and those who sit in the back of the room get C's or lower. He concludes that all college students should sit in the front of the room. <u>inductive argument;</u>

    <u>small sample</u>

We can now examine manipulative techniques writers use to get readers to accept conclusions they might otherwise reject. To simplify matters, I have divided these persuasive techniques into two types: emotional appeals and logical fallacies.

■ EMOTIONAL APPEALS IN ARGUMENTS

Emotional appeals are acceptable in persuasive writing, as long as logical evidence is present that balances the discussion. We also need to distinguish between legitimate appeals to the emotions and illegitimate ones. An illegitimate appeal attempts to control our emotions by spurious means; the writer plays on emotions that are either not relevant or appropriate to the argument, or the emotional appeal diverts one's attention from the real argument. A legitimate appeal relates directly and appropriately to the argument.

When you examine a piece of writing or a promotional piece, ask yourself: How good is this argument or product *without the appeal?* Is there any evidence besides the appeal? Strip away the fluff from the argument and examine the claim *for itself,* unobscured by emotion or sentiment. Be aware that the more emotional the appeal, the weaker the argument. This section examines several types of emotional appeals, alphabetized for easy reference.

Appeal to
Authority

A writer who uses the **appeal to authority** allows the claim to rest solely on the fact that a supposed authority is behind it. The authority may not be identified or may be highly biased.

- I read in a recent journal that a scientific study showed no correlation between a low-carbohydrate diet and high cholesterol. This is good news because now I can follow the Atkins diet and eat all the red meat, butter, and sour cream that I want. (Studies like this come out all the time, offering conflicting evidence on nutrition. Before accepting such an argument, wait until more evidence is in.)
- Linus Pauling, a chemist from Stanford University who won both the Nobel Prize for science and the Nobel Peace Prize, believed that massive doses of vitamin C could prevent cancer. (The fact that a famous scientist believes something doesn't make it so, nor in this case did the rest of the scientific and medical community accept his theory. Also, Pauling was a chemist, not a medical doctor or cancer specialist.)

Appeal to Fear   The appeal to fear makes us concerned about what will happen if we adopt (or fail to adopt) a certain course, or what will happen if we don't adopt a certain course. The public has been justifiably worried about the threat of impending terrorist attacks, though cynics have questioned if the timing of such announcements like those issued in the summer of 2004 was politically motivated. A typical headline read, "Al Qaeda Aims to Disrupt Vote, Ridge Warns" (*Los Angeles Times*, July 9, 2004). The government is faced with a dilemma in a case like this: Ignoring a legitimate terrorist threat might jeopardize public safety, while issuing constant warnings keeps everyone in a perpetual state of jitteriness. Here is another example:

- If the Springfield City Council doesn't stop medical marijuana from being distributed, pretty soon you'll have a whole bunch of drug addicts moving here and pretending they're sick just to get the drug.

This advertisement for a tracking device called Angel Alert appeared in the July 2004 issue of *Parents*, a magazine devoted to articles on child

More than 2,000 children are reported missing in the U.S. everyday.

Angel Alert enables you to keep a constant CONNECTION with yours.

raising. While stranger abductions and missing children are scary and are undoubtedly a serious problem, notice how the language at the top of the ad and the shadowy figures of adults targeting or surrounding the little girl in the accompanying photograph appeal to fear.

| Appeal to Patriotism | This appeal obviously relates to love of one's country, often implying an accusation that citizens who oppose a policy are not patriotic. |

- If you really loved the United States, you would support American foreign policy.
- Common bumpersticker during the Vietnam War: "America: Love it or leave it."

| Appeal to Pity or Sympathy | Should we adopt a policy simply because we feel sorry for someone? An **appeal to sympathy or pity** asks us to suspend our critical judgment because we pity a victim of sad circumstances or because we can identify with someone else's troubles. |

- The fact that Emma Jones hasn't paid her rent for six months is no reason for her landlord to evict her. Her husband died, she recently found out that she suffers from high blood pressure, and she has three children to support on her salary as a Wal-Mart sales clerk.
- A recent *Wall Street Journal* editorial on Martha Stewart's legal troubles included this paragraph: "Maybe there's some rough justice in putting Miss Stewart in an orange jumpsuit for fibbing about the circumstances of that [stock] sale with her broker. Manifestly the jury thought so. But in a case ostensibly brought on behalf of sticking up for the forgotten 'little guy,' we'd like to think prosecutors might have weighed the price paid by the truly innocent here: all the Martha Stewart Living shareholders, employees, executives, and so forth whose livelihoods have suffered tremendously since this case first broke into the headlines and whose futures, like their company, are now in limbo. And it's not just Miss Stewart's company; Kmart, a big buyer of Martha's products, is going to take a hit too." (Quoted in "Martha Stewart Misgivings," *The Wall Street Journal,* March 8, 2004.)

| Appeal to Prejudice | Like the appeal to fear, the **appeal to prejudice** inflames negative feelings, beliefs, or stereotypes about racial, ethnic, or religious groups or gender or sexual orientations. Emotion replaces reasoned discourse. |

- Letting so many immigrants into this country is a mistake. They take jobs away from Americans who are out of work, and they don't share our traditional values.
- Why would a man ever want to become a nurse? After all, women are the traditional caregivers in our culture.

Appeal to Tradition

An **appeal to tradition** asks us to accept a practice because it has always been done that way or because it represents some long-standing, venerable tradition.

- The Roman Catholic Church has forbidden women to become priests for nearly 2,000 years. Why should the church abandon this long-standing practice?
- The Democratic party has always stood up for the little guy.

Bandwagon Appeal

The **bandwagon appeal** rests on the assumption that everyone likes to be on the winning side or doing what everyone else is doing. The origin of this metaphorically named appeal comes from the fact that lots of people ride on the bandwagon during a parade.

- Eighty percent of Mapleton residents support the petition for the city to build a new football stadium. That's why I'm voting yes on Measure 11 on the November ballot.
- It's inconceivable that the United States still has the death penalty. All the nations in the European Union abolished this barbaric practice years ago.

Bandwagon appeals often use phrases like "everyone agrees," "we all know that," and so forth as a substitute for reasons or other evidence to support the claim.

- Everyone knows that pornography is the main cause of rape.
- Of course, you can see the undeniable logic of requiring all residents to pay for garbage service, whether they use it or not.

Look for evidence, not appeals to join the crowd. The crowd can be wrong. A related appeal tries to bully the reader into accepting an idea.

- Certainly no one sitting in this room would be foolish enough to vote against allowing the annual rodeo to be held in Woodside again this year.

Flattery

A writer who uses **flattery** tries to put us into a group of people that we admire and might hope to identify with, whether we share their convictions or not.

- Every well-educated person knows that James Joyce was one of the most important writers of the twentieth century.
- Men with good taste buy their clothes at Buffalo Shirt Company.

We like to think of ourselves as being well educated or having good taste, and the writer hopes to arouse this emotion in us with this appeal.

Just Plain Folks   This appeal lies in the desire of the subject (usually a politician) to have himself or herself perceived as just an "ordinary citizen" or **just plain folks.** It is the opposite of snob appeal.

- Despite the fact that John Edwards, Democratic vice presidential nominee in the 2004 election, made millions of dollars as a trial lawyer suing large corporations before he ran for the U.S. Senate, during the campaign he made much of his small-town roots, his father's blue-collar job in North Carolina, and the fact that he was the first person in his family to go to college. All of these things, of course, were true; nonetheless, the intent was to use the just-plain-folks appeal.
- When Bob Dole, Republican presidential candidate, was preparing to announce his candidacy in 1987, his media consultants chose Russell, Kansas, Dole's hometown for "the perfect backdrop." They chose Ol' Dawson's drugstore, where Dole had worked during his youth. (Journalists pointed out that this site had symbolic overtones. We know it as the just-plain-folks appeal.)
- When Democrat Joseph E. Kernan ran for governor of Indiana in 2004, his campaign used this billboard advertisement to demonstrate that the candidate was a regular guy, just like his constituents. The candidate is depicted touring a manufacturing facility where hard hats are required for workers. Donning his own hard hat as he talks to factory workers is a subtle way of using the just-plain-folks appeal.

Ridicule

This appeal asks the reader to dismiss an idea by subjecting it to ridicule rather than by analyzing its inherent weaknesses.

- The mayor's proposal to impose a license fee on all bicycles owned by city residents sounds like something an eight-year-old kid would come up with.
- Only irresponsible people would vote to oppose the Rockport City Council's proposed tree-trimming requirement.

A related tactic allows humor to substitute for supporting evidence.

Testimonial

Television and magazine advertisements abound with **testimonial** appeals whereby famous people—actors, athletes, celebrities, or other notable figures—are paid enormous sums of money to endorse a particular product. Heather Locklear touts L'Oreal hair color, and Michael Jordan has reaped millions for endorsing Nike products.

It's possible that Locklear and Jordan truly do know from personal experience that these products are excellent, but not all endorsements are so reliable. A recent pharmaceutical company ad for Prinivil, a high-blood pressure medication, featured baseball legend, Cal Ripken, Jr., otherwise known as the "Iron Man." The ad's slogan is "Pressure Under Control." The implication, of course is that Ripken takes Prinivil to control his blood pressure. But the tiny print at the bottom of the ad states: "Cal Ripken, Jr., is not hypertensive and is not taking Prinivil." Here, the testimonial is not a personal endorsement, but an attempt to show that the medicine is strong and hard-working, just as Ripken was on the field. The ad is misleading, but only if the unwary reader ignores the fine print.

Transfer

This emotional appeal is most commonly associated with advertising. By using **transfer,** the writer (or advertiser) deliberately plants the idea that favorable impressions about one thing will transfer or carry over to something else. Ironically, the *association* of the image is almost more important than the product itself. Advertisers identify this phenomenon as "selling the sizzle, not the steak." A glance through *Cosmopolitan, GQ, Marie Claire, Self,* and similar glossy magazines will yield many examples of transfer. (Note that transfer operates both with the appeals of flattery and just plain folks.)

Sometimes attempts to use transfer are so clumsy or transparently deceptive that they backfire. One such case occurred when Governor Pete Wilson of California announced that he would run in the 1995 Republican presidential primaries. Wilson gave his announcement speech in the shadow of the Statue of Liberty, the American symbol of welcome for immigrants. By choosing this site, Wilson hoped that the tolerance and generosity associated with Lady Liberty would be transferred to himself for the assembled crowd (and, of course, for that evening's television viewers). But political commentators saw through the ruse and reported the hypocrisy: Wilson had angered immigration supporters by supporting two anti-immigration propositions.

Practice Exercise 2

Using the information in the preceding section, study these examples and identify the emotional appeal each represents. For easier reference, the appeals are listed here:

- Appeal to authority
- Appeal to fear
- Appeal to patriotism
- Appeal to pity or sympathy
- Appeal to prejudice
- Appeal to tradition
- Bandwagon appeal
- Flattery
- Just plain folks
- Ridicule
- Testimonial
- Transfer

1. By the year 2030, if we continue to admit immigrants, especially from Mexico and Central America, at the same level we do today, whites will constitute only 51 percent of the U.S. population. That will mean the death of American culture as we know it.

   Appeal(s): <u>appeal to prejudice; appeal to fear</u>

2. The government should not have forced the Citadal, a military college in South Carolina, to admit women. The Citadel has always been a men's college, and it should just have been allowed to stay that way.

   Appeal(s): <u>appeal to tradition</u>

3. In 1999, an American fisherman rescued eight-year-old Elián Gonzales from a leaky boat off the coast of Florida. His mother and several other refugees had died trying to escape from Cuba. During the conflict over whether to return the boy to his father in Cuba, this argument was current: Elisabeth Gonzales gave her life to bring the little boy to our shores. To force the little boy to return to Cuba, with its repressive Communist system, can't possibly be in the child's best interests.

   Appeal(s): <u>appeal to pity or sympathy</u>

4. Between February and March 2004, 3,955 gay and lesbian couples were married in San Francisco. The California State Supreme Court later invalidated those marriages. While the marriages were taking place, many letters to the editor weighed in on the controversy, both for and against. Here is one such letter (paraphrased): People are ashamed of San Francisco Mayor Gavin Newsom's order to allow gay marriages to take place at City Hall. My friends around the country call San Francisco San Fran-sicko!

   Appeal(s): <u>ridicule</u>

5. Letter to the editor (paraphrased): Of course, gays and lesbians should be allowed to marry, and San Francisco Mayor Gavin Newsom is to be commended for engaging in civil disobedience on this issue. In the nineteenth century Henry David Thoreau committed civil disobedience and went to jail for refusing to pay a poll tax to finance a war he opposed. During the 1960s Southern blacks engaged in sit-ins to get segregation laws overturned. Newsom is simply following in the footsteps of these brave Americans.

   Appeal(s): appeal to tradition

6. If God wanted homosexuals to marry, he would have created Adam and Steve instead of Adam and Eve.

   Appeal(s): appeal to prejudice; ridicule

7. Clearly, the nation's new "get-tough" welfare laws have wreaked havoc on recipients. Forcing people who aren't equipped to deal with the real world and who have a limited education and no job experience by cutting off their benefits after two years will just increase the number of homeless on the streets.

   Appeal(s): appeal to pity or sympathy; appeal to fear

8. Let's face it. Sixty-five percent of the American people in a recent poll voiced concern about the direction in which the country was headed. That shows that things need to change in this country!

   Appeal(s): bandwagon appeal

9. In spring 2001 President George W. Bush gave two speeches on national parks. In one, President Bush stood before a magnificent giant sequoia in Sequoia National Park; the other occurred in the Florida Everglades, where the backdrop was a grove of sawgrass and mangrove.

   Appeal(s): transfer

10. "Neoconservatives widely predicted an easy occupation [of Iraq] followed by an immediate peace, followed by a 'flourishing democracy which would cause a domino effect across the region creating democracies elsewhere,' said Peter Singer, a national security fellow at the Brookings Institution. 'And then the very first foreign policy position taken by this new democratic Iraq, run by their exile friends, would be to recognize Israel, and that would somehow end the Arab-Israeli conflict, and bunnies would dance in the streets, and we would find life on Mars.'" (Quoted in Carolyn Lochhead, "Bush Speech Alarms Even War Enthusiasts," *San Francisco Chronicle.* May 26, 2004.)

   Appeal(s): ridicule

11. Paint store clerk to author: "Why did you choose Benjamin Moore paint to use on your bookcases?"
Customer: "I heard it's the best paint on the market."
Clerk: "You made the right decision. Benjamin Moore paint is definitely the best paint available. You can't go wrong choosing it."

Appeal(s): _flattery_

12. During the impeachment trial of President Bill Clinton, Democratic Senator Dale Bumpers from Arkansas urged his Senate colleagues to drop the impeachment hearings, arguing that the Clintons "have been about as decimated as a family can get." Bumpers continued: "The relationship between husband and wife, father and child, has been incredibly strained, if not destroyed. There's been nothing but sleepless nights, mental agony for this family for almost five years." (Quoted in "Ex-Senator Pleads with His Old Friends to Acquit," *San Francisco Chronicle,* January 22, 1999.)

Appeal(s): _appeal to sympathy or pity_

13. Drew Sheneman is the editorial cartoonist for the *Star-Ledger,* a newspaper published in Newark, New Jersey. This cartoon, which caricatures Vice President Richard Cheney, appeared on the editorial page during the 2004 presidential race.

Appeal(s): _appeal to ridicule; appeal to fear_

Paid for by the Committee to Re-Elect Bush/Cheney (If you know what's good for you)

Sheneman, Drew. Copyright © 2004 by Tribune Media Services.
Reprinted with permission.

14. Letter to the editor (paraphrased): Those so-called homeless people who hold up signs at intersections saying "Will Work for Food" are just a bunch of scam artists and slackers. What they really mean is "Will Gladly Take Your Money." Work is the last thing on their minds!

Appeal(s): _appeal to prejudice_ _____

■ LOGICAL FALLACIES: PART 1

The second type of manipulative technique in arguments is the **logical fallacy,** an error in reasoning that also invalidates an argument. Because these fallacies are difficult, I have divided twelve of the most basic fallacies into two sections arranged alphabetically; a practice exercise follows each section. It should be noted that, like emotional appeals, not all fallacies are purposely intended to dupe the unwary reader. Many writers lapse into them as a result of ignorance or sloppy thinking.

Ad Hominem Argument

Ad hominem in Latin means "to the man." This fallacy can take two forms: The first is to attack the person's personality traits rather than his or her position on an issue. For example, calling George W. Bush "stupid" and "arrogant" or John Kerry "cold" and "cerebral" is unfair if these characterizations are irrelevant to their positions on the issues. The second form attacks the character and reputation of a person because of whom he or she associates with (guilt by association), rather than on the basis of his or her actions. Here are some exceptions:

- Letter to the editor (paraphrased): Bill Clinton had a lot of nerve taking a moral stand promoting stem cell research. What a hypocrite! His own scandals and sexual adventures tell me that he had no business lecturing Americans on moral issues.
- During the Vietnam War, Vice President Spiro Agnew characterized intellectuals (who were generally opposed to President Nixon's war policies) with this famous alliterative phrase—"nattering nabobs of negativism"—thereby attacking their collective character rather than the principles they stood for.
- Letter to the editor (paraphrased): Republican Senator Bill Frist of Tennessee should never have been nominated to take over as Senate Majority Leader. His father and brother founded HCA, the hospital corporation that is now in a lot of legal trouble for various wrongdoings.

Begging the Question

When a writer **begs the question,** he or she asserts as true that which has yet to be proved. This unproved "truth" then becomes the basis of the discussion. A simpler way of understanding this fallacy is to think of it as a circular argument: The writer assumes to be true that which it is his duty to prove. The classic example of this fallacy is this question: When did you stop beating your wife? Either a yes or a no answer confirms that the person either has beaten his wife or still beats her, when in fact that charge needs to be established. Here are two more examples:

- Who is the best person to censor controversial articles in the campus newspaper? (In phrasing the question like this, the writer begs the question, assuming without proof that censorship of the campus newspaper is desirable in the first place.)
- During a murder trial, the prosecuting attorney asks the jury, "Does it make sense to release this murderer so that he can commit the same atrocities again and again? We need to lock this person up for a very long time so that he can never kill someone again." (This argument begs the question, since the very purpose of a trial is to prove whether the defendant actually committed the murder.)

Cause–Effect Fallacies	Fallacies involving cause–effect relationships can be divided into two types.

False Cause

This first type results either from citing a false or a remote cause to explain a situation or from oversimplifying the cause of a complicated issue.

- In the 1950s researchers pointed to public swimming pools as a source of the polio virus, noting that children who contracted polio had swum in public pools. (Note: Since thousands of city children swam in public pools, there were bound to be outbreaks of polio among them.) In fact, it wasn't the pools that caused the disease; the virus was spread by an infected person's sneezing or coughing.
- It is obvious that Sam Anderson would grow up to be an axe murderer. According to an interview I read, he was subjected to a rigid toilet-training regimen when he was a toddler. (The remoteness of this "cause" makes the conclusion improbable or questionable.)
- Billboard ad for ABC Television: "Before TV, Two World Wars. After TV, Zero." (This ad makes it sound as if the ABC network was responsible for world peace.)

Post Hoc, Ergo Propter Hoc

In Latin, this second kind of cause–effect fallacy means "After this, therefore because of this." The fallacy suggests that because event B occurred after event A, event A caused event B; in other words, the writer makes a connection solely because of chronology. This fallacy accounts for many silly superstitions, for example, when someone breaks a mirror and then blames that action for seven years of bad luck.

- Yesterday I forgot to take my vitamins, and this morning I woke up with a cold. That proves that taking vitamins prevents colds.
- Every time a Republican gets into the White House, the U.S. experiences a recession. That's why I'm not voting Republican in this election.

One problem with cause-and-effect arguments is that sometimes it's difficult to determine which is the cause and which is the effect. For example, research into the effects of excessive television on children has led to two conclusions: (1) children who watch a lot of television tend to be more aggressive, and (2) preschool children who watch a lot of TV tend to have problems paying attention. But which is the cause and which is the effect? As one recent editorial argued, "Maybe more aggressive kids are drawn more to TV. Ditto for the April study about preschoolers who watch hours of TV tending to have attention-span problems later on. It's possible that children with a propensity toward attention problems are drawn more to that jumpy onscreen world in the first place." (Quoted in "Kids' Brains in the Balance," *Los Angeles Times,* June 4, 2004.)

Either-Or Fallacy

Sometimes called *false dilemma,* the **either-or fallacy** discusses an issue as if there are only two alternatives available, thereby ignoring other alternatives. Rejecting one choice requires one to accept the other. Here are some examples:

- Rap star and fashion mogul P. Diddy's 2004 campaign slogan to encourage young adults to vote: Vote or die!
- A married woman should stay home and devote herself to raising her children. If she wants a career, she should forget about having children. (This fallacy ignores a middle ground or other alternatives, such as working part time, working at home, or the husband and wife taking turns with child care duties.)

Evasion

Evasion is a fallacy that occurs when a speaker or writer evades or ignores the question by talking around it.

- A reporter asks Mayor Sanchez how he proposes to solve the homeless problem. The mayor answers: "We must find a solution to the problem of homeless people on our streets. This is a complicated problem that I am taking very seriously."
- In March 2003, just prior to declaring war on Iraq, George W. Bush was asked why he thought "so many people around the world take a different view of the threat that Saddam Hussein poses than you and your allies." Bush replied "I've seen all kinds of protests since I've been the president.

I remember the protests against trade. There was [sic] a lot of people who didn't feel like free trade was good for the world. I completely disagree. I think free trade is good for both wealthy and impoverished nations. That didn't change my opinion about trade." (Quoted in William Finnegan, "The Economics of Empire," *Harper's Magazine,* May 2003.)

Practice Exercise 3

Study the following arguments carefully. Then decide which of these fallacies each argument represents:

- Ad hominem argument
- Begging the question
- False cause

- Post hoc, ergo propter hoc
- Either-or fallacy (false dilemma)
- Evasion

1. The Lytton band of Pomo Indians has proposed building a gigantic casino in San Pablo with 2,500 slot machines. Because more and more people have become addicted to gambling, I am opposed to this project.

   Fallacy: <u>begging the question</u>

2. The voters of the Red River Valley should vote against Congressman Lewis when he runs for reelection. He recently was accused of having an affair, and he is rumored to have smoked marijuana in college. He can't possibly represent our community's environmental concerns.

   Fallacy: <u>ad hominem argument</u>

3. The president of XYZ Widget Company reports: "The recent settlement between management and the labor union was a huge mistake. Giving in to the union's demands for a wage increase has resulted in low production figures."

   Fallacy: <u>post hoc, ergo propter hoc</u>

4. Iran and North Korea are part of the Axis of Evil because their leaders are vicious.

   Fallacy: <u>begging the question</u>

5. Letter to the editor (paraphrased): Has anyone else noticed that all of these schoolyard killings have occurred in suburban areas and that minorities are never responsible for such acts? This tells me that the suburbs breed violence more than inner cities.

   Fallacy: <u>false cause</u>

6. Because having a common language is an essential requirement of any democratic government, I'm planning on voting for Proposition 227, which will eliminate bilingual education in my state's schools.

   Fallacy: <u>begging the question</u>

7. I saw Madonna give an open-mouth kiss to Britney Spears and Christina Aguilera on the MTV Video Music Awards. And her little daughter, Lourdes, was wearing an outfit that said "Boy Toy." Madonna isn't a good spokesperson for personal values. That's why I'm not going to buy any of her books for my children.

   Fallacy: ad hominem argument

8. "Sugar is dead. . . . Every day that passes, and we do not allow farmers to grow industrial hemp means agricultural workers are unemployed. And our land lies fallow." (Quoted in Leslie Guttman, "Hemp—It's Rope, Not Dope," San Francisco Chronicle, May 28, 1999.)

   Fallacy: either-or fallacy (false dilemma)

9. In 2002 Oregon's Measure 23 asked voters to approve a single-payer or universal health care system. Supporters of the measure, which was defeated in the election, had argued that the big medical and health insurance companies were pouring a lot of money into the campaign to defeat the measure. They concluded that if big corporations opposed it, it must have been a good bill.

   Fallacy: ad hominem argument (guilt by association)

10. In August 1997 the Democratic National Committee was under investigation for questionable fund-raising practices. When asked for his reaction to recent revelations about the alleged laundering of foreign money into the DNC coffers, President Clinton responded, "I was sick at heart" and "disappointed."

    Fallacy: evasion

11. As I see it, residents can deal with the threats of rolling electrical blackouts either by conserving more or by building more nuclear power plants.

    Fallacy: either-or fallacy (false dilemma)

12. After Evansville allowed pornographic movie theaters and bookstores to do business downtown, violent crime decreased by twenty-five percent. This proves that restrictions on pornography rather than pornography itself is a cause of such crimes.

    Fallacy: post hoc, ergo propter hoc

13. In an interview on ABC's news magazine 20/20, Tatum O'Neal, former wife of tennis star John McEnroe, claimed that during their marriage he had taken steroids and used both marijuana and cocaine during the years he was playing in championship tournaments. Asked to respond, McEnroe wrote in a press release, "I am very disappointed in Tatum's statements. I had hoped that after all these years, she would see things

more accurately." (Quoted in Bruce Jenkins, "McEnroe Dodges Questions about Drugs," *San Francisco Chronicle,* June 27, 2002.)

Fallacy: <u>evasion</u>

14. When a reporter asked actor Alec Baldwin about Bill Clinton's sexual escapades, Baldwin was quoted in the *New York Daily News* as saying: "Sexual promiscuity has always been the medicine of choice for the chief executive of the United States. What would you rather have him do: take drugs?" (March 16, 1998.)

Fallacy: <u>either-or fallacy (false dilemma)</u>

■ LOGICAL FALLACIES: PART 2

False Analogy   As you will recall from Chapter 4 in Part 2, an analogy discusses one subject in terms of another, completely different subject. Although it does not carry the same force as factual evidence or good reasons, arguing by analogy can be effective and persuasive in supporting an argument. An analogy can break down, however, and become a **false analogy** if there are fewer similarities than differences, if the resemblance is remote or ambiguous, or if there is no connection between the two subjects at all. For example, consider this argument:

- Every red-blooded American serviceman knows that gays should be banned from the military. In the military we're like one big family living in close quarters, and a homosexual just wouldn't fit in.

This argument rests on the dubious idea that people living in military quarters are comparable to a family. To see why the analogy is false, we have to see where it breaks down and if there are more dissimilarities than similarities. Consider this analysis:

- One chooses to enter the military. The United States has a voluntary military, not a draft. However, one cannot choose what family he or she is born into.
- The argument implies in the military there is no privacy, whereas family members enjoy such a luxury.
- Members of the military wouldn't be "comfortable" with gays around, which implies, contradictorily, that gays couldn't "fit in" to a family, either.

In sum, when you examine these inconsistencies, the only real connection between the military and a family is that both are social institutions.

- In 2003, recording artists protested the plan by the Recording Industry Association of America (RIAA) to sue consumers caught downloading music on sites like Morpheus and Kazaa. The RIAA had filed suits against 261 people who had downloaded more than 1,000 files onto their computers because they had violated copyright laws. Alternative musician and Grammy nominee DJ Moby was quoted on his Web site as saying, in response to the RIAA's actions: "File sharing is a reality, and it would seem that the labels would do well to learn how to incorporate it into their business models somehow. Record companies suing 12-year-old girls for file sharing is kind of like horse-and-buggy operators suing Henry Ford." (Quoted in Moby Tour Diary Updates, September 10, 2003. Accessed at www.moby.com.)

Try to explain why this argument rests upon a false analogy.

It is important to note that not all analogies used in persuasive writing are false, and in fact, as noted earlier, analogies can be both effective and cogent—as long as the similarities between the two things being compared are greater than their differences. To illustrate, in 1987 a group of parents from Minneapolis (a city with one of the highest Native American populations in the country), called Concerned American Indian Parents, designed a poster distributed to local high schools. They were protesting the practice in some high schools of calling their athletic teams the "Indians." The poster depicted the banner of the real Cleveland Indians baseball team, along with three other hypothetical banners for the Pittsburgh Negroes, the Kansas City Jews, and the San Diego Caucasians. The slogan at the bottom of the poster read, "Maybe now you know how Native Americans feel." One of the schools that received the poster, Southwest Secondary School in Minneapolis, announced that it had changed the name of one of its teams from the Indians to the Lakers, demonstrating the compelling power of a good analogy.

Oversimplification

The fallacy of **oversimplification** can involve either reducing a complicated issue to overly simple terms or suppressing information that would strengthen the argument.

- Strikes should be illegal because they inconvenience innocent people.
- Human DNA has 23 chromosomes, while dogs have 39. Therefore, dogs are more complex than humans. (This argument oversimplifies the differences between humans and dogs and rests on a simplistic definition of the word *complex*.)

Rationalization

A **rationalization** is a self-serving but incorrect reason to justify one's position. It uses reasons that sound plausible but that are actually false.

- A student received a D in his college chemistry course. When asked by his parents why he received such a low grade, the student responded that he didn't like the instructor.
- It would be bad for my health if I stopped smoking. First, I would gain a lot of weight, and that would cause a strain on my heart, which might lead to high blood pressure. Anyway, science is surely bound to find a cure for cancer one of these days.

Red Herring

This colorfully named fallacy comes from the practice of dragging a fish across a trail to throw dogs off the scent of the fox. The fallacy works in a similar way: The writer who uses the **red herring** fallacy presents another argument that is irrelevant to the real question, thus throwing the discussion off the track.

- It doesn't make sense for people to get so upset about violence on television. All they have to do is look around at the larger society, and they'll see that violence is all around them. Why don't these critics worry about that issue? (The real issue under discussion is violence on television, not violence in the larger society.)
- SUV owners are getting a bad rap. Environmentalists and safety experts complain about the SUV's poor fuel economy and propensity to roll over in an accident. What these critics should really be concerned about is traffic congestion and the need for better mass transit in our cities.

Slippery Slope

The metaphoric name of the **slippery slope fallacy** will help you remember it. It suggests that one step in the wrong direction will lead to increasingly dire occurrences.

- The New York law prohibiting drivers from talking on cell phones while driving provoked this typical response: Denying drivers in New York the right to talk on cell phones is a bad idea. The next thing you know, New York's legislature will be passing laws forbidding drivers to listen to the radio, change the radio station, eat a Big Mac, or talk to their passengers while driving.
- In an NBC interview, Governor Arnold Schwarzenegger said that California's law against same-sex marriages needs to be obeyed, adding "we cannot have . . . mayors go and hand out licenses for various different things. Maybe the next thing is another city that hands out licenses for assault weapons, and someone else hands out licenses for selling drugs." (Quoted in Kirk Semple, "Schwarzenegger Backs Amending Presidential Rule," *New York Times*, February 22, 2004.) Since marriage licenses are obviously not in the same category as assault weapons or illegal drugs, Schwarzenegger's argument rests on the slippery slope fallacy.

Two Wrongs Make a Right

The **two wrongs make a right** fallacy is commonly used to defend wrongdoing and make it appear legitimate because others engage in the same practice. In other words, the writer accuses the opposition of holding the same views or behaving in the same way.

- During the campaign fund-raising investigations of 1997, President Clinton admitted that the Democratic National Committee had been guilty of certain abuses (money laundering, illegal contributions by foreigners, and so forth), but argued that the Republican National Committee had done exactly the same thing. (In fact, the Republicans were in a sticky position concerning the Senate hearings; they risked looking ridiculous if they came down too hard on the Democrats for practices that both parties had been guilty of using for years.)

Practice Exercise 4	Study the following arguments carefully. Then decide which of these fallacies each represents:

- False analogy
- Oversimplification
- Rationalization

- Red herring
- Slippery slope
- Two wrongs make a right

1. A university fund-raiser routinely sent her personal mail, including bills and gifts, using the university's postage, arguing that the university didn't pay her enough; thus the free postage helped compensate her for the higher salary she thought she deserved.

   Fallacy: _rationalization_

2. If doctors are allowed to consult reference books, medical journals, and World Wide Web sites, why can't we medical students use our medical textbooks or Web sites during tests?

   Fallacy: _false analogy_

3. Letter to the editor (paraphrased): For all those bleeding-heart liberals who gripe about the death of the tobacco bill, I say that the idea that a tax increase will stop people from smoking is way out in left field. If the administration really wanted to protect kids, it would do something about all the illegal drugs available to our young people. Children don't die from smoking cigarettes, but plenty die from using illegal drugs.

   Fallacy: _red herring_

4. A dog breeder refused to reimburse a customer, who had purchased a pedigreed German shepherd that later was found to have a serious defect requiring corrective surgery. The breeder argued: "You wouldn't expect your doctor to reimburse you if your child needed surgery, would you?"

   Fallacy: _false analogy_

5. Letter to the editor (paraphrased) after the U.S. Supreme Court over-turned Texas's sodomy law: If the Supreme Court says that you have the right to do whatever kind of sexual practice you want in your home, then you have the right to commit adultery, to practice bigamy or polygamy, all in the privacy of your own home. And as for gay mar-riage, if homosexuals are allowed to marry, what's to prevent me from marrying my sister, or marrying my dog, or even marrying myself?!

    Fallacy: <u>slippery slope</u>

6. All this talk about conserving electricity and buying more fuel-efficient cars is beside the point. What we really should be concerned with is becoming independent in our energy needs so that we don't have to go begging for oil from OPEC nations.

    Fallacy: <u>red herring</u>

7. I don't care whether file-sharing and swapping music online is wrong; most CDs cost between $15 and $18, and that's too expensive for college students who are already on a tight budget.

    Fallacy: <u>rationalization</u>

8. In 1996, a Massachusetts bill required, among other provisions, that tobacco companies reveal the additives in each cigarette brand, in particular "ammonia-based compounds that tobacco critics say boost nicotine delivery and make cigarettes more potent." Peggy Carter, a spokeswoman for RJR Nabisco, the parent company of R.J. Reynolds Tobacco Co., challenged the bill, arguing: "They wouldn't ask Coke, Pepsi or the Colonel to divulge their soft-drink or chicken recipe, so why should we be deprived of trade-secret privileges?" (Quoted in Barbara Carton, "State Demands List of Contents for Cigarettes," *The Wall Street Journal."* August 2, 1996.)

    Fallacy: <u>false analogy</u>

9. The controversy over cloning human beings and using stem cells for medical research is misguided. People really ought to be concerned about the disregard for human life that pro-abortion types represent.

    Fallacy: <u>red herring; oversimplification</u>

10. I don't see anything wrong with using the office copy machine to make copies of my personal income tax forms. Just yesterday I saw Joan Wilson downstairs in the duplicating room Xeroxing that mystery novel she's been writing on the side.

    Fallacy: <u>two wrongs make a right</u>

11. I'm opposed to those supermarket discount club cards. I don't trust the supermarket chains to keep my purchases private. What if health insur-

ance companies got data on shoppers' buying habits? The next thing you know, we'll have the food police poking through our garbage cans looking for sour cream containers, candy bar and Twinkie wrappers, and empty liquor bottles. Then insurance companies might deny us health benefits just because we have unhealthy diets!

Fallacy: <u>slippery slope</u>

12.   In June 2002, the Ninth Circuit U.S. Court of Appeals ruled the Pledge of Allegiance unconstitutional because the phrase "under God" violates the principle of separation of church and state. One argument against the ruling went like this: By outlawing the phrase "under God," the court is promoting atheism.

Fallacy: <u>oversimplification</u>

13.   At crocodile hunter Steve Irwin's reptile farm in Beerwah, Australia, Irwin outraged observers with this animal stunt shown on a TV news show: He held his one-month-old son in one hand and in the other dangled a piece of chicken in front of a large crocodile. When angry letters and phone calls swamped the television station, Irwin responded that he wanted to get his child used to crocodiles since they live in crocodile country. (" 'Crocodile Hunter' in Hot Water after Feeding Stunt with Infant Son," *San Jose Mercury News,* January 3, 2004.)

Fallacy: <u>rationalization</u>

14.   Letter to the editor (paraphrased): Concerning the prisoner abuse scandal at Iraq's Abu Ghraib prison, I was appalled and outraged at the photographs of American soldiers tormenting Iraqi prisoners. But before we label these American military personnel as torturers, we need to remember the photographs of Americans hanging from a bridge who had been murdered by Iraqis.

Fallacy: <u>two wrongs make a right</u>

15.   French scientists inserted jellyfish genes into a rabbit embryo to create a bunny that emitted a green glow in the dark. Supporters of this sort of tinkering with nature by manipulating an organism's genes defended it, saying that dog breeders manipulate mating all the time to produce dogs with desirable qualities, so why can't biotech breeders create glowing bunnies?

Fallacy: <u>false analogy</u>

■ APPEALS AND FALLACIES IN ADVERTISING

We are all exposed to advertisements every day, almost everywhere we look—on billboards, on television, on the radio, on the Web, even in stadiums and arenas. These ads, for the most part, are designed to get us to consume—to buy soap, to shop at Wal-Mart or Macy's, to eat at Joe's Café, to drink Budweiser beer. In effect, advertisements are mini-arguments that use both words and images to persuade us to action.

When examining advertisements critically, start with the same criteria that you use when analyzing a photograph. Consider:

- The subject—Who (or what) is being depicted?
- The action—What is happening and what is the significance of what's happening?
- The arrangement—What is in the foreground and what is in the background? Does one figure or object dominate? Are the background elements of interest?
- The people—What are they wearing? Does the clothing they're wearing reveal anything about their status or occupation? What emotions or feelings are they displaying?

Next, consider the copy (or text) in the ad:

- What does the text in the ad say?
- What tone is used?
- What emotional or symbolic overtones does the copy convey? Is there a more neutral word that could have been used to convey the same idea?

Because an advertisement combines text, called ad copy, with images, it's important to understand how they work together to create an argument. You should look for the strategies of persuasion that you read about in Chapter 8, as well as the material you read earlier in this chapter:

- What does the advertiser want me to do, think, or buy?
- How is the image in the advertisement designed for further this end?
- How is the text in the advertisement designed to further this end?
- What emotional appeals is the advertisement using—authority? fear? patriotism? pity or sympathy?
- Is the advertisement committing any fallacies, such as *post hoc, ergo propter hoc* (suggesting a cause–effect relationship where there really isn't one), false analogy (making an invalid comparison), oversimplification (reducing a complicated issue to a single term or omitting inconvenient information)?

Most readers are familiar with advertisements for cosmetics and beauty products, which often feature models chosen for their sex appeal and in various stages of undress. The advertiser—by using the appeals of flattery and transfer and a questionable cause–effect relationship—hopes to entice the consumer to accept an implied claim: using the product will miraculously endow the consumer with the same appeal the model enjoys. Advertisements for other items, from liquor and cigarettes to consumer goods and clothing, may also use these implied claims and emotional appeals.

Here are two advertisements for you to examine. The first is a billboard advertising Chivas Regal, an expensive brand of scotch whisky, directed toward the Latino consumer. This billboard appeared on Sunset Boulevard in West Hollywood. The area is largely commercial, with night clubs, restaurants, and hip clothing stores. After studying the layout of the advertisement according to the criteria listed at the beginning of this section, identify the claim that is put forth and determine whether the advertisement contains a logical fallacy or emotional appeal.

What claim is this advertisement making and what type of claim does it represent? Drinking Chivas Regal scotch will bring you the same level of emotional satisfaction that is depicted on the billboard—a claim of value. It shows an attractive Latino couple dancing, perhaps doing the tango, a romantic dance. The couple exudes intimacy, happiness, and sexual magnetism. The slogan is a takeoff on the common cliché, "This is the good life," here translated into "the Chivas life," suggesting a life rich in personal satisfaction.

Does the advertisement use an emotional appeal or a logical fallacy? The advertisement relies on the appeal of transfer (a person who drinks Chivas will experience the same gratification depicted). Finally, there is the underlying *post hoc, ergo propter hoc* fallacy: The advertisement presents a dubious link between drinking an expensive brand of scotch and sex.

This second advertisement is a public-service billboard advertisement sponsored by the Center to Prevent Handgun Violence. It appeared in a middle-class, urban area of Los Angeles.

What claim is this advertisement making and what type of claim does it represent? Guns should not be kept in the home where children might find them—a claim of policy. The photo suggests that a child's natural curiosity might lead him or her to examine a gun in the same way he or she examines any new and interesting object.

What evidence does the sign use to support the claim? The evidence is a pseudo-statistic, "A child a day is killed with a handgun"; no source is provided for this fact, nor does the ad indicate whether these 365 children are killed while playing with or examining a gun.

What is the ad advocating? Is its message clear? The advertising copy at the bottom raises a curious question: If children are obviously the "wrong hands," then whose hands are "right" for gun ownership? When looked at this way the claim seems muddled: Is the sign arguing that guns should not be kept in the house at all (even locked up), or is it arguing that children are sometimes the innocent or unintended victims of gun ownership?

Does the advertisement use an emotional appeal or a logical fallacy? The photo accompanying the text plays on our sympathy: The baby is extremely photogenic and exhibits a baby's natural curiosity. There is an appeal to fear—though in this case the fear seems a reasonable one.

Practice Exercise 5

Study these two billboard advertisements and then answer the questions that follow. The first is a billboard advertisement for Palm Pilot, a popular brand of personal organizer. It was located on Highway 101 near San Francisco International Airport, an area with a high density of high-tech companies.

A.

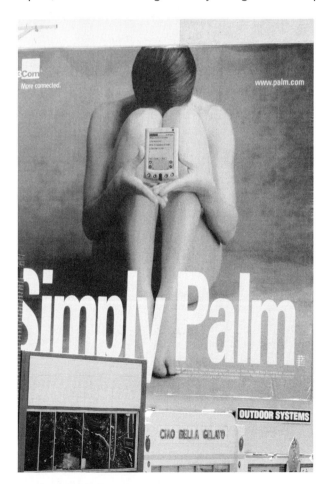

1. What is happening in the photo? What is the significance of what is happening? A naked woman is holding a Palm Pilot in her upraised hands (palms up); her head is resting against her knees. The photo seems to suggest that all one needs in life is a Palm Pilot. The device is more essential even than clothing.

2. What type of claim is represented in this advertisement? Claim of value.

3. Who is the audience for the advertisement? The advertisement is pitched toward an adult audience, to consumers who have not yet purchased a PDA.

4. Comment on the slogan The slogan "Simply Palm" is reinforced by the woman's upraised palms holding the Palm Pilot, thereby using a play on words. The phrase is short and snappy and therefore memorable. The slogan is also aptly demonstrated by the woman's nakedness.

5. Is there any emotional appeal or logical fallacy evident in the advertisement?   In this ad, the viewer is meant to apprehend the woman's nakedness as suggesting the *possibility* of sex, thereby suggesting a doubtful link between sexual experience and the experience of using a Palm Pilot. If the sexual link were not intended, why would the woman be naked? The fact that the woman's identity is stripped (her face is not revealed) reinforces the dominance of the Palm Pilot in her existence.

B.   This billboard for Pom pomegranate juice was displayed on Robertson Boulevard in West Hollywood, a neighborhood of middle-class to upper-class houses, expensive home design firms, and stores selling fine antiques, art objects, and other expensive items.

1. What type of claim is represented in this advertisement?   <u>The bill-</u>
   <u>board represents both a claim of policy and a claim of fact. If you</u>
   <u>drink Pom juice, you might live a long and healthy life. Pomegranate</u>
   <u>juice contains antioxidants, which promote good health. The word</u>
   <u>"might" is important because it makes the claim only a possibility,</u>
   <u>not a fact. Words like these are called "weasel words"; they are</u>
   <u>there, but they don't really register. Weasel words allow the ad-</u>
   <u>vertiser to make claims sound stronger than they really are.</u>

2. Who is the audience for this advertisement? What clues in the ad help
   you determine your answer?   <u>The advertisement is directed toward</u>
   <u>a wealthy audience. (Pom is expensive and is usually found in high-</u>
   <u>end supermarkets catering to a wealthy clientele.) The ad copy also</u>
   <u>appeals to a relatively well-educated audience who would be familiar</u>
   <u>with the nutritional claim linking consumption of foods high in</u>
   <u>antioxidants with preventing cancer and heart disease.</u>

3. Comment on the shape of the bottle and on the design of the word "POM." <u>The bottle resembles an abstract version of a curvaceous</u> <u>woman's body. The heart-shaped "O" in the word "Pom" reinforces</u> <u>the link between drinking Pom and maintaining a healthy heart.</u>

4. What support or evidence is offered to reinforce the claim? Is there any emotional appeal or logical fallacy evident in the advertisement? <u>The</u> <u>ad uses an appeal to tradition, implying that ancient people knew</u> <u>the healthy properties of pomegranate juice. It uses hyperbole.</u>

■ POLITICAL CARTOONS

Cartoons are a staple of newspaper editorial pages. Using exaggeration in the form of caricature, irony, and parody, cartoons comment humorously on the issues of the day, often presenting a stark vision of an issue stripped down to its essential elements. Study the cartoon below by Walt Handelsman, the editorial cartoonist for Long Island's *Newsday*. This cartoon appeared in May 2003. It points up the sad reality this representative college graduate faces. Armed with a diploma (in this case, a degree in the old cliché "rocket science"), he finds his ambitions thwarted by a bleak job market.

C.

Copyright © 2003 by Tribune Media Services. Reprinted with permission.

Practice Exercise 6

Examine the cartoons on this page and the next.

A. The first is by Ann Telnaes, an editorial cartoonist who won the Pulitzer Prize in 2001. Study the cartoon carefully; in particular examine the setting, the people depicted, and their dress.

Copyright © 2003 by Tribune Media Services. Reprinted with permission.

1. What is the subject of this cartoon?   The cartoon depicts a woman attempting to breastfeed her baby in a public place.

2. What thesis or argument does the cartoon embody?   Female breasts can be used for advertising purposes and on magazine covers (a customer is reading *Cosmo*), women can dress in scanty clothing, and men can wear tank tops in public places, but the public regards unfavorably a mother performing a natural human activity.

3. What point of view does this cartoon represent? <u>The cartoon points</u>

<u>up the hypocrisy of our attitudes toward the female body and</u>

<u>represents a feminist viewpoint.</u>

B.   This cartoon is by Gary Markstein, editorial cartoonist for *The Milwaukee Journal Sentinel*. Study the figures, the setting, and the situation described.

Copyright © Gary Markstein. Copley News Service.
Reprinted by permission.

1. What is the subject of this cartoon?   <u>The cartoon depicts an elderly</u>

<u>man who, because of high gas and prescription drug prices, is</u>

<u>forced to withdraw a large sum of money from his savings account.</u>

<u>Point out the large stack of bills that the teller is handing the</u>

<u>customer.</u>

2. What thesis or argument does the cartoon embody? <u>The cartoon</u>

<u>highlights the plight of elderly people who, forced to live on a</u>

<u>fixed income, suffer disproportionately from high energy and drug</u>

<u>prices.</u>

3. What emotion does the cartoon appeal to?   <u>It appeals to our</u>

<u>sympathy.</u>

■ BIAS AND OTHER DECEPTIVE TECHNIQUES

In this final portion of Chapter 9, we will look briefly at some other deceptive techniques used in persuasion. The particular topics discussed in this section are bias—both in print and in graphic material—misuse of authority, slanting, and distortion.

Bias

Bias occurs when a writer favors one side over the other, writing from a subjective viewpoint colored by—and possibly distorted by—his or her political, economic, social, ethnic, racial, or religious views. It also occurs by the writer's selecting carefully chosen details that reinforce that viewpoint. Knowing the background of a writer—not merely his or her qualifications for serving as an authority—can alert readers to subtle or not-so-subtle attempts to manipulate our thinking. Bias also seems easier to detect when reading a writer whose ideas you don't agree with. Writing that conforms to one's worldview seems right and natural, but it is likely to be just as biased as writing that contains objectionable ideas. So, as a critical reader, you must work hard to subject writing that reinforces your perspective to the same level of scrutiny as you do writing you disagree with.

Although total objectivity is not humanly possible, in a factual news article we should expect that a writer will attempt to be fair and to exercise careful judgment about what material to select and what material to omit. In persuasive writing, however, the writer has more leeway. Because the writer's purpose is to argue from a subjective point of view, we should not expect objectivity, which is associated with exposition. To some extent, then, bias is a necessary consequence of persuasive writing.

Further, the critical reader must not suppose that bias always assumes a sinister motive, and we must distinguish between *acceptable* (or fair) and *unacceptable* (or unfair) *bias*. Unacceptable bias is based on racial, ethnic, religious, or political intolerance or prejudice or on one's own economic self-interest. It may result from the writer's omitting relevant facts or from distorting the truth.

Further, if bias is evident, we must decide whether or not the writer is otherwise **credible,** or believable. To do so consider:

- Does the writer have expertise in the subject?
- What is the basis for the writer's ideas?
- Has the writer revealed any personal experience that lends credibility to the point of view?

Assuming that the writer does a decent job of presenting evidence (as discussed in the previous chapter), then one can entertain the argument, perhaps even accept it. In contrast, an article that shows unacceptable bias will include one or more of the manipulative techniques you have studied, for example slanted language (using euphemisms or sneer words), specious arguments, unproven claims, emotional appeals, logical fallacies, and the like.

Let us illustrate with a simple example: Suppose your English teacher tells you in a conference that your last essay received a D because it was weak. She recommends more specific development in the form of examples, analysis, or explanation, and more careful proofreading to catch careless errors. This evaluation would be an example of fair bias, because your instructor's credibility is backed up by her expertise (by virtue of her academic background and teaching experience). Your teacher's preference for clear, well-developed, adequately supported, and grammatical prose is consistent with criteria endorsed by other college English teachers. However, if your instructor gave your essay a D because you wrote about professional football, which she knows or cares nothing about, that would be *unfair* bias, the result of personal prejudice, a position not necessarily shared by other teachers.

Bias in the Media

The mass media in America are often accused of bias. Conservatives blast *The New York Times,* National Public Radio, CBS, and CNN for their liberal bias. Conservatives also claim that the American mass media in general is biased toward a liberal perspective. Liberals, for their part, deride Fox News, the *Washington Times,* and *New York Post,* among other publications and many talk radio stations for pushing a conservative agenda. Of course, both sides are often mistaken or overstate their case. For example, *The Wall Street Journal* is often cited as a newspaper with a conservative bent. To be sure, the unsigned editorials on the paper's daily editorial page do reflect a conservative point of view; however, every day the newspaper runs signed editorials reflecting a wide variety of perspectives (liberal, conservative, and middle-of-the-road), making this charge both untrue and unfair.

Sorting out these claims and counterclaims of liberal and conservative bias is not only difficult, it's also a waste of time. Because bias is inevitable both in the mass media in general and in persuasive writing in particular, a better approach is to put into practice the critical reading skills presented in this text: you need to maintain a skeptical stance toward claims and evidence, evaluate the piece according to the criteria discussed in Chapter 8, and most important, take a little time to investigate on your own. You can get help from your college librarian or use the vast resources available on the World Wide Web (see Chapter 10) to corroborate the truth of what you have read. A few minutes in your library's reference section or at the computer may turn up a wealth of pertinent information to help you decide if bias (fair or unfair) is present and whether the argument accords with your worldview. In summary, it's not sufficient to accept claims because they happened to make their way into the editorial pages of a prestigious newspaper or periodical; you must evaluate them critically with all the tools you possess. Let us examine two obvious examples of political bias, the first conservative, the second liberal.

An Example of Conservative Bias

The excerpt below is the opening three paragraphs of a *Wall Street Journal* editorial, one of an occasional series of columns titled "American Conservatism." (Note that the title forewarns the reader about the writer's bias— a good sign). The author, James Piereson, is executive director of the John M. Olin Foundation.

> The Capital Research Center recently reported that in 2002 Teresa Heinz Kerry presided over the disbursement of more than $65 million in grants through various Heinz family philanthropies. A large proportion of these grants went to liberal advocacy groups such as the Natural Resources Defense Council and the League of Conservation Voters, which promote further regulation of business and higher taxes on the American people. Thus do the Heinz philanthropies join George Soros, Ted Turner, the Ford Foundation and scores of other donors in funding left-wing causes.
>
> This report is simply the latest sign that organized philanthropy, like the academic world, remains firmly in the grip of orthodox liberalism. Among the largest foundations in the United States, liberal foundations have been well represented by such stalwarts as the Ford, Rockefeller and MacArthur foundations, the Carnegie Corporation and the Pew Charitable Trusts—which list combined assets of some $25 billion and annual expenditures of more than $1.2 billion. By contrast, there is not now, nor has there been in the recent past, a conservatively oriented foundation with sufficient assets to make this list. These liberal foundations alone outspend the main conservative foundations by a factor of at least 10 to 1. When smaller foundations—like the Heinz Foundations—are added to the list, the disparity is more like 20 to 1.
>
> Yet this imbalance in resources is one that conservative donors have always faced, and have succeeded in overcoming to a surprising degree. In the immediate future, however, conservative philanthropy will face a challenge that may prove far more daunting.
>
> James Piereson, "You Get What You Pay For," *The Wall Street Journal.* July 21, 2004

How can you evaluate or verify these claims? First, examine the claims themselves and look for examples of manipulation.

- Claim 1: Teresa Heinz Kerry (wife of 2004 Democratic presidential candidate John Kerry) disbursed $65 million in grants to liberal advocacy groups and other left-wing causes.

- Claim 2: Liberal foundations have more assets than conservative foundations.
- Claim 3: Groups like the Natural Resources Defense Council and the League of Conservation Voters promote regulating business and higher taxation.

The first claim suggests guilt by association and words intended to convey a negative connotation (especially "left-wing"), as if liberal advocacy groups that work to save the environment and regulate business are bad while conservative foundations that have the opposite goals by implication are good. The second claim is not so easy to refute, though a check on various World Wide Web sites yielded a great deal of helpful information. The John M. Olin Foundation, according to two reliable sources, has assets of approximately $90 million (not exactly small change), which is used to promote a variety of conservative causes and to fund professorships at elite American universities. Interestingly, the Olin Foundation home page does not list its assets, though it does offer a mission statement. (See www.jmof.org/.)

Also doing a search on Google for "conservative foundations" turned up a list of several organizations, among them the Lynde and Harry Bradley Foundation, which has assets of over $532 million; the Joseph Coors Foundation; and several others. You can check these out for yourself. For the third claim, go to the Web sites of the Natural Resources Defense Council, www.nrdc.org, and the League of Conservation Voters, www.lcf.org, to find out what these two groups stand for. Do they seem to promote the agenda Piereson suggests? Finally, note that in the third paragraph Piereson provides no explanation for this seeming contradiction: If the situation for conservative foundations is so dire, then how have they "succeeded in overcoming" this "imbalance in resources"?

An Example of Liberal Bias

On the other side of the political spectrum, there is *Harper's Magazine,* which publishes articles on politics, culture, literature, and social trends. At the beginning of each issue, its editor, Lewis H. Lapham, writes a column in which he comments on the social issues of the day. Lapham writes unapologetically from a liberal point of view; he expresses his views on the day's issues in straightforward, often eloquent language. In one such column published in 2002 (before the U.S. invasion of Iraq), Lapham writes that he has been "questioning the premises of our new-found war on terrorism." He then alludes to the fact that some readers—he doesn't say how many—had cancelled their subscriptions to the magazine because of his sentiments. In the piece, Lapham praises the United States for its role in ensuring victory during World War II. Then at the heart of the essay, he writes,

[I]t occurs to me that the victories over Germany and Japan presented the United States with a world-encircling supremacy that bore the stamp of an inherited estate. Although I don't know if anybody has written a book on the subject, I expect that many of the country's subsequent blunders overseas (in Cuba, Iran, and Chile as well as in Vietnam) can be attributed to the stupidity implicit in the assumption that fortune's child can do anything he pleases, that God is always with us and the world is made of painted scenery.

If America's once certain virtue now seems to me closer to a fiction than a fact, it's not because we deserve to be blamed for all the world's misfortune but because the makers of America's foreign policy over the course of the last fifty years have embraced a dream of power almost as vainglorious as the one that rallies the disciples of Osama bin Laden to the banner of jihad. For what reason do we possess the largest store of weapons known to the history of mankind if not to kill as many people as we declare to be our enemies? Why then should our enemies not kill us? Taking into account Washington's repeated experiments with the bombing of civilian populations as a form of propaganda meant to sell the splendor of democracy, how does it come to pass that our ranking geopoliticians fail to notice that explosions are hard to copyright? If the logic of globalization allows Chinese bicycle mechanics to manufacture cheap knockoffs of first-run Arnold Schwarzenegger films, what prevents a nonunion crew of Saudi Arabian terrorists from making a low-budget version of the Pentagon's "Operation Enduring Freedom"?

The events furnishing the headlines in recent months—the civil war in Israel as well as the attacks on New York and Washington—speak to the rising surge of violence in the world, and at the turn of a new millennium we might wish to ask ourselves on what ethical ground we defend our American freedom and prosperity. Nobody disputes the fact of our military predominance, but with what moral and intellectual force do we confront the hostility of a world populated by increasing numbers of people who bear us no good will and who maybe can find their way to weapons as terrible as our own?

Lewis Lapham, "Innocents Abroad," Harper's Magazine, June 2002

What is Lapham's claim? In short, he is saying that America has squandered the virtue it gained from helping to defeat the enemy in World War II. Convinced that we are "fortune's child," we have demonstrated a feeling of superiority. This attitude, coupled with our superior firepower, makes us targets of terrorists—all for legitimate reasons. The claims of value are made forcefully; they reflect a decidedly biased and skeptical view of America's preeminence in the world.

Is the bias fair or unfair? There is no one answer to that question; it depends on one's vision of the United States' position in the world. But unlike the bias in the previous example, one cannot turn to outside sources or to the World Wide Web to evaluate the worth of these claims. They are too intensely subjective and too closely allied to his particular worldview. Conservatives might label Lapham un-American for what he writes. Would this be a fair criticism? And wouldn't labeling him as un-American merely confirm exactly what he is saying? One must answer these questions for oneself. (For a similar worldview, but expressed in an entirely different style, see Margaret Atwood's short piece at the end of Chapter 6, "The View from the Backyard.")

To sum up, discovering a writer's hidden agenda is one of the most difficult tasks in critical reading. One solution is to read widely. When you become familiar with editorial writers' beliefs by reading their columns over time, you will have a better grasp of their politics. Also pay attention to biographical headnotes when they are provided, for they may tell you something about the writer's positions on the issues and certainly about his or her authority. Last, when reading persuasive prose, ask this question: What does the writer stand to gain (or lose) by my accepting (or rejecting) this argument?

Practice Exercise 7

Study these opening paragraphs from an editorial criticizing California's new law banning soft-drink machines from public school campuses in an effort to help students maintain healthy lifestyles. The writer of the editorial, David Martosko, is director of research at the Center for Consumer Freedom, www.ConsumerFreedom.com.

California, in the person of state Sen. Deborah Ortiz, D-Sacramento, has declared war. Not on drugs, gangs or guns. Not on teenage pregnancy, school dropout rates or violent Hollywood movies. This war is being waged against 12-ounce cans of soda pop. Ortiz won't declare victory until all things fizzy are banished from our schoolchildren's line of sight.

Obesity warriors such as Ortiz—the same legislator who wants food menus with endless nutrition warnings (do we really need to be warned that ice cream contains sugar and fat?)—believe they have a mandate to teach us all the basics about health and nutrition. Parents, under the wishful impression that keeping their kids physically fit is their job (not the government's) stand corrected.

David Martosko, "Soft Drink Ban Based on Bad Science,"
San Francisco Chronicle, June 19, 2003

1. Identify the bias in the editorial. The writer is anti-government regulation. He argues that the government has no business telling parents what their children should eat or drink and that parents must take the responsibility for their children's well-being.

2. How is the bias conveyed? Look for examples of slanted language.

   <u>"declared war," "obesity warriors," "endless nutrition warnings,"</u>

   <u>"have a mandate"</u>

3. What point is Martosko making by comparing the soft-drink ban to other problems facing teenagers (dropout rates, teenage pregnancy, etc.)? <u>The intent is to trivialize or ridicule Senator Ortiz's cam-</u>

   <u>paign by suggesting that drinking soda pop is not a very serious</u>

   <u>problem compared to the others he mentions.</u>

4. Does the name Center for Consumer Freedom have a positive or negative connotation? <u>Positive; the name suggests that the organiza-</u>

   <u>tion promotes individual choice and suggests a rebuke of govern-</u>

   <u>ment intrusion into personal decisions like what to drink.</u>

5. Investigate this organization. Go to the World Wide Web and type in www.ConsumerFreedom.com. Scroll down to the bottom of the page and click on "About Us." What does this group stand for? <u>This group</u>

   <u>is a nonprofit coalition supported by restaurant operators and food</u>

   <u>and beverage companies. It seeks to promote personal responsibility</u>

   <u>and to protect consumer choices. In other words, it's a trade organi-</u>

   <u>zation to help the industry, not a consumer-protection group, as the</u>

   <u>name misleadingly implies.</u>

Bias in Visual Material

In the same way that bias can appear in textual material, bias can also occur in visual material. Bias is especially evident in the political cartoons that one finds on the editorial page of every newspaper (See pp. 346–348 for examples of political cartoons; can you identify the cartoonists' biases?) But charts and graphs can also show bias. One egregious—and rather ingenious—use of bias in graphic material occurred in the spring of 2004 when President Bush unveiled his proposed $2.4 trillion budget. The figures included a projected deficit of $521 billion, at the time the highest deficit in U.S. history, one that disturbed even Bush's fellow Republicans. Typically, in presentations like these, monetary surpluses are indicated graphically using green or black ink, and deficits are indicated in red ink. The English language bears these distinctions out: We may say that a business is either "operating in the black" or "drowning in red ink." On this occasion, the Bush team provided a chart showing the deficit numbers in green ink rather than the traditional red, presumably so that they wouldn't look so bad. Analysts saw through the ruse and duly reported it. In this case, the bias was reflected in the color, not the language.

Thus, graphic material needs to be scrutinized carefully. As with the accompanying text, when examining charts and graphs, ask these questions:

- What is the claim being put forth?
- Are there any unstated assumptions?
- Is the graph drawn so that data are represented fairly?
- Is the information complete?
- Is the source of the data clearly indicated?
- Is any bias evident?

Practice Exercise 8

Study this graph, which accompanied an article entitled "War Looms Large in Latino Vote."

Latino Voters

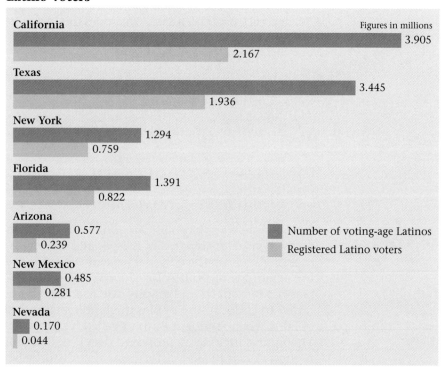

Chart shows projected population for Latinos of voting age and the number of registered voters in key electoral states in 2004.
Source: United States Hispanic Leadership Institute, Chronicle Graphics, *The San Francisco Chronicle,* May 5, 2004. Reprinted with permission.

Now answer these questions:

1. What is the primary claim represented in the graph? What type of claim is it? <u>The number of Latinos who are registered to vote is signifi-</u>

   <u>cantly smaller than the number of Latinos eligible to vote. Claim</u>

   <u>of fact.</u>

2. Which state has the largest number of registered Latino voters in proportion to the number of Latino residents? (To calculate this, divide the number of registered Latino voters by the number of voting-age Latinos. Move the decimal point over two places; this is the ratio, or percentage, of voters.) <u>New York</u>

   Which has the least? <u>Nevada</u>

3. What argument can be inferred from this graph? <u>If the unregistered</u>

   <u>Latino residents registered and voted, they could make a signifi-</u>

   <u>cant impact on the 2004 elections.</u>

4. What information is not included in the graph? What questions does the chart raise?   <u>What are the rates of voter registration for other</u>

   <u>ethnic groups for U.S. citizens as a whole? What is the breakdown</u>

   <u>by political party for registered Latino voters? What party would</u>

   <u>benefit if more Latinos registered to vote? How many Latino</u>

   <u>residents over 18 are citizens and, thus, entitled to vote?</u>

5. Is there any evidence of bias in this chart? <u>Answers will vary. Though</u>

   <u>the information seems straightforward, the figures show that</u>

   <u>Latinos are not making the impact that they could be making on the</u>

   <u>issues. Latinos tend to vote Democratic; therefore, Democrats</u>

   <u>would probably be more likely to court the Latino vote than</u>

   <u>Republicans.</u>

6. Do a search on Google or any other search engine you prefer to find out what the United States Hispanic Leadership Institute stands for. The address is www.ushli.com.

Misuse of Authority

In Chapter 8, you learned that one criterion of a good argument is a reliable authority. But authority can also be misused, for example, when the high-sounding names of "research organizations" are used to hood-wink the unwary reader or consumer. A particularly blatant instance of **misuse of authority** occurred in 1992 when *The New York Times* pub-lished an article reporting that chocolate contains cavity-fighting prop-erties. This startling announcement made headlines across the country. A few days later, however, it was revealed that the announcement had come from a newsletter published by the Princeton Dental Resource Center and distributed to dentists' offices. This organization, of course, is meant to sound as if it is affiliated with Princeton University; it is not. As it turns out, the Princeton Dental Resource Center is actually a front for the M&M/Mars Candy Company.

Slanting

From the discussion of connotation and denotation in Chapter 6, you may recall that a writer's word choice has significant power to influence the reader's perceptions. **Slanting** is a way of presenting information in such a way that it will sway the audience. It may be subtle, or it may involve more obvious misrepresentation to create either a positive or a negative impression in the reader's mind. We will examine two types of slanting.

Slanting by Means of Word Choice

First, slanting can be achieved simply by a writer's employing a carefully chosen word. For example, in a favorable editorial published in *The Wall Street Journal,* the unnamed writer praised a proposal by former secretary of education Lamar Alexander to give $1,000 scholarships to low- and moderate-income parents, which would allow them to send their chil-dren to a school of their own choice. The plan was called a "G.I. Bill for Kids." The *Journal* editorial homed in on the inevitable opposition from teachers' unions. (Some background: A voucher refers to a sum of money that parents can use to send their child to any school of their choice, private or religious or public. Voucher systems exist in only a handful of districts [Milwaukee is one such district], and voters have turned down school-choice initiatives in several state elections over the past few years.) The editorial writer states (italics are mine):

> The administration program is further evidence that empowering parents with choice is an idea whose time has come. Support for choice cuts across income, political and racial lines. Its major opponent is the *entrenched edu-cation bureaucracy that benefits from the status quo.*

The writer goes on to discuss a ballot initiative on vouchers, which the teachers' unions had opposed: "*Educrats* did everything they could to block the initiative." (Quoted in "The Education Revolution," *The Wall Street Journal,* June 25, 1992.)

The italicized words are slanted and as a result misrepresent the position of teachers who have two primary arguments against voucher plans: they fear (1) that public funds will be siphoned away from already troubled public schools and leave them in even worse shape than they are in now, and (2) that only middle-class parents will be financially able to take advantage of vouchers, leaving only poor children in public school districts and leading to a loss of diversity.

These two words are the culprits: "bureaucracy," with its implications of endless red tape and unbending rules and regulations, and "educrat," a sneer word you won't find in the dictionary, which combines the first syllables of *educator* and the last syllable of *bureaucrat.* Thus the editorial writer creates a negative impression in the reader's mind and depicts teachers and their unions as being more concerned with serving their narrow self-interests than with supporting a quality education for all children.

Slanting in Public Opinion Polls

In an informative article on political polls, "How to Tell If Political Polls Are about Truth, or Consequences" (*Los Angeles Times,* January 30, 2000), Janet Wilson first explains how polls are conducted.

> If polled properly, statisticians say, as few as 1,000 people can accurately reflect opinions of 185 million Americans. The most widely accepted method of sampling people is through random-digit dialing, which means everyone has an equal chance of being interviewed.
>
> Using area codes and exchanges in geographically stratified areas, computers generate more than 3,000 phone numbers to make up for hang-ups, refusals, those who aren't home, non-residences, and other dead-ends. Computer-generated dialing is vital, especially in California, which leads the nation in unlisted telephone numbers.
>
> Weighted formulas are used to make sure men and women, minorities and age groups are represented in the same proportion in which they appear in the general population. For political surveys, pollsters ask questions regarding voting history and intention to vote to identify likely or highly probable voters.

Next, the article looks at how the wording of a poll's questions can yield different results. Study these three sample questions on the issue of affirmative action.

1. Do you favor or oppose affirmative action programs to help women and minorities get better jobs and education?
2. Do you favor or oppose affirmative action programs that use quotas to help women and minorities get jobs or education?

3. Do you favor or oppose programs to rectify discrimination in jobs and education against women and minorities?

Did your answer change with each question?

Which question is designed to elicit the most favorable response?

<u>Question 1</u>

Which question is designed to elicit a slightly less favorable response?

<u>Question 3</u>

Which question is designed to elicit the most negative response?

<u>Question 2</u>

Finally, the article lists other types of polls (unlike the previously described reliable polls) to show that not all polls are created equally or are equally trustworthy.

Push Polls

Used by partisan political pollsters for their clients who are running for office. They are intended to push voters away from one candidate and toward another.

Dial-in Polls

Unscientific and not true polling. The sample is distorted because the respondents have to call in.

"Frugging"

The practice by special-interest groups or political parties of sending out questionnaires on a particular topic, often coupled with a plea for money. The results, also unscientific, are sometimes presented as poll findings.

"Sugging"

The practice of companies' sending out questionnaires and then trying to sell something to the respondents. Again, this is not a real poll.

Internet Polls

Though sometimes amusing to read and increasingly popular, these are not true polls because the respondents are not selected randomly. Some Internet polls are labeled "for entertainment only" which, at a minimum, indicates they are unscientific.

Distortion

Distortion means twisting facts or misrepresenting one's position or one's opponent's position. Here are two brief examples. The first is a paraphrased version of a letter by a pro-life activist.

> Editor—I have just read your article about women in China aborting their female fetuses after their sonogram reveals the sex of their unborn child. What's the big deal? I wish someone who is in favor of abortion would tell me why selectively aborting female babies is wrong. Isn't it simply the mother's choosing not to have a female child? And isn't this what the pro-abortion movement is all about?

Some women in China do indeed abort their female fetuses (and commit infanticide), a result of China's stringent one-child-per-family policy. However, in connecting abortion as it is practiced in North America and in Europe with abortion as it is practiced in China, this writer unfairly distorts the position of abortion supporters.

Here is a second example. During the 2000 presidential campaign, both candidates made education—specifically, improving public education in the United States—a top priority. When the National Assessment of Educational Progress (NAEP) released statistics on reading scores in February 1999, Al Gore called a press conference to announce that scores had improved and that this "great progress" was a direct result of the Clinton–Gore education program. In fact, eighth-grade reading scores did improve a little between 1992 and 1998 (during Clinton and Gore's tenure), but according to Diane Ravitch, an education specialist and author of several books on the subject, there was "no net gain" for fourth- or twelfth-graders. Ravitch continues:

> Far from the "amazing" progress that political appointees were describing, improvements in reading were slight at best. The vice-president had used the event to generate headlines about successes that didn't happen; worse, he attempted to claim credit for what little progress the nation was making; worse still, he left the impression that NAEP scores can be used to promote the political program of whoever happens to be in office, this despite the fact that Congress (at the behest of the Reagan administration) took considerable pains to try to insulate NAEP from political manipulation of every sort.

> Quoted in Diane Ravitch, "Education: See All the Spin,"
> *The Washington Post National Weekly Edition*, March 29, 1999

▣ CHAPTER EXERCISES

The following selections address various types of distortion in the media. As you read, consider how an American worldview and ethnocentrism affect news coverage, influence television commercials, and encourage "mutant" statistics.

Selection 1

Norman Solomon is a media critic who writes a weekly syndicated column focusing on media and politics. His columns are available at www.fair.org/mediabeat. His latest book is *The Habits of Highly Deceptive Media* (Common Courage Press, 1999). This spoof of a news story was published in *Utne*.

WASHINGTON—There were unconfirmed reports yesterday that the United States is not the center of the world.

The White House had no immediate comment on the reports, which set off a firestorm of controversy in the nation's capital.

Speaking on background, a high-ranking State Department official doubted the reports would turn out to be true. "If that were the case," he said, "don't you think we would have known about it a long time ago?"

On Capitol Hill, leaders of both parties were quick to rebut the assertion. "That certain news organizations would run with such a poorly sourced and obviously slanted story tells us that the liberal media are still up to their old tricks, despite the current crisis," a GOP lawmaker fumed. A prominent Democrat, also speaking on condition of anonymity, said that classified briefings to congressional intelligence panels disproved such claims long ago.

Scholars at leading think tanks were more restrained, and some said there was a certain amount of literal truth to the reports. But they pointed out that while the claim might be accurate in a narrow sense, it was taken out of context and could damage national unity at a time when the United States could ill afford such a disruption.

The claim evidently originated in a piece by a Lebanese journalist in a Beirut magazine. It was picked up by a pair of left-leaning daily newspapers in London. From there, the story quickly made its way across the Atlantic via the Internet.

"It shows how much we need seasoned, professional gatekeepers to separate the journalistic wheat from the chaff before it gains wide attention," remarked the managing editor of a major U.S. television network news program. "This is the kind of stuff you see on ideologically driven Web sites, but that hardly means it belongs on the evening news." A news-magazine editor agreed, calling the reports "the worst kind of geographical correctness."

None of the major cable networks devoted much air time to the story. At one outlet, a news executive's memo told staffers that any reference to the controversy should include mention of the fact that the United States continues to lead the globe in scientific discoveries. At a more conservative network, anchors and correspondents reminded viewers that English is widely acknowledged to be the international language—and more people speak English in the United States than in any other nation.

While government officials voiced acute skepticism about the notion that the United States is not the center of the world, they declined to comment on the record. Meanwhile, an informal survey of intellectuals with ties to influential magazines of political opinion, running the gamut from *The Weekly Standard* to

The New Republic, indicated that the report was unlikely to gain much currency among Washington's media elite.

"The problem with this kind of shoddy impersonation of reporting is that it's hard to knock down because there are grains of truth," one editor commented. "Sure, who doesn't know that our country includes only a small percentage of the planet's land mass and population?"

Another well-known American journalist speculated that the controversy will soon pass: "Moral relativism remains a pernicious force in our society, but overall it holds less appeal than ever, even on American college campuses. It's not just that we're the only superpower—we happen also to be the light unto the nations and the key to the world's fate. People who can't accept that reality are not going to have much credibility."

Norman Solomon, "News Flash!" Utne (www.fair.org)

Selection 2

Elayne Rapping writes about television—coverage of the news, advertising, news magazines, game shows—as a reflection of our larger culture. This excerpt is from her book *The Looking Glass World of Nonfiction TV.*

One of the most powerful and misunderstood features of TV commercials—and programs—is the way in which form itself, rather than mere content, communicates meaning. Most analysts of advertising are content to point out the absurdities of the overt messages. Of course the use of a new toothpaste or shampoo is not going to lead directly to true love. Of course the purchase of the proper breakfast cereal or fabric softener will not make husbands and children suddenly appreciate and express adoration for their wives and mothers. But advertisements are not linear or rational in method. They create meaning through juxtaposition of like and unlike, real and fictional elements. They take "certain elements, things or people from the ordinary world" and rearrange and alter them "in terms of a product's myth to create a new world, the world of the advertisement." They function much as dreams and poetry do. They combine elements of reality with wish fulfillment fantasies in a way which touches us where our desires are deepest, and most unfulfilled. If, as Althusser[1] says, "Ideology represents the imaginary relationship of individuals to their real conditions of existence," then TV commercials are ideology of the first order.

Examples of typical TV commercials bear this out. Everyone has a favorite example of a "really good" commercial. Usually it is visually startling. The series of Chanel perfume ads, run regularly during the Christmas season, are as good as any. There's the sexually suggestive one in which a physically beautiful man

---

[1]Leon Althusser is the author of *Lenin and Philosophy and Other Essays* (1971).

dives into a luxurious pool and comes up between the legs of a physically beautiful woman. The images of luxury and sensual perfection combine with pure eroticism to connect the product with an ideal of sensual pleasure and luxury unavailable to all but a few jetsetters. There's the more romantic ad in which a montage of sophisticated urban images—ultramodern glass highrises, soaring airplanes, and such—are intercut with brief scenes between a man and woman, dressed in sophisticated elegance, mouthing the "John," "Mary," romantic clichés of 1930s Hollywood. In the background, the Ink Spots sing "I Don't Want to Set the World on Fire," from the same romantic era. In all, it makes no linear sense. But the feeling and the promise are crystal clear. Older viewers, most likely to be buying Chanel for Christmas, will be reminded of the romance and glamour of their youths, as interpreted and remembered by Hollywood.

For younger viewers, the most effective ads are equally suggestive, but in a different way. The 501 Levi commercials are as artistically impressive as anything they sponsor, including most of the music videos they so strongly resemble. Street scenes of hip kids—having fun, being cool, hanging out—are shot in a funky "video *verite*" style that contrasts with the sophistication of the Chanel ads. The text reinforces the visual message: if you buy 501 jeans, you'll be as cool and laid back as most teenagers dream of being. "And now my hard to please woman's havin' a hard time pleasin' me," sings the proud but ever so casual owner of the 501s.

Elayne Rapping, *The Looking Glass World of Nonfiction TV*

Selection 3

Joel Best is the author of *Damned Lies and Statistics,* the title of which is a take-off on Mark Twain's famous line: "There are three kinds of lies: lies, damned lies and statistics." The word *innumeracy* in the second paragraph means, as he writes, "difficulties grasping the meanings of numbers and calculations." The word is akin to *illiteracy,* which means difficulties grasping printed material.

Not all statistics start out bad, but any statistic can be made worse. Numbers—even good numbers—can be misunderstood or misinterpreted. Their meanings can be stretched, twisted, distorted, or mangled. These alterations create what we can call *mutant statistics*—distorted versions of the original figures.

Many mutant statistics have their roots in innumeracy. Remember that innumeracy—difficulties grasping the meanings of numbers and calculations—is widespread. The general public may be innumerate, but often the advocates promoting social problems are not any better. They may become confused about a number's precise meaning; they may misunderstand how the problem has been defined, how it has been measured, or what sort of sampling has been used. At the same time, their commitment to their cause and their enthusiasm for promoting the problem ("After all, it's a big problem!") may lead them to "improve" the statistic, to make the numbers seem more dramatic, even more compelling. Some mutant statistics may be products of advocates' cynicism, of their deliberate attempts to distort information in order to make their claims more convincing; this seems particularly likely when mutation occurs at the hands of large institutions that twist information into the form most favorable to their vested interests. But mutation can also be a product of sincere, albeit muddled interpretations by innumerate advocates.

Once someone utters a mutant statistic, there is a good chance that those who hear it will accept it and repeat it. Innumerate advocates influence their audiences: the media repeat mutant statistics; and the public accepts—or at least does not challenge—whatever numbers the media present. A political leader or a respected commentator may hear a statistic and repeat it, making the number seem even more credible. As statistics gain wide circulation, number laundering occurs. The figures become harder to challenge because everyone has heard them, everyone assumes the numbers must be correct. Particularly when numbers reinforce our beliefs, prejudices, or interests ("Of course that's true!"), we take figures as facts, without subjecting them to criticism.

Consider one widely circulated statistic about the dangers of anorexia nervosa (the term for eating dangerously little in an effort to be thin). Anorexia usually occurs in young women, and some feminists argue that it is a response to societal pressures for women to be beautiful, and cultural standards that equate slenderness with beauty. Activists seeking to draw attention to the problem estimated that 150,000 American women were anorexic, and noted that anorexia could lead to death. At some point, feminists began reporting that each year 150,000 women *died* from anorexia. (This was a considerable exaggeration; only about 70 deaths per year are attributed to anorexia.) This simple transformation—turning an estimate for the total number of anorexic women into the annual number of fatalities—produced a dramatic, memorable statistic. Advocates repeated the erroneous figure in influential books, in newspaper columns, on talk shows, and so on. There were soon numerous sources for the mistaken number. A student searching for material for a term paper on anorexia, for instance, had a good chance of encountering—and repeating—this wildly inaccurate statistic, and each repetition helped ensure that the mutant statistic would live on.

Yet it should have been obvious that something was wrong with this figure. Anorexia typically affects *young* women. In the United States each year, roughly 8,500 females aged 15–24 die from all causes; another 47,000 women aged 25–44 also die. What were the chances, then, that there could be 150,000 deaths from anorexia each year? But, of course, most of us have no idea how many young women die each year ("It must be a lot. . . ."). When we hear that anorexia kills 150,000 young women per year, we assume that whoever cites the number must know that it is true. We accept the mutant statistic, and may even repeat it ourselves.

Joel Best, "Mutant Statistics," *Damned Lies and Statistics*

CHAPTER 10

Evaluating Web Sites

"What do you mean, 'no internet access'? What kind of heaven is this, anyhow?"

CHAPTER OBJECTIVES

This final chapter of Part 4 examines the effects of the information revolution on critical reading skills and ends with practice exercises in which you will do an in-depth appraisal of some World Wide Web sites. Specifically, you will learn about:

- The differences between reading online and reading print

- Search engines and how to use them

- Assessing Web sites

- Web sites that will help you develop your critical reading skills

- Web sites for online reading

- How others see us—foreign news sources

First, a warning: Some of the information you read in this chapter by, say, 2008, may sound as antiquated as doilies on tables or telephones with rotary dials. The Internet is changing so rapidly that even the most innovative technology can quickly become obsolete. And a decade ago, in the early 1990s, no one had ever heard of 'zines, blogs, cable wireless modems, megabytes, gigabytes, terabytes, or pedabytes. I have tried to choose Web sites to include in this chapter that are likely to be accessible for the life of this edition. But the warning holds: URLs listed here may have moved, or they may have expired.

■ READING ONLINE VERSUS READING PRINT

There is no question that the World Wide Web has truly revolutionized the way information is disseminated and retrieved; ironically, that advantage is also its main drawback. The Web has exacerbated the problem of information overload, and we may feel overwhelmed by the glut of information available to us. In addition, turning to the Web first, as many people now do, rather than to traditional research tools in the library as a source of information, requires new warnings and new criteria for judging the worth of what we read. Despite the convenience of information available with a single mouse click at any time of the day or night, there are crucial differences between reading material on the printed page and reading material on a computer screen. Here is a summary of these differences as I see them:

- ***Reading print on the Web is more difficult than reading a printed text.*** Researchers at Ohio State University found that college students who read essays on a computer screen "found the text harder to understand, less interesting and less persuasive than students who read the same essay on paper."[1] These results were the same no matter how much computer experience students had.

- ***Concentrating is more difficult.*** There are two reasons for this problem: The colorful waving, blinking, flashing, or pulsating banner ads or other elements are distracting to the reader, just as they are meant to be. More important, the use of hyperlinks, the technique that allows the Web surfer to move from one link to another to another and so on, is *antithetical to the act of sustained reading* and, by extension, to concentration. The Web surfer zips from one site to the next, skimming and scanning, sampling here, clicking there. This is a different sort of reading! Only the most dedicated, focused reader can withstand the temptation not to move quickly from link to link.

- ***Technology is seductive****.* The novelty of finding what we are looking for on a Web site with blazing speed may cause us to suspend our critical judgment. That, coupled with the sheer quantity of material available on a subject, makes sorting out the good from the bad even more difficult. It takes concentration to ignore the dazzle and the glitz; it takes concentration to work through a series of sites until you find exactly what you want.

These factors suggest that the critical reader must be even more vigilant while reading and gathering information on the Web than while reading traditional print sources. Another important difference between material you'll find online and material you'll find in print is editorial control. While some sites that appear online, such as newspapers and magazines, are carefully edited and checked, many sites are not. Trying to sort out the fair from the unfair, the true from the false takes time, skill, and a healthy skepticism. Unbiased information can be found on sites maintained by nonprofit public interest groups (for example, the League of Women Voters), and most organizations involved in political and social issues now maintain Web sites. The important point is this: The critical reading skills you studied in Chapters 8 and 9 with conventional reading material will also help you appraise Web material.

■ SEARCH ENGINES

The following list of search engines is not meant to be comprehensive, but they are all highly regarded, and they all work a little differently.

---

[1]More information from this study can be read at www.ncpa.org/pi/edu/pd090700e.html, "Reading Comprehension: Cellulose Over Silicon," sponsored by the National Center for Policy Analysis.

Spend some time with a few until you find the two or three that work best for you.

For a comprehensive search, make sure to try your search terms in two or three search engines: Search engines use different methods to retrieve relevant sites, so different search engines are likely to provide different sites in a different order.

Also, be aware that search engines list sponsored links (that is, advertisements for links) as well as unsponsored ones. Make sure you know which is which when perusing the "hits" a search engine returns.

Popular Search Engines

www.google.com

www.yahoo.com (technically yahoo is a directory)

www.altavista.com

www.askjeeves.com (www.ask.com)

www.northernlight.com

www.lycos.com

www.go.com

http://a9.com

www.teoma.com

http://search.msn.com/

www.wired.com

www.wisenut.com

Whichever search engines you use to locate material, you will get a better result by taking a few minutes to learn proper search techniques, like refining and narrowing searches and doing advanced searches. If you want to get information on a particular subject—for example, the War on Terror—some search engines suggest that you type the phrase in quotation marks to keep the words together ("war on terror"); otherwise, you'll get a zillion sites on "war" and another zillion on "terror." Others, through their Advanced Search options, allow you to customize your search by clicking on "exact phrase."

Conducting a search on the phrase for "war on terror" on the most popular search engine—Google, www.google.com, yielded the results shown in the following screenshot:

For images from
the "War on Terror,"
click here

For lists of groups
discussing the
"War on Terror,"
click here

For news reports
from the "War on
Terror," click here

Select "Advanced Search"
to narrow your search further

Search terms
(in quotation marks)

Total number of "hits"

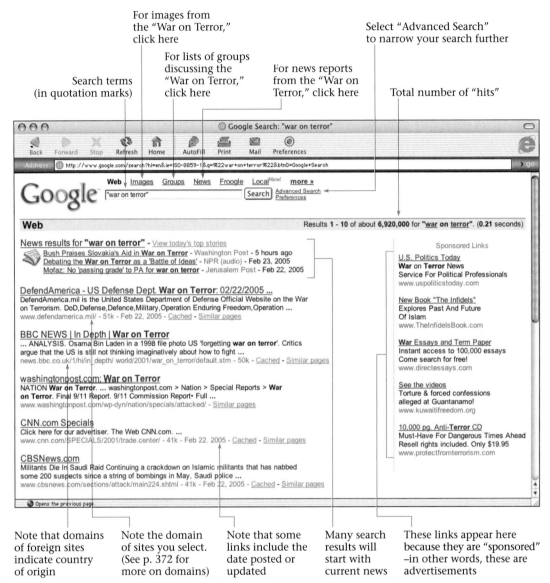

Note that domains
of foreign sites
indicate country
of origin

Note the domain
of sites you select.
(See p. 372 for
more on domains)

Note that some
links include the
date posted or
updated

Many search
results will
start with
current news

These links appear here
because they are "sponsored"
–in other words, these are
advertisements

Source: Reprinted by permission of Google Inc.

In addition to regular search engines, another useful tool is the so-called meta-search engine, which queries several search engines for information and presents a compilation of Web sites.[2] Meta-search engines allow you to obtain information from a variety of regular search engines by visiting only one site. Here is a list of the most widely known meta-search engines:

[2]An overview of meta-search engines and a guide to using them prepared by the UC Berkeley staff is available at www.lib.berkeley.edu/TeachingLib/Guides/Internet/MetaSearch.html.

www.metacrawler.com
www.dogpile.com
www.surfwax.com
www.teoma.com
www.vivisimo.com
www.ixquick.com
www.copernic.com

■ ASSESSING WEB SITES

Consider these three observations about the World Wide Web:

- *Editorial scrutiny is not a given.* Undoubtedly, the Internet has democratized information and expanded access to that information. However, the typical magazine or newspaper article, for example, is pored over by editors and copy editors before it arrives in your mailbox or at the newsstand. But with the Web (except for those sites sponsored by media outlets, news organizations, and nonprofit or research organizations), editorial scrutiny and fact checking is not a requirement. The reader has to perform his or her own scrutiny and check facts for accuracy.

- *The Web is a paradox, at once egalitarian and anarchistic.* Anyone can create a Web site; indeed, thousands of new sites are added each week. If you are experienced in navigating Web sites, you are aware that anyone with an opinion or interest—no matter how trustworthy, no matter how crackpot—can create a site, resulting in an overabundance of terrifically useful material—and an overabundance of junk. In essence, the Web represents an anarchic nation, with no rules or strictures as to what can be published. (The instances of sites that have been shut down are infinitesimal compared to the millions of sites available.) These twin characteristics—egalitarianism and anarchy—are at once the Web's greatest virtues (no censorship) and its greatest handicap (no external objective analysis for fairness, bias, evidence, and the like).

- *Web sites are not commercial-free, so you must be alert to sales pitches.* Health care sites are particularly prone to disguises for what turns out to be pure marketing hype. The site may appear to provide unbiased information until you look further and discover that you are meant to send money for a newsletter or for a product. For example, when I used the search engine http://www.metacrawler.com to get information on insomnia (a common complaint of college students), out of the first 20 sites, 15 carried the domain suffix *com*. Typing in "insomnia" + "information" in the search box turned up several clinical sites sponsored by institutions or universities.

Because of these three issues, it's crucial that when evaluating Web sites, you use all the skills you have already studied—establishing the authority writing, identifying claims, evidence, and instances of manipulative appeal, logical fallacies, and bias. Here are some additional suggestions for appraising sites:

- First, note the site's domain. The term *domain* refers to a group of networked computers that share a common address depending on what type of site it is. The domain is indicated by means of a particular suffix, such as **.com** (pronounced "dot-com"), **.org,** or **.edu.**[3] Familiarize yourself with these suffixes and pay attention to them when you are searching for information. Here is a list of the common domains:

  - **gov:** government agency; e.g., www.cia.gov (the official site for the Central Intelligence Agency)
  - **edu:** educational institution; e.g., www.lanecc.edu/ (Lane Community College, Eugene, Oregon)
  - **org:** usually a nonprofit organization; e.g., www.alz.org (a voluntary health organization dedicated to research on the treatment and eventual cure for Alzheimer's)
  - **com:** commercial company; e.g., www.amazon.com (online seller of books, music, and other consumer products)
  - **mil:** military institutions; e.g., www.ngb.army.mil/ (the National Guard)
  - **net:** network organizations; e.g. www.comcast.net (broadband Internet Service Provider and cable company)
  - **it** (Italy), **uk** (United Kingdom), **mx** (Mexico), **ca** (Canada), **th** (Thailand) (examples of domains designating particular countries)

  Knowing that a particular Web site is a commercial site, rather than a site run by a nonprofit organization or educational institution is important if you want unbiased information or information not linked to a particular product.

- Next, consider these questions: Who sponsors the site? Is the sponsor identified clearly? What does the organization stand for? One way to find out a sponsor's identity if it is not apparent on the site is to click on the "About Us" feature common on Web sites' home pages. For example, typing in "vocabulary improvement" in Google's search box turned up several sites, the first of which was www.verbaladvantage.com. This com-

[3]Other domain suffixes currently available are **.biz** (for businesses); **.aero** (airlines, airports, reservation systems); **.coop** (for business cooperatives such as credit unions); **.info** (for all uses); **.museum** (for accredited worldwide museums); **.name** (for individuals); and **.pro** (for professionals such as physicians and attorneys).

mercial outfit advertises its Verbal Advantage products on radio stations across the country. At the top of the screen is a button labeled "About Us," and clicking on this leads to a page where the company describes its mission and offers its products for sale. However, not all commercial sites identify their sponsors so clearly, and you may have to scroll down to the very bottom of the page to locate the information.

- Then, consider whether the information the site offers is current. How frequently is the site updated? Is a date provided? Sometimes you scroll down to the very bottom of a site only to find out that what you assumed is current is really several years old.
- Finally, ask if the sponsor of the site is trying to sell you something. You may open a Web address looking for factual information, only to discover that the site is touting a product.

■ THE ANATOMY OF A WEB SITE

Study the screenshot on the next page, which shows the home page of the Web site sponsored by the World Wildlife Federation. Notice these elements:

- the panda logo
- the domain (.org)
- FAQs (frequently asked questions)
- the search box for locating information in the top right corner and a second search box for locating news
- About WWF (their version of "About Us")
- the solicitation for donations (in the top pulldown menu and in the left vertical menu)
- the appeal for volunteers (in the top pulldown menu and in the left vertical menu)
- where to shop for environmentally friendly products
- date last updated
- Contact Us
- URL in the bottom left corner

  1. Which elements suggest that this Web site is not strictly informational?

     the solicitation for donations, the appeal for volunteers, and the

     shopping information

Link to home page

URL, including domain (nonpartisan organization)

About us

Sponsor

Appeal for volunteers and donations

Frequently Asked Questions

Search box

News search box

Membership appeal

Date last updated

How to navigate site

How to reach World Wildlife Foundation

Appeal for volunteers and donations

Lead article

2. Why does the World Wildlife Federation use the panda as its representative symbol or logo? <u>Pandas are cute, and they have universal</u>

<u>appeal. Also their existence in China is threatened, making them</u>

<u>the perfect animal for drawing viewers in.</u>

Practice Exercise 1

To locate reliable information about sleep disorders, I used Google and typed in these words "sleep" + "information." Here are three sites that came up in the first batch. Which do you think would offer the most reliable information about sleeping problems?

1. www.shuteye.com/   This is a commercial site sponsored by an ethical drug company called Sanofi-Synthelabo, a European manufacturer of ethical pharmaceuticals, best known for its sleep-aid product Ambien.
2. www.mckinley.uiuc.edu/Handouts/sleepguide.html   This site, which offers information on various sleep disorders, is sponsored by the McKinley Health Center, Student Affairs, University of Illinois at Urbana-Champaign.
3. www.nlm.nih.gov/medlineplus/sleepdisorders.html   This site is sponsored by the National Library of Medicine and the National Institutes of Health, a U.S. government agency.

   <u>Either the University of Illinois or the NIH site offers unbiased</u>

   <u>scientific information. Although www.shuteye.com does offer</u>

   <u>information about sleep disorders and sleep solutions, it is also</u>

   <u>trying to sell you something by means of a free trial offer for a</u>

   <u>prescription sleep-aid.</u>

Practice Exercise 2

Do a little research on an illness that a family member has or has had. Be as specific as possible in your search; in other words, instead of searching for information on *diabetes,* narrow the type down, for example, to *Type-2 diabetes* or *adult-onset diabetes.* In the search box, type in the term. Choose three sites that look promising. Open each one and look to see if the current date is displayed or if there is an indication of the date the material was last updated. Assess whether or not the site's information is current enough to be useful, and compare content among the sites.

■ WEB SITES FOR CRITICAL READING SKILLS

Web sites sponsored by UCLA, UC–Berkeley, and Cornell University offer guidance for students doing Web research, in much greater detail than space allows in this text. Whether for your own edification and amusement or for compiling research for a course, they are all worth studying in some depth:

www.library.ucla.edu/libraries/college/help/critical/index.htm
www.lib.berkeley.edu/TeachingLib/Guides/Internet/Evaluate.html

These two sites sponsored by Cornell University pertain specifically to Web sites:

www.library.cornell.edu/olinuris/ref/research/webcrit.html
www.library.cornell.edu/olinuris/ref/research/webeval.html

This site, also sponsored by Cornell, titled "Critically Analyzing Information Sources," shows students how to evaluate print material:

www.library.cornell.edu/olinuris/ref/research/skill26.htm

■ WEB SITES FOR ONLINE READING

There is something wonderfully liberating about sitting at one's desk in Memphis or in the campus library in Des Moines and being able to find out what is going on in Seattle or Alaska or Iraq. The Web offers everyone the opportunity to read information online for free.[4] In 1999 the *Columbia Journalism Review,* the publication of Columbia University's prestigious School of Journalism, published a list of the 26 best American newspapers.[5] Here are the top 10 from the *CJR* list, along with their ranking, location, and ownership. I have included Internet addresses.

[4]Note: Most newspapers offer that day's content for free. However, the trend among some newspapers is to charge for reading archived material. *The New York Times* and the *Los Angeles Times* charge a small fee for reading articles; *The Wall Street Journal* interactive edition has some free material, but a subscription is required for complete online access.

[5]As of fall 2004, the *Columbia Journalism Review* has not updated this list. For recent articles on state of journalism in the United States, go to their home page at www.cjr.org/.

RANK	NEWSPAPER	LOCATION	OWNERSHIP
1	*New York Times* www.nytimes.com	New York, NY	New York Times
2	*Washington Post* www.washingtonpost.com	Washington, D.C.	Washington Post
3	*Wall Street Journal* online.wsj.com/public/us	New York, NY	Dow Jones
4.	*Los Angeles Times* www.latimes.com	Los Angeles, CA	Times Mirror
5	*Dallas Morning News* www.dallasnews.com	Dallas, TX	A. H. Belo
6	*Chicago Tribune* www.chicagotribune.com	Chicago, IL	Tribune
6 (tie)	*Boston Globe* www.boston.com/globe/	Boston, MA	New York Times
8	*San Jose Mercury News* www.mercurynews.com/mld/mercurynews/	San Jose, CA	Knight Ridder
9	*St. Petersburg Times* www.stpetersburgtimes.com/	St. Petersburg, FL	Independent
10	*Baltimore Sun* www.baltimoresun.com/	Baltimore, MD	Times Mirror

In addition to newspapers, many major North American magazines and periodicals have Web sites, which you can locate easily by typing in the name in the search box of your favorite search engine. Other publications, however, are strictly Web-based. Here are some of the most popular:

- www.salon.com   Salon.com publishes essays, articles, commentary, and reviews.
- www.slate.com   Slate.com publishes a variety of articles on political and social issues.
- www.wired.com   Wired.com is an especially good source for current technological information.
- www.cnn.com   Cable News Network sponsors one of the best on-line sites for current events and news from around the nation and the world.
- www.theonion.com   The Onion is an irreverent humor site, which has won several Webby awards.
- www.nationalgeographic.com   This Web site sponsored by the venerable National Geographic organization is an excellent education resource.

- aldaily.com/   Arts and Letters Daily is a comprehensive site devoted to the arts, cultural events, essays, commentary, reviews, and much more.
- www.topix.net   This relatively recent site is a clearing house for news from the Internet.
- www.discover.com   This is the online version of their monthly magazine, which offers articles on science for the general audience.
- www.motherjones.com   This online site offers articles on a wide variety of subjects with a liberal bent.

■ HOW OTHERS SEE US—FOREIGN NEWS SOURCES

With the magic of the Internet, we can now read newspapers that were previously inconvenient or difficult to obtain. Perusing sites of foreign newspapers and news agencies gives the reader a different slant on the news and allows him or her to see how other countries perceive America. Here are seven to get you started:

- www.bbc.co.uk/   The home page for the BBC, the leading source for news in Great Britain
- www.guardian.co.uk/guardian   The online edition of one of Britain's most well-respected newspapers
- www.aljazeera.com   The International English Edition of Aljazeera, the Qatar-based Middle Eastern news agency
- www.alarabiya.net/english.aspx   Based in Media City, Dubai, another source for news in the Middle East
- http://mondediplo.com/   The English language edition of France's leading newspaper, *Le Monde*
- www.economist.com/   A reliable source that also publishes a highly regarded weekly print magazine
- www.pressdisplay.com/pressdisplay/viewer.aspx   A source for leading newspapers around the world, many of which have English-language editions

Do not be limited by this list. Come up with your own list of favorite periodical sites and 'zines.

The following four practice exercises are designed to give you an opportunity to perform various Web-based tasks on a variety of current controversial issues. Consider the advice on assessing Web sites, as well as the critical reading skills you studied in Chapters 8 and 9, as you work your way through these exercises.

**Practice
Exercise 3**

The issue of teaching creationism in the nation's public schools has been in the news in recent months. Science teachers teach evolutionary theory, while some fundamentalist groups advocate the teaching of creation theory, or an updated version called Intelligent Design.[6] The following sites explore both sides of this controversy:

> A debate on the issues sponsored by the University of Missouri Law School is available at www.law.umkc.edu/faculty/projects/ftrials/conlaw/evolution.htm
>
> People for the American Way, "Public Wants Evolution, Not Creationism, in Science Class, New National Poll Shows," at www.pfaw.org/pfaw/general/default.aspx?oid=1903

1. In your own words, state the points each site makes. How are the points of view expressed in these articles similar? How do they differ?
2. What type of evidence does each article rely on to make its point? Is it fair, accurate, sufficient, and relevant?
3. Do these Web sites lean in a particular political direction? Is either an impartial source? How can you tell?

**Practice
Exercise 4**

Here is another pair of articles covering two sides of a divisive issue—gay marriage and the proposed constitutional amendment defining marriage as a union between a man and a woman. Read both and answer the questions that follow.

> The Heritage Foundation, "One Man, One Woman: The Constitutional Amendment," at www.heritage.org/Press/Commentary/ed031604c.cfm
>
> The Center for American Progress "Feeding the Base; Soiling the Constitution," at www.americanprogress.org/site/pp.asp?c=biJRJ8OVF&b=34900

1. State in your own words the point each author is trying to put forth. Do they refute each other's positions?
2. What type of evidence does each article rely on to support their claim? Does either source appear unbiased? How does each Web site try to make their article seem legitimate and "official"?
3. Do you accept each argument? Why or why not? What other information do you need?
4. Again, look carefully at the Web sites hosting these articles: www.heritage.org and www.americanprogress.org. Are their respective biases easy to detect? Do the names of the organization make it easier or more difficult to detect political affiliation?

[6]For another overview of evolutionary theory and resources for teaching and understanding the controversy, go to http://evolution.Berkeley.edu/.

**Practice
Exercise 5**

Below is a list of political Web sites, including those mentioned above. Look through these sites and try to ascertain how upfront each is about its political leanings. Which would you feel comfortable about using for a source if you were writing a research paper? Can a site about politics ever be completely free of bias? You may want to consider some of the following:

- Clear explanation of the organization's mission
- News of the day
- Evidence of slanted language
- Frequency of updates
- Appeals to donate money

The Center for American Progress	www.americanprogress.org
The Heritage Foundation	www.heritage.org
People for the American Way	www.pfaw.org
The American Enterprise Online	www.taemag.com
MoveOn.org	www.moveon.org/front/
The Brookings Institution	www.brook.edu/
Progressive Policy Institute	www.ppionline.org/
Club for Growth	www.clubforgrowth.org/

**Practice
Exercise 6**

Using the Web sites listed in Practice Exercise 5, find opposing articles on a political issue. List any you would use if you were writing a research paper and explain why. Then search the Web for more information on the issue. Look through a number of sites. List three or four that appear to present impartial information (and that aren't selling something). In addition, list the sponsor of the site, the sponsor's authority to convey the information, and the date the site was last updated. Here are some suggestions for issues:

- Immigration policy
- Outsourcing of jobs
- Drilling for oil in the Alaska National Wildlife Refuge
- Sex and violence in the media
- Global warming

You may use one of these or come up with an issue of your own choosing.

Reading Essays and Articles

OUTLINE

■ INTRODUCTION TO READING ESSAYS

Why Read Essays in the First Place?

The essay is the staple of college courses where the assigned textbook is an anthology. The essay form has several advantages: It is short, it can be read in one sitting, and it can be discussed in one or two class meetings. Students acquire analytical tools more easily by studying short pieces of nonfiction prose, which they can then transfer to book-length nonfiction works.

Often students are unsure of their instructors' expectations with essay assignments. Part 5 will give you ample practice in various essay-reading skills. You will learn a great deal from your reading assignments if you allow sufficient time to complete each assignment. The truism that practice makes perfect surely applies here. The more experience you get reading your assignments attentively, the more competent you will become and the more you will enjoy preparing your assignments. Besides learning more about the day's current issues and gathering interesting information, an added bonus might be higher grades. There is no advantage in *not* reading. Students who seldom read on their own, who speed through their assignments, or who sit in the back of the classroom or look down, pretending to be engrossed in the text and hoping to avoid being called on, miss a significant part of the college intellectual experience.

The Characteristics of an Essay

The essays here exemplify the characteristics that you learned about in Chapters 1 to 5 in Parts 1 and 2. The essay form derives from the seventeenth-century French writer Michel de Montaigne. His short pieces were an *attempt* to explain his observations of human behavior and customs. (In French, the verb *essayer* means "to attempt.") Today, an **essay** describes a sustained piece of nonfiction prose with a myriad of purposes and characteristics. Like the paragraph, an essay contains or suggests a main idea, which is called the **thesis;** the essay has a direction; and it has development, unity, and coherence. Unlike the paragraph, however, whose short length limits its scope, the essay is more varied in length, organization, and methods of development. Typically, essays published by professional writers run between 500 and 5,000 words, but length is not an important criterion for defining the form.

Essays may be a personal narrative, a description of a scene or an emotion, a presentation of scientific information, a personal confession, an emotional plea to resolve a controversy, a satire on a practice or custom that the writer wants to mock, an explanation of a social or political issue, or an examination of a problem and its repercussions. In short, the essay is infinitely adaptable. It may represent any of the four modes of discourse—narration, description, exposition, or persuasion—singly or in combination, though one mode usually predominates. If you recall the practice essays you read in Parts 1, 2, and 3, you can see that the form is a diverse instrument for communicating ideas.

The remarks of two professional writers shed further light on the essay form. In *A Writer's Companion,* Richard Marius says that the essay "inevitably has about it the scent of an argument," by which he means that even in narrative and descriptive essays, there is an underlying persuasive intent. In the prologue to *The Best American Essays* (Third College Edition), essayist Annie Dillard has this to say about the essay:

> The essay is, and has been, all over the map. There's nothing you cannot do with it; no subject matter is forbidden, no structure is proscribed. You get to make up your own structure every time, a structure that arises from the materials and best contains them. The material is the world itself, which, so far, keeps on keeping on. The thinking mind will analyze, and the creative imagination will link instances, and time itself will churn out scenes—scenes unnoticed and lost, or scenes remembered, written, and saved.

Annie Dillard, "The Essay's Unlimited Possibilities,"
Quoted in *The Best American Essays,* Robert Atwan, Editor, Third College Edition

The Parts of an Essay

The essay can be divided into three parts: the beginning (the introduction); the middle (the body or supporting paragraphs); and the end (the conclusion). We will look at these structural parts one by one. Try to separate each essay you read into these three parts by asking at what point the introduction ends and the body paragraphs begin and at what point the body paragraphs give way to the conclusion. The importance of this skill cannot be emphasized enough. Rather than drowning in a sea of words, seeing the logical progression of ideas will help you distinguish the main points from the support. Often, making a brief outline of the component parts will help you see the overall structure, just as an aerial view of a city reveals its layout better than a ground-level view does. And annotating while you read, demonstrated later in this section, allows you to master the content.

The Introduction

Writing teachers often tell their students that the opening paragraph of their essays should grab the reader's attention, that they should use some sort of hook to entice the reader to continue reading. Beginning college readers should be aware of these devices as well. There are no particular rules governing the hook—only the writer's estimation of how to invite us into the world of that particular essay topic. The introduction may directly state the essay's **thesis**—the main idea—or it may merely be suggested, in which case the thesis is **implied.** Few professional writers use the obvious direct-announcement approach for a thesis.

Given the diverse form of the essay, finding the thesis poses some difficulty because writers are under no obligation to adhere to a formula. Where should you look for the thesis? A writer may provide a thesis somewhere near the beginning of the essay, often following an opening paragraph or two (which provides the hook), introducing the general subject, setting the scene, establishing a problem to be solved—in other words, orienting us to the topic. These paragraphs may include a personal anecdote or a short narrative, they may provide historical background, or they may present a problematic issue. The techniques at the writer's disposal are many and varied. After this section, the writer *may* state a thesis. (Some textbooks refer to this type of opening as a funnel pattern.)

To illustrate the funnel pattern, study these three opening paragraphs:

> In his famous story of the outlaw wolf Lobo, Earnest Thompson Seton held that the wolf walked on the backs of sheep at night to attack the goats around which the flock clustered, not because he was hungry for goats, but so that the sheep would scatter and the wolves could pick them off at their leisure over the following weeks. Seton described his own meticulous care in putting out poison to kill the wolf. He melted cheese and kidney fat in a china dish, cut it with a bone knife "to avoid the taint of metal," and injected strychnine and cyanide into chunks of the bait. All the while, he wore gloves "steeped in the hot blood of a heifer." Carrying the baits in a rawhide bag which was bathed in blood and always suspended from a rope, he dropped baits over a ten mile circuit; the next day, he returned to find that the wolf had gathered up baits, piled them in the trail, and defecated on them. The wolf methodically sprung the traps he buried in the trail, too. "The old king was too cunning for me," confessed Seton.
>
> Such stories crowd our view of wolves, but their proclamation that wolves are sagacious is largely an interpretation born of storytelling. The artful tracker reconstructs a hunt from tracks, and often fills the gaps between what he knows with speculations about how a wolf thought.
>
> We really know very little about what a wolf plans or thinks. However, those who spend time observing wolves see plenty of evidence that the mind of the wolf is complex, purposeful, and full of feeling.
>
> Peter Steinhart, "Thinking Like a Wolf," *The Company of Wolves*

Write the sentence that represents the thesis in the space. Then, as you did for main-idea sentences in Chapter 1, underline the topic once and the controlling idea twice.

"... those who spend time observing wolves see plenty of evidence that the mind of the wolf is complex, purposeful, and full of feeling."

Do not expect every essay you read, however, to use the funnel pattern, and don't expect a bell to sound when you reach the thesis. In adult prose, few writers announce that a particular sentence is meant to represent the main idea.

Practice Exercise 1

To test your reading acumen and your ability to identity the thesis, I selected seven introductory sections for essays from one anthology in my bookshelf,

The McGraw-Hill Reader, a college textbook for composition students, and from one of the Best American Essays series published each year. Read each carefully and then follow these instructions: First, write the mode of discourse (narration, description, exposition, or persuasion) that you predict will occur in the essay as a whole. If you are unsure, write a question mark. Second, write the thesis statement or main idea, if one is represented, in your own words. If there is no thesis stated or implied, write another question mark.

A.   Mortimer Adler was editor of the *Encyclopedia Britannica's Great Books* project and a thinker dedicated to the premise that all people should be conversant with the world's great thinkers. The piece was published in 1941 when a literary masterpiece could indeed be bought for "less than a dollar."

You know you have to read "between the lines" to get the most out of anything. I want to persuade you to do something equally important in the course of your reading. I want to persuade you to "write between the lines." Unless you do, you are not likely to do the most efficient kind of reading.

I contend, quite bluntly, that marking up a book is not an act of mutilation but of love.

You shouldn't mark up a book which isn't yours. Librarians (or your friends) who lend you books expect you to keep them clean, and you should. If you decide that I am right about the usefulness of marking books, you will have to buy them. Most of the world's great books are available today, in reprint editions, at less than a dollar.

Mortimer Adler, "How to Mark a Book," *The Saturday Review of Literature*

Mode of discourse: persuasion, exposition

Thesis statement: Although some insist that marking up a book

mutilates it, doing so is beneficial if the reader is to make the

most efficient use of time spent reading.

B.   David Gelernter is professor of computer science at Yale University.

Over the last decade an estimated $2 billion has been spent on more than 2 million computers for America's classrooms. That's not surprising. We constantly hear from Washington that the schools are in trouble and that computers are a godsend. Within the education establishment, in poor as well as rich schools, the machines are awaited with nearly religious awe. An inner-city principal bragged to a teacher friend of mine recently that his school "has a computer in every classroom . . . despite being in a bad neighborhood!"

Computers should be in the schools. They have the potential to accomplish great things. With the right software, they could help make science tangible or teach neglected topics like art and music. They help students form a concrete idea of society by displaying onscreen a version of the city in which they live—a picture that tracks real life moment by moment.

In practice, however, computers make our worst educational nightmares come true. While we bemoan the decline of literacy, computers discount words in favor of pictures and pictures in favor of video. While we fret about the decreasing cogency of public debate, computers dismiss linear argument and promote fast, shallow romps across the information landscape. While we worry abut basic skills, we allow into the classroom software that will do a student's arithmetic or correct his spelling.

David Gelernter, "Unplugged: The Myth of Computers in the Classroom"

Mode of discourse: <u>Persuasion</u>

Thesis statement: <u>Although computers have great potential to help</u> <u>our students, they have an adverse impact on the important skills</u> <u>of reading, writing, and thinking.</u>

C. Peter Elbow is a writing instructor who revolutionized the teaching of writing with his concept of freewriting.

The most effective way I know to improve your writing is to do freewriting exercises regularly. At least three times a week. They are sometimes called "automatic writing," "babbling," or "jabbering" exercises. The idea is simply to write for ten minutes (later on, perhaps fifteen or twenty). Don't stop for anything. Go quickly without rushing. Never stop to look back, to cross something out, to wonder how to spell something, to wonder what word or thought to use, or to think about what you are doing. If you can't think of a word or a spelling, just use a squiggle or else write, "I can't think of it." Just put down something. The easiest thing is just to put down whatever is in your mind. If you get stuck it's fine to write "I can't think of what to say, I can't think of what to say" as many times as you want; or repeat the last word you wrote over and over again; or anything else. The only requirement is that you *never* stop.

What happens to a freewriting exercise is important. It must be a piece of writing which, even if someone reads it, doesn't send any ripples back to you. It is like writing something and putting it in a bottle in the sea. The teacherless class helps your writing by providing maximum feedback. Freewritings help you by providing no feedback at all. When I assign one, I invite the writer to let me read it. But also tell him to keep it if he prefers. I read it quickly and make no comments at all and I do not speak with him about it. The main thing is that a freewriting must never be evaluated in any way; in fact there must be no discussion or comment at all.

Peter Elbow, "Freewriting," Writing Without Teachers

Mode of discourse: <u>exposition</u>

Thesis statement: <u>Freewriting exercises are the most effective way</u>

<u>to improve your writing.</u>

D.   N. Scott Momaday is a Kiowa, a Native American writer and poet.

A single knoll rises out of the plain in Oklahoma, north and west of the Wichita Range. For my people, the Kiowas, it is an old landmark, and they gave it the name Rainy Mountain. The hardest weather in the world is there. Winter brings blizzards, hot tornadic winds arise in the spring, and in summer the prairie is an anvil's edge. The grass turns brittle and brown, and it cracks beneath your feet. There are green belts along the rivers and creeks, linear groves of hickory and pecan, willow and witch hazel. At a distance in July or August the steaming foliage seems almost to writhe in fire. Great green and yellow grasshoppers are everywhere in the tall grass, popping up like corn to sting the flesh, and tortoises crawl about on the red earth, going nowhere in the plenty of time. Loneliness is an aspect of the land. All things in the plain are isolate; there is no confusion of objects in the eye, but *one* hill or *one* tree or *one* man. To look upon that landscape in the early morning, with the sun at your back, is to lose the sense of proportion. Your imagination comes to life, and this, you think, is where Creation was begun.

N. Scott Momaday, The Way to Rainy Mountain

Mode of discourse: <u>description</u>

Thesis statement: <u>The plain near Rainy Mountain in Oklahoma is so</u>

<u>open and isolated that one simultaneously loses his sense of pro-</u>

<u>portion and develops a new imagination.</u>

E.   Robert Coles is a psychologist best known for his nonfiction studies of children, *Children of Crisis.*

Not so long ago children were looked upon in a sentimental fashion as "angels," or as "innocents." Today, thanks to Freud and his followers, boys and girls are understood to have complicated inner lives; to feel love, hate, envy and rivalry in various and subtle mixtures; to be eager participants in the sexual and emotional politics of the home, neighborhood and school. Yet some of us parents still cling to the notion of childhood innocence in another way. We do not see that our children also make ethical decisions every day in their own lives, or realize how attuned they may be to moral currents and issues in the larger society.

Robert Coles, "I Listen to My Parents and I Wonder What They Believe"

Mode of discourse: <u>exposition/persuasion</u>

Thesis statement: <u>Contrary to the myth that children are</u>

<u>innocents, they make ethical decisions and reflect the larger</u>

<u>moral concerns of their society.</u>

F.   Deborah Tannen is a linguist who specializes in the subject of communication between men and women.

I was addressing a small gathering in a suburban Virginia living room—a women's group that had invited men to join them. Throughout the evening, one man had been particularly talkative, frequently offering ideas and anecdotes, while his wife sat silently beside him on the couch. Toward the end of the evening, I commented that women frequently complain that their husbands don't talk to them. This man quickly concurred. He gestured toward his wife and said, "She's the talker in our family." The room burst into laughter; the man looked puzzled and hurt. "It's true," he explained. "When I come home from work I have nothing to say. If she didn't keep the conversation going, we'd spend the whole evening in silence."

This episode crystallizes the irony that although American men tend to talk more than women in public situations, they often talk less at home. And this pattern is wreaking havoc with marriage.

Deborah Tannen, "Sex, Lies and Conversation:
Why Is It So Hard for Men and Women to Talk to Each Other?"

Mode of discourse: <u>exposition</u>

Thesis statement: <u>The problems men and women have communicating</u>

<u>with each other negatively impact marriage.</u>

G.   William Bennett served as the nation's drug "czar" and as Secretary of Education.

A few months ago I lunched with a friend who now lives in Asia. During our conversation the topic turned to America as seen through the eyes of foreigners. My friend had observed that while the world still regards the United States as the leading economic and military power on earth, this same world no longer beholds us with the moral respect it once did, as a "shining city on a hill." Instead, it sees a society in decline.

Recently, a Washington, D.C., cabdriver—a graduate student from Africa—told me that when he receives his degree, he is returning to his homeland. His reason? He doesn't want his children to grow up in a country where his daughter will be an "easy target" for young men and where his son might also be a target for violence at the hands of other young males. "It is more civilized where I come from," he said.

Last year an article in the *Washington Post* described how exchange students adopt the lifestyle of American teens. Paulina, a Polish high-school student studying in the United States, said that when she first came here she was amazed at the way teenagers spent their time. "In Warsaw, we would come home after school, eat with our parents and then do four or five hours of homework. Now I go to Pizza Hut and watch TV and do less work in school. I can tell it is not a good thing to get used to."

I have an instinctive aversion to foreigners harshly judging my nation; yet, I must concede that much of what they say is true. Something has gone wrong with us.

William Bennett, "What Really Ails America," *Reader's Digest*

Mode of discourse: <u>persuasion</u>

Thesis statement: <u>Contemporary American society is in serious</u>

<u>trouble, and other countries are right to judge us critically.</u>

The Body Paragraphs

The supporting paragraphs constitute the bulk of the essay, developing and exploring the thesis and its implications by whatever methods the writer considers appropriate. You might want to review the methods of development and organizational patterns in Chapters 3, 4, and 5, since body paragraphs in the essays you read very likely will employ many of these elements. As each paragraph moves the ideas forward, writers use these devices to ensure coherence: *transitions*, both within as well as between paragraphs; *parallel phrases, clauses, or sentences;* and *repetition of key words or phrases.* The careful writer also organizes the body paragraphs logically, typically arranging them in a least-important-to-most-important order, especially in persuasive writing.

The Conclusion

An essay's conclusion is usually short—perhaps only a paragraph or two. To find the conclusion, look for the spot where the supporting ideas give way to a summary, a restatement of the main idea, a logical deduction to be drawn from the evidence, a solution or recommendation, a warning for the future, or a challenge. Again, the conclusion's form and length depend on the purpose, subject, and audience.

How to Read an Essay

Armed with this overview of the essay's characteristics and form, you can now tackle your assigned readings. The following suggestions constitute what your English teachers ideally hope their students will do to prepare for class discussion. For each assignment, set aside at minimum an hour preparing, perhaps two hours if the essay is long or difficult. First, read the essay through without stopping. At this stage you can underline any unfamiliar vocabulary words. Read the piece again, more slowly the second time, to put the pieces together. Be sure to read with a pencil in your hand, as you learned in the introduction to the text, and annotate the text like this: Note the main points; write a question mark for material that you do not understand, that needs clarification, or that you disagree with. Also, during this second reading you should look up the troublesome words and allusions.

Finally, review these questions to see if you can answer them in your own words. Although your other English texts may provide discussion or critical-thinking questions after each selection, these questions are extensive and versatile enough to help you with any nonfiction material you are assigned, whether in this textbook or in another course. They constitute the sorts of things your instructors want you to look for when you read. Eventually, the process will become automatic so that you will not have to refer to them before each assignment. If a passage eludes your understanding, make a note of it so that you can raise the point in class discussion. This process enables you to be responsible for your own learning and to master a most worthwhile skill—the ability to analyze difficult prose, which will serve you well in all your academic courses.

■ ANALYZING ESSAYS: QUESTIONS TO ASK

1. Who is the author? In most anthologies, as in this text, the writer is identified by a brief biographical source note or headnote, along with where the material was originally published. This information helps you determine the writer's authority to write, the intended audience, purpose in writing, and point of view or possible bias.

2. This question follows from the first. Who is the audience? Are the writer's ideas aimed toward the general reading public, or do the vocabulary and subject matter suggest that the writer is appealing to a narrower group with specialized knowledge? What clues does the author provide that identify whom he or she is writing for? If the piece comes from a magazine or periodical, is it a mainstream vehicle, like *Time, Newsweek, The New Yorker,* or *Vanity Fair,* or is it a

source apt to appeal to a more specialized audience, for example, *Scientific American, Mother Jones, Yankee Magazine,* or *Foreign Affairs*?

3. What is the writer's purpose? Remember that purpose is closely related to mode of discourse. Is there a secondary purpose as well?

4. What is the thesis? Where is it located? Is its placement appropriate for the writer's purpose and subject? Can you restate the thesis in your own words?

5. What are the main parts of the essay? Note the divisions between introduction, body, and conclusion. How do these parts fit together?

6. Because we read to learn new information, what did you learn? What are the essay's main ideas? What are the major supporting points for the thesis?

7. What inferences did you draw? What conclusions? What has the essay done to educate you about the world? How do the essay's ideas accord with what you already know? What further information do you need?

8. Aside from unfamiliar words—which you should add to your vocabulary notebook as suggested in Part 1—are any words used in unusual ways? Any metaphors or similes? Any strongly connotative words? Is the writer's word choice appropriate for the purpose, audience, and content?

9. Was the essay accompanied by any illustrations? If so, how do the illustrations help reinforce the writer's message?

▣ *PRACTICE ESSAY*

Preposterous: What Has Happened to the Rhinoceros Is as Hard to Fathom as the Beast Itself

Stephen Jay Gould

Stephen Jay Gould was the consummate scientific writer on the topic of evolution. He received his Ph.D. from Columbia University in 1967, and he was Agassiz professor of zoology at Harvard University until his death in 2002. In addition, he served as curator of invertebrate paleontology for Harvard's Museum of Comparative Zoology. Nine collections of his essays on scientific subjects have been published. His 1989 essay, "The Creation Myths of Cooperstown," was selected for inclusion in The Best American Essays of the Century. *The essay reprinted here, which has been annotated for you, is from a column Gould published in* The Sciences.

Rhinos—despite   1
their preposterous
appearance & image
as vestiges of a lost
world, survival of 5
remaining species in
Africa & Asia is
threatened

From numerous versifications in books for children, rhinoceroses have acquired a one-word definition in a near rhyme: preposterous. The five living species of rhinoceroses, viewed as tanklike vestiges of a prehistoric past, and barely hanging on as threatened populations in their African and Asian homes, do convey an image of superannuated heavyweights from a lost world where brawn could overcome stupidity and ensure survival.

Fossil records   2
show that the an-
cestors of today's
rhinos were ecolog-
ically successful—
wide territorial
range with lots of
varied species.
Modern rhinos are
"a vestige within a
vestige." Numbers
have now shrunk to
3 groups

Modern rhinoceroses do represent a remnant of past glory: they were once maximally prosperous, rather than preposterous. Their enormously successful fossil forebears included Paraceratherium, the largest land mammal of all time—eighteen feet high at the shoulder and a browser of treetops. Their extensive ecological range included small and lithe running forms no bigger than a goat (the hyracodontines), and rotund river dwellers that looked like hippopotamuses (the teleoceratines). Moreover, modern rhinoceroses are a vestige within a vestige. The formerly dominant order of odd-toed hoofed mammals has now dwindled to three groups: the rhinoceroses and the tapirs, each barely hanging on, and the horses, given an artificial boost and a new lease on life by human needs for transport and human foibles for warfare and wagering.

Rhinos pose a   3
dilemma: The dis-
tinctive horn de-
fines the species
but also is the cause
of their imminent
demise. Poachers
value horns because
they are believed to
have curative
powers, esp. for
male sexual
impotence

A dilemma, in technical terms, is a problem with two logical solutions, each untenable or unpleasant. We speak of being caught on the "horns of a dilemma," in reference, I suppose, to the crescent moon with its two points, or horns (or perhaps to the devil himself). The dilemma of the rhinoceroses also rests upon two aspects of their distinctive and defining horns. On one point, horns mark the rhinoceros's fascination as both preposterous and alluring—a sign of fame and therefore a desired trophy for Western hunters. On the other point, horns inspire legends of utility for alleviating various human ills, particularly sexual impotence in males—and the few remaining horns have therefore become a prize for poachers and a substance nearly beyond price in Eastern pharmaceuticals.

Gould cannot   4
serve as a dispas-
sionate analyst
when reading about
magnificent animals
being slaughtered
because a single
part is put to some
frivolous and

We all have a personal breaking point, where moral indignation swamps dispassionate analysis. I can read about human desecration of animals with reasonable equanimity in the face of great sadness, but I fall into predominant anger when I encounter the numerous stories of magnificent creatures slaughtered in vast numbers for single parts deemed desirable (often so frivolously) or useful (often so fallaciously) to humans: elephants only for their tusks, buffaloes for their tongues, nightingales for the same organ (for use in Roman banquets) and gorillas because some people will buy ashtrays made of large primate paws. Rhinoceroses,

specious use. The rhino's distinctive horn is the cause of their destruction

sadly, are victims of this same outrage: their most distinctive evolution- ary markers become the brands of their destruction.

Unfortunately, **5** naturalists in the past collected specimens without regard for the bigger picture. Photo shows horns collected by Agassiz in 1877 & modern specimens in the 30s. These specimens are morally equivalent of something truly preposterous

I wish I could portray naturalists as perennial opponents of such exploitation. We certainly function in this manner today, but our past does not always measure up to current practices. In a former age, one that viewed nature as an unlimited bounty and men as masters of all, natu- ralists often collected in a wanton manner—as though scientific study demanded a mass transport from live in the field to dead in a museum drawer. Rosamond Purcell's photograph [see page 395] depicts just some of the specimens in a "miscellaneous bin" of rhinoceros horns in the collection of my own institution, the Museum of Comparative Zoology at Harvard. These specimens range from horns bought by the museum director Alexander Agassiz from Ward's of London in 1877 to animals shot by hunters on safari and donated to the museum as late as 1936. Detached horns, often severed with pieces of surrounding skin. The part that dooms the whole. A strangely beautiful picture of elegance separated from a symbol of ungainliness. Do we not witness here the moral equiv- alent of preposterous?

ANALYSIS OF PRACTICE ESSAY

Here are some suggested responses to the nine questions for analyzing essays (see pages 390–391).

1. *Who is the author?* The headnote clearly identifies Gould as having been associated with one of the country's best universities. His extensive experience teaching and doing research is supported by extensive publications. Therefore, he can likely be considered an authority whose observations are credible.

2. *Who is the audience?* "Preposterous" was published in a bimonthly journal called *The Sciences,* sponsored by the New York Academy of Sciences, an independent, nonprofit organization, whose purpose is "to advance the understanding of science, technology, and medi- cine, and to stimulate new ways to think about how their research is applied in society and the world." (See their home page at www. nyas.org, which summarizes their mission like this: "Since 1817, the New York Academy of Sciences has been bringing together sci- entists of different disciplines from around the world. Their pur- pose is to advance the understanding of science, technology, and medicine, and to stimulate new ways to think about how their re- search is applied in society and the world.") The audience for this

publication, therefore, is probably more interested in scientific subjects than the general reader would be, though there are several clues that Gould is not writing for a scientific audience, as the answer to the next question suggests.

3.   *What is the writer's purpose?* Gould's purpose is to condemn the practice of slaughtering "magnificent animals" because one part is considered desirable by people, especially when the use is both "frivolous" and "fallacious."

4.   *What is the thesis? Where is it located?* The thesis comes in the first two sentences of paragraph 4. Its placement is appropriate because paragraphs 1 to 3 examine the circumstances regarding this admittedly preposterous-looking animal. Once viewed as a vestige of a lost world, today their survival in Asia and Africa is threatened because poachers hunt them illegally to harvest their horns.

5.   *What are the main parts of the essay?* Though this essay is only five paragraphs long, it can be broken down like this:

Introduction: Paragraph 1

>   Background information—contrast between ecological success of rhinos evident from fossil records and their current status as a threatened species

Body: Paragraphs 2–4

>   Further explanation of the rhinoceros's "past glory," the dilemma the rhinoceros's horns present, and author's statement of personal anguish over the practice of killing animals for a single desirable part

Conclusion: Paragraph 5

>   The role natural scientists have played in this desecration

6.   *What did you learn from the essay?* The answer to this question depends on the individual and his or her worldview. One might surely think twice, however, about buying a product made from an animal if its use is inessential (a fur coat is one example).

7.   *What inferences and conclusions can you draw?* The rhinoceros may be a preposterous-looking animal, as Gould suggests from the references to children's books, but the threatened existence of this animal is only one example of human exploitation of nature for our own frivolous ends. Nor does Gould exempt earlier generations of natural scientists from his accusations, and he implies in paragraph 5 that museum collections, in this case of rhinoceros horns, are the result of their habit of "wanton" collecting of specimens.

8.   *Is the language unusual?* Although Gould is a scientist, his style is measured, nuanced, and occasionally poetic. Look again, for example, at his writing in paragraph 3, in his connecting the horns of the dilemma the rhinoceros presents to the rhinoceros's actual horns and to the symbolic horns of the devil, thereby suggesting

that the practice of killing rhinos for their horns is evil. In paragraph 5, Gould concludes with three sentence fragments expressing the sadness with which he views the collection of horns at the Museum of Comparative Zoology at Harvard: "Detached horns, often severed with pieces of surrounding skin. The part that dooms the whole. A strangely beautiful picture of elegance separated from a symbol of ungainliness."

9. *Was the essay accompanied by any illustrations?* This photo accompanied the text in its original publication.

This photograph helps reinforce Gould's observations in the essay by showing rhinoceros horns that were ripped from animals by the Western hunters referred to in paragraph 5. In several cases, the tissue that was removed with the horn can still be seen.

■ WRITING PARAPHRASES

To paraphrase means to restate a writer's ideas in your own words. In the next section, you will learn how to write a summary. A necessary element in writing a summary is the paraphrase. To show you how this is accomplished, here are five suggestions. One or two sentences from Gould's essay are followed by a paraphrase.

1. Use synonyms for key words without changing the meaning.

    Original sentence:

    Modern rhinoceroses do represent a remnant of past glory.

    Paraphrase:

    The rhinoceros today signifies a vestige of its former magnificence.

2. Change the order of ideas within the original sentence.

    Original sentence:

    Their extensive ecological range included small and lithe running forms no bigger than a goat (the hyracodontines), and rotund river dwellers that looked like hippopotamuses (the teleoceratines).

    Paraphrase:

    The forebears of the modern rhinoceros covered a wide territory, ranging from large river dwellers, somewhat like the modern hippopotamus, to smaller forms the size of goats that were nimble runners.

3. Omit unimportant details or excess verbiage.

    In the preceding example, the terms "hyracodontines" and "teleoceratines" have been dropped.

4. Combine ideas and sentences.

    Original sentences:

    I wish I could portray naturalists as perennial opponents of such exploitation. We certainly function in this manner today, but our past does not always measure up to current practices.

    Paraphrase:

    Although natural scientists today are more careful not to exploit the animal populations they study, unfortunately in the past naturalists did not always oppose such exploitation.

5. Maintain the same tone and style as the original passage.

    Original sentence:

    We all have a personal breaking point, where moral indignation swamps dispassionate analysis.

    Paraphase:

    Everyone has a threshold where the sense of moral outrage overwhelms the ability to analyze a problem without prejudice.

Your instructor may require you to write paraphrases of short passages, or you may incorporate the paraphrase process into writing summaries (as well as writing research papers in other courses). Whatever the assignment, writing a paraphrase is an excellent way to check the accuracy of your comprehension.

◼ WRITING SUMMARIES

Why Write Summaries?

A colleague has described a summary as a distillation of ideas. As she put it, "We can reduce a large number of grapes into a very small, but potent glass of wine. The grapes are still there, but in a different, more condensed and powerful form." In other words, a summary is a condensed version of an essay, article, or book; it presents the writer's thesis, the supporting ideas, and the conclusion—in other words, only the important information. Writing summaries provides many intellectual benefits: A summary is a good measure of your reading and writing skills. Like a paraphrase, it requires that you understand a passage accurately. It forces you to weigh the relative worth of ideas, deciding what is essential and what is inessential, what to retain and what to omit. It forces you to discern the arrangement of ideas, and it requires you to restate these ideas concisely, accurately, and fairly, without intruding your own opinion or judgment or distorting the thinking. Finally, it helps you avoid plagiarism (copying). Your ability to restate the main ideas of a passage is a true indicator of how well you understand it.

How long should a summary be? If your instructor does not require you to conform to a particular length, you can use this formula as a guide: A summary of an essay or article should be roughly between 5 and 15 percent of the original. Some instructors ask that a summary be no more than a single typed page, double-spaced, or roughly 200 to 250 words, depending on the length of the assigned essay. Gould's essay is quite short, only 634 words long, meaning that a summary of it should be no more than 100 words.

How to Write a Summary

Follow these suggestions to write an effective summary:

- Read through the passage at least twice so that you have a good understanding of the content. Look up any unfamiliar words.
- Underline important words, phrases, and sentences. Determine where the piece breaks into sections. Annotate the article, noting main ideas and key supporting statements, as I have done for the Gould piece.
- On a separate sheet of paper, write down the main point of each section (or of each paragraph in the case of a short piece like "Preposterous"). Leave plenty of space between each point to make changes or to add material.
- Maintain the balance between main ideas and supporting details in the original. Since you will not have space to include all of the supporting details, choose those that best support the main points.
- Paraphrase the writer's ideas as much as possible, but do not change key terms. For example, in writing a summary of "Preposterous," it would not be plagiarizing to use words or phrases from the essay like "fossil

forebears," "poachers," or "male sexual impotence." In other words, do not strain for synonyms for words that form the basis of the essay.

- Insert transitional words or phrases as necessary to show the relationship between ideas.
- Prepare a final draft by rewriting your sentences. Check to see that your summary is accurate and free of your own ideas and opinions. (Note, however, that many instructors assign a summary-response paper, in which you would be asked both to summarize an essay and then to evaluate it by explaining your objections, criticisms, or other observations. In that case, your instructor is asking for your point of view. If you are unsure about an assignment, ask for clarification.)
- Your summary's first sentence should include the author's name and the essay title, as well as the essay's main idea. Use the present tense throughout. If you use quotations, do so sparingly.
- Do a word count, making sure that your summary is the appropriate length. If it is too long, cut unnecessary verbiage or supporting examples.

■ SAMPLE SUMMARY

Stephen Jay Gould's essay, "Preposterous," examines the plight of the rhinoceros. Though often characterized in children's books as preposterous in appearance, in prehistoric times these magnificent creatures thrived in a variety of environments. Today, however, their survival is threatened. Poachers kill them because their horns are reputed to cure sexual impotence, or they are collected as trophies. Gould finds this practice morally repugnant; he abandons his scientific objectivity when he encounters stories of animals slaughtered for a single part, especially for frivolous or fallacious reasons. What is truly preposterous is not the animal, but our wanton killing of them. (99 words)

⌐ ON THE WEB

Purdue University's Web site has one of the oldest and best Online Writing Laboratories (OWL) in the nation. Its OWL offers hundreds of handouts on all the elements of writing an essay, including how to write a summary and how to avoid plagiarism. For more help with these and other topics, go to: owl.English.purdue.edu/.

■ TWELVE ESSAYS AND ARTICLES FOR FURTHER PRACTICE

Selection 1

An Ethnic Trump
Gish Jen

This article, first published in Essence, *and reprinted in* The New York Times, *looks at cultural identity and the hard work that parents of biracial children face. Gish Jen is known primarily as a fiction writer; she is the author of* Typical American *(1991),* Mona in the Promised Land *(1999),* Who's Irish? *(1999), and most recently,* The Love Wife *(2004).*

Preview Questions

1. The word *trump* is central to the meaning of this essay. If you are unsure of its definition, look it up in the dictionary before reading the piece.

2. Luke, the small child whose mixed racial heritage causes his parents anguish, has several reactions to the comments and taunts of his classmates and friends. Note these carefully as you read the essay; then evaluate the way his parents respond to his concerns.

1   That my son, Luke, age 4, goes to Chinese-culture school seems inevitable to most people, even though his father is of Irish descent. In America, certain ethnicities are seen as more ethnic than others: Chinese, for example, trumps Irish. This has something to do with the relative distance of certain cultures from mainstream America, but it also has to do with race. As we all know, it is not only certain ethnicities that trump others but certain colors: Black trumps White, for example, always and forever; a mulatto is not a kind of White person, but a kind of Black person.

2   And so it is, too, that my son is considered a kind of Asian person, whose destiny is to embrace Asian things: the Chinese language, Chinese food, Chinese New Year. No one cares whether he speaks Gaelic or wears green on St. Patrick's Day, for though Luke's skin is fair and his features mixed, people see his straight black hair and *know* who he is.

3   But is this how we should define ourselves, by other people's perceptions? My husband, Dave, and I had originally hoped for Luke to grow up embracing his whole complex heritage. We had hoped to pass on to him values and habits of mind that had survived in both of us.

4   Then one day Luke combed his black hair and said he was turning it yellow. Another day, a mother I knew said her son had invited all blond-haired children like himself to his birthday party. And yet another day, Luke was happily scooting around the Cambridge Common playground when a pair of older boys, apparently brothers, blocked his way. "You're

Chinese!" they shouted, leaning on the hood of Luke's scooter car. "You are! You're Chinese!" Even when I intervened, they kept shouting. Luke answered, "No, I'm not!" to no avail; the boys didn't seem to hear him. Then the boys' mother called to them from some distance away, and though her voice was no louder than Luke's, they left obediently.

5   Behind them opened a great, rippling quiet, like the wash of a battleship.

6   Luke and I immediately went over things he could say if anything like that happened again. I told him he was 100-percent American, even though I knew from my own childhood in Yonkers, New York, that these words would be met only with derision. It was a sorry chore. Since then I have not asked him about the incident, hoping, that he has forgotten about it, and wishing I could, too. I wish I could forget the sight of those kids' fingers on the hood of Luke's little car. I wish I could forget their loud attack, but also Luke's soft defense: "No, I'm not!"

7   Chinese school. After dozens of phone calls, I was elated to discover the Greater Boston Chinese Cultural Association in nearby West New-ton, Massachusetts. The school takes children at 3, has a wonderful sense of community and is housed in a center paid for, in part, by karaoke fund-raising events. (Never mind what the Japanese meant to the Chinese in the old world. In this world, people donate $200 apiece for a chance at the mike, and the singing goes on all night.) At the school, there are even vendors who bring home-style Chinese food to sell after class, stuff you can't get in a restaurant. Dave and I couldn't wait for Luke's second class and a chance to buy more *bao* for our freezer.

8   But in the car on the way to the class, Luke announced that he didn't want to go to Chinese school anymore. He said the teacher talked mostly about ducks and bears, and he wasn't interested in ducks and bears. I knew this was true. Luke was interested only in whales and ships. What's more, I knew we wouldn't push him to take swimming lessons if he didn't want to, or music. Chinese school was a wonderful thing, but weren't we making it somehow nonoptional? Was that right? Hadn't we always said that we didn't want our son to see himself as more Chinese than Irish?

9   Yet we didn't want to deny his Chinese heritage, either. And if there were going to be incidents on the playground, we wanted him to at least know what Chinese meant. So when Luke said again that he didn't want to go to Chinese school, I said, "Oh, really?" Later on we could try to teach him to define himself irrespective of race. For now, he was going to Chinese school. I exchanged glances with Dave. And then together, in a most casual manner, we squinted at the road and kept going.

A. Comprehension

Choose the answer that best completes each statement. Do not refer to the selection while doing this exercise.

1. Jen writes that not only do certain ethnicities "trump" others but also certain
   (a) neighborhoods.
   (b) (skin colors.)
   (c) cultural values.
   (d) hair colors.

2. Jen states that she and her husband wanted their son, Luke, to
   (a) learn what being Chinese meant.
   (b) consider himself American.
   (c) (accept both sides of his cultural heritage.)
   (d) learn to stand up for himself against bigotry.

3. When a pair of older boys on a playground taunted Luke about being Chinese, he responded by
   (a) retaliating against them.
   (b) getting beaten up.
   (c) running home.
   (d) (denying their accusations.)

4. Telling Luke that he was 100 percent American was, according to Jen,
   (a) (wishful thinking on her part.)
   (b) a deliberate lie.
   (c) a useful way to help Luke understand his heritage.
   (d) the way she dealt with her own youthful problems concerning race.

5. With regard to Chinese school, Jen and her husband decided to
   (a) allow Luke to leave.
   (b) (make Luke continue attending.)
   (c) allow Luke to attend less frequently.
   (d) let Luke make up his own mind about whether to continue or not.

B. Vocabulary

For each italicized word from the selection, write the best definition according to the context in which it appears. You may refer to the selection to answer the questions in this section and in all the remaining sections.

1. Chinese . . . *trumps* Irish [paragraph 1]:   dominates in the sense of

   establishing one's identity

2. *to no avail* [4]:   with no result, of no use

3. these words would be met only with *derision* [6]:   contempt, ridicule

4. *irrespective* of race [9]:   without regard for, regardless of

C. Inferences

Complete the following questions.

1. From paragraphs 6 and 7, we can infer that Luke's parents sent him to Chinese school so that he could learn
   (a) to speak Chinese.
   (b) about the Chinese side of his heritage.
   (c) to defend himself against future playground attacks.
   (d) a martial art.
2. The fundamental conflict that Jen examines in this article is between
   (a) the labels placed on us by the larger society and the cultural heritage our parents hope to instill in us.
   (b) the heritage we hope to identify with and the heritage we actually do identify with.
   (c) Chinese and American cultural values.
   (d) the wish to remain identified with one's cultural background and the wish to assimilate into the larger culture.
3. When Jen writes in paragraph 2 that her son's "destiny is to embrace Asian things," what is the origin of this destiny?   It is based on his

   appearance and on other people's perceptions of his race.
4. Why does Luke say in paragraph 4 that he was turning his hair yellow?

   Because he wanted to be more like the blond boys who had been

   invited to a birthday party he had been excluded from
5. In the last two sentences of the article, Jen suggests that she and her husband
   (a) disagreed about the best way to teach him.
   (b) had nothing more to say about the subject.
   (c) did not want to argue in front of their child.
   (d) were only feigning casualness and were, in fact, concerned.

D. Structure

Complete the following questions.

1. When Jen says that "Chinese trumps Irish" and "Black trumps White . . . always and forever," she means that
   (a) Whites and Blacks must learn to get along.
   (b) race is the most important element in the way people perceive others.
   (c) being Black or being Chinese allows one to outrank Whites.
   (d) one's race is more important than one's cultural or ethnic heritage.

2. At the beginning of paragraph 3, Jen asks a rhetorical question (one asked only for effect)—"But is this how we should define ourselves, by other people's perceptions?" If she did answer it, would she say yes or no?   <u>no</u>

E. Questions for Discussion and Analysis

1. What instance of prejudice have you observed and/or experienced firsthand? To what extent was your experience the result of race?

2. What should parents of biracial children do to educate and protect their children?

ON THE WEB

- The issue of biracial adoption has been controversial in recent years. Do some research, using your favorite Internet search engine, on policies regarding biracial adoption in your home state.
- Gish Jen's 1998 novel *Typical American* tells the story of a young man from China, Yifeng, who comes to America to study engineering. His plan is to return to China; however, he soon finds himself becoming Americanized. Use a search engine to locate reviews of this book to see if it is one you might enjoy reading for pleasure.

Selection 2   # On Leavened Bread
Salman Rushdie

Salman Rushdie is a contemporary writer who was born in India in 1947. He is best known for his controversial novel, The Satanic Verses *(1988). Muslim fundamentalists attacked the novel: They believed that Rushdie had committed blasphemy by modeling a character on the Prophet Mohammed. Iran's Ayatollah Khomeini issued a* fatwa, *a religious edict calling for the murder of Rushdie, forcing him to live in hiding for many years. After Khomeini's death, the Iranian government eventually lifted the* fatwa. *You can see Rushdie in a cameo role playing himself in the 2001 film,* Bridget Jones's Diary.

Preview Questions

1. Do not let the names of the breads mentioned in the essay intimidate you. Leavened bread, mentioned in the title, refers to bread

that is made to rise by adding a leavening agent like yeast, in contrast to Indian breads, which are flat. *Chapati, phulka, tandoori nan, Peshawari nan, feshmi roti, shirmal,* and *paratha,* mentioned in the first paragraph, are all traditional Indian flat breads, meaning that, because they contain no yeast, they do not rise. The two breads mentioned in paragraph 5 are European: *ciabatta* is a rough Italian bread; *brioche* is a sweet light French bread.

2. As you read this essay, you will see that Rushdie is talking about different types of bread both literally and metaphorically. His relishing of traditional Indian breads and his new-found pleasure in eating spongy white bread in England are actually suggestive of something deeper. See if you can identify what he means.

3. Pay special attention to paragraph 4, and keep in mind that Rushdie is writing about a discovery he makes at the onset of puberty, at the age of around thirteen.

1   There was leavened bread in Bombay, but it was sorry fare: dry, crumbling, tasteless—unleavened bread's paler, unluckier relative. It wasn't "real." Real bread was the chapati, or phulka, served piping hot; the tandoori nan, and its sweeter Frontier variant, the Peshawari nan; and, for luxury, the feshmi roti, the shirmal, the paratha. Compared with these aristocrats, the leavened white loaves of my childhood seemed to merit the description that Shaw's immortal dustman, Alfred Doolittle, dreamed up for people like himself: they were, in truth, "the undeserving poor."[1]

2   My first inkling that there might be more to leavened bread than I knew came while I was visiting Karachi, Pakistan, where I learned that a hidden order of nuns, in a place known as the Monastery of the Angels, baked a mean loaf. To buy it, you had to get up at dawn—that is, a servant had to get up at dawn—and stand in line outside a small hatch in the monastery's wall. The nun's baking facilities were limited, the daily run was small, and this secret bakery's reputation was high. Only the early bird caught the loaf. The hatch would open, and a nun would hand the bread out to the waiting populace. Loaves were strictly rationed. No bulk buying was permitted. And the price, of course, was high. (All this I knew only by hearsay, for I never got up at such as unearthly hour to see for myself.)

3   The nuns' bread—white, crusty, full of flavor—was a small revelation, but it was also, on account of its unusual provenance, eccentric. It came

---

[1]The reference here is to the play *Pygmalion* by George Bernard Shaw, which was later made into a Broadway musical and the film *My Fair Lady.* It concerns Eliza Doolittle, a flower-stall clerk, and Henry Higgins's attempts to rid her of her cockney accent. Alfred Doolittle, mentioned here, is Eliza's father. A dustman in England is a garbage collector.

from beyond the frontiers of the everyday, a mystery trailing an anecdote behind it. It was almost—well, fictional. (Later, it became fictional, when I put the monastery in my novel "Midnight's Children.") Now, in the matter of bread such extraordinariness is not good. You want bread to be part of your daily life. You want it to be ordinary. You want it to be there. You don't want to get up in the middle of the night and wait by a hatch in a wall. So, while the Angels' bread was tasty, it felt like an aberration, a break in the natural order. It didn't really change my mind.

4   Then, aged thirteen and a half, I flew to England. And, suddenly, there it was, in every shopwindow. The White Crusty, the Sliced and the Unsliced. The Small Tin, the Large Tin, the Bloomer. The abandoned, plentiful promiscuity of it. The soft, pillowy mattressiness of it. The well-sprung bounciness of it between your teeth. Hard crust and soft center: the sensuality of that perfect textural contrast. I was done for. In the whorehouses of the bakeries, I was serially, gluttonously, irredeemably unfaithful to all those chapatis next door, waiting for me back home. East was East, but yeast was West.

5   This, remember was long before British bread counters were enlivened by the European invasion, long before ciabatta and brioche; this was 1961. But the love affair that began then has never lost its intensity; the new exotic breads have served only to renew the excitement.

6   I should add that there was a second discovery, almost as thrilling; that is, water. The water back home was dangerous and had to be thoroughly boiled. To be able to drink water from the tap was a privilege indeed. I have never forgotten that when I first arrived in these immeasurably wealthy and powerful lands I found the first proofs of my good fortune in loaf and glass. Since that time, a regime of bread and water has never sounded like a hardship to me.

A. Comprehension

Choose the answer that best completes each statement. Do not refer to the selection while doing this exercise.

1. The leavened bread from Rushdie's childhood in Bombay was
    (a) of excellent quality.
    (b) of very poor quality.
    (c) bought only by aristocrats.
    (d) nearly impossible to buy.
2. Rushdie found the bread baked at the Monastery of the Angels in Karachi "eccentric" because of its
    (a) unusual origin.
    (b) resemblance to the traditional Indian breads of this youth.
    (c) strange color and flavor.
    (d) weird shape and texture.

3. According to the author, bread should be
    (a) made only at home.
    (b) served with every meal.
    (c) (ordinary and easily available.)
    (d) difficult to obtain and therefore more desirable.

4. The author characterizes the white leavened bread he encountered in England as almost
    (a) miraculous.
    (b) (seductive.)
    (c) mysterious.
    (d) addictive.

5. The safe water in England was, to Rushdie, another indication of England's
    (a) immense influence in the colonial world.
    (b) (immeasurable wealth and power.)
    (c) concern with the environment.
    (d) advanced technology.

B. *Vocabulary*

For each italicized word from the selection, write the dictionary definition most appropriate for the context. You may refer to the selection to answer the questions in this section and in all the remaining sections.

1. it was *sorry* fare [paragraph 1]:   of poor quality

2. nuns . . . baked a *mean* loaf (slang or informal meaning) [2]:

    excellent

3. its unusual *provenance* [3]:   place of origin

4. it felt like an *abberation* [3]:   deviation from the normal

5. the abandoned, plentiful *promiscuity* [4]: Here used ironically and humorously to mean   indiscriminate presence, availability

6. *irredeemably* unfaithful [4]: describing one who is impossible to

    reform

C. *Structure*

Complete the following questions.

1. The author's literal purpose is to
    (a) (explain the differences between Indian unleavened bread and Western leavened bread.)
    (b) classify types of bread.

      (c) explore his pleasurable sensory discoveries of different kinds of bread.

      (d) convince us that leavened breads are superior to unleavened types.

2.   This essay is about more than just bread. In your own words, explain Rushdie's deeper purpose in writing this essay. <u>To show his coming</u>

   <u>of age and his moving into the wider world; to show his excitement</u>

   <u>at coming into contact with unfamiliar Western culture</u>

3.   Rushdie strongly implies in paragraph 2 that

      (a) the Monastery of Angels' bread was a well-kept secret.

      (b) Rushdie's family was sufficiently rich that they could afford to send a servant to buy the monastery's bread.

      (c) the monastery's white bread was superior to the bread he later discovered in England.

      (d) the nuns were probably English.

D. Language

Complete the following questions.

1.   In paragraph 1 Rushdie uses two metaphors to contrast the white unleavened bread of Bombay and the "real" Indian breads, such as chapali, tandoori nan, and paratha. White leavened breads are imaginatively compared to <u>poor people.</u>

   Traditional Indian breads are imaginatively compared to <u>aristocrats.</u>

2.   In paragraph 1, Rushdie describes leavened bread from his childhood as "dry, crumbling, tasteless." In paragraph 3, he describes the monastery bread he ate in Karachi as "white, crusty, full of flavor."

   These phrases are

   (a) denotative.

   (b) connotative.

   (c) examples of bakers' jargon.

   (d) euphemisms.

3.   Consider the words "eccentric" and "mystery" in paragraph 3. How would you characterize their use?

   (a) denotative.

   (b) connotative with positive overtones.

   (c) connotative with negative overtones.

   (d) clichés.

4.   At the heart of the essay, in paragraph 4, Rushdie imaginatively compares the English variety of white bread to <u>a prostitute who seduces</u>

   <u>a young boy and makes him lose his virginity.</u>

   The word "mattressiness," also in paragraph 4, refers specifically to which quality of English bread? <u>its softness, its puffy quality</u>

5. The emotional atmosphere that this essay suggests is
    (a) playful, amusing.
    (b) nostalgic, melancholy.
    (c) earnest, serious.
    (d) philosophic, questioning.

E. *Questions for Discussion and Analysis*

1. Examine a food that, as bread does for Salman Rushdie, reveals something more profound about the culture that produces it.

2. Explore the concept of food as a trigger for memory. What foods serve this function for you?

ON THE WEB

Using Google or your favorite search engine, investigate what happened to Salman Rushdie as a result of the publication of *The Satanic Verses* in 1989. You will get several good leads by typing in "Salman Rushdie" and "fatwa," which is the term for a religious edict or ruling in the Islamic faith.

Selection 3   # The Truck: Hitching Through Hell
Ryszard Kapuściński

Poland's most respected reporter, Ryszard Kapuściński, was born in 1932 in Pinsk, in what is now Belarus. Like all good reporters, he is fascinated with politics and with exotic places. He has traveled all over the world, but especially in Africa, reporting on everyday affairs, wars, revolutions, coups, and the end of imperialism. He has written several books about Africa. This selection, originally titled "Salim," appeared first in The New Yorker *and then in a collection of accounts from his travels in Africa,* Shadow of the Sun *(2001). Kapuściński lives in Warsaw, Poland. Mauritania, where the events described take place, lies on the Atlantic Ocean in northwest Africa. This essay was translated from the Polish by Klara Glowczewska.*

Preview Questions

1. Kapuściński describes a harrowing incident in this essay. As you read it, note the description of his emotional state and his reaction

to the events unfolding around him. What qualities does Kapuściński exhibit that are the qualities a good reporter traveling in difficult places should possess?

2. What universal human condition is strongly implied in this account? Is Kapuściński's view of life essentially optimistic or pessimistic?

1   In the darkness, I suddenly spotted two glaring lights. They were far away and moved about violently, as if they were the eyes of a wild animal thrashing about in its cage. I was sitting on a stone at the edge of the Ouadane oasis, in the Sahara, northeast of Nouakchott, the Mauritanian capital. For an entire week now I had been trying to leave this place—to no avail. It is difficult to get to Ouadane, but even more difficult to depart. No marked or paved road leads to it, and there is no scheduled transport. Every few days—sometimes weeks—a truck will pass, and if the driver agrees to take you with him, you go; if not, you simply stay, waiting who knows how long for the next opportunity.

2   The Mauritanians who were sitting beside me stirred. The night chill had set in, a chill that descends abruptly and, after the burning hell of the sun-filled days, can be almost piercingly painful. It is a cold from which no sheepskin or quilt can adequately protect you. And these people had nothing but old, frayed blankets, in which they sat tightly wrapped, motionless, like statues.

3   A black pipe poked out from the ground nearby, a rusty and salt-encrusted compressor-pump mechanism at its tip. This was the region's sole gas station, and passing vehicles always stopped here. There is no other attraction in the oasis. Ordinarily, days pass uneventfully and unchangeably, resembling in this the monotony of the desert climate: the same sun always shines, hot and solitary, in the same empty, cloudless sky.

4   At the sight of the still-distant headlights, the Mauritanians began talking among themselves. I didn't understand a word of their language. It's quite possible they were saying: "At last! It's finally coming! We have lived to see it!"

5   It was recompense for the long days spent waiting, gazing patiently at the inert, unvarying horizon, on which no moving object, no living thing that might rouse you from the numbness of hopeless anticipation, had appeared in a long time. The arrival of a truck—cars are too fragile for this terrain—didn't fundamentally alter the lives of the people. The vehicle usually stopped for a moment and then quickly drove on. Yet even this brief sojourn was vital and important to them: it injected variety into their lives, provided a subject for later conversation, and, above all, was both material proof of the existence of another world and a bracing confirmation that that world, since it had sent them a mechanical envoy, must know that they existed.

6   Perhaps they were also engaged in a routine debate: will it—or won't it—get here? For traveling in these corners of the Sahara is a risky

adventure, an unending lottery, perpetual uncertainty. Along these road-less expanses full of crevices, depressions, sinkholes, protruding boulders, sand dunes and rocky mounds, loose stones and fields of slippery gravel, a vehicle advances at a snail's pace—several kilometers an hour. Each wheel has its own drive, and each one, meter by meter, turning here, stopping there, going up, down, or around, searches for something to grip. Most of the time, these persistent efforts and exertions, which are accompanied by the roar of the straining and overheated engine and by the bone-bruising lunges of the swaying platform, finally result in the truck's moving forward.

7   But the Mauritanians also knew that sometimes a truck could get hopelessly stuck just a step away from the oasis, on its very threshhold. This can happen when a storm moves mountains of sand onto the track. In such an event, either the truck's occupants manage to dig out the road, or the driver finds a detour—or he simply turns around and goes back where he came from. Another storm will eventually move the dunes farther and clear the way.

8   This time, however, the electric lights were drawing nearer and nearer. At a certain moment, their glow started to pick out the crowns of date palms that had been hidden under the cover of darkness, and the shabby walls of mud huts, and the goats and cows asleep by the side of the road, until, finally, trailing clouds of dust behind it, an enormous Berliet truck drew to a halt in front of us, with a clang and thud of metal. Berliets are French-made trucks adapted for roadless desert terrain. They have large wheels with wide tires, and grilles mounted atop their hoods. Because of their great size and prominent shape of the grille, from a distance they resemble the fronts of old steam engines.

9   The driver—a dark-skinned, barefoot Mauritanian in an ankle-length indigo djellabah—climbed down from the cab using a ladder. He was, like the majority of his countrymen, tall and powerfully built. People and animals with substantial body weight endure tropical heat better, which is why the inhabitants of the Sahara usually have a magnificently statuesque appearance. The law of natural selection is also at work here: in these extremely harsh desert conditions, only the strongest survive to maturity.

10   The Mauritanians from the oasis immediately surrounded the driver. A cacophony of greetings, questions, and well-wishings erupted. This went on and on. Everybody was shouting and gesticulating, as if haggling in a noisy marketplace. After a while they began to point at me. I was a pitiful sight—dirty, unshaven, and, above all, wasted by the nightmarish heat of the Sahara summer. An experienced Frenchman had warned me earlier: it will feel as if someone were sticking a knife into you. Into your back, into your head. At noon, the rays of the sun beat down with the force of a knife.

11   The driver looked at me and at first said nothing. Then he motioned toward the truck with his hand and called out to me: "*Yalla!* (Let's go!

We're off!)" I climbed into the cab and slammed the door shut. We set off immediately.

12   I had no sense of where we were going. Sand flashed by in the glow of the headlights, shimmering with different shades, laced with strips of gravel and shards of rock. The wheels reared up on granite ledges or sank down into hollows and stony fissures. In the deep, black night one could see only two spots of light—two bright, clearly outlined orbs sliding over the surface of the desert. Nothing else was visible.

13   Before long, I began to suspect that we were driving blind, on a short-cut to somewhere, because there were no demarcation points, no signs, posts, or any other traces of a roadway. I tried to question the driver. I gestured at the darkness around us and asked: "Nouakchott?"

14   He looked at me and laughed. "Nouakchott?" He repeated this dreamily, as if it were the Hanging Gardens of Semiramis that I was asking him about—so beautiful but, for us lowly ones, too high to reach. I concluded from this that we were not headed in the direction I desired, but I did not know how to ask him where, in that case, we were going. I desperately wanted to establish some contact with him, to get to know him even a little. "Ryszard," I said, pointing at myself. Then I pointed at him. He understood. "Salim," he said, and laughed again. Silence fell. We must have come upon a smooth stretch of desert, for the Berliet began to roll along more gently and quickly (exactly how fast, I don't know, since all the instruments were broken). We drove on for a time without speaking, until finally I fell asleep.

15   A sudden silence awoke me. The engine had stopped, the truck stood still. Salim was pressing on the gas pedal and turning the key in the ignition. The battery was working—the starter too—but the engine emitted no sound. It was morning, and already light outside. He began searching around the cab for the lever that opens the hood. This struck me as at once odd and suspicious: a driver who doesn't know how to open the hood? Eventually, he figured out that the latches that need to be released were on the outside. He then stood on a fender and began to inspect the engine, but he peered at its intricate construction as if he were seeing it for the first time. He would touch something, try to move something, but his gestures were those of an amateur. Every now and then he would climb into the cab and turn the key in the ignition, but the engine remained dead silent. He located the toolbox, but there wasn't much in it. He pulled out a hammer, several wrenches, and screwdrivers. Then he started to take the engine apart.

16   I stepped down from the cab. All around us, as far as the eye could see, was desert. Sand, with dark stones scattered about. Nearby, a large black oval rock. (In the hours following noon, after being warmed by the sun, it would radiate heat like a steel-mill oven.) A moonscape, delineated by a level horizon line: the earth ends, and then there's nothing but sky and more sky. No hills. No sand dunes. Not a single leaf. And, of

course, no water. Water! It's what instantly comes to mind under such circumstances. In the desert, the first thing man sees when he opens his eyes in the morning is the face of his enemy—the flaming visage of the sun. The sight elicits in him a reflexive gesture of self-preservation: he reaches for water. Drink! Drink! Only by doing so can he ever so slightly improve his odds in the desert's eternal struggle—the desperate duel with the sun.

17   I resolved to look around for water, for I had none with me. I found nothing in the cab. But I did discover some: attached with ropes to the bed of the truck, near the rear, underneath, were four goatskins, two on the left side and two on the right. The hides had been rather poorly cured, then sewn together in such a way that they retained the animal's shape. One of the goat's legs served as a drinking spout.

18   I sighed with relief, but only momentarily. I began to calculate. Without water, you can survive in the desert for twenty-four hours; with great difficulty, forty-eight or so. The match is simple. Under these conditions, you secrete in one day approximately ten liters of sweat, and to survive you must drink a similar amount of water. Deprived of it, you will immediately start to feel thirsty. Genuine, prolonged thirst in a hot and dry climate is an exhausting, ravaging sensation, harder to control than hunger. After a few hours of it you become lethargic and limp, weak and disoriented. Instead of speaking, you babble, ever less cogently. That same evening, or the next day, you get a high fever and quickly die.

19   If Salim doesn't share his water with me, I thought, I will die today. Even if he does, we will have only enough left for one more day—which means we will both die tomorrow, the day after at the latest.

20   Trying to stop these thoughts, I decided to observe him closely. Covered with grease and sweating, Salim was still taking the engine apart, unscrewing screws and removing cables, but with no rhyme or reason, like a child furiously destroying a toy that won't work. On the fenders, on the bumper, lay countless springs, valves, compression rings, and wires; some had already fallen to the ground. I left him and went around to the other side of the truck, where there was still some shade. I sat down on the ground and leaned my back against the wheel.

21   Salim.

22   I knew nothing about the man who held my life in his hands. Or, at least, who held it for this one day. I thought, if Salim chases me away from the truck and the water—after all, he had a hammer in his hand and probably a knife in his pocket, and, on top of that, enjoyed a significant physical advantage—if he orders me to leave and march off into the desert, I won't last even until nightfall. And it seemed to me that was precisely what he might choose to do. He would thereby extend his life, after all—or, if help arrives in time, he might even save it.

23   Clearly Salim was not a professional driver, or at any rate, not a driver of a Berliet truck. He also didn't know the area well. (On the other hand,

can one really know the desert, where successive storms and tempests constantly alter the landscape, moving mountains of sand to ever different sites and transposing features of the landscape with impunity?) It is common practice in these parts for someone with even a small financial windfall to immediately hire another with less money to carry out his tasks for him. Maybe the rightful driver of this truck had hired Salim to take it in his stead to one of the oases. And hereabouts no one will ever admit to not knowing or not being capable of something. If you approach a taxi driver in a city, show him an address, and ask him if he knows where it is, he will say yes without a second's hesitation. And it is only later, when you are driving all over the city, round and round, that you fully realize he has no idea where to go.

24   The sun was climbing higher and higher. The desert, that motionless, petrified ocean, absorbed its rays, grew hotter, and began to burn. The hour was approaching when everything would become a hell—the earth, the sky, us. The Yoruba are said to believe that if a man's shadow abandons him, he will die. All the shadows were beginning to shrink, dwindle, fade. The dread afternoon hours were almost upon us, the time of day when people and objects have no shade, exist and yet do not exist, reduced to a glowing, incandescent whiteness.

25   I thought that this moment had arrived, but suddenly I noticed before me an utterly different sight. The lifeless, still horizon—so crushed by the heat that it seemed nothing could ever issue forth from it—all at once sprang to life and became green. As far as the eye could see stood tall, magnificent palm trees, entire groves of them along the horizon, growing thickly, without interruption. I also saw lakes—yes, enormous blue lakes, with animated, undulating surfaces. Gorgeous shrubs also grew there, with wide-spreading branches of a fresh, intense, succulent, deep green. All this shimmered continuously, sparkled, pulsated, as if it were wreathed in a light mist, soft-edged and elusive. And everywhere—here, around us, and there, on the horizon—a profound, absolute silence reigned: the wind did not blow, and the palm groves had no birds.

26   "Salim!" I called. "Salim!"

27   A head emerged from under the hood. He looked at me.

28   "Salim!" I repeated once more, and pointed.

29   Salim glanced where I had shown him, unimpressed. In my dirty, sweaty face he must have read wonder, bewilderment, and rapture—but also something else besides, which clearly alarmed him, for he walked up to the side of the truck, untied one of the goatskins, took a few sips, and wordlessly handed me the rest. I grabbed the rough leather sack and began to drink. Suddenly dizzy, I leaned my shoulder against the truck bed so as not to fall. I drank and drank, sucking fiercely on the goat's leg and still staring at the horizon. But as I felt my thirst subsiding, and the madness within me dying down, the green vista began to vanish. Its colors faded and paled, it contours shrank and blurred. By the time I had

emptied the goatskin, the horizon was once again flat, empty, and life-less. The water, disgusting Saharan water—warm, dirty, thick with sand and sludge—extended my life but took away my vision of paradise. The crucial thing, though, was the fact that Salim himself had given me the water to drink. I stopped being afraid of him. I felt I was safe—at least, until the moment when we would be down to our last sip.

30   We spent the second half of the day lying underneath the truck, in its faint, bleached shade. In this world circled all about with flaming horizons, Salim and I were the only life. I inspected the ground within my arm's reach, the nearest stones, searching for some living thing, any-thing that might twitch, move, slither. I remembered that somewhere on the Sahara there lives a small beetle which the Tuareg call Ngubi. When it is very hot, according to legend, Ngubi is tormented by thirst, desperate to drink. Unfortunately, there is no water anywhere, and only burning sand all around. So the small beetle chooses an incline—this can be a sloping fold of sand—and with determination begins to climb to its summit. It is an enormous effort, a Sisyphean task, because the hot and loose sand constantly gives way, carrying the beetle down with it, right back to where he began his toils. Which is why, before too long, the beetle starts to sweat. A drop of moisture collects at the end of his abdomen and swells. Then Ngubi stops climbing, curls up, and plunges his mouth into that very bead.

31   He drinks.

32   Salim has several biscuits in a paper bag. We drink the second goat-skin of water. Two remain. I consider writing something. (It occurs to me that this is often done at such moments.) But I don't have the strength. I'm not really in pain. It's just that everything is becoming empty. And within this emptiness another one is growing.

33   Then, in the darkness, two glaring lights. They are far away and move about violently. Then the sound of a motor draws near, and I see the truck, hear voices in a language I do not understand. "Salim!" I say. Several dark faces, resembling his, lean over me.

A. Comprehension

Choose the answer that best completes each statement. Do not refer to the selection while doing this exercise.

1. Travel in Mauritania is particularly difficult because
   (a) the roads are badly maintained and fuel is expensive.
   (b) there are no paved roads and no scheduled transportation.
   (c) there are few skilled mechanics to repair the nation's public transit vehicles.
   (d) there is not enough demand for public transit to maintain a regu-lar fleet.

2. Besides giving the Mauritanians something to talk about, the arrival of the truck near the Ouadane oasis also signified that
    (a) someone in authority had taken their request for transportation seriously.
    (b) they could finally leave for the city to find jobs.
    (c) the sand from a recent storm had been cleared from the tracks.
    (d) the outside world recognized their existence.
3. Which of these was *not* mentioned as a reason that travel in the Sahara is risky?
    (a) The roads are unsafe and filled with dangerous rocks and other obstacles.
    (b) There is always the threat of highway robbers stealing one's possessions.
    (c) A truck can easily get stuck in the sand and wait days for rescue.
    (d) The heat is punishing, so being stranded might result in death.
4. Kapuściński's first suspicions of Salim's status as a driver occurred when he discovered that Salim
    (a) had brought no map.
    (b) spoke no English or Polish.
    (c) had forgotten to bring food or water.
    (d) did not know how to open the truck's hood.
5. Kapuściński writes that a person can survive in the Sahara without water for 24 hours and, with great difficulty, for only
    (a) 36 hours.
    (b) 48 hours.
    (c) four days.
    (d) five days.

B. Vocabulary

For each italicized word from the selection, write the best definition according to the context in which it appears. You may refer to the selection to answer the questions in this section and in all the remaining sections.

1. it was *recompense* [paragraph 5]: compensation, amends

2. the *inert,* unvarying horizon [5]: unmoving, motionless

3. a *cacophony* of greetings [10]: jarring, discordant sound

4. there were no *demarcation* points [13]: referring to a boundary line, distinct limit

5. a moonscape, *delineated* by a level horizon [16]: drawn, depicted

6. soft-edged and *elusive* [25]: evading capture or perception

C. Inferences

On the basis of the evidence in the essay, mark these statements as follows: PA (probably accurate), PI (probably inaccurate), or NP (not in the passage).

1. _NP_ Kapuściński was concerned that his family did not know his whereabouts.
2. _PA_ The writer had not realized that finding a ride to Nouakchott would be so difficult.
3. _PA_ Kapuściński's health had suffered during his stay in Mauritania.
4. _NP_ Salim's lack of mechanical experience is representative of drivers in the Sahara.
5. _PI_ Salim did not assume that the disabled truck would be rescued and shared his goatskin bags of water only out of pity for Kapuściński.
6. _PA_ If the truck had not arrived when it did, Kapuściński probably would not have lived very long.

D. Language

Complete the following questions.

1. In describing the truck in paragraph 5 as a "mechanical envoy," Kapuściński uses
   (a) irony.
   (b) personification.
   (c) a metaphor.
   (d) a simile.
2. When he describes the movements of the truck in paragraph 6 as "bone-bruising lunges," is the writer being literal or figurative? literal
3. Look again at paragraphs 10, 16, and 24, and locate a figure of speech in each. State what is compared to what.

   Paragraph 10: The rays of the sun

   are compared to a knife sticking into a person.

   Paragraph 16: The desert traveler's attempt to find enough water

   is compared to an eternal duel with the sun.

   Paragraph 16: The sun's radiating heat

   is compared to a steel-mill oven

   Paragraph 24: The desert

   is compared to a motionless, petrified ocean.

4. Here are two allusions from the essay. Look them up and explain what they mean.

Paragraph 14: The Hanging Gardens of Semiramis are famous gardens built in Babylon by its founder, Queen Semiramis; they are one of the Seven Wonders of the Ancient World. <u>The capital city of</u>

<u>Nouakchott was as out of reach as these ancient gardens and not</u>

<u>possible for such lowly people as these travelers to reach.</u>

Paragraph 30: A little beetle called Ngubi continuously climbs a sand dune, a Sisyphean task, to achieve one drop of sweat, which it drinks to save itself. <u>The Greek mythological figure Sisyphus received the</u>

<u>eternal punishment to roll a rock up to the top of a large hill, only</u>

<u>to see it roll down again; it means a difficult task performed con-</u>

<u>tinuously with no apparent result.</u>

E. Questions for Discussion and Analysis

1. What are some techniques and devices Kapuściński uses to make the reader feel as if he or she is present in the Saharan landscape?

2. What are the primary human emotions embodied in Kapuściński's experience?

ON THE WEB

Try these two Web sites for information about Mauritania and travel to other destinations.

- Around the World in 80 Clicks: http://www.traveladventures.org
- www.lonelyplanet.com From the home page, type "Mauritania" in the search box. Click on "site," not "store."
- Using Google or your favorite search engine, type in "Mauritania" + "travel" and read more about this remote and exotic African nation.

IN THE BOOKSTORE

- *Things Fall Apart* (1958), by Nigerian writer Chinua Achebe is undoubtedly the most widely read novel from Africa. By focusing on one Ibo village in Nigeria, Achebe details the cultural upheaval that occurred after the arrival of European colonialists and Christian missionaries. The title is an allusion to a poem by William Butler Yeats and here refers to the fracturing of African society ("things fall apart") that occurs if the villagers adopt European ways.

Selection 4

Faux Chicken & Phony Furniture: Notes of an Alien Son
Andrei Codrescu

Andrei Codrescu is a Romanian-born poet, nonfiction writer, and professor of English at Louisiana State University in Baton Rouge. However, he is probably best known as a commentator on National Public Radio's "All Things Considered." First published in The Nation, *this article explores some of the paradoxes associated with the immigrant experience, using his mother's initial infatuation with American products as its starting point. Codrescu is the author of* The Hole in the Flag: An Exile's Story of Return and Revolution *(1991).*

Preview Questions

1. The word *Faux* in the title means "fake" and usually has a positive connotation. In this context, Codrescu is using the word to refer to supermarket chickens, which are shot full of hormones and raised in cages. Ironically, they have less flavor than the free-range chickens his mother bought in Romania, by American standards, a very poor country.

2. Another word that is central to your understanding of this essay is *paradox,* usually described as "a seeming contradiction." Be sure that you can explain the paradoxes inherent in the experiences of Codrescu's mother as she gradually accepted her new life in America.

1   My mother, ever a practical woman, started investing in furniture when she came to America from Romania. Not just any furniture. Sears furniture. Furniture that she kept the plastic on for 15 years before she had to conclude, sadly, that Sears wasn't such a great investment. In Romania, she would have been the richest woman on the block.

2   Which brings us to at least one paradox of immigration. Most people come here because they are sick of being poor. They want to eat and they want something to show for their industry. But soon enough it becomes evident to them that these things aren't enough. They have eaten and they are full, but they have eaten alone and there was no one with whom to make toasts and sing songs. They have new furniture with plastic on it, but the neighbors aren't coming over to ooh and aah. If American neighbors or less recent immigrants do come over, they smile condescendingly at the poor taste and the pathetic greed. And so the

greenhorns find themselves poor once more: This time they are lacking something more elusive than salami and furniture. They are bereft of a social and cultural milieu.

3   My mother, who was middle class by Romanian standards, found herself immensely impoverished after her first flush of material well-being. It wasn't just the disappearance of her milieu—that was obvious—but the feeling that she had, somehow, been had. The American supermarket tomatoes didn't taste at all like the rare genuine item back in Romania. American chicken was tasteless. Mass-produced furniture was built to fall apart. Her car, the crowning glory of her achievements in the eyes of folks back home, was only three years old and already beginning to wheeze and groan. It began to dawn on my mother that she had perhaps made a bad deal: She had traded in her friends and relatives for ersatz tomatoes, fake chicken, phony furniture.

4   Leaving behind your kin, your friends, your language, your smells, your childhood, is traumatic. It is a kind of death. You're dead for the home folk and they are dead to you. When you first arrive on these shores you are in mourning. The only consolations are these products, which were imbued with religious significance back at home. But when these things turn out not to be the real things, you begin to experience a second death, brought about by betrayal. You begin to suspect that the religious significance you attached to them was only possible back home, where these things did not exist. Here, where they are plentiful, they have no significance whatsoever. They are inanimate fetishes, somebody else's fetishes, no help to you at all. When this realization dawned on my mother, she began to rage against her new country. She deplored its rudeness, its insensitivity, its outright meanness, its indifference, the chase after the almighty buck, the social isolation of most Americans, their inability to partake of warm, genuine fellowship, and, above all, their deplorable lack of awe before what they had made.

5   This was the second stage of grief for her old self. The first, leaving her country, was sharp and immediate, almost tonic in its violence. The second was more prolonged, more damaging, because no hope was attached to it. Certainly not the hope of return.

6   And here, thinking of return, she began to reflect that perhaps there had been more to this deal than she'd first thought. True, she had left behind a lot that was good, but she had also left behind a vast range of daily humiliations. If she was ordered to move out of town she had to comply. If a party member took a dislike to her she had to go to extraordinary lengths to placate him because she was considered petit bourgeois and could easily have lost her small photo shop. She lived in fear of being denounced for something she had said. And worst of all, she was a Jew, which meant that she was structurally incapable of obtaining any justice in her native land. She had lived by the grace of an immensely complicated web of human relations, which was kept in place by a thousand small concessions, betrayals, indignities, bribes, little and big lies.

7   At this point, the ersatz tomatoes and the faux chicken did not appear all that important. An imponderable had made its appearance, a bracing, heady feeling of liberty. If she took that ersatz tomato and flung it at the head of the agriculture secretary of the United States, she would be making a statement about the disastrous effects of pesticides and mechanized farming. Flinging that faux chicken at Barbara Mandrell would be equally dramatic and perhaps even media-worthy. And she'd probably serve only a suspended sentence. What's more, she didn't have to eat those things, because she could buy organic tomatoes and free-range chicken. Of course, it would cost more, but that was one of the paradoxes of America: To eat as well as people in a Third World country eat (when they eat) costs more.

8   My mother was beginning to learn two things: one, that she had gotten a good deal after all, because in addition to food and furniture they had thrown in freedom; and two, America is a place of paradoxes—one proceeds from paradox to paradox like a chicken from the pot into the fire.

A. Comprehension

Choose the answer that best completes each statement. Do not refer to the selection while doing this exercise.

1. According to Codrescu, most immigrants come to the United States to escape
   (a) political persecution.
   (b) religious persecution.
   (c) poverty and lack of opportunity.
   (d) the dislocation that results from years of civil wars.
2. Because immigrating is so traumatic, newcomers often console themselves by
   (a) acquiring American products.
   (b) making plans to return home.
   (c) preserving their language and culture.
   (d) becoming politically active in their adopted homeland.
3. Codrescu compares the immigrant experience of leaving their homelands to
   (a) a release.
   (b) a second chance at life.
   (c) an intermediate stage.
   (d) a kind of death.
4. One paradox about living in America concerns food, specifically, that
   (a) one can eat better in America than in Romania.
   (b) the pesticide-free, hormone-free food that one can buy cheaply in Romania is expensive in America.

(c) American food is more nutritious than food available in Third
World countries.

(d) ordinary Americans do not eat as well as ordinary Romanians.

5. Eventually, Codrescu's mother realized that in this country she could
escape religious and political persecution and enjoy

(a) her family's economic success.

(b) acceptance by her neighbors.

(c) better-quality food.

(d) her liberty.

B. Vocabulary

For each italicized word from the selection, choose the best definition according to the context in which it appears. You may refer to the selection to
answer the questions in this section and in all the remaining sections.

1. one *paradox* of immigration [paragraph 2]:

(a) result.

(b) seeming contradiction.

(c) fault.

(d) unexplained event.

2. they smile *condescendingly* [2]: Describing an attitude that is

(a) guilt-producing.

(b) greedy and selfish.

(c) patronizingly superior.

(d) punishing, reproachful.

3. lacking something more *elusive* [2]:

(a) difficult to describe.

(b) harmful.

(c) corrupting.

(d) confirming one's status.

4. they are *bereft* [2]:

(a) bewildered by.

(b) in mourning for.

(c) enslaved by.

(d) lacking something necessary.

5. *ersatz* tomatoes (pronounced er´ - zäts) [3]: Describing something that

(a) lacks nutritional value.

(b) is an inferior imitation.

(c) is juicy and succulent.

(d) is of excellent quality.

6. she was considered *petit bourgeois* [6]: A member of

(a) the ruling class.

(b) the proletariat, or working class.

(c) the lower middle class, including tradespeople and shop owners.

(d) the professional class, including physicians and lawyers.

C. Inferences

On the basis of the evidence in the essay, mark these statements as follows: PA (probably accurate), PI (probably inaccurate), or NP (not in the passage).

1. <u>PA</u> For Codrescu's mother, being able to purchase furniture from Sears Roebuck represented the pinnacle of success.
2. <u>NP</u> Codrescu's mother eventually grew fond of hormone-filled super-market chicken.
3. <u>PI</u> Codrescu's mother eventually realized that life in Romania was more stable and more enjoyable than life in the United States

D. Structure

Complete the following questions.

1. The author's purpose is to
   (a) examine the paradox of immigration and the emotional stages immigrants experience.
   (b) criticize Americans for not being more welcoming to recent immigrants.
   (c) explain his mother's decision to emigrate from Romania.
   (d) explain how recent arrivals can avoid trauma after immigrating.
2. Look again at paragraph 2. Although Codrescu is seemingly interested in his mother's Sears Roebuck furniture, what more significant concept did her furniture represent to her? <u>unimagined wealth and an</u>

   <u>advanced level of taste</u>
3. Near the end of paragraph 2, Codrescu writes, "And so the greenhorns find themselves poor once more." What does he mean by "poor"?

   <u>culturally impoverished, having poor taste</u>
4. Look again at paragraph 7, where Codrescu describes the possibility of throwing ersatz tomatoes at the agricultural secretary or at Barbara Mandrell. What is he referring to? <u>In the United States one has</u>

   <u>the freedom to protest against anything.</u>

   Are these examples literal or metaphoric? <u>metaphoric</u>
5. The tone of this article can be best described as
   (a) arrogant, snobbish.
   (b) unsympathetic, callous.
   (c) sympathetic, compassionate.
   (d) impartial, objective.

E. *Questions for Discussion and Analysis*

1. Explain in your own words the stages that immigrants experience, focusing in particular on the paradoxes his mother encountered with American culture.

2. On the basis of the information the author includes in paragraph 4, do you think Codrescu's mother was justified or not in her rage against Americans? Explain.

3. Consider the relationship between living in a materialistic culture and having the freedom to think and to express one's opinions without fear of punishment. Does the pull of consumerism have a negative impact on this freedom?

⌂ ON THE WEB

- Further information about Andrei Codrescu is available at his home page: http://literati.net/Codrescu/.
- You can listen to Andrei Codrescu's observations about life in America at the Web site for National Public Radio, which can be accessed at www.npr.org/. On the home page, type in "Andrei Codrescu" in the search box.

Selection 5

The Law of the Few
Malcolm Gladwell

As a young child, Malcolm Gladwell and his family emigrated from the West Indies to Ontario, Canada. After graduating from the University of Toronto, he became a staff writer at The Washington Post, *covering business and science. Since 1996, he has been a staff writer at* The New Yorker. *This selection is reprinted from his best-selling book* The Tipping Point *(2000), which examines the premise that ideas, behavior, and messages can spread just the way infectious diseases do. This particular excerpt examines "a select group of people—salesmen [who have] the skills to persuade us when we are unconvinced of what we are hearing."*

Preview Questions

1. If you watch the evening news on one of the major television channels, whether commercial network or cable, you may not be aware that barely imperceptible facial expressions on the part of

the news announcer may reveal his or her biases. Are you aware of any particular biases evident in the news programs you watch?

2. What particular traits do successful salespeople have that makes their pitches difficult to resist? Think, for example, of an item (a CD player, a DVD player, a car, or some similar consumer product) that you bought from a salesperson because of his or her manner.

1   The question of what makes someone—or something—persuasive is a lot less straightforward than it seems. We know it when we see it. But just what "it" is is not always obvious. Consider the following two examples, both drawn from the psychological literature. The first is an experiment that took place during the 1984 presidential campaign between Ronald Reagan and Walter Mondale. For eight days before the election, a group of psychologists led by Brian Mullen of Syracuse University videotaped the three national nightly news programs, which then, as now, were anchored by Peter Jennings at ABC, Tom Brokaw at NBC, and Dan Rather at CBS.[1] Mullen examined the tapes and excerpted all references to the candidates, until he had 37 separate segments, each roughly two and a half seconds long. Those segments were then shown, with the sound turned off, to a group of randomly chosen people, who were asked to rate the facial expressions of each newscaster in each segment. The subjects had no idea what kind of experiment they were involved with, or what the newscasters were talking about. They were simply asked to score the emotional content of the expressions of these three men on a 21-point scale, with the lowest being "extremely negative" and the highest point on the scale "extremely positive."

2   The results were fascinating. Dan Rather scored 10.46—which translates to an almost perfectly neutral expression—when he talked about Mondale, and 10.37 when he talked about Reagan. He looked the same when he talked about the Republican as he did when he talked about the Democrat. The same was true for Brokaw, who scored 11.21 for Mondale and 11.50 for Reagan. But Peter Jennings of ABC was much different. For Mondale, he scored 13.38. But when he talked about Reagan, his face lit up so much he scored 17.44. Mullen and his colleagues went out of their way to try to come up with an innocent explanation for this. Could it be, for example, that Jennings is just more expressive in general than his colleagues? The answer seemed to be no. The subjects were also shown control segments of the three newscasters, as they talked about unequivocally happy or sad subjects (the funeral of Indira Gandhi; a breakthrough in treating a congenital disease). But Jennings didn't score any higher on the happy subjects or lower on the sad subjects than his counterparts. In fact, if anything, he seemed to be the least expressive of the three. It also isn't the case that Jennings is simply someone who has a happy expression on his face all the time. Again, the opposite seemed to be true. On the

[1]In spring 2005, Rather and Brokaw retired from their respective networks.

"happy" segments inserted for comparison purposes, he scored 14.13, which was substantially lower than both Rather and Brokaw. The only possible conclusions, according to the study, is that Jennings exhibited a "significant and noticeable bias in facial expression" toward Reagan.

3   Now here is where the study gets interesting. Mullen and his colleagues then called up people in a number of cities around the country who regularly watch the evening network news and asked them who they voted for. In every case, those who watched ABC voted for Reagan in far greater numbers than those who watched CBS or NBC. In Cleveland, for example, 75 percent of ABC watchers voted Republican, versus 61.9 percent of CBS or NBC viewers. In Williamstown, Massachusetts, ABC viewers were 71.4 percent for Reagan versus 50 percent for the other two networks; in Erie, Pennsylvania, the difference was 73.7 percent to 50 percent. The subtle pro-Reagan bias in Jennings's face seems to have influenced the voting behavior of ABC viewers.

4   As you can imagine, ABC News disputes this study vigorously. ("It's my understanding that I'm the only social scientist to have the dubious distinction of being called a 'jackass' by Peter Jennings," says Mullen.) It is hard to believe. Instinctively, I think, most of us would probably assume that the causation runs in the opposite direction, that Reagan supporters are drawn to ABC because of Jennings's bias, not the other way around. But Mullen argues fairly convincingly that this isn't plausible. For example, on other, more obvious levels—like, for example, story selection—ABC was shown to be the network most hostile to Reagan, so it's just as easy to imagine hard-core Republicans deserting ABC news for the rival networks. And to answer the question of whether his results were simply a fluke, four years later, in the Michael Dukakis–George Bush campaign, Mullen repeated his experiment, with the exact same results. "Jennings showed more smiles when referring to the Republican candidate than the Democrat," Mullen said, "and again in a phone survey, viewers who watch ABC were more likely to have voted for Bush."

5   Here is another example of the subtleties of persuasion. A large group of students were recruited for what they were told was a market research study by a company making high-tech headphones. They were each given a headset and told that the company wanted to test to see how well they worked when the listener was in motion—dancing up and down, say, or moving his or her head. All of the students listened to songs by Linda Ronstadt and the Eagles, and then heard a radio editorial arguing that tuition at their university should be raised from its present level of $587 to $750. A third were told that while they listened to the taped radio editorial they should nod their heads vigorously up and down. The next third were told to shake their heads from side to side. The final third were the control group. They were told to keep their heads still. When they were finished, all the students were given a short questionnaire, asking them questions about the quality of the songs and the effect of the shaking. Slipped in at the end was the question the

experimenters really wanted an answer to: "What do you feel would be an appropriate dollar amount for undergraduate tuition per year?"

6   The answers to that question are just as difficult to believe as the answers to the newscasters poll. The students who kept their heads still were unmoved by the editorial. The tuition amount that they guessed was appropriate was $582—or just about where tuition was already. Those who shook their heads from side to side as they listened to the editorial—even though they thought they were simply testing headset quality—disagreed strongly with the proposed increase. They wanted tuition to fall on average to $467 a year. Those who were told to nod their heads up and down, meanwhile, found the editorial very persuasive. They wanted tuition to rise, on average, to $646. The simple act of moving their heads up and down—ostensibly for another reason entirely—was sufficient to cause them to recommend a policy that would take money out of their own pockets. Somehow nodding, in the end, mattered as much as Peter Jennings's smiles did in the 1984 election.

7   There are in these two studies, I think, very important clues as to what makes someone like Tom Gau[2]—or, for that matter, any of the Salesmen in our lives—so effective. The first is that little things can, apparently, make as much of a difference as big things. In the headphone study, the editorial had no impact on those whose heads were still. It wasn't particularly persuasive. But as soon as listeners started nodding, it became very persuasive. In the case of Jennings, Mullen says that someone's subtle signals in favor of one politician or another usually don't matter at all. But in the particular, unguarded way that people watch the news, a little bias can suddenly go a long way. "When people watch the news, they don't intentionally filter biases out, or feel they have to argue against the expression of the newscaster," Mullen explains. "It's not like someone saying: this is a very good candidate who deserves your vote. This isn't an obvious verbal message that we automatically dig in our heels against. It's much more subtle and for that reason much more insidious, and that much harder to insulate ourselves against."

8   The second implication of these studies is that nonverbal cues are as or more important than verbal cues. The subtle circumstances surrounding how we say things may matter more than what we say. Jennings, after all, wasn't injecting all kinds of pro-Reagan comments in his newscasts. In fact, as I mentioned, ABC was independently observed to have been the most hostile to Reagan. One of the conclusions of the authors of the headphones study—Gary Wells of the University of Alberta and Richard Petty of the University of Missouri—was that "television advertisements would be most effective if the visual display created repetitive vertical movement of the television viewers' heads (e.g.,

[2]Tom Gau is a Southern California financial planner and, according to Gladwell's discussion in the passage preceding this one, is a "mesmerizing" salesman who could sell "absolutely anything."

bouncing ball)." Simple physical movements and observations can have a profound effect on how we feel and think.

9   The third—and perhaps most important—implication of these studies is that persuasion often works in ways that we do not appreciate. It's not that smiles and nods are subliminal messages. They are straightforward and on the surface. It's just that they are incredibly subtle. If you asked the head nodders why they wanted tuition to increase so dramatically—tuition that would come out of their own pockets—none of them would say, because I was nodding my head while I listened to that editorial. They'd probably say that it was because they found the editorial particularly insightful or intelligent. They would attribute their attitudes to some more obvious, logical cause. Similarly the ABC viewers who voted for Reagan would never, in a thousand years, tell you that they voted that way because Peter Jennings smiled every time he mentioned the President. They'd say that it was because they liked Reagan's policies, or they thought he was doing a good job. It would never have occurred to them that they could be persuaded to reach a conclusion by something so arbitrary and seemingly insignificant as a smile or a nod from a newscaster. If we want to understand what makes someone like Tom Gau so persuasive, in other words, we have to look at much more than his obvious eloquence. We need to look at the subtle, the hidden, and the unspoken.

A. Comprehension

Choose the answer that best completes each statement. Do not refer to the selection while doing this exercise.

1. The participants in Brian Mullen's study at Syracuse University were asked to examine tapes of television newscasters, specifically, to score
    (a) their mannerisms as they delivered the news.
    (b) their dress and hairstyles.
    (c) bias in their spoken words.
    (d) their facial expressions.

2. People who voted for Reagan in larger numbers watched the evening news on
    (a) CNN.
    (b) NBC.
    (c) ABC.
    (d) CBS.

3. Another study asked students to nod or shake their heads while being asked a question concerning
    (a) the presidential candidate they planned to vote for.
    (b) an appropriate amount for college tuition.
    (c) ways to improve food in campus dining facilities.
    (d) an amount for a proposed increase in student financial aid.

4. Gladwell states that, in the student study, what made the difference in students' responses was the
    (a) wording of the question they were asked to respond to.
    (b) persuasive quality of the editorial.
    (c) (shaking or nodding of their heads.)
    (d) attitude and bias of the researchers conducting the study.
5. Gladwell concludes that, in determining how we feel, think, and react,
    (a) (nonverbal clues are more important than verbal clues.)
    (b) verbal clues are more important than nonverbal clues.
    (c) verbal and nonverbal clues are equally important.
    (d) more research needs to be done before one can decide whether nonverbal or verbal clues are more persuasive.

B. Vocabulary

For each italicized word from the selection, choose the best definition according to the context in which it appears. You may refer to the selection to answer the questions in this section and in all the remaining sections.

1. *unequivocally* happy or sad subjects [paragraph 2]:
    (a) (clearly and unambiguously.)
    (b) observably.
    (c) relatively.
    (d) unpredictably.
2. the *dubious* distinction [4]:
    (a) praiseworthy.
    (b) honorable.
    (c) (doubtful.)
    (d) untrustworthy.
3. simply a *fluke* [4]:
    (a) miracle.
    (b) (chance occurrence.)
    (c) predictable event.
    (d) difference of opinion.
4. *ostensibly* for another reason [6]:
    (a) predictably.
    (b) unintentionally.
    (c) clearly.
    (d) (supposedly.)
5. much more *insidious* [7]:
    (a) persuasive, convincing.
    (b) (treacherous, intending to trap.)
    (c) causing worry or concern.
    (d) subtle, difficult to detect.

6. harder to *insulate* ourselves [7]:
   (a) (shield, isolate.)
   (b) educate, receive instruction.
   (c) persuade, encourage.
   (d) defend, guard.

C. *Inferences*

On the basis of the evidence in the essay, mark these statements as follows:
PA (probably accurate), PI (probably inaccurate), or NP (not in the passage).

1. _NP_ If the Syracuse psychologists had studied the newscasters'
   voices rather than their facial expressions, the results would
   have been quite different.
2. _PA_ Peter Jennings of ABC News was probably unaware that his facial expressions demonstrated pro-Reagan bias.
3. _PI_ The proof or evidence that Peter Jennings's bias toward Reagan
   swayed voters' sympathies is not well documented and therefore doesn't represent a firm conclusion.
4. _NP_ After Mullen's results were published, ABC warned Jennings to
   act more neutral when he reported on Republican candidates.
5. _PA_ The beginning of paragraph 6 suggests that the researchers
   were surprised at the results of the student research study.

D. *Structure*

1. Gladwell's purpose in writing, specifically, is to
   (a) instruct readers in ways to resist salespeople's attempt to persuade
       them.
   (b) (illustrate how little things can influence our responses.)
   (c) demonstrate how two separate research studies were conducted.
   (d) warn readers to be alert to bias when watching the evening news.
2. Look again at the second half of paragraph 2. What is its purpose?

   to offer evidence that Jennings really was biased toward Reagan

3. With respect to paragraph 2, which *two* of these functions does paragraph 3 serve?
   (a) (It confirms that researchers were right about Jennings' bias toward
       Reagan.)
   (b) (It confirms that Jennings' bias influenced voter behavior.)
   (c) It underscores the importance of the study.
   (d) It explains why Ronald Reagan won the 1984 election.

4. Gladwell suggests in paragraphs 7 and 8 that the persuasive nonverbal clues he describes in the essay
   (a) threaten our rights to free expression and thought.
   (b) will change the way advertisers display their wares on television.
   (c) are a little frightening because they are so subtle.
   (d) are immediately obvious to those who bother to look for them.

E. Questions for Discussion and Analysis

1. If you have the time, videotape three television networks' evening programs for two or three days. (Some suggestions are the Big Three networks—ABC, CBS, and NBC—or CNN, Fox News, or MSNBC.) Then
   watch the segments dealing with Republican and Democrat politicians. Do you detect any of the subtle biases Gladwell reports on?

2. What implications for advertising do the research studies described
   here have?

🖱 ON THE WEB

- Malcolm Gladwell's *New Yorker* articles can be accessed at
  http://www.gladwell.com. Click on the New Yorker archives.
- The 2004 presidential election was both one of the most closely con-
  tested and polarizing in recent history. Further, television—news reports as well as advertising—has become a more significant factor in
  the way people receive their news and determine their opinions
  about the candidates. As a result, the question of bias—whether liberal or conservative—has become ever more important to evaluate.
  Using Google or your favorite search engine, type "presidential election" + "TV coverage" + "bias" into the search box. (If your search
  engine requires it, use quotation marks around the phrases.) You
  might want to restrict your search to a particular election year (1972,
  2000, and 2004 are all good choices.) See what the various sites you
  look at reveal about television's treatment of the candidates, the issues, the debates, the poll results, and any other related matters.

Selection 6   # How Flowers Changed the World
                   Michael Pollan

*Michael Pollan is a writer of nonfiction material for which he has won numer-
ous awards, among them, the Reuters-World Conservation Union Global Award
for Excellence in Environmental Journalism. This selection comes from his recent book,* The Botany of Desire: A Plant's Eye View of the World *(2001),*

in which he explains, in unusually vivid and poetic language, the reciprocal relationship between human beings and plants. The book is divided into four parts—the apple, the tulip, marijuana, and the potato—each of which satisfies a fundamental human desire. This excerpt is from the section called "The Tulip."

Preview Questions

1. Before you read the selection, consider the role of plants, and particularly of flowers, in our world. Besides pleasing us with their beauty and scent, what other uses might flowers have?

2. In an unabridged dictionary, look up these two Greek gods, Apollo and Dionysus, and their related adjectives, *Apollonian* and *Dionysian*. Doing so will help you understand better Pollan's conclusion.

1   Once upon a time, there were no flowers—two hundred million years ago, to be only slightly more precise. There were plants then, of course, ferns and mosses, conifers and cycads, but these plants didn't form true flowers or fruit. Some of them reproduced asexually, cloning themselves by various means. Sexual reproduction was a relatively discreet affair usually accomplished by releasing pollen onto the wind or water; by sheer chance some of it would find its way to other members of the species, and a tiny, primitive seed would result. This prefloriferous world was a slower, simpler, sleepier world than our own. Evolution proceeded more slowly, there being so much less sex, and what sex there was took place among close-by and closely related plants. Such a conservative approach to reproduction made for a biologically simpler world, since it generated relatively little novelty or variation. Life on the whole was more local and inbred.

2   The world before flowers was sleepier than ours because, lacking fruit and large seeds, it couldn't support many warm-blooded creatures. Reptiles ruled, and life slowed to a crawl whenever it got cold; little happened at night. It was a plainer-looking world, too, greener even than it is now, absent all the colors and patterns (not to mention scents) that flowers and fruits would bring into it. Beauty did not yet exist. That is, the way things looked had nothing to do with desire.

3   Flowers changed everything. The angiosperms, as botanists call the plants that form flowers and then encased seeds, appeared during the Cretaceous period, and they spread over the earth with stunning rapidity. "An abominable mystery" is how Charles Darwin described this sudden and entirely evitable event. Now, instead of relying on wind or water to move genes around, a plant could enlist the help of an animal by striking a grand coevolutionary compact: nutrition in exchange for transportation. With the advent of the flower, whole new levels of complexity come

into the world: more interdependence, more information, more communication, more experimentation.

4   The evolution of plants proceeded according to a new motive force: attraction between different species. Now natural selection favored blooms that could rivet the attention of pollinators, fruits that appealed to foragers. The desires of other creatures became paramount in the evolution of plants, for the simple reason that the plants that succeeded at gratifying those desires wound up with more offspring. Beauty had emerged as a survival strategy.

5   The new rules speeded the rate of evolutionary change. Bigger, brighter, sweeter, more fragrant: all these qualities were quickly rewarded under the new regime. But so was specialization. Since bestowing one's pollen on an insect that might deliver it to the wrong address (such as the blossoms of unrelated species) was wasteful, it became an advantage to look and smell as distinctive as possible, the better to command the undivided attention of a single, dedicated pollinator. Animal desire was thus parsed and subdivided, plants specialized accordingly, and an extraordinary flowering of diversity took place, much of it under the signs of coevolution and beauty.

6   With flowers came fruit and seeds, and these, too, remade life on Earth. By producing sugars and proteins to entice animals to disperse their seed, the angiosperms multiplied the world's supply of food energy, making possible the rise of large warm-blooded mammals. Without flowers, the reptiles, which had gotten along fine in a leafy, fruitless world, would probably still rule. Without flowers, we would not be.

7   So the flowers begot us, their greatest admirers. In time human desire entered into the natural history of the flower, and the flower did what it has always done: made itself still more beautiful in the eyes of this animal, folding into its very being even the most improbable of our notions and tropes. Now came roses that resembled aroused nymphs, tulip petals in the shape of daggers, peonies bearing the scent of women. We in turn did our part, multiplying the flowers beyond reason, moving their seeds around the planet, writing books to spread their fame and ensure their happiness. For the flower it was the same old story, another grand coevolutionary bargain with a willing, slightly credulous animal—a good deal on the whole, though not nearly as good as the earlier bargain with the bees.

8   And what about us? How did we make out? We did very well by the flower. There were, of course, the pleasures to the senses, the sustenance of their fruit and seeds, and the vast store of new metaphor. But we gazed even farther into the blossom of a flower and found something more: the crucible of beauty, if not art, and maybe even a glimpse into the meaning of life. For look into a flower, and what do you see? Into the very heart of nature's double nature—that is, the contending energies of creation and dissolution, the spiring toward complex form and

the tidal pull away from it. Apollo and Dionysus were names the Greeks gave these two faces of nature, and nowhere in nature is their contest as plain or as poignant as it is in the beauty of a flower and its rapid passing. There, the achievement of order against all odds and its blithe abandonment. There, the perfection of art and a blind flux of nature. There, somehow, both transcendence *and* necessity. Could that be it—right there, in a flower—the meaning of life?

A. *Comprehension*

Choose the answer that best completes each statement. Do not refer to the selection while doing this exercise.

1. In the period of history before there were flowers,
    (a) plants had a more difficult time reproducing and flourishing.
    (b) plants were primitive and reproduced more conservatively.
    (c) plants as we know them today did not exist.
    (d) plants produced fruits and flowers but lacked colorful variations.
2. Angiosperms is the word botanists use to describe plants that
    (a) comprise the moss, fern, conifer, and cycad families.
    (b) reproduce asexually by releasing pollen into the wind or water.
    (c) form flowers and encased seeds.
    (d) live only for one season and then die.
3. Animals helped cause the development of more complex types of flowers because, by eating the flowers, they ensured that
    (a) only the strongest species of flowers would survive.
    (b) only the strongest species of animals would survive.
    (c) the genes of the flowers would be dispersed over a wide area.
    (d) pollen would be available for pollination by certain insects.
4. In terms of natural selection in plants, pollinators generally favored flowers that
    (a) attracted them because of their appearance and distinctive smell.
    (b) were dispersed over a large geographic area, making them accessible.
    (c) reproduced rapidly, making them available in large numbers.
    (d) were specialized, in that the pollen of one type of flower depended on a particular type of pollinator.
5. The author concludes by saying that when one looks into a flower, he or she gets a glimpse into
    (a) the origin of the universe.
    (b) proof that evolutionary development is more than just a scientific theory.
    (c) objects that ensure human pleasure and happiness.
    (d) creation and dissolution, the duality of nature.

B. Vocabulary

For each italicized word from the selection, write the dictionary definition most appropriate for the context.

1.   reproduced *asexually* [paragraph 1]: without involving sexual reproduction

2.   a relatively *discreet* affair [1]: modest, inconspicuous

3.   a grand coevolutionary *compact* [3]: agreement, bargain

4.   the desires became *paramount* [4]: of chief concern or importance

5.   animal desire was *parsed* [5]: broken down into component parts, analyzed

6.   the flowers *begot* us [7]: fathered, produced

7.   a willing, slightly *credulous* animal [7]: inclined to believe

8.   nowhere is their contest as plain or as *poignant* [8]: emotionally affecting, profoundly moving

C. Inferences

On the basis of the evidence in the essay, mark these statements as follows: PA (probably accurate), PI (probably inaccurate), or NP (not in the passage).

1.   _PA_ Cloning is another term for asexual reproduction.
2.   _PA_ The development of more complex varieties of flowers allowed for the evolution of more complex forms of animal life, beyond dinosaurs.
3.   _NP_ The dinosaurs died out because they ate poisonous angiosperms.
4.   _PI_ To survive, certain species of reptiles eat flowers.
5.   _PI_ Charles Darwin understood the reason that flowers spread over the earth so rapidly and described the phenomenon clearly.
6.   _PA_ The advent of flowers made human existence possible.

D. Structure

Complete the following questions.

1.   Pollan's purpose in writing is specifically to

    (a) prove that evolutionary theory is scientifically sound, not merely theoretical.
    (b) examine the role of flowers both in terms of nature and of human civilization.
    (c) show the reader the real meaning of life.
    (d) explain the interdependence between flowers and animals.

2. What are the *two* primary methods of development throughout the selection?
    (a) analogy.
    (b) example and illustration.
    (c) informative process.
    (d) cause and effect.

3. Read the first half of paragraph 7 again. What agent accounts for the flower making "itself still more beautiful in the eyes of this animal"? What is Pollan specifically referring to?   People propagated flowers so that they would develop particular characteristics.

4. Paraphrase this sentence from paragraph 8: "We did very well by the flower."   Flowers benefited human beings in several ways.

5. What method of development is evident in this sentence from paragraph 7: "Now came roses that resembled aroused nymphs, tulip petals in the shape of daggers, peonies bearing the scent of women"?
    (a) steps in a process
    (b) cause and effect
    (c) analogy
    (d) examples

6. Explain in your own words the connection Pollan makes between flowers, "the crucible of beauty," and "the two faces of nature," referring to Apollo and Dionysus.   In flowers, Pollan sees the twin forces of the Apollonian, with its pull toward order and reason, and the Dionysian, with its pull toward the irrational, the sensory, and the frenzied.

E. Questions for Discussion and Analysis

1. Explain the specific roles of pollinators, animals, and human beings in the evolution of flowers.

2. Consider this sentence from paragraph 2: "Beauty did not yet exist." Is Pollan being merely fanciful, or can this statement be defended rationally?

🖱 ON THE WEB

In seventeenth-century Holland, there erupted a speculative frenzy over tulips that rivaled the dot-com bubble of the late 1990s in the United States. Called "tulipomania," this speculative bubble is a classic example of irrational exuberance. Using Google or your favorite search engine, investigate two or three Web sites dealing with the subject of tulipomania or speculative bubbles like the dot-com frenzy of the late 1990s.

📖 IN THE LIBRARY

Charles MacKay's classic study of speculative bubbles, *Extraordinary Popular Delusions And The Madness Of Crowds* (1841), contains a chapter on tulipomania.

Selection 7 | # In the Laboratory with Agassiz
Samuel H. Scudder

Samuel H. Scudder (1837–1911) graduated from Williams College in 1857 and entered the Lawrence Scientific School at Harvard University to study under the famous naturalist Jean Louis R. Agassiz. (We now use the term biologist rather than naturalist.) Scudder's chosen field was entomology (the study of insects), and in fact, he later became one of his era's most important American experts in that field. But Professor Agassiz had other ideas for his young scholar as he began his graduate study of natural science. As Scudder relates in this classic essay, Agassiz set him to work describing a specimen of a disgusting fish, with surprising results. Later in his career in 1877, Scudder was elected to the National Academy of Sciences.

Preview Questions

1. If you have taken a college course in natural science (biology, physiology, or zoology), consider the method of instruction and the kind of laboratory work you were asked to perform. How was information conveyed to you? What instructional materials did you have? What was the role of instructor? How big was your class?
2. What are the most important qualities of a good teacher?
3. Is self-discovery more beneficial for long-term learning than learning material from lectures?

1   It was more than fifteen years ago that I entered the laboratory of Professor Agassiz, and told him I had enrolled my name in the scientific school as a student of natural history. He asked me a few questions about my object in coming, my antecedents generally, the mode in which I afterwards proposed to use the knowledge I might acquire, and finally, whether I wished to study any special branch. To the latter I replied that while I wished to be well grounded in all departments of zoölogy, I purposed to devote myself specially to insects.

2   "When do you wish to begin?" he asked.

3   "Now," I replied.

4   This seemed to please him, and with an energetic "Very well," he reached from a shelf a huge jar of specimens in yellow alcohol.

5   "Take this *fish*," said he, "and look at it; we call it a Hæmulon; by and by I will ask what you have seen."

6   With that he left me, but in a moment returned with explicit instructions as to the care of the object entrusted to me.

7   "No man is fit to be a naturalist," said he, "who does not know how to take care of specimens."

8   I was to keep the fish before me in a tin tray, and occasionally moisten the surface with alcohol from the jar, always taking care to replace the stopper tightly. Those were not the days of ground glass stoppers, and elegantly shaped exhibition jars; all the old students will recall the huge, neckless glass bottles with their leaky, wax-besmeared corks, half eaten by insects and begrimed with cellar dust. Entomology was a cleaner science than ichthyology,[1] but the example of the professor, who had unhesitatingly plunged to the bottom of the jar to produce the fish, was infectious; and though his alcohol had "a very ancient and fish-like smell," I really dared not show any aversion within these sacred precincts, and treated the alcohol as though it were pure water. Still I was conscious of a passing feeling of disappointment, for gazing at a fish did not commend itself to an ardent entomologist. My friends at home, too, were annoyed, when they discovered that no amount of eau de cologne would drown the perfume which haunted me like a shadow.

9   In ten minutes I had seen all that could be seen in that fish, and started in search of the professor, who had however left the museum; and when I returned, after lingering over some of the odd animals stored in the upper apartment, my specimen was dry all over. I dashed the fluid over the fish as if to resuscitate the beast from a fainting-fit, and looked with anxiety for a return of the normal, sloppy appearance. This little excitement over, nothing was to be done but return to a steadfast gaze at my mute companion. Half an hour passed,—an hour,—another hour; the fish began to look loathsome. I turned it over and around; looked it in the face,—ghastly; from behind, beneath, above, sideways, at a three quarters view,—just as ghastly. I was in despair; at an early hour I concluded

[1]Entomology is the study of insects; ichthyology is the study of fish.

that lunch was necessary; so, with infinite relief, the fish was carefully re-placed in the jar, and for an hour I was free.

10   On my return, I learned that Professor Agassiz had been at the mu-seum, but had gone and would not return for several hours. My fellow-students were too busy to be disturbed by continued conversation. Slowly I drew forth that hideous fish, and with a feeling of desperation again looked at it. I might not use a magnifying glass; instruments of all kinds were interdicted. My two hands, my two eyes, and the fish; it seemed a most limited field. I pushed my finger down its throat to feel how sharp the teeth were. I began to count the scales in the different rows until I was convinced that that was nonsense. At last a happy thought struck me—I would draw the fish; and now with surprise I began to discover new features in the creature. Just then the professor returned.

11   "That is right," said he; "a pencil is one of the best of eyes. I am glad to notice, too, that you keep your specimen wet and your bottle corked."

12   With these encouraging words, he added,—

13   "Well, what is it like?"

14   He listened attentively to my brief rehearsal of the structure of parts whose names were still unknown to me; the fringed gill-arches and mov-able operculum; the pores of the head, fleshy lips, and lidless eyes; the lateral line, the spinous fins, and forked tail; the compressed and arched body. When I had finished, he waited as if expecting more, and then, with an air of disappointment,—

15   "You have not looked very carefully; why," he continued, more earnestly, "you haven't even seen one of the most conspicuous features of the animal, which is as plainly before your eyes as the fish itself; look again, look again!" and he left me to my misery.

16   I was piqued; I was mortified. Still more of that wretched fish! But now I set myself to my task with a will, and discovered one new thing after another, until I saw how just the professor's criticism had been. The afternoon passed quickly, and when, toward its close, the professor inquired,—

17   "Do you see it yet?"

18   "No," I replied, "I am certain I do not, but I see how little I saw before."

19   "That is next best," said he, earnestly, "but I won't hear you now; put away your fish and go home; perhaps you will be ready with a better answer in the morning. I will examine you before you look at the fish."

20   This was disconcerting; not only must I think of my fish all night, studying, without the object before me, what this unknown but most visible feature might be; but also, without reviewing my new discover-ies, I must give an exact account of them the next day. I had a bad mem-ory; so I walked home by Charles River in a distracted state, with my two perplexities.

21   The cordial greeting from the professor the next morning was reas-suring; here was a man who seemed to be quite as anxious as I, that I should see for myself what he saw.

22   "Do you perhaps mean," I asked, "that the fish has symmetrical sides with paired organs?"

23   His thoroughly pleased, "Of course, of course!" repaid the wakeful hours of the previous night. After he had discoursed most happily and enthusiastically—as he always did—upon the importance of this point, I ventured to ask what I should do next.

24   "Oh, look at your fish!" he said, and left me again to my own devices. In a little more than an hour he returned and heard my new catalogue.

25   "That is good, that is good!" he repeated; "but that is not all; go on;" and so for three long days he placed that fish before my eyes, forbidding me to look at anything else, or to use any artificial aid. "Look, look, look," was his repeated injunction.

26   This was the best entomological lesson I ever had,—a lesson, whose influence has extended to the details of every subsequent study; a legacy the professor has left to me, as he has left it to many others, of inestimable value, which we could not buy, with which we cannot part.

27   A year afterward, some of us were amusing ourselves with chalking outlandish beasts upon the museum blackboard. We drew prancing starfishes; frogs in mortal combat; hydra-headed worms; stately crawfishes, standing on their tails, bearing aloft umbrellas; and grotesque fishes with gaping mouths and staring eyes. The professor came in shortly after, and was as amused as any, at our experiments. He looked at the fishes.

28   "Hæmulons, every one of them," he said; "Mr.—— drew them."

29   True; and to this day, if I attempt a fish, I can draw nothing but Hæmulons.

30   The fourth day, a second fish of the same group was placed beside the first, and I was bidden to point out the resemblances and differences between the two; another and another followed, until the entire family lay before me, and a whole legion of jars covered the table and surrounding shelves; the odor had become a pleasant perfume; and even now, the sight of an old, six-inch, worm-eaten cork brings fragrant memories!

31   The whole group of Hæmulons was thus brought in review; and, whether engaged upon the dissection of the internal organs, the preparation and examination of the bony frame-work, or the description of the various parts, Agassiz' training in the method of observing facts and their orderly arrangement was ever accompanied by the urgent exhortation not to be content with them.

32   "Facts are stupid things," he would say, "until brought into connection with some general law."

33   At the end of eight months, it was almost with reluctance that I left these friends and turned to insects; but what I had gained by this outside experience has been of greater value than years of later investigation in my favorite groups.

A. Comprehension

Choose the answer that best completes each statement. Do not refer to the selection while doing this exercise.

1. At Agassiz's initial interview, Scudder announced his intention to specialize in the study of
    (a) butterflies.
    (b) fish.
    (c) insects.
    (d) all branches of zoology.
2. Professor Agassiz was particularly strict about the way his students
    (a) prepared their laboratory notes.
    (b) handled and stored their specimens.
    (c) handled and organized their instruments.
    (d) arranged the specimens in their trays.
3. Agassiz directed Scudder to examine the fish
    (a) through a microscope.
    (b) with a set of instruments.
    (c) by dissecting it.
    (d) only with his hands and his eyes.
4. The conspicuous feature that Scudder finally observed in his specimen fish was its
    (a) unusual pattern and number of scales.
    (b) lidless eyes.
    (c) fringed gill-arches.
    (d) symmetrical structure.
5. Observing facts and their orderly arrangement was only part of Agassiz's lesson to Scudder. More important was the lesson of
    (a) developing a lifelong interest in ichthyology.
    (b) learning how to record the facts accurately.
    (c) connecting the facts and observations to a general law.
    (d) studying the structure of every living organism.

B. Vocabulary

For each italicized word from the selection, write the dictionary definition most appropriate for the context. You may refer to the selection to answer the questions in this section and in all the remaining sections.

1. he asked me about my *antecedents* [paragraph 1]:   ancestors
2. with *explicit* instructions [6]:   clearly expressed
3. I dared not show any *aversion* [8]:   repugnance
4. instruments . . . were *interdicted* [10]:   prohibited

5. I was *piqued* [16]: <u>irritated, full of resentment</u>

6. this was *disconcerting* [20]: <u>upsetting, frustrating</u>

7. "Look, look, look" was his repeated *injunction* [25]: <u>command, order</u>

8. a *legacy* the professor has left to me [26]: <u>something handed down</u>

9. of *inestimable* value [26]: <u>invaluable, impossible to determine</u>

10. urgent *exhortation* [31]: <u>strong argument or advice</u>

C. *Inferences*

On the basis of the evidence in the essay, mark these statements as follows: PA (probably accurate), PI (probably inaccurate), or NP (not in the passage).

1. <u>NP</u> Scudder's interest in natural science was the result of his father's influence.

2. <u>PA</u> Professor Agassiz chose a fish for Scudder to study, knowing that he was probably not familiar with it.

3. <u>PI</u> Scudder was delighted with Agassiz's assignment and pursued his study of the fish with great enthusiasm.

4. <u>PI</u> Agassiz left Scudder alone to observe his fish because he was too busy with his other commitments to be of much help.

5. <u>PA</u> The conspicuous feature that Scudder had initially missed pertained to the structure of the fish.

D. *Structure*

Complete the following questions.

1. Scudder's purpose in writing is specifically to
    (a) explain the origin of his love of science.
    (b) (show how a scientist must learn to observe.)
    (c) argue for a change in the way science is taught in college.
    (d) tell an amusing and entertaining story.
2. Scudder's attitude toward Professor Agassiz can be best described as
    (a) (respectful and serious.)
    (b) hostile, angry.
    (c) indifferent, neutral.
    (d) resentful, irritated.
3. Look again at paragraph 8. The phrase "sacred precincts" refers literally to
    (a) the campus of Harvard University.
    (b) Agassiz's office.
    (c) (Agassiz's laboratory.)
    (d) the field of natural science.

4. Read paragraphs 14 and 15 again, which emphasize the idea that
   (a) most scientific observation is boring and dry.
   (b) observing an organism like a fish is a good way to learn the scientific method.
   (c) observing the individual parts of the fish was less important than observing the whole.
   (d) Agassiz treated Scudder, as a new student, with scorn.

5. When Agassiz told his students, "Facts are stupid things," what exactly did he mean? <u>Facts are worthless unless they are</u>

   <u>connected with some larger principle.</u>

E. Questions for Discussion and Analysis

1. Consider your chosen field of study. How might Agassiz's "repeated injunction" to "look, look, look" be of some benefit for your academic work?

2. What kind of student did Scudder appear to be? What are his primary characteristics?

ON THE WEB

- One of the best Web sites available on science is this one sponsored by San Francisco's Exploratorium: http://www.exploratorium.edu. The site offers tours, exhibits, scientific experiments, games, and a wealth of information for laypersons and specialists alike.
- In Google, click on "Images" and then type in "Samuel H. Scudder." There you will find drawings of the famous hæmulon fish.

Selection 8

The Insufficiency of Honesty
Stephen L. Carter

Stephen L. Carter is the William Nelson Cromwell Professor of Law at Yale University. He is also the author of several books, among them Reflections of an Affirmative Action Baby *(1991);* The Culture of Disbelief: How American Law and Politics Trivialize Religious Devotion *(1994); and his most recent book, a thriller titled* The Emperor of Ocean Park *(2002). This selection first appeared in the February 1996 issue of* The Atlantic Monthly; *it also appears in his 1996 book* Integrity.

Preview Questions

1. Is honesty always the best policy? Can you think of a situation where telling the truth resulted in hurt feelings or loss of trust and faith?

2. Look up the word *integrity* in an unabridged dictionary. Then consider how it differs from the word *honesty*. Are these abstract qualities the same or somehow different?

1   A couple of years ago I began a university commencement address by telling the audience that I was going to talk about integrity. The crowd broke into applause. Applause! Just because they had heard the word "integrity": that's how starved for it they were. They had no idea how I was using the word, or what I was going to say about integrity, or, indeed, whether I was for it or against it. But they knew they liked the idea of talking about it.

2   Very well, let us consider this word "integrity." Integrity is like the weather: everybody talks about it but nobody knows what to do about it. Integrity is that stuff that we always want more of. Some say that we need to return to the good old days when we had a lot more of it. Others say that we as a nation have never really had enough of it. Hardly anybody stops to explain exactly what we mean by it, or how we know it is a good thing, or why everybody needs to have the same amount of it. Indeed, the only trouble with integrity is that everybody who uses the word seems to mean something slightly different.

3   For instance, when I refer to integrity, do I mean simply "honesty?" The answer is no; although honesty is a virtue of importance, it is a different virtue from integrity. Let us, for simplicity, think of honesty as not lying; and let us further accept Sissela Bok's definition of a lie: "any intentionally deceptive message which is *stated*." Plainly, one cannot have integrity without being honest (although, as we shall see, the matter gets complicated), but one can certainly be honest and yet have little integrity.

4   When I refer to integrity, I have something very specific in mind. Integrity, as I will use the term, requires three steps: discerning what is right and what is wrong; acting on what you have discerned, even at personal cost; and saying openly that you are acting on your understanding of right and wrong. The first criterion captures the idea that integrity requires a degree of moral reflectiveness. The second brings in the ideal of a person of integrity as steadfast, a quality that includes keeping one's commitments. The third reminds us that a person of integrity can be trusted.

5   The first point to understand about the difference between honesty and integrity is that a person may be entirely honest without ever engaging in the hard work of discernment that integrity requires: she may tell us quite truthfully what she believes without ever taking the time to figure out whether what she believes is good and right and true. The problem may be as simple as someone's foolishly saying something that

hurts a friend's feelings; a few moments of thought would have revealed the likelihood of the hurt and the lack of necessity for the comment. Or the problem may be more complex, as when a man who was raised from birth in a society that preaches racism states his belief in one race's inferiority as a fact, without ever really considering that perhaps this deeply held view is wrong. Certainly the racist is being honest—he is telling us what he actually thinks—but his honesty does not add up to integrity.

Telling Everything You Know

6   A wonderful epigram sometimes attributed to the filmmaker Sam Goldwyn goes like this: "The most important thing in acting is honesty; once you learn to fake that, you're in." The point is that honesty can be something one *seems* to have. Without integrity, what passes for honesty often is nothing of the kind; it is fake honesty—or it is honest but irrelevant and perhaps even immoral.

7   Consider an example. A man who has been married for fifty years confesses to his wife on his deathbed that he was unfaithful thirty-five years earlier. The dishonesty was killing his spirit, he says. Now he has cleared his conscience and is able to die in peace.

8   The husband has been honest—sort of. He has certainly unburdened himself. And he has probably made his wife (soon to be his widow) quite miserable in the process, because even if she forgives him, she will not be able to remember him with quite the vivid image of love and loyalty that she had hoped for. Arranging his own emotional affairs to ease his transition to death, he has shifted to his wife the burden of confusion and pain, perhaps for the rest of her life. Moreover, he has attempted his honesty at the one time in his life when it carries no risk; acting in accordance with what you think is right and risking no loss in the process is a rather thin and unadmirable form of honesty.

9   Besides, even though the husband has been honest in a sense, he has now twice been unfaithful to his wife: once thirty-five years ago, when he had his affair, and again when, nearing death, he decided that his own peace of mind was more important than hers. In trying to be honest he has violated his marriage vow by acting toward his wife not with love but with naked and perhaps even cruel self-interest.

10   As my mother used to say, you don't have to tell people everything you know. Lying and nondisclosure, as the law often recognizes, are not the same thing. Sometimes it is actually illegal to tell what you know, as, for example, in the disclosure of certain financial information by market insiders. Or it may be unethical, as when a lawyer reveals a confidence entrusted to her by a client. It may be simple bad manners, as in the case of a gratuitous comment to a colleague on his or her attire. And it may be subject to religious punishment, as when a Roman Catholic priest breaks the seal of the confessional—an offense that carries automatic excommunication.

11   In all the cases just mentioned, the problem with telling everything you know is that somebody else is harmed. Harm may not be the intention, but it is certainly the effect. Honesty is most laudable when we risk harm to ourselves; it becomes a good deal less so if we instead risk harm to others when there is no gain to anyone other than ourselves. Integrity may counsel keeping our secrets in order to spare the feelings of others. Sometimes, as in the example of the wayward husband, the reason we want to tell what we know is precisely to shift our pain onto somebody else—a course of action dictated less by integrity than by self-interest. Fortunately, integrity and self-interest often coincide, as when a politician of integrity is rewarded with our votes. But often they do not, and it is at those moments that our integrity is truly tested.

Error

12   Another reason that honesty alone is no substitute for integrity is that if forthrightness is not preceded by discernment, it may result in the expression of an incorrect moral judgment. In other words, I may be honest about what I believe, but if I have never tested my beliefs, I may be wrong. And here I mean "wrong" in a particular sense: the proposition in question is wrong if I would change my mind about it after hard moral reflection.

13   Consider this example. Having been taught all his life that women are not as smart as men, a manager gives the women on his staff less-challenging assignments than he gives the men. He does this, he believes, for their own benefit: he does not want them to fail, and he believes that they will if he gives them tougher assignments. Moreover, when one of the women on his staff does poor work, he does not berate her as harshly as he would a man, because he expects nothing more. And he claims to be acting with integrity because he is acting according to his own deepest beliefs.

14   The manager fails the most basic test of integrity. The question is not whether his actions are consistent with what he most deeply believes but whether he has done the hard work of discerning whether what he most deeply believes is right. The manager has not taken this harder step.

15   Moreover, even within the universe that the manager has constructed for himself, he is not acting with integrity. Although he is obviously wrong to think that the women on his staff are not as good as the men, even were he right, that would not justify applying different standards to their work. By so doing he betrays both his obligation to the institution that employs him and his duty as a manager to evaluate his employees.

16   The problem that the manager faces is an enormous one in our practical politics, where having the dialogue that makes democracy work can seem impossible because of our tendency to cling to our views even when we have not examined them. As Jean Bethke Elshtain has said, borrowing

from John Courtney Murray, our politics are so fractured and contentious that we often cannot even reach *disagreement.* Our refusal to look closely at our own most cherished principles is surely a large part of the reason. Socrates thought the unexamined life not worth living. But the unhappy truth is that few of us actually have the time for constant reflection on our views—on public or private morality. Examine them we must, however, or we will never know whether we might be wrong.

17   None of this should be taken to mean that integrity as I have described it presupposes a single correct truth. If, for example, your integrity-guided search tells you that affirmative action is wrong, and my integrity-guided search tells me that affirmative action is right, we need not conclude that one of us lacks integrity. As it happens, I believe—both as a Christian and as a secular citizen who struggles toward moral understanding—that we *can* find true and sound answers to our moral questions. But I do not pretend to have found very many of them, nor is an exposition of them my purpose here.

18   It is the case not that there aren't any right answers but that, given human fallibility, we need to be careful in assuming that we have found them. However, today's political talk about how it is wrong for the government to impose one person's morality on somebody else is just mindless chatter. *Every* law imposes one person's morality on somebody else, because law has only two functions: to tell people to do what they would rather not or to forbid them to do what they would.

19   And if the surveys can be believed, there is far more moral agreement in America than we sometimes allow ourselves to think. One of the reasons that character education for young people makes so much sense to so many people is precisely that there seems to be a core set of moral understandings—we might call them the American Core—that most of us accept. Some of the virtues in this American Core are, one hopes, relatively noncontroversial. About 500 American communities have signed on to Michael Josephson's program to emphasize the "six pillars" of good character: trustworthiness, respect, responsibility, caring, fairness, and citizenship. These virtues might lead to a similarly noncontroversial set of political values: having an honest regard for ourselves and others, protecting freedom of thought and religious belief, and refusing to steal or murder.

Honesty and Competing Responsibilities

20   A further problem with too great an exaltation of honesty is that it may allow us to escape responsibilities that morality bids us bear. If honesty is substituted for integrity, one might think that if I say I am not planning to fulfill a duty, I need not fulfill it. But it would be a peculiar morality indeed that granted us the right to avoid our moral responsibilities simply by stating our intention to ignore them. Integrity does not permit such an easy escape.

21   Consider an example. Before engaging in sex with a woman, her lover tells her that if she gets pregnant, it is her problem, not his. She says that she understands. In due course she does wind up pregnant. If we believe, as I hope we do, that the man would ordinarily have a moral responsibility toward both the child he will have helped to bring into the world and the child's mother, then his honest statement of what he intends does not spare him that responsibility.

22   This vision of responsibility assumes that not all moral obligations stem from consent or from a stated intention. The linking of obligations to promises is a rather modern and perhaps uniquely Western way of looking at life, and perhaps a luxury that only the well-to-do can afford. As Fred and Shulamit Korn (a philosopher and an anthropologist) have pointed out, "If one looks at ethnographic accounts of other societies, one finds that, while obligations everywhere play a crucial role in social life, promising is not preeminent among the sources of obligation and is not even mentioned by most anthropologists." The Korns have made a study of Tonga, where promises are virtually unknown but the social order is remarkably stable. If life without any promises seems extreme, we Americans sometimes go too far the other way, parsing not only our contracts but even our marriage vows in order to discover the absolute minimum obligation that we have to others as a result of our promises.

23   That some societies in the world have worked out evidently functional structures of obligation without the need for promise or consent does not tell us what *we* should do. But it serves as a reminder of the basic proposition that our existence in civil society creates a set of mutual responsibilities that philosophers used to capture in the fiction of the social contract. Nowadays, here in America, people seem to spend their time thinking of even cleverer ways to avoid their obligations, instead of doing what integrity commands and fulfilling them. And all too often honesty is their excuse.

A. Comprehension

Choose the answer that best completes each statement. Do not refer to the selection while doing this exercise.

1. According to Carter, which of the following statements best explains the relationship between honesty and integrity?
    (a) Honesty is part of integrity, but integrity requires discernment, while honesty does not.
    (b) Honesty and integrity are so similar in meaning that it is pointless to try to distinguish between them.
    (c) Integrity is honesty with a social and moral conscience.
    (d) Integrity is similar to honesty but requires a stronger commitment to telling the truth.

2. Carter writes that integrity requires three steps. Which of the following is *not* included among them?
    (a) Distinguishing between what is right and what is wrong.
    (b) Acting upon this distinction, even if it costs you personally.
    (c) Always saying what is right and what is wrong even if it hurts another.
    (d) Stating openly that you are acting on your distinction between what is right and what is wrong.

3. According to Carter, honesty is the right course of action only when
    (a) we save our own good reputations despite the harm it may do to others.
    (b) it serves our self-interest.
    (c) it causes harm to ourselves and spares others from being harmed.
    (d) we are forced to disclose everything we know, for example, in a court of law.

4. A manager gives his female employees easier tasks because he is certain they will fail if he gives them harder tasks. Carter says that the manager lacks integrity because he has
    (a) not examined his beliefs to be sure they were right in the first place.
    (b) been dishonest with his employees.
    (c) remained true to his own beliefs, even if others do not agree with him.
    (d) made a generalization based on insufficient evidence.

5. A society functions best when its citizens believe in the importance of
    (a) making legal contracts to govern every aspect of human relationships.
    (b) being honest, even if it means abdicating one's responsibilities.
    (c) keeping promises.
    (d) recognizing the importance of responsibility rather than mere promises.

B. Vocabulary

For each italicized word from the selection, write the best definition according to the context in which it appears. You may refer to the selection to answer the questions in this section and in all the remaining sections.

1. *discerning* what is right and what is wrong [paragraph 4]:   telling the difference between

2. the first *criterion* [4]:   standard for judging

3. a person of integrity as *steadfast* [4]:   firmly resolute

4. a *gratuitous* comment [10]:   unnecessary

5. honesty is most *laudable* [11]:   <u>praiseworthy</u>

6. he does not *berate* her [13]:   <u>rebuke</u>

7. our politics are so . . . *contentious* [16]:   <u>controversial, quarrelsome</u>

8. given human *fallibility* [18]:   <u>the capability of making an error</u>

9. an *exaltation* of honesty [20]:   <u>a raise in status</u>

10. *parsing* . . . our contracts [22]:   <u>breaking down into separate parts</u>

    <u>and explaining each one</u>

C. Inferences

Complete the following questions.

1. Carter suggests that, when discussing honesty and integrity, what is most important is
    (a) (to avoid unnecessarily harming another person.)
    (b) to recognize that not everyone knows what these terms mean.
    (c) to be true to one's beliefs no matter what the consequences.
    (d) not to disclose everything unless one is forced to.
2. Look again at the end of paragraph 5, from which the reader can infer that
    (a) racists usually act honestly based on their beliefs.
    (b) (racists have not examined the validity of their beliefs, no matter how honest they think they are being.)
    (c) racists are born, not made.
    (d) everyone is racist to some degree or other.
3. The hypothetical story of the dying man who confesses his past infidelity to his wife confirms Carter's observation that
    (a) (his honesty derived from self-interest, not from integrity.)
    (b) it was important for him to confess to wrongdoings before dying.
    (c) deathbed confessions are seldom a good idea.
    (d) he was probably punishing his wife for a miserable marriage.
4. A man who tells a woman that any resulting pregnancy from their relationship is her problem, not his,
    (a) (is not absolved of responsibility just because he has been honest about his feelings.)
    (b) is not responsible morally either for her or for the child.
    (c) has shown integrity by being forthright from the beginning.
    (d) is guilty of the worst sort of sexual exploitation.

D. Structure

Complete the following questions.

1. Carter never explicitly defines the word *integrity,* perhaps because
   (a) he does not clearly understand the word's meaning himself.
   (b) the examples he uses throughout the essay suggest and clarify the word's meaning.
   (c) everyone knows what *integrity* and *honesty* mean.
   (d) the word is impossible to define accurately.

2. Why does Carter include paragraphs 17 and 18? What do they add to his discussion?   They serve as a concession and show that he is not

   establishing himself as a moral authority.

3. The tone of this essay can be best described as
   (a) reflective, thoughtful.
   (b) impartial, objective.
   (c) scholarly, pedantic.
   (d) uncertain, ambivalent.

E. Questions for Discussion and Analysis

1. What is your personal definition of integrity?

2. Is Carter condoning lying? Concerning the hypothetical husband who confesses to an adulterous affair on his deathbed, what would have been the right course of action if his wife had asked him if he had ever been unfaithful to her?

3. Examine an incident in your life when your behavior showed honesty but not integrity.

 AT THE MOVIES

The 1999 British movie *The Winslow Boy,* directed by playwright David Mamet, is an excellent film that embodies Carter's concept of integrity. When a 14-year-old boy is accused of stealing a small amount of money at his school, his family sacrifices a great deal to prove his accusers wrong and to restore his honor. The film stars Rebecca Pidgeon, Gemma Jones, and Guy Edwards II as Ronnie Winslow, the accused boy.

Selection 9   # Harmless Lying
Sissela Bok

Reprised from the fourth edition of this text, "Harmless Lying" seems especially pertinent today in an era when public lying has proliferated in corporate America, in government, and in the media. From her 1978 book, Lying: Moral Choice in Public and Private Life, *this selection examines something everybody probably admits to doing at least occasionally—telling white lies. Sissela Bok is Senior Visiting Fellow at Harvard University's Center for Population and Development Studies. She is also the author of several other books, among them* Secrets: On the Ethics of Concealment and Revelation *(1982);* Alva Myrdal: A Daughter's Memoir *(1991); and with Gerald Dworkin and Ray Frey,* Euthanasia and Physician-Assisted Suicide *(1998). Note: The book from which this selection comes was written in the post-Watergate era, to which Bok refers in the concluding paragraph. The Watergate scandal and ensuing cover-up are often cited as the catalysts for public's increasing cynicism and distrust in the U.S. government.*

Preview Questions

1. Consider the matters of honesty and integrity that Stephen Carter examines in the previous selection as you read this piece.
2. Does lying ever have utilitarian value? That is, can you justify lies—white lies or more serious lies—either because they are innocuous or because they actually bring about a benefit?

1   White lies are at the other end of the spectrum of deception from lies in a serious crisis. They are the most common and the most trivial forms that duplicity can take. The fact that they are so very common provides their protective coloring. And their very triviality, when compared to more threatening lies, makes it seem unnecessary or even absurd to condemn them. Some consider all well-intentioned lies, however momentous, to be white; in this book, I shall adhere to the narrower usage: a white lie, in this sense, is a falsehood not meant to injure anyone, and of little moral import. I want to ask whether there are such lies; and if there are, whether their cumulative consequences are still without harm; and, finally, whether many lies are not defended as "white" which are in fact harmful in their own right.

2   Many small subterfuges may not even be intended to mislead. They are only "white lies" in the most marginal sense. Take, for example, the many social exchanges: "How nice to see you!" or "Cordially Yours." These and a thousand other polite expressions are so much taken for granted that if someone decided, in the name of total honesty, not to employ them, he might well give the impression of an indifference he

did not possess. The justification for continuing to use such accepted formulations is that they deceive no one, except possibly those unfamiliar with the language.

3   A social practice more clearly deceptive is that of giving a false excuse so as not to hurt the feelings of someone making an invitation or request: to say one "can't" do what in reality one may not *want* to do. Once again, the false excuse may prevent unwarranted inferences of greater hostility to the undertaking than one may feel. Merely to say that one can't do something, moreover, is not deceptive in the sense that an elaborately concocted story can be.

4   Still other white lies are told in an effort to flatter, to throw a cheerful interpretation on depressing circumstances, or to show gratitude for unwanted gifts. In the eyes of many, such white lies do no harm, provide needed support and cheer, and help dispel gloom and boredom. They preserve the equilibrium and often the humaneness of social relationships, and are usually accepted as excusable so long as they do not become excessive. Many argue, moreover, that such deception is so helpful and at times so necessary that it must be tolerated as an exception to a general policy against lying. Thus Bacon observed:

> Doth any man doubt, that if there were taken out of men's minds vain opinions, flattering hopes, false valuations, imaginations as one would, and the like, but it would leave the minds of a number of men poor shrunken things, full of melancholy and indisposition, and unpleasing to themselves?

5   Another kind of lie may actually be advocated as bringing a more substantial benefit, or avoiding a real harm, while seeming quite innocuous to these who tell the lies. Such are the placebos given for innumerable common ailments, and the pervasive use of inflated grades and recommendations for employment and promotion.

6   A large number of lies without such redeeming features are nevertheless often regarded as so trivial that they should be grouped with white lies. They are the lies told on the spur of the moment, for want of reflection, or to get out of a scrape, or even simply to pass the time. Such are the lies told to boast or exaggerate, or on the contrary to deprecate and understate; the many lies told or repeated in gossip; Rousseau's lies told simply "in order to say something"; the embroidering on facts that seem too tedious in their own right; and the substitution of a quick lie for the lengthy explanations one might otherwise have to provide for something not worth spending time on.

7   Utilitarians often cite white lies as the *kind* of deception where their theory shows the benefits of common sense and clear thinking. A white lie, they hold, is trivial; it is either completely harmless, or so marginally harmful that the cost of detecting and evaluating the harm is much greater than the minute harm itself. In addition, the white lie can often

actually be beneficial, thus further tipping the scales of utility. In a world with so many difficult problems, utilitarians might ask: Why take the time to weigh the minute pros and cons in telling someone that his tie is attractive when it is an abomination, or of saying to a guest that a broken vase was worthless? Why bother even to define such insignificant distortions or make mountains out of molehills by seeking to justify them?

8   Triviality surely does set limits to when moral inquiry is reasonable. But when we look more closely at practices such as placebo-giving, it becomes clear that all lies defended as "white" cannot be so easily dismissed. In the first place, the harmlessness of lies is notoriously disputable. What the liar perceives as harmless or even beneficial may not be so in the eyes of the deceived. Second, the failure to look at an entire practice rather than at their own isolated case often blinds liars to cumulative harm and expanding deceptive activities. Those who begin with white lies can come to resort to more frequent and more serious ones. Where some can tell a few white lies, others may tell more. Because lines are so hard to draw, the indiscriminate use of such lies can lead to other deceptive practices. The aggregate harm from a large number of marginally harmful instances may, therefore, be highly undesirable in the end—for liars, those deceived, and honesty and trust more generally.

9   Just as the life-threatening cases showed the Kantian analysis,[1] to be too rigid, so the cases of white lies show the casual utilitarian calculation to be inadequate. Such a criticism of utilitarianism does not attack its foundations, because it does not disprove the importance of weighing consequences. It merely shows that utilitarians most often do not weigh enough factors in their quick assumption that white lies are harmless. They often fail to look at *practices* of deception and the ways in which these multiply and reinforce one another. They tend to focus, rather, on the individual case, seen from the point of view of the individual liar.

10   In the post-Watergate period, no one need regard a concern with the combined and long-term effects of deception as far-fetched. But even apart from political life, with its peculiar and engrossing temptations, lies tend to spread. Disagreeable facts come to be sugar-coated, and sad news softened or denied altogether. Many lie to children and those who are ill about matters no longer peripheral but quite central, such as birth, adoption, divorce, and death. Deceptive propaganda and misleading advertising abound. All these lies are often dismissed on the same grounds of harmlessness and triviality used for white lies in general.

---

[1]The term "Kantian analysis" refers to a tenet of the philosophy of Immanuel Kant, the eighteenth-century German philosopher who espoused what he called a *categorical imperative*. This tenet states that human reason produces an absolute statement of moral action. The moral imperative is unconditional; that is, it is apart from personal motive or desire.

A. *Comprehension*

Choose the answer that best completes each statement. Do not refer to the selection while doing this exercise.

1.   Bok defines white lies as
(a)   serious falsehoods with significant moral consequences.
(b) harmless lies used only to flatter others or to cover up one's errors.
(c) falsehoods not meant to injure anyone and of little moral import.
(d) trivial examples of common civility that we all see through.

2.   Many people believe that white lies preserve social relationships, and they accept them as excusable
(a) if they deal with a trivial subject.
(b) as long as they do not become excessive.
(c) if they are easily perceived as lies.
(d) if they are easier than telling the truth.

3.   The author defines utilitarians as people who believe that white lies
(a) are never acceptable, even to avoid hurting others' feelings.
(b) destroy mutual trust between two people.
(c) are trivial, harmless, and sometimes even beneficial.
(d) are a way to alleviate boredom or to make dull facts more interesting.

4.   Which of the following are *two* concerns Bok expresses about white lies?
(a) The deceived person may not perceive such lies as harmless.
(b) Liars often have trouble keeping their lies straight.
(c) Lying is no longer seen as morally wrong.
(d) Liars become blind to the cumulative harm of lying, which in turn leads to more deceptive practices.
(e) Liars develop a reputation for lying so that nothing they say can be trusted.

5.   The problem with dismissing white lies as harmless is that we also consider other lies harmless like
(a) misleading advertising.
(b) political campaign promises.
(c) lies told to avoid hurting others' feelings.
(d) elaborate excuses to get out of doing something we don't want to do.

B. *Vocabulary*

For each italicized word from the selection, write the dictionary definition most appropriate for the context. You may refer to the selection to answer the questions in this section and in all the remaining sections.

1.   the most trivial forms that *duplicity* can take [paragraph 1]:

deliberate deception

2. of little moral *import* [1]: <u>significance</u>

3. Many small *subterfuges* [2]: <u>evasive tactics</u>

4. may prevent *unwarranted* inferences [3]: <u>unjustified</u>

5. They preserve the *equilibrium* [4]: <u>balance</u>

6. seeming quite *innocuous* [5]: <u>harmless</u>

7. for *want* of reflection [6]: <u>lack</u>

8. to *deprecate* and understate [6]: <u>belittle</u>

9. *Utilitarians* often cite white lies [7]: <u>believers in what is practical</u>

   <u>over what is ethical</u>

10. The *aggregate* harm [8]: <u>total</u>

C. Inferences

Complete the following questions.

1. From the essay as a whole, what inference can you make about Bok's opinion concerning the commonly accepted definition of white lies as well intentioned and having little moral import. <u>She does not</u>

   <u>accept this definition, pointing to the harm the lie does to the</u>

   <u>person lied to and the possibility that such lies lead to further</u>

   <u>deceits.</u>

2. According to paragraphs 2 and 3, which lie is more harmful: saying how nice it is to see someone again or saying that we can't do something we don't want to do? <u>It is more harmful to say that we</u>

   <u>can't do something we simply don't want to do.</u>

3. From what Bok suggests in paragraph 8, why should we look at the whole pattern of lying rather than simply isolated examples of white lies? <u>Looking at only isolated examples shields liars from seeing</u>

   <u>the cumulative harmful effects of their lies.</u>

4. From what Bok implies in paragraph 10, why have we become accustomed to and tolerant of misleading advertising, sugar-coated facts, and deceptive propaganda? <u>We lump such instances in with white</u>

   <u>lies, which we perceive as harmless.</u>

D. Structure

Complete the following questions.

1. The writer's purpose is to
   (a) provide a reasonable definition of white lies.
   (b) examine contemporary attitudes about white lies and our reasons for telling them.
   (c) question the ethics and examine the effects of telling white lies.
   (d) cite specific instances when telling white lies is preferable to telling the truth.
2. The last sentence of paragraph 1, in relation to the essay as a whole, serves as
   (a) a transition.
   (b) a statement of the writer's purpose in writing.
   (c) supporting evidence.
   (d) a rhetorical question asked only for effect.
3. Which method of development is most evident in the section from paragraphs 2–6?
   (a) comparison
   (b) contrast
   (c) definition
   (d) classification
   (e) steps in a process
4. The author's tone can be best described as
   (a) self-righteous, "holier-than-thou."
   (b) complaining, aggrieved.
   (c) objective, impartial.
   (d) serious, philosophical.
5. Which of the following is the most reasonable conclusion we can draw from this essay?
   (a) White lies are acceptable if they save others from being hurt.
   (b) The circumstances when we tell white lies should be limited, and we should think about their repercussions before we tell them.
   (c) Everyone tells white lies; it's simply human nature.
   (d) White lies are often more convenient and less harmful in the long run than telling the truth.

E. Questions for Discussion and Analysis

1. Do you agree with Bok's assertion about the cumulative dangers of telling white lies? Why or why not? Cite an example of someone you know whom you have caught lying. How did it affect your relationship, if at all?

2. How has this essay changed your perception about white lies in particular and about lying in general?

🖱 ON THE WEB

The last paragraph of Bok's essay refers to our era as the "post-Watergate period." If you are unfamiliar with the Watergate scandal, which occurred during Richard Nixon's second term as president in 1972–1973, go to Google or your favorite search engine and do some research on this scandal.

Selection 10

Talk Show Telling Versus Authentic Telling: The Effects of the Popular Media on Secrecy and Openness

Evan Imber-Black

Honesty and its relationship to integrity and lying (white lies) were the subjects of the two preceding essays. In this selection we turn to the other extreme—the baring of truths, no matter how personal or unsavory, on the many talk shows that titillate the home viewers of daytime television. This selection is reprinted from The Secret Life of Families: Truth-Telling, Privacy, and Reconciliation in a Tell-All Society *(1998) by Evan Imber-Black, a practicing family therapist in New York. Currently, she is also Director of Program Development of the Ackerman Institute for the Family and professor of psychiatry at the Albert Einstein College of Medicine.*

Preview Questions

1. Television talk shows are a staple of daytime television, their popularity a testament to some viewers' apparently insatiable need to learn people's intimate secrets. Do you regularly view television talk shows? If so, can you characterize your reactions to the parade of misery they thrive on displaying?

2. What do you think are the motives of guests who appear on television talk shows and reveal personal secrets in front of millions of people in the viewing audience?

Well, my guests today say that they can't bear to keep their secrets locked inside of them any longer. And they've invited their spouse or lover to come on national television to let them hear the secrets for the first time.

—*Montel Williams*

1   The young woman entered my therapy room slowly, with the usual hesitation of a new client. I settled her in a chair, expecting to begin the

low-key question-and-answer conversation that usually takes the entire first session. Almost before she could pronounce my name, she began telling me a deeply personal and shameful secret. In an effort to slow her down and start to build a relationship that might be strong enough to hold her enormous pain, I gently asked her what made her think it was all right to tell me things so quickly. "I see people doing it on *Oprah* all the time," she replied.

2   Throughout history human beings have been fascinated by other people's secrets. In great literature, theater, and films we view how people create and inhabit secrets and cope with the consequences of planned or unplanned revelation. Life-changing secrets are central to such ancient dramas such as *Oedipus* or Shakespeare's *Macbeth,* as well as to twentieth-century classics such as Ibsen's *A Doll's House,* Eugene O'Neill's *Long Day's Journey into Night,* Arthur Miller's *Death of a Salesman* and *All My Sons,* or Lorraine Hansberry's *A Raisin in the Sun.* Like me, you may remember the poignancy of the sweet secrets in the O. Henry tale "Gifts of the Magi," where a wife secretly cuts and sells her hair to buy her husband a watch chain for Christmas, while he, unbeknownst to her, sells his watch in order to buy silver combs for her hair. Contemporary popular films, such as *Ordinary People, The Prince of Tides,* or *The Wedding Banquet,* also illustrate the complexity of secrets and their impact on every member of a family. Literary and dramatic portrayals of perplexing secrets and their often complicated and messy resolutions help us to remember that keeping and opening secrets is not simple. Perhaps most important, they help us appreciate our own deep human connection to the dilemmas of others.

3   Since the advent of television, however, we have begun to learn about other people's secrets and, by implication, how to think about our own secrets in a very different way. Exploiting our hunger for missing community, both afternoon talk shows and evening magazine shows have challenged all of our previously held notions about secrecy, privacy, and openness. While such shows have been around for nearly thirty years, in the 1980s something new began to appear: Celebrities began to open the secrets in their lives on national television. As we heard about Jane Fonda's bulimia, Elizabeth Taylor's drug addiction, or Dick Van Dyke's alcoholism—formerly shameful secrets spoken about with aplomb—centuries of stigma seemed to be lifting. Other revelations enabled us to see the pervasiveness of wife battering and incest. The unquestioned shame and secrecy formerly attached to cancer, adoption, homosexuality, mental illness, or out-of-wedlock birth began to fall away.

4   This atmosphere of greater openness brought with it many benefits. In my therapy practice I experienced an important shift as the people I worked with displayed a greater ease in raising what might never have been spoken about a decade earlier. Frightening secrets lost some of their power to perpetuate intimidation. Those who had been silenced began to find their voices and stake their claim as authorities on their own lives.

5   But as the arena of the unmentionable became smaller and smaller, a more dangerous cultural shift was also taking place: the growth of the simplistic belief that telling a secret, regardless of context, is automatically beneficial. This belief, promulgated by television talk shows and media exposés, has ripped secrecy and openness away from their necessary moorings in connected and empathic relationships. Painful personal revelations have become public entertainment, used to sell dish soap and to manufacture celebrity.

6   If cultural norms once made shameful secrets out of too many happenings in human life, we are now struggling with the reverse assumption: that opening secrets—no matter how, when, or to whom—is morally superior and automatically healing. The daily spectacle of strangers opening secrets in our living rooms teaches us that no distinctions need be drawn, no care need be taken, no thought given to consequences.

Talk Show Telling

7   From a *Sally Jessy Raphael* show in 1994, we hear and see the following conversation:

> SALLY: *Let's meet David and Kelly. They're newlyweds. They got married in December. . . . As newlyweds, what would happen if he cheated on you? What would you do?*
> KELLY: *I don't know.*
>   [Before David begins to speak, the print at the bottom of the screen reads, "Telling Kelly for the first time that he's cheating on her," thus informing the audience of the content of the secret before Kelly is told.]
> DAVID: *I called Sally and told the producer of the show that I was living a double life. . . . I had a few affairs on her.*
> SALLY *(TO KELLY): Did you know about that?*
>   [Camera zooms in on Kelly's shocked and pained expression; she is speechless and in tears, and she shakes her head while members of the audience chuckle.]
> SALLY: *Kelly, how do you feel? On the one hand, listen to how awful and bad this is. On the other hand, he could have just not ever told you. He loves you so much that he wanted to come and get this out. . . .*

8   In the late 1960s the *Phil Donahue Show* began a new media format for sharing interesting information and airing issues. This shifted in the late 1970s and 1980s to celebrity confessions and the destruction of taboos. In the 1990s talk TV brings us the deliberate opening of secrets that one person in a couple or a family has never heard before. In a cynical grab for ratings and profits, the format of such shows has changed rapidly from one where guests were told ahead of time that they were going to hear a secret "for the first time on national television" to one

where guests are invited to the show under some other ruse. These programs are referred to as "ambush" shows.

9   According to former talk show host Jane Whitney, "Practically anyone willing to 'confront' someone—her husband's mistress, his wife's lover, their promiscuous best friend—in a televised emotional ambush could snare a free ticket to national notoriety. *Those who promised to reveal some intimate secret to an unsuspecting loved one got star treatment"* (italics added). Presently there are over thirty talk shows on every weekday. Forty million Americans watch these shows, and they are syndicated in many other countries. Even if you have never watched a talk show, you live in an environment where assumptions about secrets have been affected by talk show telling.

10   Opening painful secrets on talk TV shows promotes a distorted sense of values and beliefs about secrecy and openness. While viewers are drawn into the sensational content of whatever secret is being revealed, the impact on relationships after the talk show is over is ignored. Indeed, when there has been severe relationship fallout, or even tragedy following the opening of a secret, talk show hosts and producers claim they have no responsibility, intensifying the belief that secrets can be recklessly opened.

11   The audience encourages further revelations through applause. As viewers, we get the message over and over that opening a secret, regardless of consequences, gains attention and approval. Loudly applauded, cheered, jeered, and fought over, secrets are in fact trivialized. On talk shows, a secret of sexual abuse equals a secret about family finances equals a secret about being a Nazi equals a secret of paternity.

12   Once a secret is revealed, both the teller and the recipient are immediately vulnerable to the judgmental advice and criticism of strangers. Blaming and taking sides abound. Not a moment elapses for reflection on the magnitude and gravity of what has occurred. Every secret is instantly reduced to a one-dimensional problem that will yield to simplistic solutions.

13   Soon after a secret is opened, the host goes into high gear with some variation of the message that opening the secret can have only good results. Sally Jessy Raphael tells the young wife who has just discovered the secret of her husband's affairs in front of millions of unasked-for snoopers, "He loves you so much that he wanted to come and get this out." The message to all is that telling a secret, in and of itself, is curative. There is no place for ambivalence or confusion. Indeed, guests are often scolded for expressing doubt or hesitation about the wisdom of national disclosure of the intimate aspects of their lives.

14   The host's position as a celebrity can frame the content of a given secret and the process of telling as either normal or abnormal, good or bad. When Oprah Winfrey joins guests who are exposing secrets of sexual abuse or cocaine addiction with revelations of her own, the telling becomes hallowed. No distinctions are drawn between what a famous

person with a lot of money and power might be able to speak about without consequences and what an ordinary person who is returning to their family, job, and community after the talk show might be able to express. Conversely, some hosts display initial shock, dismay, and negativity toward a particular secret, its teller, or its recipient. When a guest on the *Jerry Springer Show* who has just discovered that a woman he had a relationship with is a transsexual hides in embarrassment and asks the host what he would do, Springer responds, "Well, I certainly wouldn't be talking about it on national TV!" A context of disgrace is created, only to be transformed at the next commercial break into a context of understanding and forgiveness.

15   Toward the end of any talk show on which secrets have been revealed, a mental health therapist enters. A pseudo-therapeutic context is created. The real and difficult work that is required after a secret opens disappears in the smoke and mirrors of a fleeting and unaccountable relationship with an "expert" who adopts a position of superiority and assumed knowledge about the lives of people he or she has just met. While we are asked to believe that there are no loose ends when the talk show is over, the duplicitousness of this claim is evident in the fact that many shows now offer "aftercare," or real therapy, to deal with the impact of disclosing a secret on television.

16   The time needed even to begin to deal adequately with any secret is powerfully misrepresented on talk television. In just under forty minutes on a single *Montel Williams* show, a man told his wife he was in a homosexual relationship; a woman told her husband she was having an affair with his boss; another woman told her boyfriend that she was a transsexual; a wife revealed to her husband that they were $20,000 in debt; and a woman told her boyfriend that she had just aborted their pregnancy. An ethos of "just blurt it out" underpins these shows.

17   Talk show telling also erases age-appropriate boundaries between parents and children. Children are often in the audience hearing their parents' secrets for the first time. On one show an eight-year-old boy heard his aunt reveal that he had been abandoned by his mother because she "didn't want" him. Children may also be onstage revealing a secret to one parent about the other parent, without a thought given to the guilt children experience when they are disloyal to a parent. The impact on these children, their sense of shame and embarrassment, and what they might encounter when they return to school the next day is never considered.

18   Ultimately, talk show telling transforms our most private and intimate truths into a commodity. Shows conclude with announcements: "Do you have a secret that you've never told anyone? Call and tell us"; "Have you videotaped someone doing something they shouldn't do? Send us the tape." A juicy secret may get you a free airplane trip, a limousine ride, an overnight stay in a fancy hotel. While no one forces anyone to go on a talk show, the fact that most guests are working-class

people who lack the means for such travel makes talk show telling a deal with the devil.

A. *Comprehension*

Choose the answer that best completes each statement. Do not refer to the selection while doing this exercise.

1. Television talk shows have changed the way we regard
    (a) the concepts of secrecy, privacy, and openness.
    (b) what we consider appropriate behavior in front of millions of viewers.
    (c) the benefits of confessing our sins and mistakes in public.
    (d) talk show hosts as therapists and psychiatrists.

2. Imber-Black lists several facts regarding talk shows that began to change in the 1980s. Which was *not* mentioned?
    (a) Celebrities began airing their own secrets on national television.
    (b) Secrets, such as homosexuality, alcoholism, mental illness, or cancer, which used to be considered shameful, were no longer stigmatized.
    (c) Talk show guests considered an appearance on a program as cheap psychological therapy.
    (d) Social problems were revealed to be more pervasive than we had known.

3. Imber-Black is particularly concerned that a cultural shift has occurred, one which suggests that telling secrets in public is
    (a) a way to improve television ratings.
    (b) automatically beneficial and results in automatic healing.
    (c) a form of therapy superior to traditional means, such as psychoanalysis or psychological counseling.
    (d) a good way to sell products and to boost ratings.

4. Programs on which a secret about a guest is revealed for the first time before a television audience are called
    (a) assault shows.
    (b) instant therapy shows.
    (c) entrapment shows.
    (d) ambush shows.

5. Imber-Black concludes that revealing secrets in the talk show format allows no room for
    (a) ambivalence, confusion, reflection, or true understanding of a secret's impact.
    (b) equal time so that the "victim" can tell his or her side of the story.
    (c) audience discussion of the secrets revealed.
    (d) learning the final impact on the people involved in revealing and hearing the secret.

B. Vocabulary

For each italicized word from the selection, write the best definition according to the context in which it appears. You may refer to the selection to answer the questions in this section, and in all the remaining sections.

1. the *poignancy* of the sweet secrets [paragraph 2]: the quality of being profoundly moving or emotionally affecting

2. secrets spoken about with *aplomb* [3]: self-confident assurance

3. to *perpetuate* intimidation [4]: prolong

4. *promulgated* by talk shows [5]: officially put into effect

5. their necessary *moorings* [5]: elements that provide stability or security

6. some other *ruse* [8]: a crafty strategy, a subterfuge

7. the telling becomes *hallowed* [14]: revered, established as holy

8. the *duplicitousness* of the claim [15]: deceit

C. Inferences

Complete the following questions.

1. Read paragraph 2 carefully again. In light of Imber-Black's comments about the practice of revealing secrets on national television, list three elements regarding secrets—mentioned in paragraph 2—that are missing from today's media format. Some secrets should be maintained, not revealed to the world at large. Keeping and revealing secrets is not easy. Resolutions are often messy and complicated.

2. From paragraph 3, write the phrase that Imber-Black uses to explain today's penchant for baring secrets on television. "our hunger for missing community"

3. Reread the excerpt from a Sally Jessy Raphael program in paragraph 7. What is your reaction to the way Raphael interprets the motive for the young husband's confession of adultery—that "he loves you so much that he wanted to come and get this out"? Open question, but most students should see the cynical lie at its heart.

4. What does the discussion in the section comprising paragraphs 11 through 15 suggest about the format of most television talk shows?

<u>They follow a preset script.</u>

5. At the end of paragraph 18, Imber-Black writes, "most guests are working-class people who lack the means for such travel." What inference can you draw from this remark? <u>One might infer that the</u>

<u>guests are just as cynical as the network producers: They can get</u>

<u>a free vacation just for spilling their secrets. Also it's unlikely</u>

<u>that talk-show guests are unaware of how they will be treated and</u>

<u>therefore know what they are getting into.</u>

D. Structure

Complete the following questions.

1. The purpose of paragraph 2 is specifically to
   (a) show how talk-shows' treatment of secrets is different from their treatment in literature.
   (b) list several works with the keeping and telling of secrets as their theme.
   (c) show that the subject of secrets is legitimate and beneficial in literature.
   (d) prove that the author is well-read on the subject of secrecy.
2. Paragraph 4 in relation to the essay as a whole serves as a
   (a) conclusion to what has gone before.
   (b) statement of main idea.
   (c) concession, an admission of some positive effects.
   (d) discussion of changes in the way therapy is practiced today.
3. As evidence for her criticisms of today's talk shows, Imber-Black relies on
   (a) examples from actual talk shows and analysis of consequences.
   (b) her own biases and preconceived notions.
   (c) the testimony of victims of ambush programs.
   (d) summaries of research studies.
4. Read paragraph 5 again. Then list two of Imber-Black's objections to revealing secrets on national television. <u>The assumption is that</u>

<u>revealing a secret conveys automatic benefits. People's secrets</u>

<u>are equated with public entertainment. The talk-show format</u>

<u>destroys the connections to those we are close to.</u>

5. Which of the following quotations from the essay *best* states its thesis?
    (a) "Every secret is instantly reduced to a one-dimensional problem that will yield to simplistic solutions."
    (b) "Painful personal revelations have become public entertainment, used to sell dish soap and to manufacture celebrity."
    (c) "Opening painful secrets on talk TV shows promotes a distorted sense of values and beliefs about secrecy and openness."
    (d) "Ultimately, talk-show telling transforms our most private and intimate truths into a commodity."

E. Questions for Discussion and Analysis

1. What is the role of television in a tell-all society? In other words, was the advent of television talk shows the cause of our need to reveal or merely a reflection of a larger social trend?

2. As Imber-Black suggests in paragraph 2, if the problem of maintaining and disclosing secrets has been so important in literature throughout the ages, why couldn't one argue that the talk-show format is simply an updated, twenty-first-century version of the same phenomenon? What is so reprehensible about the talk shows described in the essay?

ON THE WEB

- Get some other opinions about the worth of television talk shows. Using Google or your favorite search engine, type in "television talk shows" + criticism or "television talk shows" + opinion.
- For a comprehensive history of the evolution of television talk shows in the United States, go to: www.museum.tv/archives/etv/T/htmlT/talkshows/talkshows.htm.

Selection 11

Los Angeles Against the Mountains
John McPhee

*Pulitzer Prize–winner John McPhee is one of the great modern American masters of nonfiction prose. He has turned his considerable writing talents to a wide array of subjects during his long and distinguished career, among them handmade canoes (*The Survival of the Birch Bark Canoe*, 1975); the state of Alaska (*Coming into the Country*, 1976); growing oranges in Florida (*Oranges*, 1967); and a unique wilderness area of New Jersey (*The Pine Barrens*, 1967). More recently, McPhee has been writing about nature and*

geological formations, for example, Basin and Range *(1980);* Assembling California *(1993); and* The Control of Nature *(1989), from which this selection is taken.*

Preview Questions

1. Should homeowners be allowed to build houses in unsafe areas, that is, areas prone to mudslides, flooding, or wildfires?
2. Throughout this selection, McPhee's point of view is evident only through his selection of pertinent detail. As you read it, note these telling details to determine his viewpoint toward the Genofiles and their decision to rebuild their house.

1   In Los Angeles versus the San Gabriel Mountains, it is not always clear which side is losing. For example, the Genofiles, Bob and Jackie, can claim to have lost and won. They live on an acre of ground so high that they look across their pool and past the trunks of big pines at an aerial view over Glendale and across Los Angeles to the Pacific bays. The setting, in cool dry air, is serene and Mediterranean. It has not been everlastingly serene.

2   On a February night some years ago, the Genofiles were awakened by a crash of thunder—lightning striking the mountain front. Ordinarily, in their quiet neighborhood, only the creek beside them was likely to make much sound, dropping steeply out of Shields Canyon on its way to the Los Angeles River. The creek, like every component of all the river systems across the city from mountains to ocean, had not been left to nature. Its banks were concrete. Its bed was concrete. When boulders were running there, they sounded like a rolling freight. On a night like this, the boulders should have been running. The creek should have been a torrent. Its unnatural sound was unnaturally absent. There was, and had been, a lot of rain.

3   The Genofiles had two teen-age children, whose rooms were on the uphill side of the one-story house. The window in Scott's room looked straight up Pine Cone Road, a cul-de-sac, which, with hundreds like it, defined the northern limit of the city, the confrontation of the urban and the wild. Los Angeles is overmatched on one side by the Pacific Ocean and on the other by some very high mountains. With respect to these principal boundaries, Los Angeles is done sprawling. The San Gabriels, in their state of tectonic youth, are rising as rapidly as any range on earth. Their loose inimical slopes flout the tolerance of the angle of repose. Rising straight up out of the megalopolis, they stand ten thousand feet above the nearby sea, and they are not kidding with this city. Shedding, spalling,[1] self-destructing, they are disintegrating at

---

[1]Breaking into chips or fragments.

a rate that is also among the fastest in the world. The phalanxed communities of Los Angeles have pushed themselves hard against these mountains, an aggression that requires a deep defense budget to contend with the results. Kimberlee Genofile called to her mother, who joined her in Scott's room as they looked up the street. From its high turnaround, Pine Cone Road plunges downhill like a ski run, bending left and then right and then left and then right in steep christiania turns for half a mile above a three-hundred-foot straightaway that aims directly at the Genofiles' house. Not far below the turnaround, Shields Creek passes under the street, and there is a kink in its concrete profile that had been plugged by a six-foot boulder. Hence the silence of the creek. The water was now spreading over the street. It descended in heavy sheets. As the young Genofiles and their mother glimpsed it in the all but total darkness, the scene was suddenly illuminated by a blue electrical flash. In the blue light they saw a massive blackness, moving. It was not a landslide, not a mudslide, not a rock avalanche; nor by any means was it the front of a conventional flood. In Jackie's words, "It was just one big black thing coming at us, rolling, rolling with a lot of water in front of it, pushing the water, this big black thing. It was just one big black hill coming toward us."

4   In geology, it would be known as a debris flow. Debris flows amass in stream valleys and more or less resemble fresh concrete. They consist of water mixed with a good deal of solid material, most of which is above sand size. Some of it is Chevrolet size. Boulders bigger than cars ride long distances in debris flows. Boulders grouped like fish eggs pour downhill in debris flows. The dark material coming toward the Genofiles was not only full of boulders; it was so full of automobiles it was like bread dough mixed with raisins. On its way down Pine Cone Road, it plucked up cars from driveways and the street. When it crashed into the Genofiles' house, the shattering of safety glass made terrific explosive sounds. A door burst open. Mud and boulders poured into the hall. We're going to go, Jackie thought. Oh, my God, what a hell of a way for the four of us to die together.

5   The parents' bedroom was on the far side of the house. Bob Genofile was in there kicking through white satin draperies at the paneled glass, smashing it to provide an outlet for water, when the three others ran in to join him. The walls of the house neither moved nor shook. As a general contractor, Bob had built dams, department stores, hospitals, six schools, seven churches, and this house. It was made of concrete block with steel reinforcement, sixteen inches on center. His wife had said it was stronger than any dam in California. His crew had called it "the fort." In those days, twenty years before, the Genofiles' acre was close by the edge of the mountain brush, but a developer had come along since then and knocked down thousands of trees and put Pine Cone Road up the slope. Now Bob Genofile was thinking, I hope the roof holds. I hope the roof is strong enough to hold. Debris was flowing over it. He told Scott

to shut the bedroom door. No sooner was the door closed than it was battered down and fell into the room. Mud, rock, water poured in. It pushed everybody against the far wall. "Jump on the bed," Bob said. The bed began to rise. Kneeling on it—on a gold velvet spread—they could soon press their palms against the ceiling. The bed also moved toward the glass wall. The two teen-agers got off, to try to control the motion, and were pinned between the bed's brass railing and the wall. Boulders went up against the railing, pressed into their legs, and held them fast. Bob dived into the muck to try to move the boulders, but he failed. The debris flow, entering through windows as well as doors, continued to rise. Escape was still possible for the parents but not for the children. The parents looked at each other and did not stir. Each reached for and held one of the children. Their mother felt suddenly resigned, sure that her son and daughter would die and she and her husband would quickly follow. The house became buried to the eaves. Boulders sat on the roof. Thirteen automobiles were packed around the building, including five in the pool. A din of rocks kept banging against them. The stuck horn of a buried car was blaring. The family in the darkness in their fixed tableau watched one another by the light of a directional signal, endlessly blinking. The house had filled up in six minutes, and the mud stopped rising near the children's chins. . . .

6   It was assumed that the Genofiles were dead. Firemen and paramedics who came into the neighborhood took one glance at the engulfed house and went elsewhere in search of people needing help. As the family remained trapped, perhaps an hour went by. They have no idea.

7   "We didn't know why it had come or how long it was going to last."

8   They lost all sense of time. The stuck horn went on blaring, the directional signal eerily blinking. They imagined that more debris was on the way.

9   "We didn't know if the whole mountain was coming down."

10   As they waited in the all but total darkness, Jackie thought of the neighbors' children. "I thought, Oh my gosh, all those little kids are dead. Actually, they were O.K. And the neighbors thought for sure we were all gone. All our neighbors thought we were gone."

11   At length, a neighbor approached their house and called out, "Are you alive?"

12   "Yes. But we need help."

13   As the debris flow hit the Genofiles' house, it also hit a six-ton truck from the L.A.C.F.C.D., the vigilant bureau called Flood. Vigilance was about all that the L.A.C.F.C.D. had been able to offer. The patrolling vehicle and its crew of two were as helpless as everyone else. Each of the crewmen had lived twenty-six years, and each came close to ending it there. Minutes before the flow arrived, the truck labored up Pine Cone Road—a forty-one-per-cent grade, steep enough to stiff a Maserati. The two men meant to check on a debris basin at the top. Known as Upper Shields, it

was less than two years old, and had been built in anticipation of the event that was about to occur. Oddly enough, the Genofiles and their neighbors were bracketed with debris basins—Upper Shields above them, Shields itself below them, six times as large. Shields Debris Basin, with its arterial concrete feeder channels, was prepared to catch fifty thousand tons. The Genofiles' house looked out over Shields as if it were an empty lake, its shores hedged about with oleander. When the developer extended Pine Cone Road up into the brush, the need for Upper Shields was apparent. The new basin came in the nick of time but—with a capacity under six thousand cubic yards—not in the nick of space. Just below it was a chain-link gate. As the six-ton truck approached the gate, mud was oozing through. The basin above had filled in minutes, and now, suddenly, boulders shot like cannonballs over the crest of the dam, with mud, cobbles, water, and trees. Chris Terracciano, the driver, radioed to headquarters, "It's coming over." Then he whipped the truck around and fled. The debris flow came through the chain-link barrier as if the links were made of paper. Steel posts broke off. As the truck accelerated down the steep hill, the debris flow chased and caught it. Boulders bounced against it. It was hit by empty automobiles spinning and revolving in the muck. The whole descending complex gathered force with distance. Terracciano later said, "I thought I was dead the whole way." The truck finally stopped when it bashed against a tree and a cement-block wall. The rear window shattered. Terracciano's partner suffered a broken leg. The two men crawled out through the window and escaped over the wall.

14   Within a few miles, other trapped patrols were calling in to say, "It's coming over." Zachau went over—into Sunland. Haines went over—into Tujunga. Dunsmuir went over—into Highway Highlands. As bulldozers plow the streets after events like these, the neighborhoods of northern Los Angeles assume a macabre resemblance to New England villages under deep snow: the cleared paths, the vehicular rights-of-way, the parking meters buried within the high banks, the half-covered drift-girt homes. A street that is lined with palms will have debris berms ten feet up the palms. In the Genofiles' front yard, the drift was twelve feet deep. A person, without climbing, could walk onto the roof. Scott's bedroom had a few inches of space left at the top, Kimberlee's had mud on the ceiling. On the terrace, the crushed vehicles, the detached erratic wheels suggested bomb damage, artillery hits, the track of the Fifth Army. The place looked like a destroyed pillbox. No wonder people assumed that no one had survived inside.

15   There was a white sedan under the house eaves crushed to half its height, with two large boulders resting on top of it. Near the pool, a Volkswagen bug lay squashed. Another car was literally wrapped around a tree, like a C-clamp, its front and rear bumpers pointing in the same direction. A crushed pickup had boulders all over it, each a good deal heavier than anything a pickup could carry. One of the cars in the swimming pool was upside down, its tires in the air. A Volkswagen was on

top of it. Bob Genofile—owner, contractor, victim—walked around in rubber boots, a visored construction cap, a foul-weather jacket, studying the damage, mostly guessing at what he couldn't see. A big, strongly built, leonine man with prematurely white hair, he looked like a middle linebacker near the end of a heavy day. He wondered if the house was still on its foundation, but there was no telling in this profound chaos, now hardening and cracking like bad concrete. In time, as his house was excavated from the inside, he would find that it had not budged. Not one wall had so much as cracked. He was uninsured, but down in the rubble was a compensation of greater value then insurance. Forever, he could say, as he quietly does when he tells the story, "I built it, man."

16   Kimberlee's birthday came two days after the debris. She was a college student, turning nineteen, and her father had a gift for her that he was keeping in his wallet. "I had nineteen fifty-dollar bills to give her for her birthday, but my pants and everything was gone."

17   Young Scott, walking around in the wreckage, saw a belt sticking out of the muck like a night crawler after the rain. He pulled at it, and the buried pants came with it. The wallet was still in the pants. The wallet still contained what every girl wants for her birthday: an album of portraits of U.S. Grant, no matter if Ulysses is wet or dry.

18   The living room had just been decorated, and in six minutes the job had been destroyed—"the pale tangerines and greens, Italian-style furniture with marble, and all that." Jackie Genofile continues the story: "We had been out that night, and, you know, you wear your better jewelry. I came home like an idiot and put mine on the dresser. Bob put his on the dresser. Three weeks later, when some workers were cleaning the debris out of the bedroom, they found his rings on the floor. They did not find mine. But—can you believe it?—a year and a half later Scott was down in the debris basin with one of his friends, and the Flood Control had these trucks there cleaning it out, and Scott saw this shiny thing, and he picked it up, and it was my ring that Bob had given me just before the storm."

19   Before the storm, they had not in any way felt threatened. Like their neighbors, they were confident of the debris basins, of the concrete liners of the nearby stream. After the storm, neighbors moved away. Where Pine Cone Road swung left or right, the debris had made centrifugal leaps, breaking into houses. A hydrant snapped off, and arcing water shot through an upstairs window. A child nearly drowned inside his own house. The family moved. "Another family that moved owned one of the cars that ended up in our pool," Jackie told me. "The husband said he'd never want to live here again, you know. And she was in real estate."

20   After the storm, the Genofiles tended to wake in the night, startled and anxious. They still do. "I wake up once in a while really uptight," Bob said. "I can just feel it—go through the whole thing, you know."

21   Jackie said that when rain pounds on a roof, anywhere she happens to be, she will become tense. Once, she took her dog and her pillow and went to sleep in Bob's office—which was then in Montrose, down beyond Foothill Boulevard.

22   Soon after the storm, she said, "Scotty woke up one night, and he had a real high temperature. You see, he was sixteen, and he kept hearing the mud and rock hitting the window. He kept thinking it was going to come again. Kim used to go four-wheeling, and cross streams, and she had to get out once, because they got stuck, and when she felt the flow of water and sand on her legs, she said, she could have panicked."

23   Soon after the storm, the family gathered to make a decision. Were they going to move or were they going to dig out their house and rebuild it? Each of them knew what might have happened. Bob said, "If it had been a frame house, we would be dead down in the basin below."

24   But it was not a frame house. It was a fort. "The kids said rebuild. So we rebuilt."

25   As he sat in his new living room telling the story, Bob was dressed in a Pierre Cardin jumper and pants, and Jackie was beside him in a pale-pink jumpsuit by Saint Germain. The house had a designer look as well, with its railings and balconies and Italianate marbles under the tall dry trees. It appeared to be worth a good deal more than the half-million dollars Bob said it might bring. He had added a second story and put all the bedrooms there. The original roof spreads around them like a flaring skirt. He changed the floor-length window in the front hall, filling the lower half of it with cement block.

26   I asked what other structural changes he had made.

27   He said, "None."

28   The Genofiles sued Los Angeles County. They claimed that Upper Shields Debris Basin had not been cleaned out and that the channel below was improperly designed. Los Angeles settled for three hundred and thirty-seven thousand five hundred dollars.

29   From the local chamber of commerce the family later received a Beautification Award for Best Home. Two of the criteria by which houses are selected for this honor are "good maintenance" and "a sense of drama."

A. Comprehension

Choose the answer that best completes each statement. Do not refer to the selection while doing this exercise.

1. The Genofiles' house is located
   (a) near a flood plain and the Los Angeles River.
   (b) in a valley near the San Andreas Fault.
   (c) near a rock quarry.
   (d) high up in the San Gabriel Mountains.
2. The Genofiles' house was nearly destroyed by
   (a) a mudslide.
   (b) a rock avalanche.
   (c) a debris flow.
   (d) flooding from heavy rain.

3. Along with the damage caused by enormous boulders and mud, damage to the building and the pool was also caused by
    (a) automobiles.
    (b) pool and patio furniture.
    (c) fallen trees.
    (d) broken glass.
4. The neighborhood, and especially the Genofiles' property, suffered terrible damage because
    (a) the county had permitted residences to be built in a floodplain.
    (b) the area's debris basins had failed.
    (c) the storm produced much more rain than usual.
    (d) the vegetation had been removed and the house was poorly built.
5. When the Genofiles redesigned and rebuilt their house, all of the bedrooms were
    (a) underground.
    (b) on the first floor.
    (c) on the second floor.
    (d) in an area they called "the fort."

B. Vocabulary

For each italicized word from the selection, choose the best definition according to the context in which it appears. You may refer to the selection to answer the questions in this section and in all the remaining sections.

1. Their loose *inimical* slopes [paragraph 3]:
    (a) hostile, like an enemy
    (b) covered with dense vegetation
    (c) steep, precipitous
    (d) natural appearing
2. *flout* the tolerance [3]:
    (a) are an example of
    (b) abandon
    (c) defy, ignore
    (d) redefine, give new meaning to
3. The *phalanxed* communities [3]:
    (a) devoted to military pursuits
    (b) composed of a close-knit body of people
    (c) aggressive in their pursuit of money
    (d) built with an awareness of environmental hazards
4. in their fixed *tableau* [5]:
    (a) characteristic roles
    (b) obsessions and fixations
    (c) a picture with elements seemingly frozen
    (d) physical positions

5. assume a *macabre* resemblance [14]: Suggesting something
   (a) strikingly similar
   (b) weird, alien-looking
   (c) picturesque, scenic, quaint
   (d) (chilling, reminding one of death)
6. a strongly built, *leonine* man [15]: Resembling
   (a) a bear
   (b) a wolf
   (c) (a lion)
   (d) a leopard

C. Inferences

On the basis of the evidence in the essay, mark these statements as follows: PA (probably accurate), PI (probably inaccurate), or NP (not in the passage).

1. _PA_ The creek next to the Genofiles house is lined with concrete probably to restrict and channel its flow during heavy rainstorms.
2. _PI_ When McPhee writes that "Los Angeles is overmatched on one side by the Pacific Ocean and on the other by very high mountains," he means that nature, represented by the ocean and by the mountains, is no longer a threat in the form of natural disasters.
3. _NP_ The Genofiles had a geological survey done of the property and the surrounding area before they built their house.
4. _PA_ The debris flow that invaded the Genofiles' house was filled only with mud, rocks, and boulders.
5. _PA_ If the family had died, it would have been from the mud flowing in through the windows, which rose as high as the ceilings.

D. Structure

Complete the following questions.

1. McPhee's purpose in writing is specifically to use one family's experience to
   (a) (show the folly of building houses near the disintegrating San Gabriel Mountains.)
   (b) show their stubbornness and courage in the face of a life-threatening natural disaster.
   (c) argue for more stringent building regulations in Los Angeles, so that houses could not be built in areas prone to floods or debris flows.
   (d) show how urban development can be made to work even in the face of the power of raw nature.

2. Identify the *three* primary methods of development in paragraph 4.
    (a) (informative process)
    (b) contrast
    (c) (definition)
    (d) comparison
    (e) (example)
    (f) classification

3. Paraphrase these two sentences from paragraph 3:

    "With respect to these principle boundaries [the Pacific Ocean and the mountains], Los Angeles is done sprawling."

    <u>Bounded on one side by the ocean and on the other by mountains,</u>

    <u>Los Angeles has no more room to grow.</u>

    "The phalanxed communities of Los Angeles have pushed themselves hard against these mountains, an aggression that requires a deep defense budget to contend with the results."

    <u>Because Los Angeles communities have extended their develop-</u>

    <u>ment right up against the mountains, the city and its residents</u>

    <u>must spend a lot of money protecting their property from</u>

    <u>inevitable disasters.</u>

4. Look again at the second sentence from question 3. What is McPhee implying in his choice of words like "phalanxed," "aggression," and "a deep defense budget"?

    <u>He is implying that the decision to build houses in such an area is</u>

    <u>like an act of war between the residents and the natural elements</u>

    <u>they must contend with.</u>

5. In paragraph 5, McPhee describes the construction of the Genofiles' house like this: "It was made of concrete block with steel reinforcement, sixteen inches on center. His wife had said it was stronger than any dam in California. His crew had called it 'the fort.'" Why does he include these sentences?

    <u>The house was constructed well, but its location made it</u>

    <u>vulnerable to the debris flow that hit it.</u>

6. Look again at the details at the beginning of paragraph 18 concerning the décor of the house and also the details at the beginning of paragraph 25 concerning the designer clothing and home interior. Why does McPhee include these details?

<u>Answers will vary, but perhaps these details show that the</u>

<u>Genofiles are concerned with appearance (designer labels and</u>

<u>elegant furnishings) to the detriment of facing the reality that</u>

<u>they live in a very dangerous place.</u>

7. Look again at the information in paragraph 29, which is an example of
    (a) understatement.
    (b) hyperbole, or exaggeration for effect.
    (c) an emotional appeal.
    (d) (irony.)

E. Questions for Discussion and Analysis

1. What is your impression of the Genofiles based on McPhee's description of them in this selection?

2. What motivates people to build houses in areas that are known to be unsafe—for example, on the coast of Florida in the path of dangerous hurricanes, in high-fire areas of the Western United States, or in mountainous regions like the San Gabriel Mountains, which, as McPhee says, are "disintegrating at a rate that is also among the fastest in the world"?

ON THE WEB

Using Google or your favorite search engine, do some research on a natural disaster that occurred recently in your state (a forest fire, a hurricane, an avalanche, or the like). To what extent was the property damage the result of human intrusion into dangerous areas?

Selection 12   ## Photo Essay "Psy-Ops Patrol,"
U.S. Department of Defense, Defend America

The U.S. Department of Defense, in addition to its official home page at www.defenselink.mil/, sponsors an elaborate series of photo essays under the rubric "Defend America." The images in this particular photo essay, of which six are reprinted here, show the work of the Psy-Ops Patrol (Charlie Company, 9th Psychological Operations Battalion) and the work these soldiers were performing in Iraq. The photos were taken in August 2004, during a time of increasing unrest and violence in that country: Several foreign technical and aid workers from the United States, Britain, Italy, Poland, and Egypt, among others, had been kidnapped; several had been beheaded, the images posted by their perpetrators on the Internet; rebellious groups staged suicide car bombings nearly every day; and Shiite clerics were urging citizens to resist the occupiers. In short, control of the war-torn country was breaking down, and the insurgency against the American occupiers seemed to be gaining strength.

More photo essays can be accessed at the Defend America Web site, available at www.defendamerica.mil/. Click on "Photo Essays," which will provide you with a large assortment to study.

Photo 1
Iraqi children catch candy from a member of Charlie Company, 9th Psychological Operations Battalion out of Fort Bragg, N.C., during a patrol in Mosul, Iraq, August 16, 2004.

Photo 2
Iraqi boys run next to a HMMWV of Charlie Company, 9th Psychological
Operations Battalion out of Fort Bragg, N.C., during a patrol in Mosul, Iraq,
August 16, 2004.

Photo 3
An Iraqi boy pretends to drive
a HMMWV of Charlie Com-
pany, 9th Psychological Operations Battalion out of Fort
Bragg, N.C., during a patrol in
Mosul, Iraq, August 16, 2004.

Photo 4
Staff Sgt. Patrick Boyer, with Charlie Company, 9th Psychological Operations
Battalion out of Fort Bragg, N.C., hands a cab driver a newspaper during a
patrol in Mosul, Iraq, August 16, 2004.

Photo 5
Sgt. 1st Class Dain Christensen,
Charlie Company, 9th Psychological Operations Battalion
out of Fort Bragg, N.C., gives
a ball to an Iraqi boy during a
patrol in Mosul, Iraq, August
16, 2004.

Photo 6

Sgt. Carl Kipp, of Charlie Company, 9th Psychological Operations Battalion out of Fort Bragg, N.C., tosses a ball to Iraqi kids during a patrol in Mosul, Iraq, August 16, 2004.

Questions for Analysis

1. The soldiers in the unit depicted in these photographs are part of the 9th Psychological Operations Battalion, commonly referred to as "Psy-Ops Patrol." What does the name "Psy-Ops Patrol" connote to you? After studying these photographs, what do you think the Psy-Ops Patrol's purpose is?

2. These photographs were taken in 2004, during the insurgency (the continued violence against American soldiers and Iraqi sympathizers) but before the national elections in January 2005. Of what significance are these photographs in their portrayal of life in Iraq in the aftermath of the war? What is the most significant message they convey?

3. Who is the audience for these photographs? Are they intended for Iraqi civilians or for Americans at home? What audience would be most likely to access this Web site?

4. The entire photo essay consisted of nine photos, six of which are reprinted for you. Five of these six involve children. What activities are depicted in these pictures? What are these activities involving interaction between American soldiers and Iraqi children meant to show?

5. What emotions or feelings do the faces of the children show? Does their dress reveal anything about them—their economic status? What is their demeanor? What do they seem to be thinking? Do these photos reveal their thinking about or attitude toward the soldiers?

6. How might photographs like those in this collection pertain to the War on Terror? What larger purpose do they serve? What image of America are they intended to show?

7. If you are unsure of its meaning, look up the word *propaganda* in a dictionary. In relation to the strict definition of the term, are these photographs propagandistic or not? Explain your thinking?

8. During the Vietnam War, American soldiers attempted to win the "hearts and minds" of the civilian population. The same phrase, "winning their hearts and minds," was a recurring slogan during the American invasion of Iraq and its subsequent occupation. How might photographs like these serve to dispel the images of brutality and violence that are broadcast on the evening television news or in our daily newspapers?

The complete collection of photos can be viewed online at

www.defendamerica.mil/photoessays/aug2004/p081904c3.html.

P A R T

Reading and Studying Textbook Material

■ THE STRUCTURE OF MODERN TEXTBOOKS

Reading textbooks requires a different approach than reading articles or essays. When you read a textbook, your purpose is to extract information on which you will very likely be tested. By its nature, academic discourse is intended to convey information, and therefore such writing tends to avoid the subtleties, figurative language, and rhetorical flourishes with which other nonfiction writers strive to endow their prose. This is not to say, however, that you should ignore the structure of textbooks. As you saw in Chapters 3, 4, and 5, textbook writers use the same methods of development and patterns of organization in their writing for the same reasons that other nonfiction writers do—to help the reader stay on track. Since you have undoubtedly gained some skill in recognizing these devices, both your comprehension and your ability to remember what you read should be stronger now than when you began this course.

In fact, textbook material should present less of a problem for you than other kinds of nonfiction prose, simply because textbook authors set down their ideas in the most straightforward and organized manner possible. More important, modern textbooks are embellished with all sorts of helpful information, which you may remember from the introduction to this text. For example, a typical textbook chapter begins with an outline or preview of the chapter's contents. Within the chapter the relative importance of ideas is shown graphically with an assortment of typefaces and type sizes, as will be illustrated herein. Key terms are printed in boldface or italics. Often key terms are pulled out of the text and defined in the margin. The typical chapter ends with a self-quiz, questions for discussion or review, or a summary—and sometimes all three. (Frequently, textbooks also have a Web site, where additional study or quiz questions are provided.) Finally, the pages of modern textbooks contain charts, graphs, tables, illustrations, photographs, and sometimes even cartoons to provide visual relief, to enhance, or to explain further the main points. All of these devices serve to make your study time, if not painless, then at least more efficient.

■ MAKING EFFICIENT USE OF STUDY TIME

Given the high cost of a college education today and the fact that so many students need to work part-time to survive, it becomes ever more important to make the most efficient use possible of your study time. This section offers some suggestions to accomplish this. The three most common ways students get into academic trouble are trying to do too much, procrastinating, and spending too much time on electronic gizmos.

The most apparent hindrance to students' doing well is their over-estimation of what they can realistically accomplish in a semester or quarter. The student who takes too many classes and works too many hours finds that a few weeks into the semester, things start to slide. Finding it difficult to keep up with the academic load and the job requirements (not to mention other demands on one's time like commuting, laundry, and household chores), he slacks off, gets behind with studying (and rest), and ends up dropping courses or receiving lower grades than he might otherwise receive. Before registering for classes, keep in mind the numbers of hours you plan to work, if necessary, and devise a reasonable schedule that will enable you to balance school and work.

Most colleges suggest that students devote two to three hours a week studying *for each hour you spend in class*. A student who takes 15 units should probably expect to study a minimum of 30 hours a week. If she has a job commitment of 20 hours a week (or half of a standard 40-hour work week), she is courting disaster because now her work week will be 65 hours per week, and this figure does not include time spent commuting, doing laundry, cooking, or doing other household chores. At the beginning of the semester or quarter, make a *realistic* appraisal of your class requirements (class time, lab hours, homework) and adjust your schedule.

A second obstacle to student success is procrastination. The student may put off studying until the night before a test, but once she finally buckles down, it is usually too late. It is virtually impossible to do a month's or two months' worth of studying the night before an exam. Good students complete their assignments when they are assigned and review frequently before major exams. You can take advantage of slack times by studying while you are waiting for the bus or by going to the library between classes.

The third hindrance that interferes with students' best intentions is a more recent phenomenon: the numerous technological distractions that we as a consumer society use to occupy (or waste) our time. A semester or so ago, one of my students, after receiving a failing grade at the midterm, confessed to spending 6 hours a day playing video games, and more on the weekend. Seriously limiting the amount of time you spend surfing the Internet, playing video games, or—the ultimate time-waster—watching television will free up your time to complete your assignments when they are due. All of these suggestions will help you avoid the last-minute panic that afflicts so many students at test time.

Even if you set aside the appropriate amount of time to study for your classes, you may still not be studying efficiently. The best way of studying is to apply a method of previewing and reviewing. One such method—SQ3R—is introduced in the next section to provide specific suggestions for, in effect, devising a system to learn as you go.

■ THE SQ3R STUDY METHOD

Various study skills techniques are taught today in high school and college courses, for example, PQ3R, PQ4R,[1] SQ4R, and SQ3R. All derive from a system developed by Francis P. Robison, and all involve the basic principle that students often omit from their study time: preview (or survey) and review. The SQ3R method detailed here stands for:

S	Survey
Q	Question
R	Read
R	Recite
R	Review

The SQ4R methods add an extra "R" step—"Rite" or "Write," meaning that one should take notes after reading. If you prefer, you can add note-taking during the reciting. Above all, whatever system you use when you read textbook assignments should be flexible and appropriate for your learning style.

Here is a step-by-step explanation of the SQ3R method:

Before you begin to read a textbook chapter, **survey** its contents. Quickly go through the chapter and

- Read and think about the chapter title.
- Read the outline, overview, or introduction.
- Read the main heads and subheads and become familiar with the size and appearance of the various headings.
- Make a note of any key terms or vocabulary defined in the margins.
- Read the chapter summary.
- Read through review questions or questions for discussion.

The survey step, which should take 5 to 10 minutes, provides you with a framework, an overview of the chapter's contents before you actually read it. In this way, you will have a focus for your reading, and you can fit the various parts of the chapter into a coherent whole.

The **question** and **read** steps are done simultaneously. Section by section, begin reading the text. Turn each major heading and subheading into a question that you will answer as you read. For example, the reading selection in this part is titled "Memory." In the first section of the excerpt you will encounter these headings:

Memory (chapter title)
Three Stages of Memory: An Information-Processing View
(first level heading)
   Sensory Register (second-level heading)

[1]The "P" stands for "Preview" in these two systems.

Short-Term Memory (second-level heading)
 **Rehearsal in Short-Term Memory: Overcoming STM's
 Limited Life Span** (third level heading)
 **Chunking in Short-Term Memory: Overcoming STM's
 Limited Capacity** (third-level heading)
Long-Term Memory (second-level heading)
 and so on

This layout shows that the first-level headings contain the second-level headings, which in turn contain the third-level headings. As you work through each section, during the question step, turn each heading into a question that can't be answered with yes or no. For example, the first heading might become "What are the three stages of memory?" Then read the section to find the answer. For the second heading, ask "What does the term *sensory register* mean?" Then read that section to find the answer. Two questions you might ask yourself for the third and fourth sections are "How does *short-term memory* differ from *long-term memory?*" and "How does *rehearsal* aid in improving short-term memory?" You'll find the answers to these questions by reading the sections.

The reading step will take up the bulk of your study session with each chapter, but you can go through it efficiently once you have laid the groundwork with the survey and question steps. After you read each section and locate the information that answers each question, **recite** the important points, using your own words as much as possible. This ensures that you truly understand the material and are not just parroting it back. Be sure to study any accompanying graphs and charts as an aid to comprehending the concepts. (For more on interpreting graphs and charts, see pp. 291–293.) Continue in this way until you reach the end of the chapter.

Probably the most crucial element in the SQ3R method is the final step, **review.** Do not succumb to the temptation to review the next day. Immediately reviewing the material you have just studied helps you fix the concepts in your mind and retain them better. To review, you should go through the chapter again, noting the main points in each section and studying again any terminology that is either boldfaced or printed in the margins. Also complete any self-quizzes and try to answer the questions for review or for discussion at the end of the chapter (and on the Web site).

**Applying the
SQ3R Method**

To put these theoretical suggestions into practice, reprinted here is a selection from an introductory psychology text. Begin surveying this selection by reading the Prologue, noting the key terms in the right margin, and looking over the sections labeled "Review" and "Check Your Learning." Then continue on with the question, read, recite, and review steps. You may wish to annotate the text with a pencil (not a colored highlighter) as you complete this assignment.

■ A TEXTBOOK SELECTION FOR PRACTICE

Memory

Benjamin B. Lahey
(From Chapter 7, *Psychology: An Introduction,* 8th edition)

PROLOGUE

If we are to benefit from our experiences, we must be able to remember them. If you weren't able to remember anything tomorrow that you read in this chapter today, there would be no point in reading it. Remembering what you learn is as important as learning it in the first place.

Alexander Luria, a prominent Russian physician during the 1930s, was widely known for his research on the brain. One day, a young man (referred to as S) came to his hospital office, complaining that his memory was *too good*. He often recalled experiences in such vivid detail that he could not shake them from his consciousness. They lingered in a distracting, haunting way that impaired his ability to concentrate on his current circumstances. Because the man was clearly distraught, Luria agreed to study his problem.

Over many years, Luria tested S's memory in a number of ways. The best known of these tests involved showing S a sheet of paper containing four columns of a dozen numbers each. After viewing the numbers for a few minutes, S was able to write them out from memory without error. Moreover, without looking at the numbers again, he was able to refer to a mental image of them and tell Luria the numbers in any sequence requested. He could "read" a mental image of the numbers across the rows, down the columns, and across diagonals with apparent ease. Months later, S could still reproduce the table of numbers with few errors. In one series of experiments, he was even able to recall complex verbal material in detail after more than 15 years had elapsed.

Luria was never able to help S, but S himself found a way to make his life more comfortable. After losing many other kinds of jobs, he decided to go on stage as a "memory expert." He was able to astound audiences with his ability to recall information and was able to earn a comfortable living.

Most of us are not troubled by remembering too much—quite the opposite! Most college students would like to be able to remember a lot more every time they take a test. Learning about S might help us feel a little better about our own memories, but most of us would still like to be able to remember more.

This chapter describes the ways in which the human memory works and discusses the reasons that we forget. New information that we learn can be thought of as passing through three stages in the human memory. The first stage holds information for very brief intervals—often less than a second. The next stage retains information longer, but only a little longer—up to about a half a minute. The third stage seems to hold information indefinitely. These three stages of memory operate according to different rules and mostly serve different functions. But because information must pass through each stage to reach the most permanent memory story, they work together as three linked stages in the memory process.

Forgetting appears to occur for different reasons in the three stages of memory. In the first stage, information is lost because it decays quickly over time unless it moves to the next stage. Forgetting in the second stage also occurs because of the simple passage of time unless something is done to protect the information. But memory traces are frequently lost in the second stage because of interference from other memories. For example, if you look up a number in the telephone book, you may forget it if you try to remember what you planned to say.

The third stage of memory is called long-term memory. Information that reaches this stage seems to stay there permanently. Nonetheless, we are often unable to recall information from long-term memory for several reasons. Interference from similar memories is a common reason for being unable to recall long-term memories. In addition, long-term memories tend to change over time, making the information inaccurate. Finally, we are sometimes unable to recall some very unpleasant or threatening memories.

It's not yet known how the memory trace is stored in the brain, but several theories have been proposed. As you will see, our best clues about the biological basis of memory have come from the study of persons with a severe form of memory loss called *amnesia.*

THREE STAGES OF MEMORY: AN INFORMATION-PROCESSING VIEW

In recent years, psychologists have attempted to develop theories of memory using the computer as a model. These *information-processing* theories of memory are based on the apparent similarities between the operation of the human brain and that of the computer. This is not to say that psychologists believe that brains and computers operate in exactly the same way. Clearly they do not, but enough general similarity exists to make the information-processing model useful. Before looking at specific theories, let's look briefly at the general information-processing model and its terminology.

In the information-processing model, information can be followed as it moves through the following operations: input, storage, and retrieval. At each point in the process, a variety of *control mechanisms* (such as attention, storage, and retrieval) operate. Information enters the memory system through the sensory receptors. This is like your entering a term paper into your computer by typing on the keyboard. Attention operates at this level to select information for further processing. The raw sensory information that is selected is then represented—or **encoded**—in a form (sound, visual image, meaning) that can be used in the next stages of memory.

Other control mechanisms might then transfer selected information into a more permanent memory storage, like saving your term paper on a computer disk. When the stored information is needed, it is *retrieved* from memory. Before printing out your paper, you must first locate your file on the disk and retrieve it. Unfortunately, with both computers and human memory, some information may be lost or become irretrievable.

Some information needs to be stored in memory for only brief periods of time, whereas other information must be tucked away permanently. When we look at a cookbook to see how much tomato paste to add to chicken cacciatore, we need to remember that bit of information for only a few seconds. However, we must remember our social security numbers and our siblings' names for our entire lifetimes. The influential **stage theory of memory** (Atkinson & Shiffrin, 1968; Baddeley, 1999) assumes that we humans have a three-stage memory that meets our need to store information for different lengths of time. We seem to have one memory store that holds information for exceedingly brief intervals, a second memory store that holds information for no more than 30 seconds unless it's "renewed," and a third, more permanent memory store. Each of these memories operates according to a different set of rules and serves a somewhat different purpose. Because information must pass through each stage of memory to get to the next, more permanent one, these memory stores are best thought of as three closely linked "stages" of memory, rather than three separate memories. The three stages are known as the sensory register, short-term memory, and long-term memory (see fig. 7.1).

Sensory Register

The first stage of memory—the **sensory register**—is a very brief one, designed to hold an exact image of each sensory experience until it can be fully processed. We apparently retain a copy of each sensory experience in the sensory register long enough to locate and focus on relevant bits of information and transfer them into the next stage of memory. For visual information, this "snapshot" fades very quickly, probably lasting about one-quarter of a second in most cases. For auditory information, a vivid image of what we hear is retained for about the same length of time, one-quarter of a second (Cowan, 1987), but a weaker "echo" is retained for up to 4 seconds (Tarpy & Mayer, 1978).

encode
(en cōd´) To represent information in some form in the memory system.

stage theory of memory
A model of memory based on the idea that we store information in three separate but linked memories.

sensory register
The first stage of memory, in which an exact image of each sensory experience is held briefly until it can be processed.

FIGURE 7.1
Stage model of
memory.

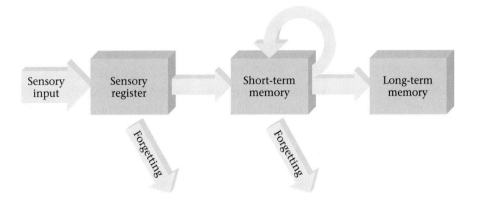

The information stored in the sensory register does not last long, but it's apparently a complete replica of the sensory experience. This fact was demonstrated in an important experiment by George Sperling (1960). Sperling presented research participants with an array of 12 letters in three horizontal rows of four letters each. He showed the participants these letters for ¹⁄₂₀ of a second and then asked them to recall all of the letters in one of the three rows. He did not tell them ahead of time which row he would ask them to recall. Instead, he signaled to them using a tone. A high-pitched tone indicated the first row, a medium tone indicated the second row, and a low tone indicated the third row. If the tone was presented very soon after the presentation of the array of letters, the participants could recall most of the letters in the indicated row. But if the delay was more than one-quarter of a second, the participants recalled an average of just over one letter per row, indicating how quickly information is lost in the sensory register.

Visual information in the sensory register is lost and replaced so rapidly with new information that we seldom are aware we even have such a memory store. Sometimes the longer-lasting, echolike traces of auditory information can be noticed, though. Most of us have had the experience of being absorbed in reading when a friend speaks. If we divert our attention from the book quickly enough, we can "hear again" what was said to us by referring to the echo of the auditory sensation stored in the sensory register.

Short-Term Memory

**short-term
memory (STM)**
The second stage of
memory in which
five to nine bits of
information can be
stored for brief periods of time.

When a bit of information is selected for further processing, it's transferred from the sensory register into **short-term memory**, or **STM**. It's not necessary to intentionally transfer information to STM; generally, just paying attention to the information is enough to transfer it. You might not intentionally try to memorize the price of your dinner, but you will be able to recognize that you were given the wrong amount of change. Once information has been transferred to short-term memory, a variety of control processes may be applied. Rehearsal and chunking are two important examples of these control processes.

Rehearsal in Short-Term Memory: Overcoming STM's Limited Life Span

As the name implies, short-term memory (STM) is good for only temporary storage of information. In general, information is lost from STM in less than half a minute unless it's "renewed," and it is often lost in a few seconds (Ellis & Hunt, 1993). Fortunately, information can be renewed in STM by mental repetition, or **rehearsal**, of the information. When a grocery list is rehearsed regularly in this way, it can be held in STM for relatively long periods of time. If the list is not rehearsed, however, it's soon lost. Rehearsing the information stored in STM has been compared to juggling eggs: The eggs stay in perfect condition as long as you keep juggling them, but as soon as you stop juggling, they are lost.

rehearsal
Mental repetition of information to retain it longer in short-term memory.

Our first reliable estimate of the limited life span of information in STM was provided by an experiment conducted by Lloyd and Margaret Peterson (1959). The participants were shown a single combination of three consonants (such as LRP) and asked to remember it as they counted backward for brief intervals (0 through 19 seconds) and then were asked to recall the letters. As shown in figure 7.2, the participants were able to remember the three consonants less than 20 percent of the time after only 12 seconds has passed. These findings make it clear that memories are impermanent in STM unless kept alive by rehearsal.

The information stored in STM can be of many different types of memories: the smell of a perfume, the notes of a melody, the taste of a fruit, the shape of a nose, the finger positions in a guitar chord, or a list of names. But we humans have a preference for transforming information into sounds, or *acoustic codes,* whenever possible for storage in STM. If I asked you to memorize a list of letters (*B, P, V, R, M, L*), you would most likely memorize them by their "names" (bee, pee, vee, etc.) rather than by the shapes of the letters. We know this because most people say they do it this way and because the errors people make are most likely to be confusions of similar sounds (recalling *zee* instead of *bee*) rather than confusions of similar shapes (recalling *O* instead of *Q*, or *R* instead of *P*) (Reynolds & Flagg, 1983). We probably use acoustic codes in STM as much as possible because it's easier to rehearse by mentally talking to ourselves than by mentally repeating the images of sights, smells, and movements. Nonetheless, STM can store any form of information that can enter the brain through the senses.

Chunking in Short-Term Memory: Overcoming STM's Limited Capacity

Perhaps the most important thing to know about STM is that its storage capacity is quite limited. The exact capacity differs slightly for different kinds of information, but as psychologist George Miller (1956) put it, it's constant enough to call it the *magic number: seven plus or minus (±)*

FIGURE 7.2

Rehearsal. The accuracy of recall for a single group of three consonants declines rapidly when subjects are prevented from rehearsing by being asked to count backward.

Source: R. L. Peterson and M. J. Peterson, "Short Term Retention of Individual Items" in *Journal of Experimental Psychology* 58:193–198, 1959.

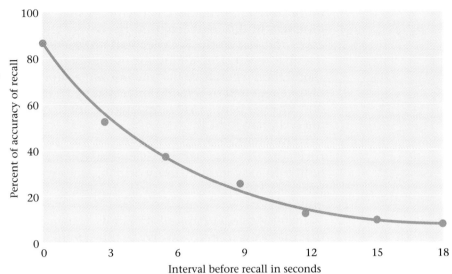

two. Estimates of the span of STM are obtained by asking research participants to memorize simple lists (of randomly ordered numbers, letters, and unrelated words) of different lengths. The length of the list that the participants can recall half the time is considered to represent the capacity of STM (Miller, 1956). Rarely are we able to hold more than five to nine bits of information in STM, regardless of the nature of that information. This is a very limited capacity, indeed.

In addition to temporarily storing information, STM serves another important function, which further limits its already small capacity—it serves as our *working memory* (Baddeley, 1992: 1999). This means that space in STM is used when old memories are temporarily brought out of long-term memory to be used or updated. Space in STM is also used when we think about this information (Morris, 1986). This is why you cannot remember the telephone number of the hardware store, which you just looked up, if you begin thinking about your purchase before you dial—thinking takes up space in STM and forces out the numbers. The fact that thinking uses STM also explains why it is difficult to think about problems that involve more than 7 ± 2 issues. We keep forgetting some of the aspects of complex problems because they exceed the limited capacity of STM. In such situations, writing out all the issues on paper helps keep them straight while you are thinking.

One advantage of the small storage capacity of the STM is that it's easy to "search" through it. When we try to remember something in STM, we apparently examine every item that is stored there. Experiments conducted by Saul Sternberg (1969) confirm that we exhaustively search STM every time we try to recall something. Sternberg's experiments even give us an estimate of how long it takes us to examine each bit of stored information. Participants were asked to memorize lists of numbers of different lengths. They were then shown a number and asked if it was in the list they had just memorized. When individuals had just memorized a long list of numbers, it took them longer to respond than when they had memorized a short list. In fact, the amount of time required to respond increased by a rather constant .04 of a second for each item in STM. Apparently, that's how long it takes to examine each item in STM.

Fortunately, there are some effective ways to get around the limited capacity of STM. One way is to learn the information well enough to transfer it into long-term memory, which, as we will see shortly, has no real space limitation. Another way is to put more information into the 7 ± 2 units of STM.

chunks
Units of memory.

George Miller (1956) calls the units of memory **chunks**. Although it's true that we can hold only five to nine chunks in STM, we can often put more than one bit of information into each chunk. If you were to quickly read the following list of 12 words once,

east	winter
spring	lateral
fall	north
dorsal	ventral
west	summer
medial	south

you probably would not be able to recall it perfectly 10 second later, because 12 chunks normally exceed the capacity of STM. But if you reorganized the words into 3 chunks (points of a compass, seasons, and anatomical directions) and memorized those, you could remember the list quite easily. This strategy would work for you only if you were able to regroup the list into meaningful chunks, however. If you did not know the four anatomical directions, it would do you no good to memorize these terms because you could not generate the four directions when you recalled them.

Other chunking strategies can also be used to expand the amount of information that can be stored in STM. It's no accident that social security numbers (as well as bank account numbers and telephone numbers) are broken up by hyphens. Most people find it easier to remember numbers in chunks (319-555-0151) than as a string of single digits.

In summary, STM is a stage of memory with limited capacity in which information—often stored in acoustic codes—is lost rapidly unless it's rehearsed. The capacity of STM can be expanded by increasing the amount of information in each chunk to be learned. But, no matter how good a job we do of chunking and rehearsing, STM is not a good place to store information for long periods of time. Such information must be transferred to long-term memory for more permanent storage.

Long-Term Memory

**long-term
memory (LTM)**
The third stage of
memory, involving
the storage of infor-
mation that is kept
for long periods of
time.

Long-term memory, or **LTM,** is the storehouse for information that
must be kept for long periods of time. But LTM is not just a more durable
version of STM; the stage model of memory suggest it's a different kind
of memory altogether.

LTM differs form STM in four major ways: (1) the way in which information is recalled, (2) the form in which information is stored in memory, (3) the reasons that forgetting occurs, and (4) the physical location
of these functions in the brain. Let's look at each of these four differences between STM and LTM separately:

1. Because the amount of information stored in LTM is so vast, we cannot scan the entire contents of LTM when we are looking for a bit of
   information, as we do in STM. Instead, LTM has to be *indexed.* We retrieve information from LTM using *cues,* much as we use a call number to locate a book in the library. This retrieval can be an intentional
   act (such as "What was the name of the secretary in Accounts Receiv-
   able?") or an unintentional one, as when hearing a particular song
   brings back memories of a lost love. In either case, only information
   relevant to the cue is retrieved, rather than the entire contents of LTM.

2. LTM differs from STM in the kind of information that is most easily
   stored. You will recall that information is usually stored in STM in
   terms of the physical qualities of the experience (what we saw, did,
   tasted, touched, or heard), with a special emphasis on acoustic codes.
   Although sensory memories can be stored in LTM, information is
   stored in LTM primarily in terms of its meaning, or *semantic codes*
   (Cowan, 1988).

3. LTM also differs from STM in the way forgetting occurs. Unlike STM,
   where information that is not rehearsed or processed appears to drop
   out of the system, information stored in LTM is not just durable but
   actually appears to be permanent. In a dramatic demonstration of
   LTM, Bahrick (1984) tested memory for Spanish using individuals
   who had studied the language in high school 50 years ago. Bahrick's
   participants retained much of their knowledge of Spanish, even after
   a period of 50 years. Not all psychologists agree that memories in LTM
   are permanent, but there is a great deal of evidence supporting this
   view. If memories in LTM are indeed permanent, this means that
   "forgetting" occurs in LTM not because the memory is erased but because we are unable to retrieve it for some reason (Baddelely, 1999).

4. Each stage of memory is handled by a different part of the brain. STM
   is primarily a function of the frontal lobes of the cerebral cortex
   (Buckner & Barch, 1999; Fuster, 1995; William & Goldman-Rakic,
   1995), whereas information that is stored in LTM is first integrated in
   the hippocampus and then transferred to the areas of the cerebral
   cortex involved in language and perception for permanent storage
   (Nadel & Jacobs, 1998).

We will describe these differences in more detail in the final section of this chapter.

Types of Long-Term Memory: Procedural, Episodic, and Semantic

Tulving (1972, 1985, 1987) has proposed the existence of three kinds of long-term memory storage, each with distinctly different properties, and each probably based on different brain mechanisms. I think I can best explain the differences among these kinds of LTM by telling you another one of my stories. Recently, I came across a photograph taken of me on my fourteenth birthday in my home in St. Petersburg, Florida. I was holding my birthday present—my first guitar. I took guitar lessons for a while and played in several mediocre rock bands until my junior year in college. Then I sold my guitar and concentrated on my studies. About 15 years ago, however, I bought another guitar, and playing guitar once again became a part of my life. That's the story; now for the three types of LTM:

1. When I picked up my new guitar in the music store, I found that I could still play the basic chords, even though I had not played them in years. That is a long-term **procedural memory**—memory for skills and other procedures. Memories of how to ride a bicycle, to cook, or to kiss are procedural memories.

2. Although I did not stop to think about it, I also obviously remembered what a guitar was. I knew what it was when I saw it, knew what it was used for, and so on. In other words, I had not forgotten the semantic memory of the meaning of *guitar*. **Semantic memory** is memory for meaning. When you remember what a father is, what pudding is, and what the phrase "peace of mind" means, you are recalling meaning from long-term semantic memory.

3. Until my memory was jogged by finding the old photograph, however, it had been years since I had remembered when and where I had gotten my first guitar. **Episodic memory** is the kind of LTM that stores information about experiences that took place at specific times and in specific places.

The LTM mechanisms are apparently able to store procedural and semantic memories quite effectively, but LTM handles episodic information much less well. I immediately knew what a guitar was (semantic) and how to play it (procedural), but it took a photograph to recall the time and place of getting my first guitar (episodic). A great deal of research has been done to show the greater ability of LTM to store semantic than episodic memories. A clever study of the memorization of sentences by J. D. S. Sachs (1967) clearly illustrates this point. The experimenter had research participants listen to passages containing a number of different sentences. After intervals of different lengths, she asked the individuals to listen to more sentences and tell her whether

procedural memory
Memory for motor movements and skills.

semantic memory
(se-man´tik) Memory for meaning without reference to the time and place of learning.

episodic memory
(epīsod´ik) Memory for specific experiences that can be defined in terms of time and space.

they were exactly the same as one of the sentences in the passage. Some of the test sentences were the same, but some were changed either in physical form or in meaning. For example, an original sentence in the passage such as "Jenny chased Melissa" might be changed to "Melissa was chased by Jenny" (change in physical structure, but not meaning) or to "Melissa chased Jenny" (change in both physical structure and meaning). Sachs found that the participants could tell quite well if a sentence had been changed in either way, as long as the test interval was within the span of STM (about 30 seconds). However, at longer intervals, they were only accurate in detecting changes in meaning. Apparently, the meaning of the sentences (semantic memory) was held in LTM, whereas details about their physical structure (episodic memory) were forgotten when they were lost from STM.

declarative memory
Semantic and episodic memory.

In spite of these apparent differences, some psychologists group semantic memory and episodic memory together under the heading **declarative memory** (see fig. 7.3, p. 496). Semantic and episodic memories are quite different, but they are alike in an important way as well: They are easily described (declared) in words. For example, I would have no difficulty telling you what a guitar is. This is in contrast to *procedural memory,* which can be accessed only through performance—as in when I play a song on my guitar (Squire, 1987). It is difficult, if not impossible, to describe verbally how to play a song on the guitar without playing it. This distinction between procedural and declarative memories will be important to our discussion of amnesia later in the chapter.

Organization in Long-Term Memory

We noted earlier that it's possible to make more efficient use of the limited capacity of STM by organizing information into larger chunks (Miller, 1956). Organization of information is also important for LTM, but it's probably not related to a need to save capacity, because LTM has essentially unlimited capacity. Rather, organization helps to facilitate the retrieval of information from the vast amount stored in LTM. The retrieval task in LTM is vastly different from that in STM: Instead of 7 ± 2 items that can be easily searched, LTM stores such an extensive amount of information that it almost certainly must be *organized* in some fashion. For instance, it's sometimes inconvenient that the 60-odd books in my office are not organized on my bookshelves, but I can still find what I am looking for by searching long enough. It would be impossible, on the other hand, to find the same book in the university library if the books were as unorganized and randomly placed on the shelves as mine. Like LTM, the library needs an organized way of storing and retrieving a huge amount of information.

Evidence for the organization of LTM has been available for some time. When research participants memorize new lists of items that could be categorized, they tend to recall them in related groups. For example, Weston Bousfield (1953) asked individuals to memorize a list of 60 words

FIGURE 7.3
Semantic and epi-
sodic memory are
sometimes grouped
together under the
term *declarative
memory* because
both can be easily
described (declared)
in words. In con-
trast, procedural
memories are dif-
ficult to describe
because they
involve skills that
can be seen only
when performed.

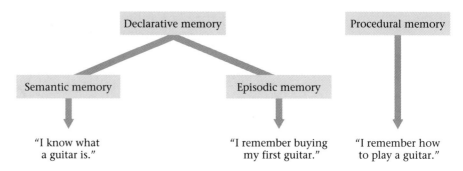

that could be conceptually grouped into four categories: animals, vegetables, names, and professions (*muskrat, blacksmith, panther, baker, wild-
cat, Howard, Jason, printer,* and so on). Even though the words were
presented in random order, participants recalled in categorical group-
ings significantly more often than would be expected by chance. Apparently, the words were stored in LTM according to organized categories.

In addition, there is clear evidence that recall from LTM is better when
we impose more organization on the information that is stored there.
Gordon Bower's Stanford University research group (Bower & Clark,
1969) asked participants to memorize 12 lists of 10 words, such as the
following:

boy	rag
boat	wheel
dog	hat
wagon	house
ghost	milk

Half of the individuals were given the usual instructions to memorize
the lists of words in any order, but the others were asked to "make up
stories" containing all of the words in the list—to organize them into a
single story. For example, the previous list could be memorized as "The
boy with the hat pulled his dog and his boat in his wagon with the
crooked wheel. He saw a rag hanging on a house that he thought was a
ghost. It scared him so much that he spilled his milk." The group that
organized the words into stories recalled an amazing 90 percent of the
words, whereas the other group recalled only 15 percent!

The organization of memory in LTM has been characterized as an *associative network* by some theorists (Ellis & Hunt, 1993; Raaijmakers &
Schiffrin, 1992). According to this view, memories are associated, or
linked together, through experience. Your experience forms links between that special song and memories of your summer vacation, or be-

tween algebra and that unbearable teacher. Researchers have studied the operation of associative networks by asking research participants to answer general knowledge questions. For instance, suppose you were asked to answer the question "Is a canary a bird?" How do you access your store of information to answer correctly? An influential network model known as the *spreading activation model* (Collins and Loftus, 1975) attempts to explain this process. According to Collins and Loftus, we form links between various concepts and their characteristics based on our experience. When we are asked a question, representations of the concepts or characteristics are activated. As shown in figure 7.4, the question would activate separate memory representations of *canary* and *bird*. The model then assumes that this activation spreads out along previously formed links to other representations. In the case of *canary* and *bird,* which are very closely associated for many people, the lines of activation spreading from these representations meet quickly, and a decision can be made. If representations are not as closely associated, it takes a longer time to respond. If you were asked whether or not a penguin is a bird, your answer would probably be slower than in the canary example.

Experimental support for the spreading activation model can be seen in a clever study (Meyer & Schvaneveldt, 1971). Research participants watched while groups of letters were flashed on a computer screen. Some of the letter groups spelled out real words, but others (such as *plame* and *blop*) just looked like words. The participants were asked to respond by hitting a "yes" button when a real word was shown and a "no" button when a made-up "word" was shown. The important part of this study is the time it took them to hit the button each time a real word was shown. The researchers found that the participants' reaction times were much

FIGURE 7.4
An example of the associative links that are hypothesized to exist among bits of information stored in long-term memory in the spreading activation theory.

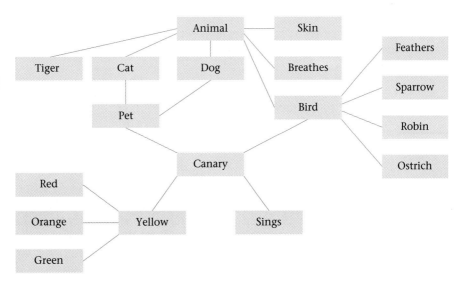

faster for words that had been shown immediately preceded by a related word (*bread-butter*) than by an unrelated word (*nurse-butter*).

What does this mean for the spreading activation model of long-term memory? According to this theory, activation of *bread* would spread along the network to related items, including *butter*. Therefore, *butter* would be partially activated even before the word appeared on the screen, producing a very fast reaction time. Thus, these results support the spreading activation model.

Retrieval of Long-Term Memories

Students are very familiar with the frustration that comes from knowing that you know something but being totally incapable of retrieving it (until, of course, you step outside the exam room!). Research on types of retrieval, on serial learning, and on the tip-of-the-tongue phenomenon provide us with the important insights into the retrieval process in long-term memory.

Three Ways of Testing Retrieval: Recall, Recognition, and Relearning.

Psychologists have distinguished three ways of measuring memory retrieval that differ from one another in important ways. In the **recall method**, you are asked to recall information with few, if any, cues: Whom did George W. Bush defeat for the presidency of the United States in 2000? This is a recall method of assessing your memory for that fact.

In the **recognition method**, you are asked to recognize the correct information from among alternatives. The same question could be asked as a recognition question:

In 2000, George W. Bush defeated _____ for the presidency of the United States.

   a. Bob Dole   c. Pat Buchanan
   b. Al Gore   d. Jimmy Carter

Generally, we can "remember" more when tested by the recognition rather than the recall method, because recognition tasks provide more cues for retrieving information from long-term memory. Our greater ability to recognize rather than to recall remembered information was demonstrated vividly in an experiment on everyday memory to which we can all relate (Bahrick, Bahrick & Wittlinger, 1975). Two years after graduation from high school, college students were found to be able to *recall* an average of 60 percent of the names of the students in their class when looking at their photographs. However, when they were shown their yearbook pictures and asked to *recognize* the corresponding names from a list, they could match names correctly 90 percent of the time.

The **relearning** (or *savings*) **method** is the most sensitive of all three of the methods of evaluating memory. Even when you can neither recall nor recognize information, it may be possible to measure some memory of the

recall method
A measure of memory based on the ability to retrieve information from long-term memory with few cues.

recognition method
A measure of memory based on the ability to select correct information from among the options provided.

relearning method
A measure of memory based on the length of time it takes to relearn forgotten material.

information using the relearning method. In this method, you relearn previously memorized information. If the relearning takes less time than the original learning, then the information has been "remembered" in this sense. For instance, at some point in your life, you probably learned how to find the area of a right triangle. You might be unable to remember how to do that now, but you could relearn the method much faster than it took you to learn it the first time. Your enhanced ability to relearn the technique shows that the memory was never completely "lost."

Serial Learning.   In some types of retrieval tasks, the order in which we memorize a list is as important as the items in the list. It would be useless to memorize the steps in defusing a bomb if you were not able to remember them in the right order! When psychologists have studied memory for serial lists (lists of words, numbers, and the like that must be recalled in a certain order), a surprisingly consistent finding has emerged. The recall of items in the serial lists is often better for items at the *beginning* and *end* of the list than in the middle. This is called the **serial position effect**. Many explanations have been suggested for this effect, but it's perhaps best explained in terms of the differences between short-term and long-term memory. The last items in a list are remembered well because they are still in STM, whereas the first items in a list are remembered well because they can be rehearsed enough times to transfer them firmly into LTM.

serial position effect
The finding that immediate recall of items listed in a fixed order is often better for items at the beginning and end of the list than for those in the middle.

Two experiments provide strong support for this explanation. First, Vito Modigliani and Donald Hedges of Simon Fraser University (1987) have shown that better recall for items at the beginning of lists is indeed related to greater opportunities for rehearsal. In a second experiment on the serial position effect (Glanzer & Cunitz, 1966), research participants attempted to memorize a list of 15 items. As shown in figure 7.5 (p. 500), the serial position effect was clearly found when the individuals were asked to recall the list immediately after learning it. That is, recall was better for items at both the beginning and the end of the list. But when the participants were asked to recall the list after a delay of 30 seconds—just beyond the limits of STM—the serial position effect was only half there. Recall was better at the beginning of the list—presumably because those items were rehearsed more and stored in LTM—but not at the end of the list, probably because the participants could not hold the last items in STM that long. The serial position effect shows that we are simultaneously using both STM and LTM in an attempt to soak up and retain as much of what's going on as possible.

The Tip of the Tongue Phenomenon.   We have all had the maddening experience of trying to recall a fact that we can *almost* remember—it's on the "tip of my tongue." Fortunately, there is a lesson in this on the nature of retrieval from LTM. The tip-of-the-tongue phenomenon was investigated by Harvard University psychologists Roger Brown and David

FIGURE 7.5
When recall of a serial list of 15 items is tested immediately after the presentation of the last item, participants recall the first and last items better than the middle items. But when the test is delayed by 30 seconds, fewer of the last items are recalled, suggesting that at least some of the last items in the list were stored only in short-term memory.

Sources: Data from M. Glanzer and A. R. Cunitz, "Two Storage Mechanisms in Free Recall," *Journal of Verbal Learning and Verbal Behavior,* 5:351–360, 1966 Academic Press; and R. M. Tarpy and R. F. Mayer, *Foundations of Learning & Memory,* © 1978 Scott, Foresman.

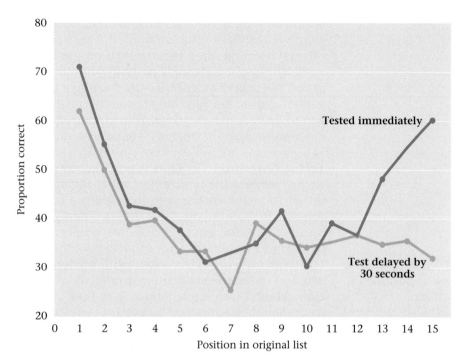

McNeil (1966) by giving definitions of uncommon words to college students and asking them to recall the words. For example, they might be read the definition of *sampan* ("a small boat used in shallow water in Asia that is rowed from behind using a single oar"). Often, the students could recall the word *sampan*. Sometimes, though, they could not quite recall the word, and the researchers were able to create the tip-of-the-tongue sensation in these students. When this happened, the students found that they were able to recall some information about the word ("It starts with *s*" or ("It sounds like *Siam*") or recall something about the thing the word referred to ("It looks a little like a junk"), even when they could not retrieve the word. Then, moments later, the word would pop into memory for some students, proving that it was there all the time but just could not be retrieved for the moment. Studies suggest that about half of the things that we can't remember, but are on the tip of our tongues, are recalled within a minute or so (Schachter, 1999), but you can drive yourself nuts for hours trying to remember the other half!

Levels of Processing: An Alternative to the Stage Model

The model suggesting that there are three separate stages of memory (sensory register, STM, and LTM) has been enormously helpful in making

levels of processing model
An alternative to the stage theory of memory stating that the distinction between short-term and long-term memory is a matter of degree rather than different kinds of memory and is based on how incoming information is processed.

sense of the complex phenomenon of memory. Fergus Craik and Robert Lockhart (1972) have proposed an alternative **levels of processing model**, however, suggesting that the distinction between short-term and long-term memory is a matter of *degree* rather than separate stages. In brief, Craik and Lockhart believe that there is only one memory store beyond the sensory register. The durability of stored information depends on how well it is processed as it is being encoded for memory. Information will be kept only briefly if it's processed at a *shallow* level, but it will be kept much longer if it's processed at a *deeper* level. Thus, the differences that we have just examined between STM and LTM are not, in this view, differences between two different memory systems operating according to different principles. Rather, these differences are the results of different levels of processing during the encoding process. Furthermore, according to Craik and Lockhart, there is a continuum of levels of processing, ranging from very shallow to very deep, rather than just two types of storage (short and long).

What is the difference between deep and shallow processing? One way of putting it is to say that shallow processing involves the encoding of superficial perceptual information, whereas deep processing encodes meaning (Ellis, 1987). Consider the following list of adjectives:

soft

swift

warm

sharp

witty

bright

clean

beautiful

If you were to ask 10 acquaintances to process this list in a superficial way ("Look at each word for 5 seconds; then circle the adjectives containing the letter *i*") and ask 10 other acquaintances to process it in a deep way ("Look at each word for 5 seconds; then circle the adjectives that describe you"), which group do you think would remember more of the words, if, without warning, you asked them to recall the list 10 minutes later? Craik and Lockhart's levels of processing view correctly predicts that the individuals who processed the words deeply by thinking about their meanings (the second group) will recall more of the words—not because they had stored the words in a different memory (LTM vs. STM) but because information processed more deeply is stored more permanently.

elaboration
(e-lab-or-rā´shun)
The process of creating associations between a new memory and existing memories.

Deep processing also involves greater *elaboration* of memories during the encoding phase than does shallow processing. **Elaboration**, in this sense, means creating more associations between the new memory and existing memories (Ellis, 1987; Ellis & Hunt, 1993). For example, if you read a paragraph in a textbook and spend a few minutes relating its contents to what you had learned in the previous chapters or to your own life, you are elaborating the memory—linking it to existing memories. We have already seen how the associative network model assumes that these links are vital to your ability to use stored information. Therefore, deeply processing the new information in this way will improve your memory of the paragraph and your ability to use the information later. In contrast, simply going through the motions of rereading a paragraph several times without really thinking about it is a much less successful study technique. What is also interesting about this view of deep processing is that even superficial perceptual information can be richly elaborated, such as by relating a new telephone number to existing memories about the person you are calling. Many studies suggest that one of the best ways to promote the elaboration of new memories to improve their later recall is to relate the new information to *yourself* (Symons & Johnson, 1997). Because your perceptions of yourself are well-elaborated and accessible in memory, linking new information to yourself is an excellent way to improve memory through deep processing. The next time you read a textbook (from English literature to physics), try relating every new fact or concept to yourself in some way—it should improve your memory for that information later (Symons & Johnson, 1997).

The levels of processing view probably will not replace the STM/LTM stage model. This is not to say that the levels of processing view of memory is unimportant, however. It is a useful reminder to us that information that is learned in a shallow, rote manner will not be around in our memories very long. If you want to retain information for a long time and have the ability to retrieve it easily, you need to take the time and effort to understand and elaborate the information as you learn it.

Review

We can think of human memory as being composed of three different, but related stages of memory. The sensory register holds a replica of the visual, auditory, or other sensory input for a very brief interval while relevant information is selected for further processing. Short-term memory holds information, generally as acoustic codes, for about a half minute unless it's renewed through rehearsal. The capacity of short-term memory is quite limited unless information is organized into larger chunks. Long-term memory stores information primarily in terms of its meaning, or semantic codes. Its capacity is very large, and memories stored there seem to be permanent. The store of information in LTM is so vast that it must be organized to facilitate retrieval of information. Current theories suggest that the organization is primarily in terms of categories of meaning or associative networks.

The division of memory into a distinct STM and LTM has been questioned by some theorists, however. They suggest, instead, that the duration that information can be held in memory depends on the *depth* at which it's processed, not the *stage* of memory in which it's held. Information that is processed deeply—more richly elaborated—during the encoding process is stored more permanently than information that is processed in a shallow way.

Check Your Learning

To be sure that you have learned the key points from the preceding section, try to answer each question. If you give an incorrect answer to any question, return to the page given next to the correct answer to see why your answer was not correct. Remember that these questions cover only some of the important information in this section; it is important that you make up your own questions to check your learning of other facts and concepts.

1. The _____ assumes that we humans have a three-stage memory, which meets our need to store information for different lengths of time.
   a) lateral processing theory of memory
   c) psychoanalytic theory of memory
   b) stage theory of memory
   d) progression theory of memory

2. The first stage of memory is the _____, which holds an exact image of each sensory experience for a very brief time until it can be fully processed.
   a) short-term memory
   c) sensory register
   b) primary store
   d) initial memory store

3. The _____ is used to store information temporarily and to think while holding information in "working memory."
   a) short-term memory
   c) sensory memory
   b) long-term memory
   d) primary store

4. Long-term memory is similar to short-term memory in terms of the way in which information is recalled, the reason forgetting occurs, and the form in which information is usually stored.
   a) true
   b) false

5. The _____ is a memory model suggesting that the distinction between short-term and long-term memory is a matter of degree rather than separate stages.

Thinking Critically about Psychology

1. Episodic memories are less durable than semantic memories in long-term memory. This is sometimes inconvenient, but is it also advantageous in some ways?

2. Can you think of some episodic memories that have stayed especially clear through the years? What is it about those events that has caused them to be so durable?

Additional Questions

1. Turn to Figure 7.2 (p. 491) and study the text in the second full paragraph on p. 490. What do the numbers along the vertical line (or axis) represent? <u>They represent the percentage of items accurately recalled.</u>

2. What do the numbers along the horizontal axis of the line graph represent? <u>They represent the number of seconds that elapsed before the consonants were remembered.</u>

3. Summarize what this graph depicts. <u>The graph depicts the decline in accuracy when subjects were asked to remember three consonants without rehearsing them. Their accuracy of recall declined rapidly as the seconds went by.</u>

4. What did the researchers do to ensure that the subjects did not cheat and rehearse the three consonants they were learning? <u>The subjects were asked to count backward by threes. It's virtually impossible to try to remember anything while performing this task.</u>

5. What conclusion can we draw about short-term memory from this graph? <u>Short-term memory is truly short term. It does not allow us to remember information unless we rehearse it (by reviewing it a few times).</u>

6. Now look at Figure 7.3 (p. 496) and study the diagram. Supply another example from your own experience for *semantic memory, episodic memory,* and *procedural memory.* <u>Answers will vary.</u>

7

Reading Short Stories

OUTLINE

Literature, Aristotle wrote, serves to delight and to instruct. The four short stories in Part 7 provide you with an opportunity to round out your reading experience, to give you pleasure, and to enhance your understanding of the human experience. Each story is followed by some general questions for discussion and analysis. However, they are by no means meant to exhaust the possibilities. Here are some general questions on plot, character, and theme that you can ask yourself after you read each story.

■ QUESTIONS ABOUT PLOT

1. How are the incidents that make up the plot related to each other? Is there a cause–effect relationship implied?
2. What is the conflict in the story? Who or what is responsible for it?
3. Is the conflict resolved, and if it is, is it resolved satisfactorily?
4. Do the events in the story suggest an additional interpretation, one that perhaps the reader can see but that the characters cannot?

■ QUESTIONS ABOUT CHARACTER

1. How is each character defined in terms of his or her "essence" (or main trait), behavior, and motivation?
2. How are the characters revealed to us—through direct comment by the narrator, through interaction with other characters, through their own words, or through their behavior?
3. Why do the characters act as they do? Are their actions consistent with what has been revealed about them?
4. What is your response to each character?
5. Does any character stand for something greater than the individual?

■ QUESTIONS ABOUT THEME

1. What is the theme, and how is it embodied in the story?
2. What do we learn about human existence, human behavior, and human nature from the story?

◾ FOUR STORIES FOR PRACTICE

Selection 1	## How Much Land Does a Man Need?

Leo Tolstoy

Count Leo Tolstoy (1828–1910) remains one of the most important figures in literature. He wrote two of the greatest novels in Western literature, War and Peace *(1869) and* Anna Karenina *(1877). Although he was a member of the Russian landowning class, he was always troubled by his position as a landowner; in his later years, he renounced all physical comforts and embarked on a new philosophy based on a simplified form of Christianity. (The reference on the next page to Pahóm's lying on top of the stove is puzzling to a non-Russian. Russian stoves, which resembled beehives, were the center of the main living area, and several people could sit or lie on them to enjoy their warmth.)*

1

An elder sister came to visit her younger sister in the country. The elder was married to a tradesman in town, the younger to a peasant in the village. As the sisters sat over their tea talking, the elder began to boast of the advantages of town life: saying how comfortably they lived there, how well they dressed, what fine clothes her children wore, what good things they ate and drank, and how she went to the theatre, promenades, and entertainments.

The younger sister was piqued, and in turn disparaged the life of a tradesman, and stood up for that of a peasant.

"I would not change my way of life for yours," said she. "We may live roughly, but at least we are free from anxiety. You live in better style than we do, but though you often earn more than you need, you are very likely to lose all you have. You know the proverb, 'Loss and gain are brothers twain.' It often happens that people who are wealthy one day are begging their bread the next. Our way is safer. Though a peasant's life is not a fat one, it is a long one. We shall never grow rich, but we shall always have enough to eat."

The elder sister said sneeringly:

"Enough? Yes, if you like to share with the pigs and the calves! What do you know of elegance or manners! However much your goodman may slave, you will die as you are living—on a dung heap—and your children the same."

"Well, what of that?" replied the younger. "Of course our work is rough and coarse. But, on the other hand, it is sure, and we need not bow down to anyone. But you, in your towns, are surrounded by temptations; to-day all may be right, but to-morrow the Evil One may tempt your husband with cards, wine, or women, and all will go to ruin. Don't such things happen often enough?"

Pahóm, the master of the house, was lying on the top of the stove and he listened to the women's chatter.

"It is perfectly true," thought he. "Busy as we are from childhood tilling mother earth, we peasants have no time to let any nonsense settle in our heads. Our only trouble is that we haven't land enough. If I had plenty of land, I shouldn't fear the Devil himself!"

The women finished their tea, chatted a while about dress, and then cleared away the tea-things and lay down to sleep.

But the Devil had been sitting behind the stove, and had heard all that was said. He was pleased that the peasant's wife had led her husband into boasting, and that he had said that if he had plenty of land he would not fear the Devil himself.

"All right," thought the Devil. "We will have a tussle. I'll give you land enough; and by means of that land I will get you into my power."

2

Close to the village there lived a lady, small landowner who had an estate of about three hundred acres.[1] She had always lived on good terms with the peasants until she engaged as her steward an old soldier, who took to burdening the people with fines. However careful Pahóm tried to be, it happened again and again that now a horse of his got among the lady's oats, now a cow strayed into her garden, now his calves found their way into her meadows—and he always had to pay a fine.

Pahóm paid up, but grumbled and, going home in a temper, was rough with his family. All through that summer, Pahóm had much trouble because of this steward, and he was even glad when winter came and the cattle had to be stabled. Though he grudged the fodder when they could no longer graze on the pasture-land, at least he was free from anxiety about them.

In the winter the news got about that the lady was going to sell her land and that the keeper of the inn on the high road was bargaining for it. When the peasants heard this they were very much alarmed.

"Well," thought they, "if the innkeeper gets the land, he will worry us with fines worse than the lady's steward. We all depend on that estate."

So the peasants went on behalf of their Commune, and asked the lady not to sell the land to the innkeeper, offering her a better price for it themselves. The lady agreed to let them have it. Then the peasants tried to arrange for the Commune to buy the whole estate, so that it might be held by them all in common. They met twice to discuss it, but could not settle the matter; the Evil One sowed discord among them and they could not agree. So they decided to buy the land individually, each according to his means; and the lady agreed to this plan as she had to the other.

---

[1] 120 desyatíns. The desyatína is properly 2.7 acres; but in this story round numbers are used.

Presently Pahóm heard that a neighbor of his was buying fifty acres, and that the lady had consented to accept one half in cash and to wait a year for the other half. Pahóm felt envious.

"Look at that," thought he, "the land is all being sold, and I shall get none of it." So he spoke to his wife.

"Other people are buying," said he, "and we must also buy twenty acres or so. Life is becoming impossible. That steward is simply crushing us with his fines."

So they put their heads together and considered how they could manage to buy it. They had one hundred rúbles laid by. They sold a colt and one half of their bees, hired out one of their sons as a laborer and took his wages in advance; borrowed the rest from a brother-in-law, and so scraped together half the purchase money.

Having done this, Pahóm chose out a farm of forty acres, some of it wooded, and went to the lady to bargain for it. They came to an agreement, and he shook hands with her upon it and paid her a deposit in advance. Then they went to town and signed the deeds; he paying half the price down, and undertaking to pay the remainder within two years.

So now Pahóm had land of his own. He borrowed seed, and sowed it on the land he had bought. The harvest was a good one, and within a year he had managed to pay off his debts both to the lady and to his brother-in-law. So he became a landowner, ploughing and sowing his own land, making hay on his own land, cutting his own trees, and feeding his cattle on his own pasture. When he went out to plough his fields, or to look at his growing corn, or at his grass-meadows, his heart would fill with joy. The grass that grew and the flowers that bloomed there seemed to him unlike any that grew elsewhere. Formerly, when he had passed by that land, it had appeared the same as any other land, but now it seemed quite different.

3

So Pahóm was well-contented, and everything would have been right if the neighboring peasants would only not have trespassed on his corn-fields and meadows. He appealed to them most civilly, but they still went on: now the Communal herdsmen would let the village cows stray into his meadows, then horses from the night pasture would get among his corn. Pahóm turned them out again and again, and forgave their owners, and for a long time he forbore to prosecute any one. But at last he lost patience and complained to the District Court. He knew it was the peasants' want of land, and no evil intent on their part, that caused the trouble, but he thought:

"I cannot go on overlooking it or they will destroy all I have. They must be taught a lesson."

So he had them up, gave them one lesson, and then another: and two or three of the peasants were fined. After a time Pahóm's neighbors began to bear him a grudge for this, and would now and then let their cattle on to his land on purpose. One peasant even got into Pahóm's wood at night and cut down five young lime trees for their bark. Pahóm passing through the wood one day noticed something white. He came nearer and saw the stripped trunks lying on the ground, and close by stood the stumps where the trees had been. Pahóm was furious.

"If he had only cut one here and there it would have been bad enough," thought Pahóm, "but the rascal has actually cut down a whole clump. If I could only find out who did this, I would pay him out."

He racked his brain as to who it could be. Finally he decided: "It must be Simon—no one else could have done it." So he went to Simon's homestead to have a look round, but he found nothing, and only had an angry scene. However, he now felt more certain than ever that Simon had done it, and he lodged a complaint. Simon was summoned. The case was tried, and retried, and at the end of it all Simon was acquitted, there being no evidence against him. Pahóm felt still more aggrieved, and let his anger loose upon the Elder and the Judges.

"You let thieves grease your palms," said he. "If you were honest folk yourselves you would not let a thief go free."

So Pahóm quarrelled with the Judges and with his neighbors. Threats to burn his building began to be uttered. So though Pahóm had more land, his place in the Commune was much worse than before.

About this time a rumor got about that many people were moving to new parts.

"There's no need for me to leave my land," thought Pahóm. "But some of the others might leave our village and then there would be more room for us. I would take over their land myself and make my estate a bit bigger. I could then live more at ease. As it is, I am still too cramped to be comfortable."

One day Pahóm was sitting at home when a peasant, passing through the village, happened to call in. He was allowed to stay the night, and supper was given him. Pahóm had a talk with this peasant and asked him where he came from. The stranger answered that he came from beyond the Vólga, where he had been working. One word led to another, and the man went on to say that many people were settling in those parts. He told how some people from his village had settled there. They had joined the Commune, and had had twenty-five acres per man granted them. The land was so good, he said, that the rye sown on it grew as high as a horse, and so thick that five cuts of a sickle made a sheaf. One peasant, he said, had brought nothing with him but his bare hands, and now he had six horses and two cows of his own.

Pahóm's heart kindled with desire. He thought:

"Why should I suffer in this narrow hole, if one can live so well elsewhere? I will sell my land and my homestead here, and with the money I will start afresh over there and get everything new. In this crowded place one is always having trouble. But I must first go and find out all about it myself."

Towards summer he got ready and started. He went down the Vólga on a steamer to Samára, then walked another three hundred miles on foot, and at last reached the place. It was just as the stranger had said. The peasants had plenty of land: every man had twenty-five acres of Communal land given him for his use, and any one who had money could buy, besides, at a rúble an acre as much good freehold land as he wanted.

Having found out all he wished to know, Pahóm returned home as autumn came on, and began selling off his belongings. He sold his land at a profit, sold his homestead and all his cattle, and withdrew from membership in the Commune. He only waited till the spring, and then started with his family for the new settlement.

4

As soon as Pahóm and his family reached their new abode, he applied for admission into the Commune of a large village. He stood treat to the Elders and obtained the necessary documents. Five shares of Communal land were given him for his own and his sons' use: that is to say 125 acres (not all together, but in different fields) besides the use of the Communal pasture. Pahóm put up the buildings he needed, and bought cattle. Of the Communal land alone he had three times as much as at his former home, and the land was good corn-land. He was ten times better off than he had been. He had plenty of arable land and pasturage, and could keep as many head of cattle as he liked.

At first, in the bustle of building and settling down, Pahóm was pleased with it all, but when he got used to it he began to think that even here he had not enough land. The first year, he sowed wheat on his share of the Communal land and had a good crop. He wanted to go on sowing wheat, but had not enough Communal land for the purpose, and what he had already used was not available; for in those parts wheat is only sown on virgin soil or on fallow land. It is sown for one or two years, and then the land lies fallow till it is again overgrown with prairie grass. There were many who wanted such land and there was not enough for all; so that people quarreled about it. Those who were better off wanted it for growing wheat, and those who were poor wanted it to let to dealers, so that they might raise money to pay their taxes. Pahóm wanted to sow more wheat, so he rented land from a dealer for a year. He sowed much wheat and had a fine crop, but the land was too far from the village—the wheat had to be carted more than ten miles. After a time Pahóm noticed that some peasant-dealers were living on separate farms and were growing wealthy; and he thought:

"If I were to buy some freehold land and have a homestead on it, it would be a different thing altogether. Then it would all be nice and compact."

The question of buying freehold land recurred to him again and again.

He went on in the same way for three years, renting land and sow-ing wheat. The seasons turned out well and the crops were good, so that he began to lay money by. He might have gone on living contentedly, but he grew tired of having to rent other people's land every year, and having to scramble for it. Wherever there was good land to be had, the peasants would rush for it and it was taken up at once, so that unless you were sharp about it you got none. It happened in the third year that he and a dealer together rented a piece of pasture-land from some peas-ants; and they had already ploughed it up, when there was some dis-pute and the peasants went to law about it, and things fell out so that the labor was all lost.

"If it were my own land," thought Pahóm, "I should be indepen-dent, and there would not be all this unpleasantness."

So Pahóm began looking out for land which he could buy; and he came across a peasant who had bought thirteen hundred acres, but hav-ing got into difficulties was willing to sell again cheap. Pahóm bargained and haggled with him, and at last they settled the price at 1,500 rúbles, part in cash and part to be paid later. They had all but clinched the mat-ter when a passing dealer happened to stop at Pahóm's one day to get a feed for his horses. He drank tea with Pahóm and they had a talk. The dealer said that he was just returning from the land of the Bashkírs, far away, where he had bought thirteen thousand acres of land, all for 1,000 rúbles. Pahóm questioned him further, and the tradesman said:

"All one needs do is to make friends with the chiefs. I gave away about one hundred rúbles' worth of silk robes and carpets, besides a case of tea, and I gave wine to those who would drink it; and I got the land for less than a penny an acre."[2] And he showed Pahóm the title-deeds, saying:

"The land lies near a river, and the whole prairie is virgin soil."

Pahóm plied him with questions, and the tradesman said:

"There is more land there than you could cover if you walked a year, and it all belongs to the Bashkírs. They are as simple as sheep, and land can be got almost for nothing."

"There now," thought Pahóm, "with my one thousand rúbles, why should I get only thirteen hundred acres, and saddle myself with a debt besides? If I take it out there, I can get more than ten times as much for the money."

5

Pahóm inquired how to get to the place, and as soon as the tradesman had left him, he prepared to go there himself. He left his wife to look after the homestead, and started on his journey taking his man with him. They stopped at a town on their way and bought a case of tea, some wine, and other presents, as the tradesman had advised. On and on they

---

[2]Five kopéks for a desyatína.

went until they had gone more than three hundred miles, and on the seventh day they came to a place where the Bashkírs had pitched their tents. It was all just as the tradesman had said. The people lived on the steppes, by a river, in felt-covered tents.[3] They neither tilled the ground, nor ate bread. Their cattle and horses grazed in herds on the steppe. The colts were tethered behind the tents, and the mares were driven to them twice a day. The mares were milked, and from the milk kumiss[4] was made. It was the women who prepared kumiss, and they also made cheese. As far as the men were concerned, drinking kumiss and tea, eating mutton, and playing on their pipes, was all they cared about. They were all stout and merry, and all the summer long they never thought of doing any work. They were quite ignorant, and knew no Russian, but were good-natured enough.

As soon as they saw Pahóm, they came out of their tents and gathered round their visitor. An interpreter was found, and Pahóm told them he had come about some land. The Bashkírs seemed very glad; they took Pahóm and led him into one of the best tents, where they made him sit on some down cushions placed on a carpet, while they sat round him. They gave him some tea and kumiss, and had a sheep killed, and gave him mutton to eat. Pahóm took presents out of his cart and distributed them among the Bashkírs, and divided the tea amongst them. The Bashkírs were delighted. They talked a great deal among themselves, and then told the interpreter to translate.

"They wish to tell you," said the interpreter, "that they like you, and that it is our custom to do all we can to please a guest and to repay him for his gifts. You have given us presents, now tell us which of the things we possess please you best, that we may present them to you."

"What pleases me best here," answered Pahóm, "is your land. Our land is crowded and the soil is exhausted; but you have plenty of land and it is good land. I never saw the like of it."

The interpreter translated. The Bashkírs talked among themselves for a while. Pahóm could not understand what they were saying, but saw that they were much amused and that they shouted and laughed. Then they were silent and looked at Pahóm while the interpreter said:

"They wish me to tell you that in return for your presents they will gladly give you as much land as you want. You have only to point it out with your hand and it is yours."

The Bashkírs talked again for a while and began to dispute. Pahóm asked what they were disputing about, and the interpreter told him that some of them thought they ought to ask their Chief about the land and not act in his absence, while others thought there was no need to wait for his return.

---

[3]A kibítka is a movable dwelling, made up of detachable wooden frames, forming a round, and covered over with felt.
[4]Fermented mare's milk.

6

While the Bashkírs were disputing, a man in a large fox-fur cap appeared on the scene. They all became silent and rose to their feet. The interpreter said, "This is our Chief himself."

Pahóm immediately fetched the best dressing-gown and five pounds of tea, and offered these to the Chief. The Chief accepted them, and seated himself in the place of honor. The Bashkírs at once began telling him something. The Chief listened for a while, then made a sign with his head for them to be silent, and addressing himself to Pahóm, said in Russian:

"Well, let it be so. Choose whatever piece of land you like; we have plenty of it."

"How can I take as much as I like?" thought Pahóm. "I must get a deed to make it secure, or else they may say, 'It is yours,' and afterwards may take it away again."

"Thank you for your kind words," he said aloud. "You have much land, and I only want a little. But I should like to be sure which bit is mine. Could it not be measured and made over to me? Life and death are in God's hands. You good people give it to me, but your children might wish to take it away again."

"You are quite right," said the Chief. "We will make it over to you."

"I heard that a dealer had been here," continued Pahóm, "and that you gave him a little land, too, and signed title-deeds to that effect. I should like to have it done in the same way."

The Chief understood.

"Yes," replied he, "that can be done quite easily. We have a scribe, and we will go to town with you and have the deed properly sealed."

"And what will be the price?" asked Pahóm.

"Our price is always the same: one thousand rúbles a day."

Pahóm did not understand.

"A day? What measure is that? How many acres would that be?"

"We do not know how to reckon it out," said the Chief. "We sell it by the day. As much as you can go round on your feet in a day is yours, and the price is one thousand rúbles a day."

Pahóm was surprised.

"But in a day you can get round a large tract of land," he said.

The Chief laughed.

"It will all be yours!" said he. "But there is one condition: If you don't return on the same day to the spot whence you started, your money is lost."

"But how am I to mark the way that I have gone?"

"Why, we shall go to any spot you like, and stay there. You must start from that spot and make your round, taking a spade with you. Wherever you think necessary, make a mark. At every turning, dig a hole and pile up the turf; then afterwards we will go around with a plough from hole to hole. You may make as large a circuit as you please, but before the sun sets you must return to the place you started from. All the land you cover will be yours."

Pahóm was delighted. It was decided to start early next morning. They talked a while, and after drinking some more kumiss and eating some more mutton, they had tea again, and then the night came on. They gave Pahóm a feather-bed to sleep on, and the Bashkírs dispersed for the night, promising to assemble the next morning at daybreak and ride out before sunrise to the appointed spot.

7

Pahóm lay on the feather-bed, but could not sleep. He kept thinking about the land.

"What a large tract I will mark off!" thought he. "I can easily do thirty-five miles in a day. The days are long now, and within a circuit of thirty-five miles what a lot of land there will be! I will sell the poorer land, or let it to peasants, but I'll pick out the best and farm it. I will buy two oxteams, and hire two more laborers. About a hundred and fifty acres shall be ploughland, and I will pasture cattle on the rest."

Pahóm lay awake all night, and dozed off only just before dawn. Hardly were his eyes closed when he had a dream. He thought he was lying in that same tent and heard somebody chuckling outside. He wondered who it could be, and rose and went out, and he saw the Bashkír Chief sitting in front of the tent holding his sides and rolling about with laughter. Going nearer to the Chief, Pahóm asked: "What are you laughing at?" But he saw that it was no longer the Chief, but the dealer who had recently stopped at his house and had told him about the land. Just as Pahóm was going to ask, "Have you been here long?" he saw that it was not the dealer, but the peasant who had come up from the Vólga, long ago, to Pahóm's old home. Then he saw that it was not the peasant either, but the Devil himself with hoofs and horns, sitting there and chuckling, and before him lay a man barefoot, prostrate on the ground, with only trousers and a shirt on. And Pahóm dreamt that he looked more attentively to see what sort of a man it was that was lying there, and he saw that the man was dead, and that it was himself! He awoke horror-struck.

"What things one does dream," thought he.

Looking round he saw through the open door that the dawn was breaking.

"It's time to wake them up," thought he. "We ought to be starting."

He got up, roused his man (who was sleeping in his cart), bade him harness; and went to call the Bashkírs.

"It's time to go to the steppe to measure the land," he said.

The Bashkírs rose and assembled, and the Chief came too. Then they began drinking kumiss again, and offered Pahóm some tea, but he would not wait.

"If we are to go, let us go. It is high time," said he.

8

The Bashkírs got ready and they all started: some mounted on horses, and some in carts. Pahóm drove in his own small cart with his servant and took a spade with him. When they reached the steppe, the morning red was beginning to kindle. They ascended a hillock (called by the Bashkírs a *shikhan*) and dismounting from their carts and their horses, gathered in one spot. The Chief came up to Pahóm and stretching out his arm towards the plain:

"See," said he, "all this, as far as your eye can reach is ours. You may have any part of it you like."

Pahóm's eyes glistened: it was all virgin soil, as flat as the palm of your hand, as black as the seed of a poppy, and in the hollows different kinds of grasses grew breast high.

The Chief took off his fox-fur cap, placed it on the ground and said:

"This will be the mark. Start from here, and return here again. All the land you go round shall be yours."

Pahóm took out his money and put it on the cap. Then he took off his outer coat, remaining in his sleeveless under-coat. He unfastened his girdle and tied it tight below his stomach, put a little bag of bread into the breast of his coat, and tying a flask of water to his girdle, he drew up the tops of his boots, took the spade from his man, and stood ready to start. He considered for some moments which way he had better go—it was tempting everywhere.

"No matter," he concluded, "I will go towards the rising sun."

He turned his face to the east, stretched himself, and waited for the sun to appear above the rim.

"I must lose no time," he thought, "and it is easier walking while it is still cool."

The sun's rays had hardly flashed above the horizon, before Pahóm, carrying the spade over his shoulder, went down into the steppe.

Pahóm started walking neither slowly nor quickly. After having gone a thousand yards he stopped, dug a hole, and placed pieces of turf one on another to make it more visible. Then he went on; and now that he had walked off his stiffness he quickened his pace. After a while he dug another hole.

Pahóm looked back. The hillock could be distinctly seen in the sunlight, with the people on it, and the glittering tires of the cart-wheels. At a rough guess Pahóm concluded that he had walked three miles. It was growing warmer; he took off his under-coat, flung it across his shoulder, and went on again. It had grown quite warm now; he looked at the sun, it was time to think of breakfast.

"The first shift is done, but there are four in a day, and it is too soon yet to turn. But I will just take off my boots," said he to himself.

He sat down, took off his boots, stuck them into his girdle, and went on. It was easy walking now.

"I will go on for another three miles," thought he, "and then turn to the left. This spot is so fine, that it would be a pity to lose it. The further one goes, the better the land seems."

He went straight on for a while, and when he looked round, the hillock was scarcely visible and the people on it looked like black ants, and he could just see something glistening there in the sun.

"Ah," thought Pahóm, "I have gone far enough in this direction, it is time to turn. Besides I am in a regular sweat, and very thirsty."

He stopped, dug a large hole, and heaped up pieces of turf. Next he untied his flask, had a drink, and then turned sharply to the left. He went on and on; the grass was high, and it was very hot.

Pahóm began to grow tired: he looked at the sun and saw that it was noon.

"Well," he thought, "I must have a rest."

He sat down, and ate some bread and drank some water; but he did not lie down, thinking that if he did he might fall asleep. After sitting a little while, he went on again. At first he walked easily: the food had strengthened him; but it had become terribly hot and he felt sleepy, still he went on, thinking: "An hour to suffer, a life-time to live."

He went a long way in this direction also, and was about to turn to the left again, when he perceived a damp hollow: "It would be a pity to leave that out," he thought. "Flax would do well there." So he went on past the hollow, and dug a hole on the other side of it before he turned the corner. Pahóm looked towards the hillock. The heat made the air hazy: it seemed to be quivering, and through the haze the people on the hillock could scarcely be seen.

"Ah!" thought Pahóm, "I have made the sides too long; I must make this one shorter." And he went along the third side, stepping faster. He looked at the sun: it was nearly half-way to the horizon, and he had not yet done two miles of the third side of the square. He was still ten miles from the goal.

"No," he thought, "though it will make my land lop-sided, I must hurry back in a straight line now. I might go too far, and as it is I have a great deal of land."

So Pahóm hurriedly dug a hole, and turned straight towards the hillock.

9

Pahóm went straight towards the hillock, but he now walked with difficulty. He was done up with the heat, his bare feet were cut and bruised, and his legs began to fail. He longed to rest, but it was impossible if he meant to get back before sunset. The sun waits for no man, and it was sinking lower and lower.

"Oh dear," he thought, "if only I have not blundered trying for too much! What if I am too late?"

He looked towards the hillock and at the sun. He was still far from his goal, and the sun was already near the rim.

Pahóm walked on and on; it was very hard walking but he went quicker and quicker. He pressed on, but was still far from the place. He began running, threw away his coat, his boots, his flask, and his cap, and kept only the spade which he used as a support.

"What shall I do," he thought again. "I have grasped too much and ruined the whole affair. I can't get there before the sun sets."

And this fear made him still more breathless. Pahóm went on running, his soaking shirt and trousers stuck to him and his mouth was parched. His breast was working like a blacksmith's bellows, his heart was beating like a hammer, and his legs were giving way as if they did not belong to him. Pahóm was seized with terror lest he should die of the strain.

Though afraid of death, he could not stop. "After having run all that way they will call me a fool if I stop now," thought he. And he ran on and on, and drew near and heard the Bashkírs yelling and shouting to him, and their cries inflamed his heart still more. He gathered his last strength and ran on.

The sun was close to the rim, and cloaked in mist looked large, and red as blood. Now, yes now, it was about to set! The sun was quite low, but he was also quite near his aim. Pahóm could already see the people on the hillock waving their arms to hurry him up. He could see the fox-fur cap on the ground and the money on it, and the Chief sitting on the ground holding his sides. And Pahóm remembered his dream.

"There is plenty of land," thought he, "but will God let me live on it? I have lost my life, I have lost my life! I shall never reach that spot!"

Pahóm looked at the sun, which had reached the earth: one side of it had already disappeared. With all his remaining strength he rushed on, bending his body forward so that his legs could hardly follow fast enough to keep him from falling. Just as he reached the hillock it suddenly grew dark. He looked up—the sun had already set! He gave a cry: "All my labor has been in vain," thought he, and was about to stop, but he heard the Bashkírs still shouting, and remembered that though to him, from below, the sun seemed to have set, they on the hillock could still see it. He took a long breath and ran up the hillock. It was still light there. He reached the top and saw the cap. Before it sat the Chief laughing and holding his sides. Again Pahóm remembered his dream, and he uttered a cry: his legs gave way beneath him, he fell forward and reached the cap with his hands.

"Ah, that's a fine fellow!" exclaimed the Chief. "He has gained much land!"

Pahóm's servant came running up and tried to raise him, but he saw that blood was flowing from his mouth. Pahóm was dead!

The Bashkírs clicked their tongues to show their pity.

His servant picked up the spade and dug a grave long enough for Pahóm to lie in, and buried him in it. Six feet from his head to his heels was all he needed.

Questions for Discussion and Analysis

1. How important is the presence of the Devil, or the Evil One, in the story? Does Pahóm have free will, or are his actions and his downfall predetermined by the Devil's intervention? Is there any evidence that Pahóm's destruction is inevitable?

2. What disguises does the Devil assume throughout the story?

3. How do you interpret the behavior of the Bashkírs? How does their presence in the story influence our attitude toward Pahóm?

4. Is there any evidence of foreshadowing?

5. "How Much Land Does a Man Need?" is a parable, a story that imparts a moral truth. How would you state that moral truth?

Selection 2   # Girl
Jamaica Kincaid

Born in 1946 on the West Indian island of Antigua, Jamaica Kincaid is regarded highly as a short story writer. Her stories have been published in The New Yorker *and other literary magazines. "Girl" appeared in her first collection of short stories,* At the Bottom of the River, *which was nominated for the prestigious PEN/Faulkner Award. Her most recent book,* The Autobiography of My Mother, *was nominated for the National Book Critics Circle Award.*

Wash the white clothes on Monday and put them on the stone heap; wash the color clothes on Tuesday and put them on the clothesline to dry; don't walk barehead in the hot sun; cook pumpkin fritters in very hot sweet oil; soak your little cloths right after you take them off; when buying cotton to make yourself a nice blouse, be sure that it doesn't have gum on it, because that way it won't hold up well after a wash; soak salt fish overnight before you cook it; is it true that you sing benna in Sunday school?; always eat your food in such a way that it won't turn someone else's stomach; on Sundays try to walk like a lady and not like the slut you are so bent on becoming; don't sing benna in Sunday school; you mustn't speak to wharf-rat boys, not even to give directions; don't eat fruits on the street—flies will follow you; *but I don't sing benna on Sundays at all and never in Sunday school;* this is how to sew on a button; this is how to make a buttonhole for the button you have just sewed on; this is how to hem a dress when you see the hem coming down and so to prevent yourself from looking like the slut I know you are so bent on becoming; this is how you iron your father's khaki shirt so that it doesn't have a crease; this is how you iron your father's khaki pants so that they don't have a crease; this is how you grow okra—far from the house, because okra tree harbors red ants; when you are growing dasheen, make sure it gets plenty of water or else it makes your throat itch when you are eating it; this is how you sweep a corner; this is how you sweep a whole house; this is how you sweep a yard; this is how you smile to someone you don't like very much; this is how you smile to someone you don't like at all; this is how you smile to someone you like completely; this is how you set a table for tea; this is how you set a table for dinner; this is how you set a table for dinner with an important guest; this is how you set a table for lunch; this is how you set a table for breakfast; this is how to behave in the presence of men who don't know you very well, and this way they won't recognize immediately the slut I have warned you against becoming; be sure to wash every day, even if it is with your own spit; don't squat down to play marbles—you are not a boy, you know; don't pick people's flowers—you might catch something; don't throw stones at blackbirds, because it might not be a blackbird at all; this is how to make a bread pudding; this is how to make doukona; this is how to make pepper pot; this is how to make a good medicine for a cold; this is how to make a good medicine to throw away a child before it even becomes a child; this is how to catch a fish; this is how to throw back a fish you don't like, and that way something bad won't fall on you; this is how to bully a man; this is how a man bullies you; this is how to love a man, and if this doesn't work there are other ways, and if they don't work don't feel too bad about giving up; this is how to spit up in the air if you feel like it, and this is how to move quick so that it doesn't fall on you; this is how to make ends meet; always squeeze bread to make sure it's fresh; *but what if the baker won't let me feel the bread?;* you mean to say that after all you are really going to be the kind of woman who the baker won't let near the bread?

Questions for Discussion and Analysis

1. Who is the narrator in the story? Who is speaking in the sentences printed in italics?

2. What is the significance of the title? Why isn't the "girl" named?

3. From the many instructions given by the narrator, what conclusions can you draw about the role of women in her culture?

4. Of what particular significance are the instructions to set a table in five different ways?

5. What tension or conflict, if any, do you detect in the story?

6. What is the dramatic effect of the story's style—the fact that the entire story represents only a single sentence?

7. Comment on the final exchange between the two characters. What is the impact of the speaker's final question?

Selection 3

In a Grove
Ryunosuke Akutagawa

Ryunosuki Akutagawa (1892–1927), who was born in Tokyo, was adopted at a young age by an uncle after his mother became insane. Her insanity haunted him for the rest of his life. As a child, he developed a love of ghost stories popular at the time. After graduating from Tokyo Imperial University, Akutagawa began publishing short stories. His best-known tale is "Rashomon," which was later made into a film of the same name (1950; directed by the famous Japanese director Akira Kurosawa); he published several collections of stories that were immensely popular in Japan. In his later years, Akutagawa's popularity declined as he developed health problems and paranoia about the possibility that he had inherited his mother's insanity. "In a Grove" presents the testimony of seven people who witnessed a woman's rape and the murder of her husband, who was a samurai. Because all of these witnesses' testimony is contradictory, it is best to read the story at least twice to separate the truth from illusion, insofar as that is possible in this unusual story.

The Testimony of a Woodcutter Questioned By a High Police Commissioner

Yes, sir. Certainly, it was I who found the body. This morning, as usual, I went to cut my daily quota of cedars, when I found the body in a grove in a hollow in the mountains. The exact location? About 150 meters off the Yamashina stage road. It's an out-of-the-way grove of bamboo and cedars.

The body was lying flat on its back dressed in a bluish silk kimono and a wrinkled head-dress of the Kyoto style. A single sword-stroke had pierced the breast. The fallen bamboo-blades around it were stained with bloody blossoms. No, the blood was no longer running. The wound had dried up, I believe. And also, a gad-fly was stuck fast there, hardly noticing my footsteps.

You ask me if I saw a sword or any such thing?

No, nothing, sir. I found only a rope at the root of a cedar near by. And . . . well, in addition to a rope, I found a comb. That was all. Apparently he must have made a battle of it before he was murdered, because the grass and fallen bamboo-blades had been trampled down all around.

"A horse was near by?"

No, sir. It's hard enough for a man to enter, let alone a horse.

The Testimony of a Traveling Buddhist Priest Questioned By a High Police Commissioner

The time? Certainly, it was about noon yesterday, sir. The unfortunate man was on the road from Sekiyama to Yamashina. He was walking toward Sekiyama with a woman accompanying him on horseback, who I have since learned was his wife. A scarf hanging from her head hid her face from view. All I saw was the color of her clothes, a lilac-colored suit. Her horse was a sorrel with a fine mane. The lady's height? Oh, about four feet five inches. Since I am a Buddhist priest, I took little notice about her details. Well, the man was armed with a sword as well as a bow and arrows. And I remember that he carried some twenty odd arrows in his quiver.

Little did I expect that he would meet such a fate. Truly human life is as evanescent as the morning dew or a flash of lightning. My words are inadequate to express my sympathy for him.

The Testimony of a Policeman Questioned By a High Police Commissioner

The man that I arrested? He is a notorious brigand called Tajomaru. When I arrested him, he had fallen off his horse. He was groaning on the bridge at Awataguchi. The time? It was in the early hours of last night. For the record, I might say that the other day I tried to arrest him, but unfortunately he escaped. He was wearing a dark blue silk kimono and a large plain sword. And, as you see, he got a bow and arrows somewhere. You say that this bow and these arrows look like the ones owned by the dead man? Then Tajomaru must be the murderer. The bow wound with leather strips, the black lacquered quiver, the seventeen arrows with hawk feathers—these were all in his possession I believe. Yes, sir, the horse is, as you say, a sorrel with a fine mane. A little beyond the stone bridge I found the horse grazing by the roadside, with his long rein dangling. Surely there is some providence in his having been thrown by the horse.

Of all the robbers prowling around Kyota, this Tajomaru has given the most grief to the women in town. Last autumn a wife who came to the mountain back of the Pindora of the Toribe Temple, presumably to pay a visit, was murdered along with a girl. It has been suspected that it was his doing. If this criminal murdered the man, you cannot tell what he may have done with the man's wife. May it please your honor to look into this problem as well.

The Testimony of an Old Woman Questioned
By a High Police Commissioner

Yes, sir, that corpse is the man who married my daughter. He does not come from Kyoto. He was a samurai in the town of Kokufu in the province of Wakasa. His name was Kanasawa no Takehiko, and his age was twenty-six. He was of a gentle disposition, so I am sure he did nothing to provoke the anger of others.

My daughter? Her name is Masago, and her age is nineteen. She is a spirited, fun-loving girl, but I am sure she has never known any man except Takehiko. She has a small, oval, dark-complected face with a mole at the corner of her left eye.

Yesterday Takehiko left for Wakasa with my daughter. What bad luck it is that things should have come to such a sad end! What has become of my daughter? I am resigned to giving up my son-in-law as lost, but the fate of my daughter worries me sick. For heaven's sake leave no stone unturned to find her. I hate that robber Tajomaru, or whatever his name is. Not only my son-in-law, but my daughter . . . (Her later words were drowned in tears.)

Tajomaru's Confession

I killed him, but not her. Where's she gone? I can't tell. Oh, wait a minute. No torture can make me confess what I don't know. Now things have come to such a head, I won't keep anything from you.

Yesterday a little past noon I met that couple. Just then a puff of wind blew, and raised her hanging scarf, so that I caught a glimpse of her face. Instantly it was again covered from my view. That may have been one reason; she looked like a Bodhisattva. At that moment I made up my mind to capture her even if I had to kill her man.

Why? To me killing isn't a matter of such great consequence as you might think. When a woman is captured, her man has to be killed anyway. In killing, I use the sword I wear at my side. Am I the only one who kills people? You, you don't use your swords. You kill people with your power, with your money. Sometimes you kill them on the pretext of working for their good. It's true they don't bleed. They are in the best of health, but all the same you've killed them. It's hard to say who is a greater sinner, you or me. (An ironical smile.)

But it would be good if I could capture a woman without killing her man. So, I made up my mind to capture her, and do my best not to kill him. But it's out of the question on the Yamashina stage road. So I managed to lure the couple into the mountains.

It was quite easy. I became their traveling companion, and I told them there was an old mound in the mountain over there, and that I had dug it open and found many mirrors and swords. I went on to tell them I'd buried the things in a grove behind the mountain, and that I'd like to sell them at a low price to anyone who would care to have them. Then . . . you see, isn't greed terrible? He was beginning to be moved by my talk before he knew it. In less than half an hour they were driving their horse toward the mountain with me.

When he came in front of the grove, I told them that the treasures were buried in it, and I asked them to come and see. The man had no objection—he was blinded by greed. The woman said she would wait on horseback. It was natural for her to say so, at the sight of a thick grove. To tell you the truth, my plan worked just as I wished, so I went into the grove with him, leaving her behind alone.

The grove is only bamboo for some distance. About fifty yards ahead there's a rather open clump of cedars. It was a convenient spot for my purpose. Pushing my way through the grove, I told him a plausible lie that the treasures were buried under the cedars. When I told him this, he pushed his laborious way toward the slender cedar visible through the grove. After a while the bamboo thinned out, and we came to where a number of cedars grew in a row. As soon as we got there, I seized him from behind. Because he was a trained, sword-bearing warrior, he was quite strong, but he was taken by surprise, so there was no help for him. I soon tied him up to the roof of a cedar. Where did I get a rope? Thank heaven, being a robber, I had a rope with me, since I might have to scale a wall at any moment. Of course it was easy to stop him from calling out by gagging his mouth with fallen bamboo leaves.

When I disposed of him, I went to his woman and asked her to come and see him, because he seemed to have been suddenly taken sick. It's needless to say that this plan also worked well. The woman, her sedge hat off, came into the depths of the grove, where I led her by the hand. The instant she caught sight of her husband, she drew a small sword. I've never seen a woman of such violent temper. If I'd been off guard, I'd have got a thrust in my side. I dodged, but she kept slashing at me. She might have wounded me deeply or killed me. But I'm Tajomaru. I managed to strike. I managed to strike down her small sword without drawing my own. The most spirited woman is defenseless without a weapon. At last I could satisfy my desire for her without taking her husband's life.

Yes, . . . without taking his life. I had no wish to kill him. I was about to run away from the grove, leaving the woman behind in tears, when she frantically clung to my arm. In broken fragments of words, she asked that either her husband or I die. She said it was more trying than death to have her shame known to two men. She gasped out that she wanted to be the wife of whichever survived. Then a furious desire to kill him seized me. (Gloomy excitement.)

Telling you in this way, No doubt I seem a crueler man than you. But that's because you didn't see her face. Especially her burning eyes at that moment. As I saw her eye to eye, I wanted to make her my wife even if I were to be struck by lightning. I wanted to make her my wife. . . this single desire filled my mind. This was not only lust, as you might think. At that time if I'd had no other desire than lust, I'd surely not have minded knocking her down and running away. Then I wouldn't have stained my sword with his blood. But the moment I gazed at her face in the dark grove, I decided not to leave there without killing him.

But I didn't like to resort to unfair means to kill him. I untied him and told him to cross swords with me. (The rope that was found at the root of the cedar is the rope I dropped at the time.) Furious with anger, he drew his thick sword. And quick as thought, he sprang at me ferociously, without speaking a word. I needn't tell you how our fight turned out. The twenty-third stroke . . . please remember this. I'm impressed with this fact still. Nobody under the sun has ever clashed swords with me twenty strokes. (A cheerful smile.)

When he fell, I turned toward her, lowering my blood-stained sword. But to my great astonishment she was gone. I wondered to where she had run away. I looked for her in the clump of cedars. I listened, but heard only a groaning sound from the throat of the dying man.

As soon as we started to cross swords, she may have run away through the grove to call for help. When I thought of that, I decided it was a matter of life and death to me. So, robbing him of his sword, and bow and arrows, I ran out to the mountain road. There I found her horse still grazing quietly. It would be a mere waste of words to tell you the later details, but before I entered town I had already parted with the sword. That's all my confession. I know that my head will be hung in chains anyway, so put me down for the maximum penalty. (A defiant attitude.)

The Confession of a Woman Who Has Come to the Shimizu Temple

That man in the blue silk kimono, after forcing me to yield to him, laughed mockingly as he looked at my bound husband. How horrified my husband must have been! But no matter how hard he struggled in agony, the rope cut into him all the more tightly. In spite of myself I ran stumblingly toward his side. Or rather I tried to run toward him, but the man instantly knocked me down. Just at that moment I saw an indescribable light in my husband's eyes. Something beyond expression . . . his eyes make me shudder even now. That instantaneous look of my husband, who couldn't speak a word, told me all his heart. The flash in his eyes was neither anger nor sorrow . . . only a cold light, a look of loathing. More struck by the look in his eyes than by the blow of the thief, I called out in spite of myself and fell unconscious.

In the course of time I came to, and found that the man in blue silk was gone. I saw only my husband still bound to the root of the cedar. I raised myself from the bamboo-blades with difficulty, and looked into his face; but the expression in his eyes was just the same as before

Beneath the cold contempt in his eyes, there was hatred. Shame, grief, and anger . . . I don't know how to express my heart at that time. Reeling to my feet, I went up to my husband.

"Takejiro," I said to him, "since things have come to this pass, I cannot live with you. I'm determined to die, . . . but you must die, too. You saw my shame. I can't leave you alive as you are."

This was all I could say. Still he went on gazing at me with loathing and contempt. My heart breaking, I looked for his sword. It must have been taken by the robber. Neither his sword nor his bow and arrows were to be seen in the grove. But fortunately my small sword was lying at my feet. Raising it over head, once more I said, "Now give me your life. I'll follow you right away."

When he heard those words, he moved his lips with difficulty. Since his mouth was stuffed with leaves, of course his voice could not be heard at all. But at a glance I understood his words. Despising me, his look said only, "Kill me." Neither conscious nor unconscious, I stabbed the small sword through the lilac-colored kimono into his breast.

Again at this time I must have fainted. By the time I managed to look up, he had already breathed his last—still in bonds. A streak of sinking sunlight streamed through the clump of cedars and bamboos, and shone on his pale face. Gulping down my sobs, I untied the rope from his dead body. And . . . and what has become of me since I have no more strength to tell you. Anyway I hadn't the strength to die. I stabbed my own throat with the small sword, I threw myself into a pond at the foot of the mountain, and I tried to kill myself in many ways. Unable to end my life, I am still living in dishonor. (A lonely smile.) Worthless as I am, I must have been forsaken even by the most merciful Kwannon. I killed my own husband. I was violated by the robber. Whatever can I do? Whatever can I . . . I . . . (Gradually violent sobbing.)

The Story of the Murdered Man, as Told Through a Medium

After violating my wife, the robber, sitting there, began to speak comforting words to her. Of course I couldn't speak. My whole body was tied fast to the root of a cedar. But meanwhile I winked at her many times, as much to say "Don't believe the robber." I wanted to convey some such meaning to her. But my wife, sitting dejectedly on the bamboo leaves, was looking hard at her lap. To all appearance, she was listening to his words. I was agonized by jealousy. In the meantime the robber went on with his clever talk, from one subject to another. The robber finally made his bold, brazen proposal. "Once your virtue is stained, you won't get along well with your husband, so won't you be my wife instead? It's my love for you that made me be violent toward you."

While the criminal talked, my wife raised her face as if in a trance. She had never looked so beautiful as at that moment. What did my beautiful wife say in answer to him while I was sitting bound there? I am lost in space, but I have never thought of her answer without burning with anger and jealousy. Truly she said, . . . "Then take me away with you wherever you go."

This is not the whole of her sin. If that were all, I would not be tormented so much in the dark. When she was going out of the grove as if in a dream, her hand on the robber's, she suddenly turned pale, and pointed at me tied to the root of the cedar, and said, "Kill him! I cannot marry you as long as he lives." "Kill him!" she cried many times, as if she had gone crazy. Even now these words threaten to blow me headlong into the bottomless abyss of darkness. Has such a hateful thing come out of a human mouth ever before? Have such cursed words ever struck a human ear, even once? Even once such a . . . (A sudden cry of scorn.) At these words the robber himself turned pale. "Kill him," she cried, clinging to his arms. Looking hard at her, he answered neither yes nor no. . . . but hardly had I thought about his answer before she had been knocked down into the bamboo leaves. (Again a cry of scorn.) Quietly folding his arms, he looked at me and said, "What will you do with her? Kill her or save her? You have only to nod. Kill her?" For these words alone I would like to pardon his crime.

While I hesitated, she shrieked and ran into the depths of the grove. The robber instantly snatched at her, but he failed even to grasp her sleeve.

After she ran away, he took up my sword, and my bow and arrows. With a single stroke he cut one of my bonds. I remember his mumbling, "My fate is next." Then he disappeared from the grove. All was silent after that. No, I heard someone crying. Untying the rest of my bonds, I listened carefully, and I noticed that it was my own crying. (Long silence.)

I raised my exhausted body from the root of the cedar. In front of me there was shining the small sword which my wife had dropped. I took it up and stabbed it into my breast. A bloody lump rose to my mouth, but I didn't feel any pain. When my breast grew cold, everything was as silent as the dead in their graves. What profound silence! Not a single bird-note was heard in the sky over this grave in the hollow of the mountains. Only a lonely light lingered on the cedars and mountain. By and by the light gradually grew fainter, till the cedars and bamboo were lost to view. Lying there, I was enveloped in deep silence.

Then someone crept up to me. I tried to see who it was. But darkness had already been gathering round me. Someone . . . that someone drew a small sword softly out of my breast in its invisible hand. At the same time once more blood flowed into my mouth. And once and for all I sank down into the darkness of space.

Questions for Discussion and Analysis

1. Of what symbolic importance is the story's setting in a forest (a grove of cedars)?

2. In what ways does "In a Grove" suggest the theme of falsity and falsehood? In assembling seven conflicting testimonies, what is

Akutagawa suggesting about the nature of truth and our ability or inability to distinguish between truth and fiction?

3. Throughout the course of the story, three people confess to murdering the samurai husband. Study these confessions carefully. What are their motivations for confessing? What does each gain from admitting to the murder?

4. In what ways does the testimony of the woodcutter contradict that of the other participants?

5. Consider the testimony of Tajomaru, who claims to have murdered the samurai. Why is he so willing to discuss his role in the rape and murder? Why does he adopt a defiant stance and ask for the "maximum penalty"?

6. The Buddhist priest, another witness, claims not to have noticed many details. How does his testimony conflict with this assertion?

7. What clues in the policeman's testimony reveal his ineptitude?

8. Why does the old woman, the young woman's mother, claim her daughter "has never known any man except Takehiko"? Why might she need to make such a statement?

9. Why does Masago go into such detail about what she sees in her husband's eyes?

10. What statements of the murdered husband, as revealed through the medium, seem questionable or even unbelievable?

11. Why does the story conclude ambiguously, with no clear indication of the murderer's identity?

Selection 4   # Chicxulub

T. C. Boyle

T. C. Boyle is one of the most imaginative fiction writers in America today. Known for his inventive, often zany, use of language and absorbing plots, Boyle has seemingly broken new ground with each of his 16 books of fiction. Of particular note are After the Plague *(2001),* The Tortilla Curtain *(1995),* Drop City *(2003), and* The Inner Circle *(2004). Boyle has a Ph.D. from the University of Iowa and an MFA from the University of Iowa Writer's Workshop. Since 1978, he has taught creative writing at the University of Southern California. In addition to his novels, he regularly publishes short fiction in such periodicals as* The New Yorker, Harper's, Esquire, Playboy, McSweeney's, *and* Granta. *A wealth of material about Boyle and his works is available on his Web site: www.tcboyle.com.*

The title of this story, "Chicxulub," is a Mayan word used to identify a crater in Mexico's Yucatán Peninsula caused by a giant meteor that crashed into the Earth 65 million years ago. Geologists cite this meteor as the cause of the dinosaurs' demise; it also establishes the boundary between the age of reptiles and the age of mammals. Complete information about the Chicxulub meteor can be found at www.lpl.arizona.edu/SIC/impact_cratering/Chicxulub/ Chicx_title.html.

My daughter is walking along the roadside late at night—too late, really, for a seventeen-year-old to be out alone, even in a town as safe as this— and it is raining, the first rain of the season, the streets slick with a fine immiscible glaze of water and petrochemicals, so that even a driver in full possession of her faculties, a driver who hadn't consumed two apple Martinis and three glasses of Hitching Post pinot noir before she got behind the wheel of her car, would have trouble keeping the thing out of the gutters and the shrubbery, off the sidewalk and *the highway median,* for Christ's sake. . . . But that's not really what I want to talk about, or not yet, anyway.

Have you heard of Tunguska? In Russia?

This was the site of the last known large-body impact on Earth's surface, nearly a hundred years ago. Or that's not strictly accurate—the meteor, which was an estimated sixty yards across, never actually touched down. The force of its entry—the compression and superheating of the air beneath it—caused it to explode some twenty-five thousand feet above the ground, but then the term "explode" hardly does justice to the event. There was a detonation—a flash, a thunderclap—with the combustive power of eight hundred Hiroshima bombs. Thirty miles away, reindeer in their loping herds were struck dead by the blast wave, and the clothes of a hunter another thirty miles beyond that burst into flame even as he was poleaxed to the ground. Seven hundred square miles of Siberian forest were leveled in an instant. If the meteor had struck just five hours later, it would have exploded over St. Petersburg and annihilated every living thing in that glorious, baroque city. And this was only a rock. And it was only sixty yards across.

My point? You'd better get down on your knees and pray to your gods, because each year this big spinning globe we ride intersects the orbits of some twenty million asteroids, at least a thousand of which are more than half a mile in diameter.

But my daughter. She's out there in the dark and the rain, walking home. Maureen and I bought her a car, a Honda Civic, the safest thing on four wheels, but the car was used—pre-owned, in dealerspeak—and as it happens it's in the shop with transmission problems and, because she just had to see her friends and gossip and giggle and balance slick multicolored clumps of raw fish and pickled ginger on conjoined chopsticks at the mall, Kimberly picked her up and Kimberly will bring her home. Maddy has a cell phone and theoretically she could have called us, but she didn't—or that's how it appears. And so she's walking. In the rain. And Alice K. Petermann, of 16 Briar Lane, white, divorced, a Realtor with Hyperion, who has picked at a salad and left her glasses on the bar, loses control of her vehicle.

It is just past midnight. I am in bed with a book, naked, and hardly able to focus on the clustered words and rigid descending paragraphs, because Maureen is the bathroom slipping into the sheer black negligee I bought her at Victoria's Secret for her birthday, and her every sound— the creak of the medicine cabinet on its hinges, the tap running, the susurrus of the brush at her teeth—electrifies me. I've lit a candle and am waiting for Maureen to step into the room so that I can flick off the light. We had cocktails earlier, and a bottle of wine with dinner, and we sat close on the couch and shared a joint in front of the fire, because our daughter was out and we could do that with no one the wiser. I listen to the little sounds from the bathroom, seductive sounds, maddening. I am ready. More than ready. "Hey," I call, pitching my voice low, "are you coming or not? You don't expect me to wait all night do you?"

Her face appears in the doorway, the pale lobes of her breasts and the dark nipples visible through the clinging black silk. "Oh, are you waiting for me?" she says, making a game of it. She hovers at the door, and I can see a smile creep across her lips, the pleasure of the moment, drawing it out. "Because I thought I might go down and work in the garden for a while—it won't take long, a couple of hours, maybe. You know, spread a little manure, bank up some of the mulch on the roses. You'll wait for me, won't you?"

Then the phone rings.

We stare blankly at each other through the first two rings and then Maureen says, "I'd better get it," I say, "No, no, forget it—it's nothing. It's nobody."

But she's already moving.

"Forget it!" I shout, and her voice drifts back to me—"What if it's Maddy"—then I watch her put her lips to the receiver and whisper, "Hello?"

The night of the Tunguska explosion the skies were unnaturally bright across Europe—as far away as London people strolled in the parks past midnight and read novels out of doors while the sheep kept right on grazing and the birds stirred uneasily in the trees. There were no stars visible, no moon—just a pale, quivering light, as if all the color had been bleached out of the sky. But, of course, that midnight glow and the fate of those unhappy Siberian reindeer were nothing compared to what would have happened if a larger object had invaded the Earth's atmosphere. On average, objects greater than a hundred yards in diameter strike the planet once every five thousand years, and asteroids half a mile across thunder down at intervals of three hundred thousand years. Three hundred thousand years is a long time in anybody's book. But if—

when—such a collision occurs, the explosion will be in the million-megaton range and will cloak the atmosphere in dust, thrusting the entire planet into a deep freeze and effectively stifling all plant growth for a period of a year or more. There will be no crops. No forage. No sun.

There had been an accident, that is what the voice on the other end of the line is telling my wife, and the victim is Madeline Biehn, of 1337 Laurel Drive, according to the I.D. the paramedics found in her purse. (The purse, with a silver clasp that has been driven half an inch into the flesh under her arm by the force of the impact, is a little thing, no bigger than a hardcover book, with a ribbon-thin strap, the same purse all the girls carry, as if it were part of a uniform.) Is this her parent or guardian speaking?

I hear my wife say, "This is her mother." And then, the bottom dropping out of her voice, "Is she—?"

Is she? They don't answer such questions, don't volunteer information, not over the phone. The next ten seconds are thunderous, cataclysmic, my wife standing there numbly with the phone in her hand as if it were some unidentifiable object she'd found in the street while I fumble out of bed to search for my pants—and my shoes, where are my shoes? The car keys? My wallet? This is the true panic, the loss of faith and control, the punch to the heart, and the struggle for breath. I say the only thing I can think to say, just to hear my own voice, just to get things straight: "She was in an accident. Is that what they said?"

"She was hit by a car. She's—they don't know. In surgery."

"What hospital? Did they say what hospital?"

My wife is in motion now, too. The negligee ridiculous, unequal to the task, and she jerks it over her head and flings it to the floor even as she snatches up a blouse, shorts, flip-flops—anything, anything to cover her nakedness and get her out the door. The dog is whining in the kitchen. There is the sound of rain on the roof, intensifying, hammering at the gutters. I don't bother with shoes—there are no shoes, shoes do not exist—and my shirt hangs limply from my shoulders misbuttoned, sagging, tails hanging loose, and we're in the car now and the driver's-side wiper is beating out of synch and the night closing on us like a fist.

And then there's Chicxulub. Sixty-five million years ago, an asteroid (or perhaps a comet—no one is quite certain) collided with the Earth on what is now the Yucatán Peninsula. Judging from the impact crater, which is a hundred and twenty miles wide, the object—this big flaming ball—was some six miles across. When it came down, day became night and that night extended so far into the future that at least seventy-five per cent of all known species were extinguished, including the dinosaurs in nearly all their forms and array and some ninety per cent of the oceans' plankton, which in turn devastated the pelagic food chain. How fast was it travelling? The nearest estimates put it at fifty-four thousand miles an hour, more than sixty times the speed of a bullet. Astrophysicists call such objects "civilization enders," and calculate the chances that a disaster of this magnitude will occur during any individual's lifetime at roughly one in ten thousand, the same odds as dying in an auto accident in the next six months—or, more tellingly, living to be a hundred in the company of your spouse.

All I see is windows, an endless grid of lit windows climbing one above the other into the night, as the car shoots into the Emergency Vehicle Only lane and slides in hard against the curb. Both doors fling open simultaneously. Maureen is already out on the sidewalk, already slamming the door behind her and breaking into a trot, and I'm right on her heels, the keys still in the ignition and the lights stabbing at the pale underbelly of a diagonally parked ambulance—and they can have the car, anybody can have it and keep it forever, if they'll just tell me that my daughter is all right. "Just tell me," I mutter, out of breath, "just tell me and it's yours," and this is a prayer, the first in a long discontinuous string, addressed to whoever or whatever might be listening. Overhead, the sky is having a seizure, black above, quicksilver below, the rain coming down in windblown arcs, and I wouldn't even notice but for the fact that we are suddenly—instantly—wet, our hair knotted and clinging and our clothes stuck like flypaper to the slick tegument of our skin.

In we come, side by side, through the doors that jolt back from us in alarm, and all I can think is that the hospital is a death factory and that we have come to it like the walking dead, haggard, sallow, shoeless. "My daughter," I say to the nurse at the admittance desk, "she's —they called. You called. She's been in an accident."

Maureen is at my side, tugging at the fingers of one hand as if she were trying to remove an invisible glove. "A car. A car accident."

"Name?" the nurse asks. About this nurse: she's young, Filipina, with opaque eyes and the bone structure of a cadaver; every day she sees death and it blinds her. She doesn't see us. She sees a computer screen; she sees the TV monitor mounted in the corner and the shadows that pass there; she sees the walls, the floor, the naked light of the fluorescent tube. But not us. Not us.

For one resounding moment that thumps in my ears and then thumps again, I can't remember my daughter's name—I can picture her leaning into the mound of textbooks spread out on the dining-room table, the glow of the overhead light making a nimbus of her hair as she glances up at me with a glum look and half a rueful smile, as if to say, *It's all in a day's work for a teen-ager, Dad, and you're lucky you're not in high school anymore*, but her name is gone.

"Maddy," my wife says. "Madeline Biehn."

I watch, mesmerized, as the nurse's fleshless fingers maneuver the mouse, her eyes locked on the screen before her. A click. Another click.

The eyes lift to take us in, even as they dodge away again. "She's still in surgery," she says.

"Where is it?" I demand. "What room? Where do we go?"

Maureen's voice cuts in then, elemental, chilling, and it's not a question she's posing, not a statement or demand, but a plea: "What's wrong with her?"

Another click, but this one is just for show, and the eyes never move from across the screen. "There was an accident," the nurse says. "She was brought in by the paramedics. That's all I can tell you."

It is then that I become aware that we are not alone, that there are others milling around the room—other zombies like us, hurriedly dressed and streaming water till the beige carpet is black with it—and why, I wonder, do I despise this nurse more than any human being I've ever encountered, this young woman not much older than my daughter, with her hair pulled back in a bun and a white cap like a party favor perched atop it, *who is just doing her job*? Why do I want to reach across the counter that separates us and awaken her to a swift, sure knowledge of hate and fear and pain? Why?

"Ted," Maureen says, and I feel her grip at my elbow, and then we're moving again—hurrying, sweeping, practically running—out of this place, down a corridor under the glare of the lights that are a kind of death in themselves, and into a worse place, a far worse place.

The thing that disturbs me about Chicxulub, aside from the fact that it erased the dinosaurs and wrought catastrophic and irreversible change, is the deeper implication that we, and all our works and worries and attachments, are so utterly inconsequential. Death cancels our individuality, we know that, yes, but ontogeny recapitulates phylogeny, and the kind goes on, human life and culture succeed us. That, in the absence of God, is what allows us to accept death of the individual. But when you throw Chicxulub into the mix—or the next Chicxulub, the Chicxulub that could come howling down to obliterate all and everything even as your eyes skim the lines of this page—where does that leave us?

"You're the parents?" We are in another room, gone deeper now, the loudspeakers murmuring their eternal incantations—*Dr. Chandrosoma to Emergency, Dr. Bell, Paging Dr. Bell*—and here is another nurse, grimmer, older, with lines like the strings of a tobacco pouch pulled tight around her lips. She's addressing us, me and my wife, but I have nothing to say, either in denial or affirmation. If I claim Maddy as my own—and I'm making deals again—then I'm sure to jinx her, because those powers that might or might not be, those gods of the infinite and the minute, will see how desperately I love her and they'll take her way just to spite me for refusing to believe in them. *Voodoo, Hoodoo, Santería, Bless me, Father, for I have sinned.* I hear Maureen's voice, emerging from a locked vault, the single whispered monosyllable, and then: "Is she going to be all right?"

"I don't have that information," the nurse says, and her voice is neutral, robotic even. This is not her daughter. Her daughter's at home, asleep in a pile of Teddy bears, pink sheets, fluffy pillows, the night-light glowing like the all-seeing eye of a sentinel.

I can't help myself. It's that neutrality, that maddening clinical neutrality, and can't anybody take any responsibility for anything? "What information *do* you have?" I say, and maybe I'm too loud, maybe I am. "Isn't that your job, for Christ's sake—to know what's going on here? You call us up in the middle of the night—our daughter's hurt, she's been in an accident, and you tell me you don't have *any fucking information?*"

People turn their heads, eyes burn into us. They're slouched in orange plastic chairs, stretched out on the floor, praying, pacing, their lips moving in silence. They want information, too. We all want information. We want news, good news: it was all a mistake, minor cuts and bruises—contusions, that's the word—and your daughter, son, husband, grandmother, first cousin twice removed will be walking through that door over there any minute. . . .

The nurse drills me with a look, and then she's coming out from behind the desk, a short woman, dumpy—almost a dwarf—and striding briskly to a door, which swings open on another room, deeper yet. "If you'll just follow me, please," she says.

Suddenly sheepish, I duck my head and comply, two steps behind Maureen. This room is smaller, an examining room, with a set of scales and charts on the walls and its slab of a table covered with a sheet of antiseptic paper. "Wait here," the nurse tells us, already shifting her weight to make her escape. "The doctor will be in in a minute."

"What doctor?" I want to know. "What for? What does he want?"

But the door has already drawn closed.

I turn to Maureen. She's standing there in the middle of the room, afraid to touch anything or to sit down or even to move for fear of breaking the spell. She's listening for footsteps, her eyes fixed on the door. I hear myself murmur her name, and then she's in my arms, sobbing, and I know I should hold her, know that we both need it, the human contact, the love and support, but all I feel is the burden of her—there is nothing and no one that can make this better, can't she see that? I don't want to console or be consoled. I don't want to be touched. I just want my daughter back.

Maureen's voice comes from so deep in her throat I can barely make out what she's saying. It takes a second to register, even as she pulls away from me, her face crumpled and red, and this is her prayer, whispered aloud: "She's going to be all right, isn't she?"

"Sure," I say, "sure she is. She'll be fine. She'll have some bruises, that's for sure, maybe a couple of broken bones even . . ." and I trail off, trying to picture it, the crutches, the cast, the Band-Aids, the gauze: our daughter returned to us in a halo of shimmering light.

"Maybe she broke her arm—she could break her arm. That would— Or her leg, even her leg. But why would she be in surgery so long? Why? Why would that be?"

I don't have an answer to that. I don't want to have an answer.

"It was a car," Maureen says. "A car, Ted. A car hit her."

The room seems to tick and buzz with the fading energy of the larger edifice, and I can't help thinking of the categories of wires strung inside the walls, the cables bringing power to the X-ray lab, the EKG and EEG machines, the life support systems, and of the myriad pipes and the fluids that they drain.

A car. Three thousand pounds of steel, chrome, glass, iron.

"What was she even doing walking like that? She knows better than that."

My wife nods, the wet ropes of her hair beating at her shoulders like the flails of the penitents. "She probably had a fight with Kimberly—I'll bet that's it. I'll bet anything."

"Where is the son of a bitch?" I snarl. "This doctor—where is he?"

We are in that room, in that purgatory of a room, for a good hour or more. Twice I thrust my head out the door to give the nurse an annihilating look, but there is no news, no doctor, nothing. And then, at quarter past two, the inner door swings open, and there he is, a man too young to be a doctor, an infant with a smooth bland face and hair that rides a wave up off his brow, and he doesn't have to say a thing, not a word, because I can see what he's bringing us and my heart seizes with the shock of it. He looks to Maureen, looks to me, then drops his eyes. "I'm sorry," he says.

When it comes, the meteor will punch through the atmosphere and strike the Earth in a single second, vaporizing on impact and creating a fireball that will in that moment achieve temperatures of sixty thousand degrees Kelvin, or ten times the surface reading of the sun. If it is Chicxulub-size and it hits one of our landmasses, some two hundred thousand cubic kilometers of the Earth's surface will be thrust up into the atmosphere, even as the thermal radiation of the blast sets fire to the Earth's cities and forests. This will be succeeded by seismic and volcanic activity on a scale unknown in human history, and then the dark night of cosmic winter. If it should land in the sea, as the Chicxulub meteor did, it would spew superheated water into the atmosphere, instead, extinguishing the light of the sun and triggering the same scenario of seismic catastrophe and eternal winter, while simultaneously sending out a rippling ring of water three miles high to rock the continents as if they were saucers in a dishpan.

So what does it matter? What does anything matter? We are powerless. We are bereft. And the gods—all the gods of all the ages combined—are nothing but a rumor.

The gurney is the focal point in a room of gurneys, people laid out as if there'd been a war, the beaked noses of the victims poking up out of the maze of sheets like a series of topographic blips on a glaciated plain. These people are alive still, fluids dripping into their veins, machines monitoring their vital signs, nurses hovering over them like ghouls, but they'll be dead soon, all of them. That much is clear. But *the* gurney, the one against the black wall with the sheet pulled up over the impossibly small and reduced form—this is all that matters. The doctor leads us across the room, speaking in a low voice of internal injuries, ruptured spleen, trauma, the brain stem, and I can barely control my feet.

Can I tell you how hard it is to lift this sheet? Thin percale, and it might as well be made of lead, iron, iridium, might as well be the repository of all the dark matter in the universe. The doctor steps back, hands folded before him. The entire room or triage ward or whatever it is holds its breath. Maureen moves in beside me till our shoulders are touching, till I can feel the flesh and the heat of her pressing into me, and I think of this child we made together, this thing under the sheet, and the hand clenches at the end of my arm, the fingers there, prehensile, taking hold. The sheet draws back millimeter by millimeter, the slow striptease of death—and I can't do this, I can't—until Maureen lunges forward and jerks the thing off in a single violent motion.

It takes us a moment—the shock of the bloated and discolored flesh, the crusted mat of blood at the temple and the rag of the hair, this obscene violation of everything we know and expect and love—before the surge of joy hits us. Maddy is a redhead, like her mother, and though she's seventeen, she's as rangy and thin as a child, with oversized hands and feet, and she never did pierce the smooth sweet run of flesh beneath her lower lip. I can't speak. I'm rushing still with the euphoria of this new mainline drug I've discovered, soaring over the room, the hospital, the whole planet. Maureen says it for me: "This is not our daughter."

Our daughter is not in the hospital. Our daughter is asleep in her room beneath the benevolent gaze of the posters on the wall—Britney and Brad and Justin—her things are scattered around her as if laid out for a rummage sale. Our daughter has in fact gone to Hana Sushi at the mall, as planned, and Kimberley has driven her home. Our daughter has, unbeknownst to us or anyone else, fudged the rules a bit—the smallest thing in the world, nothing really, the sort of thing every teen-ager does without thinking twice. She has loaned her I.D. to her second-best friend, Kristi Cherwin, because Kristi is sixteen and Kristi wants to see—is dying to see—the movie at the Cineplex with Brad Pitt in it, the one rated NC-17. Our daughter doesn't know that we've been to the hospital, doesn't know about Alice K. Petermann and the pinot noir and the glasses left on the bar, doesn't know that even now the phone is ringing at the Cherwins'.

I am sitting on the couch with a drink, staring into the ashes of the fire. Maureen is in the kitchen with a mug of Ovaltine, gazing vacantly out the window where the first streaks of light have begun to limn the trunks of the trees. I try to picture the Cherwins—they've been to the house a few times, Ed and Lucinda—and I draw a blank until a backlit scene from the past presents itself, a cookout at their place, the adults gathered around the grill with gin-and-tonics, the radio playing some forgotten song, the children, our daughters, riding their bikes up and down the cobbled drive, making a game of it, spinning, dodging, lifting the front wheels from the ground even as their hair fans out behind them and the sun crashes through the trees. Flip a coin ten times and it could turn up heads ten times in a row—or not once. The rock is coming, the new Chicxulub, hurtling through the dark and the cold to remake our fate. But not tonight. Not for me.

For the Cherwins, it's already here.

Questions for Discussion and Analysis

1. Comment on the structure of this story. What is the effect of the alternating sections describing the events of the evening as experienced by the narrator and his wife, Maureen, and the two meteorological events? What does the story gain by the narrative's four interruptions?

2. Describe the impact of the car accident and the news that his daughter has been injured on the narrator and Maureen. What emotions do they experience as they make their way to the hospital?

3. Look up the word *catharsis* in an unabridged dictionary. In what way does the word apply to the end of the story?

4. Comment on this passage from the story: "So what does it matter? What does anything matter? We are powerless. We are bereft. And the gods—all the gods of all ages combined—are nothing but a rumor." What, ultimately, is Boyle's theme in this story? What does the story say about human certainty, about our faith in higher powers?

5. Of what larger significance is the meteor that crashed into Tunguska in Russia and Chicxulub that crashed into the Yucatán Peninsula? What do these events have to do with the human experiences in the story? Specifically, how are the meteor Chicxulub and the accident that killed Kristi Cherwin linked?

Permissions Acknowledgments

Photos

Page 59: © Lauren Chelec Cafritz; **88:** © Barbara S. Salz; **150:** © Jerry Bauer; **176:** © Jim Gipe/Pivot Media; **219:** George C. Beresford/Getty Images; **262:** © Gary W. Meek/Gary W. Meek Photography, Inc.; **292:** © Royalty-Free/Corbis; **298:** Thememoryhole.org/Getty Images; **299:** © Bettmann/Corbis; **300:** AP/Wide World Photos; **321:** Courtesy of Franzus Company LLC; **324:** AP/Wide World Photos; **341:** Bill Aron/PhotoEdit; **342:** Mary Kate Denny/PhotoEdit; **343:** Bonnie Kamin/PhotoEdit; **345:** Bill Aron/PhotoEdit; **391:** © Wally McNamee/Corbis; **395:** By Rosamond Purcell © 1994; **399:** © Jerry Bauer; **403:** © Christopher Felver/Corbis; **408:** AP/Wide World Photos; **418:** Photo Courtesy of Andrei Codrescu; **423:** © Jerry Bauer; **431:** © Shannon McIntyre Photography; **436:** Courtesy of the Bishop Museum; **443:** Photo by Gail Zucker; **451:** Photo courtesy of Harvard Center for Population and Development Studies; **457:** Photo by Ashnell Tyson; **466:** AP/Wide World Photos; **476, 477, 478, 479:** U.S. Army photo by Sgt. Jeremiah Johnson; **507:** Hulton Archive/Getty Images; **519:** © Jerry Bauer; **521:** Photo provided by AaN Press; **528:** Photograph by Spencer Boyle

Text and Line Art

Ackerman, Diane. From *A Natural History of the Senses.* Copyright © 1990 by Diane Ackerman. Reprinted by permission of Random House, Inc.

Acocella, Joan. From "Under the Spell" by Joan Acocella. *The New Yorker,* July 31, 2000. Copyright © 2000 by Joan Acocella. Reprinted by permission.

Akutagawa, Ryunosuke, translated by Takashi Kojima. From "In a Grove" in *Rashomon and Other Stories.* Copyright © 1952 by Liveright Publishing Corporation. Reprinted with permission from Liveright Publishing Corporation.

Altick, Richard D., and Lunsford, Andrea L. From Preface to *Critical Reading,* 6th Edition. Copyright © 1984. Reprinted with permission from Heinle, a division of Thomson Learning.

The American Heritage Dictionary of English Language, 3rd Edition. Copyright © 1996 by Houghton Mifflin Company. Adapted and reproduced by permission of Houghton Mifflin Company.

Atwood, Margaret. "The View from the Backyard." *The Nation,* 1986. Reprinted with permission from McClelland and Stewart.

Bennett, William. From "What Really Ails America." *Reader's Digest,* August 1984. Reprinted with the permission of the author.

Bernard, Andrew. From *Madame Bovary, C'Est Moi: The Great Characters of Literature and Where They Came From.* Copyright © 2004 by Andrew Bernard. Reprinted by permission of W.W. Norton & Company, Inc.

Best, Joel. From *Damned Lies and Statistics.* Copyright © 2001 by The Regents of the University of California. Reprinted with permission.

Bok, Sissela. From *Lying: Moral Choices in Public and Private Lives.* Copyright © 1978 by Sissela Bok. Reprinted by permission of Pantheon Books, a division of Random House, Inc.

Boulding, Kenneth. From *The Image: Knowledge in Life and Society.* Copyright © 1963 by University of Michigan Press. Reprinted by permission of University of Michigan Press.

Bourdain, Anthony. From "Don't Eat Before Reading This" by Anthony Bourdain. *The New Yorker.* Reprinted by permission of Anthony Bourdain.

Boyle, Peter. From "The Ames Strain." *The New Yorker,* November 12, 2001. Reprinted with permission.

Boyle, T. Coraghessan. From "Chicxulub" in *Tooth and Claw.* First appeared in *The New Yorker.* Copyright © 2004 by T. Coraghessan Boyle. Reprinted by permission of Viking Penguin, a division of Penguin Group (USA) Inc.

Carter, Stephen L. From "The Insufficiency of Honesty." *The Atlantic Monthly,* February 1996. Originally published as part of a book entitled, *Integrity* by Stephen L. Carter, which was published by Basic Books in 1996. Reprinted with permission.

Codrescu, Andrei. "Faux Chicken & Phony Furniture: Notes of an Alien Son." Reprinted with permission from the December 12, 1994, issue of *The Nation.*

Della Femina, Jerry. From "They've Got Us Where They Want Us." *The Washington Post National Weekly Edition Reprinted,* October 9, 2000. Reprinted by permission.

DeVito, Joseph A. Exercise adapted from *General Semantics: Guide and Workbook* by Joseph A. DeVito. This test is based on those developed by William Honey (1973), *Communication and Organizational Behavior,* 3rd Edition, Homewood, IL: Irwin. Reprinted with permission from Joseph DeVito.

Elliot, Jason. From *An Unexpected Light: Travels from Afghanistan.* Copyright © 2000 by James Elliot. Reprinted by permission from St. Martin's Press, LLC.

Ewald, Paul. From *Plague Time: How Stealth Infections Cause Cancer, Heart Disease, and Other Deadly Ailments.* Copyright © 2000 by Paul Ewald. Reprinted by permission from The Free Press, a Division of Simon & Schuster Adult Publishing Group.

Freeman, Jr., Castle. "Surviving Deer Season." *The Atlantic Monthly,* December 1995. Reprinted with permission.

Garber, Marjorie. "Dog Days." *The New Yorker,* August 8, 1996, pp. 72–73. Reprinted with permission.

Del Castillo Guilbault, Rose. "Book of Dreams: The Sears Roebuck Catalog." *The San Francisco Chronicle,* February 28, 1993. Reprinted by permission.

Gelernter, David. From *Unplugged: The Myth of Computers in the Classroom.* Copyright © 1994. Reprinted by permission from The New Republic.

Gladwell, Malcolm. From *The Tipping Point.* Copyright © 2000 by Malcolm Gladwell. Reprinted by permission from Little, Brown and Co., Inc..

Glanzer, M. and Cunitz, A.R. From "Two Storage Mechanisms in Free Recall." *Journal of Verbal Learning and Verbal Behavior* (now *Journal of Memory & Language*), Volume 5. Copyright © 1996, Reprinted by permission from Elsevier.

Gordon, Nicholas. "Happiness Is Like a Sunny Day" by Nicholas Gordon from www.poemsforfree.com/happi7.html. Reprinted by permission of the author.

Gould, Stephen Jay. From "Preposterous: What Has Happened to the Rhinoceros Is as Hard to Fathom as the Beast Itself." *The Sciences,* July–August 1996. Published by the New York Academy of Sciences. Reprinted by permission of the estate of Stephen Jay Gould.

Hillenbrand, Laura. From *Seabiscuit: An American Legend.* Copyright © 2001 by Laura Hillenbrand. Reprinted by permission from Random House, Inc.

Hunt, Albert R. From "Public Ambivalence on Gay Unions." *The Wall Street Journal,* December 18, 2003. Copyright © 2003 by Dow Jones & Co. Inc. Reproduced with permission of Dow Jones & Co. Inc.

Imber-Black, Evan. From *The Secret Life of Families.* Copyright © 1998 by Evan Imber-Black. Reprinted by permission from Bantam Books, a division of Random House, Inc.

Iyer, Pico. From "In Praise of the Humble Comma." *Time,* June 13, 1988. Copyright © 1988 by Time, Inc. Reprinted by permission.

Jacoby, Jeff. From "Fishing for Sport Is Cruel, Inhumane." *The Boston Globe,* May 11, 2003. Reprinted by permission.

Jen, Gish. From "An Ethnic Trump." First published in *The New York Times Magazine.* Copyright © 1996 by Gish Jen. Reprinted by permission of the author.

Kapuściński, Ryszard. Translated by Klara Glowczewska. From *The Shadow of the Sun.* Originally published in *The New Yorker.* Copyright © 2001 by Klara Glowczewska. Reprinted by permission of Alfred A. Knopf, a division of Random House, Inc.

Kincaid, Jamaica. "Girl" from *At the Bottom of the River.* Copyright © 1983 by Jamaica Kincaid. Reprinted by permission of Farrar, Straus and Giroux, LLC.

Kottak, Conrad Phillip. From *Anthropology: The Exploration of Human Diversity,* 10th Edition. Copyright © 2004 by McGraw-Hill. Reprinted by permission of The McGraw-Hill Companies.

Lahey, Benjamin B. From *Psychology: An Introduction,* 8th Edition. Copyright © 2004 by The McGraw-Hill Companies. Reprinted by permission of The McGraw-Hill Companies.

Langewiesche, William. From *American Ground: Unbuilding the World Trade Center.* The McGraw-Hill Companies. Copyright © 2002 by William Langewiesche. Reprinted by permission from The McGraw-Hill Companies.

Lapham, Lewis. "Innocents Abroad." *Harper's,* June 2002. Reprinted with permission.

LaSalle, Mick. From "Ask Mick LaSalle." *The San Francisco Chronicle.* Copyright © 2003 by The San Francisco Chronicle. Reproduced by permission.

Levine, Arthur. From "College— More Than Serving Time." *The Wall Street Journal,* December 21, 1993. Copyright © 1993 by Dow Jones & Co. Inc. Reproduced with permission of Dow Jones & Co. Inc.

Levison, Iain. From *A Working Stiff's Manifesto: A Memoir.* Copyright © 2002. Reprinted by permission from Soho Press.

Lorenzoni, Fr. Larry N., S.D.B. From Letter to the editor, *The San Francisco Chronicle,* December 5, 2003. Reprinted by permission of Fr. Larry Lorenzoni.

Mackey, Sandra. From *The Saudis: Inside the Desert Kingdom.* Copyright © 2003, 1987 by Sandra Mackey. Reprinted by permission of W.W. Norton & Company, Inc.

Mader, Sylvia S. From *Biology,* 8th Edition. Copyright © 2004 by The McGraw-Hill Companies. Reprinted by permission of The McGraw-Hill Companies.

Margolin, Malcolm. From *Ohlone Way: Indian Life in the San Francisco-Monterey Bay Area.* Copyright © 1978 by Heyday Books. Reprinted by permission from Heyday Books.

Martosko, David. From "Soft Drink Ban Based on Bad Science." *The San Francisco Chronicle,* June 19, 2003. Copyright © 2003 by The San Francisco Chronicle. Reproduced with permission.

Masson, Jeffrey and McCarthy, Susan. From *When Elephants Weep.* Copyright © 1995 by Jeffrey Masson and Susan McCarthy. Reprinted by permission of Dell Publishing, a division of Random House, Inc.

McConnell, Campbell, and Brue, Stanley. From *Economics.* Copyright © 2002 by McGraw-Hill Irwin. Reprinted by permission from The McGraw-Hill Companies.

McMurtry, Larry. From *Walter Benjamin at the Dairy Queen: Reflections at Sixty and Beyond.* Copyright © 1999 by Larry McMurtry. Reprinted by permission of Simon & Schuster Adult Publishing Group.

McPhee, John. From "Los Angeles Against the Mountains" in *The Control of Nature.* Copyright © 1989 by John McPhee. Reprinted by permission of Farrar, Straus and Giroux, LLC.

Mehta, Suketu. From "Mumbai: A Lover's Embrace" by Suketu Mehta. Copyright © 1997 by Suketu Mehta. Reprinted by permission of William Morris Agency, Inc. on behalf of the author.

Murphy, Cullen. "In Praise of Snow." *The Atlantic Monthly,* January 1995, p. 48. Reprinted with permission.

Obama, Barack. From *Dreams from My Father.* Copyright © 1995 by Barack Obama. Reprinted by permission from Times Books, a division of Random House, Inc.

Orr, David. Published in "The Speed of Sound." *EarthLight,* Spring 2001. Was later reprinted in the January–February 2002 issue of Utne.

Orwell, George. From "Some Thoughts on the Common Toad" in *Shooting an Elephant and Other Essays.* Copyright © 1936 by George Orwell. Reprinted by permission of Bill Hamilton as the Literary Executor of the Estate of the Late Sonia Brownell Orwell and Secker & Warburg Ltd. Copyright © 1950 by Sonia Brownell Orwell and renewed 1978 by Sonia Pitt-Rivers. Reprinted by permission of Harcourt, Inc.

Piereson, James. From "You Get What You Pay For." *The Wall Street Journal,* July 21, 2004. Copyright © 2004 by Dow Jones & Co. Inc. Reproduced with permission of Dow Jones & Co. Inc.

Plath, Sylvia. From *Metaphors from Crossing the Water* by Sylvia Plath. Copyright © 1960 by Ted Hughes.

Reprinted by permission of HarperCollins Publishers Inc. and Faber and Faber.

Pollan, Michael. From *The Botany of Desire.* Copyright © 2001 by Michael Pollan. Reprinted by permission from Random House, Inc.

Rapping, Elayne. From *The Looking Glass World of NonFiction TV.* Reprinted by permission from South End Press.

Ravitch, Diane. From *The Language Police.* Copyright © 2003, 2004 by Diane Ravitch. Reprinted by permission from Alfred A. Knopf, a division of Random House, Inc.

Ridley, Matt. From *Genome: The Autobiography of a Species in 23 Chapters.* Reprinted by permission of HarperCollins Publishers, Inc.

Ringle, Ken. "A Thousand Years of Bad Memories." *The Washington Post National Weekly Edition,* October 29–November 4, 2001. Published as "The Crusaders Giant Footprints." Copyright © 2001 by The Washington Post. Reprinted with permission.

Rosenbaum, James E. From "It's Time to Tell the Kids: If You Don't Do Well in High School, You Won't Do Well in College (or on the Job)." *The American Educator,* the quarterly journal of the American Federation of Teachers, AFL-CIO. Spring 2004. Reprinted by permission.

Rubin, Avi. From "The Perils of Electronic Voting." *San Jose Mercury* News, August 8, 2004. Copyright © 2004 Tribune Media Services. Reprinted with permission

Rushdie, Salman. From *Step Across This Line.* Originally published in *The New Yorker.* Copyright © 2002 by Salman Rushdie. Reprinted by permission of Random House, Inc.

Sayle, Murray. From "Letter from Hiroshima: Did the Bomb End the War?" by Murray Sayle. *The New Yorker,* July 31, 1995. Reprinted by permission.

Schapiro, Mark. "Muddy Waters" by Mark Schapiro as appeared in *Utne Reader,* November/December 1974. Reprinted by permission of the author. Mark Schapiro is a freelance writer based in New York. His work appears in *Harper's, The Atlantic Monthly, The Nation,* and other publications.

Solomon, Norman. From "News Flash!" by Norman Solomon. Copyright © 2002. Reprinted by permission of the author. www.normansolomon.com

Specter, Michael. From "No Place to Hide." Originally appeared in *The New Yorker,* November 27, 2000. Copyright © 2000 by Michael Specter. Reprinted by permission of International Creative Management, Inc.

Staples, Brent. From "Treat the Epidemic Behind Bars Before It Hits the Streets." *The New York Times,* June 22, 2004. Copyright © 2004 by The New York Times Co. Reprinted with permission.

INDEX